Computer Architecture

Computer Architecture
Single and Parallel Systems

Mehdi R. Zargham
Southern Illinois University

PRENTICE HALL, Upper Saddle River, New Jersey 07458

Library of Congress Cataloging-in-Publishing Data

Zargham, Mehdi R.
   Computer architecture : Single and parallel systems / Mehdi R. Zargham
      p. cm.
   Includes index.
   ISBN 0-13-010661-5
   1. Computer architecture.   I. Title
   QA76.9.A73Z36   1995
   004.2'56--dc20
                                                                   95-22198
                                                                              CIP

Acquisitions editor: Alan Apt
Editorial/production supervision: TKM Productions
Cover design: Wendy Alling Judy
Buyer: Donna Sullivan

©1996 by Prentice-Hall, Inc.
Simon & Schuster / A Viacom Company
Upper Saddle River, New Jersey 07458

All rights reserved. No part of this book may
be reproduced, in any form or by any means,
without permission in writing from the publisher.

Printed in the United States of America
10 9 8 7 6 5 4 3 2 1

ISBN 0-13-010661-5

Prentice-Hall International (UK) Limited, *London*
Prentice-Hall of Australia Pty. Limited, *Sydney*
Prentice-Hall Canada Inc., *Toronto*
Prentice-Hall Hispanoamericana, S.A., *Mexico*
Prentice-Hall of India Private Limited, *New Delhi*
Prentice-Hall of Japan, Inc., *Tokyo*
Simon & Schuster Asia Pte. Ltd., *Singapore*
Editora Prentice-Hall do Brasil, Ltda., *Rio de Janeiro*

*To my father and brother-in-law,
Ardeshir Zargham and Kazunari Ohsone,
my wife, son, and daughter,
Tomoko, Brian, and Emilia.*

Contents

PREFACE XIX

CHAPTER 1 CLASSIFICATION OF DESIGNS 1

Introduction 1

Significant Historical Computers *1*
Computer Generations *2*

1.2 Taxonomies of Parallel Architectures 4

1.3 Performance and Quality Measurements 12

1.4 Outline of the Following Chapters 14

References 15

Problems 16

CHAPTER 2 VON NEUMANN ARCHITECTURE 18

2.1 Introduction 18

2.2 Design of a Simple Microcomputer Using VHDL 20

2.3 Control Unit 27

Hardwired Control Unit 27
Microprogrammed Control Unit 32
Microinstruction Word Design 33

2.4 Instruction Set Design 37

Size of Opcode 37
Type of Operation 38
Type of Operand Fields 39
   Immediate Addressing 39
   Direct Addressing 39
   Indirect Addressing 39
   Displacement Addressing 40
   Stack Addressing 40
Number of Operands per Operation 40

2.5 Arithmetic Logic Unit 43

2.5.1 Addition 43

Full Adder 43
Ripple Carry Adder 44
Carry Lookahead Adder 45
Carry Select Adder 48
Carry Save Adder 49
Binary-coded Decimal Number Addition 49
Serial Adder 51

2.5.2 Multiplication 52

Shift-and-Add Multiplication 53
Booth's Technique 54
Array Multiplier 57

2.5.3 Floating-point Representation 61

Floating-point Addition 63
Floating-point Multiplication 65

2.6 Memory System Design 66

Contents

2.6.1 Memory Hierarchy   66
2.6.2 Memory Cell and Memory Unit   69
2.6.3 Interleaved Memory   71
2.6.4 Associative Memory   72
2.6.5 Cache Memory   74

Cache Operation   76
Basic Cache Organization   77
   Associative Mapping   77
   Direct Mapping   78
   Set-associative Mapping   80
Replacement Strategies   81
   Random Replacement   82
   Least Frequently Used   82
   Least Recently Used   82
Example: i486 Microprocessor Cache Structure   82
Cache Performance   83

2.6.6 Virtual Memory   85

Paging   85
   First In, First Out   88
   Least Recently Used   89
Segmentation   89
   First Fit   90
   Best Fit   90
   Worst Fit   91
Example: i486 Microprocessor Addressing Mechanism   91

2.7 Interrupts and Exceptions   93

References   95

Problems   97

CHAPTER 3   PIPELINING   102

3.1 Introduction   102

3.1.1 Pipeline Structure   102
3.1.2 Pipeline Performance Measures   103
3.1.3 Pipeline Types   105

3.2 Instruction Pipeline 106

3.2.1 Improving the Throughput of an Instruction Pipeline 108

The Fetching Problem   *108*
The Bottleneck Problem   *109*
The Issuing Problem   *109*
    Structural Hazard   109
    Data Hazard   109
      Tomasulo's Method   113
      Scoreboard Method   115
    Control Hazard   117
      Branch Prediction   120
      Delayed Branching   123
      Multiple Prefetch   123

3.2.2 Further Throughput Improvement of an Instruction Pipeline 124

Superscalar   *124*
Superpipeline   *124*
Very Long Instruction Word (VLIW)   *125*

3.3 Arithmetic Pipeline 125

3.4 Pipeline Control: Scheduling 128

Reservation Table   *128*
Latency   *128*

3.4.1 Scheduling Static Pipelines 129

Forbidden List   *129*
Collision Vectors   *129*
State Diagram   *129*
Average Latency   *130*
Minimum Average Latency   *130*

3.4.2 Scheduling Dynamic Pipelines 131

Forbidden Lists   *131*
Collision Vectors and Collision Matrices   *131*
State Diagram   *132*

3.4.3 Decreasing the MAL of a Pipeline Using Delay Insertion 133

References 136

Problems 137

CHAPTER 4 RISC VERSUS CISC ARCHITECTURE 139

4.1 Introduction 139

4.2 Causes for Increased Architectural Complexity 140

Support for High-level Languages 140
Migration of Functions from Software into Hardware 140
Upward Compatibility 140

4.3 Why RISC 140

Effect of VLSI 141

4.4 RISC Design versus CISC Design 145

4.5 Case Studies 145

4.5.1 Case Study I: Motorola 88110 Microprocessor 146

4.5.2 Case Study II: Intel Pentium Microprocessor 158

4.5.3 Case Study III: Alpha AXP Microprocessor 164

4.5.4 Case Study IV: PowerPC Microprocessor 172

4.5.5 Summary of the Case Studies 180

References 181

Problems 183

CHAPTER 5 INTERCONNECTION NETWORKS 184

5.1 Introduction 184

5.2 Network Topology 185

5.2.1 Static Networks 185

Shared Bus 185
Linear Array 186
Ring 186

Binary Tree   *186*
Fat Tree   *187*
Shuffle-Exchange   *188*
Two-Dimensional Mesh   *190*
n-Cube or Hypercube   *198*
n-Dimensional Mesh   *202*
k-Ary n-Cube   *204*
Routing in n-Dimensional Meshes and k-Ary n-Cubes   *204*
    Network Latency   *207*

5.2.2 Dynamic Networks   209

Nonblocking Networks   *214*
Rearrangeable Networks   *216*
    Construction of Rearrangeable Networks   *216*
Blocking Networks   *218*
    Multistage Cube Network   *219*
    Omega Network   *224*

5.3 Interconnection Design Decisions   226

Operation Mode   *226*
Switching Methodology   *226*
Network Topology   *226*
Control Strategy and Functional Characteristics of the Switch   *227*

References   228

Problems   229

CHAPTER 6   MULTIPROCESSORS AND MULTICOMPUTERS   237

6.1 Introduction   237

6.2 Multiprocessors   239

6.2.1 Common Interconnection Networks   240

Shared Bus   *240*
Multiple Bus   *242*
Crossbar Switch   *242*
Ring   *245*

6.2.2 Cache Coherence Schemes   246

Hardware-Based Schemes   248
  Snoopy Cache Protocol   248
    Write-Invalidate Snoopy Cache Protocol   248
    Write-Update Snoopy Cache Protocol   251
  Directory Protocols   252
    Centralized Directory Protocols   252
    Distributed Directory Protocols   254
  Software-based Schemes   257

6.3 Multicomputers   257

6.3.1 Common Interconnection Networks   258

K-Ary n-Cubes and n-Dimensional Meshes   258
n-Cube Network (Hypercube)   258
n-Dimensional Mesh Network   259
Crossbar Network   260
Fat-tree Network   261

6.4 Multiprocessors versus Multicomputers   263

6.5 Multi-Multiprocessors   263

References   267

Problems   269

CHAPTER 7 PARALLEL PROGRAMMING AND PARALLEL ALGORITHMS   272

7.1 Introduction   272

7.2 Programming Models   273

7.2.1 Parallel Programming on Multiprocessors   273

Process Creation   274
Synchronization   274
  Lock and Unlock   275
  Wait and Signal (or Increment and Decrement)   279
  Fetch&Add   280
  Barrier   281
  Deadlock   283

7.2.2 Parallel Programming on Multicomputers   284

7.3 Parallel Computation   285

7.3.1 Partitioning   285

7.3.2 Assignment or Scheduling   287

7.4 Algorithm Structures   288

7.4.1 Synchronous Structure   288

7.4.2 Asynchronous Structure   290

7.4.3 Pipeline Structure   292

7.5 Data Parallel Algorithms   294

Elementwise Operations   295
Broadcasting   295
Reduction   297
Parallel Prefix   297
Permutation   298

7.6 Analyzing Parallel Algorithms   300

7.6.1 Speedup   300

Cost   302

7.6.2 Factors Affecting Speedup   303

Algorithm Penalty   303
Concurrency   303
Granularity   303

7.7 Examples   304

7.7.1 Asynchronous Algorithms for Multiprocessors   304

Matrix Multiplication   304
Quicksort   305
Gaussian Elimination   306

7.7.2 Synchronous Algorithms for Multicomputers   309

Matrix Multiplication   309

References   312

Problems   313

CHAPTER 8   DATA FLOW AND SYSTOLIC ARRAY ARCHITECTURES   318

8.1 Introduction   318
8.2 Data Flow Architecture   318
8.2.1 Basic Structure of a Data Flow Computer   322
8.3 Systolic Arrays   324
8.3.1 Basic Terminology and Proposed Arrays of Processors   326

Hexagonal Array   *327*
Pipelined Array   *329*
Semibroadcast Array   *329*
Wavefront Array   *330*
Broadcast Array   *331*

8.3.2 Mapping Algorithm to Systolic Architecture   332

Steps of the Mapping Procedure   *334*

References   339
Problems   340

CHAPTER 9   FUTURE HORIZONS FOR ARCHITECTURE   341

9.1 Introduction   341
9.2 Neural Networks   342
9.2.1 Fundamentals of Neurophysiology   343

Information-Processing in the Nervous System   *345*

9.2.2 Artificial Neural Networks   346

Taxonomy of ANN Models   *347*
Supervised Learning   *349*
    Reinforcement Learning   350
    Unsupervised Learning   351
    Adaptive Linear Neurons   352
    Training an Adaline Network   354

Madaline Networks   *355*
Classical Perceptron   *356*
    Training Multilayer Perceptrons   357
    Back-propagation Training Rule   358
        XOR Example   360
        Comments on Back-propagation Algorithm   363
Hopfield Network   *364*
    Example of a Hopfield Network Application   366

9.2.3 Implementation of ANNs   370

9.3 Multiple-Valued Logic   371

9.4 Fuzzy Logic   374

9.4.1 Fuzzy Sets   376

Fuzzy Relation   *379*

9.4.2 Linguistic Variables and Fuzzy Rules   380

9.4.3 Control System   381

9.4.4 Architecture of a Fuzzy Logic Accelerator   389

References   391

Problems   394

APPENDIX A   BASIC COMPONENTS OF VLSI DESIGN   401

A.1 Introduction   401

A.2 Basic VLSI Components and Fabrication Techniques   403

The MOS Transistor   *403*
The Inverter   *405*

A.3 Layout-level Description   406

References   412

Problems   412

Contents   xvii

APPENDIX B COMBINATIONAL AND SEQUENTIAL CIRCUITS 413

B.1 Combinational Circuits 413

Multiplexer and Demultiplexer 413
Decoder and Encoder 416
Programmable Logic Array 419

B.2 Sequential Circuits 421

Design of a Sequential Circuit by Using PLA 426

References 429

Problems 430

APPENDIX C HARDWARE DESCRIPTION LANGUAGE: VHDL 432

C.1 Introduction 432

C.2 VHDL Views 435

C.3 Design Entity 440

C.4 Declaration of Items within a Design Entity 443

C.4.1 Types 443
C.4.2 Objects 445
C.4.3 Component 446
C.4.4 Attributes 447

C.5 Expressions 447

C.5.1 Logical Operators 447
C.5.2 Relational Operators 448
C.5.3 Arithmetic Operators 448

C.6 Sequential Statements 449

C.6.1 Assignment Statements 449

- C.6.2 Wait Statements 451
- C.6.3 If Statements 453
- C.6.4 Case Statements 454
- C.6.5 Loop Statement 454

C.7 Concurrent Statements 455
- C.7.1 Process Statements 456
- C.7.2 Block Statements 458
- C.7.3 Concurrent Signal Assignment 460
- C.7.4 Conditional Signal Assignment 460
- C.7.5 Selected Signal Assignment 460

References 461

Problems 461

Index 463

Preface

"For in and out, above, about, below,
'Tis nothing but a Magic Shadow-show,
Play'd in a Box whose Candle is the Sun,
Round which we Phantom Figures come and go."
                                    Omar Khayyam

Computer architecture is changing rapidly and has advanced a great deal in a very short time. Progress in increasing the number of transistors on a single chip continues to augment the computational power of computer systems. Today, a single chip performs operations 100,000 times faster than a computer that would have been as large as a movie theater forty years ago. As a result of these improvements, it has become increasingly economical to construct large parallel computers using small system processors. Today, parallel computers are found in many universities and industries. For these reasons we have entered a period in which there is an unprecedented need for books on the architecture and utilization of modern computers.

This book is based on many senior and graduate level courses in computer architecture that I have taught at Southern Illinois University at Carbondale. Its primary objective is to provide a foundation for understanding and evaluating the design principles incorporated in modern computers. A secondary objective is to present basic techniques for designing parallel systems and parallel algorithms. With this two-fold approach, the text organizes and links a wide spectrum of related topics in both a systematic and reader-friendly manner. The book emphasizes "the why of things" as its organizing principle. As such, each section begins with the reasons for using a technique (or mechanism) for doing a specific task and is followed with a detailed description of the steps of that method. The book explains each technique in a simple manner by providing numerical examples and illustrations. Sometimes segments of codes (written in pseudo C or pseudo VHDL) are used to clarify the description of the steps of different methods. However, these codes stress more on concepts rather than syntax of the language; they are not intended to provide executable codes.

This book is designed to be used as a textbook for seniors and/or graduate students in computer science and electrical engineering. It is intended for use in a course (or a sequence of two courses with some supplemental materials) on computer architecture. Because the book is self contained, it could also serve as a graduate level articulation course in computer architecture—that is, as a text for students at the graduate level (CS or non-CS majors) with no prior background in computer organization. Furthermore, it could also be used as a survey text by computer scientists, computer designers, application engineers, and computer professionals in their respective lines of work. The ideal prerequisites for this book would be at least one undergraduate course in digital logic design and an additional course in programming with a high level language (preferably C language).

The coverage in this book can be divided into three sections. The first part (chapters 1 to 4) provides a foundation for understanding and evaluating the design principles incorporated in a single processor. The second part (chapters 5 to 9) presents basic techniques for designing parallel systems and parallel algorithms. It also examines systems based on artificial neural networks and fuzzy set theory. The last part (appendices A to C) provides background materials on a variety of topics, including MOS transistors, VLSI layout design, combinational circuits and sequential circuits. It also describes VHDL—at present the most important leading-edge hardware description language.

Chapter 1 provides a brief history of the development of computer architecture. It then classifies a wide range of modern machines and introduces the basic concepts used in measuring the performance and quality of these architectures. Chapter 2 describes the main elements of a von Neumann machine, including design of the control unit, instruction set, arithmetic logic unit, and memory unit. Students with some background in computer architecture can skip over this chapter or use it for a cursory review. Chapter 3 details the design of instruction and arithmetic pipelines. Chapter 4 discusses the properties of RISC and CISC architectures. In addition, it includes case studies that focus on the architecture of several microprocessors, such as Motorola 88110, Intel Pentium, Alpha AXP, and PowerPC. The explanation of these microprocessors can be skipped without loss of continuity.

Chapter 5, which is independent of the previous chapters, deals with several aspects of the interconnection networks used in modern (and theoretical) computers. It classifies different types of networks and describes the property of each network. Chapter 6 details the architectures of multiprocessors, multicomputers, and multi-multiprocessors. Chapter 7 discusses the issues involved in parallel programming and development of parallel algorithms for multiprocessors and multicomputers. Chapter 8 describes the structure of two parallel architectures: data flow machines and systolic arrays. Finally, Chapter 9 discusses two constituents of soft computing currently offering the greatest potential for future architecture of machines with specialized applications. They are artificial neural networks and fuzzy set theory. Part or all of chapters 7, 8, and 9 can be skipped, without loss of continuity.

Finally, I hope this book is useful to readers. I would like to hear from you about any mistakes or misstatements I need to correct or any improvements I might make. Please send your comments to:

mehdi@cs.siu.edu.

Mehdi R. Zargham

Acknowledgments

The author is grateful to many individuals for their guidance and valuable comments during the long process of developing this book. In particular, I wish to thank Mohammad Ashtijou, Jiang-Hsing Chu, Morteza Daneshdoost, Kenneth J. Danhof, Bidyut Gupta, Andy Haas, Lydia Hazel, Wen-Chi Hou, Dimitrios Kagaris, Lional M. Ni, David Rokh, Mohammad R. Sayeh, Spyros Tragoudas, Yaakov L. Varol, Lofti A. Zadeh, Bahman Zargham, and anonymous referees for their valuable and helpful suggestions. I would also like to thank many of my graduate students for their comments, including Mehmet A. Cer, Tim DeClue, Leishi Hu, Vinay Mogali, Daniel Nikovski, and Jing Zhang. I am grateful to everyone at Prentice-Hall and production staff—especially to my editors Alan Apt, Tom McElwee, and Ralph Pescatore for their efforts in the production of this book. I would like to express gratitude to my dear wife and parents for their unlimited patience, support, and encouragement throughout the years.

1

Classification of Designs

1.1 INTRODUCTION

To fulfill their purpose, most buildings must be divided into rooms of various proportions that are connected by halls, doors, and stairs. The organization and proportions are the duty of the architect. But the architecture of a building is more than engineering: it must also express a fundamental desire for beauty, ideals, and aspirations. This is analogous to the architectural design of computers.

Computer architecture is concerned with the selection of basic building blocks (such as processor, memory, and input/output subsystems) and the way that these blocks interact with each other. A computer architect selects and interconnects the blocks based on making trade-offs among a set of criteria, such as visible characteristics, cost, speed, and reliability. The architecture of a computer should specify what functions the computer performs and even the speed and data items with which those functions are accomplished.

Computer architecture is changing rapidly and has advanced a great deal in a very short time. As a result, computers are becoming more powerful and more flexible each year. Today, a single chip performs operations 100,000 times faster than a computer that would have been as large as a movie theater 40 years ago.

Significant historical computers. John Atanasoff and his assistant, Clifford Berry, are credited with building the first electronic computer at Iowa State University in 1939, which they named the ABC (Atanasoff–Berry Computer). It was not large compared to the computers that would soon follow, and it was built solely for the purpose of solving tedious physics equations, not for general purposes. Today, it would be called a calculator, rather than a computer. Still, its design was based on binary arithmetic, and its memory consisted of capacitors that were periodically refreshed, much like modern dynamic random access memory (RAM).

A second important development occurred during World War II when John Mauchly from University of Pennsylvania, who knew that the U.S. government was interested in building a computer for military purposes, received a grant from the U.S. Army for just that reason. With the help of J. Presper Eckert, he built the ENIAC (Electronic Numerical Integrator and Calculator). Mauchly and Eckert were unable to complete the ENIAC until 1946, a year after the war was over. One reason may have been its size and complexity. The ENIAC contained over 18,000 vacuum tubes and weighed 30 tons. It was able to perform around 5000 additions per second. Although the ENIAC is important from a historical perspective, it was hugely inefficient because each instruction had to be programmed manually by humans working outside the machine.

In 1949, the world's first stored-program computer, called the Electronic Delay Storage Automatic Calculator (EDSAC), was built by Maurice Wilkes of England's Cambridge University. This computer used about 3000 vacuum tubes and was able to perform around 700 additions per second. The EDSAC was based on the discovery of the mathematician John von Neumann. Von Neumann discovered the concept of storing program instructions in memory along with the data on which those instructions operate. The design of EDSAC was a vast improvement over the prior machines (such as the ENIAC) that required rewiring to be reprogrammed.

In 1951, the Remington-Rand Corporation built the first commercialized derivative of the EDSAC, called the UNIVersal Automatic Computer (UNIVAC I). The UNIVAC I was sold to the U.S. Bureau of the Census, where it was used 24 hours a day, seven days a week. Similar to EDSAC, this machine was also made of vacuum tubes; however, it was able to perform nearly 4000 additions per second.

Computer generations. The UNIVAC I and the machines that were built within the period of late 1940s and mid 1950s are often referred to as the first generation of computers. In 1955, near the end of the first-generation period, the IBM 704 was produced and became a commercial success. The IBM 704 used parallel binary arithmetic circuits and a floating-point unit to significantly boost arithmetic speed-up over traditional arithmetic logic units (ALU). Although the IBM 704 had advanced arithmetic operations, the input/output (I/O) operations were still slow, thus bottlenecking the ALU from computing independently of slow I/O operations. To reduce the bottleneck, I/O processors (later called *channels*) were introduced in subsequent models of the IBM 704 and its successor, the IBM 709. I/O processors were used to process reading and printing of data from and to the slow I/O devices. An I/O processor could print blocks of data from main memory while the ALU could continue working. Because the printing occurred while the ALU continued to work, this process became known as a *spool* (simultaneous print operation on line).

From 1958 to 1964, the second generation of computers was developed based on transistor technology. The transistor, which was invented in 1947, was a breakthrough that enabled the replacement of vacuum tubes. A transistor could perform most of the functions of a vacuum tube, but was much smaller in size, much faster, and much more energy efficient. As a result, a second generation of computers emerged. During this phase, IBM reengineered its 709 to use transistor technology and named it the IBM 7090. The 7090 was able to calculate close to 500,000 additions per second. It was very successful and IBM sold about 400 units.

In 1964, the third generation of computers was born. This new generation was based on *integrated circuit* (IC) technology, which was invented in 1957. An IC device is a tiny chip of silicon that hosts many transistors and other circuit components. The silicon chip is encased in a sturdy ceramic (or other nonconductive) material. Small metallic legs that extrude from the IC plug into the computer's circuit board, connecting the encased chip to the computer. Through the last three decades, refinements of this device have made it possible to construct faster and more flexible computers. Processing speed has increased by an order of magnitude each year. In fact, the ways in which computers are structured, the procedures used to design them, the trade-offs between hardware and software, and the design of computational algorithms have all been affected by the advent and development of integrated circuits and will continue to be greatly affected by the coming changes in this technology.

An IC may be classified according to the number of transistors or gates imprinted on its silicon chip. Gates are simple switching circuits that, when combined, form the more complex logic circuits that allow the computer to perform the complicated tasks now expected. Two basic gates in common usage, for example, are the NAND and NOR gates. These gates have a simple design and may be constructed from relatively few transistors. Based on the circuit complexity, ICs are categorized into four classes: SSI, MSI, LSI, and VLSI. SSI (small-scale integration) chips contain 1 to 10 gates; MSI (medium-scale integration) chips contain 10 to 100 gates; LSI (large-scale integration) chips contain 100 to 100,000 gates; and VLSI (very large-scale integration) chips include all ICs with more than 100,000 gates. The LSI and VLSI technologies have moved computers from the third to new generations. The computers that were developed within 1972 to 1990 are referred to as the fourth generation of computers; from 1991 to present is referred to as fifth generation.

Today, a VLSI chip can contain millions of transistors. They are expected to contain more than 100 million transistors by the year 2000. One main factor contributing to this increase in integrated circuits is the effort that has been invested in the development of computer-aided design (CAD) systems for IC design. CAD systems are able to simplify the design process by hiding the low-level circuit theory and physical details of the device, thereby allowing the designer to concentrate on functionality and ways of optimizing the design.

The progress in increasing the number of transistors on a single chip continues to augment the computational power of computer systems, in particular that of the small systems (personal computers and workstations). Today, as a result of improvements in these small systems, it is becoming more economical to construct large systems by utilizing small systems processors. This allows some large systems companies to use the high-performance, inexpensive processors already on the market so that they do not have to spend thousands or millions of dollars for developing traditional large systems processor units. (The term *performance* refers to the effective speed and the reliability of a device.) The large systems firms are now placing more emphasis on developing systems with multiple processors for certain applications or general purposes. When a computer has multiple processors, they may operate simultaneously, parallel to each other. Functioning this way, the processors may work independently on different tasks or process different parts of the same task. Such a computer is referred to as a *parallel computer* or *parallel machine*.

There are many reasons for this trend toward parallel machines, the most common of which is to increase overall computer power. Although the advancement of semiconductor and VLSI technology has substantially improved the performance of single-processor machines, these machines are still not fast enough to perform certain applications within a reasonable time period, such as biomedical analysis, aircraft testing, real-time pattern recognition, real-time speech recognition, and systems of partial differential equations. Another reason for the trend is the physical limitations in VLSI technology and the fact that basic physical laws limit the maximum speed of the processor's clock, which governs how quickly instructions can be executed. One gigahertz (one clock cycle every billionth of a second) may be an absolute limit that can be obtained for clock speed.

In addition to faster speed, some parallel computers provide more reliable systems than do single-processor machines. If a single processor on the parallel system fails, the system can still operate (at a slightly diminished capacity), whereas if the processor on a uniprocessor system fails, the whole system fails. Parallel computers have built-in redundancy, meaning that many processors may be capable of performing the same task. Computers with a high degree of redundancy are more reliable and robust and are said to be fail-safe machines. Such machines are used in situations where failure would be catastrophic. Computers that control shuttle launches or monitor nuclear power production are good examples.

The preceding advantages of parallel computers have led many companies to design such systems. Today, numerous parallel computers are commercially available, and there will be many more in the near future. The following section represents a classification of such machines.

1.2 TAXONOMIES OF COMPUTER ARCHITECTURES

One of the most well known taxonomies of computer architectures is called Flynn's taxonomy. Michael Flynn [FLY 72] classifies architectures into four categories based on the presence of single or multiple streams of instructions and data. (An instruction stream is a set of sequential instructions to be executed by a single processor, and the data stream is the sequential flow of data required by the instruction stream.) Flynn's four categories are as follows;

1. **SISD** (single instruction stream, single data stream). This is the von Neumann concept of serial computer design in which only one instruction is executed at any time. Often, SISD is referred to as a serial scalar computer. All SISD machines utilize a single register, called the *program counter*, that enforces serial execution of instructions. As each instruction is fetched from memory, the program counter is updated to contain the address of the next instruction to be

fetched and executed in serial order. Few, if any, pure SISD computers are currently manufactured for commercial purposes. Even personal computers today utilize small degrees of parallelism to achieve greater efficiency. In most situations, they are able to execute two or more instructions simultaneously.

2. **MISD** (multiple instruction stream, single data stream). This implies that several instructions are operating on a single piece of data. There are two ways to interpret the organization of MISD-type machines. One way is to consider a class of machines that would require that distinct processing units receive distinct instructions operating on the same data. This class of machines has been challenged by many computer architects as impractical (or impossible), and at present there are no working examples of this type. Another way is to consider a class of machines in which the data flows through a series of processing units. Highly pipelined architectures, such as systolic arrays and vector processors, are often classified under this machine type. Pipeline architectures perform vector processing through a series of stages, each of which performs a particular function and produces an intermediate result. The reason that such architectures are labeled as MISD systems is that elements of a vector may be considered to belong to the same piece of data, and all pipeline stages represent multiple instructions that are being applied to that vector.

3. **SIMD** (single instruction stream, multiple data stream). This implies that a single instruction is applied to different data simultaneously. In machines of this type, many separate processing units are invoked by a single control unit. Like MISD, SIMD machines can support vector processing. This is accomplished by assigning vector elements to individual processing units for concurrent computation. Consider the payroll calculation (hourly wage rate * hours worked) for 1000 workers. On an SISD machine, this task would require 1000 sequential loop iterations. On an SIMD machine, this calculation could be performed in parallel, simultaneously, on 1000 different data streams (each representing one worker).

4. **MIMD** (multiple instruction stream, multiple data stream). This includes machines with several processing units in which multiple instructions can be applied to different data simultaneously. MIMD machines are the most complex, but they also hold the greatest promise for efficiency gains accomplished through concurrent processing. Here concurrency implies that not only are multiple processors operating simultaneously, but multiple programs (processes) are being executed in the same time frame, concurrent to each other, as well.

Flynn's classification can be described by an analogy from the manufacture of automobiles. SISD is analogous to the manufacture of an automobile by just one person doing all the various tasks, one at a time. MISD can be compared to an assembly line where each worker performs one specialized task or set of specialized tasks on the results of the previous worker's accomplishment. Workers perform the same specialized task for each result given to them by the previous worker, similar to an automobile moving down an assembly line. SIMD is comparable to several workers performing the same tasks concurrently. After all workers are finished, another task is given to the

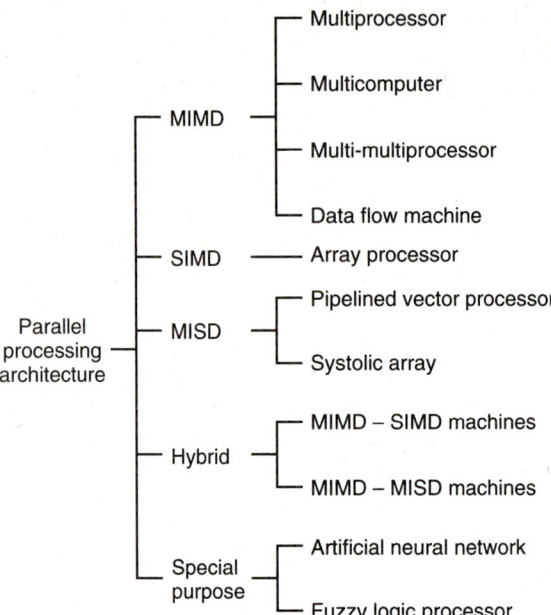

Figure 1.1 Classification of parallel processing architectures.

workers. Each worker constructs an automobile by himself doing the same task at the same time. Instructions for the next task are given to each worker at the same time and from the same source. MIMD is like SIMD except that the workers do not perform the same task concurrently; each constructs an automobile independently following his own set of instructions.

Flynn's classification has proved to be a good method for the classification of computer architectures for almost three decades. This is evident by its widespread use by computer architects. However, advancements in computer technologies have created architectures that cannot be clearly defined by Flynn's taxonomy. For example, it does not adequately classify vector processors (SIMD and MISD) and hybrid architectures. To overcome this problem, several taxonomies have been proposed [DAS 90, HOC 87, SKI 88, BEL 92]. Most of these proposed taxonomies preserve the SIMD and MIMD features of Flynn's classification. These two features provide useful shorthand for characterizing many architectures.

Figure 1.1 shows a taxonomy that represents some of the features of the proposed taxonomies. This taxonomy is intended to classify most of the recent architectures, but is not intended to represent a complete characterization of all parallel architectures.

As shown in Figure 1.1, the MIMD class of computers is further divided into four types of parallel machines: multiprocessors, multicomputers, multi-multiprocessors, and data flow machines. For the SIMD class, it should be noted that there is only one type, called array processors. The MISD class of machines is divided into two types of architectures: pipelined vector processors and systolic arrays. The remaining parallel architectures are grouped under two classes: hybrid machines and special-purpose processors. Each of these architectures is explained next.

Sec. 1.2 Taxonomies of Computer Architectures

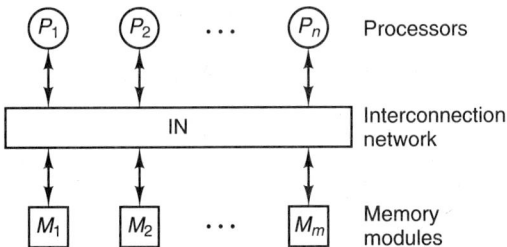

Figure 1.2 Block diagram of a multiprocessor.

The *multiprocessor* can be viewed as a parallel computer consisting of several interconnected processors that can share a memory system. The processors can be set up so that each is running a different part of a program or so that they are all running different programs simultaneously. A block diagram of this architecture is shown in Figure 1.2. As shown, a multiprocessor generally consists of n processors and m memory modules (for some $n > 1$ and $m > 0$). The processors are denoted as $P_1, P_2, \ldots,$ and P_n, and the memory modules as $M_1, M_2, \ldots,$ and M_m. The interconnection network (IN) connects each processor to some subset of the memory modules. A transfer instruction causes data to be moved from each processor to the memory to which it is connected. To pass data between two processors, a programmed sequence of data transfers, which moves the data through intermediary memories and processors, must be executed.

In contrast to the multiprocessor, the *multicomputer* can be viewed as a parallel computer in which each processor has its own local memory. In multicomputers the main memory is privately distributed among the processors. This means that a processor only has direct access to its local memory and cannot address the local memories of other processors. This local, private addressability is an important characteristic that distinguishes multicomputers from multiprocessors. A block diagram of this architecture is shown in Figure 1.3. In this figure, there are n processing nodes (PNs), and each PN consists of a processor and a local memory. The interconnection network connects each PN to some subset of the other PNs. A transfer instruction causes data to be moved from each PN to one of the PNs to which it is connected. To move data between two PNs that cannot be directly connected by the interconnection network, the data must be passed through intermediary PNs by executing a sequence of data transfers.

The *multi-multiprocessor* combines the desired features of multiprocessors and multicomputers. It can be viewed as a multicomputer in which each processing node is a multiprocessor.

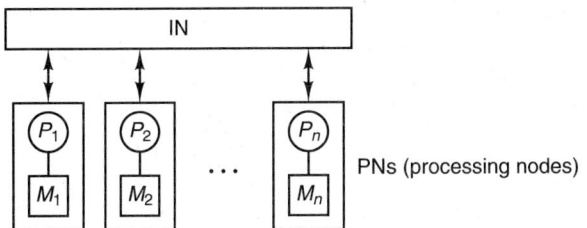

Figure 1.3 Block diagram of a multicomputer.

In the *data flow* architecture an instruction is ready for execution when data for its operands have been made available. Data availability is achieved by channeling results from previously executed instructions into the operands of waiting instructions. This channeling forms a flow of data, triggering instructions to be executed. Thus instruction execution avoids the controlled program counter type of flow found in the von Neumann machine.

Data flow instructions are purely self-contained; that is, they do not address variables in a global shared memory. Rather, they carry the values of variables with themselves. In a data flow machine, the execution of an instruction does not affect other instructions ready for execution. In this way, several ready instructions may be executed simultaneously, thus leading to the possibility of a highly concurrent computation.

Figure 1.4 is a block diagram of a data flow machine. Instructions, together with their operands, are kept in the instruction and data memory (I&D). Whenever an instruction is ready for execution, it is sent to one of the processing elements (PEs) through the arbitration network. Each PE is a simple processor with limited local storage. The PE, upon receiving an instruction, computes the required operation and sends the result through the distribution network to the destination in the memory.

Figure 1.5 represents the generic structure of an array processor. An *array processor* consists of a set of processing nodes (PNs) and a scalar processor that are operating under a centralized control unit. The control unit fetches and decodes instructions from the main memory and then sends them either to the scalar processor or the processing nodes, depending on their type. If a fetched instruction is a scalar instruction, it is sent to the scalar processor; otherwise, it is broadcast to all the PNs. All the PNs execute the same instruction simultaneously on different data stored in their local

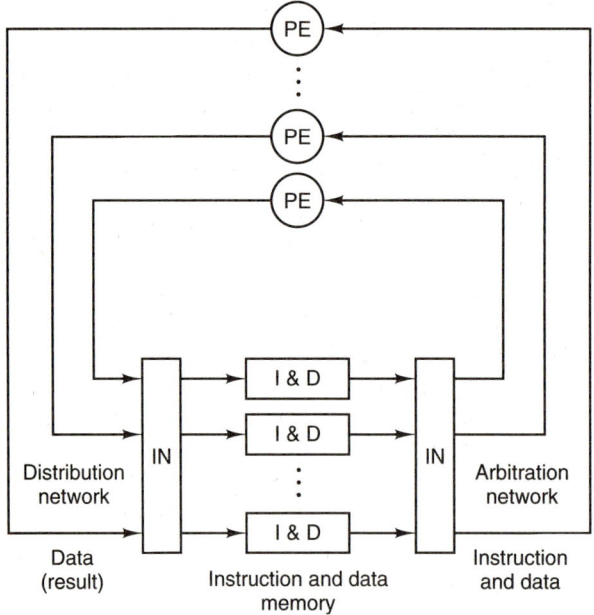

Figure 1.4. Block diagram of a data flow machine.

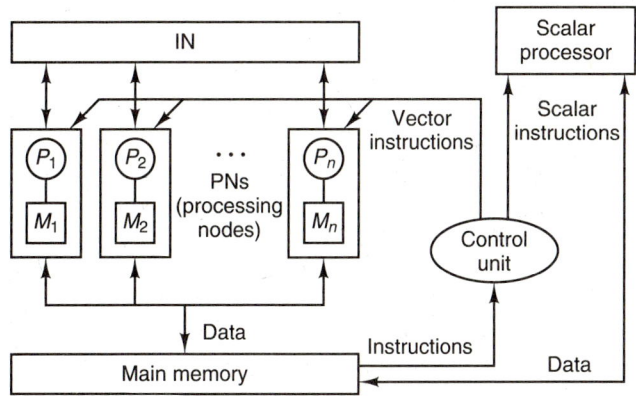

Figure 1.5. Block diagram of an array processor.

memories. Therefore, an array processor requires just one program to control all the PNs in the system, making it unnecessary to duplicate program codes at each PN. For example, an array processor can be defined in terms of a grid in which each intersection represents a PN and the lines between intersections are communication paths. Each PN in the array can send (receive) data to (from) the four surrounding PNs. A processor, known as a control unit, handles the decisions on what operation the PNs are to do during each processing cycle, as well as data transfer between the PNs.

The idea behind an array processor is to exploit parallelism in a given problem's data set rather than to parallelize the problem's sequence of instruction execution. Parallel computation is realized by assigning each processor to a data partition. If the data set is a vector, then a partition would simply be a vector element. Array processors increase performance by operating on all data partitions simultaneously. They are able to perform arithmetic or logical operations on vectors. For this reason, they are also referred to as vector processors.

A *pipelined vector processor* is able to process vector operands (streams of continuous data) effectively. This is the primary difference between an array or vector processor and a pipelined vector processor. Array processors are instruction driven, while pipelined vector processors are driven by streams of continuous data. Figure 1.6 repre-

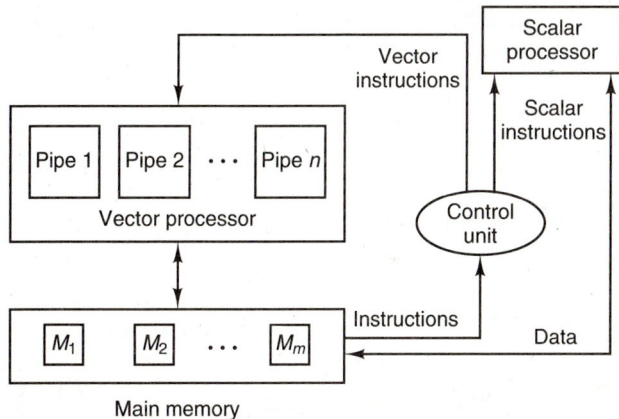

Figure 1.6 Block diagram of a pipelined vector processor.

sents the basic structure of a pipelined vector processor. There are two main processors: a scalar processor and a vector processor. Both rely on a separate control unit to provide instructions to execute. The vector processor handles execution of vector instructions by using pipelines, and the scalar processor deals with the execution of scalar instructions. The control unit fetches and decodes instructions from the main memory and then sends them either to a scalar processor or vector processor, depending on their type.

Pipelined vector processors make use of several memory modules to supply the pipelines with a continuous stream of data. Often a vectorizing compiler is used to arrange the data into a stream that can then be used by the hardware.

Figure 1.7 represents a generic structure of a systolic array. In a *systolic array* there are a large number of identical processing elements (PEs). Each PE has limited local storage, and in order not to restrict the number of PEs placed in an array, each PE is only allowed to be connected to neighboring PEs through interconnection networks. Thus all PEs are arranged in a well-organized pipelined structure, such as a linear or two-dimensional array. In a systolic array the data items and/or partial results flow through the PEs during execution time consisting of several processing cycles. At each processing cycle, some PEs perform the same relatively simple operation (like multiplication and addition) on their data items and send these items and/or partial results to other neighboring PEs.

Hybrid architectures incorporate features of different architectures to provide better performance for parallel computations. In general, there are two types of parallelism for performing parallel computations: control parallelism and data parallelism. In control parallelism, two or more operations are performed simultaneously on different processors. In data parallelism, the same operation is performed on many data partitions by many processors simultaneously. MIMD machines are ideal for the implementation of control parallelism. They are suited for problems that require different operations to be performed on separate data simultaneously. In an MIMD computer, each processor independently executes its own sequence of instructions. On the other hand, SIMD machines are ideal for implementation of data parallelism. They are suited for problems in which the same operation can be performed on different portions of the data simultaneously. MISD machines are also suited for data parallelism. They support vector processing through pipeline design.

In practice, the greatest rewards have come from data parallelism. This is because data parallelism exploits parallelism in proportion to the quantity of data involved in the computation. However, sometimes it is impossible to exploit fully the data parallelism inherent in many application programs, and so it becomes necessary

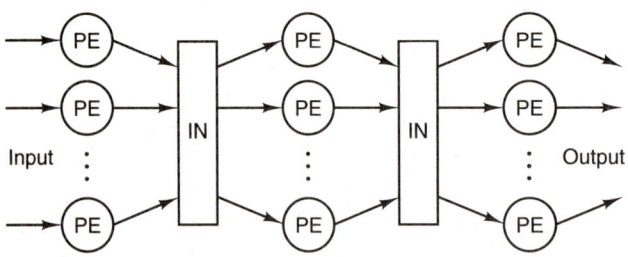

Figure 1.7 Block diagram of a systolic array.

to use both control and data parallelism. For example, some application programs may perform best when divided into subparts that each make use of data parallelism, and all subparts together make use of control parallelism in the form of a pipeline. One group of processors gathers data and performs some preliminary computations. The processors then pass their result to a second group of processors that do more intense computations on the result. The second group then passes their result to a third group of processors, where the final result is obtained. Thus a parallel computer that incorporates features of both MIMD and SIMD (or MISD) architectures is able to solve a broad range of problems effectively.

An example of a *special-purpose device* is an artificial neural network (ANN). Artificial neural networks consist of a large number of processing elements operating in parallel. They are promising architectures for solving some of the problems that the von Neumann computer performs poorly, such as emulating natural information and recognizing patterns. These problems require enormous amounts of processing to achieve humanlike performance. ANNs utilize one technique for obtaining the processing power required: using large numbers of processing elements operating in parallel. They are capable of learning, adaptive to changing environments, and able to cope with serious disruptions.

Figure 1.8 represents a generic structure of an artificial neural network. Each PE mimics some of the characteristics of the biological neuron. It has a set of inputs and one or more outputs. A numerical weight is assigned to each input. This weight is analogous to the synaptic strength of a biological neuron. All the inputs of a PE are multiplied by their weights and are then summed to determine the activation level of the neuron. Once the activation level is determined, a function, referred to as *activation function*, is applied to produce the output signal. The combined outputs from a preceding layer become the inputs for the next layer, where they are again summed and evaluated. This process is repeated until the network has been traversed and some decision is reached.

Unlike von Neumann design, in which the primary element of computation is the processor, in ANNs it is the connectivity between the PEs. For a given problem, we would like to determine the correct values for the weights in order that the network be able to perform necessary computation. Often, finding the proper values for weights is done by iterative adjustment of the weights in a manner to improve network performance. The rule of adjustment of the weights is referred to as a *learning rule,* and the whole process of obtaining the proper weights is called *learning.*

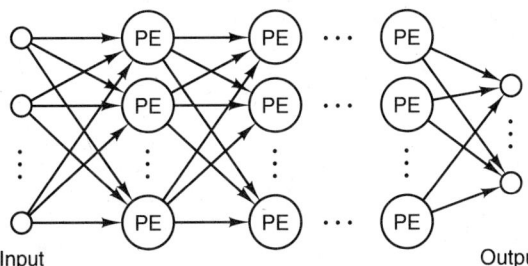

Figure 1.8 Block diagram of an artificial neural network.

Another example of a special-purpose device results from the design of a processor based on fuzzy logic. Fuzzy logic is concerned with formal principles of *approximate reasoning,* while classical two-valued logic (true or false) is concerned with *formal principles of reasoning.* Fuzzy logic attempts to deal effectively with the complexity of human cognitive processes, and it overcomes some of the inconveniences associated with classical two-valued logic, which tends not to reflect true human cognitive processes. It is making its way through many applications, ranging from home appliances to decision support systems. Although software implementation of fuzzy logic in itself provides good results for some applications, dedicated fuzzy processors, called fuzzy logic accelerators, are required for implementing high-performance applications.

1.3 PERFORMANCE AND QUALITY MEASUREMENTS

The performance of a computer refers to its effective speed and its hardware and software reliability. In general, it is unreasonable to expect that a single number could characterize performance. This is because the performance of a computer depends on the interactions of a variety of its components and the fact that different users are interested in different aspects of a computer's ability.

One measurement that is commonly used to represent the performance of a computer is MIPS (million instructions per second). MIPS represents the speed of a computer by indicating the number of "average instructions" that it can execute per second [SER 86]. To understand the meaning of average instruction, let's consider the inverse of the MIPS measure, that is, the execution time of an average instruction. The execution time of an average instruction can be calculated by using frequency and execution time for each instruction class. By tracing the execution of a large number of benchmark programs, it is possible to determine how often an instruction is likely to be used in a program. As an example, let's assume that Figure 1.9 represents the frequency of instructions (IF) that occurs in a program. Note that the execution time of the instructions of each class is represented in terms of cycles per instruction (CPI). The CPI denotes the number of clock cycles that a processor requires to execute a particular instruction. Different processors may require different numbers of clock cycles to execute the same type of instruction. Assuming that a clock cycle takes τ nanoseconds, the execution time of an instruction can be expressed as CPI $* \tau$ nanoseconds. Now, considering Figure 1.9, the execution time of an average instruction can be represented as

$$\sum_{\text{all } i} (IF_i * CPI_i * \tau), \quad \text{where } i \text{ is an instruction class.}$$

Thus

$$MIPS = \frac{1}{\sum (IF_i * CPI_i * \tau)} * 1000.$$

Instruction Class	Instruction Frequency % (IF)	Cycles per Instruction (CPI)	Weighted CPI (IF * CPI)
Load and store	30.4	1.5	0.456
Integer add and subtract	10.0	1	0.1
Integer multiply and divide	3.8	10	0.38
Floating-point add and subtract	9.5	7	0.665
Floating-point multiply and divide	6.5	15	0.975
Logical	3.0	1	0.03
Branch	20.0	1.5	0.3
Compare, shift system	16.8	2	0.336
		Cycles per average instruction =	3.242

Execution time of an average instruction
(for when $\tau = 10$) = 3.242 * 10 = 32.42 nanoseconds.

MIPS = (1/32.42) * 1000 = 30.845.

Figure 1.9. Example for calculating MIPS rate.

In this expression, a reasonable MIPS rating is obtained by finding the average execution time of each class of instructions and weighting that average by how often each class of instructions is used.

When a computer can perform more than one billion instructions per second, BIPS (billion instructions per second) is used as a performance measurement. BIPS can be defined in a similar way as MIPS.

Although the MIPS rating can give us a rough idea of how fast a computer can operate, it is not a good representative for computers that perform scientific and engineering computation, such as vector processors. For such computers it is important to measure the number of floating-point operations that they can execute per second. To indicate such a number, FLOPS (floating-point operations per second) notation is often used. Megaflops (MFLOPS) stands for millions of floating-point operations per second, and gigaflops(GFLOPS) stands for billions of floating-point operations per second.

MIPS and FLOPS figures are useful for comparing members of the same architectural family. They are not a good representative for comparing computers with different instruction sets and different clock cycles. This is because programs may be translated into different numbers of instructions on different computers.

Besides MIPS and FLOPS, other measurements are often used to obtain a better picture of the system. The most commonly used are *throughput, utilization, response time, memory bandwidth, memory access time,* and *memory size.*

Throughput of a processor is a measure that indicates the number of programs (tasks or requests) that the processor can execute per unit of time.

Utilization of a processor refers to the fraction of time the processor is busy executing programs. It is the ratio of busy time and total elapsed time over a given period.

Response time is the time interval between the time that a request is issued for service and the time that the service is completed. Sometimes response time is referred to as *turnaround time*.

Memory bandwidth indicates the number of memory words that can be accessed per unit time.

Memory access time is the average time that it takes the processor to access the memory, usually expressed in terms of nanoseconds (ns).

Memory size indicates the capacity of the memory, usually expressed in terms of megabytes (Mbytes). It is an indication of the volume of data that the memory can hold.

In addition to the preceding performance measurements, a number of quality factors also have influence over the success of a computer. Some of these factors are *generality, ease of use, expandability, compatibility, and reliability*.

Generality is a measure that determines the range of applications for an architecture. Some architectures are good for scientific purposes and some for business applications. The architecture is more marketable when it supports a variety of applications.

Ease of use is a measure of how easy it is for the system programmer to develop software (such as operating system and compiler) for the architecture.

Expandability is a measure of how easy it is to add to the capabilities of an architecture, such as processors, memory, and I/O devices.

Compatibility is a measure of how compatible the architecture is with previous computers of the same family.

Reliability is a measure that indicates the probability of faults or the mean time between errors.

These measures and properties are usually used to characterize the capability of computer systems. Every year, these measures and properties are enhanced with better hardware and software technology, innovative architectural features, and efficient resources management.

1.4 OUTLINE OF THE FOLLOWING CHAPTERS

Chapter 2 describes the typical implementation techniques used in von Neumann machines. The main elements of a data path, as well as the hardwired and microprogramming techniques for implementing control functions, are discussed. Next, a hierarchical memory system is presented. The architectures of a memory cell, interleaved memory, an associative memory, and a cache memory are given. Virtual memory is also discussed. Finally, interrupts and exception events are addressed.

Chapter 3 details the various types of pipelined processors in terms of their advantages and disadvantages based on such criteria as processor overhead and implementation costs. Instruction pipelining and arithmetic pipelining, along with methods for maximizing the utilization of a pipeline, are discussed.

Chapter 4 discusses the properties of RISC (reduced instruction set computer) and CISC (complex instruction set computer) architectures. In addition, the main elements of several microprocessors are explained.

Chapter 5 deals with several aspects of the interconnection networks used in modern (and theoretical) computers. Starting with basic definitions and terms relative to networks in general, the coverage proceeds to static networks, their different types and how they function. Next, several dynamic networks are analyzed. In this context, the properties of nonblocking, rearrangeable, and blocking networks are mentioned. Some elements of network designs are also explored to give the reader an understanding of their complexity.

Chapter 6 details the architectures of multiprocessors, multicomputers, and multi-multiprocessors. To present some of the most common interconnections used, the architectures of some state-of-the-art parallel computers are discussed and compared.

Chapter 7 discusses the issues involved in parallel programming and the development of parallel algorithms for multiprocessors and multicomputers. Various approaches to developing a parallel algorithm are explained. Algorithm structures, such as synchronous structure, asynchronous structure, and pipeline structure, are described. A few terms related to performance measurement of parallel algorithms are presented. Finally, examples of parallel algorithms illustrating different structures are given.

Chapter 8 describes the structure of two parallel architectures: data flow machines and systolic arrays. For each class of architectures, various design methodologies are represented. A general method is given for mapping an algorithm to a systolic array.

Chapter 9 examines the neuron, together with the dynamics of neural processing, and surveys some of the well-known proposed artificial neural networks. Also, it describes the basic features of the multiple-valued logic. Finally, it explains the use of fuzzy logic in control systems and discusses an architecture for this theory.

REFERENCES

[BEL 92] BELL, G., "Ultracomputers: A Teraflop before Its Time," *Commun. ACM*, 35(8); Aug 1992, p8 pp. 26–47.

[DAS 90] DASGUPTA, S., "A Hierarchical Taxonomic System for Computer Architectures," *Computer,* 23(3), 1990, pp. 64–74.

[FLY 72] FLYNN, M. J., "Some Computer Organizations and Their Effectiveness," *IEEE Trans. Computers,* 21(9), 1972, pp. 948–960.

[HOC 87] HOCKNEY, R. W., "Classification and Evaluation of Parallel Computer Systems," *Springer-Verlag Lecture Notes in Computer Science*, No. 295, 1987, pp. 13–25.

[SER 86] SERLIN, OMRI, "MIPS, Dhrystones, and Other Tales," *Datamation*, 32, June 1986, pp. 112–118.

[SKI 88] SKILLICORN, D. B., "A Taxonomy for Computer Architectures," *Computer* 21(11), 1988, pp. 46–57.

PROBLEMS

1.1. What characterizes the differences between the generations of computers described in this chapter?

1.2. Classify each of the following computing systems according to Flynn's taxonomy.
   a. A personal computer using the Intel Pentium processor.
   b. Your university's primary computer system.
   c. Your department's local area network.
   d. Your department's parallel machine(s).
   e. A computer that forecasts weather by dividing Earth into 10-square-mile divisions and simulates weather patterns.
   f. NASA launch control computer.

1.3. What justification can be made for the expansion or modification of Flynn's taxonomy?

1.4. Why do some computer scientists believe that a MISD computer is impossible?

1.5. What purpose does the program counter serve in the classic von Neumann machine?

1.6. Define the terms *parallelism* and *concurrency,* noting what makes them different.

1.7. Identify at least one design feature in each computer system design discussed in this chapter that sets the design apart from the others.

1.8. What advantage might be gained by giving multiple processors local memory, as shown in Figure 1.3?

1.9. How does a multiprocessor machine differ from a multicomputer machine?

1.10. What is parallelism in a data set and how can this be used to increase computer performance?

1.11. In what ways is a systolic array machine similar to a pipelined vector processor and an array processor?

1.12. Create an analogy from automobile manufacturing to represent a data flow machine. Would you anticipate problems with a data flow machine handling data structures?

1.13. Describe a data structure and the operations to be performed on the data structure that could take advantage of both control parallelism and data parallelism.

1.14. Write two types of applications in which artificial neural networks have been either successful or believed to be successful.

1.15. Write two types of applications in which fuzzy logic has been either successful or believed to be successful.

1.16. Let's assume that the following table represents the frequency of instructions that occur in a program. The CPI denotes the number of clock cycles that a processor requires to execute a particular instruction. What is the MIPS rating when a clock cycle takes τ nanoseconds? Show your work.

Instruction Class	Instruction Frequency % (IF)	Cycles per Instruction (CPI)
Load and store	28.5	2
Integer add and subtract	12.0	1
Integer multiply and divide	4.5	8
Floating-point add and subtract	8.5	7
Floating-point multiply and divide	7.5	12
Logical	5.0	1
Branch	18.0	1.5
Compare and shift system	16.0	2

2
Von Neumann Architecture

2.1 INTRODUCTION

Computer architecture has undergone incredible changes in the past 20 years, from the number of circuits that can be integrated onto silicon wafers to the degree of sophistication with which different algorithms can be mapped directly to a computer's hardware. One element has remained constant throughout the years, however, and that is the von Neumann concept of computer design.

The basic concept behind the von Neumann architecture is the ability to store program instructions in memory along with the data on which those instructions operate. Until von Neumann proposed this possibility, each computing machine was designed and built for a single predetermined purpose. All programming of the machine required the manual rewiring of circuits, a tedious and error-prone process. If mistakes were made, they were difficult to detect and hard to correct.

Von Neumann architecture is composed of three distinct components (or subsystems): a central processing unit (CPU), memory, and input/output (I/O) interfaces. Figure 2.1 represents one of several possible ways of interconnecting these components.

1. The CPU, which can be considered the heart of the computing system, includes three main components: the *control unit* (CU), one or more *arithmetic logic units* (ALUs), and various *registers*. The control unit determines the order in which instructions should be executed and controls the retrieval of the proper operands. It interprets the instructions of the machine. The execution of each instruction is

Sec. 2.1   Introduction

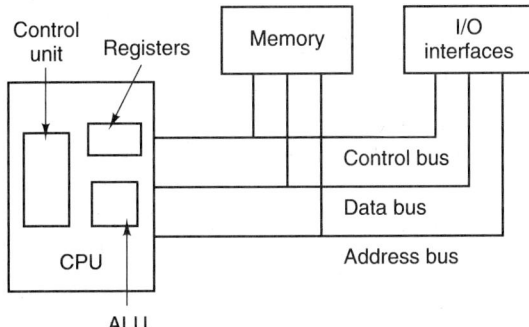

Figure 2.1 Basic computer components.

determined by a sequence of control signals produced by the control unit. In other words, the control unit governs the flow of information through the system by issuing control signals to different components. Each operation caused by a control signal is called a microoperation (MO). ALUs perform all mathematical and Boolean operations. The registers are temporary storage locations to quickly store and transfer the data and instructions being used. Because the registers are often on the same chip and directly connected to the CU, the registers have faster access time than memory. Therefore, using registers both as the source of operands and as the destination of results will improve the performance. A CPU that is implemented on a single chip is called a *microprocessor.*

2. The computer's *memory* is used to store program instructions and data. Two of the commonly used type of memories are *RAM* (random-access memory) and *ROM* (read-only memory). RAM stores the data and general-purpose programs that the machine executes. RAM is temporary; that is, its contents can be changed at any time and it is erased when power to the computer is turned off. ROM is permanent and is used to store the initial boot-up instructions of the machine.

3. The *I/O interfaces* allow the computer's memory to receive information and send data to output devices. Also, they allow the computer to communicate to the user and to secondary storage devices like disk and tape drives.

The preceding components are connected to each other through a collection of signal lines known as a *bus*. As shown in Figure 2.1, the main buses carrying information are the *control bus, data bus,* and *address bus.* Each bus contains several wires that allow for the parallel transmission of information between various hardware components. The address bus identifies either a memory location or an I/O device. The data bus, which is bidirectional, sends data to or from a component. The control bus consists of signals that permit the CPU to communicate with the memory and I/O devices.

The execution of a program in a von Neumann machine requires the use of the three main components just described. Usually, a software package, called an *operating system*, controls how these three components work together. Initially, a program has to be loaded into the memory. Before being loaded, the program is usually stored on a secondary storage device (like a disk). The operating system uses the I/O interfaces to retrieve the program from secondary storage and load it into the memory.

Once the program is in memory, the operating system then schedules the CPU to begin executing the program instructions. Each instruction to be executed must first be retrieved from memory. This retrieval is referred to as an *instruction fetch*. After an instruction is fetched, it is put into a special register in the CPU, called the *instruction register* (IR). While in the IR, the instruction is decoded to determine what type of operation should be performed. If the instruction requires operands, these are fetched from memory or possibly from other registers and placed into the proper location (certain registers or specially designated storage areas known as *buffers*). The instruction is then performed, and the results are stored back into memory and/or registers. This process is repeated for each instruction of the program until the program's end is reached.

This chapter describes the typical implementation techniques used in von Neumann machines. The main components of a von Neumann machine are explained in the following sections. To make the function of the components in the von Neumann architecture and their interactions clear, the design of a simple microcomputer is discussed in the next section. In later sections, various design techniques for each component are explained in detail. Elements of a datapath, as well as the hardwired and microprogramming techniques for implementing control functions, are discussed. Next, a hierarchical memory system is presented. The architectures of a memory cell, interleaved memory, an associative memory, and a cache memory are given. Virtual memory is also discussed. Finally, interrupts and exception events are addressed.

2.2 DESIGN OF A SIMPLE MICROCOMPUTER USING VHDL

A computer whose CPU is a microprocessor is called a *microcomputer*. Microcomputers are small and inexpensive. Personal computers are usually microcomputers. Figure 2.2 represents the main components of a simple microcomputer. This microcomputer contains a CPU, a clock generator, a decoder, and two memory modules. Each memory module consists of 8 words, each of which has 8 bits. (A *word* indicates how much data a computer can process at any one time.) Since there are two memory modules, this microcomputer's memory consists of a total of sixteen 8-bit memory words. The address bus contains 4 bits in order to address these 16 words. The three least significant bits of the address bus are directly connected to the memory modules, whereas the most significant (leftmost) bit is connected to the select line of the decoder (S). When this bit is 0, M0 is chosen; when it is 1, M1 is chosen. (See Appendix B for information on decoders.) In this way, the addresses 0 to 7 (**0**000 to **0**111) refer to the words in memory module M0, and the addresses 8 to 15 (**1**000 to **1**111) refer to memory module M1. Figure 2.3 represents a structural view of our microcomputer in VHDL. (See Appendix C for information on VHDL. If you are not familiar with VHDL, you can skip this figure and also later VHDL descriptions.) The structural view describes our system by declaring its main components and connecting them with a set of signals. The structure_view is divided into two parts: the declaration part, which appears before the keyword *begin*, and the design part, which appears after *begin*. The declara-

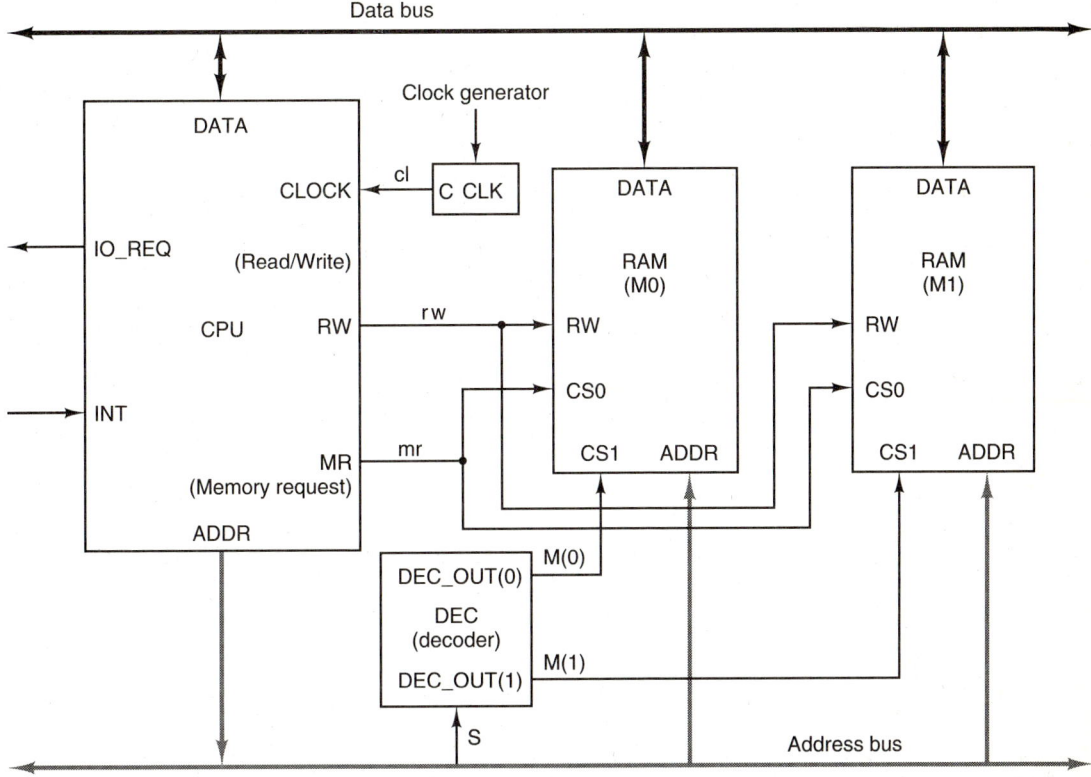

Figure 2.2 A simple microcomputer system.

tion part consists of four component statements and two signal statements. Each component statement defines the input/output ports of each component of the microcomputer. The signal statements define a series of signals that are used for interconnecting the components. For example, the 2–bit signal M is used to connect the outputs of the decoder to the chip select (CS) lines of the memory modules. The design part includes a set of component instantiation statements. A component instantiation statement creates an instance of a component. An instance starts with a label followed by the component name and a portmap. Each entry of the portmap refers to one of the component's ports or a locally declared signal. A port of a component is connected to a port of another component if they have the same portmap entry. For instance, the CPU and memory unit M0 are connected because they both contain DATA as a portmap entry.

Figure 2.4 describes the function (behavioral_view) of a memory module called random-access memory (RAM). In this figure, the variable memory stands for a memory unit consisting of 8 words, each of which has 8 bits. The while statement determines whether the RAM is selected or not. The RAM is selected whenever both signals CS0 and CS1 are 1. The case statement determines whether a datum should be read from the memory into the data bus (RW = 0) or written into memory from the data bus (RW = 1). When the signal RW is 0, the contents of the address bus (ADDR) are

```
architecture structure_view of microprocessor is
   component CPU
    port (DATA: inout tri_vector (0 to 7);
          ADDR: out bit_vector(3 downto 0);
          CLOCK, INT: in bit;
          MR, RW, IO_REQ: out bit);
   end component;
   component RAM
    port (DATA: inout tri_vector(0 to 7);
          ADDR: in bit_vector(2 downto 0);
          CS0, CS1, RW: in bit);
   end component;
   component DEC
    port (DEC_IN: in bit; DEC_OUT: out bit_vector(0 to 1));
   end component;
   component CLK
    port (C: out bit);
   end component;
   signal M: bit_vector(0 to 1);
   signal cl, mr, rw: bit;
begin
   PROCESSOR: CPU portmap (DATA, ADDR, cl, INT, mr, rw,
                           IO_REQ);
   M0: RAM portmap (DATA, ADDR(2 downto 0), mr, M(0), rw);
   M1: RAM portmap (DATA, ADDR(2 downto 0), mr, M(1), rw);
   DECODER: DEC portmap (ADDR(3), M);
   CLOCK: CLK portmap (cl);
end structure_view;
```

Figure 2.3 Structural representation of a simple microcomputer.

```
architecture behavioral_view of RAM is
begin
   process
      type memory_unit is array(0 to 7) of bit_vector(0 to 7);
      variable memory: memory_unit;
   begin
      while (CS0 = '1' and CS1 = '1') loop
         case RW is                   --RW = 0 means read operation
                                      --RW = 1 means write operation
            when '0' => DATA <= memory(intval(ADDR)) after 50 ns;
            when '1' => memory(intval(ADDR)) <= DATA after 60 ns;
         end case;
         wait on CS0, CS1, DATA, ADDR, RW;
      end loop;
      wait on CS0, CS1;
   end process;
end behavioral_view;
```

Figure 2.4 Behavioral representation of an 8-by-8 RAM.

Sec. 2.2   Design of a Simple Microcomputer Using VHDL   23

converted to an integer value, which is used as an index to determine the memory location that the data must be read from. Then the contents of the determined memory location are copied onto the data bus (DATA). In a similar manner, when the signal RW is 1, the contents of the data bus are copied into the proper memory location. The process statement constructs a process for simulating the RAM. The wait statement within the process statement causes the process to be suspended until the value of CS0 or CS1 changes. Once a change appears in any of these inputs, the process starts all over again and performs the proper function as necessary.

Figure 2.5 represents the main components of the CPU. These components are the data path, the control unit, and several registers referred to as the register file. The data path consists of the arithmetic logic unit (ALU) and various registers. The CPU communicates with memory modules through the memory data register (MDR) and the memory address register (MAR). The program counter (PC) is used for keeping the

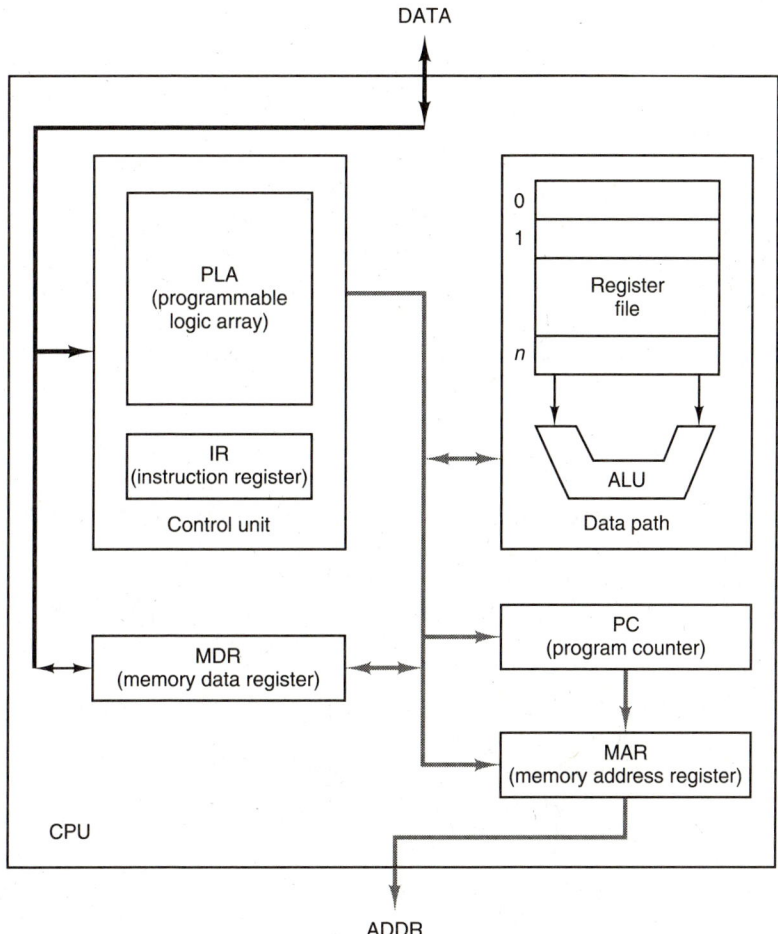

Figure 2.5 A simple CPU.

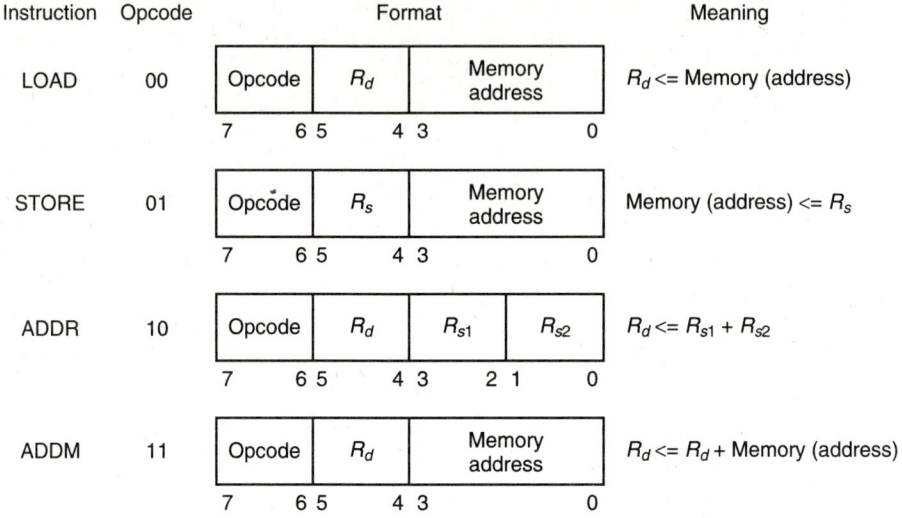

Figure 2.6 Instruction formats of a simple CPU.

address of the next instruction that should be executed. The instruction register (IR) is used for temporarily holding an instruction while it is being decoded and executed.

To express the function of the control unit, we will assume that our microcomputer has only four different instructions. Each instruction has a format as follows:

Opcode	Operand	...	Operand

The *opcode* (stands for operation code) field determines the function of the instruction, and the *operand* fields provide the addresses of data items. Figure 2.6 represents the opcode and the type of operands for each instruction. The *LOAD* instruction loads a memory word into a register. The *STORE* instruction stores a register into a memory word. The *ADDR* instruction adds the contents of two registers and stores the result in a third register. The *ADDM* instruction adds the contents of a register and a memory word and stores the result in the register.

To understand the role of the control unit, let us examine the execution of a simple program in our microcomputer. As an example, consider a program that adds two numbers at memory locations 13 and 14 and stores the result at memory location 15. Using the preceding instructions, the program can be written as

```
LOAD   1,13    -- R1 <= Memory (13)
ADDM   1,14    -- R1 <= R1 + Memory (14)
STORE  1,15    -- Memory (15) <= R1
```

Sec. 2.2 Design of a Simple Microcomputer Using VHDL   25

Let's assume that locations 13 and 14 contain values 4 and 2, respectively. Also, assume that the program is loaded into the first three words of memory. Thus, the contents of memory in binary are:

0	00 01 1101
1	11 01 1110
2	01 01 1111
13	00000100
14	00000010
15	

Memory

Figure 2.7 outlines the steps the computer will take to execute the program. Initially, the address of the first instruction (i.e., 0) is loaded into the program counter (PC). Next the contents of the PC are copied into the memory address register (MAR) and from there to the address bus. The control unit requests a read operation from the

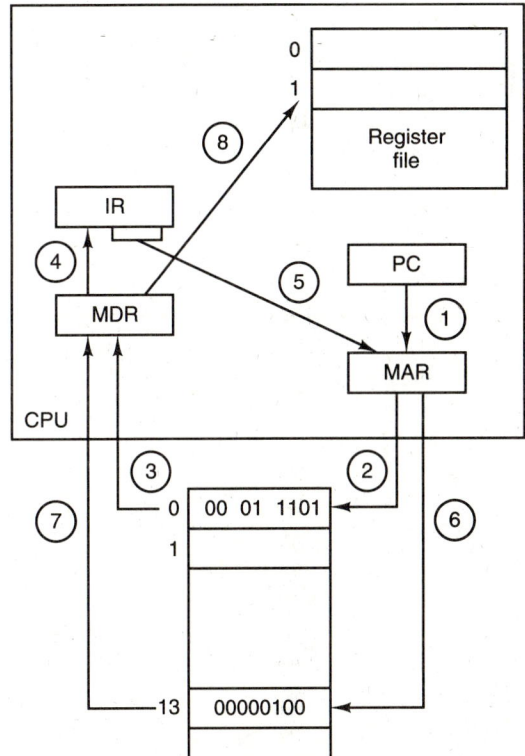

Figure 2.7 Flow of addresses and data for execution of the LOAD instruction.

memory unit. At the same time, the contents of the PC are incremented by 1 to point to the next instruction. The memory unit picks up the address of the requested memory location (that is, 0) from the address bus and, after a certain delay, it transfers the contents of the requested location (that is, 00011101) to the memory data register (MDR) through the data bus. Then the contents of the MDR are copied into the instruction register (IR). The IR register is used for decoding the instruction. The control unit examines the leftmost 2 bits of the IR and determines that this instruction is a load operation. It copies the rightmost 4 bits of the IR into the MAR, such that it now contains 1101, which represents address 13 in decimal. The contents of memory location 13 are retrieved from the memory and stored in MDR in a similar manner to retrieving the instruction LOAD from memory. Next the contents of MDR are copied into the register R_1. At this time the execution of the LOAD instruction is complete.

The preceding process continues until all the instructions are executed. At the end of execution, the value 6 is stored in memory location 15.

In general, the execution process of an instruction can be divided into three main phases, as shown in Figure 2.8. The phases are *instruction fetch, decode_opfetch,* and *execute_opwrite*. In the fetch instruction phase, an instruction is retrieved from the memory and stored in the instruction register. The sequence of actions required to carry out this process can be grouped into three major steps.

1. Transfer the contents of the program counter to the memory address register and increment the program counter by 1. The program counter now contains the address of the next instruction to be fetched.

2. Transfer the contents of the memory location specified by the memory address register to the memory data register.

3. Transfer the contents of the memory data register to the instruction register.

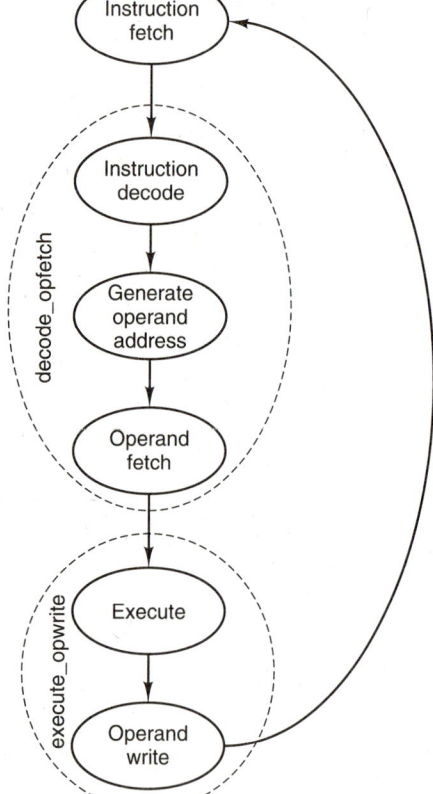

Figure 2.8 Main phases of an instruction execution process.

In the decode_opfetch phase, the instruction in the instruction register is decoded, and if the instruction needs an operand, it is fetched and placed into the desired location.

The last phase, execute_opwrite, performs the desired operation and then stores the result in the specified location. Sometimes no further action is required after the decode_opfetch phase. In these cases, the execute_opwrite phase is simply ignored. For example, a load instruction completes execution after the decode_opfetch phase.

The three phases described must be processed in sequence. Figure 2.9 presents a VHDL process for controlling the sequence of the phases. The function of each phase is described by a VHDL process. Figure 2.10 represents the steps involved in the instruction fetch phase. The function of decode_opfetch phase is presented in Figure 2.11. As shown in Figure 2.11, a case statement decodes a given instruction in the IR to direct the execution process to the proper routine. Figure 2.12 shows the process of the execute_opwrite phase. Take a moment to look over these figures to become familiar with instruction execution phases in the von Neumann architecture.

In the following sections, various design techniques for each component of the von Neumann architecture are explained.

2.3 CONTROL UNIT

In general, there are two main approaches for realizing a control unit: the *hardwired* circuit and *microprogram* design.

Hardwired control unit. The hardwired approach to implementing a control unit is most easily represented as a sequential circuit based on different states in a machine; it issues a series of control signals at each state to govern the computers operation. (See Appendix B for information on sequential circuits.) As an example,

```
control_state: process (inst_fetch, decode_opfetch,
                    execute_opwrite, CLOCK)
  begin
     if ((CLOCK = '1') and (not CLOCK'stable)) then
        if ((not inst_fetch) and (not decode_opfetch) and
              (not execute_opwrite)) then
           case (next_state) is
              when "inst_fetch_st" => inst_fetch <= true;
                    next_state := 'decode_opfetch_st';
              when "decode_opfetch_st" => decode_opfetch <= true;
                    next_state := 'execute_opwrite_st';
              when "execute_opwrite_st" => execute_opwrite <= true;
                    next_state := 'inst_fetch_st';
           end case;
        end if;
     end if;
  end process control_state;
```

Figure 2.9 Process for controlling the sequence of phases.

```
inst_fetch_state: process
   begin
     wait on inst_fetch until inst_fetch;
     MAR <= PC;
     ADDR <= MAR after 15 ns;   --set the address for desired memory location
     MR <= '1' after 25 ns;     --sets CS0 of each memory module to 1
     RW <= '0' after 20 ns;     --read from memory
     wait for 100 ns;           --required time to read a data from memory
     MDR <= tri_vector_to_bit_vector (DATA); --since DATA has a tri_vector
                                --type is converted to MDR
                                --type which is bit_vector
     MR <= '0';
     IR <= MDR after 15 ns;
     for i in 0 to 3 loop       --increment PC by one
        if PC (i) = '0' then
           PC (i) := '1';
          exit;
        else
           PC (i) := '0';
        end if
     end loop;
     inst_fetch <= false;
end process inst_fetch_state;
```

Figure 2.10 Function of the instruction fetch phase.

consider the design of a hardwired circuit for the load instruction of the simple microcomputer mentioned previously. This instruction has the format:

LOAD R_d, Address

As such, it would load the contents of a memory word into register R_d. Figure 2.13 represents the main registers and the control signals involved in this operation. The control signals are RW, MR, LD, AD, LA, WR, SR_0 and SR_1. The function of each is defined as follows:

RW: perform read/write operation from/to memory
 (RW = 0 means read, and RW = 1 means write).
MR: enable the chip select terminal (CS0) of the memory.
LD: load data from data bus (DATA) to MDR.
AD: load address from MAR to address bus (ADDR).
LA: load the rightmost 4 bits of IR to MAR.
WR: perform read/write operation from/to register file
 (WR = 0 means read, and WR = 1 means write).
SR_0 and SR_1: select 2 bits of the IR as the address of
 register file.

Sec. 2.3 Control Unit 29

```
decode_opfetch_state: process
begin
   wait on decode_opfetch until decode_opfetch;
   case (IR (7 downto 6)) is
                                    --LOAD
      when "00" => MAR <= IR (3 downto 0);
         ADDR <= MAR after 15 ns;
         MR <= '1' after 25 ns;
         RW <= '0' after 20 ns;
         wait for 100 ns;    --suppose 100 ns is
                             --required to read a
                             --datum from memory
         MDR <= tri_vector_to_bit_vector (DATA);
         MR <= '0';
         reg_file (intval (IR(5 downto 4))) <= MDR;
                             --copy MDR to the
                             --destination register
                             --STORE
      when "01" => MDR <= reg_file (intval (IR (5 downto 4)));
         DATA <= MDR after 20 ns;
         MAR <= IR (3 downto 0);
         ADDR <= MAR after 15 ns;
         MR <= '1' after 25 ns;
         RW <= '1' after 20 ns;
         wait for 110 ns;    --suppose 110 ns is required
                             --to store a datum in memory
         MR <= "0";
                             --ADDR
      when "10" => ALU_REG1 <= reg_file (intval(IR(3 downto 2)));
         ALU_REG2 <= reg_file (intval(IR(1 downto 0)));
         add_op <= true after 20 ns;
                             --ADDM
      when "11" => ALU_REG1 <= reg_file (intval(IR(5 downto 4)));
         MAR <= IR (3 downto 0);
         ADDR <= MAR after 15 ns;
         MR <= '1' after 25 ns;
         RW <= '0' after 20 ns;
         wait for 100 ns;    --suppose 100 ns is required
                             --to read a
                             --datum from memory
         MDR <= tri_vector_to_bit_vector (DATA);
         MR <= '0';
         ALU_REG2 <= MDR;
         add_op <= true;
   end case;
   decode_opfetch <= false;
end process decode_opfetch_state;
```

Figure 2.11 Function of the decode_opfetch phase.

```
execute_opwrite_state: process
begin
   wait on execute_opwrite until execute_opwrite;
      if add_op then
         reg_file(intval(IR(5 downto 4))) := ADD(ALU_REG1, ALU_REG2);
         add_op <= false;
      end if;
      execute_opwrite <= false;
end process execute_opwrite_state;
```

Figure 2.12 Function of the execute_opwrite phase.

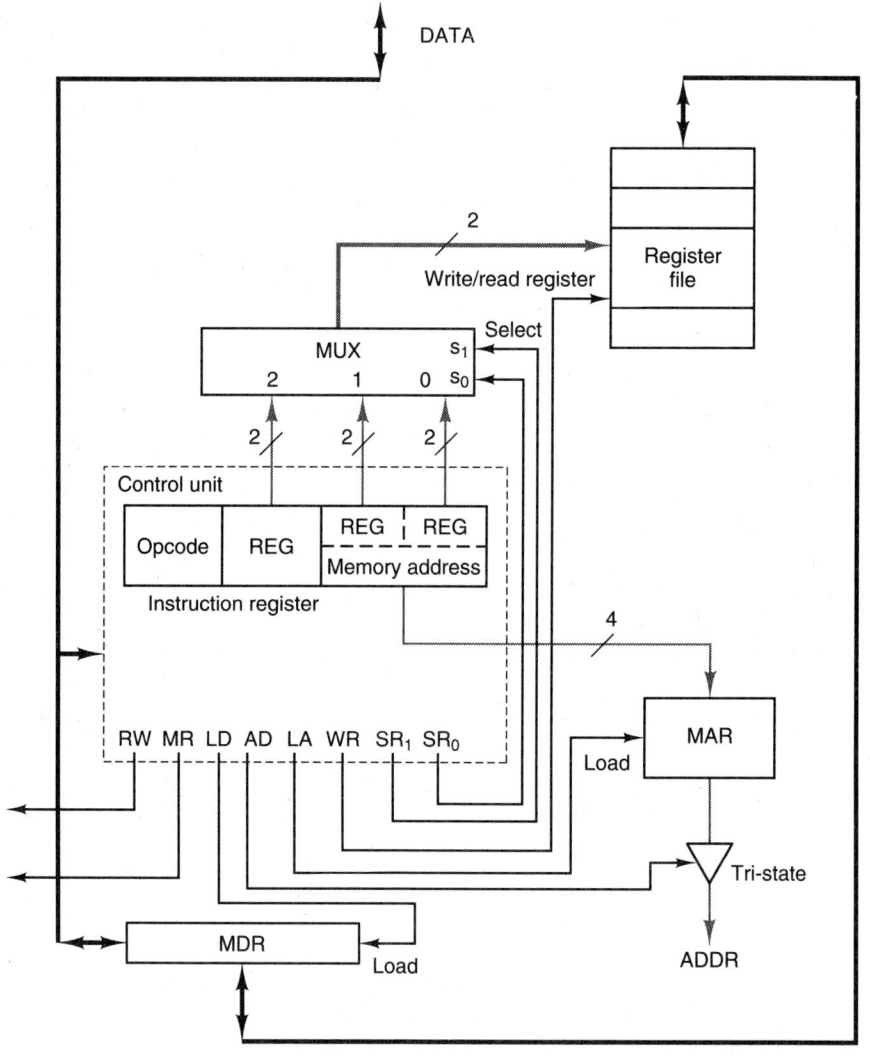

Figure 2.13 Control signals for some portions of the simple CPU in Figure 2.5.

Sec. 2.3 Control Unit

The load operation starts by loading the 4 least significant bits of the instruction register (IR) into the memory address register (MAR). Then the desired data are fetched from memory and loaded into the memory data register (MDR). Next the destination register R_d is selected by setting s_0 and s_1 (select lines of the multiplexer, or MUX) to 0 and 1, respectively. The operation is completed by transferring the contents of the MDR to the register selected by SR_0 and SR_1.

Figure 2.14 represents a state diagram for the load operation. In this state diagram, the state S_0 represents the initial state. A transition from a state to another state is represented by an arrow. To each arrow a label in the form of X/Z is assigned; here X and Z represent a set of input and output signals, respectively. When there is no input signal or output signal, X or Y is represented as "-". A transition from S_0 to S_1 occurs whenever the leftmost 2 bits of IR are '00' and the signal decode_opfetch is true. (Note that although values of the signal decode_opfetch are represented as true and false, these values would actually be logical values 1 and 0, respectively, in a real implementation of this machine.) The signal decode_opfetch is set to true whenever the execution process of an instruction enters the decode_opfetch phase. When transition from S_0 to S_1 occurs, the control signal LA is set to 1, causing the rightmost 4 bits of IR to be loaded into the MAR. A transition from S_1 to S_2 causes the contents of MAR to be loaded on the address bus. The transition from S_2 to S_3 causes the target data to be read

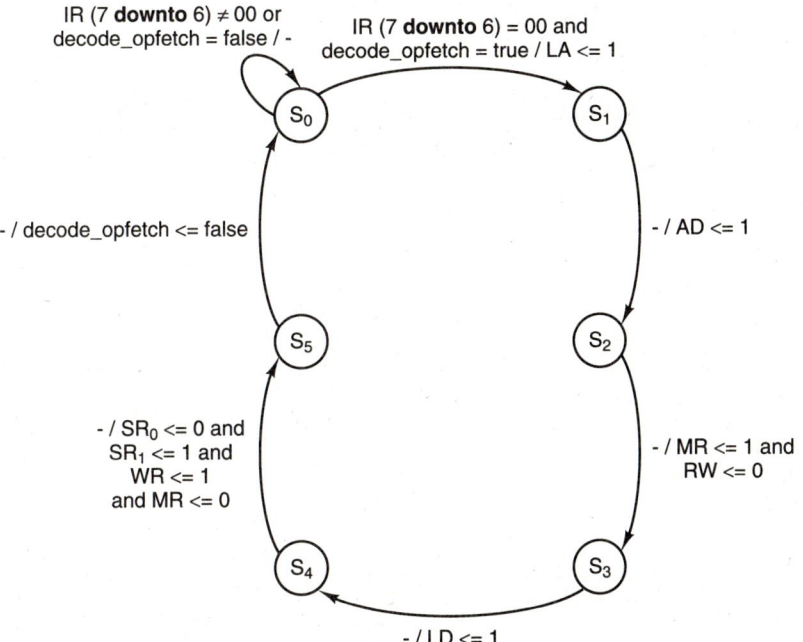

LA <= 1 ≡ MAR <= IR (3 **downto** 0)
AD <= 1 ≡ ADDR <= MAR
LD <= 1 ≡ MDR <= DATA
SR_0 <= 0 and SR_1 <= 1 and WR <= 1 ≡ reg_file (IR (5 **downto** 4)) <= MDR

Figure 2.14 State diagram for the load operation.

from the memory and loaded on the data bus. Note that it is assumed that a clock cycle (which causes the transition from S_2 to S_3) is enough for reading a datum from memory. A transition from S_3 to S_4 copies the data on the data bus into MDR. The transition from S_4 to S_5 sets the select lines of the multiplexer (MUX) to 1 and 0. This causes the third and fourth bits (from left) of IR to be selected as an address to the register file. By setting WR = 1, the contents of MDR are copied into the addressed register. A transition from S_5 to S_0 completes the load operation by setting the signal decode_opfetch to false.

The state diagram of Figure 2.14 can be used to implement a hardwired circuit. Usually a programmable logic array (PLA) (defined in Appendix B) is used for designing such a circuit. Figure 2.15 represents the main components involved in such a design. When the size of the PLA becomes too large, it is often decomposed to several smaller-sized PLAs in order to save space on the chip.

One main drawback with the preceding approach (which is often mentioned in the literature) is that it is not flexible. In other words, a later change in the control unit requires the change of the whole circuit. The rationale for considering this a drawback is that a complete instruction set is usually not definable at the time that a processor is being designed, and a good design must allow certain operations, defined by some later user, to be executed at a very high speed. However, because microprocessor design changes so rapidly today, the lifetime of any particular processor is very short, making flexibility less of an issue. In fact, most of today's microprocessors are based on the hardwired approach.

Microprogrammed control unit. To solve the inflexibility problem with a hardwired approach, in 1951 Wilkes invented a technique called microprogramming [WIL 51]. Today, while microprogramming has become less important as a widespread design method, the concept remains quite important. Hayes says that a microprogram design "resembles a computer within a computer; it contains a special memory from which it fetches and executes control information, in much the same manner as the CPU fetches and executes instructions from the main memory" [HAY 93].

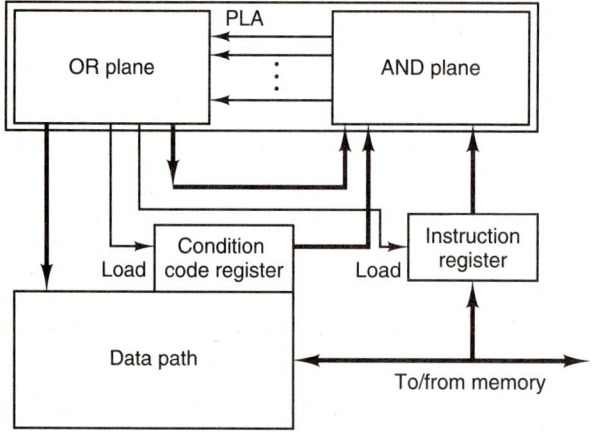

Figure 2.15 Structure of a CPU based on hardwired control unit design.

Sec. 2.3 Control Unit

In microprogramming, each machine instruction translates into a sequence of microinstructions that triggers the control signals of the machine's resources; these signals initiate fundamental computer operations. Microinstructions are bit patterns stored in a separate memory known as microcode storage, which has an access time that is much faster than that of main memory. The evolution of microprogramming in the 1970s is linked to the introduction of low-cost and high-density memory chips made possible by the advance of semiconductor technology. Figure 2.16 shows the main components involved in a microprogrammed machine. The microprogram counter points to the next microinstruction for execution, which, upon execution, causes the activation of some of the control signals. In Figure 2.16, instead of having direct connections from microcode storage and condition code registers to the decoder, a control circuit maps these connections to a smaller number of connections. This reduces the size of microcode storage. Because the microinstructions are stored in a memory, it is possible to add or change certain instructions without changing any circuit. Thus the microprogramming technique is much more flexible than the hardwired approach. However, it is potentially slower because each microinstruction must be accessed from microcode storage.

Microinstruction Word Design. The following criteria should be considered in designing a microinstruction format.

1. Minimization of the microcode storage word size (microword).
2. Minimization of the microprogram size.
3. Maximization of the flexibility of adding or changing microinstructions.
4. Maximization of the concurrency of the microoperations.

In general, a microword contains two fields, the microoperation field and the next address field. One extreme design for the microoperation field is to assign a bit to

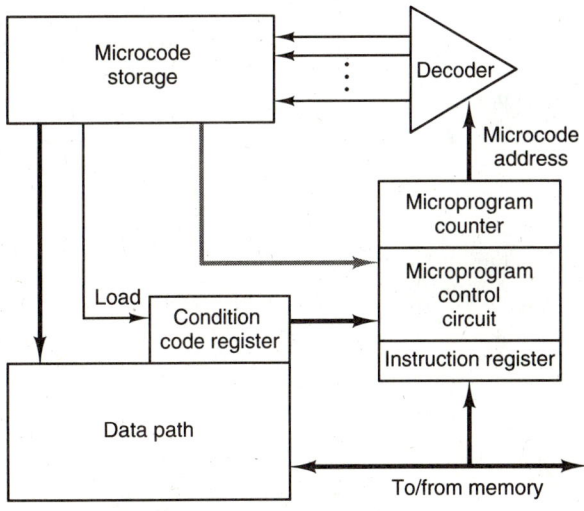

Figure 2.16 Structure of a CPU based on microprogrammed control unit design.

each control signal; this is called *horizontal* design, because many bits are usually needed, resulting in a wide, or horizontal, microoperation field. In this type of design, whenever a microword is addressed the stored 1's in the microoperation field will cause the invocation of corresponding control signals.

Another extreme design for the microoperation field is to have a few highly encoded subfields; this is called *vertical* design, because relatively few bits are needed, resulting in a narrower microoperation field. Each subfield may invoke only one control signal within a certain group of control signals. This is done by assigning a unique code to each control signal. For example, to a subfield with 2 bits, a unique code of 00, 01, 10, or 11 can be assigned to each control signal in a group with a maximum of three control signals. Note that one of the codes in each subfield is reserved for no operation (i.e., for when you do not want to invoke any signals within a group). The distinction between the concept of horizontal and vertical designs becomes more clear upon investigating the design of a microprogram for the load instruction of our simple microcomputer. This instruction has a format such as

```
LOAD R_d Address
```

This instruction loads the contents of a memory word into register R_d. Figure 2.13 shows the main registers and the control signals involved in this operation. The operation starts by loading the 4 least significant bits of the instruction register (IR) into the memory address register (MAR). Then the desired data are fetched from memory and loaded into the memory data register (MDR). Next the destination register R_d is selected by setting S_0 and S_1 (select lines of the multiplexor) to 0 and 1, respectively. The operation is completed by transferring the contents of the MDR to the selected register.

Figure 2.17 shows the preceding steps as a series of microinstructions that is stored in a microcode storage based on a horizontal design (i.e., a bit is assigned to each control signal). In addition to the eight control signals of Figure 2.13, there are two other control signals, ST and DO. The ST signal causes the load operation to start whenever signal START becomes 1. The DO signal indicates the completion of the load operation and causes the control unit to bring to an end the decode_opfetch phase. Initially, the contents of the MSAR register (microcode storage address register) are set to 0. Hence the contents of microword 0 appear on the control signals. That is, ST is set to 1 and the other signals are set to 0. When a load instruction is detected, START is set to 1. At this point, both signals ST and START are 1, and as a result the rightmost bit of MSAR is set to 1. Therefore, microword 1 is selected and, as a result, control signal LA is set to 1. This process continues until the last microcode, 6, is selected. At that time DO is set to 1, which completes the load operation.

An alternative to the preceding design is shown in Figure 2.18. This figure represents a vertical microprogram for the same load operation. Note that in this design each microword has 8 bits, in comparison to the former horizontal design in which each microword had 13 bits. The microoperation of each microword consists of two subfields: F_1 and F_2. F_1 has 2 bits that are used to invoke one of the control signals SR_0, WR, and MR, at any given time. In F_1, the codes 00, 01, 10, and 11 are assigned to no

Sec. 2.3 Control Unit

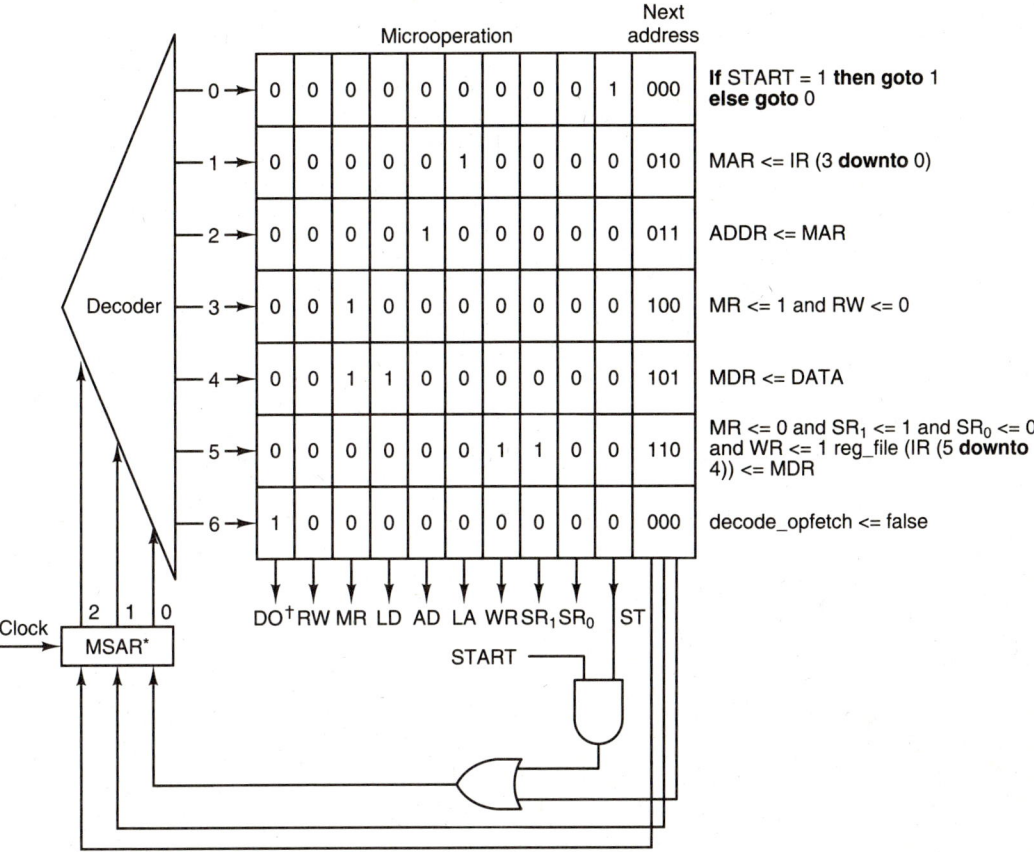

+ **If** (IR (7 **downto** 6) = 00 and decode_opfetch = true) **then**
  START <= 1;
else
  START <= 0;
end if;
* MSAR stands for microcode storage address register.
† DO stands for decode_opfetch; DO = 1 is equivalent to decode_opfetch <= false.

Figure 2.17 Horizontal microprogram for the load operation.

operation, SR_0, WR, and MR, respectively. F_2 has 3 bits that are used to invoke one of the control signals SR_1, AD, LD, RW, DO, LA, and ST, at any given time. In F_2, the codes 000, 001, 010, 011, 100, 101, 110, and 111 are assigned to no operation, SR_1, AD, LD, RW, DO, LA, and ST, respectively.

An advantage of vertical microprogramming (VM) over horizontal microprogramming (HM) is that VM uses relatively shorter microinstructions. Nevertheless, horizontal microprogramming is more powerful because it does not enforce any constraint for modifying the set of microinstructions of an instruction. Some of the advantages of HM over VM are:

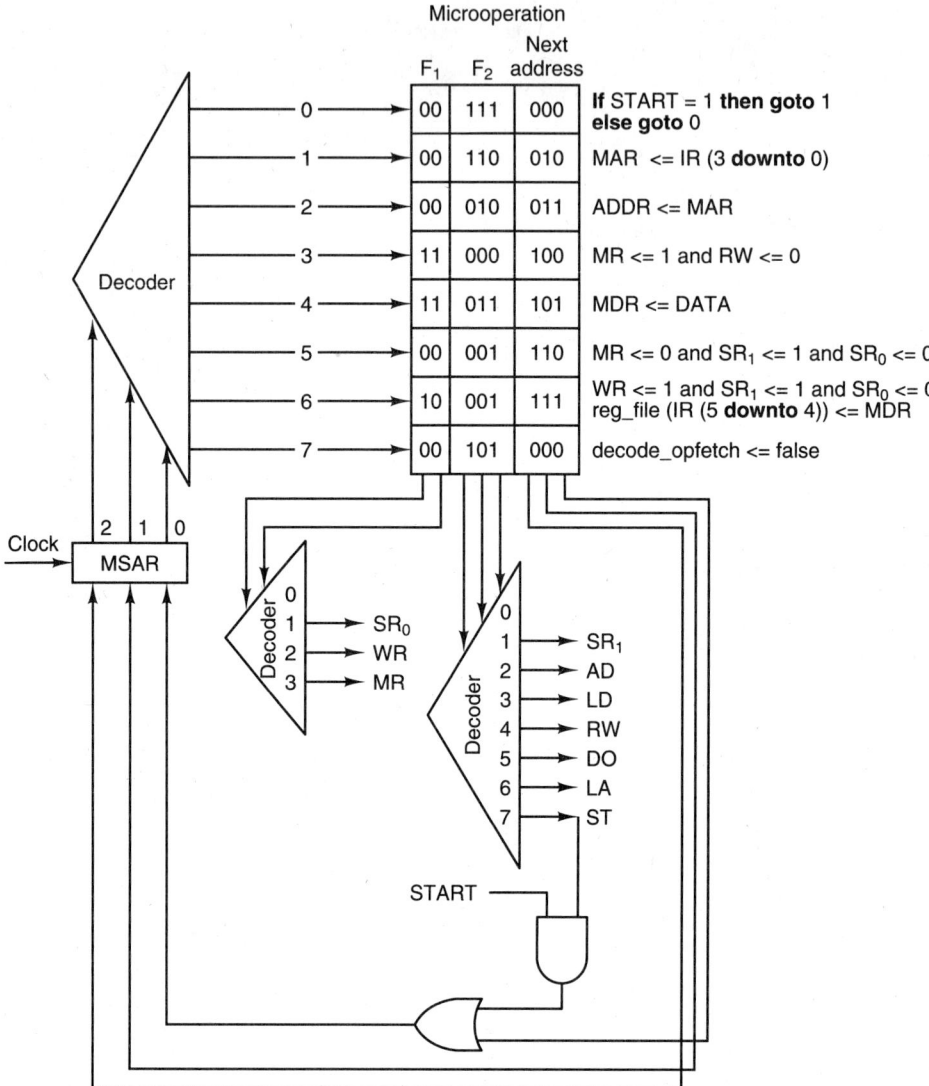

Figure 2.18 Vertical microprogram for the load operation.

1. Simultaneous execution of control signals within the same microinstruction (i.e., any combination of control signals can be triggered at the same time)
2. Relatively short microinstruction executing time. VM requires a longer execution time because of the delays associated with decoding the encoded microinstruction subfields.

The characteristics of VM and HM have a direct impact on the structures of computer systems. Therefore, when adopting one of the two techniques, computer architects must be aware of the attributes of each method. For instance, if many components of the CPU are required to be operated simultaneously, HM is more appropriate. HM always allows full use of parallelism. On the other hand, if the emphasis is on less hardware cost and a smaller set of microinstructions, VM would be more suitable. In practice, usually a mix of both approaches is chosen.

2.4 INSTRUCTION SET DESIGN

The design of an instruction set is one of the most important aspects of processor design. The design of the instruction set is highly complex because it defines many of the functions performed by the CPU and therefore affects most aspects of the entire system. Each instruction must contain the information required by the CPU for execution.

With most instruction sets, more than one instruction format is used. Each instruction format consists of an opcode field and 0 to 3 operand fields, as follows:

Opcode	Operand	...	Operand

The opcode (stands for operation code) field determines the function of the instruction, and the operand fields provide the addresses of data items (or sometimes the data items themselves). Designing this type of instruction format requires answers to the following questions:

How many instructions are provided?
What type of operations are provided?
How many operand fields and what type of operands are allowed in each instruction?

A number of conflicting factors complicate the task of instruction set design. As a result, there are no simple answers to these questions, as the following discussion demonstrates.

Size of opcode. The question of how many instructions are provided is directly related to the size of the opcode. The opcode size reflects the number of instructions that can be provided by an architecture; as the number of bits in the opcode increases, the number of instructions will also increase. Having more instructions reduces the size of a program. Smaller programs tend to reduce the storage space and execution time. This is because a sequence of basic instructions can be reinterpreted as equivalent to one advanced instruction. For example, if an instruction set (all the instructions provided by an architecture) includes a multiplication operation, only one instruction is needed in the program to multiply instead of a sequence of add and shift instructions. To summarize, if there are only a few simple instructions to choose from, then many are required, making longer programs to perform a task. If many instructions are available, then fewer are needed, because each instruction will accomplish a longer part of the task. Fewer program instructions means a shorter program.

Although increasing the number of bits in the opcode reduces the program size, ultimately a price must be paid for such an increase. Eventually, the addition of an extra bit to the opcode field will result in increased storage space for a program, despite the initial program size reduction.

Furthermore, increasing the number of instructions will add more complexity to the processor design, which increases the cost. A larger set of instructions requires a more extensive control unit circuit and complicates the process of microprogramming design if microprogramming is used. Additionally, it is ideal to have the whole CPU design on a single chip, since a chip is much faster and less expensive than a board of chips. If design complexity increases, more gates will be needed to successfully implement the design, which could make it impossible to fit the whole design on a single chip.

From this discussion, it can be concluded that the size of an instruction set directly affects even the most fundamental issues involved in processor design. A small and simple instruction set offers the advantage of uncomplicated hardware designs, but also increases program size. A large and complex instruction set decreases program storage needs, but also increases hardware complexity. One trend in computer design is to increase the complexity of the instruction set by providing special instructions that are able to perform complex operations. Recent machines falling within such trends are termed *complex instruction set computers* (**CISC**s). The CISC design approach emphasises reducing the number of instructions in the program and, as a result, increases overall performance.

Another trend in computer design is to simplify the instruction set rather than make it more complex. As a result, the terminology *reduced instruction set computer* (**RISC**) has been introduced for this type of design. The basic concept of the RISC design approach is based on the observation that in a large number of programs many complex instructions are seldom used. It has been shown that programmers or compiler writers often use only a subset of the instruction set. Therefore, in contrast to CISC, the RISC design approach employs a simpler instruction set to improve the rate at which instructions can be executed. It emphasizes reducing the average number of clock cycles required to execute an instruction, rather than reducing the number of instructions in the program. In RISC design, most instructions are executed within a single cycle. This innovative approach to computer architecture is covered in more detail in Chapters 3 and 4.

Type of operation. It is important to have an instruction set that is compatible with previous processors in the same series or even with different brands of processors. Compatibility allows the user to run the existing software on the new machine. Therefore, there is a tendency to support the existing instruction set and add more instructions to it in order to increase performance (i.e., instruction set size is increasing). However, the designer should be very careful when adding an instruction to the set because, once programmers decide to use the instruction and critical programs include the instruction, it may become hard to remove it in the future.

Sec. 2.4 Instruction Set Design

Although instruction sets vary among machines, most of them include the same general types of operations. These operations can be classified as follows:

Data transfer. For transferring (or copying) data from one location (memory or register) to another location (register or memory), such as load, store, and move instructions.

Arithmetic. For performing basic arithmetic operations, such as increment, decrement, add, subtract, multiply, and divide.

Logical. For performing Boolean operations such as NOT, AND, OR, and exclusive-OR. These operations operate on bits of a word as bits rather than as numbers.

Control. For controlling the sequence of instruction execution there exist instructions such as jump, branch, skip, procedure call, return, and halt.

System. These types of operations are generally privileged instructions and are often reserved for the use of the operating system, as in system calls and memory management instructions.

Input/output (I/O). For transferring data between the memory and external I/O devices. The commonly used I/O instructions are input (read) and output (write).

Type of operand fields. An instruction format may consist of one or more operand fields, which provide the address of data or data themselves. In a typical instruction format the size of each operand is quite limited. With this limited size, it is necessary to refer to a large range of locations in main memory. To achieve this goal, a variety of addressing modes have been employed. The most commonly used addressing modes are *immediate, direct, indirect, displacement,* and *stack.* Each of these techniques is explained next.

Immediate Addressing. In immediate addressing the operand field actually contains the operand itself, rather than an address or other information describing where the operand is. The immediate addressing is the simplest way for an instruction to specify an operand. This is because, upon execution of an instruction, the operand is immediately available for use, and hence it does not require an extra memory reference to fetch the operand. However, it has the disadvantage of restricting the range of the operand to numbers that can fit in the limited size of the operand field.

Direct Addressing. In direct addressing, also referred to as absolute addressing, the operand field contains the address of the memory location or the address of the register in which the operand is stored. When the operand field refers to a register, this mode is also referred to as *register direct addressing.* This type of addressing requires only one memory (or register) reference to fetch the operand and does not require any special calculation for obtaining the operand's address. However, it provides a limited address space depending on the size of operand field.

Indirect Addressing. In indirect addressing the operand field specifies which memory location or register contains the address of the operand. When the operand field refers to a register, this mode is also referred to as *register indirect addressing.* In this addressing mode the operand's address space depends on the word length of the memory or the register length. That is, in contrast to direct addressing, the operand's address space is not limited to the size of the operand field. The main drawback of this addressing mode is that it requires two references to fetch the operand, one memory (or register) reference to get the operand's address and a second memory reference to get the operand itself.

Displacement Addressing. Displacement addressing combines the capabilities of direct addressing and register indirect addressing. It requires that the operand field consists of two subfields and that at least one of them is explicit. One of the subfields (which may be implicit in the opcode) refers to a register whose content is added to the value of the other subfield to produce the operand's address. The value of one of the subfields is called the *displacement* from the memory address which is denoted by the other subfield. The term displacement is used because the value of the subfield is too small to reference all the memory locations. Three of the most common uses of this addressing mode are *relative addressing, base register addressing,* and *indexed addressing.*

For relative addressing, one of the subfields is implicit and refers to the program counter (PC). That is, the program counter (current instruction address) is added to the operand field to produce the operand's address. The operand field contains an integer called the displacement from the memory address indicated by the program counter.

For base register addressing, the referenced register, referred to as the *base register,* contains a memory address, and the operand field contains an integer called the displacement from that memory address. The register reference may be implicit or explicit. The content of the base register is added to the displacement to produce the operand's address. Usually, processors contain special base registers; if they do not, general-purpose registers are used as base registers.

For indexed addressing (or simply indexing), the operand field references a memory address, and the referenced register, referred to as the *index register,* contains a positive displacement from that address. The register reference may be implicit or explicit. The memory address is added to the index register to produce the operand's address. Usually, processors contain special index registers; if they do not, general-purpose registers are used as index registers.

Stack Addressing. A stack can be considered to be a linear array of memory locations. Data items are added (removed) to (from) the top of the stack. Stack addressing is in fact an implied form of register indirect addressing. This is so that, at any given time, the address of the top of the stack is kept in a specific register, referred to as the *stack register.* Thus the machine instructions do not need to include the operand field because, implicitly, the stack register provides the operand's address. That is, the instructions operate on the top of the stack. For example, to execute an add instruction, two operands are popped off the top of the stack, one after another, the addition is performed, and the result is pushed back onto the stack.

Number of operands per operation. A question that a designer must answer is how many operands (operand fields) might be needed in an instruction. The

Sec. 2.4 Instruction Set Design 41

number of operands ranges from none to two or more. The relative advantages and disadvantages of each case are discussed next.

1. When there is no operand for most of the operations, the machine is called a *stack machine*. A stack machine uses implicit specification of operands; therefore, the instruction does not need a field to specify the operand. The operands are stored on a stack. Most instructions implicitly use the top operand in the stack. Only the instructions PUSH and POP access memory. For example, to perform the expression $Z = X + Y$, the following sequence of operations may be used:

```
PUSH X      --load top of stack X
PUSH Y      --load top of stack Y
ADD         --add top most two operands of stack
POP Z       --store top of stack in Z
```

In general, the evaluation of an expression is based on a simple model in this type of machine. Also, instructions have a short format (the number of bits in opcode field determines the size of most instructions). However, these good points are tempered by the following drawbacks:

    a. It does not allow the use of registers (beside top of stack), which is needed for generating an efficient code and reducing the execution time of a program.
    b. It makes fast implementations of programs difficult.

2. When there is one operand, the machine usually has a register called the *accumulator*, which contains the second operand. In this type of machine, most operations are performed on the operand and the accumulator with the result stored in the accumulator. There are some instructions for loading and storing data in accumulators. For example, for the expression $Z = X + Y$, the code is

```
LOAD_ACC X    --load accumulator X
ADD Y         --adds the contents of
              --accumulator to Y
              --and store result in accumulator
STORE Z       --store accumulator in Z
```

Similar to a stack machine, the advantages are a simple model for expression evaluation and short instruction formats. The drawbacks are also like those of the stack machine, that is, a lack of registers besides the accumulator, which affects good code performance. Since there is only one register, the performance degrades by accessing memory most of the time.

3. When there are two or three operands, usually the machine has two or more registers. Typically, arithmetic and logical operations require one to three operands. Two- and three-operand instructions are common because they require a relatively short instruction format. In the two-operand type of instruction, one operand is often used both as a source and a destination. In three-operand instructions, one operand is used as a destination and the other two as sources.

In general, the machines with two- or three-operand instructions are of two types: those with a load-store design, and those with a memory-register design. In a load-store machine, only load and store instructions access memory, and the rest of the instructions usually perform an operation on registers. For example, for $Z = X + Y$, the code may be

```
LOAD  R1, X
LOAD  R2, Y
ADD   R1, R2
STORE R1, Z
```

The advantages of this type of design are as follows:

a. Few memory accesses; that is, performance (speed) increases by accessing registers most of the time.
b. Short instruction formats, because fewer bits are required for addressing a register than they are for addressing memory (on the grounds that the register address space is much smaller than memory address space).
c. Instructions may have a fixed length.
d. Instructions often take the same number of clock cycles for execution.
e. Registers provide a simple model for compilers to generate good object code.

However, because most of the instructions access registers, fewer addressing modes can be encoded in a single instruction. In other words, instruction encoding is inefficient, and hence sometimes a sequence of instructions is needed to perform a simple operation. For example, to add the contents of a memory location to a register may involve the execution of two instructions: a LOAD and an ADD. This type of machine usually provides more instructions than the memory-register type.

In a memory-register type of machine, usually one operand addresses a memory location while the other operands (one or two) address registers. For example, for $Z = X + Y$, the code may be:

```
LOAD  R1, X
ADD   R1, Y
STORE R1, Z
```

In comparison with the load-store machine, the memory-register machine has the advantage that data can be accessed from memory without first loading them into a register. Another benefit is that the number of addressing modes that can be encoded in a single instruction increases; as a result, on average, less instructions are needed to encode a program. The drawbacks are the following:

a. The instructions have variable lengths, which increases the complexity of design.
b. Most of the time the operands are fetched from memory.

    c. There are fewer registers than in load-store machines due to the increase in the number of addressing modes encoded in an instruction.

4. Finally, there may be two or more memory addresses for an instruction. An advantage of this scheme is that it does not waste registers for temporary storage. However, this scheme results in too many memory accesses, causing the instructions to become more complex in size and work (utilizing zero to three memory operands and zero to three memory accesses).

2.5 ARITHMETIC LOGIC UNIT

The arithmetic logic unit (ALU) is arguably the most important part of the central processing unit (CPU). The ALU performs the decision-making (logical) and arithmetic operations. It works in combination with a number of registers that hold the data on which the logical or mathematical operations are to be performed.

For decision-making operations, the ALU can determine if a number equals zero, is positive or negative, or which of two numbers is larger or smaller. These operations are most likely to be used as criteria to control the flow of a program. It is also standard for the ALU to perform basic logic functions such as AND, OR, and exclusive-OR.

For arithmetic operations, the ALU often performs functions such as addition, subtraction, multiplication, and division. There are a variety of techniques for designing these functions. In this section, some well-known basic and advanced techniques for some of these functions are discussed. These same techniques can be applied to the more complex mathematical operations, such as raising numbers to powers or extracting roots. These operations are customarily handled by a program that repetitively uses the simpler functions of the ALU; however, some of the newer ALUs have been experimenting with more proficient ways of hardwiring more complex mathematical operations directly into the circuit. The trade-off is a more complex ALU circuit for much faster operation results.

2.5.1 Addition

Many of the ALU's functions reduce to a simple addition or series of additions [DEE 74]. As such, by increasing the speed of addition, we might increase the speed of the ALU and, similarly, the speed of the overall machine. Adder designs range from very simple to very complex. Speed and cost are directly proportional to the complexity. The discussions that follow will explore full adders, ripple carry adders, carry lookahead adders, carry select adders, carry save adders, binary-coded decimal adders, and serial adders.

    Full adder. A full adder adds three 1-bit inputs. Two of the inputs are the two significant bits to be added (denoted x, y), and the other input is the carry from the lower significant bit position (denoted C_{in}), producing a sum (denoted S) bit and a carry (denoted C_{out}) bit as outputs. Figure 2.19 presents the truth table, the Boolean

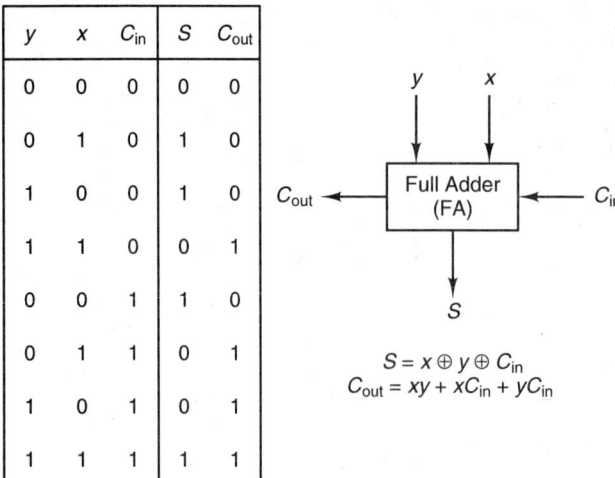

Figure 2.19 Truth table, Boolean expressions, and block diagram for a full adder.

expressions, and a block diagram for a full adder. The full adder will be one of the basic building blocks for the more complex adders to follow.

Ripple carry adder. One of the most basic addition algorithms is the ripple carry addition algorithm. This algorithm is also easily implemented with full adders. The principle of this algorithm is similar to that of paper and pencil addition. Let $x_3 x_2 x_1 x_0$ and $y_3 y_2 y_1 y_0$ represent two 4-bit binary numbers. To add these numbers on paper, we would add x_0 and y_0 to determine the first digit of the sum. The resulting carry, if any, is added with x_1 and y_1 to determine the next digit of the sum, and similarly for the ensuing carry with x_2 and y_2. This process continues until x_3 and y_3 are added. The final carry, again if any, will become the most significant digit. One way to implement this process is to connect several full adders in series, one full adder for each bit of the numbers to be added. Figure 2.20 presents a ripple carry adder for adding two 4-bit binary numbers ($x_3 x_2 x_1 x_0$ and $y_3 y_2 y_1 y_0$). As shown in Figure 2.20, to ensure that the correct sum is calculated, the output carry of a full adder is connected to the input carry of the next full adder, and the rightmost carry in (C_0) is wired to a constant 0.

The ripple carry adder is a parallel adder because all operands are presented at the same time. The adder gets its name because the carry must ripple through all the full adders before the final value is known. Although this type of adder is very easy and inexpensive to design, it is the slowest adder. This is due to the fact that the carry has to propagate from the least significant bit (LSB) position to the most significant bit

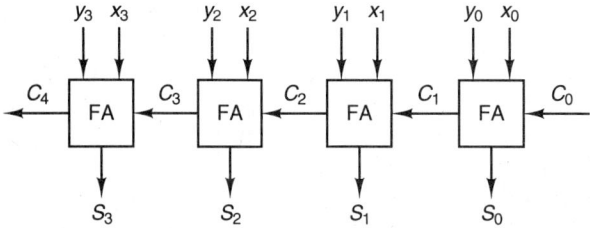

Figure 2.20 Block diagram of a 4-bit ripple carry adder.

(MSB) position. However, since the ripple carry adder has a simple design, it is sometimes used as small adder cell in building larger adders.

The ripple carry adder can also be used as a subtractor. Subtraction of two binary numbers can be performed by taking the 2's complement of the subtrahend and adding it to the minuend [MAN 91]. (The 2's complement of an n-bit binary number N is defined as $2^n - N$ [MAN 91].) For example, given two binary numbers $X = 01001$ and $Y = 00011$, the subtraction $X - Y$ can be performed as follows:

```
                        X =              01001
2's complement of       Y =    +         11101
                                       -------
                               1         00110
discard the carry;     X - Y  =          00110
```

It is also possible to design a subtractor in a direct manner. In this way, each bit of the subtrahend is subtracted from its corresponding significant minuend bit to form a difference bit. When the minuend bit is 0 and the subtrahend bit is 1, a 1 is borrowed from the next significant position. Just as there are full adders for designing adders, there are full subtractors for designing subtractors. The design of such full subtractors is left as an exercise for the reader (see Problems section).

Carry lookahead adder. This technique increases the speed of the carry propagation in a ripple carry adder. It produces the input carry bit directly, rather than allowing the carries to ripple from full adder to full adder. Figure 2.21 presents a block diagram for a carry lookahead adder that adds two 4-bit integers. In this figure, the carry blocks generate the carry inputs for the full adders. Note that the inputs to each carry block are only the input numbers and the initial carry input (C_0). The Boolean expression for each carry block can be defined by using the carry-out expression of a full adder. For example,

$$C_{i+1} = x_i y_i + C_i (x_i + y_i). \qquad (2.1)$$

Thus, C_1 can be generated as

$$C_1 = x_0 y_0 + C_0 (x_0 + y_0).$$

In a similar way, C_2 can be generated as

$$C_2 = x_1 y_1 + C_1 (x_1 + y_1)$$
$$= x_1 y_1 + [x_0 y_0 + C_0 (x_0 + y_0)] (x_1 + y_1).$$

To simplify the expression for each C_i, often two notations g and p are used. These notations are defined as

$$g_i = x_i y_i,$$
$$p_i = x_i + y_i$$

Therefore, expression (2.1) can be written as:

$$C_{i+1} = g_i + p_i C_i. \qquad (2.2)$$

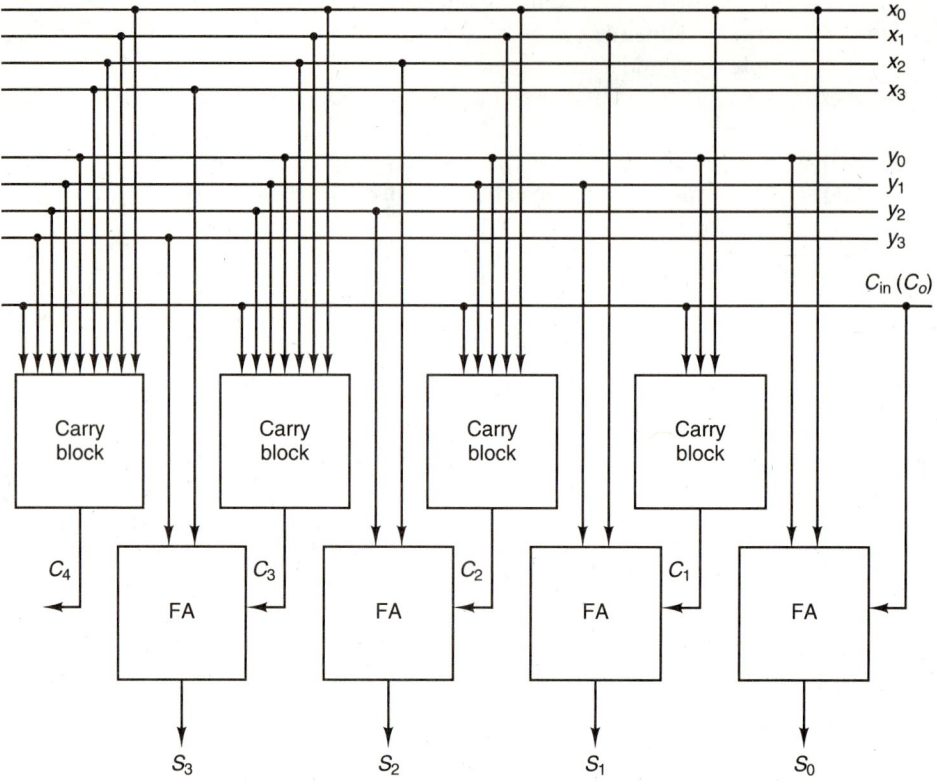

Figure 2.21 Block diagram of a 4-bit carry lookahead adder.

The notation g stands for generating a carry; that is, C_{i+1} is 1 whenever g_i is 1. The notation p stands for propagating the input carry to output carry; that is, when C_i and p_i are 1's, C_{i+1} becomes 1.

Using these notations, we get

$$C_1 = g_0 + C_0 p_0,$$
$$C_2 = g_1 + p_1 g_0 + p_1 p_0 C_0,$$
$$C_3 = g_2 + p_2 g_1 + p_2 p_1 g_0 + p_2 p_1 p_0 C_0,$$
$$C_4 = g_3 + p_3 g_2 + p_3 p_2 g_1 + p_3 p_2 p_1 g_0 + p_3 p_2 p_1 p_0 C_0.$$

Now we can draw the logic diagram for each carry block. As an example, Figure 2.22 presents the logic diagram for generating C_4. Note there is an AND gate and an OR gate with fan-in of 5 (i.e., they have five inputs). Also, the signal p_3 needs to drive four AND gates (i.e., the OR gate that generates p_3 needs to have at least fan-out of 4). In general, adding two n-bit integers requires an AND gate and an OR gate with fan-in of $n + 1$. It also requires the signal p_{n-1} to drive n AND gates. In practice, these requirements might not be feasible for $n > 5$. In addition to these requirements, Figures

Sec. 2.5   Arithmetic Logic Unit   47

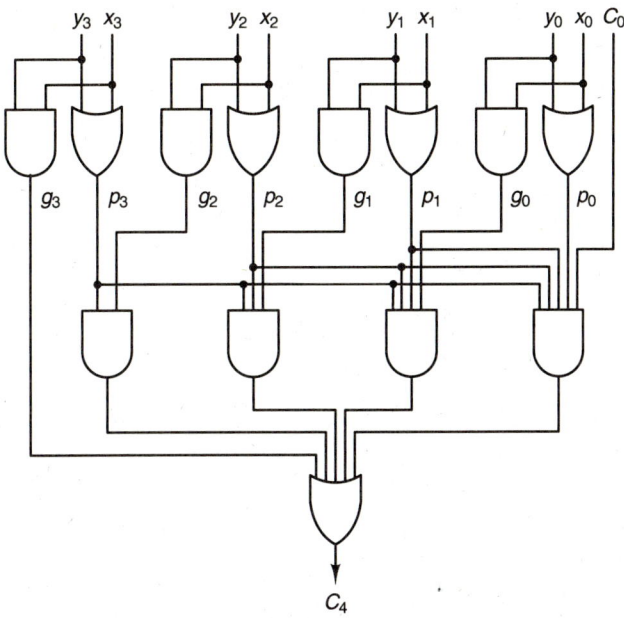

Figure 2.22 Logic diagram for generating carry C_4.

2.21 and 2.22 do not support a modular design for a large n. A modular design requires a structure in which similar parts can be used to build adders of any size.

To solve the preceding problems, we limit the fan-in and fan-out to a certain number depending on technology. This requires more logic levels to be added to the

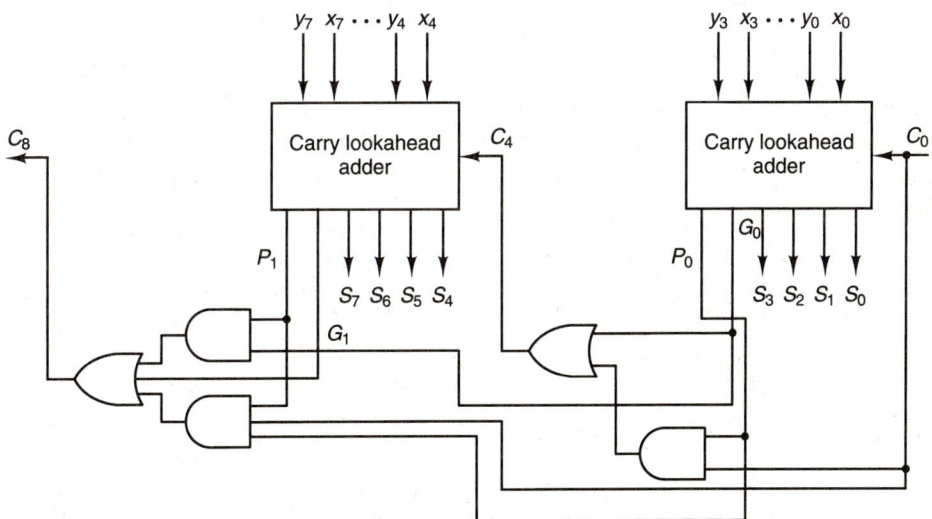

Figure 2.23 Block diagram for an 8-bit carry lookahead adder.

lookahead circuitry. For example, if we limit the fan-in to 4 in the preceding example, more gate delay will be needed in order to compute C_4. To do this, we define two new terms, denoted as group generate G_0 and group propagate P_0, where

$$G_0 = g_3 + p_3 g_2 + p_3 p_2 g_1 + p_3 p_2 p_1 g_0,$$

$$P_0 = p_3 p_2 p_1 p_0.$$

Thus we get

$$C_4 = G_0 + P_0 C_0.$$

Figure 2.23 presents a block diagram for a carry lookahead adder that adds two 8-bit numbers. In this figure, C_8 is computed similarly to C_4:

$$C_8 = G_1 + P_1 G_0 + P_1 P_0 C_0,$$

where $G_1 = g_7 + p_7 g_6 + p_7 p_6 g_5 + p_7 p_6 p_5 g_4,$ and $P_1 = p_7 p_6 p_5 p_4.$

Although the carry lookahead adder is faster than the ripple carry adder, it requires more space on the chip due to more circuitry.

Carry select adder. The carry select adder uses redundant hardware to speed up addition. The increase in speed is created by calculating the high-order half of the sum for both possible input carries, once assuming an input carry of 1 and once assuming an input of 0. When the calculation of the low-order half of the sum is complete and the carry is known, the proper high-order half can be selected.

Assume that two 8-bit numbers are to be added. The low-order 4 bits might be added using a ripple carry adder or a carry lookahead adder (see Figure 2.24). Simul-

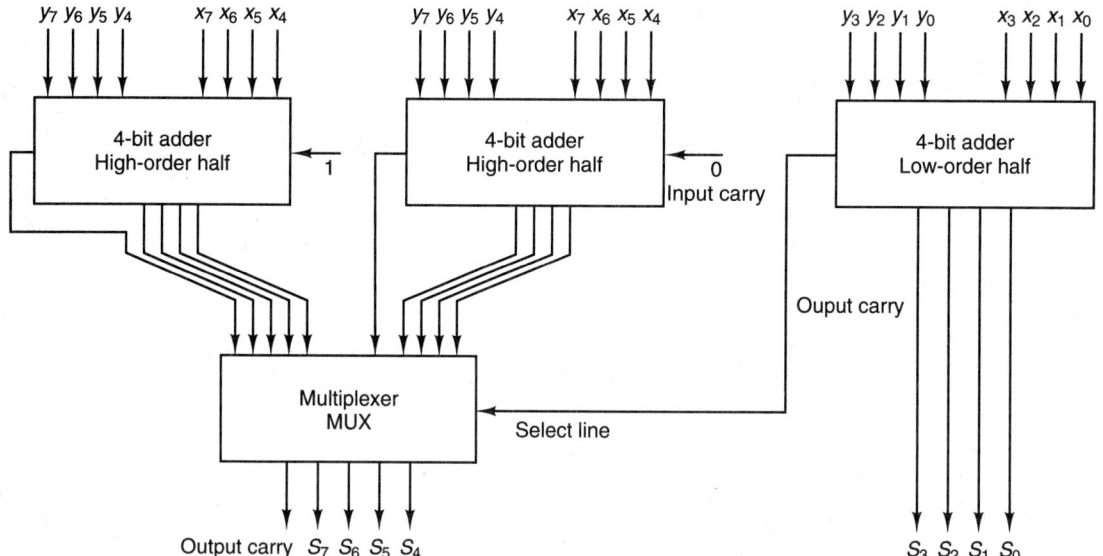

Figure 2.24 Block diagram of an 8-bit carry select adder.

Sec. 2.5   Arithmetic Logic Unit

taneously, the high-order bits will be added once, assuming an input carry of 1 and once assuming an input carry of zero. When the output carry of the low-order bits is known, it can be used to select the proper bit pattern for the sum. Obviously, more adders are needed; therefore, more space is required on the chip [HEN 90]. By limiting the number of bits added at one time, the carry select adder overcomes the carry look-ahead adders complexity in high-order carry calculations.

Carry save adder.   This type of adder is useful when more than two numbers are added. For example, when there are four numbers (X, Y, Z, and W) to be added, the carry save adder first produces a sum and a saved carry for the first 3 numbers. Assuming that $X = 0101$, $Y = 0011$, and $Z = 0100$, the produced sum and saved carry are

```
       0101        X
       0011        Y
   +   0100        Z
       ----
       0010        sum
       1010        saved carry
```

In the next step, the sum, the saved carry, and the fourth number (W) are added in order to produce a new sum and a new saved carry. Assuming that $W = 0001$,

```
       0010        sum
       1010        saved carry
   +   0001        W
       ----
       1001        new sum
       0100        new saved carry
```

In the last step, a carry lookahead adder is used to add the new sum and the new saved carry. Putting all these steps together, a multioperand adder (often used in multiplier circuits to accumulate partial products) can be designed. For example, Figure 2.25 presents a block diagram for adding four numbers. Notice that this design includes two carry save adders, each having a series of full adders.

Figure 2.26 shows how to use only one carry save adder (one level) to add a set of numbers. First, three numbers are applied to the inputs X, Y, and Z. The sum and carry generated by these three numbers are fed back to the inputs X and Y, and then added to the fourth number, which is applied to Z. This process continues until all the numbers are added.

Binary-coded decimal number addition.   So far we have only considered addition of binary numbers. However, sometimes the numbers are represented in binary-coded decimal (BCD) form. In such cases, rather than converting the numbers to binary form and then using a binary adder to add them, it is more efficient to use a decimal adder. A decimal adder adds two BCD digits in parallel and produces a sum in BCD form. Given the fact that a BCD digit is between 0 and 9, whenever the sum exceeds 9 the result is corrected by adding the value 6 to it. For example, in the

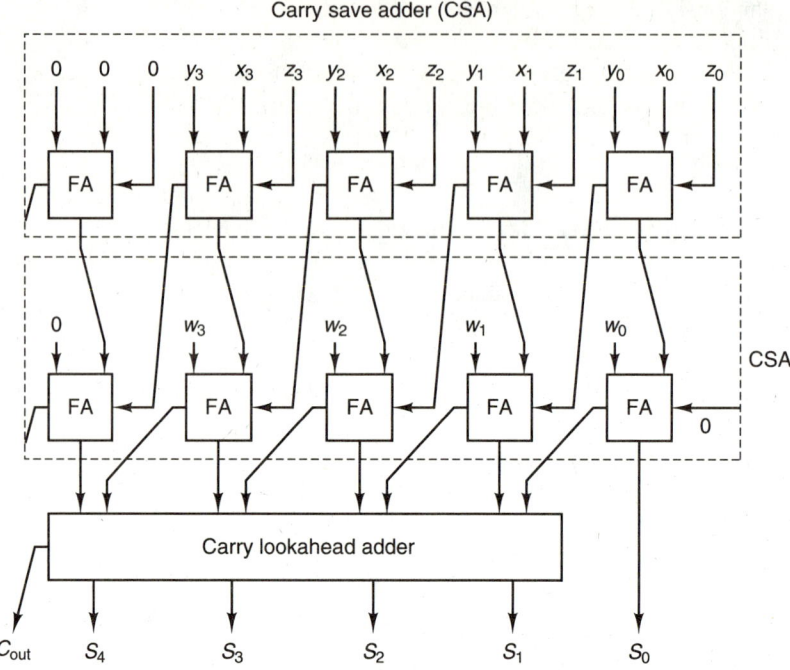

Figure 2.25 Block digram of an adder for adding four 4-bit numbers.

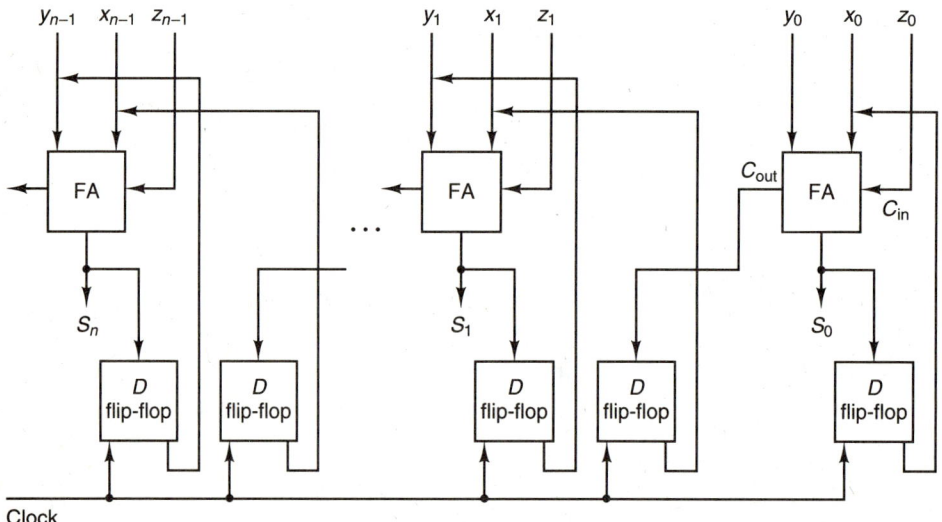

Figure 2.26 Block diagram of an n-bit carry save adder for adding a set of numbers.

Sec. 2.5 Arithmetic Logic Unit

following addition, the sum of 4 (0100) and 7 (0111) is greater than 9; in this case the corresponding intermediate sum digit is corrected by adding 6 to it:

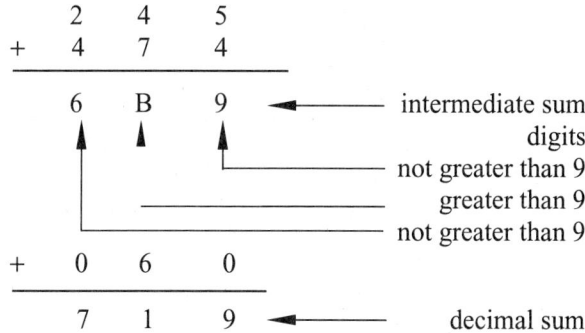

Figure 2.27 shows a decimal adder based on 4-bit adder. In addition to two 4-bit adders, the adder includes some gates to perform logic correction for intermediate sum digits that are equal to or greater than 10 (1010); we add value 6 to these digits.

Serial adder. The serial adder performs the addition step by step from the least significant bit to the most significant bit. The output will be produced bit by bit. As is shown in Figure 2.28, a serial adder consists of only a full adder and a D flip-flop. The D flip-flop is used to propagate the carry of sum of ith input bits to the sum of $(i+1)$th input bits. Compared to the ripple carry adder, the serial adder is even slower, but it is simpler and inexpensive.

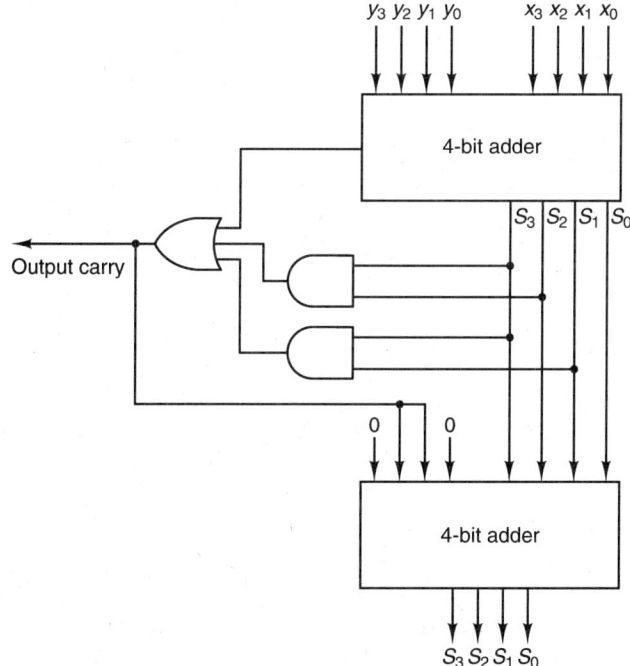

Figure 2.27 Block diagram of a 4-bit binary-coded decimal adder.

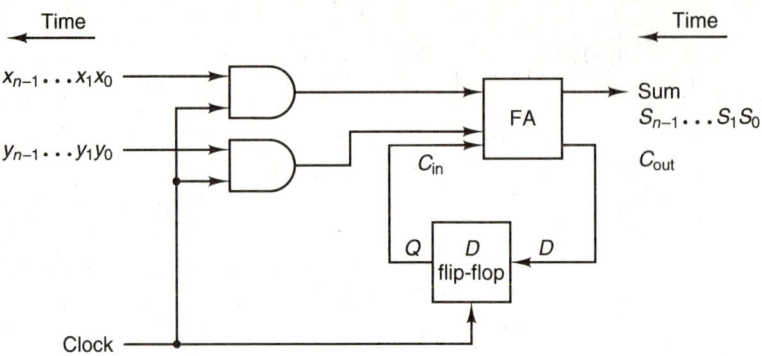

Figure 2.28 Block diagram of a serial adder.

2.5.2 Multiplication

After addition and subtraction functions, multiplication is one of the most important arithmetic functions. Statistics suggest that in some large scientific programs multiplication occurs as frequently as addition and subtraction. Multiplication of two n-bit numbers (or binary fractions) in its simplest form can be done by addition of n partial products.

Wallace showed that the partial products can be added in a fast and economical way using an architecture called a *Wallace tree* [WAL 64]. The Wallace tree adds the partial products by using multilevels of carry save adders. Assuming that all partial products are produced simultaneously, in the first level the Wallace tree groups the numbers into threes and uses a carry save adder to add the numbers in each group. Thus the problem of adding n numbers reduces to the problem of adding $2n/3$ numbers. In the second level, the $2n/3$ resulting numbers are again grouped into three and added by carry save adders. This process continues until there are only two numbers left to be added. (Often the carry lookahead adder is used to add the last two numbers.) Since each level reduces the number of terms to be added by a factor of 1.5 (or a little less when the number of terms is not a multiple of three), the multiplication can be completed in a time proportional to $\log_{1.5} n$.

For example let's consider multiplication of two unsigned 4-bit numbers as shown next:

				x_3	x_2	x_1	x_0	
				$* y_3$	y_2	y_1	y_0	
0	0	0	0	$x_3 y_0$	$x_2 y_0$	$x_1 y_0$	$x_0 y_0$	$\rightarrow M_1$
0	0	0	$x_3 y_1$	$x_2 y_1$	$x_1 y_1$	$x_0 y_1$	0	$\rightarrow M_2$
0	0	$x_3 y_2$	$x_2 y_2$	$x_1 y_2$	$x_0 y_2$	0	0	$\rightarrow M_3$
0	$x_3 y_3$	$x_2 y_3$	$x_1 y_3$	$x_0 y_3$	0	0	0	$\rightarrow M_4$

As is shown in Figure 2.29, the inputs to the carry save adders are M_1, M_2, M_3, and M_4. Also, Figure 2.29 shows how to generate M_1. M_1 consists of 8 bits where the

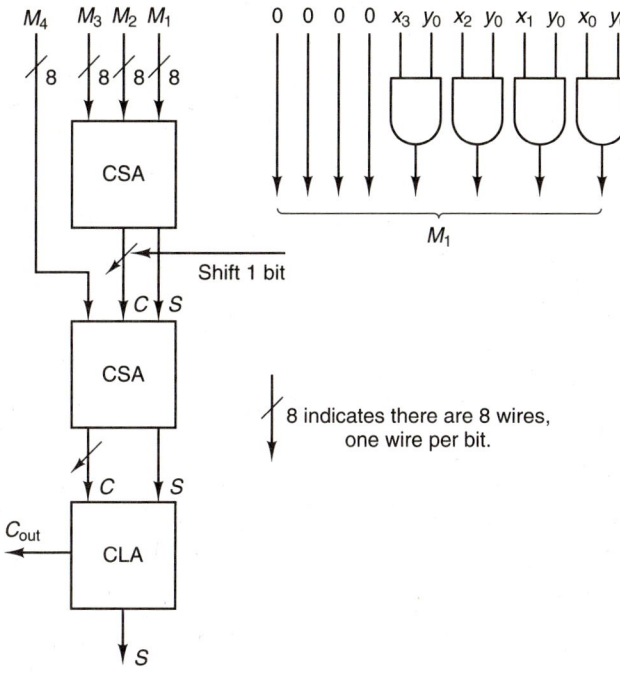

Figure 2.29 Block diagram of a 4-bit multiplier using carry save adders

leftmost 4 bits are 0 and the rightmost 4 bits are x_0y_0, x_1y_0, x_2y_0, and x_3y_0. M_2, M_3, and M_4 can be generated in a similar way.

The discussion that follows will explore different techniques for multiplication, such as *shift-and-add, Booth's technique,* and *array multiplier.*

Shift-and-add multiplication. Shift-and-add multiplication, also called the pencil-and-paper method, is a simple but slow method. This method adds the multiplicand Y to itself X times, where X denotes the multiplier. Assume that X and Y are n-bit 2's complement numbers that are stored in n-bit registers Q and M, respectively. Also, assume that there are an n-bit register A and a 1-bit register S. Furthermore, let registers S, A, and Q be connected to each other as shown:

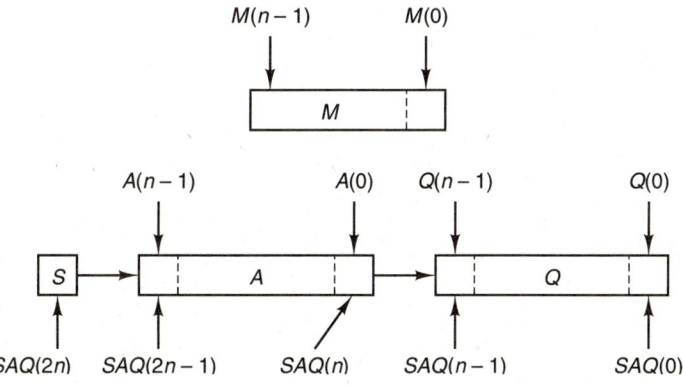

By putting three registers *S*, *A*, and *Q* together, a larger register, *SAQ*, is constructed for storing the partial products and final result. The following code represents the steps of shift-and-add multiplication.

```
A = 0; S = 0;              --Initialize the registers A and S.
M = Y;                     --M contains multiplicand.
Q = X;                     --Q contains multiplier.
if(Q(n-1) = '1') then      --If the multiplier is negative, then
    M = -M;                --replace the contents of M and Q
    Q = -Q;                --with their 2's complement.
end if;                    --In this way the contents of Q will
                           --always be positive.
S = M(n-1);                --Set S equal to the sign of M.
for i in 1 to n loop       --Add the contents of M to A,
    if(Q(0) = '1') then    --Q times.
        A = M + A;
    end if;
    for j in 1 to 2n loop
                           --Shift SAQ register 1 to the
        SAQ(j-1) = SAQ(j); --right, and don't change S.
    end loop;              --(Register SAQ has 2n+1 bits
                           --and is concatenation of the
end loop;                  --three registers S, A, and Q.)
```

For example, let $X = 01101$ and $Y = 10111$ be two 2's complement numbers; that is, *X* and *Y* represent the decimal values 13 and -9, respectively. (Note that if we want to represent the same values of 13 and -9 in more than 5 bits we need to pad the extra bits, depending on what the sign of the value is. Positive values are padded with 0, and negative values with 1. So 13 and -9 in 8 bits are 00001101 and 11110111, respectively.) The contents of the registers *S*, *A*, and *Q* at each cycle are as follows:

Cycle	S	A	Q	Operation
	0	00000	01101	Initialization
1	1	10111	01101	Add *M* to *A*
	1	11011	10110	Shift right
2	1	11101	11011	Shift right
3	1	10100	11011	Add *M* to *A*
	1	11010	01101	Shift right
4	1	10001	01101	Add *M* to A
	1	11000	10110	Shift right
5	1	11100	01011	Shift right (result)

Booth's technique. In the shift-and-add form of a multiplier, the multiplicand is added to the partial product at each bit position where a 1 occurs in the multiplier. Therefore, the number of times that the multiplicand is added to the partial product is equal to the number of 1's in the multiplier. Also, when the multiplier is

Sec. 2.5 Arithmetic Logic Unit

negative, the shift-and-add method requires an additional step to replace the multiplier and multiplicand with their 2's complement.

To increase the speed of multiplication, Booth discovered a technique that reduces the addition steps and eliminates the conversion of the multiplier to positive form [BOO 51]. The main point of Booth's multiplication is that the string of 0's in the multiplier requires no addition, but just shifting, and the string of 1's can be treated as a number with value $L - R$, where L is the weight of the zero before the leftmost 1 and R is the weight of the rightmost 1. So, if the number is 01100, then $L = 2^4 = 16$ and $R = 2^2 = 4$. That is, the value of 01100 can be represented as $16 - 4$. Let's take a look at an example; let multiplier $X = 10011$ and multiplicand $Y = 10111$ in 2's complement representation. The multiplier X can be represented as

$$X = -2^4 + (2^2 - 2^0).$$

Thus

$$X * Y = [-2^4 + (2^2 - 2^0)] * Y = -2^4 Y + 2^2 Y - 2^0 Y.$$

Based on this string manipulation, the Booth's multiplier considers every two adjacent bits of the multiplier to determine which operation to perform. The possible operations are

X_{i+1}	X_i	Operation
0	0	Shift right
1	0	Subtract multiplicand and shift right
1	1	Shift right
0	1	Add multiplicand and shift right

For example, let $X = Q = 10011$, $Y = M = 10111$, and $-M = $ 2's complement of $Y = 01001$. Initially, a 0 is placed in front of the rightmost bit of Q. At each cycle of operation, based on the rightmost 2 bits of Q, one of the preceding operations is performed. The contents of the registers S, A, and Q at each cycle are shown next:

Cycle	S	A	Q	Operation
	0	00000	100110	Initialization Add an extra bit to Q
1	0	01001	100110	Subtract M from A, in other words add $-M$ to A
	0	00100	110011	Shift right
2	0	00010	011001	Shift right
3	1	11001	011001	Add M to A
	1	11100	101100	Shift right
4	1	11110	010110	Shift right
5	0	00111	010110	Subtract M from A
	0	00011	101011	Shift right (result)

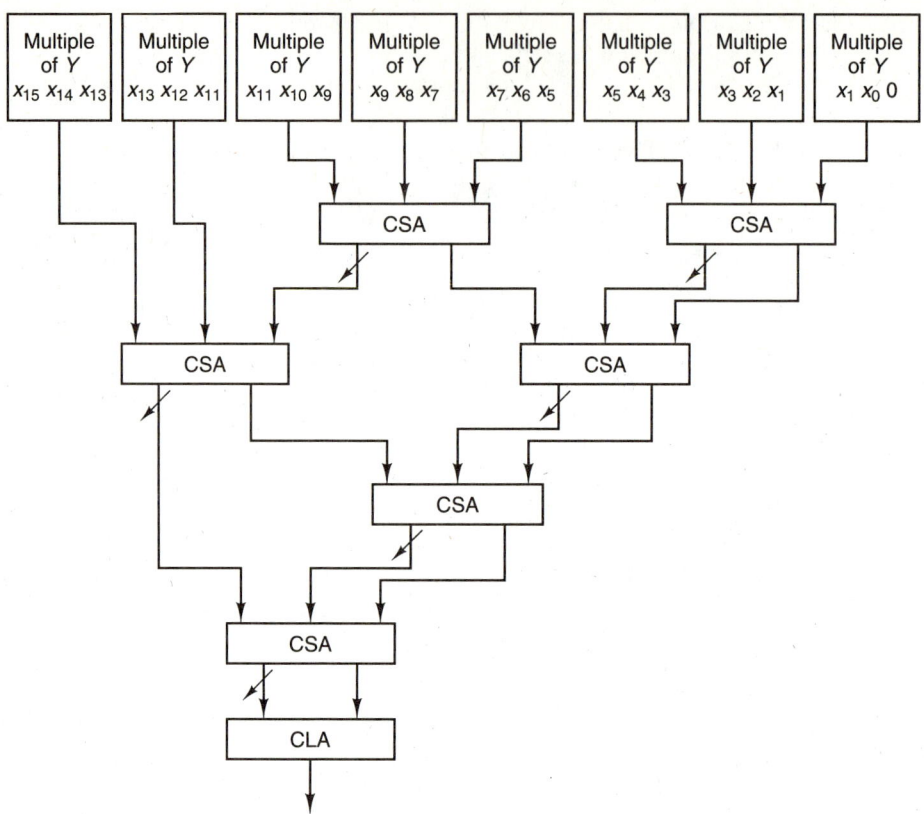

Figure 2.30 A multiplier combining a Wallace tree and Booth's technique.

Often, in practice, both Booth's technique and the Wallace tree method are used for producing fast multipliers. Booth's technique is used to produce the partial products, and the Wallace tree is used to add them. For example, assume that we want to multiply two 16-bit numbers. Let $X = x_{15} \ldots x_1 x_0$ and $Y = y_{15} \ldots y_1 y_0$ denote the multiplier and the multiplicand, respectively. Figure 2.30 represents a possible architecture for multiplying such numbers. In the first level of the tree, the partial products are produced by using a scheme similar to Booth's technique, except that 3 bits are examined at each step instead of 2 bits. (Three-bit scanning is an extension to Booth's technique. It is left as an exercise for the reader.) With a 16-bit multiplier, the 3 examined bits for producing each partial product are

$$x_1 x_0 0$$
$$x_3 x_2 x_1$$
$$x_5 x_4 x_3$$
$$x_7 x_6 x_5$$
$$x_9 x_8 x_7$$
$$x_{11} x_{10} x_9$$
$$x_{13} x_{12} x_{11}$$
$$x_{15} x_{14} x_{13}$$

Sec. 2.5 Arithmetic Logic Unit

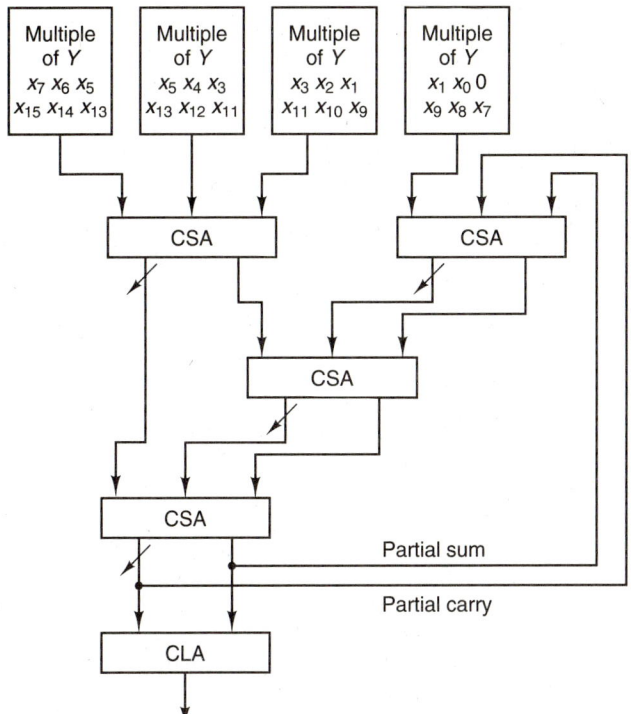

Figure 2.31 A two pass multiplier combining Wallace tree and Booth's technique.

The partial products are then added by a set of CSAs arranged in the form of a Wallace tree.

To reduce the required hardware in the preceding structure, especially for large numbers, often the final product is obtained by passing through the Wallace tree several times. For example, Figure 2.31 represents an alternative design for our example. This design requires two passes. The first pass adds the four partial products that result from the 8 least significant bits of the multiplier. In the second pass, the resulting partial sum and carry are fed back into the top of the tree to be added to the next four partial products.

Array multiplier. Baugh and Wooley have proposed a notable method for multiplying 2's complement numbers [BAU 73]. They have converted the 2's complement multiplication to an equivalent parallel array addition problem. In contrast to the conventional two's-complement multiplication, which has negative and positive partial products, Baugh–Wooley's algorithm generates only positive partial products. Using this algorithm, we can add the partial products with an array of full adders in a modular way; this is an important feature in VLSI design. With the advent of VLSI design, the implementation of an array of similar cells is very easy and economical. (In general, the placement of a set of same–sized cells, such as full adders, requires an ideal area on a chip.)

Before we study the algorithm, we should know about some of the equivalent representations of a 2's complement number. Given an n-bit 2's complement $X = (x_{n-1}, ..., x_0)$, the value of X, X_v, can be represented as

$$X_v = -x_{n-1}2^{n-1} + \sum_{i=0}^{n-2} x_i 2^i$$

or

$$X_v = -x_{n-1}2^{n-1} + (2^{n-1} - 2^{n-1}) + \sum_{i=0}^{n-2} x_i 2^i$$

$$= -(x_{n-1}-1)2^{n-1} - 2^{n-1} + \sum_{i=0}^{n-2} x_i 2^i$$

$$= (1 - x_{n-1})2^{n-1} - (1 + \sum_{i=0}^{n-2} 2^i) + \sum_{i=0}^{n-2} x_i 2^i$$

$$= (1-x_{n-1})2^{n-1} - 1 - \sum_{i=0}^{n-2} (1 - x_i)2^i$$

$$= \overline{x}_{n-1}2^{n-1} - 1 - \sum_{i=0}^{n-2} \overline{x}_i 2^i \qquad (2.3)$$

Now let the n-bit $X = (x_{n-1}, ..., x_0)$ be the multiplier, and the m-bit $Y = (y_{m-1}, ..., y_0)$ be the multiplicand. The value of the product $P = (p_{n+m-1}, ..., p_0)$ can be represented as:

$$P_v = Y_v X_v$$

$$= (-y_{m-1}2^{m-1} + \sum_{i=0}^{m-2} y_i 2^i)(-x_{n-1}2^{n-1} + \sum_{i=0}^{n-2} x_i 2^i)$$

$$= y_{m-1}x_{n-1}2^{m+n-2} + \sum_{i=0}^{m-2}\sum_{j=0}^{n-2} y_i x_j 2^{i+j}$$

$$- \sum_{i=0}^{m-2} x_{n-1}y_i 2^{n-1+i} - \sum_{i=0}^{n-2} y_{m-1}x_i 2^{m-1+i}.$$

This equation shows that P_v is formed by adding the positive partial products and subtracting the negative partial products. As shown in Figure 2.32, by placing all the negative terms in the last two rows, P_v can be computed by adding the first $n-2$ rows and subtracting the last two rows.

We would like to change the negative terms to positive in order to do simple addition instead of subtraction. The negative term

$$- \sum_{i=0}^{m-2} x_{n-1}y_i 2^{n-1+i}$$

can be rewritten as

$$- 2^{n-1}(-0 * 2^{m-1} + \sum_{i=0}^{m-2} x_{n-1}y_i 2^i).$$

Sec. 2.5 Arithmetic Logic Unit

| | | | | | | | y_{m-1} | | . | . | . | | | y_2 | y_1 | y_0 |
| | | | | | | | | | | | | x_{n-1} | . | . | . | x_2 | x_1 | x_0 |

Positive terms			$x_0 y_{m-2}$	.	.	.	$x_0 y_2$ $x_0 y_1$ $x_0 y_0$
			$x_1 y_{m-2}$	.	.	.	$x_1 y_2$ $x_1 y_1$ $x_1 y_0$

$x_{n-1}y_{m-1}$ 0 $x_{n-2}y_{m-2}$ . . . $x_{n-2}y_2$ $x_{n-2}y_1$ $x_{n-2}y_0$

0 0 $x_{n-1}y_{m-2}$ $x_{n-1}y_{m-3}$ . . $x_{n-1}y_2$ $x_{n-1}y_1$ $x_{n-1}y_0$
0 0 $x_{n-2}y_{m-1}$ $x_{n-3}y_{m-1}$ . . . $x_0 y_{m-1}$ Negative terms

P_{n+m-1} P_{n+m-2} . . . P_2 P_1 P_0

Figure 2.32 Positive and negative partial products for multiplying an *n*-bit number with an *m*-bit number.

Using (2.3), this term can be replaced with

$$2^{n-1}(-1 * 2^{m-1} + 1 + \sum_{i=0}^{m-2} \overline{x_{n-1}y_i} 2^i),$$

or

$$2^{n-1}(-1 * 2^m + 1 * 2^{m-1} + 1 + \sum_{i=0}^{m-2} \overline{x_{n-1}y_i} 2^i), \qquad (2.4)$$

which has the following values:

$0,$ when $x_{n-1} = 0,$

$2^{n-1}(-2^m + 2^{m-1} + 1 + \sum_{i=0}^{m-2} \overline{y_i} 2^i),$ when $x_{n-1} = 1.$

Therefore, (2.4) can be rewritten as

$$2^{n-1}(-2^m + 2^{m-1} + \overline{x}_{n-1} 2^{m-1} + x_{n-1} + \sum_{i=0}^{m-2} \overline{x_{n-1}y_i} 2^i).$$

So the second to last row in Figure 2.32 can be replaced by

0 $\overline{x}_{n-1}$ $\overline{x_{n-1}y}_{m-2}$ $\overline{x_{n-1}y}_{m-3}$ ... $\overline{x_{n-1}y}_2$ $\overline{x_{n-1}y}_1$ $\overline{x_{n-1}y}_0$
1 1 0 0 0 0 x_{n-1}

Similarly, the last row in Figure 2.32 can be replaced by

0 $\overline{y}_{m-1}$ $\overline{x_{n-2}y}_{m-1}$ $\overline{x_{n-3}y}_{m-1}$ ... $\overline{x_0 y}_{m-1}$
1 1 0 0 y_{m-1}

These replacements are shown in Figure 2.33. Notice that in this figure all partial products are positive. Therefore, the product P can be obtained by adding the rows; this is shown in Figure 2.34 for $m = 6$ and $n = 4$.

		y_{m-1}	.	.	.		y_2	y_1	y_0	
				x_{n-1}	.	.	.	x_2	x_1	x_0
		$x_0 y_{m-2}$		.	.	.		$x_0 y_2$	$x_0 y_1$	$x_0 y_0$
	$x_1 y_{m-2}$			.	.	.	$x_1 y_2$	$x_1 y_1$	$x_1 y_0$	
		.						.		
$\overline{x_{n-1} y_{m-1}}$	0	$x_{n-2} y_{m-2}$	.	.	.	$x_{n-2}\overline{y_2}$	$x_{n-2}\overline{y_1}$	$x_{n-2} y_0$		
$\overline{x}_{n-1}$	$\overline{x}_{n-1}\overline{y}_{m-2}$	$\overline{x}_{n-1}\overline{y}_{m-3}$	.	.	.	$\overline{x}_{n-1}\overline{y_2}$	$\overline{x}_{n-1}\overline{y_1}$	$\overline{x}_{n-1} y_0$		
$\overline{y}_{m-1}$	$\overline{x}_{n-2} y_{m-1}$	$\overline{x}_{n-3} y_{m-1}$	. . .	$\overline{x}_0 y_{m-1}$						
1			y_{m-1}			x_{n-1}				
P_{n+m-1}	P_{n+m-2}		.	.	.		P_2	P_1	P_0	

Figure 2.33 Using only positive partial products for multiplying for an *n*-bit number with an *m*-bit number.

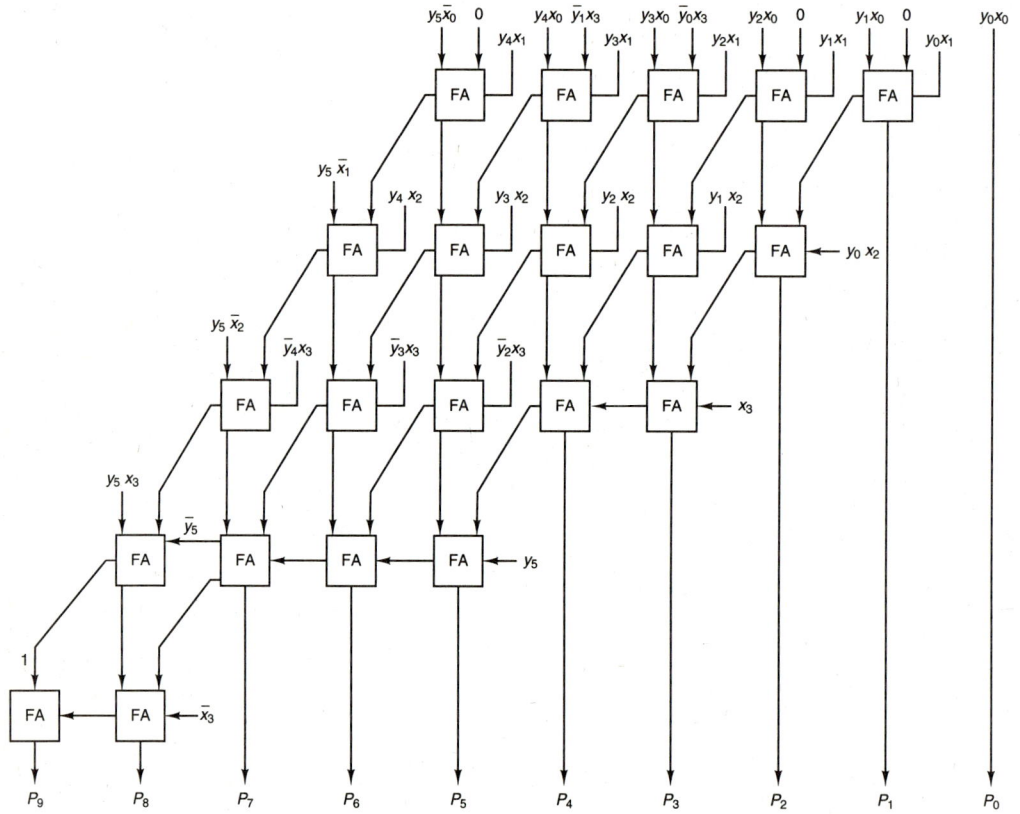

Figure 2.34 Block diagram of an array multiplier for multiplying a 4-bit number with a 6-bit number.

2.5.3 Floating-point Representation

The range of numbers available for a word is strictly limited by its size. A 32-bit word has a range of 2^{32} different numbers. If the numbers are considered as integers, it is necessary to scale the numbers of many problems in order to represent the fractions. One solution can be to increase the size of the word to get a better range. However, this solution increases the storage space and computing time. A better solution is to use an automatic scaling technique, known as the floating-point representation (also referred to as scientific notation).

In general, a floating-point number can be represented in the following form:

$$\pm m * b^e$$

where m, called the *mantissa*, represents the fraction part of the number and is normally represented as a signed binary fraction. The e represents the exponent, and the b represents the base (radix) of the exponent.

This representation can be stored in a binary word with three fields: sign, mantissa, and exponent. For example, assuming that the word has 32 bits, a possible assignment of bits to each field could be

31	30 ... 23	22 ... 0
S	Exponent	Mantissa

Notice that no field is assigned to the exponent base b. This is because the base b is the same for all the numbers, and often it is assumed to be 2. Therefore, there is no need to store the base. The sign field consists of 1 bit and indicates the sign of the number, 0 for positive and 1 for negative. The exponent consists of 8 bits, which can represent numbers 0 through 255. To represent positive and negative exponents, a fixed value, called *bias*, is subtracted from the exponent field to obtain the true exponent. In our example, assuming the bias value to be 128, the true exponents are in the range from -128 to $+127$. (The exponent -128 is stored as 0, and the exponent $+127$ is stored as 255 in the exponent field.) In this way, before storing an exponent in the exponent field, the value 128 should be added to the exponent. For example, to represent exponent $+4$, the value 132 $(128 + 4)$ is stored in the exponent field, and the exponent -12 is stored as 116 $(128 - 12)$.

The mantissa consists of 23 bits. Although the radix point (or binary point) is not represented, it is assumed to be at the left side of the most significant bit of the mantissa. For example, when $b = 2$, the floating-point number 1.75 can be represented in any of the following forms:

$+0.111 * 2^1$ | 0 | 10000001 | 11100000000000000000000 | (2.5)

$+0.0111 * 2^2$ | 0 | 10000010 | 01110000000000000000000 | (2.6)

$+0.00000000000000000000111 * 2^{21}$ | 0 | 10010101 | 00000000000000000000111 | (2.7)

To simplify the operation on floating-point numbers and increase their precision, floating-point numbers are always represented in normalized form. A floating-point number is said to be *normalized* if the leftmost bit (most significant bit) of the mantissa is 1. Therefore, in the three representations for 1.75, the first representation, which is normalized, is used. Since the leftmost bit of the mantissa of a normalized floating-point number is always 1, this bit is often not stored and is assumed to be a hidden bit to the left of the radix point. This allows the mantissa to have one more significant bit. That is, the stored mantissa m will actually represents the value $1.m$. In this case, the normalized 1.75 will have the following form:

$+ 1. 11 * 2^0$ | 0 | 10000000 | 11000000000000000000000 |

Assuming a hidden bit to the left of the radix point in our floating-point format, a nonzero normalized number represents the following value:

$$(-1)^s * (1.m) * 2^{e-128},$$ where s denotes the sign bit.

Furthermore, the format can represent the following range of numbers.
Smallest negative number: $-1.0 * 2^{-128}$

| 1 | 00000000 | 00000000000000000000000 |

Largest negative number: $-[1 + (1 - 2^{-23})] * 2^{127}$

| 1 | 11111111 | 11111111111111111111111 |

Smallest positive number: $1.0 * 2^{-128}$

| 0 | 00000000 | 00000000000000000000000 |

Largest positive number: $[1 + (1 - 2^{-23})] * 2^{127}$

| 0 | 11111111 | 11111111111111111111111 |

Computation on floating-point numbers may produce results that are either larger than the largest representable value or smaller than the smallest representable value. When the result is larger than the allowable representation, an *overflow* is said to have occurred, and when it is smaller than the allowable representation, an *underflow* is said to have occurred. Processors have certain mechanisms for detecting, handling, and signaling overflow and underflow.

The problem with the preceding format is that there is no representation for the value 0. This is because a zero cannot be normalized since it does not contain a nonzero digit. However, in practice the floating-point representations reserve a special bit pattern for 0. Often a zero is represented by all 0's in the mantissa and exponent. A good example of such bit pattern assignment for 0 is the standard formats defined by the IEEE Computer Society [IEE 85].

Sec. 2.5   Arithmetic Logic Unit

The *IEEE 754 floating-point standard* defines both a single-precision (32-bit) and a double-precision (64-bit) format for representing floating-point numbers.

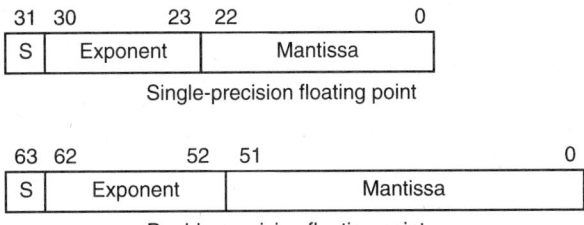

In both formats the implied exponent base *(b)* is assumed to be 2. The single-precision format allocates 8 bits for exponent, 23 bits for mantissa, and 1 bit for sign. The exponent values 0 and 255 are used for representing special values, including 0 and infinity. The value 0 is represented as all 0's in the mantissa and exponent. Depending on the sign bit the value 0 can be represented as $+0$ or -0. Infinity is represented by storing all 0's in the mantissa and 255 in the exponent. Again, depending on sign bit, $+\infty$ and $-\infty$ are possible. When the exponent is 255 and the mantissa is nonzero, a not-a-number (NaN) is represented. The NaN is a symbol for the result of invalid operations, such as taking the square root of a negative number, subtracting infinity from infinity, or dividing a zero by a zero. For exponent values from 1 through 254, a bias value 127 is used to determine the true exponent. Such biasing allows a true exponent from -126 through $+127$. There is a hidden bit on the left of the radix point for normalized numbers, allowing an effective 24-bit mantissa. Thus the value of a normalized number represented by a single-precision format is

$$(-1)^s * (1.m) * 2^{e-127}.$$

In addition to representation of positive and negative exponents, the bias notation also allows floating-point numbers to be sorted based on their bit patterns. Sorting can occur because the largest negative exponent is represented as 00000001, and the largest positive exponent is represented as 11111110. Given the fact that the exponent field is placed before the mantissa and the mantissa is normalized, numbers with bigger exponents are larger than numbers with smaller exponents. In other words, any bigger number has a larger bit pattern than a smaller number.

The double-precision format can be defined similarly. This format allocates 11 bits for exponent and 52 bits for mantissa. The exponent bias is 1023. The value of a normalized number represented by a double-precision format is

$$(-1)^s * (1.m) * 2^{e-1023}.$$

Floating-point addition. The difficulty involved in adding two floating-point numbers stems from the fact that they may have different exponents. Therefore, before the two numbers can be properly added together, their exponents must be equalized. This involves comparing the magnitude of two exponents and then *aligning* the mantissa of the number that has smaller magnitude of exponent. The alignment is

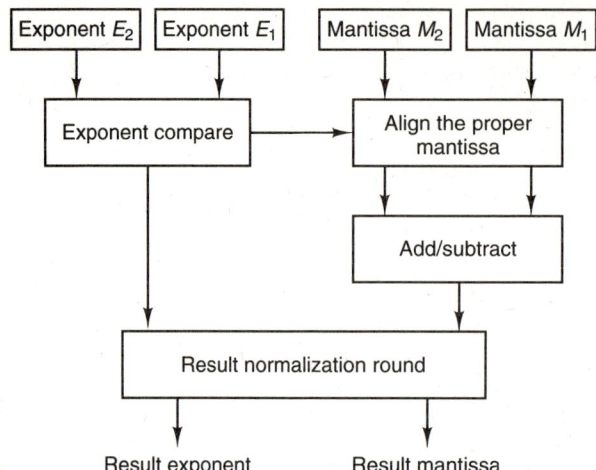

Figure 2.35 Block diagram of a floating-point adder.

accomplished by shifting the mantissa a number of positions to the right. The number of positions to shift is determined by the magnitude of difference in the exponents. For example, to add $1.1100 * 2^4$ and $1.1000 * 2^2$, we proceed as follows. The number $1.1000 * 2^2$ has a smaller exponent, so it is rewritten as $0.0110 * 2^4$ by aligning the mantissa. Now the addition can be performed as follows:

$$\begin{array}{rl} 1.1100 & * 2^4 \\ + \ 0.0110 & * 2^4 \\ \hline 10.0010 & * 2^4 \end{array}$$

Notice that the resulting number is not normalized. In general, the addition of any pair of floating-point numbers may result in an unnormalized number. In this case, the resulting number should be normalized by shifting the resulting mantissa and adjusting the resulting exponent. Whenever the exponent is increased or decreased, we should check to determine whether an overflow or underflow has occurred in this field. If the exponent cannot fit in its field, an exception is issued. (Exceptions are defined later in this chapter.) We also need to check the size of the resulting mantissa. If the resulting mantissa requires more bits than its field, we must round it to the appropriate number of bits. In the example, where 4 bits after radix point are kept, the final result will be $1.0001 * 2^5$.

Figure 2.35 represents a block diagram for floating-point addition. The result of comparison of the magnitude of two exponents directs the align unit to shift the proper mantissa. The aligned mantissa and the other mantissa are then fed to the add/subtract unit for the actual computation. (If one number has a negative sign, what should actually be performed is a subtraction operation.) The resulting number is then sent to the result normalization–round unit. The result is normalized and rounded when needed. The detail of the function of this unit is shown in Figure 2.36. (A good explanation on rounding procedure can be found in [FEL 94].)

Sec. 2.5 Arithmetic Logic Unit

Floating-point multiplication. Considering a pair of floating-point numbers represented by
$X = m_x * 2^{ex}$ and $Y = m_y * 2^{ey}$, the multiplication operation can be defined as:

$$X * Y = (m_x * m_y) * 2^{ex + ey}$$

For example, when $X = 1.000 * 2^{-2}$ and $Y = -1.010 * 2^{-1}$, the product $X * Y$ can be computed as follows:

Add the exponents:
$-2 + (-1) = -3$.

Multiply the mantissas:
```
        1.000
    * - 1.010
    ---------
         0000
         1000
         0000
         1000
    ---------
    - 1.010000
```

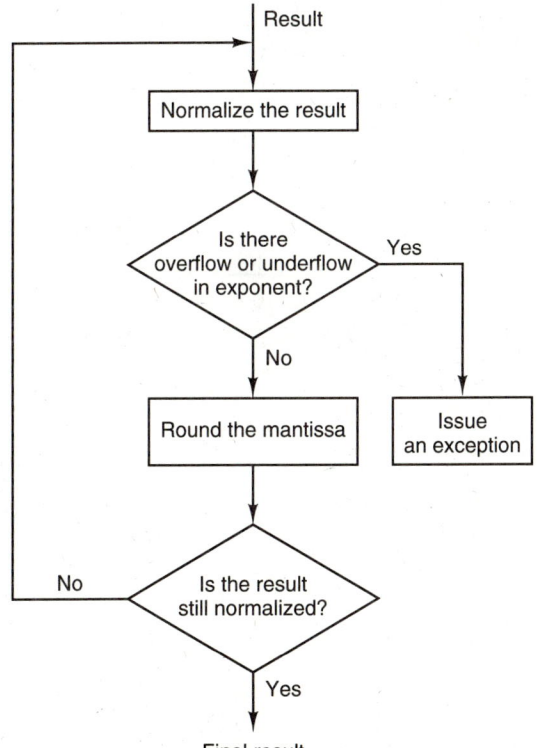

Figure 2.36 The function of the normalization-round unit in a floating-point adder.

Thus the product is $-1.0100 * 2^{-3}$. In general, an algorithm for floating-point multiplication consists of three major steps: (1) computing the exponent of the product by adding the exponents together, (2) multiplying the mantissas, and (3) normalizing and rounding the final product.

Figure 2.37 represents a block diagram for floating-point multiplication. This design consists of three units: add, multiply, and result normalization-round units. The add and multiply units can be designed similarly to the ones that are used for binary integer numbers (different methods were discussed in previous sections). The result normalization–round unit can be implemented in a similar way as the normalization–round unit in a floating-point adder, as shown in Figure 2.36.

2.6 MEMORY SYSTEM DESIGN

This section discusses the general principles and terms associated with a memory system. It also presents a review of the design of memory systems, including the use of memory hierarchy, the design of associative memories, and caches.

2.6.1 Memory Hierarchy

With increasing CPU speeds, the bottleneck in the speedup of any computer system can be associated to the memory *access time*. (The time taken to gain access to a data item assumed to exist in memory is known as the access time.) To avoid wasting precious CPU cycles in access time delay, faster memories have been developed. But the cost of such memories prohibits their exclusive use in a computer system. This leads to the need of having a memory hierarchy that supports a combination of faster (expensive) as well as slower (relatively inexpensive) memories. The fastest memories are usually smaller in capacity than slower memories. At present, the general trend of large as well as small personal computers has been toward increasing the use of memory hierarchies. The major reason for this increase is due to the way that programs operate. By statistical analysis of typical programs, it has been established that at any given interval of time the references to memory tend to be confined within local areas of memory [MAN 86]. This phenomenon is known as the property of *locality of refer-*

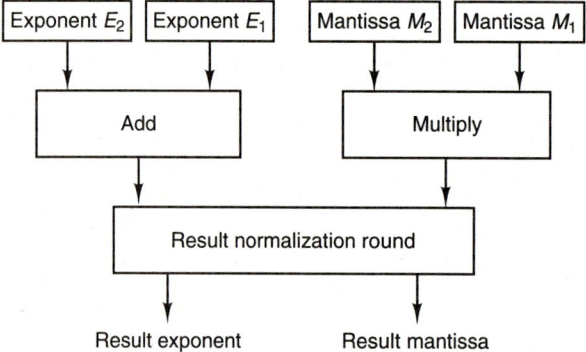

Figure 2.37 Block diagram of a floating-point multiplier.

Sec. 2.6   Memory System Design   67

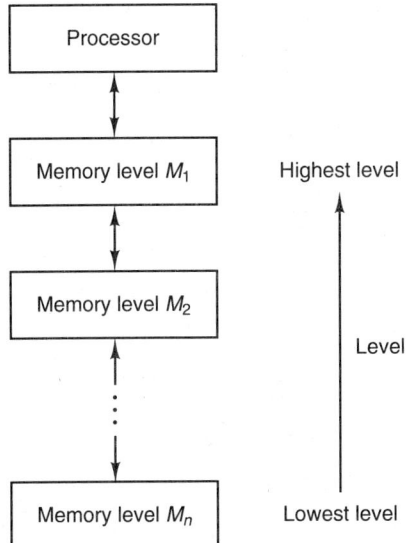

Figure 2.38 Memory hierarchy.

ence. Three concepts are associated with locality of reference: *temporal, spatial,* and *sequential.* Each of these concepts is defined next.

> **Temporal locality.** Items (data or instructions) recently referenced have a good chance to be referenced in the near future. For example, a set of instructions in an iterative loop or in a subroutine may be referenced repeatedly many times.
> **Spatial locality.** A program often references items whose addresses are close to each other in the address space. For example, references to the elements of an array always occur within a certain bounded area in the address space.
> **Sequential locality.** Most of the instructions in a program are executed in a sequential order. The instructions that might cause out-of-order execution are branches. However, branches construct about 20% to 30% of all instructions; therefore, about 70% to 80% of instructions are often accessed in the same order as they are stored in memory.

Usually, the various memory units in a typical memory system can be viewed as forming a hierarchy of memories ($M_1, M_2, ..., M_n$), as shown in Figure 2.38. As can be seen, M_1 (the highest level) is the smallest, fastest, most expensive memory unit, and is located the closest to the processor. M_2 (the second highest level) is slightly larger, slower, and less expensive and is not as close to the processor as is M_1. The same is true for M_3 to M_n. In general, as the level increases, the speed and thus the cost per byte increases proportionally, which tends to decrease memory capacity. Because of the property of locality of reference, generally data transfers take place in fixed-sized segments of words called *blocks* (sometimes called *pages* or *lines*). These transfers are between adjacent levels and are entirely controlled by the activity in the first level of the memory.

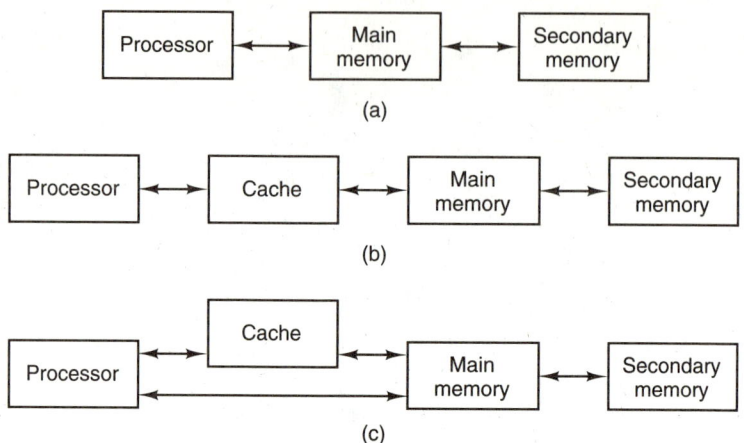

Figure 2.39 (a) Two level memory hierarchy; (b) and (c) Three level memory hierarchy.

In general, whenever there is a block in level M_i, there is a copy of it in each of the lower levels $M_{i+1}, \ldots, M_n$ [CHO 74]. Also, whenever a block is not found in M_1, a request for it is sent to successively lower levels until it is located in, say, level M_i. Since each level has limited storage capability, whenever M_i is full and a new block is to be brought in from M_{i+1}, a currently stored block in M_i is replaced using a predetermined replacement policy. These policies vary and are governed by the available hardware and the operating system. (Some replacement policies are explained later in this chapter.)

The main advantage of having a hierarchical memory system is that the information is retrieved most of the time from the fastest level M_1. Hence the average memory access time is nearly equal to the speed of the highest level, whereas the average unit cost of the memory system approaches the cost of the lowest level.

The highest two or three levels of common memory hierarchies are shown in Figure 2.39. Figure 2.39a presents an architecture in which main memory is used as the first level of memory hierarchy, and secondary memory (such as a disk) is used as the second level. Figures 2.39b and c present two alternative architectures for designing a system with three level of memories. Here a relatively large and slower main memory is coupled together with a smaller, faster memory called *cache*. The cache memory acts as a go-between for the main memory and the processor. (The organization of a cache memory is explained later in this chapter.) Figure 2.40 shows a sample curve of the cost function versus access time for different memory units.

With the advancement of technology, the cost of semiconductor memories has decreased considerably, making it possible to have large amounts of semiconductor memories installed in computer systems as main memory. As a result, most of the required data can be brought into the semiconductor memories in advance and can satisfy a major part of the memory references. Thus the impact of the speed of mass storage devices like hard disks and tapes on the overall computer system speed is lessening.

Sec. 2.6   Memory System Design

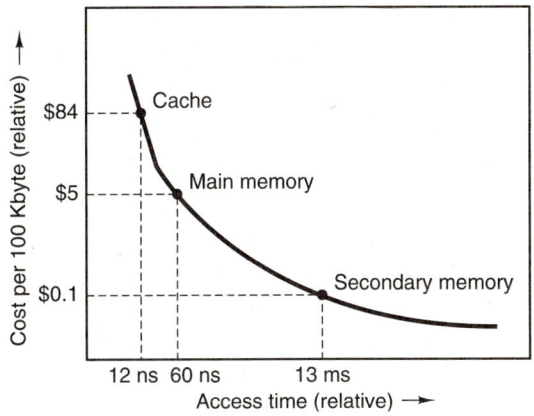

Figure 2.40 Cost function versus access time for various memory devices.

2.6.2 Memory Cell and Memory Unit

A memory cell is the building block of a memory unit. The internal construction of a random-access memory of *m* words with *n* bits per word consists of $m * n$ binary storage cells. A block diagram of a binary cell that stores 1 bit of information is shown in Figure 2.41. The select line determines whether the cell is selected (enabled). The cell is selected whenever the select line is 1. The R/W (read/write) line determines whether a read or a write operation must be performed on a selected cell. When the R/W line is 1, a write operation is performed, which causes the data on the input data line to be stored in the cell. In a similar manner, when the R/W line is 0, a read operation is performed, which causes the stored data in the cell to be sent out on the output data line.

A memory cell may be constructed using a few transistors (one to six transistors). The main constraint on the design of a binary cell is its size. The objective is to make it as small as possible so that more cells can be packed into the semiconductor area available on a chip.

A memory unit is an array of memory cells. In a memory unit, each cell may be individually addressed or a group of cells may be addressed simultaneously. Usually, a computer system has a fixed word size. If a word has *n* bits, then *n* memory cells will have to be addressed simultaneously, which enables the cells to have a common select line. A memory unit having four words with a word size of 2 is shown in Figure 2.42.

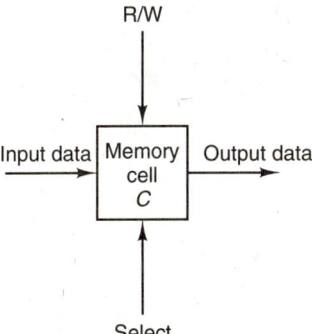

Figure 2.41 Block diagram of a binary memory cell.

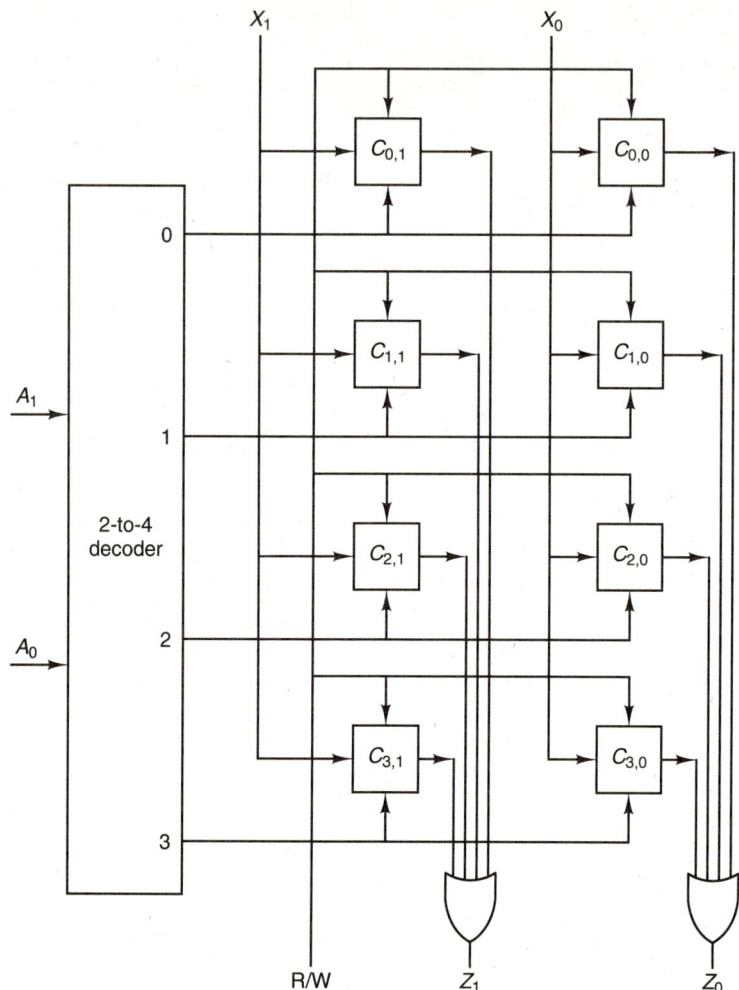

Figure 2.42 Block diagram of a 4-by-2 memory unit.

Any particular word can be selected by means of the address lines A_1 and A_0. The operation to be performed on the selected word is determined by the R/W line. For example, if the address lines A_1 and A_0 are set to 1 and 0, respectively, word 2 is selected. If the R/W line is set to 1, then the data on the input data lines X_1 and X_0 are stored in cells $C_{2,1}$ and $C_{2,0}$ respectively. Similarly, if the R/W line is set to 0, the data in cells $C_{2,1}$ and $C_{2,0}$ are sent out on the output data lines Z_1 and Z_0, respectively.

A memory unit, in which any particular word can be accessed independently, is known as a *random-access memory* (RAM). In a random-access memory the time required for accessing a word is the same for all words.

There are two types of memories, *static* (SRAM) and *dynamic* (DRAM). Static memories hold the stored data either until new data are stored in them or until the power supply is discontinued. Static memories retain the data when a word is read

Sec. 2.6 Memory System Design

from it. Hence this type of memory is said to have a *nondestructive-read property*. In contrast, the data contained in dynamic memories need to be written back into the corresponding memory location after every read operation. Thus dynamic memories are characterized by a *destructive-read property*. Furthermore, dynamic memories need to be periodically refreshed. (In a DRAM, often each bit of the data is stored as a charge in a leaky capacitor, and this requires the capacitor to be recharged within certain time intervals. When the capacitors are recharged, they are said to have been *refreshed*.) The implementation of the refreshing circuit may appear as a disadvantage for DRAM design; but, in general, a cell of a static memory requires more transistors than a cell of a dynamic memory. So the refreshing circuit is considered an acceptable and unavoidable cost of DRAM.

2.6.3 Interleaved Memory

To be able to overlap read or write accesses of several data, multiple memory units can be connected to the CPU. Figure 2.43 represents an architecture for connecting 2^m memory units (memory modules, or banks) in parallel. In this design, the memory address from the CPU, which consists of n bits, is partitioned into two sections, S_m and S_{n-m}. The section S_m is the least significant m bits of the memory address and selects one of the memory units. The section S_{n-m} is the most significant n-m bits of the memory address and addresses a particular word in a memory unit. Thus a sequence of consecutive addresses is assigned to consecutive memory units. In other words, address i points to a word in the memory unit M_j, where $j = i$ (modulo 2^m). For example, addresses $0, 1, 2, \ldots, 2^m - 1$ and 2^m are assigned to memory units $M_0, M_1, M_2, \ldots,$

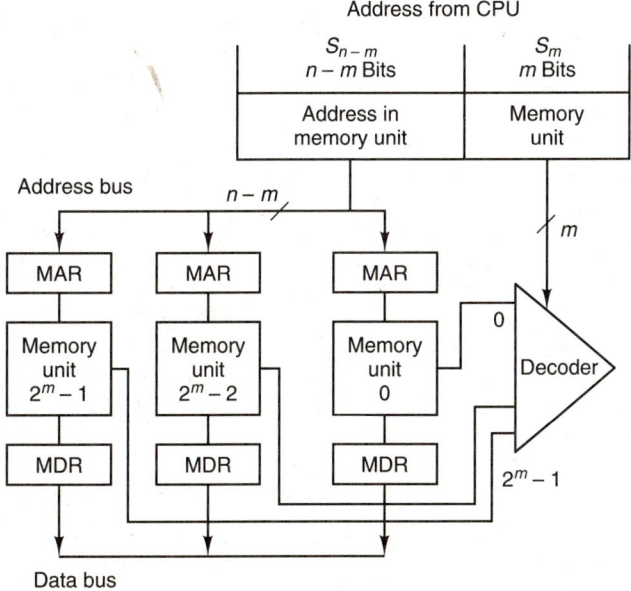

Figure 2.43 Block diagram of an interleaved memory.

M_{2^m-1} and M_0, respectively. This technique of distributing addresses among memory units is called *interleaving*. The interleaving of addresses among m memory units is called *m-way interleaving*. The accesses are said to overlap because the memory units can be accessed simultaneously.

2.6.4 Associative Memory

Unlike RAMs, in which the stored data are identified by means of a unique address assigned to each data item, the data stored in an associative memory are identified, or accessed, by the content of the data themselves. Because of the nature of data access in associative memories, such memories are also known as *content addressable memories* (CAM).

In general, a search time for a particular piece of data in a RAM having n words will take $t * f(n)$, where t is the time taken to fetch and compare one word of the memory and f is an increasing function on n. [f is an increasing function on n if and only if $f(n_1) < f(n_2)$ for all $n_1 < n_2$.] Hence, with an increase in n, the search time increases too. But in the case of a CAM having n words, the search time is almost independent of n because all the words may be searched in parallel. Only one cycle time is required to determine if the desired word is in memory, and, if present, one more cycle time is required to retrieve it.

To be able to do a parallel search by data association, each word needs to have a dedicated circuit for itself. The additional hardware associated with each word adds significantly to the cost of associative memories, and, as a result, the hardware is used only in applications for which the search time is vital to the proper implementation of the task under execution. For example, associative memories may be used, as the highest level of memory, in real-time systems or in military applications requiring a large number of memory accesses, as in the case of pattern recognition.

CAMs can be categorized into two basic types of functions. The first type describes CAMs in terms of an exact match (that is, they address data based on equality with certain key data). This type is simply referred to as an *exact match CAM*. The second type, called a *comparison CAM,* is an enhancement of the exact match. Rather than basing a search on equality alone, the search is based on a general comparison (i.e., the CAM supports various relational operators, such as greater than and less than).

All associative memories are organized by words, but they may differ depending on whether their logical organizations are fixed or variable [HAN 66]. In fixed organization, a word is divided into fixed segments in which any segment may be used for interrogation. Depending on the application, a segment of a word may further be defined as the *key segment,* and each bit of this segment *must* be used for the purpose of interrogation. In variable organization, the word may be divided into *fixed segments,* but any part of a segment may be used for the purpose of interrogation. In its most general form, the CAM will be fully interrogatable (i.e., it will allow any combination of bits in the word to be searched for).

In this section, we shall focus on fully interrogatable CAMs with exact match capacity. This will allow us to illustrate topics such as cache memory (in the following section) in which associative memories play a vital role more concretely.

Sec. 2.6 Memory System Design

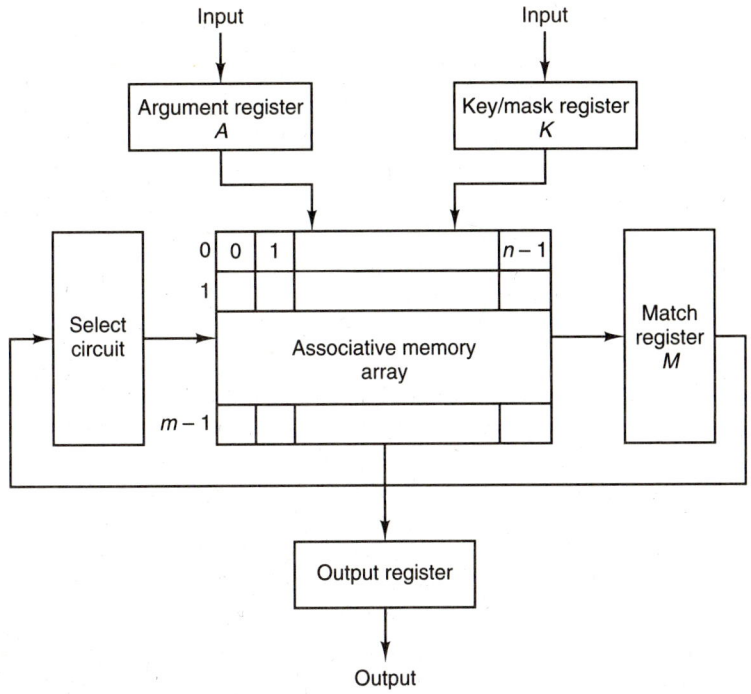

Figure 2.44 Block diagram of an associative memory.

Figure 2.44 shows a block diagram of an associative memory having m words and n bits per word. The argument register A and the key register K each have n bits, one for each bit of a word. Before the search process is started, the word to be searched is loaded into the argument register A. The segment of interest to the word is specified by the bit positions having 1's in the key register K. Once the argument and key registers are set, each word in memory is compared in parallel with the content of A. If a word matches the argument, the corresponding bit in the match register M is set. Thus, M has m bits, one for each word in memory. If more than one bit is set to 1 in M, the select circuit determines which word is to be read. For example, all the matching entries may be read out in some predetermined order [HAY 78].

The following example shows the bit settings in M for three words if the contents of A and K are as shown (assuming a word size of 8 bits).

A	01 101010	
K	11 000000	
Word 1	00 101010	Match bit = 0
Word 2	01 010001	Match bit = 1
Word 3	01 000000	Match bit = 1

Because only the two leftmost bits of K are set, words 2 and 3 are declared as a match with the given argument, whereas word 1 is not a match, although it is closer to

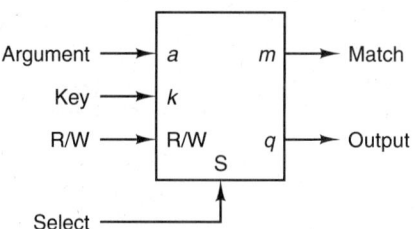

Figure 2.45 Block diagram of an associative memory cell.

the contents of A. A subsequent sequential search of words 2 and 3 will be required to access the required word.

An associative memory is made of an array of similar cells. A block diagram of one of these cells is given in Figure 2.45. It has four inputs: the argument bit a, the corresponding key bit k, the R/W line to specify the operation to be performed, and the select line S to select the particular cell for read or write. The cell has two outputs: the match bit m, which shows if the data stored in the cell match with the argument bit a, and the data output q. The match bit is set to 1 if the key bit k is 0.

Figure 2.46 shows a 4-by-2 associative memory array. When the read operation is selected, the argument is matched with the words whose select lines are set to 1. The match output of each cell is then ANDed together to generate the match bit for that particular word. When the write operation is selected, the argument bits are stored in the selected word.

The Boolean expression for each bit M_i of the match register can be derived as follows: Let W_{ij} denote the jth bit of the ith word in the memory, A_j and K_j denote the jth bit of A and K respectively, and M_i denote the ith bit of M.

Suppose that x_j is defined as $x_j = A_j W_{ij} + \overline{A_j}\overline{W_{ij}}$ for $j = 0, 1, 2, \ldots, n-1$. That is, x_j is equal to 1 if W_{ij} matches A_j; otherwise x_j is 0. Then word i matches the argument if M_i is equal to 1, where

$$M_i = (x_0 + \overline{K}_0)(x_1 + \overline{K}_1)(x_2 + \overline{K}_2)\ldots(x_{n-1} + \overline{K}_{n-1})$$

$$= \prod_{j=0}^{n-1} (x_j + \overline{K}_j)$$

$$= \prod_{j=0}^{n-1} (A_j W_{ij} + \overline{A_j}\overline{W_{ij}} + \overline{K}_j)$$

Compared to RAMs, associative memories are very expensive (require more transistors), but have much faster response time in searching. (Response time refers to the time interval between the start and finish time of the search.)

2.6.5 Cache Memory

One problem designers face in constructing a processor is the bottleneck associated with memory speeds. Because fetches from main memory require considerably more time when compared to the overall speeds in the processor, designers spend a lot of time and effort making memory speeds as fast as possible.

One way to make the memory appear faster is to reduce the number of times main memory has to be accessed. If a small amount of fast memory is installed and at

Sec. 2.6 Memory System Design

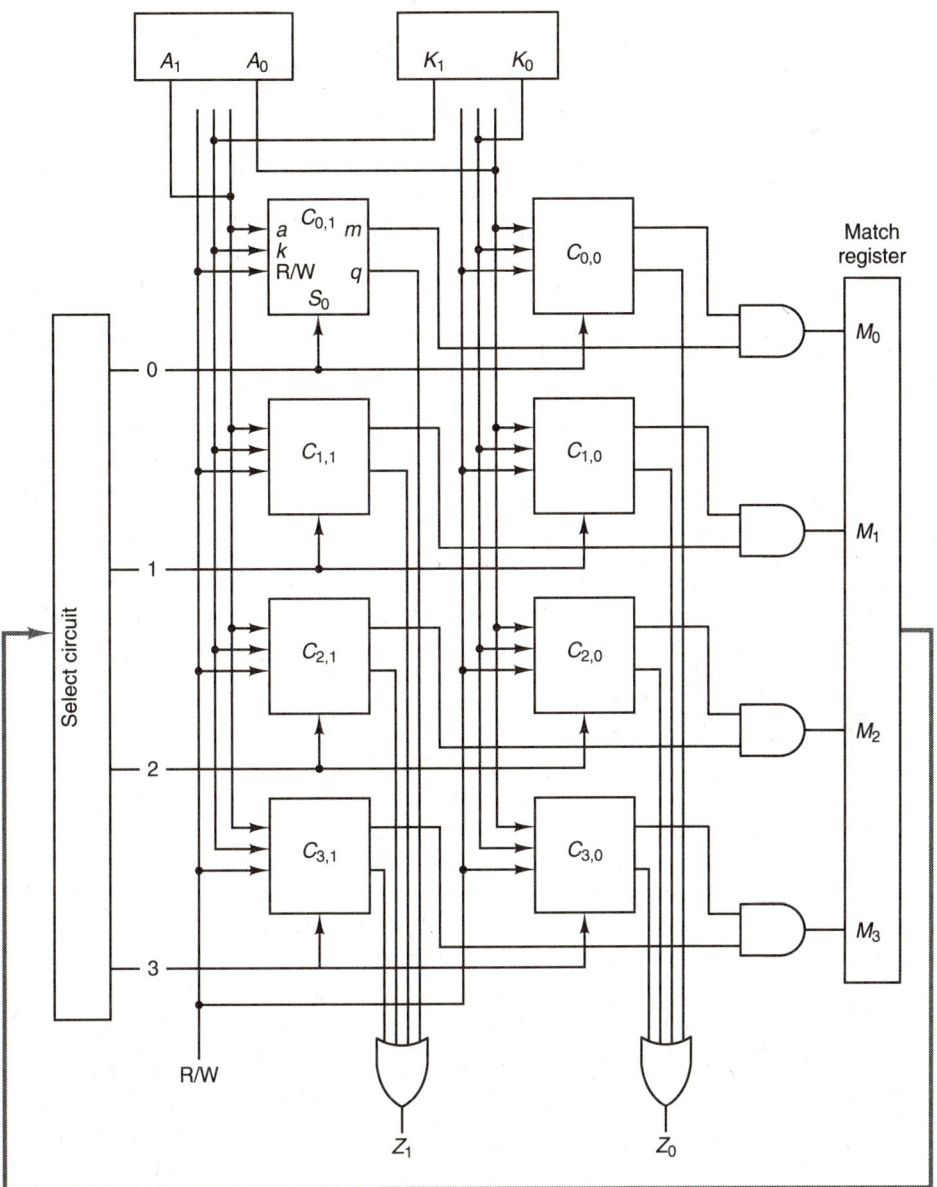

Figure 2.46 Block diagram of a 4-by-2 associative memory array.

any point in time part of a program is loaded in this fast memory, then, due to the property of locality of reference, the number of references to the main memory will be drastically reduced. Such a fast memory unit, used temporarily to store a portion of the data and instructions (from the main memory) for immediate use, is known as *cache memory*.

Because cache memory is expensive, a computer system can have only a limited amount of it installed. Therefore, in a computer system there is a relatively large and slower main memory coupled together with a smaller, faster cache memory. The cache acts as a "go-between" for the main memory and the CPU. The cache contains copies of some blocks of the main memory. Therefore, when the CPU requests a word (if the word is in the fast cache), there will be no need to go to the larger, slower main memory.

Although the cache size is only a small fraction of the main memory, a large part of the memory reference requests will be fulfilled by the cache due to the nonrandomness of consecutive memory reference addresses. As stated previously, if the average memory access time per datum approaches the access time for the cache, while the average cost per bit approaches that of the main memory, the goals of the memory hierarchy design are realized.

The performance of a system can be greatly improved if the cache is placed on the same chip as the processor. In this case, the outputs of the cache can be connected to the ALU and registers through short wires, significantly reducing access time. For example, the Intel 80486 microprocessor has an on-chip cache [CRW 90]. Although the clock speed for the 80486 is not much faster than that for the 80386, the overall system speed is much faster.

Cache operation. When the CPU generates an address for memory reference, the generated address is first sent to the cache. Based on the contents of the cache, a *hit* or a *miss* occurs. A hit occurs when the requested word is already present in the cache. In contrast, a miss happens when the requested word is not in the cache.

Two types of operations can be requested by the CPU: a read request and a write request. When the CPU generates a read request for a word in memory, the generated request is first sent to the cache to check if the word currently resides in the cache. If the word is not found in the cache (i. e., a read miss), the requested word is supplied by the main memory. A copy of the word is stored in the cache for future reference by the CPU. If the cache is full, a predetermined replacement policy is used to swap out a word from the cache in order to accommodate the new word. (A detailed explanation of cache replacement policies is given later in this chapter.) If the requested word is found in the cache (i. e., a read hit), the word is supplied by the cache. Thus no fetch from main memory is required. This speeds up the system considerably.

When the CPU generates a write request for a word in memory, the generated request is first sent to the cache to check if the word currently resides in the cache. If the word is not found in the cache (i. e. a write miss), a copy of the word is brought from the memory into the cache. Next, a write operation is performed. Also, a write operation is performed when the word is found in the cache (i. e., a write hit). To perform a write operation, there are two main approaches that the hardware may employ: *write through,* and *write back.* In the write-through method, the word is modified in both the cache and the main memory. The advantage of the write-through method is that the main memory always has consistent data with the cache. However, it has the disadvantage of slowing down the CPU because all write operations require subsequent accesses to the main memory, which are time consuming.

In the write-back method, every word in the cache has a bit associated with it, called a *dirty bit* (also called an *inconsistent bit*), which tells if it has been changed while in the cache. In this case, the word in the cache may be modified during the write operation, and the dirty bit is set. All changes to a word are performed in the cache. When it is time for a word to be swapped out of the cache, it checks to see if the word's dirty bit is set: if it is, it is written back to the main memory in its updated form.

The advantage of the write-back method is that as long as a word stays in the cache it may be modified several times and, for the CPU, it does not matter if the word in the main memory has not been updated. The disadvantage of the write-back method is that, although only one extra bit has to be associated with each word, it makes the design of the system slightly more complex.

Basic cache organization. The basic motivation behind using cache memories in computer systems is their speed. Most of the time, the presence of the cache is not apparent to the user. Since it is desirable that very little time be wasted when searching for words in a cache, usually the cache is managed through hardware-based algorithms. The translation of the memory address, specified by the CPU, into the possible location of the corresponding word in the cache is referred to as a *mapping* process.

Based on the mapping process used, cache organization can be classified into three types:

1. Associative-mapping cache
2. Direct-mapping cache
3. Set-associative mapping cache

The following sections explain these cache organizations. To illustrate these three different cache organizations, the memory organization shown in Figure 2.39c is used. In this figure, the CPU communicates with the cache as well as the main memory. The main memory stores 64K words (16-bit address) of 16 bits each. The cache is capable of storing 256 of these words at any given time. Also, in the following discussion it is assumed that the CPU generates a read request and not a write request. (The write request would be handled in a similar way.)

Associative Mapping. In an associative-mapping cache (also referred to as fully associative cache), both the address and the contents are stored as one word in the cache. As a result, a memory word is allowed to be stored at any location in the cache, making it the most flexible cache organization. Figure 2.47 shows the organization of an associative-mapping cache for a system with 16-bit addressing and 16-bit data. Note that the words are stored at arbitrary locations regardless of their absolute addresses in the main memory.

The organization of an associative-mapping cache can be viewed as a combination of an associative memory and a RAM, as shown in Figure 2.47 (all numbers are in hexadecimal). Since each associative memory cell is many times more expensive than a RAM cell, only the addresses of the words are stored in the associative part, while the data can be stored in the RAM part of the cache because only the address is used for associative search. This will not increase the access time of the cache significantly, but will result in a significant drop in cost. In this organization, when the CPU generates an address for memory reference, it is passed into the argument register and is compared, in parallel, with the address fields of all words currently stored in the cache for a matching address. Once the location has been determined, the corresponding data can be accessed from the RAM.

The major disadvantage of this method is its need for a large associative memory, which is very expensive and increases the access time of the cache.

Direct Mapping. Associative-mapping caches require associative memory for some part of their organization. Since associative memories are very expensive, an alternative cache organization, known as a *direct-mapping cache,* may be used. In this organization, RAM memories are used as the storage mechanism for the cache. This reduces the cost of the cache, but imposes limitations on its use. In a direct-mapping cache, the requested memory address is divided into two parts, an *index* field, which refers to the lower part of the address, and a *tag* field, which refers to the upper part. The index is used as an address to a location in the cache where the data are located. At this index, a tag and a data value are stored in the cache. If the tag of the requested memory address matches the tag of the cache, the data value is sent to the CPU. Otherwise, the main memory is accessed, and the corresponding data value is fetched and

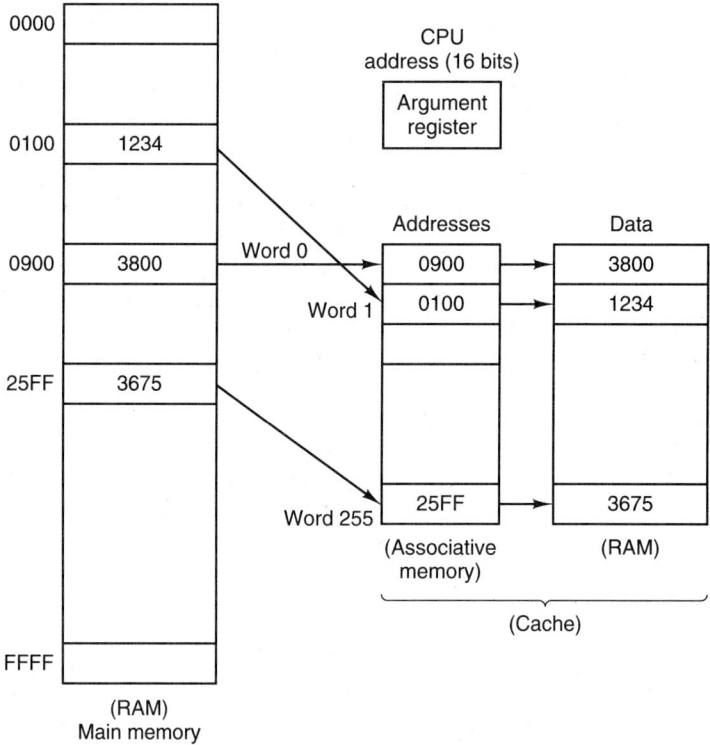

Figure 2.47 Associative-mapping cache (all numbers are in hexadecimal).

Sec. 2.6   Memory System Design   79

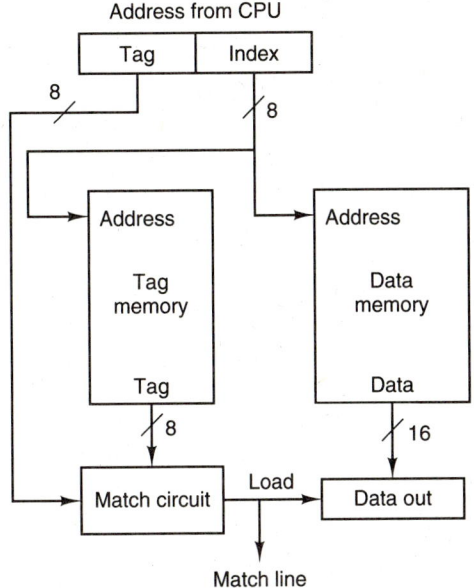

Figure 2.48   Architecture of a direct-mapping cache.

sent to the CPU. The data value, along with the tag part of its address, also replaces any word currently occupying the corresponding index location in the cache.

Figure 2.48 represents an architecture for the direct-mapping cache. The design consists of three main components: data memory, tag memory, and match circuit. The data memory holds the cached data. The tag memory holds the tag associated with each cached datum and has an entry for each word of the data memory. The match circuit sets the match line to 1, indicating that the referenced word is in the cache.

An example illustrating the direct-mapping cache operation is shown in Figure 2.49 (all numbers are in hexadecimal). In this example, the memory address consists

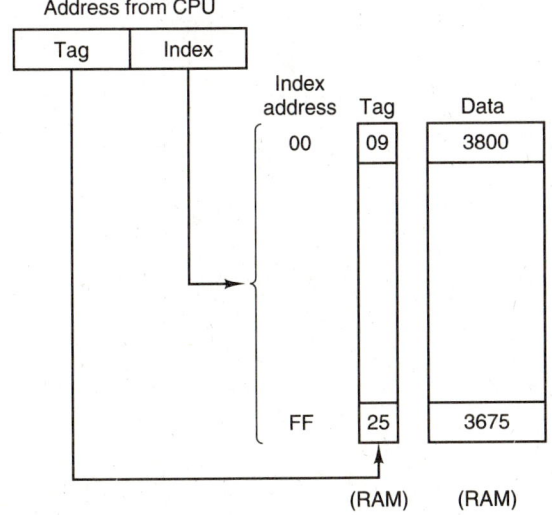

Figure 2.49   Direct-mapping cache (all numbers in hexadecimal).

of 16 bits and the cache has 256 words. The eight least significant bits of the address constitute the index field, and the remaining eight bits constitute the tag field. The 8 index bits determine the address of a word in the tag and data memories. Each word in the tag memory has 8 bits, and each word in the data memory has 16 bits. Initially, the content of address 0900 is stored in the cache. Now, if the CPU wants to read the contents of address 0100, the index (00) matches, but the tag (01) is now different. So the content of main memory is accessed, and the data word 1234 is transferred to the CPU. The tag memory and the data memory words at index address 00 are then replaced with 01 and 1234, respectively.

The advantage of direct mapping over associative mapping is that it requires less overhead in terms of the number of bits per word in the cache. The major disadvantage is that the performance can drop considerably if two or more words having the same index but different tags are accessed frequently. For example, memory addresses 0100 and 0200 both have to be put in the cache at position 00, so a great deal of time is spent swapping them back and forth. This slows the system down, thus defeating the purpose of the cache in the first place. However, considering the property of locality of reference, the probability of having two words with the same index is low. Such words are located 2^k bits apart in the main memory, where k denotes the number of bits in the index field. In our example, such a situation will only occur if the CPU requests reference to words that are 256 (2^8) words apart. To further reduce the effects of such situations often an expanded version of the direct-mapping cache, called a *set-associative cache*, is used. The following section describes the basic structure of a set-associative mapped cache.

Set-Associative Mapping. The set-associative mapping cache organization (also referred to as set-associative cache) is an extension of the direct-mapping cache. It solves the problem of direct mapping by providing storage for more than one data value with the same index. For example, a set-associative cache with m memory blocks, called m-way set associative, can store m data values having the same index, along with their tags. Figure 2.50 represents an architecture for a set-associative mapping cache with m memory blocks. Each memory block has the same structure as a direct-mapping cache. To determine that a referenced word is in the cache, its tag is compared with the tag of cached data in all memory blocks in parallel. A match in any of the memory blocks will enable (set to 1) the signal match line to indicate that the data are in the cache. If a match occurs, the corresponding data value is passed on to the CPU. Otherwise, the data value is brought in from the main memory and sent to the CPU. The data value, along with its tag, is then stored in one of the memory blocks.

An example illustrating the set-associative mapping cache operation is shown in Figure 2.51 (all numbers are in hexadecimal). This figure represents a two-way set-associative mapping cache. The content of address 0900 is stored in the cache under index 00 and tag 09. If the CPU wants to access address 0100, the index (00) matches, but the tag is now different. Therefore, the content of main memory is accessed, and the data value 1234 is transferred to the CPU. This data with its tag (01) is stored in the second memory block of the cache. When there is no space for a particular index in the cache, one of the two data values stored under that index will be replaced according to some predetermined replacement policy (discussed next).

Sec. 2.6　Memory System Design

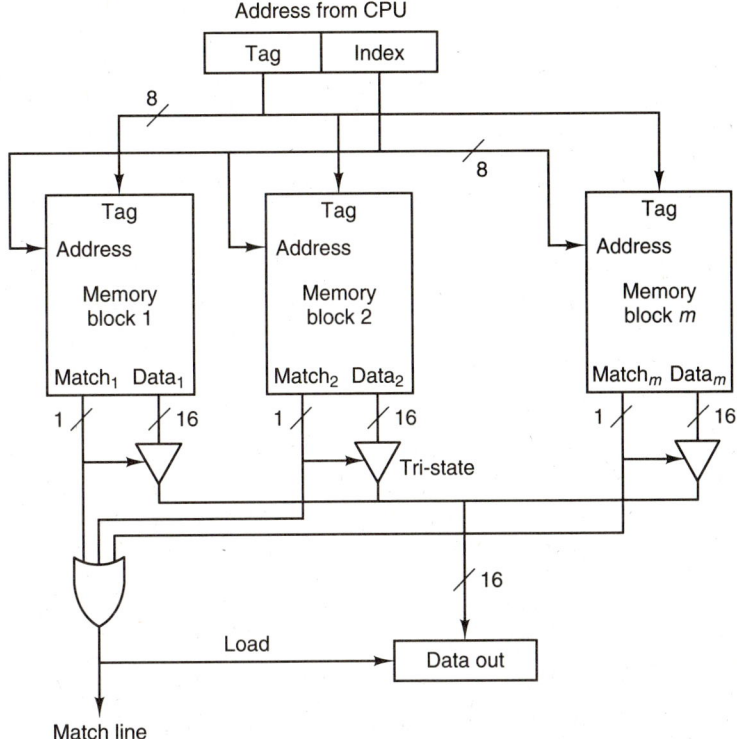

Figure 2.50　Architecture of an m-way set-associative mapping cache.

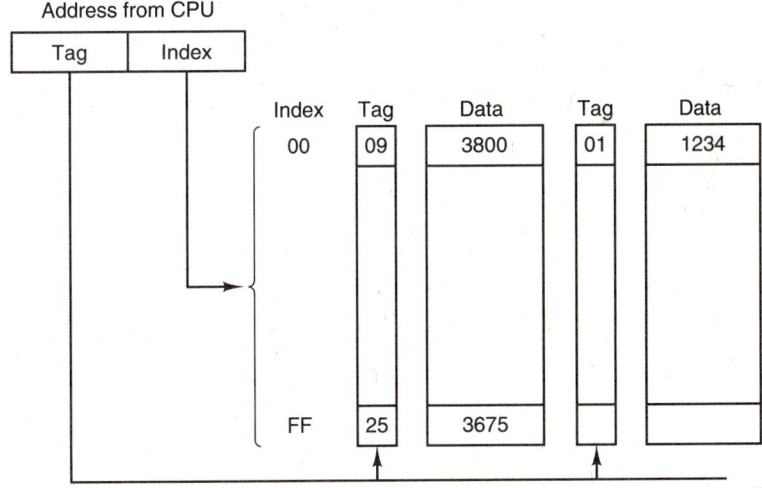

Figure 2.51　Two-way set-associative mapping cache (all numbers are in hexadecimal).

Replacement strategies. Sooner or later, cache will become full. When this occurs, a mechanism should be there to replace a word with the newly accessed data from memory. In general, there are three main strategies for determining which word should be swapped out from the cache; they are called *random, least frequently used,* and *least recently used* replacement policies. Each is explained next.

Random Replacement. This method picks a word at random and replaces that word with the newly accessed data. This method is easy to implement in hardware, and it is faster than most other algorithms. The disadvantage is that the words most likely to be used again have as much of a chance of being swapped out as a word that is likely not to be used again. This disadvantage diminishes as the cache size increases.

Least Frequently Used. This method replaces the data that are used the least. It assumes that data that are not referenced frequently are not needed as much. For each word, a counter is kept for the total number of times the word has been used since it was brought into the cache. The word with the lowest count is the word to be swapped out. The advantage of this method is that a frequently used word is more likely to remain in cache than a word that has not been used often. One disadvantage is that words that have recently been brought into the cache have a low count total, despite the fact that they are likely to be used again. Another disadvantage is that this method is more difficult to implement in terms of hardware and is thus more expensive.

Least Recently Used. This method has the best performance per cost compared with the other techniques and is often implemented in real-world systems. The idea behind this replacement method is that a word that has not been used for a long period of time has a lesser chance of being needed in the near future according to the property of temporal locality. Thus, this method retains words in the cache that are more likely to be used again. To do this, a mechanism is used to keep track of which words have been accessed most recently. The word that will be swapped out is the word that has not been used for the longest period of time. One way to implement such a mechanism is to assign a counter to each word in the cache. Each time the cache is accessed, each word's counter is incremented, and the word's counter that was accessed is reset to zero. In this manner, the word with the highest count is the one that was least recently used.

Example: i486 Microprocessor Cache Structure

To increase overall performance, the Intel *i*486 microprocessor contains an 8-Kbyte on-chip cache [INT 91]. The write-through strategy is used for writing into this cache. As shown in Figure 2.52, the cache has four-way set-associative organization. Each memory block contains a data memory with 128 lines; each line is 16 bytes. Also, each memory block contains a 128×21 memory to keep the tags. Note that it is not necessary to store the 4 least significant bits of memory addresses because each time 16 bytes are fetched into the cache. Considering Figure 2.52, the structure of the cache memory can also be expressed by saying that the 8 Kbytes of cache are logically organized as 128 sets, each containing four lines.

A valid bit is assigned to each line in the cache. Each line is either valid or nonvalid. When a system is powered up, the cache is supposed to be empty. But, in practice, it has some random data that are invalid. To discard such data, when the system is pow-

Sec. 2.6   Memory System Design

ered up, all the valid bits are set to 0. The valid bit associated with each line in the cache is set to 1 the first time the line is loaded from main memory. As long as the valid bit is 0, the corresponding lines are excluded from any search performed on the cache.

When a new line needs to be placed in the cache, a pseudo least recently used mechanism (implemented in hardware) is used to determine which line should be replaced. If there is a nonvalid line among the four possible lines, that line will be replaced. Otherwise, when all four lines are valid, a least recently used line is selected for replacement based on the value of 3 bits, r_0, r_1, and r_2, which are defined for each set of four lines in the cache. In Figure 2.52, these bits are denoted as LRU bits. The LRU bits are updated for every hit or replaced in their corresponding four lines. Let these four lines be labeled l_0, l_1, l_2, and l_3. If the most recent access was to l_0 or l_1, r_0 is set to 1. Otherwise, if the most recent access was to l_2 or l_3, r_0 is set to 0. Among l_0 and l_1, if the most recent access was to l_0, r_1 is set to 1, otherwise r_1 is set to 0. Among l_2 and l_3, if the most recent access was to l_2, r_2 is set to 1; otherwise, r_2 is set to 0.

This updating policy allows us to replace a valid line based on the following rules:

if $r_0 = 0$ and $r_1 = 0$, then replace l_0,

if $r_0 = 0$ and $r_1 = 1$, then replace l_1,

if $r_0 = 1$ and $r_2 = 0$, then replace l_2,

if $r_0 = 1$ and $r_2 = 1$, then replace l_3.

Whenever the cache is flushed all 128 three LRU bits are set to 0.

Cache performance. How well a cache performs is based on the number of times a given piece of data is matched, or found in the cache. In extreme cases, if no matches are found in the cache, then the cache must fetch everything from main memory, and cache performance is very poor. On the other hand, if everything could be held in the cache, it would match every time and never have to access main memory. Cache performance for this case would be extremely high. In reality, caches fall somewhere between these extremes. Nevertheless, as you can see, cache performance is still based on the number of matches or hits found in the cache. This probability of getting

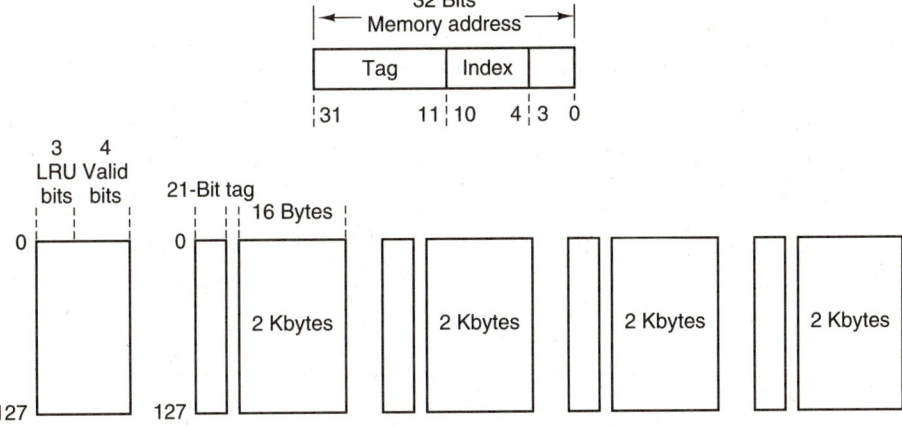

Figure 2.52   On-chip cache organization of Intel i486 microprocessor.

a match, called, *the hit ratio*, is denoted by H. During execution of a program, if N_c and N_m are the number of address references satisfied by the cache and the main memory, respectively, then H is the ratio of total addresses satisfied by the cache to the total number of addresses satisfied by both the cache and main memory. That is,

$$H = \frac{N_c}{N_c + N_m}$$

Because data in the cache can be retrieved more quickly than data in main memory, making H as close to 1 as possible is desirable. This definition of H is applicable to any two adjacent levels of a memory hierarchy; but due to the huge amount of main memory available on modern computers, it is often used in the previously described context.

In the preceding equation, if H is the probability that a hit will occur, then $1 - H$, called the *miss ratio*, is the probability that a hit will not occur. Given that t_c denotes the access time for the cache when a hit occurs, and t_m denotes the access time for the main memory in the case of a miss, then the average access time for the cache, t_a, is equal to the probability for a hit times the access time for the cache, plus the probability for a miss times the access time for main memory (because if it is not in the cache, it must be fetched from main memory). Thus

$$t_a = Ht_c + (1 - H) t_m$$

and, by substitution, we get:

$$\begin{aligned} t_a &= \frac{N_c t_c}{N_c + N_m} + \left(1 - \frac{N_c}{N_c + N_m}\right) t_m \\ &= \frac{N_c t_c + N_m t_m}{N_c + N_m}. \end{aligned}$$

This makes perfect sense, because this equation simply means the total amount of time spent addressing from the cache plus the total amount of time spent addressing from the main memory divided by the total number of requests.

In general, direct-mapping caches have larger miss ratios than set-associative caches. However, Hill [HIL 88] based on simulations on some data, has shown that the gap diminishes as the size of caches gets larger. For example, an 8-Kbyte two-way set-associative cache with line size of 32 bytes has a miss ratio difference of 0.013 in comparison with a direct-mapping cache of the same size. However, for the caches with the 32 Kbytes the difference is 0.005. The main reason for this phenomenon is that the miss ratio of all kinds of caches decreases as the cache size increases.

In comparing the direct-mapping caches with set-associative caches, it turns out that the direct-mapping caches have smaller average access times for sufficiently large cache sizes [HIL 88]. One reason is that a set-associative cache requires extra gates and hence has a longer hit access time (t_c) than a direct-mapping cache (this can be observed from their basic structure given in Figures 2.48 and 2.50). Another reason is that the gap between the direct-mapping caches miss ratio and set-associative caches miss ratio diminishes as the caches get larger. Therefore, set-associative organization

Sec. 2.6   Memory System Design

is preferred for small caches, while direct-mapping organization is preferred for large caches.

2.6.6 Virtual Memory

Another technique used to improve system performance is called *virtual memory*. As the name implies, virtual memory is the illusion of a much larger main memory size (logical view) than what actually exists (physical view). Prior to the advent of virtual memory, if a program's address space exceeded the actual available memory, the programmer was responsible for breaking up the program into smaller pieces called *overlays*. Each overlay then could fit in main memory. The basic process was to store all these overlays in secondary memory, such as on a disk, and to load individual overlays into main memory as they were needed.

This process required knowledge of where the overlays were to be stored on disk, knowledge of input/output operations involved with accessing the overlays, and keeping track of the entire overlay process. This was a very complex and tedious process that made the complexity of programming a computer even more difficult.

The concept of virtual memory was created to relieve the programmer of this burden and to let the computer manage this process. Virtual memory allows the user to write programs that grow beyond the bounds of physical memory and still execute properly. It also allows for multiprogramming, by which main memory is shared among many users on a dynamic basis. With multiprogramming, portions of several programs are placed in the main memory at the same time, and the processor switches its time back and forth among these programs. The processor executes one program for a brief period of time (called a *quantum* or *time-slice*) and then switches to another program; this process continues until each program is completed. When virtual memory is used, the addresses used by the programmer are seen by the system as *virtual addresses,* which are so called because they are mapped onto the addresses of physical memory and therefore do not access the same physical memory address from one execution of an instruction to the next.

Virtual addresses, also called *logical addresses,* are generated by the processor during the compile time and are translated into physical addresses at run time. The two main methods for achieving a virtual memory environment are *paging* and *segmentation*. Each is explained next.

Paging.   Paging is the technique of breaking a program (referred to in the following as process) into smaller blocks of identical size and storing these blocks in secondary storage in the form of *pages*. By taking advantage of the locality of reference, these pages can then be loaded into main memory, a few at a time, into blocks of the same size called *frames* and executed just as if the entire process were in memory. For this method to work properly, each process must maintain a *page table* in main memory. Figure 2.53 shows how a paging scheme works. The base register, which each process has, points to the beginning of the process's page table. Page tables have an entry for each page that the process contains. These entries usually contain a *load* field of one bit, an *address* field, and an *access* field. The load field specifies whether the page has been brought into main memory. The address field specifies the frame num-

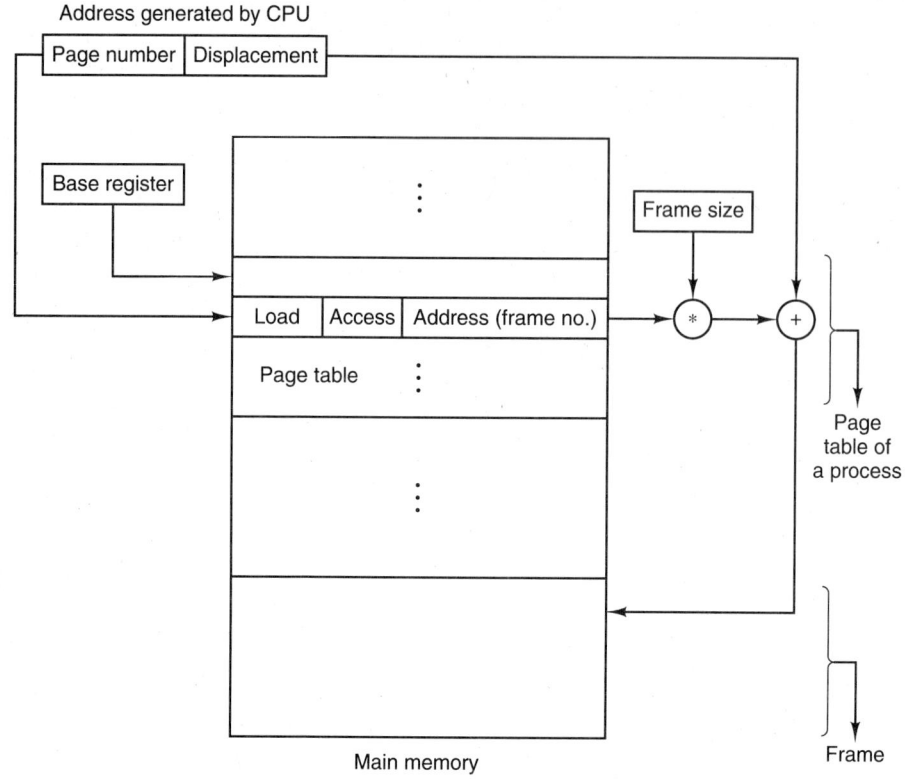

Figure 2.53 Using page table to convert a virtual address to a physical address.

ber of the frame into which the page is loaded. The address of the page within main memory is evaluated by multiplying the frame number and the frame size. (Since frame size is usually a power of 2, shifting is often used for multiplying frame number by frame size.) If a page has not been loaded, the address of the page within secondary memory is held in this field. The access field specifies the type of operation that can be performed on a block. It determines whether a block is read only, read/write, or executable.

When an access to a variable or an instruction that is not currently loaded into the memory is encountered, a *page fault* occurs, and the page that contains the necessary variable or instruction is brought into the memory. The page is stored in a free frame, if one exists. If a free frame does not exist, one of the process's own frames must be given up, and the new page will be stored in its place. Which frame is given up and whether the old page is written back to secondary storage depend on which of several page replacement algorithms (discussed later in this section) is used.

As an example, Figure 2.54 shows the contents of page tables for two processes, process 1 and process 2. Process 1 consists of three pages, P_0, P_1, and P_2, whereas process 2 has only two pages, P_0 and P_1. Assume that all the pages of process 1 have read access only and the pages of process 2 have read/write access; this is denoted by R and W in each page table. Because each frame has 4096 (4K) bytes, the physical address of

Sec. 2.6   Memory System Design   87

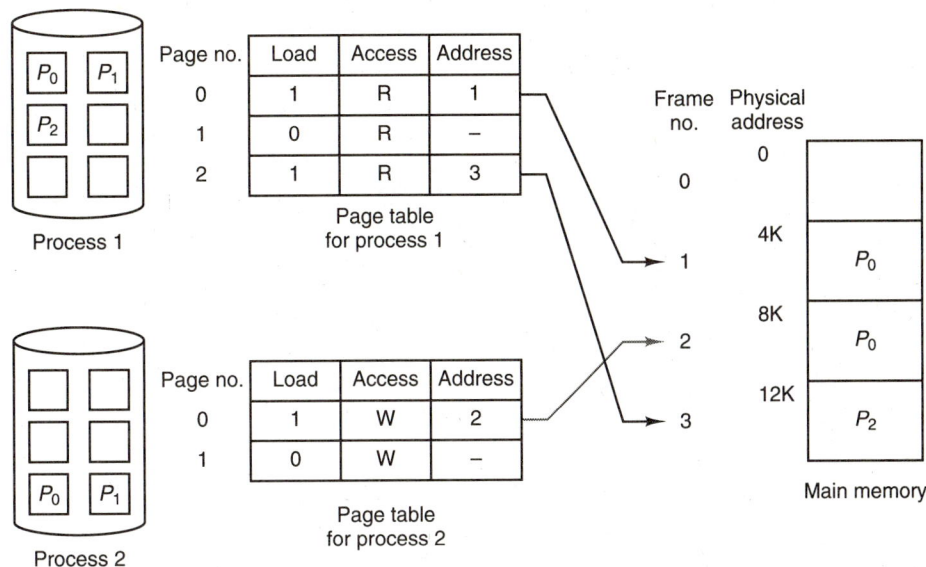

Figure 2.54 Page tables for two different processes, Process 1 and Process 2.

the beginning of each frame is computed by the product of the frame number and 4096. Therefore, given that P_0 and P_2 of process 1 are loaded into frames 1 and 3, their beginning address in main memory will be 4K = (1 * 4096) and 12K = (3 * 4096), respectively.

The process of converting a virtual address to a physical address can be sped up by using a high-speed lookup table called a *translation lookaside buffer* (TLB). The page number of the virtual address is fed to the TLB where it is translated to a frame number of the physical address. The TLB can be implemented as an associative memory that has an entry for each of the most recently or likely referenced pages. Each entry contains a page number and other relevant information similar to the page table entry, essentially the frame number and access type. For a given page number, an entry of the TLB that matches (a hit) this page number is used to provide the corresponding frame number. If a match cannot be found in the TLB (a miss), the page table of the corresponding process will be located and used to produce the frame number.

The efficiency of the virtual memory system depends on minimizing the number of page faults. Because the access time of secondary memory is much higher than the access time of main memory, an excessive number of page faults can slow the system dramatically. When a page fault occurs, a page in the main memory must be located and identified as one not needed at the present time so that it can be written back to the secondary memory. Then the requested page can be loaded into this newly freed frame of main memory.

Obviously, paging increases the processing time of a process substantially, because two disk accesses would be required along with the execution of a replacement algorithm. There is an alternative, however, which at times can reduce the number of the disk accesses to just one. This reduction is achieved by adding to the hardware an extra bit to each frame, called a *dirty bit* (also called an *inconsistent* bit). If some modification has taken place to a particular frame, the corresponding dirty bit is set to 1. If the dirty bit for frame f is 1, for example, and in order to create an available frame, f has been chosen as the frame to swap out, then two disk accesses would be required. If the dirty bit is 0 (meaning that there were no modifications on f since it was last loaded), there would be no need to write f back to disk. Because the original state of f is still on disk (remember that the frames in main memory contain copies of the pages in secondary memory) and no modifications have been made to f while in main memory, the page frame containing f can simply be overwritten by the newly requested page.

Most replacement algorithms consider the principle of locality when selecting a frame to replace. The principle of locality states that over a given amount of time the addresses generated will fall within a small portion of the virtual address space and that these generated addresses will change slowly with time. Two possible replacement algorithms are

1. First in, first out (FIFO)
2. Least recently used (LRU)

Before the discussion of replacement algorithms, you should note that the efficiency of the algorithm is based on the page size (Z) and the number of pages (N) the main memory ($M1$) can contain. If $Z = 100$ bytes and $N = 3$, then $M1 = N * Z = 3 * 100 = 300$ bytes.

Another concern with replacement algorithms is the page fault frequency (*PF*). The *PF* is determined by the number of page faults (F) that occurs in an entire execution of a process divided by F plus the number of nonfault references *(S)*: $PF = F/(S + F)$. The *PF* should be as low a percentage as possible in order to minimize disk accesses. The *PF* is affected by page size and the number of page frames.

First In, First Out. First in, first out (FIFO) is one of the simplest algorithms to employ. As the name implies, the first page loaded will be the first page to be removed from main memory. Figure 2.55a demonstrates how FIFO works as well as how the page fault frequency (*PF*) is determined by using a table. The number of rows in the table represents the number of available frames, and the columns represent each reference to a page. These references come from a given reference sequence 0, 1, 2, 0, 3, 2, 0, 1, 2, 4, 0, where the first reference is to page 0, the second is to page 1, the third is to page 2, and so on. When a page fault occurs, the corresponding page number is put in the top row, representing its precedence, and marked with an asterisk. The previous pages in the table are moved down. Once the page frames are filled and a page fault occurs, the page in the bottom page frame is removed or swapped out. (Keep in mind that this table is used only to visualize a page's current precedence. The movement of these pages does not imply that they are actually being shifted around in $M1$. A counter can be associated with each page to determine the oldest page.)

Once the last reference in the reference sequence is loaded, the *PF* can be calculated. The number of asterisks appearing in the top row equals page faults *(F)* and the items in the top row that do not contain an asterisk equals success *(S)*. Considering Fig-

Sec. 2.6   Memory System Design   89

Reference sequence

FIFO

0	1	2	0	3	2	0	1	2	4	0
0*	1*	2*	2	3*	3	0*	1*	2*	4*	0*
	0	1	1	2	2	3	0	1	2	4
		0	0	1	1	2	3	0	1	2

Maximum capacity of $M1 = 3$ frames
$F = 9, S = 2, PF = 9 / (2 + 9) = 81\%$

(a)

Reference sequence

FIFO

0	1	2	0	3	2	0	1	2	4	0
0*	1*	2*	2	3*	3	3	3	3	4*	0*
	0	1	1	2	2	2	2	2	3	4
		0	0	1	1	1	1	1	2	3
				0	0	0	0	0	1	2

Maximum capacity of $M1 = 4$ frames
$F = 6, S = 5, PF = 6 / (5 + 6) = 54\%$

(b)

Figure 2.55 Performance of the FIFO replacement technique on two different memory configurations.

ure 2.55, when $M1$ contains three frames, PF is 81% for the above reference sequence. When $M1$ contains four frames, PF reduces to 54%. That is, PF is improved by increasing the number of page frames to 4.

The disadvantage of FIFO is that it may significantly increase the time it takes for a process to execute because it does not take into consideration the principle of locality and consequently may replace heavily used frames as well as rarely used frames with equal probability. For example, if an early frame contains a global variable that is in constant use, this frame will be one of the first to be replaced. During the next access to the variable, another page fault will occur, and the frame will have to be reloaded, replacing yet another page.

Least Recently Used. The least recently used (LRU) method will replace the frame that has not been used for the longest time. In this method, when a page is referenced that is already in $M1$, it is placed in the top row and the other pages are shifted down. In other words, the most used pages are kept at the top. See Figure 2.56a. An improvement of PF is made using LRU by adding a page frame to $M1$. See Figure 2.56b. In general, LRU is more efficient than FIFO, but it requires more hardware (usually a counter or a stack) to keep track of the least and most recently used pages.

Segmentation. Another method of swapping between secondary and main memory is called *segmentation*. In segmentation, a program is broken into variable-length sections known as *segments*. For example, a segment can be a data set or a function within the program. Each process keeps a segment table within main memory that contains basically the same information as the page table. However, unlike pages,

Reference sequence

LRU

	0	1	2	0	3	2	0	1	2	4	0
	0*	1*	2*	0	3*	2	0	1*	2	4*	0*
		0	1	2	0	3	2	0	1	2	4
			0	1	2	0	3	2	0	1	2

Maximum capacity of $M1 = 3$ frames
$F = 7$, $S = 4$, $PF = 7 / (4 + 7) = 63\%$

(a)

Reference sequence

LRU

	0	1	2	0	3	2	0	1	2	4	0
	0*	1*	2*	0	3*	2	0	1	2	4*	0
		0	1	2	0	3	2	0	1	2	4
			0	1	2	0	3	2	0	1	2
					1	1	1	3	3	0	1

Maximum capacity of $M1 = 4$ frames
$F = 5$, $S = 6$, $PF = 5 / (6 + 5) = 45\%$

(b)

Figure 2.56 Performance of LRU replacement technique on two different memory configurations.

segments have variable lengths, and they can start anywhere in the memory; therefore, removing one segment from main memory may not provide enough space for another segment.

There are several strategies for placing a given segment into the main memory. Among the most well-known strategies are *first fit, best fit,* and *worst fit.* Each of these strategies maintains a list that represents the size and position of the free storage blocks in the main memory. This list is used for finding a suitable block size for the given segment. The following is an explanation.

First Fit. This strategy puts the given segment into the first suitable free storage. It searches through the free storage list until it finds a block of free storage that is large enough for the segment; then it allocates a block of memory for the segment.

The main advantage of this strategy is that it encourages free storage areas to become available at high-memory addresses by assigning segments to the low-memory addresses whenever possible. However, this strategy will produce free areas that may be too small to hold a segment. This phenomenon is known as *fragmentation.* When fragmentation occurs, eventually some sort of compaction algorithm will have to be run to collect all the small free areas into one large one. This causes some overhead, which degrades the performance.

Best Fit. This strategy allocates the smallest available free storage block that is large enough to hold the segment. It searches through the free storage list until it finds the smallest block of storage that is large enough for the segment. To prevent searching the entire list, the free storage list is usually sorted according to the increas-

Sec. 2.6 Memory System Design

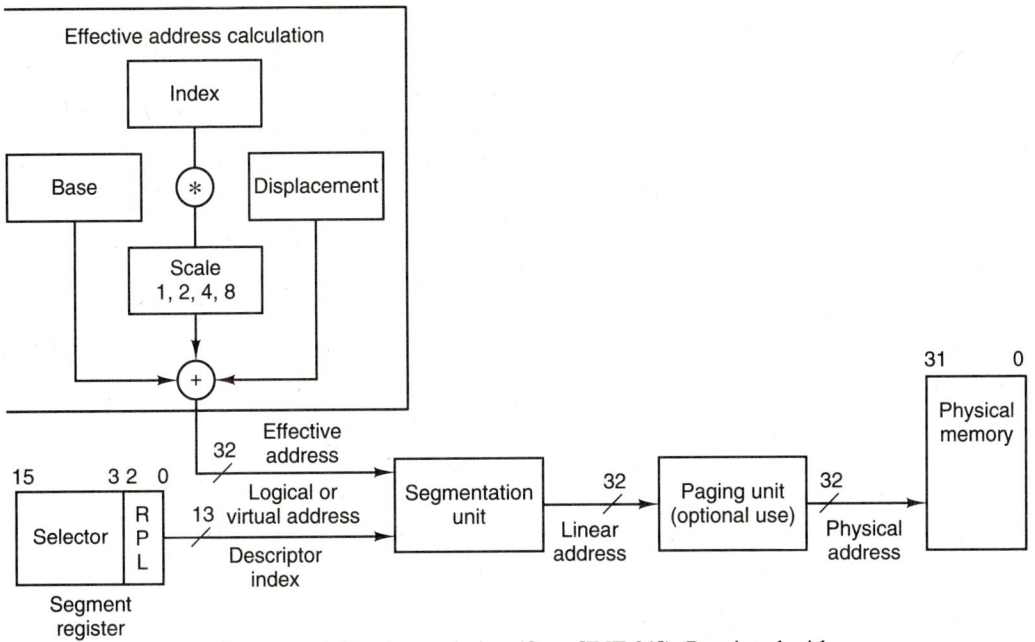

Figure 2.57 Address translation (from [INT 91]). Reprinted with permission of Intel Corporation, Copyright/Intel Corporation 1991.

ing block size. Unfortunately, like first fit, this strategy also causes fragmentation. In fact, it may create many small blocks that are almost useless.

Worst Fit. This strategy allocates the largest available free storage block for the segment. It searches the free storage list for the largest block. The list is usually sorted according to the decreasing block size. Again, the worst fit, like the other two strategies, causes fragmentation. However, in contrast to first fit and best fit, worst fit reduces the number of small blocks by always allocating the largest block for the segment.

Example: i486 Microprocessor Addressing Mechanism

The *i486* supports both segmentation and paging. It contains a segmentation unit and a paging unit. The i486 has three different address spaces: *virtual, linear,* and *physical*. Figure 2.57 represents the relationship between these address spaces. The segmentation unit translates a virtual address into a linear address. When the paging is not used, the linear address corresponds to a physical address. When paging is used, the paging unit translates the linear address into a physical address.

The virtual address consists of a 16-bit *segment selector* and a 32-bit *effective address*. The segment selector points to a table called segment descriptor (which is the same as segment table); see Figure 2.58. The descriptor contains information about a given segment. It includes the base address of the segment, the length of the segment (limit), read, write, or execute privileges (access rights), and so on. The size of a segment can vary from 1 byte to the maximum size of the main memory, 4 gigabytes (2^{32} bytes). The effective address is computed by adding some combinations of the addressing components. There are three addressing components: *displacement, base,* and *index*. The displacement is an 8-, or 32-bit immediate value following the instruction. The base is the contents of any general-purpose register and often points to the beginning of the local variable area. The index is the contents of any general-purpose register and often is used to address the elements of an array or the characters of a string. The index may be multiplied by a scale factor (1, 2, 4, or 8) to facilitate certain addressing, such as addressing arrays or structures. As shown in Figure 2.57, the effective address is computed as:

*effective address = base register + (index register * scaling) + displacement*

The segmentation unit adds the contents of the segment base register to the effective address to form a 32-bit linear address (see Figure 2.58).

The paging unit can be enabled or disabled by software control. When paging is enabled, the linear address will be translated to a physical address. The paging unit uses two levels of tables to translate a linear address into a physical address. Figure 2.59 represents these two levels of tables, a page directory that points to a page table. The page directory can have up to 1024 entries. Each page directory entry contains the address of a page table and statistical information about the table, such as read/write privilege bits, a dirty bit, and a present bit [INT 92]. (The dirty bit is set to 1 when a write to an address covered by the corresponding page occurs. The present bit indicates whether a page directory or page table entry can be used in address translation.) The starting address of the page directory is stored in a register called the page directory base address register (*CR3*, root). The upper 10 bits of the linear address are used as an index to select one of the page directory entries. Similar to the page directory, the page table allows up to 1024 entries, where each entry contains the address of a page frame and statistical information about the page. The main memory is divided into 4-Kbyte page frames. The address bits 12 to 21 of the linear address are used as an index to select one of the page table entries. The page frame address of the selected entry is concatenated with the lower 12 bits of the linear address to form the physical address.

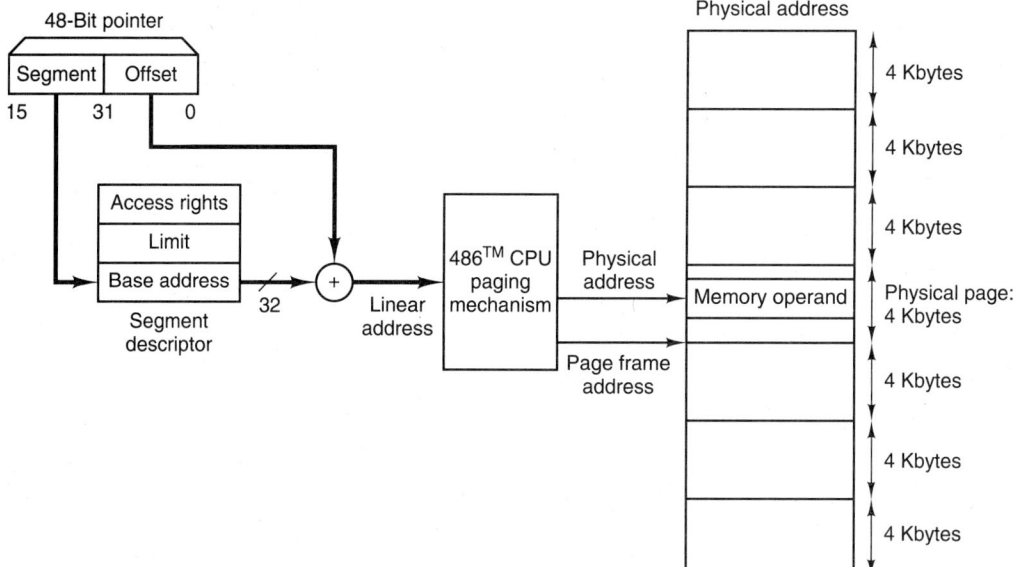

Figure 2.58 Paging and segmentation (from [INT 91]). Reprinted with permission of Intel Corporation, Copyright/Intel Corporation 1991.

Sec. 2.7   Interrupts and Exceptions   93

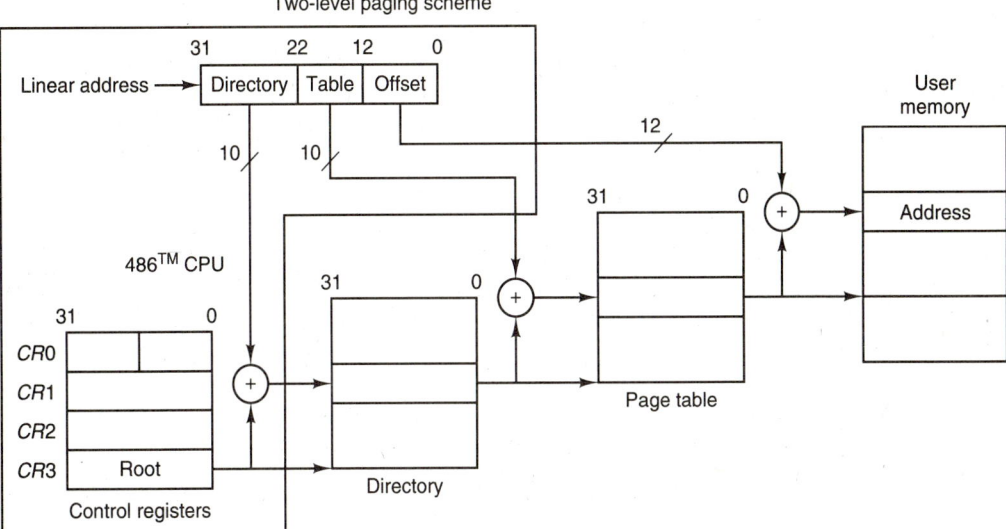

Figure 2.59 Paging mechanism (from [INT 91]). Reprinted with permission of Intel Corporation, Copyright/Intel Corporation 1991.

This paging mechanism requires access to two levels of tables for every memory reference. The access to the tables degrades the performance of the processor. To prevent this degradation, the *i*486 uses a translation lookaside buffer (TLB) to keep the most commonly used page table entries. The TLB is a four-way, set associative cache with 32 entries. Given that a page has 4 Kbytes, the 32-entry TLB can cover 128 Kbytes of main memory addresses. This size of coverage gives a hit rate of about 98% for most applications [INT 92]. That is, the processor needs to access the two tables for only 2% of all memory references. Figure 2.60 represents how the TLB is used in the paging unit.

2.7 INTERRUPTS AND EXCEPTIONS

During execution of a program, an interrupt or an exception may cause the processor to temporarily suspend the program in order to service the needs of a particular event. The event may be external to the processor or may be internal. Interrupts are used for handling asynchronous external events, such as when an external device wants to perform an I/O operation. Exceptions are used for handling synchronous internal events that occur due to instruction faults, such as divide by zero [INT 91].

Interrupts are caused by asynchronous signals applied to certain input lines, called interrupt request lines, of a processor. When an external event triggers an interrupt during execution of a program, the processor suspends the execution of the program, determines the source of the interrupt, acknowledges the interrupt, saves the state of the program (such as program counter and registers) in a stack, loads the address of the proper interrupt service routine into the program counter, and then processes the interrupt by executing the interrupt service routine. After finishing the processing of the interrupt, it resumes the interrupted program. Often, interrupts are classified into different levels of priorities. For example, disk drives are given higher priorities then keyboards. Thus, if an interrupt is being processed and a higher-priority interrupt arrives, the process of the former interrupt will be suspended and the latter interrupt will be serviced. In general, the priority levels are divided into two groups: *maskable* and *nonmaskable*. A maskable interrupt can be handled or delayed by the processor. However, nonmaskable interrupts have very high priority. Often, when a nonmaskable interrupt routine is started, it cannot be interrupted by any other interrupt. They are usually intended for catastrophic events, such as memory error detection or power failure. A typical use of a nonmaskable interrupt would be to start a power failure routine when the power goes down.

Depending on how the processor obtains the address of interrupt service routines, the maskable interrupts are further divided into three classes: *nonvectored, vectored,* and *autovectored*. In a nonvectored interrupt scheme, each interrupt request line is associated with a fixed interrupt service routine address. When an external device sends a request on one of the interrupt request lines, the processor loads the corresponding interrupt service routine address into the program counter. In contrast to nonvectored interrupt, in the vectored interrupt scheme the external device supplies a vector number from which the processor retrieves the address of the interrupt service routine. In the vectored interrupt scheme, an interrupt request line is shared among all the external devices. In this way, the number of interrupt sources can be increased independent of the number of available interrupt request lines. When the processor sends an acknowledgment for an interrupt request, the device that requested the interrupt places a vector number on the data bus (or system bus). The processor converts the vector number to a vector address that points to a vector in the memory. This vector contains the address of the interrupt service routine. The processor fetches the vector

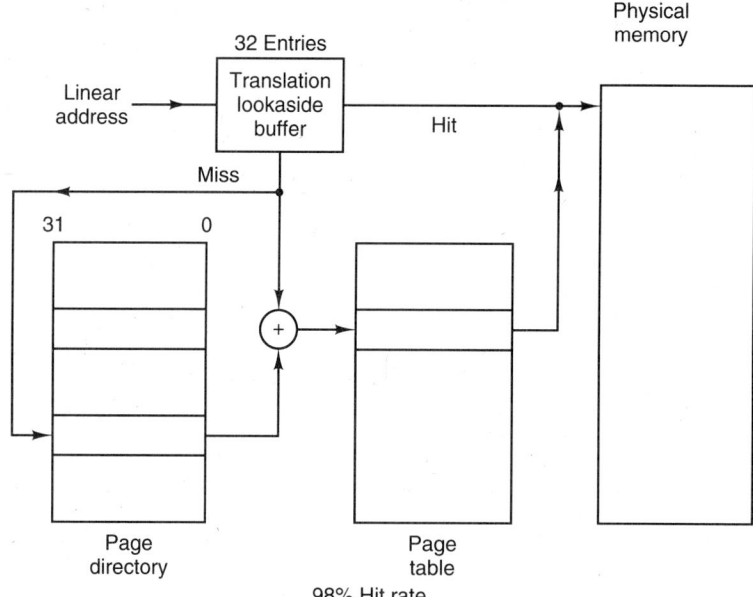

Figure 2.60 Translation lookalike buffer (from [INT 91]). Reprinted with permission of Intel Corporation, Copyright/Intel Corporation 1991.

and loads that into the program counter. Such vectors are usually stored in a specific memory space called a *vector table*. An autovectored interrupt is similar to the vectored interrupt except that in the former case an external vector number is not supplied to the processor. Instead the processor generates a vector number depending on the specific interrupt request line that the interrupt was detected on. The vector number then is converted to a vector address.

Exceptions are used to handle instruction faults [INT 91]. They are divided into three classes: *faults, traps,* and *aborts*. An exception is called a *fault* if it can be detected and serviced before the execution of a faulty instruction. For example, as a result of a programming error such as divide by zero, stack overflow, or an illegal instruction, a fault is generated.

An exception is called a *trap* if it is serviced after the execution of the instruction that requested (or caused) the exception. For example, a trap could be an exception routine defined by the user. Often a programmer uses traps as a substitute for CALL instructions to frequently used procedures in order to save some execution time.

An exception is called an *abort* when the precise location of the cause cannot be determined. Often, aborts are used to report severe errors, such as a hardware failure.

BIBLIOGRAPHIC NOTES

The reference [DAN 87] provides a good description of ALU design. [STA 87] provides a good description of cache design. [GAO 87] was used for describing interrupts. [HIL 88] presents basic structures for direct-mapping and set-associative caches and makes a good comparison between them. [POL 90] was used for floating-point addition.

REFERENCES

[BAU 73] BAUGH, C. R., AND B. A. WOOLEY, "A Two's Complement Parallel Array Multiplication Algorithm," *IEEE Trans. Computers,* C-22 (1–2), 1973, pp. 1045–1047.

[BOO 51] BOOTH, A. D., "A Signed Binary Multiplication Technique," *Quart. Mech. Applied Math.*, 4(2) 1951, pp. 236–240.

[CHO 74] CHOW, C. K. "On Optimization of Storage Hierarchies," *IBM J. of R&D*, (18)3 May 1974, pp. 194–203.

[CLA 80] CLARK, D. W, AND W. D. STRECKER, "Comments on The Case for the RISC," *Computer Architecture News*, 8(6), 1980, pp. 34–38.

[CRW 90] CRAWFORD, J. H. "The *i*486 CPU: Executing Instructions in One Clock Cycle," *IEEE Micro*. 10, February 1990, pp. 27–36.

[DAN 87] DANIEL, TABAK, *RISC Architecture*. New York: John Wiley & Sons, 1987.

[DEE 74] DEEM, WILLIAM, KENNETH MUCHOW, AND ANTHONY ZEPPA, *Digital Computers Circuits and Concepts*. Reston, VA: Reston Publishing Co., 1974.

[FEL 94] FELDMAN, J. M., AND C.T. RETTER, "Computer Architecture: A Designer's Text Based on a Generic RISC," McGraw-Hill, Inc., 1994.

[GAO 87] GAONKAR, R. S. *Microprocessor Architecture, Programming, and Applications.* New Delhi, India: Wiley Eastern Limited, 1987.

[GIM 90] GIMARC, CHARLES E., AND VELJKO M. MILUTINOVIC, "A Survey of RISC Processors and Computers of the Mid-1980s," *IEEE Computer Society Press Tutorial on RISC*, 1990, pp. 259–270.

[GRE 88] GREGORY, RICHARD, "Caching Designs Eliminate Wait States to Relieve Bottlenecks," *Computer Design*, 27, October 1988, pp. 65–73.

[HAN 66] HANLON, A. G. "Content-addressable and Associative Memory Systems—A Survey," *IEEE Trans. Electronic Computers*, EC-15(4), 1966, pp. 509–521.

[HAY 78] HAYES, J. P. *Computer Architecture and Organization.* New York: McGraw-Hill Book Co., 1978.

[HAY 93] HAYES, J. P. *Introduction to Digital Logic Design.* Reading, MA: Addison-Wesley Publishing Co., 1993.

[HEN 90] HENNESSY, JOHN L., AND DAVID A. PATTERSON *Computer Architecture, A Quantitative Approach.* Morgan Kaufmann Publishers, San Francisco, California 1990.

[HIL 88] HILL, MARK D., "A Case for Direct-mapped Caches," *Computer*, 21, December 1988, pp. 25–40.

[IEE 85] IEEE, "IEEE Standard for Binary Floating Point Arithmetic," ANSI/IEEE Std 754-1985, New York, 1985.

[INT 91] INTEL, "*i*486 Microprocessor Data Book," Intel, 1991.

[INT 92] INTEL, "Intel 486 DX Microprocessor Data Book," Intel, 1992.

[KAP 73] KAPLAN, K. R., AND R. O., WINDER, "Cache Based Computer Systems," *Computers*, 6, March 1973, pp. 30–36.

[MAN 86] MANO, M. M. *Computer System Architecture.* New Delhi, India: Prentice-Hall of India Private Limited, 1986.

[MAN 91] MANO, M. MORRIS, *Digital Design*, 2nd, ed. Englewood Cliffs, NJ: Prentice Hall, 1991.

[PAT 80] PATTERSON, D. A., AND D. R. DITZEL, "The Case for the Reduced Instruction Set Computer," *Computer Architecture News*, 8(6), October 15, 1980, pp. 25–33.

[POL 90] POLLARD, L. H., *Computer Design and Architecture.* Englewood Cliffs, NJ: Prentice Hall, 1990.

[STA 87] STALLINGS, WILLIAM, *Computer Organization and Architecture: Principles of Structure and Function.* New York: Macmillan Publishing Co., 1987.

[SUB 89] SUBRATA, DASGUPTA, *Computer Architecture—A Modern Synthesis*, Vol. 1. New York: John Wiley & Sons, 1989.

[WAL 64] WALLACE, C. S., "A Suggestion for a Fast Multiplier," *IEEE Trans Electronic Computers*, EC-13(1) 1964, pp. 14–17.

[WIL 51] WILKES, M. V. "The Best Way to Design an Automatic Calculating Machine," Report of the Manchester University Computer Inaugural Conference. Manchester, U.K.: University of Manchester, 1951 (not published until 1953).

PROBLEMS

2.1. Similar to Figure 2.7, show the flow of addresses and data for execution of the following STORE instruction:

```
STORE R, X    --X is a memory location address
```

2.2. Design a horizontal and a vertical microprogram for the store instruction given in this chapter. Determine and define the function of all control signals that you need. Use Figures 2.17 and 2.18 as a template for your design.

2.3. What are the advantages and disadvantages of the following methods in designing a control unit?

a. Hardwired versus microprogramming.

b. Vertical versus horizontal microprogramming.

2.4. Design a hardwired control unit for generating the following sequence of control signals:

```
{
issue control signals (c₁, c₂)
if S = 0 {
    issue control signals (c₁, c₃)
    }
  else
    {
    issue control signals (c₁, c₄)
    issue control signals (c₂, c₃)
    }
}
```

 issue control signals (c_1, c_2); (c_1, c_3); (c_1, c_4); (c_2, c_3))

2.5. Consider the following expression:

$$[(a * b + c) - d/f]/(a * d) + b.$$

Write a code for this expression so that a stack machine can use it. Use operators such as PUSH, POP, ADD, SUB, MUL, and DIV.

2.6. Consider a simple processor with only one register, R, and one instruction, SUBSTO (subtract and store). The instruction SUBSTO has the following format:

```
SUBSTO R, X, where X is address of a memory location.
```

Whenever this instruction is executed, the following two operations are performed:

```
R = R - M(X), where M(X) is contents of location X,
M(X) = R.
```

Use the instruction SUBSTO to write a simple program for each of the instructions LOAD, STORE, and ADD. The format and function of these instructions are defined as

```
LOAD  R, X    --R = M(X)
STORE R, X    --M(X) = R
ADD   R, X    --R = R + M(X)
```

Note: the contents of a memory location (other than x) can be assumed to have an initial value.

2.7. Design combinational circuits for a half-subtractor and a full subtractor. A half-subtractor subtracts two 1-bit inputs and produces a difference bit and a borrow bit. If the minuend bit is smaller than the subtrahend bit, the borrow bit is set to 1; otherwise, the borrow bit is set to 0. A full subtractor has three 1-bit inputs and two one-bit outputs. Two of the inputs are the two significant bits to be subtracted (minuend and subtrahend bits), and the other input is the borrow from the lower significant bit position. The outputs are the difference bit and the output borrow bit. For each circuit,

  a. Derive the truth table.

  b. Derive the Boolean expression.

  c. Draw the logic diagram.

2.8. Assume that it takes one gate delay time unit for each of the gates AND, OR, and NOT to produce the resultant Boolean value once its inputs are available. Let's also assume the fan-in of AND and OR gates to be 4.

  a. How many gate delays are required for a 4-bit ripple carry adder to add two 4-bit numbers?

  b. How many gate delays are required for a 4-bit carry lookahead adder to add two 4-bit numbers?

2.9. Considering carry lookahead adder design that was presented in this chapter, derive the Boolean expressions for C_{10}, C_{12}, and C_{16}. Assume that the fan-in is limited to 4.

2.10. A BCD adder is a circuit that adds two BCD digits and produces a sum digit also in BCD. Design such a circuit by using five full adders, two half-adders, three two-input NAND gates, and one three-input NAND gate.

2.11. Show the block diagram of a multiple-operand adder with multilevel of carry save adders (CSA's) and one carry lookahead adder (CLA). The adder can receive 10 input numbers where each number has 4 bits. Assume that each level of CSAs has D delay, and CLA has a delay of $2D$. Using such an adder, estimate the total time required to add one hundred 4-bit numbers. Show your work.

2.12. Consider the 9-bit floating-point format in figure P2.12, where the 4-bit exponent is biased by 8.

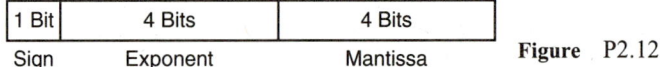

Figure P2.12

  a. Assume that the exponent base is 2, and consider only normalized representations. What are the largest positive value and the smallest negative value representable by this format? (Express your answer in base 10.) Also, specify approximately how many decimal digits of precision this format can represent.

  b. Repeat part a when the exponent base is 4.

2.13. Draw the block diagram of an array multiplier that multiplies two 3-bit positive binary numbers. Your design should use at most nine of the cells shown in Figure P2.13; no other cell or gate can be used.

2.14. Use the types of full adders shown in Figure P2.14 to design an array multiplier for multiplying two 4-bit 2's complement numbers.

Let $X = x_3x_2x_1x_0$ represent the multiplicand and $Y = y_3y_2y_1y_0$ be the multiplier. In your design use AND gates, four full adders of type 0, two of type 1, five of type 2, and one of type 3.

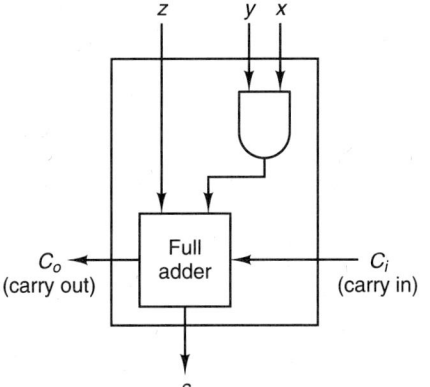

Figure P2.13

2.15. Use the shift-and-add multiplication method to multiply two 2's complement numbers $X = 1101$ (multiplier) and $Y = 1101$ (multiplicand). Show all your work.

2.16. Give a multiplication scheme similar to the shift-and-add multiplication method but that proceeds with a left-to-right scan of the multiplier.

2.17. Use Booth's algorithm to multiply $y = 11101$ (multiplicand) and $x = 11100$ (multiplier), where x and y are 2's complement numbers. Show the contents of A and Q for each step of the algorithm.

2.18. Use Booth's algorithm to multiply $y = 1.1001$ (multiplicand) and $x = 1.1101$ (multiplier), where x and y are 2's complement numbers. Show the contents of A and Q for each step of the algorithm.

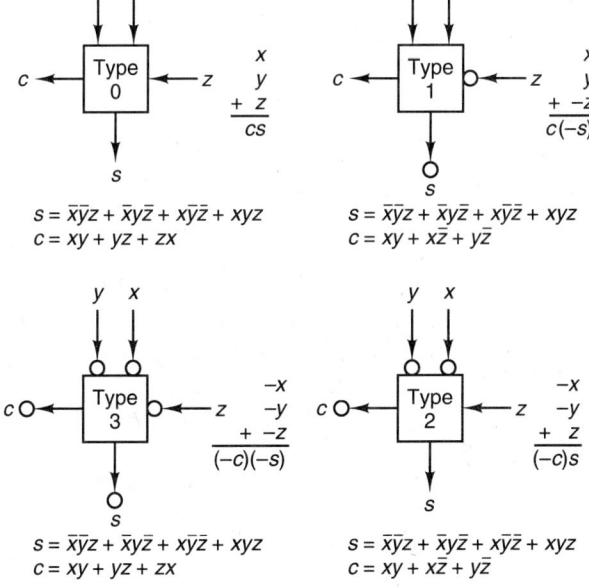

Figure P2.14

2.19. As an extension to Booth's algorithm, derive a table that represents possible operations for an overlapped 3-bit scanning multiplication system, also called a 3-bit grouping overlapped multiple-bit scanning multiplication. In such a system at every step of multiplication, we consider 3 bits of the multiplier to determine which operation to perform, and the registers are shifted two places to the right after each iteration. Use your table to multiply $y = 000111$ and $x = 111101$, where x and y are 2's complement numbers.

2.20. Using 4-by-2 memory units of the type shown in Figure P2.20, design a 16-by-4 random-access memory unit.

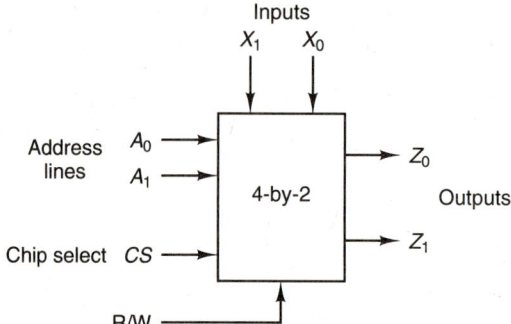

Figure P2.20

2.21. Using the associative memory cells of the type shown in Figure P2.21, design a 2-by-2 associative memory unit.

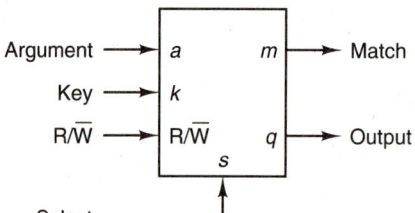

Figure P2.21

2.22. Why is set-associative cache organization better than direct-mapping and associative-mapping caches?

2.23. Consider a processor with a cache and main memory. Out of 100 requests that the processor sends to the cache, let's assume the following:

Number of address references satisfied by cache N_c is 10. Number of address references satisfied by main memory N_m is 90.

Access time for cache t_c is 10 ns.

Access time for main memory t_m is 90 ns.

   a. Compute hit ratio, H, and average access time, t_a, for these assumptions.

   b. Now let $N_c = 60$ and $N_m = 40$. Recompute H and t_a and compare the result with that in part *a*. Is there much improvement in the average access time?

   c. From the approximately 5% decrease in the hit ratio, from 0.95 to 0.90, what is the percent of increase in the average access time?

2.24. Consider a system that consists of a main memory and a cache. The main memory has 2^{16} words (from 0000 to FFFF), and each word has 16 bits. The cache has *only* the following data in it:

Main Memory Address	Data
0910	2373
2124	0A1B
0000	7345
FFFF	2100

The CPU wishes to READ the contents of the memory location 0800, which contains data value A99B. Explain what happens and what the contents of the cache will look like after the READ operation for each of the following cache organizations. Assume that the size of each is the same as the one given in Figures 2.47, 2.49, and 2.51.

a. Associative-mapping cache (associative memory part is addressed from 00 to FF).

b. Direct-mapping cache (tag part is addressed from 00 to FF).

c. Two-way set-associative mapping cache (tag of each set is addressed from 00 to FF).

2.25. Given the following reference string: 1, 4, 10, 4, 3, 6, 1, 1, 8, 6, 9, 4, 3, 3, 3, 1. What will be the number of page faults for a system that gives each process a maximum of four frames, using the following:

a. First in, first out.

b. An approximation of least frequently used that keeps a counter for each page. For each reference, the counter for that page is incremented. The page with the lowest count will be replaced. The system also uses a first in, first out algorithm to break ties.

c. Least recently used.

Show all states of the stack and counters.

2.26. Consider a two-dimensional integer array x defined as

```
integer x [50][50];
```

Also consider a paged memory system with four page frames each of size 100. What will be the number of page faults for each of the following array initialization loops when using LRU replacement policy? Assume that page frame 0 is used for the program, and the other three are initially empty.

a.
```
for (i = 0; i < 50; i++)
    for (j = 0; j < 50; j++)
        x[i][j] = 0;
```
b.
```
for (j = 0; j < 50; j++)
    for (i = 0; i < 50; i++)
        x[i][j] = 0;
```

2.27. What are the advantages and disadvantages of nonvectored and vectored interrupt schemes?

3
Pipelining

3.1 INTRODUCTION

Pipelining is one way of improving the overall processing performance of a processor. This architectural approach allows the simultaneous execution of several instructions. Pipelining is transparent to the programmer; it exploits parallelism at the instruction level by overlapping the execution process of instructions. It is analogous to an assembly line where workers perform a specific task and pass the partially completed product to the next worker.

This chapter explains various types of pipeline design. It describes different ways to measure their performance. Instruction pipelining and arithmetic pipelining, along with methods for maximizing the throughput of a pipeline, are discussed. The concepts of reservation table and latency are discussed, together with a method of controlling the scheduling of static and dynamic pipelines.

3.1.1 Pipeline Structure

The pipeline design technique decomposes a sequential process into several subprocesses, called stages or segments. A *stage* performs a particular function and produces an intermediate result. It consists of an input latch, also called a register or buffer, followed by a processing circuit. (A processing circuit can be a combinational or sequential circuit.) The processing circuit of a given stage is connected to the input latch of the next stage (see Figure 3.1). A clock signal is connected to each input latch. At each clock pulse, every stage transfers its intermediate result to the input latch of the next

Sec. 3.1   Introduction

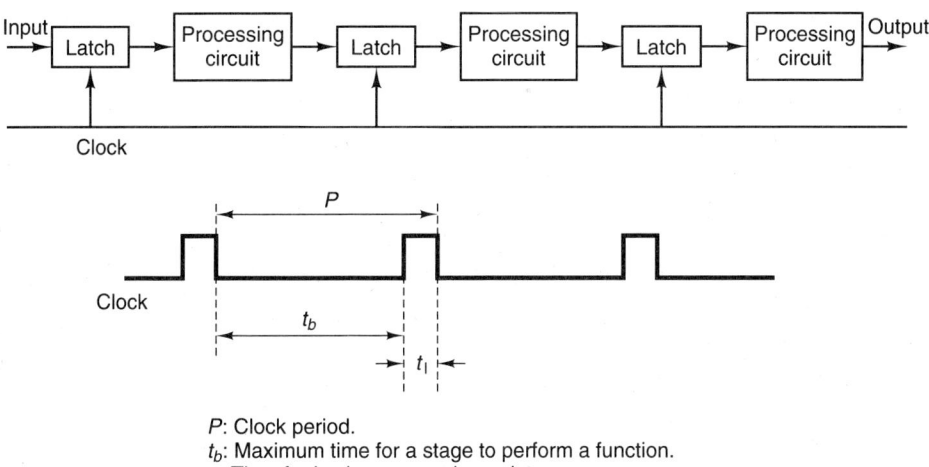

P: Clock period.
t_b: Maximum time for a stage to perform a function.
t_l: Time for latch to accept input data.

Figure 3.1   Basic structure of a pipeline.

stage. In this way, the final result is produced after the input data have passed through the entire pipeline, completing one stage per clock pulse. The period of the clock pulse should be large enough to provide sufficient time for a signal to traverse through the slowest stage, which is called the *bottleneck* (i.e., the stage needing the longest amount of time to complete). In addition, there should be enough time for a latch to store its input signals. If the clock's period, P, is expressed as $P = t_b + t_l$, then t_b should be greater than the maximum delay of the bottleneck stage, and t_l should be sufficient for storing data into a latch.

3.1.2 Pipeline Performance Measures

The ability to overlap stages of a sequential process for different input tasks (data or operations) results in an overall theoretical completion time of

$$T_{\text{pipe}} = m * P + (n - 1) * P, \tag{3.1}$$

where n is the number of input tasks, m is the number of stages in the pipeline, and P is the clock period. The term $m * P$ is the time required for the first input task to get through the pipeline, and the term $(n - 1) * P$ is the time required for the remaining tasks. After the pipeline has been filled, it generates an output on each clock cycle. In other words, after the pipeline is loaded, it will generate output only as fast as its slowest stage. Even with this limitation, the pipeline will greatly outperform nonpipelined techniques, which require each task to complete before another task's execution sequence begins. To be more specific, when n is large, a pipelined processor can produce output approximately m times faster than a nonpipelined processor. On the other hand, in a nonpipelined processor, the above sequential process requires a completion time of

$$T_{\text{seq}} = n * \sum_{i=1}^{m} \tau_i$$

where τ_i is the delay of each stage. For the ideal case when all stages have equal delay $\tau_i = \tau$ for $i = 1$ to m, T_{seq} can be rewritten as

$$T_{seq} = n * m * \tau.$$

If we ignore the small storing time t_1 that is required for latch storage (i.e., $t_1 = 0$), then

$$T_{seq} = n * m * P. \qquad (3.2)$$

Now, *speedup* (*S*) may be represented as:

$$S = T_{seq} / T_{pipe} = n * m / (m + n - 1).$$

The value S approaches m when $n \to \infty$. That is, the maximum speedup, also called ideal speedup, of a pipeline processor with m stages over an equivalent nonpipelined processor is m. In other words, the ideal speedup is equal to the number of pipeline stages. That is, when n is very large, a pipelined processor can produce output approximately m times faster than a nonpipelined processor. When n is small, the speedup decreases; in fact, for $n = 1$ the pipeline has the minimum speedup of 1.

In addition to speedup, two other factors are often used for determining the performance of a pipeline; they are *efficiency* and *throughput*. The efficiency E of a pipeline with m stages is defined as:

$$E = S / m = [n * m / (m + n - 1)] / m = n / (m + n - 1).$$

The efficiency E, which represents the speedup per stage, approaches its maximum value of 1 when $n \to \infty$. When $n = 1$, E will have the value $1/m$, which is the lowest obtainable value.

The throughput H, also called bandwidth, of a pipeline is defined as the number of input tasks it can process per unit of time. When the pipeline has m stages, H is defined as

$$H = n / T_{pipe} = n / [m * P + (n - 1) * P] = E / P = S / (mP).$$

When $n \to \infty$, the throughput H approaches the maximum value of one task per clock cycle.

The number of stages in a pipeline often depends on the tradeoff between performance and cost. The optimal choice for such a number can be determined by obtaining the peak value of a performance/cost ratio (PCR). Larson [LAR 73, HWA 93] has defined PCR as follows:

$$PCR = \frac{\text{maximum throughput}}{\text{pipeline cost}}.$$

To illustrate, assume that a nonpipelined processor requires a completion time of t_{seq} for processing an input task. For a pipeline with m stages to process the same task, a clock period of $P = (t_{seq}/m) + t_1$ is needed. (The time t_1 is the latch delay.) Thus the maximum throughput that can be obtained with such a pipeline is

$$1/P = 1/[(t_{seq}/m) + t_1].$$

Sec. 3.1 Introduction 105

The maximum throughput $1/P$ is also called the pipeline frequency. The actual throughput may be less than $1/P$ depending on the rate of consecutive tasks entering the pipeline.

The pipeline cost c_p can be expressed as the total cost of logic gates and latches used in all stages. That is, $c_p = c_g + mc_1$ where c_g is the cost of all logic stages and c_1 is the cost of each latch. (Note that the cost of gates and latches may be interpreted in different ways; for example, the cost may refer to the actual dollar cost, design complexity, or the area required on the chip or circuit board.) By substituting the values for maximum throughput and pipeline cost in the PCR equation, the following formula can be obtained:

$$\text{PCR} = 1/\{[(t_{seq}/m) + t_1](c_g + mc_1)\}.$$

This equation has a maximum value m_0, where

$$m_0 = \sqrt{\frac{(t_{seq} * c_g)}{(t_l * c_l)}}$$

Since the value m_0 maximizes PCR, this value can be used as an optimal choice for the number of stages.

3.1.3 Pipeline types

Pipelines are usually divided into two classes: instruction pipelines and arithmetic pipelines. A pipeline in each of these classes can be designed in two ways: static or dynamic. A static pipeline can perform only one operation (such as addition or multiplication) at a time. The operation of a static pipeline can only be changed after the pipeline has been drained. (A pipeline is said to be drained when the last input data leave the pipeline.) For example, consider a static pipeline that is able to perform addition and multiplication. Each time that the pipeline switches from a multiplication operation to an addition operation, it must be drained and set for the new operation. The performance of static pipelines is severely degraded when the operations change often, since this requires the pipeline to be drained and refilled each time. A dynamic pipeline can perform more than one operation at a time. To perform a particular operation on an input data, the data must go through a certain sequence of stages. For example, Figure 3.2 shows a three-stage dynamic pipeline that performs addition and multiplication on different data at the same time. To perform multiplication, the input data must go through stages 1, 2, and 3; to perform addition, the data only need to go through stages 1 and 3. Therefore, the first stage of the addition process can be performed on an input data D_1 at stage 1, while at the same time the last stage of the multiplication process is performed at stage 3 on a different input data D_2. Note that the time interval between the initiation of the inputs D_1 and D_2 to the pipeline should be such that they do not reach stage 3 at the same time; otherwise, there is a *collision*. In general, in dynamic pipelines the mechanism that controls when data should be fed to the pipeline is much more complex than in static pipelines.

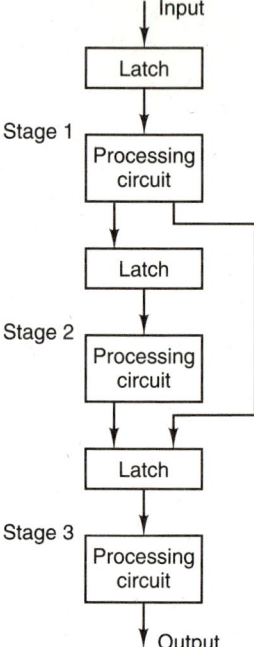

Figure 3.2 A three-stage dynamic pipeline.

3.2 INSTRUCTION PIPELINE

In a von Neumann architecture, the process of executing an instruction involves several steps. First, the control unit of a processor fetches the instruction from the cache (or from memory). Then the control unit decodes the instruction to determine the type of operation to be performed. When the operation requires operands, the control unit also determines the address of each operand and fetches them from cache (or memory). Next, the operation is performed on the operands and, finally, the result is stored in the specified location.

An instruction pipeline increases the performance of a processor by overlapping the processing of several different instructions. Often, this is done by dividing the instruction execution process into several stages. As shown in Figure 3.3, an instruction pipeline often consists of five stages, as follows:

1. **Instruction fetch (IF).** Retrieval of instructions from cache (or main memory).
2. **Instruction decoding (ID).** Identification of the operation to be performed.
3. **Operand fetch (OF).** Decoding and retrieval of any required operands.
4. **Execution (EX).** Performing the operation on the operands.
5. **Write-back (WB).** Updating the destination operands.

Sec. 3.2 Instruction Pipeline

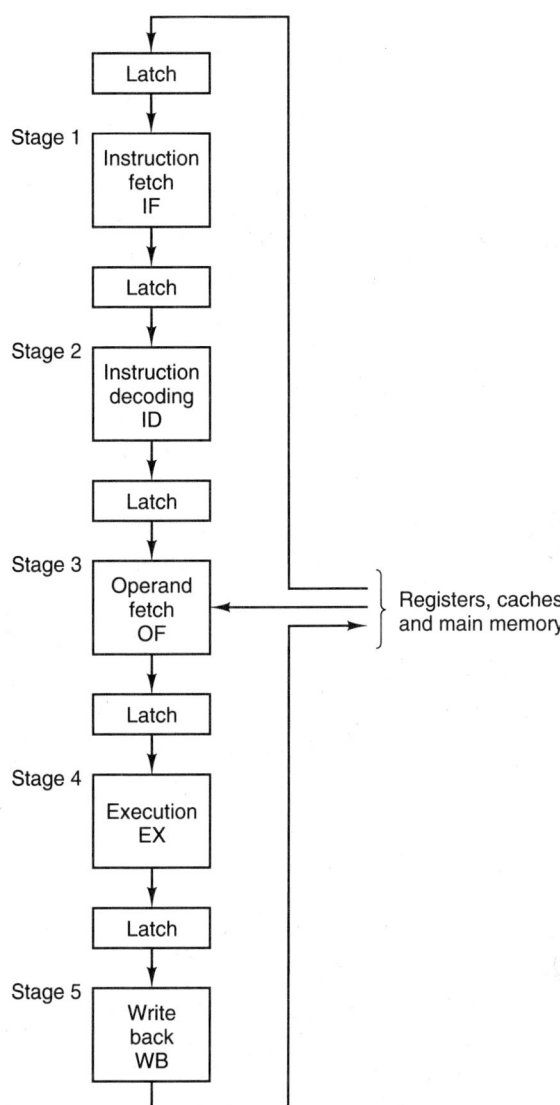

Figure 3.3 Stages of an instruction pipeline.

An instruction pipeline overlaps the process of the preceding stages for different instructions to achieve a much lower total completion time, on average, for a series of instructions. As an example, consider Figure 3.4, which shows the execution of four instructions in an instruction pipeline. During the first cycle, or clock pulse, instruction i_1 is fetched from memory. Within the second cycle, instruction i_1 is decoded while instruction i_2 is fetched. This process continues until all the instructions are executed. The last instruction finishes the write-back stage after the eighth clock cycle. Therefore, it takes 80 nanoseconds (ns) to complete execution of all the four instructions

Instruction	Cycles							
	1	2	3	4	5	6	7	8
i_1	IF	ID	OF	EX	WB			
i_2		IF	ID	OF	EX	WB		
i_3			IF	ID	OF	EX	WB	
i_4				IF	ID	OF	EX	WB

Figure 3.4 Execution cycles of four consecutive instructions in an instruction pipeline.

when assuming the clock period to be 10 ns. The total completion time can also be obtained using equation (3.1); that is,

$$T_{pipe} = m * P + (n - 1) * P$$
$$= 5 * 10 + (4 - 1) * 10 = 80 \text{ ns}.$$

Note that in a nonpipelined design the completion time will be much higher. Using equation (3.2),

$$T_{seq} = n * m * P = 4 * 5 * 10 = 200 \text{ ns}.$$

It is worth noting that a similar execution path will occur for an instruction whether a pipelined architecture is used or not; a pipeline simply takes advantage of these naturally occurring stages to improve processing efficiency. Henry Ford made the same connection when he realized that all cars were built in stages and invented the assembly line in the early 1900s. Some ideas have an enduring quality and can be applied in many different ways!

Even though pipelining speeds up the execution of instructions, it does pose potential problems. Some of these problems and possible solutions are discussed next.

3.2.1 Improving the Throughput of an Instruction Pipeline

Three sources of architectural problems may affect the throughput of an instruction pipeline. They are fetching, bottleneck, and issuing problems. Some solutions are given for each.

The fetching problem. In general, supplying instructions rapidly through a pipeline is costly in terms of chip area. Buffering the data to be sent to the pipeline is one simple way of improving the overall utilization of a pipeline. The utilization of a pipeline is defined as the percentage of time that the stages of the pipeline are used over a sufficiently long period of time. A pipeline is utilized 100% of the time when every stage is used (utilized) during each clock cycle.

Occasionally, the pipeline has to be drained and refilled, for example, whenever an interrupt or a branch occurs. The time spent refilling the pipeline can be minimized by having instructions and data loaded ahead of time into various geographically close buffers (like on-chip caches) for immediate transfer into the pipeline. If instructions and data for normal execution can be fetched before they are needed and stored in buffers, the pipeline will have a continuous source of information with which to work. Prefetch algorithms are used to make sure potentially needed instructions are available most of the time. Delays from memory-access conflicts can thereby be reduced if these algorithms are used, since the time required to transfer data from main memory is far greater than the time required to transfer data from a buffer.

The bottleneck problem. The bottleneck problem relates to the amount of load (work) assigned to a stage in the pipeline. If too much work is applied to one stage, the time taken to complete an operation at that stage can become unacceptably long. This relatively long time spent by the instruction at one stage will inevitably create a bottleneck in the pipeline system. In such a system, it is better to remove the bottleneck that is the source of congestion. One solution to this problem is to further subdivide the stage. Another solution is to build multiple copies of this stage into the pipeline.

The issuing problem. If an instruction is available, but cannot be executed for some reason, a hazard exists for that instruction. These hazards create issuing problems; they prevent issuing an instruction for execution. Three types of hazard are discussed here. They are called *structural hazard, data hazard,* and *control hazard*. A structural hazard refers to a situation in which a required resource is not available (or is busy) for executing an instruction. A data hazard refers to a situation in which there exists a data dependency (operand conflict) with a prior instruction. A control hazard refers to a situation in which an instruction, such as branch, causes a change in the program flow. Each of these hazards is explained next.

Structural Hazard. A structural hazard occurs as a result of resource conflicts between instructions. One type of structural hazard that may occur is due to the design of execution units. If an execution unit that requires more than one clock cycle (such as multiply) is not fully pipelined or is not replicated, then a sequence of instructions that uses the unit cannot be subsequently (one per clock cycle) issued for execution. Replicating and/or pipelining execution units increases the number of instructions that can be issued simultaneously. Another type of structural hazard that may occur is due to the design of register files. If a register file does not have multiple write (read) ports, multiple writes (reads) to (from) registers cannot be performed simultaneously. For example, under certain situations the instruction pipeline might want to perform two register writes in a clock cycle. This may not be possible when the register file has only one write port.

The effect of a structural hazard can be reduced fairly simply by implementing multiple execution units and using register files with multiple input/output ports.

Data Hazard. In a nonpipelined processor, the instructions are executed one by one, and the execution of an instruction is completed before the next instruction is started. In this way, the instructions are executed in the same order as the program. However, this may not be true in a pipelined processor, where instruction executions are overlapped. An instruction may be started and completed before the previous

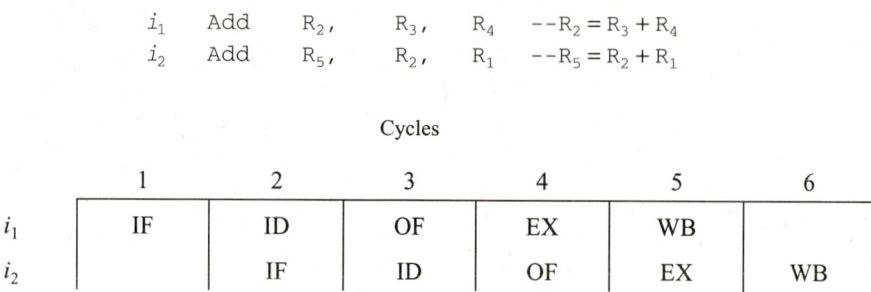

Figure 3.5 Instruction i_2 has data dependency on i_1.

instruction is completed. The data hazard, which is also referred to as the data dependency problem, comes about as a result of overlapping (or changing the order of) the execution of data-dependent instructions. For example, in Figure 3.5 instruction i_2 has a data dependency on i_1 because it uses the result of i_1 (i.e., the contents of register R_2) as input data. If the instructions were sent to a pipeline in the normal manner, i_2 would be in the OF stage before i_1 passed through the WB stage. This would result in using the old contents of R_2 for computing a new value for R_5, leading to an invalid result. To have a valid result, i_2 must not enter the OF stage until i_1 has passed through the WB stage. In this way, as is shown in Figure 3.6, the execution of i_2 will be delayed for two clock cycles. In other words, instruction i_2 is said to be *stalled* for two clock cycles. Often, when an instruction is stalled, the instructions that are positioned after the stalled instruction will also be stalled. However, the instructions before the stalled instruction can continue execution.

The delaying of execution can be accomplished in two ways. One way is to delay the OF or IF stages of i_2 for two clock cycles. To insert a delay, an extra hardware component called a pipeline interlock can be added to the pipeline. A *pipeline interlock* detects the dependency and delays the dependent instructions until the conflict is

Figure 3.6 Two ways of executing data dependent instructions

Sec. 3.2   Instruction Pipeline

i_1 Add R_2, R_3, R_4 $--R_2 = R_3 + R_4$
i_2 Add R_5, R_2, R_1 $--R_5 = R_2 + R_1$
i_3 Add R_6, R_6, R_7 $--R_6 = R_6 + R_7$
i_4 Add R_8, R_8, R_7 $--R_8 = R_8 + R_7$

Cycles

	1	2	3	4	5	6	7	8
i_1	IF	ID	OF	EX	WB			
i_3		IF	ID	OF	EX	WB		
i_4			IF	ID	OF	EX	WB	
i_2				IF	ID	OF	EX	WB

Figure 3.7   Rearranging the order of instruction execution.

resolved. Another way is to let the compiler solve the dependency problem. During compilation, the compiler detects the dependency between data and instructions. It then rearranges these instructions so that the dependency is not hazardous to the system. If it is not possible to rearrange the instructions, NOP (no operation) instructions are inserted to create delays. For example, consider the four instructions in Figure 3.7. These instructions may be reordered so that i_3 and i_4, which are not dependent on i_1 and i_2, are inserted between i_1 and i_2.

In the previous type of data hazard, an instruction uses the result of a previous instruction as input data. In addition to this type of data hazard, other types may occur in designs that allow concurrent execution of instructions. Note that the type of pipeline design considered so far preserves the execution order of instructions in the program. Later in this section we will consider architectures that allow concurrent execution of independent instructions.

There are three primary types of data hazards: RAW (read after write), WAR (write after read), and WAW (write after write). The hazard names denote the execution ordering of the instructions that must be maintained to produce a valid result; otherwise, an invalid result might occur. Each of these hazards is explained in the following discussion. In each explanation, it is assumed that there are two instructions i_1 and i_2, and i_2 should be executed after i_1.

RAW: This type of data hazard was discussed previously; it refers to the situation in which i_2 reads a data source before i_1 writes to it. This may produce an invalid result since the read must be performed after the write in order to obtain a valid result. For example, in the sequence

i_1:   Add R_2, R_3, R_4 $--R_2 = R_3 + R_4$
i_2:   Add R_5, R_2, R_1 $--R_5 = R_2 + R_1$

an invalid result may be produced if i_2 reads R_2 before i_1 writes to it.

WAR: This refers to the situation in which i_2 writes to a location before i_1 reads it. For example, in the sequence

i_1:   Add R_2, R_3, R_4 $--R_2 = R_3 + R_4$
i_2:   Add R_4, R_5, R_6 $--R_4 = R_5 + R_6$

an invalid result may be produced if i_2 writes to R_4 before i_1 reads it; that is, the instruction i_1 might use the wrong value of R_4.

WAW: This refers to the situation in which i_2 writes to a location before i_1 writes to it. For example, in the sequence

i_1:   Add R_2, R_3, R_4 $--R_2 = R_3 + R_4$
i_2:   Add R_2, R_5, R_6 $--R_2 = R_5 + R_6$

the value of R_2 is recomputed by i_2. If the order of execution were reversed, that is, i_2 writes to R_2 before i_1 writes to it, an invalid value for R_2 might be produced.

Note that the WAR and WAW types of hazards cannot happen when the order of completion of instructions execution in the program is preserved. However, one way to enhance the architecture of an instruction pipeline is to increase concurrent execution of the instructions by dispatching several independent instructions to different functional units, such as adders/subtractors, multipliers, and dividers. That is, the instructions can be executed out of order, and so their execution may be completed out of order too. Hence, in such architectures all types of data hazards are possible.

In today's architectures, the dependencies between instructions are checked statically by the compiler and/or dynamically by the hardware at run time. This preserves the execution order for dependent instructions, which ensures valid results. Many different static dependency checking techniques have been developed to exploit parallelism in a loop [LIL 94, WOL 91]. These techniques have the advantage of being able to look ahead at the entire program and are able to detect most dependencies.

Unfortunately, certain dependencies cannot be detected at compile time. For example, it is not always possible to determine the actual memory addresses of load and store instructions in order to resolve a possible dependency between them. However, during the run time the actual memory addresses are known, and thereby dependencies between instructions can be determined by dynamically checking the dependency. In general, dynamic dependency checking has the advantage of being able to determine dependencies that are either impossible or hard to detect at compile time. However, it may not be able to exploit all the parallelism available in a loop because of the limited lookahead ability that can be supported by the hardware. In practice, a combined static–dynamic dependency checking is often used to take advantage of both approaches.

Here we will discuss the techniques for dynamic dependency checking. Two of the most commonly used techniques are called *Tomasulo's method* [TOM 67] and the *scoreboard method* [THO 64, THO 70]. The basic concept behind these methods is to use a mechanism for identifying the availability of operands and functional units in successive computations.

Tomasulo's Method. Tomasulo's method was developed by R. Tomasulo to overcome the long memory access delays in the IBM 360/91 processor. Tomasulo's method increases concurrent execution of the instructions with minimal (or no) effort by the compiler or the programmer. In this method, a busy bit and a tag register are associated with registers. The busy bit of a particular register is set when an issued instruction designates that register as a destination. (The destination register, or sink register, is the register that the result of the instruction will be written to.) The busy bit is cleared when the result of the execution is written back to the register. The tag of a register identifies the unit whose result will be sent to the register (this will be made clear shortly).

Each functional unit may have more than one set (source_1 and source_2) of input registers. Each such set is called a reservation station and is used to keep the operands of an issued instruction. A tag register is also associated with each register of a reservation station. In addition, a common data bus (CDB) connects the output of the functional units to their inputs and the registers. Such a common data bus structure, called a *forwarding* technique (also referred to as *feed-forwarding*), plays a very important role in organizing the order in which various instructions are presented to the pipeline for execution. The CDB makes it possible for the result of an operation to become available to all functional units without first going through a register. It allows a direct copy of the result of an operation to be given to all the functional units waiting for that result. In other words, a currently executing instruction can have access to the result of a previous instruction before the result of the previous instruction has actually been written to an output register.

Figure 3.8 represents a simple architecture for such a method. In this architecture there are nine units communicating through a common data bus. The units include five registers, two add reservation stations called A_1 and A_2 (virtually two adders), and 2 multiply reservation stations called M_1 and M_2 (virtually two multipliers). The binary-coded tags 1 to 5 are associated with registers in the register file, 6 and 7 are associated to add stations, and 8 and 9 are associated with multiply stations. The tags are used to direct the result of an instruction to the next instruction through the CDB. For example, consider the execution of the following two instructions.

i_1 Add R_2, R_3, R_4 $--R_2 = R_3 + R_4$
i_2 Add R_2, R_2, R_1 $--R_2 = R_2 + R_1$

After issuing the instruction i_1 to the add station A_1, the busy bit of the register R_2 is set to 1, the contents of the registers R_3 and R_4 are sent to source_1 and source_2 of the add station A_1, respectively, and the tag of R_2 is set to 6 (i.e., 110), which is the tag of A_1. Then the adder unit starts execution of i_1. In the meantime, during the process of operand fetch for the instruction i_2, it becomes known that the register R_2 is busy. This means that instruction i_2 depends on the result of instruction i_1. To let the execution of i_2 start as soon as possible, the contents of tag of R_2 (i.e., 110) are sent to the tag of the source_1 of the add station A_2; therefore, tag of source_1 of A_2 is set to 6. At this time the tag of R_2 is changed to 7, which means that the result of A_2 must be transferred to R_2. Also, the contents of R_1 are sent to source_2 of A_2. Right before the adder finishes the execution of i_1 and produces the result, it sends a request signal to the CDB for

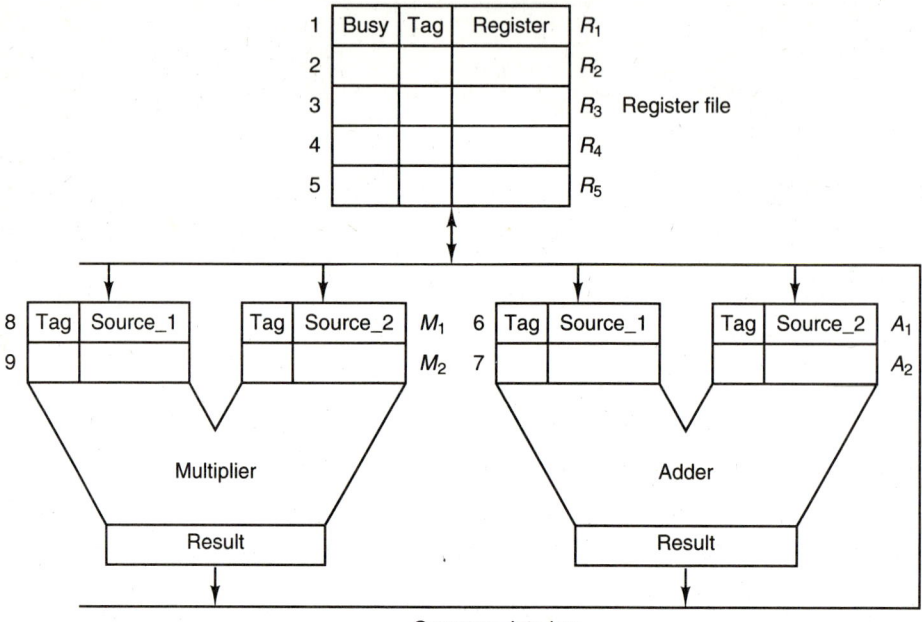

Figure 3.8 Common data bus architecture.

sending the result. (Since CDB is shared with many units, its time sharing can be controlled by a central priority circuit.) When the CDB acknowledges the request, the adder A_1 sends the result to the CDB. The CDB broadcasts the result together with the tag of A_1 (i.e., 6) to all the units. Each reservation station, while waiting for data, compares its source register tags with the tag on the CDB. If they match, the data are copied to the proper register(s). Similarly, at the same time, each register whose busy bit is set to 1 compares its tag with the tag on the CDB. If they match, the register updates its data and clears the busy bit. In this case the data are copied to source_1 of A_2. Next, A_2 starts execution and the result is sent to R_2.

As demonstrated in the preceding example, the main concepts in Tomasulo's method are the addition of reservation stations, the innovation of the CDB, and the development of a simple tagging scheme. The reservation stations do the waiting for operands and hence free up the functional units from such a task. The CDB utilizes the reservation stations by providing them the result of an operation directly from the output of the functional unit. The tagging scheme preserves dependencies between successive operations while encouraging concurrency.

Although the extra hardware suggested by the Tomasulo's method encourages concurrent execution of instructions, the programmer and/or compiler still has substantial influence on the degree of concurrency. The following two programs for computing $(A * B) + (C + D)$ illustrate this.

```
Load R1, A
Load R2, B
Load R3, C
```

Sec. 3.2   Instruction Pipeline

```
LoadR₄, D
Mul  R₅, R₁, R₂    --R₅ = R₁ * R₂
Add  R₅, R₅, R₃    --R₅ = R₅ + R₃
Add  R₄, R₅, R₄    --R₄ = R₅ + R₄
```

An alternative to this program that allows more concurrency is:

```
LoadR₁, A
LoadR₂, B
LoadR₃, C
LoadR₄, D
Mul  R₅, R₁, R₂    --R₅= R₁ * R₂
Add  R₄, R₃, R₄    --R₄= R₃ + R₄
Add  R₄, R₄, R₅    --R₄= R₄ + R₅
```

In the second set of instructions, the multiply instruction and the first add instruction can be executed simultaneously, an impossibility in the first set of instructions. Often, in practice, a combination of hardware and software techniques is used to increase concurrency.

Scoreboard Method.   The scoreboard method was first used in the high-performance CDC 6600 computer, in which multiple functional units allow instructions to be completed out of the original program order. This scheme maintains information about the status of each issued instruction, each register, and each functional unit in some buffers (or hardware mechanism) known as the *scoreboard*. When a new instruction is issued for execution, its influence on the registers and the functional units is added to the scoreboard. By considering a snapshot of the scoreboard, it can be determined if waiting is required for the new instruction. If no waiting is required, the proper functional unit immediately starts the execution of the instruction. If waiting is required (for example, one of the input operands is not yet available), execution of the new instruction is delayed until the waiting conditions are removed.

As described in [HEN 90], a scoreboard may consist of three tables: *instruction status, functional unit status,* and *destination register status.* Figure 3.9 represents a snapshot of the contents of these tables for the following program:

```
LoadR₁, A
LoadR₂, B
LoadR₃, C
LoadR₄, D
Mul  R₅, R₁, R₂    --R₅ = R₁ * R₂
Add  R₂, R₃, R₄    --R₂ = R₃ + R₄
Add  R₂, R₂, R₅    --R₂ = R₂ + R₅
```

The instruction status table indicates whether or not an instruction is issued for execution. If the instruction is issued, the table shows which stage the instruction is in. After an instruction is brought in and decoded, the scoreboard will attempt to issue an instruction to the proper functional unit. An instruction will be issued if the functional unit is free and there is no other active instruction using the same destination register;

Instruction Status

Instructions	Issued	Operand Fetch Complete	Execution Complete	Write Back Complete
Load R_1, A	yes	yes	yes	yes
Load R_2, B	yes	yes	yes	yes
Load R_3, C	yes	yes	yes	yes
Load R_4, D	yes	yes		
Mul R_5, R_1, R_2	yes	yes		
Add R_2, R_3, R_4	yes			
Add R_2, R_2, R_5				

Functional Unit Status

Unit ID	Unit Name	Busy	Destination Register R_d	Source R_{s1}	Ready	Registers R_{s2}	Ready
1	Load/Store	yes	R_4				
2	Multiplier	yes	R_5	R_1	yes	R_2	yes
3	Adder_1	yes	R_2	R_3	yes	R_4	no
4	Adder_2	no					

Destination Register Status

	R_1	R_2	R_3	R_4	R_5	R_6
Unit ID		3		1	2	

Figure 3.9 A snapshot of the scoreboard after issuing the first add instruction

otherwise, the issuing is delayed. In other words, an instruction is issued when WAW hazards and structural hazards do not exist. When such hazards exist, the issuing of the instruction and the instructions following are delayed until the hazards are removed. In this way the instructions are issued in order, while independent instructions are allowed to be executed out of order.

The functional unit status table indicates whether or not a functional unit is busy. A busy unit means that the execution of an issued instruction to that unit is not completed yet. For a busy unit, the table also identifies the destination register and the availability of the source registers. A source register for a unit is available if it does not appear as a destination for any other unit.

The destination register status table indicates the destination registers that have not yet been written to. For each such register the active functional unit that will write to the register is identified. The table has an entry for each register.

During the operand fetch stage, the scoreboard monitors the tables to determine whether or not the source registers are available to be read by an active functional unit. If none of the source registers is used as the destination register of other active functional units, the unit reads the operands from these registers and begins execution. After the execution is completed (i.e., at the end of execution stage), the scoreboard checks for WAR hazards before allowing the result to be written to the destination register. When no WAR hazard exists, the scoreboard tells the functional unit to go ahead and write the result to the destination register.

In Figure 3.9, the tables indicate that the first three load instructions have completed the execution and their operands are written to the destination registers. The last load instruction has been issued to the load/store unit (unit 1). This instruction has completed the fetch but has not yet written its operand to the register R_4. The multiplier unit is executing the instruction mul, and the first add instruction is issued to Adder_1 unit. The Adder_1 is waiting for R_4 to be written by load/store before it begins execution. This is because there is a RAW hazard between the last load and first add instructions. Note that at this time the second add cannot be issued because it uses R_2 as the source and destination register. R_2, at this time, is busy with the first add. When R_4 is written by the load/store unit, Adder_1 begins execution.

At a later time, the scoreboard changes. As shown in Figure 3.10, if Adder_1 completes execution before the multiplier, it will write its result to R_2, and the second add instruction will be issued to the Adder_2 unit. Note that if the multiplier unit has not read R_2 before Adder_1 completes execution, Adder_1 will be prevented from writing the result to R_2 until the multiplier reads its operands; this is because there is a WAR hazard between mul and the first add instructions.

The main component of the scoreboard approach is the destination register status table. This table is used to solve data hazards between instructions. Each time an instruction is issued for execution, the instruction's destination register is marked busy. The destination register stays busy until the instruction completes execution. When a new instruction is considered for execution, its operands are checked to ensure that there are no register conflicts with prior instructions still in execution.

Control Hazard. In any set of instructions, there is normally a need for some kind of statement that allows the flow of control to be something other than sequential. Instructions that do this are included in every programming language and are called *branches*. In general, about 30% of all instructions in a program are branches. This means that branch instructions in the pipeline can reduce the throughput tremendously if not handled properly. Whenever a branch is taken, the performance of the pipeline is seriously affected. Each such branch requires a new address to be loaded into the

Instruction Status

Instructions	Issued	Operand Fetch Complete	Execution Complete	Write Back Complete
Load R_1, A	yes	yes	yes	yes
Load R_2, B	yes	yes	yes	yes
Load R_3, C	yes	yes	yes	yes
Load R_4, D	yes	yes	yes	yes
Mul R_5, R_1, R_2	yes	yes	yes	
Add R_2, R_3, R_4	yes	yes	yes	yes
Add R_2, R_2, R_5	yes			

Functional Unit Status

Unit ID	Unit Name	Busy	Destination Register R_d	Source R_{s1}	Ready	Registers R_{s2}	Ready
1	Load/Store	no					
2	Multiplier	yes	R_5	R_1	yes	R_2	yes
3	Adder_1	no					
4	Adder_2	yes	R_2	R_2	yes	R_5	no

Destination Register Status

	R_1	R_2	R_3	R_4	R_5	R_6
Unit ID		4			2	

Figure 3.10 A snapshot of the scoreboard after issuing the second add instruction.

program counter, which may invalidate all the instructions that are either already in the pipeline or prefetched in the buffer. This draining and refilling of the pipeline for each branch degrade the throughput of the pipeline to that of a sequential processor. Note that the presence of a branch statement does not automatically cause the pipeline to drain and begin refilling. A branch not taken allows the continued sequential flow of uninterrupted instructions to the pipeline. Only when a branch is taken does the problem arise.

In general, branch instructions can be classified into three groups: (1) unconditional branch, (2) conditional branch, and (3) loop branch [LIL 88]. An unconditional

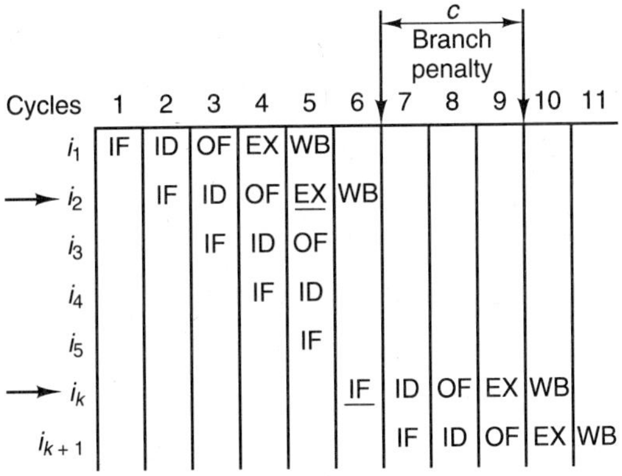

Sec. 3.2 Instruction Pipeline

```
                              |← c →|
                              Branch
                              penalty
Cycles  1   2   3   4   5   6   7   8   9   10  11
  i₁   IF  ID  OF  EX  WB
  i₂       IF  ID  OF  EX  WB
  i₃           IF  ID  OF
  i₄               IF  ID
  i₅                   IF
  iₖ                          IF  ID  OF  EX  WB
  iₖ₊₁                            IF  ID  OF  EX  WB
```

Figure 3.11 Branch penalty.

branch always alters the sequential program flow. It sets a new target address in the program counter, rather than incrementing it by 1 to point to the next sequential instruction address, as is normally the case. A conditional branch sets a new target address in the program counter only when a certain condition, usually based on a condition code, is satisfied. Otherwise, the program counter is incremented by 1 as usual. In other words, a conditional branch selects a path of instructions based on a certain condition. If the condition is satisfied, the path starts from the target address and is called a *target path*. If it is not, the path starts from the next sequential instruction and is called a *sequential path*. Finally, a loop branch in a loop statement usually jumps back to the beginning of the loop and executes it either a fixed or a variable (data-dependent) number of times.

Among the preceding branch types, conditional branches are the hardest to handle. As an example, consider the following conditional branch instruction sequence:

```
i₁
i₂ (conditional branch to iₖ)
i₃
 .
 .
 .
iₖ (target)
iₖ₊₁
```

Figure 3.11 shows the execution of this sequence in our instruction pipeline when the target path is selected. In this figure, c denotes the branch penalty, that is, the number of cycles wasted whenever the target path is chosen.

To show the effect of the branch penalty on the overall pipeline performance, the average number of cycles per instruction must be determined. Let t_{ave} denote the average number of cycles required for execution of an instruction; then

$$t_{ave} = p_b * \text{(average number of cycles per branch instruction)} + (1 - p_b) * \text{(average number of cycles per nonbranch instruction)}, \quad (3.3)$$

where p_b denotes the probability that a given instruction is a branch.

The average number of cycles per branch instruction can be determined by considering two cases. If the target path is chosen, $1 + c$ cycles (c = branch penalty) are needed for the execution; otherwise, there is no branch penalty and only one cycle is needed.

Thus average number of cycles per branch instruction $= p_t(1+c) + (1-p_t)(1)$, where p_t denotes the probability that the t target path is chosen. The average number of cycles per nonbranch instruction is 1. After the pipeline becomes filled with instructions, a nonbranch instruction completes every cycle. Thus

$$t_{ave} = p_b [p_t(1+c) + (1-p_t)(1)] + (1-p_b)(1) = 1 + cp_b p_t.$$

After analyzing many practical programs, Lee and Smith [LEE 84] have shown the average p_b to be approximately 0.1 to 0.3 and the average p_t to be approximately 0.6 to 0.7. Assuming that $p_b = 0.2$, $p_t = 0.65$, and $c = 3$, then

$$t_{ave} = 1 + 3 (0.2)(0.65) = 1.39.$$

In other words, the pipeline operates at 72% (100/1.39 = 72) of its maximum rate when branch instructions are considered.

Sometimes, the performance of a pipeline is represented in terms of throughput. The throughput, H, of a pipeline can also be expressed as the average number of instructions executed per clock cycle. Thus

$$H = 1/t_{ave} = 1/(1 + cp_b p_t).$$

To reduce the effect of branching on processor performance, several techniques have been proposed [LIL 88]. Some of the better known techniques are branch prediction, delayed branching, and multiple prefetching. Each of these techniques is explained next.

Branch Prediction. In this type of design, the outcome of a branch decision is predicted before the branch is actually executed. Therefore, based on a particular prediction, the sequential path or the target path is chosen for execution. Although the chosen path often reduces the branch penalty, it may increase the penalty in case of incorrect prediction.

There are two types of predictions, static and dynamic. In static prediction, a fixed decision for prefetching one of the two paths is made before the program runs. For example, a simple technique would be to always assume that the branch is taken. This technique simply loads the program counter with the target address when a branch is encountered. Another such technique is to automatically choose one path (sequential or target) for some branch types and another for the rest of the branch types. If the chosen path is wrong, the pipeline is drained and instructions corresponding to the correct path are fetched; the penalty is paid.

In dynamic prediction, during the execution of the program the processor makes a decision based on the past information of the previously executed branches. For example, a simple technique would be to record the history of the last two paths taken by each branch instruction. If the last two executions of a branch instruction have chosen the same path, that path will be chosen for the current execution of the branch instruction. If the two paths do not match, one of the paths will be chosen randomly.

A better approach is to associate an n-bit counter with each branch instruction. This is known as the counter-based branch prediction approach [PAN 92, HWU 89,

LEE 84]. In this method, after executing a branch instruction for the first time, its counter, C, is set to a threshold, T, if the target path was taken, or to $T-1$ if the sequential path was taken. From then on, whenever the branch instruction is about to be executed, if $C \geq T$, then the target path is taken; otherwise, the sequential path is taken. The counter value C is updated after the branch is resolved. If the correct path is the target path, the counter is incremented by 1; if not, C is decremented by 1. If C ever reaches $2^n - 1$ (an upper bound), C is no longer incremented, even if the target path was correctly predicted and chosen. Likewise, C is never decremented to a value less than 0.

In practice, often n and T are chosen to be 2. Studies have shown that 2-bit predictors perform almost as well as predictors with more number of bits. The following diagram represents the possible states in a 2-bit predictor.

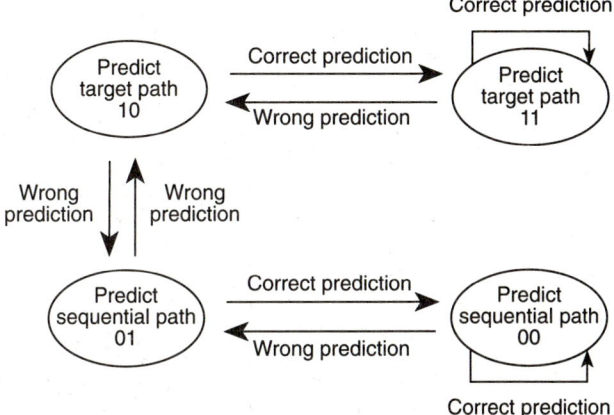

An alternative scheme to the preceding 2-bit predictor is to change the prediction only when the predicted path has been wrong for two consecutive times. The following diagram shows the possible states for such a scheme.

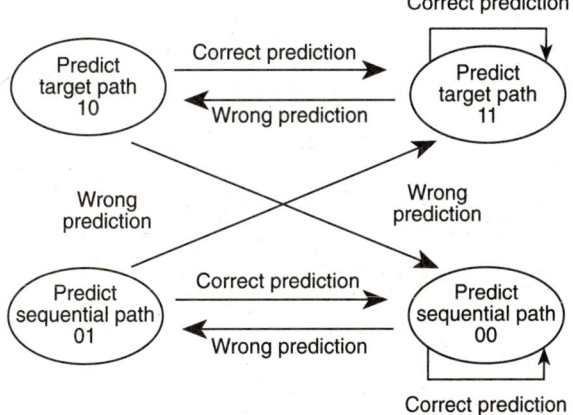

Most processors employ a small size cache memory called *branch target buffer* (BTB); sometimes referred to as *target instruction cache* (TIC). Often, each entry of this cache keeps a branch instruction's address with its target address and the history used by the prediction scheme. When a branch instruction is first executed, the processor allocates an entry in the BTB for this instruction. When a branch instruction is fetched, the processor searches the BTB to determine whether it holds an entry for the corresponding branch instruction. If there is a hit, the recorded history is used to determine whether the sequential or target path should be taken.

Static prediction methods usually require little hardware, but they may increase the complexity of the compiler. In contrast, dynamic prediction methods increase the hardware complexity, but they require less work at compile time. In general, dynamic prediction obtains better results than static prediction and also provides a greater degree of object code compatibility, since decisions are made after compile time.

To find the performance effect of branch prediction, we need to reevaluate the average number of cycles per branch instruction in equation (3.3). There are two possible cases: the predicted path is either correct or incorrect. In the case of a correctly predicted path, the penalty is d when the path is a target path (see Figure 3.12a), and the penalty is 0 when the path is a sequential path. (Note that, in Figure 3.12a, the address of target path is obtained after the decode stage. However, when a branch target buffer is used in the design, the target address can be obtained during or after the fetch stage.) In the case of an incorrectly predicted path for both target and sequential predicted paths, the penalty is c (See Figure 3.11 and Figure 3.12b). Putting it all together, we have

average number of cycles per branch instruction =

$$p_r [p_t(1+d) + (1-p_t)(1)] + (1-p_r)[p_t(1+c) + (1-p_t)(1+c)],$$

where p_r is the probability of a right prediction. Substituting this term in equation (3.3),

$$t_{ave} = p_b[p_r(p_t d + 1) + (1-p_r)(1+c)] + (1-p_b)(1)$$
$$= 1 + p_b c - p_b p_r c + p_b p_r p_t d.$$

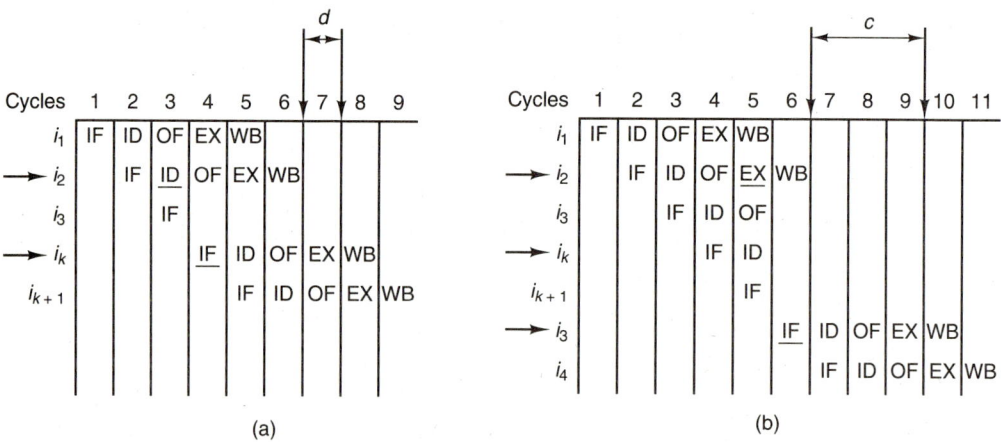

Figure 3.12 Branch penalties for when the target path is predicted: (a) The penalty for a correctly chosen target path. (b) The penalty for an incorrectly chosen target path.

Assume that $p_b = 0.2$, $p_t = 0.65$, $c = 3$, and $d = 1$. Also assume that the predicted path is correct 70% of the time (i.e., $p_r = 0.70$). Then

$$t_{ave} = 1.27.$$

That is, the pipeline operates at 78% of its maximum rate due to the branch prediction.

Delayed Branching. The delayed branching scheme eliminates or significantly reduces the effect of the branch penalty. In this type of design, a certain number of instructions after the branch instruction is fetched and executed regardless of which path will be chosen for the branch. For example, a processor with a branch delay of k executes a path containing the next k sequential instructions and then either continues on the same path or starts a new path from a new target address. As often as possible, the compiler tries to fill the next k instruction slots after the branch with instructions that are independent from the branch instruction. NOP (no operation) instructions are placed in any remaining empty slots. As an example, consider the following code:

```
i1:   Load R1, A
i2:   Load R2, B
i3:   BrZr R2, i7           --branch to i7 if R2 = 0;
i4:   Load R3, C
i5:   Add  R4, R2, R3       --R4 = R2 + R3
i6:   Mul  R5, R1, R2       --R5 = R1 * R2
i7:   Add  R4, R1, R2       --R4 = R1 + R2.
```

Assuming that $k = 2$, the compiler modifies this code by moving the instruction i_1 and inserting an NOP instruction after the branch instruction i_3. The modified code is

```
i2:   Load R2, B
i3:   BrZr R2, i7
i1:   Load R1, A
      NOP
i4:   Load R3, C
i5:   Add  R4, R2, R3
i6:   Mul  R5, R1, R2
i7:   Add  R4, R1, R2.
```

As can be seen in the modified code, the instruction i_1 is executed regardless of the branch outcome.

Multiple Prefetching. In this type of design, the processor fetches both possible paths. Once the branch decision is made, the unwanted path is thrown away. By prefetching both possible paths, the fetch penalty is avoided in the case of an incorrect prediction.

To fetch both paths, two buffers are employed to service the pipeline. In normal execution, the first buffer is loaded with instructions from the next sequential address of the branch instruction. If a branch occurs, the contents of the first buffer are invalidated, and the secondary buffer, which has been loaded with instructions from the target address of the branch instruction, is used as the primary buffer.

This double buffering scheme ensures a constant flow of instructions and data to the pipeline and reduces the time delays caused by the draining and refilling of the pipeline. Some amount of performance degradation is unavoidable any time the pipeline is drained, however.

In summary, each of the preceding simple techniques reduces the degradation of pipeline throughput. However, the choice of any of these techniques for a particular design depends on factors such as throughput requirements and cost constraints. In practice, due to these factors, it is not unusual to see a mixture of these techniques implemented on a single processor.

3.2.2 Further Throughput Improvement of an Instruction Pipeline

One way to increase the throughput of an instruction pipeline is to exploit instruction-level parallelism. The common approaches to accomplish such parallelism are called *superscalar* [IBM 90, OEH 91], *superpipeline* [JOU 89, BAS 91], and *very long instruction word (VLIW)* [COL 88, FIS 83]. Each approach attempts to initiate several instructions per cycle.

Superscalar. The superscalar approach relies on spatial parallelism, that is, multiple operations running concurrently on separate hardware. This approach achieves the execution of multiple instructions per clock cycle by issuing several instructions to different functional units. A superscalar processor contains one or more instruction pipelines sharing a set of functional units. It often contains functional units, such as an add unit, multiply unit, divide unit, floating-point add unit, and graphic unit. A superscalar processor contains a control mechanism to preserve the execution order of dependent instructions for ensuring a valid result. The scoreboard method and Tomasulo's method (discussed in the previous section) can be used for implementing such mechanisms. In practice, most of the processors are based on the superscalar approach and employ a scoreboard method to ensure a valid result. Examples of such processors are given in Chapter 4.

Superpipeline. The superpipeline approach achieves high performance by overlapping the execution of multiple instructions on one instruction pipeline. A superpipeline processor often has an instruction pipeline with more stages than a typical instruction pipeline design. In other words, the execution process of an instruction is broken down into even finer steps. By increasing the number of stages in the instruction pipeline, each stage has less work to do. This allows the pipeline clock rate to increase (cycle time decreases), since the clock rate depends on the delay found in the slowest stage of the pipeline.

An example of such an architecture is the MIPS R4000 processor. The R4000 subdivides instruction fetching and data cache access to create an eight-stage pipeline. The stages are instruction fetch first half, instruction fetch second half, register fetch, instruction execute, data cache access first half, data cache access second half, tag check, and write back.

A superpipeline approach has certain benefits. The single functional unit requires less space and less logic on the chip than designs based on the superscalar approach. This extra space on the chip allows room for specialized circuitry to achieve higher speeds, room for large caches, and wide data paths.

Very Long Instruction Word (VLIW). The very long instruction word (VLIW) approach makes extensive use of the compiler by requiring it to incorporate several small independent operations into a long instruction word. The instruction is large enough to provide, in parallel, enough control bits over many functional units. In other words, a VLIW architecture provides many more functional units than a typical processor design, together with a compiler that finds parallelism across basic operations to keep the functional units as busy as possible. The compiler compacts ordinary sequential codes into long instruction words that make better use of resources. During execution, the control unit issues one long instruction per cycle. The issued instruction initiates many independent operations simultaneously.

A comparison of the three approaches will show a few interesting differences. For instance, the superscalar and VLIW approaches are more sensitive to resource conflicts than the superpipelined approach. In a superscalar or VLIW processor, a resource must be duplicated to reduce the chance of conflicts, while the superpipelined design avoids any resource conflicts.

To prevent the superpipelined processor from being slower than the superscalar, the technology used in the superpipelined must reduce the delay of the lengthy instruction pipeline. Therefore, in general, superpipelined designs require faster transistor technology such as GaAs (gallium arsinide), whereas superscalar designs require more transistors to account for the hardware resource duplication. The superscalar design often uses CMOS technology, since this technology provides good circuit density. Although superpipelining seems to be a more straightforward solution than superscaling, existing technology generally favors increasing circuit density over increasing circuit speed. Historically, circuit density has increased at a faster rate than transistor speed. This historical precedent suggests a general conclusion that the superscalar approach is more cost effective for industry to implement.

Technological advances have allowed superscalar and superpipelining techniques to be combined, providing good solutions to many current efficiency problems found in the computing industry. Such solutions, which attempt to take advantage of the positive attributes of each design, can be studied in existing processors. One example is the alpha microprocessor [DIG 92]. This microprocessor is described in detail in Chapter 4.

3.3 ARITHMETIC PIPELINE

Some functions of the arithmetic logic unit of a processor can be pipelined to maximize performance. An arithmetic pipeline is used for implementing complex arithmetic functions like floating-point addition, multiplication, and division. These functions can be

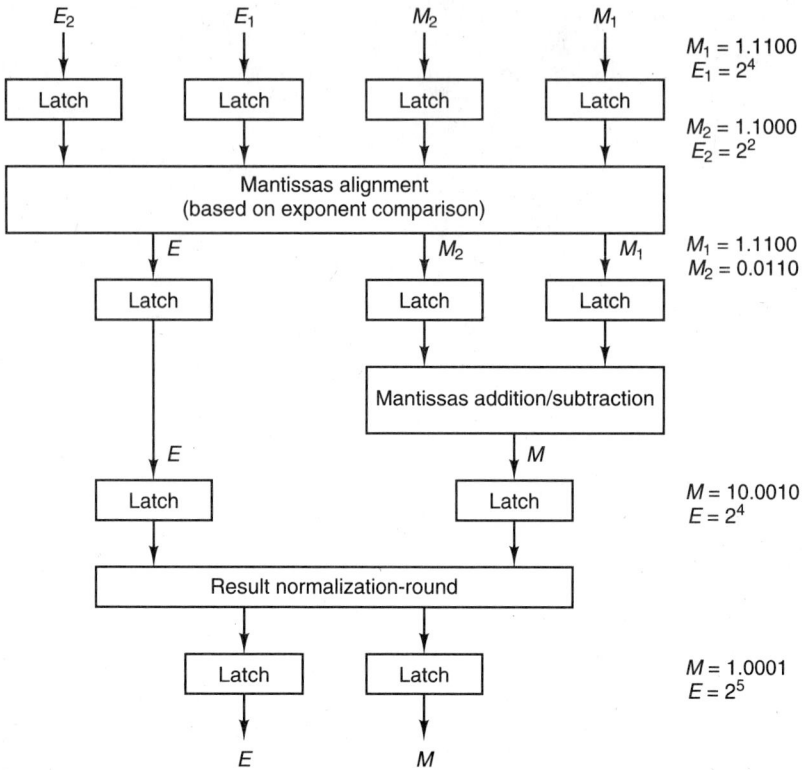

Figure 3.13 A pipelined floating-point adder.

decomposed into consecutive subfunctions. For example Figure 3.13 presents a pipeline architecture for floating-point addition of two numbers. (A nonpipelined architecture of such an adder is described in Chapter 2.) The floating-point addition can be divided into three stages: mantissas alignment, mantissas addition, and result normalization [MAN 82, HAY 78].,

In the first stage, the mantissas M_1 and M_2 are aligned based on the difference in the exponents E_1 and E_2. If $|E_1 - E_2| = k > 0$, then the mantissa with the smaller exponent is right shifted by k digit positions. In the second stage, the mantissas are added (or subtracted). In the third stage, the result is normalized so that the final mantissa has a nonzero digit after the fraction point. When necessary, this normalized adjustment is done by shifting the result mantissa and the exponent.

Another example of an arithmetic pipeline is shown in Figure 3.14. This figure presents a pipelined architecture for multiplying two unsigned 4-bit numbers using carry save adders. The first stage generates the partial products M_1, M_2, M_3, and M_4. Figure 3.14 represents how M_1 is generated; the rest of partial products can be generated in the same way. The M_1, M_2, M_3, and M_4 are added together through the two stages of carry save adders and the final stage of carry lookahead adder. (A nonpipelined architecture of such a multiplier is described in Chapter 2.)

Sec. 3.3 Arithmetic Pipeline

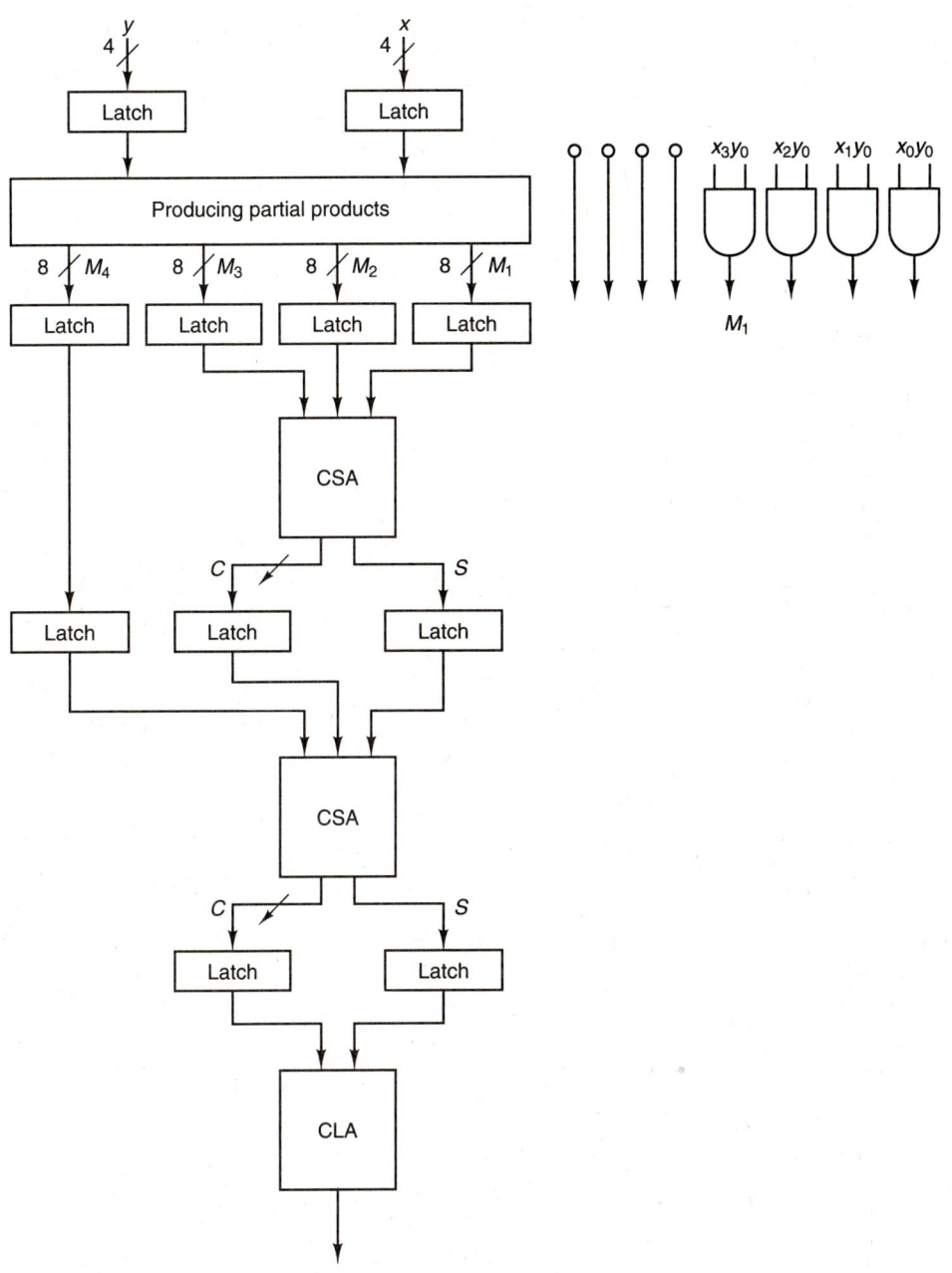

Figure 3.14 A pipelined carry save multiplier.

3.4 PIPELINE CONTROL: SCHEDULING

Controlling the sequence of tasks presented to a pipeline for execution is extremely important for maximizing its utilization. If two tasks are initiated requiring the same stage of the pipeline at the same time, a collision occurs, which temporarily disrupts execution. This section presents a method to control the scheduling of a pipeline. (A detailed explanation and analysis of pipeline scheduling are given in [KOG 81].) Before the description of such a method can be given, reservation table and latency concepts must be defined.

Reservation table. There are two types of pipelines: static and dynamic. A static pipeline can perform only one function at a time, whereas a dynamic pipeline can perform more than one function at a time. A pipeline reservation table shows when stages of a pipeline are in use for a particular function. Each stage of the pipeline is represented by a row in the reservation table. Each row of the reservation table is in turn broken into columns, one per clock cycle. The number of columns indicates the total number of time units required for the pipeline to perform a particular function. To indicate that some stage S is in use at some time t_y, an × is placed at the intersection of the row and column in the table corresponding to that stage and time. Figure 3.15 represents a reservation table for a static pipeline with three stages. The times t_0, t_1, t_2, t_3, and t_4 denote five consecutive clock cycles. The positions of ×'s indicate that, in order to produce a result for an input data, the data must go through the stages 1, 2, 2, 3, and 1, progressively. As shown later in this section, the reservation table can be used for determining the time difference between input data initiations so that collisions won't occur. (Initiation of an input data refers to the time that the data enter the first stage of the pipeline.)

Latency. The delay, or number of time units separating two initiations, is called *latency*. A collision will occur if two pieces of input data are initiated with a latency equal to the distance between two ×'s in a reservation table. For example, the table in Figure 3.15 has two ×'s with a distance of 1 in the second row. Therefore, if a second piece of data is passed to the pipeline one time unit after the first, a collision will occur in stage 2.

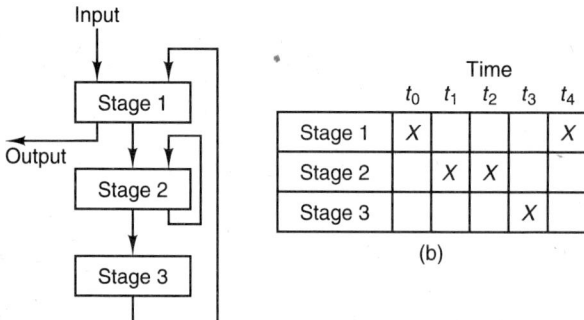

Figure 3.15 A static pipeline and its corresponding reservation table.

Sec. 3.4 Pipeline Control: Scheduling

3.4.1 Scheduling Static Pipelines

Forbidden list. Every reservation table with two or more ×'s in any given row has one or more forbidden latencies, which, if not prohibited, would allow two data to collide or arrive at the same stage of the pipeline at the same time. The forbidden list F is simply a list of integers corresponding to these prohibited latencies. With static pipelines, zero is always considered a forbidden latency, since it is impossible to initiate two jobs to the same pipeline at the same time. (However, as shown later, such initiations are possible with dynamic pipelines.) For example, the reservation table in Figure 3.15 has the forbidden list (4,1,0). Each element of this list can be figured by calculating the distance between two ×'s in a particular row.

Collision vectors. A collision vector is a string of binary digits of length $N + 1$, where N is the largest forbidden latency in the forbidden list. The initial collision vector, C, is created from the forbidden list in the following way: each component c_i of C, for $i = 0$ to N, is 1 if i is an element of the forbidden list. Otherwise, c_i is zero. Zeros in the collision vector indicate allowable latencies, or times when initiations are allowed into the pipeline.

For the preceding forbidden list (4,1,0), the collision vector is

$$\begin{array}{rccccc} C = & c_4 & c_3 & c_2 & c_1 & c_0 \\ = & (1 & 0 & 0 & 1 & 1) \\ & 4 & 3 & 2 & 1 & 0 = \text{latency.} \end{array}$$

Notice in this collision vector that latencies of 2 and 3 would be allowed, but latencies of 0, 1, and 4 would not.

State diagram. State diagrams can be used to show the different states of a pipeline for a given time slice. Once a state diagram is created, it is easier to derive schedules of input data for the pipeline that have no collisions.

To create the state diagram of a given pipeline, the initial state is always the initial collision vector. If there is a zero in position c_i, then an initiation to the pipeline is allowed after i time units or clock cycles. Figure 3.16 represents a state diagram for the pipeline of Figure 3.15. The collision vector 10011 forms the initial state. Note that the initial state has zero in positions 2 and 3. Therefore, a new datum can be initiated to the pipeline after two or three clock cycles. Each time an initiation is allowed the collision vector is shifted right i places with zeros filling in on the left. This corresponds to the passing of i time units. This new vector is then ORed with the initial collision vector to generate a new collision vector or state. ORing is necessary because the new initiation enforces a new constraint on the current status of the pipeline. Whenever a new collision vector is generated from an existing collision vector in the state diagram, an arc is drawn between them. The arc is labeled by latency i. The process of generating new collision vectors continues until no more can be generated.

Within a state diagram, any initiation of value $N + 1$ or greater will automatically go back to the initial collision vector. This is simply because the current collision vec-

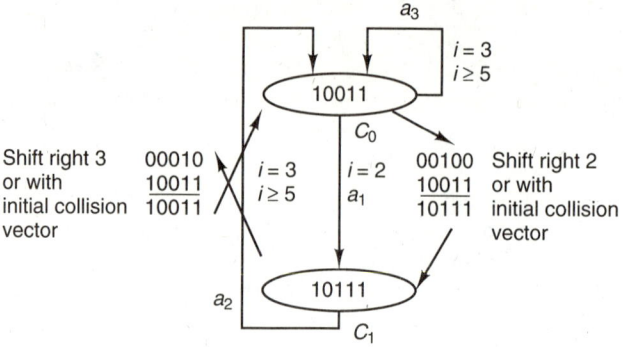

Figure 3.16 State diagram of a static pipeline.

tor is shifted right $N+1$ places with zeros filling in on the left, producing a collision vector of all zeros. When a collision vector of all zeros is ORed with the initial collision vector, the initial collision vector is the result.

Average latency. The average latency is determined for a given cycle in a state diagram. A cycle in a state diagram is an alternating sequence of collision vectors and arcs, $C_0, a_1, C_1, \ldots, a_n, C_n$, in which each arc a_i connects collision vector C_{i-1} to C_i, and all the collision vectors are distinct except the first and last. For simplicity, we represent a cycle by a sequence of latencies of its arcs. For example, in Figure 3.16 the cycle C_0, a_1, C_1, a_2, C_0, where $C_0 = (10011)$, $C_1 = (10111)$, a_1 is an arc from C_0 to C_1, and a_2 is an arc from C_1 to C_0, is represented as cycle $C = (2,3)$, where 2 and 3 are the latencies of a_1 and a_2, respectively.

The average latency for a cycle is determined by adding the latencies (right-shift values) of the arcs of the cycle and then dividing it by the total number of arcs in the cycle. For example, in Figure 3.16, the cycle $C = (2, 3)$ has the average latency

$$(2 + 3)/2 \;=\; 2.5.$$

Minimum average latency. A pipeline may have several average latencies associated with different cycles. The minimum average latency is simply the smallest such ratio. For example, the following are the average latency cycles for the state diagram in Figure 3.16:

$(2 + 3)/2 = 2.5$, from cycle C_0, a_1, C_1, a_2, C_0
$(2 + 5)/2 = 3.5$ from cycle C_0, a_1, C_1, a_2, C_0
$3/1 = 3$ from cycle C_0, a_3, C_0
$5/1 = 5$ from cycle C_0, a_3, C_0

Therefore, the minimum average latency (MAL) is 2.5. Although the cycle with the minimum average latency maximizes the throughput of the pipeline, sometimes a less efficient cycle may be chosen to reduce the implementation complexity of the pipeline's control circuit (i.e., a trade-off between time and cost.) For example, the cycle $C = (2, 3)$, which has the MAL of 2.5, requires a circuit that counts three units of

Sec. 3.4   Pipeline Control: Scheduling

time, then two units, again three units, and so on. However, if it is acceptable to initiate an input datum after every three units of time, the complexity of the circuit will be reduced. Therefore, sometimes it may be necessary to determine the smallest latency that can be used for initiating input data at all times. Such a latency is called the *minimum latency*. One way to determine the minimum latency is to choose a cycle of length 1 with the smallest latency from the state diagram. Another way is to find the smallest integer whose product with any arbitrary integer is not a member of the forbidden list. For example, for the forbidden list (4, 1, 0), the minimum latency can be determined as follows:

Minimum Latency	Times an Integer	Product	Result
1	* 1	= 1	No good
2	* 1	= 2	OK
2	* 2	= 4	No good
3	* 1	= 3	OK
3	* 2	= 6	OK
4	* 1	= 4	No good

Therefore the minimum latency for this pipeline is 3.

3.4.2 Scheduling Dynamic Pipelines

When scheduling a static pipeline, only collisions between different input data for a particular function had to be avoided. With a dynamic pipeline, it is possible for different input data requiring different functions to be present in the pipeline at the same time. Therefore, collisions between these data must be considered as well. As with the static pipeline, however, dynamic pipeline scheduling begins with the compilation of a set of forbidden lists from function reservation tables. Next the collision vectors are obtained, and finally the state diagram is drawn.

Forbidden lists.   With a dynamic pipeline, the number of forbidden lists is the square of the number of functions sharing the pipeline. In Figure 3.17 the number of functions equals 2, A and B; therefore, the number of forbidden lists equals 4, denoted as AA, AB, BA, and BB. For example, if the forbidden list AB contains integer d, then a datum requiring function B cannot be initiated to the pipeline at some later time $t + d$, where t represents the time at which a datum requiring function A was initiated. Therefore,

$$AA = (3,0),\ AB = (2,1,0),\ BA = (4,2,1,0),\ BB = (3,2,0).$$

Collision vectors and collision matrices.   The collision vectors are determined in the same manner as for a static pipeline; 0 indicates a permissible latency and a 1 indicates a forbidden latency. For the preceding example, the collision vectors are

$$C_{AA} = (0\ 1\ 0\ 0\ 1) \quad C_{BA} = (1\ 0\ 1\ 1\ 1)$$
$$C_{AB} = (0\ 0\ 1\ 1\ 1) \quad C_{BB} = (0\ 1\ 1\ 0\ 1).$$

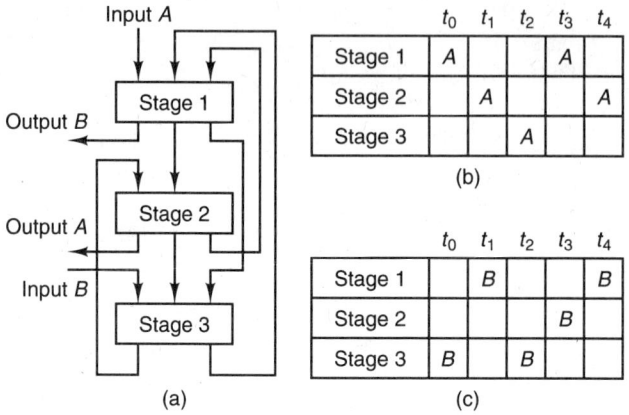

Figure 3.17 A dynamic pipeline and its corresponding reservation tables.

The collision vectors for the A function form the collision matrix M_A, that is,

$$M_A = \begin{bmatrix} C_{AA} \\ C_{AB} \end{bmatrix}.$$

The collision vectors for the B function form the collision matrix M_B:

$$M_B = \begin{bmatrix} C_{BA} \\ C_{BB} \end{bmatrix}.$$

For the above collision vectors, the collision matrices are

$$M_A = \begin{bmatrix} 01001 \\ 00111 \end{bmatrix},$$

$$M_B = \begin{bmatrix} 10111 \\ 01101 \end{bmatrix}.$$

State diagram. The state diagram for the dynamic pipeline is developed in the same way as for the static pipeline. The resulting state diagram is much more complicated than a static pipeline state diagram due to the larger number of potential collisions.

As an example, consider the state diagram in Figure 3.18. To start, refer to the collision matrix M_A. There are two types of collisions: an A colliding with another A (the top vector) or an A colliding with a B (the bottom vector.) If the first allowable latency from C_{AA} is chosen, in this case 1, the entire matrix is shifted right 1 place, with zeros filling in on the left. This new matrix is then ORed with the initial collision matrix M_A because the original forbidden latencies for function A still have to be considered in later initiations.

If the first allowable latency for vector C_{AB} in matrix M_A is chosen, in this case 3, the entire matrix is shifted right three places with zeros filling in on the left. This new matrix is then ORed with the initial collision matrix for function B, because the origi-

Sec. 3.4 Pipeline Control: Scheduling

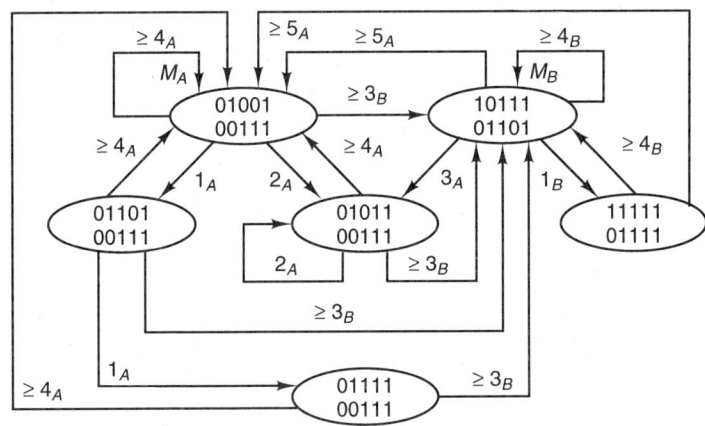

Figure 3.18 State diagram of a dynamic pipeline.

nal collisions for function B are still possible and have to be considered. This shifting and ORing continues until all possible allowable latencies are considered and the state diagram is complete.

3.4.3 Decreasing the MAL of a Pipeline Using Delay Insertion

Sometimes it is possible to modify the reservation table of a pipeline so that the overall structure is unchanged, but the overall throughput is increased (i.e., the MAL is decreased). The reservation table can be modified with the insertion of delays or dummy stages in the table. Insertion of a delay in the table reflects the insertion of a latch in front of or after the logic for a stage. For example, Figure 3.19 represents the changes in a reservation table and its corresponding pipeline before and after delay insertion.

Given a desired cycle, the technique for delay insertion places some delays in certain rows of the original reservation table. Such delays may force the marks on certain rows to be moved forward. The location of the delays is chosen such that each row of the table matches some criteria of a cycle that the designer wishes to have. To understand the process of delay insertion, consider the reservation table shown in Figure 3.20. The MAL for this reservation table is 2.5. As indicated, there is at least one row with two marks (×'s), which means that for each input there is a stage that will be used at least two times. Therefore, we wish to modify this reservation table in such a way that MAL becomes 2.

In general, the lower bound for the MAL is greater than or equal to the maximum number of marks in a row of the reservation table. The lower bound can be achieved by delay insertion, which increases the time per computation. To have a MAL = 2, we start with a cycle, say $C = (2)$, and determine the properties of a reservation table that supports it. To do this, we need to define the following parameters.

1. L_c, the latency sequence, is the sequence of time between successive data that enter the pipeline. For cycle $C = (2)$,
$$L_c = 2, 2, 2, 2, 2, \ldots.$$

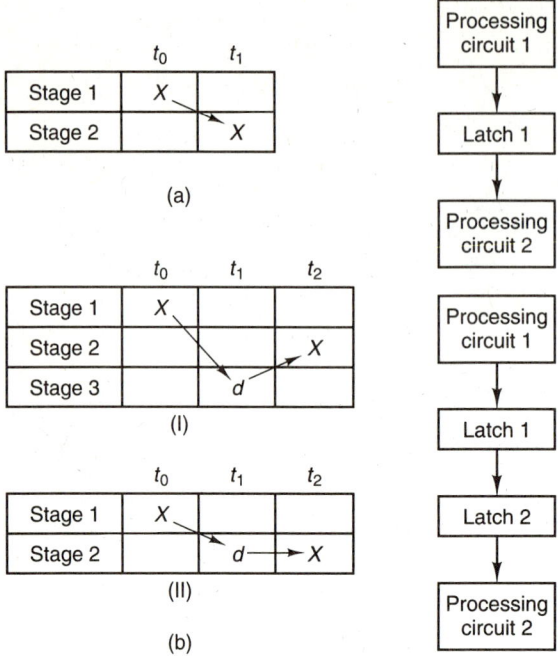

Figure 3.19 Changes in a reservation table and its corresponding pipeline before and after delay insertion. (a) Before insertion of delay. (b) Inserting a delay between the two stages. Two equivalent forms for the reservation table are shown; we select form II.

2. I_c, the initiation time sequence, is the starting time for each datum. The ith ($i>0$) element in this sequence is the starting time of the ith initiated data, so it equals the sum of the latencies between the previous initiations. For the preceding L_c,

$$I_c = 0, 2, 4, 6, 8, 10, \ldots.$$

3. G_c, the initiation interval set, is the set of all distinct intervals between initiation times. That is, $G_c = \{t_i - t_j \text{ for every } i > j\}$, where t_i and t_j are the ith and j^{th} elements in the initiation time sequence, respectively. For our example,

$$G_c = 2, 4, 6, 8, \ldots.$$

Note that G_c determines the properties that a reservation table must have in order to support cycle C. If an integer i is in G_c, any reservation table supporting cycle C cannot have two marks with distance of i time units (clocks) in any row. For example, for our cycle C, distances of 1 or 3 are possible because they are not in G_c. In general, it is easier to consider the complement of G_c. This is denoted by H_c and defined next.

4. H_c, the permissible distance set, is the complement of set G_c (i.e., $H_c = Z - G_c$, where Z is the set of all nonnegative integers). For our cycle,

$$H_c = 0, 1, 3, 5, 7, \ldots.$$

Therefore, any reservation table that supports a cycle C should have marks with distances that are allowed in H_c, that is H_c showing permissible (but not mandatory) distances between marks. In other words, if a reservation table has forbidden list F, then the cycle C is valid if

$$F \subseteq H_c \text{ or } F \cap G_c = \Phi.$$

Sec. 3.4 Pipeline Control: Scheduling

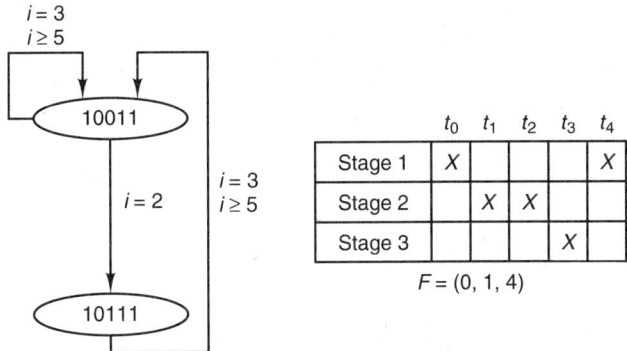

Figure 3.20 Reservation table and state diagram of a static pipeline.

Since the set H_c is infinite, it is hard to deal with in the real world. Thus we try to make it finite by considering $H_c \pmod{p}$, where p is the period of the cycle C, that is, the sum of the latencies. This is an accurate categorization of all permissible distances, since the latency sequence repeats with period p. For our example,

$$H_c \pmod{2} = \{0, 1\}.$$

To facilitate the process of testing or constructing a reservation table, the following definition and theorem are given in [KOG 81].

Definition: Two integers $i, j \in Z_p$, where Z_p is the set of all nonnegative integers less than p, are compatible with respect to $H_c \pmod{p}$ if and only if $|i - j| \pmod{p} \in H_c \pmod{p}$. A set is called a compatible class if every pair of its elements are compatible.

Theorem: Any reservation table to support cycle C must have rows with marks at the following times:

$$z_1 + i_1 p, z_2 + i_2 p, \ldots,$$

where $\{z_1, z_2, \ldots\}$ is a compatible class of $H_c \pmod{p}$ and $i_1, i_2, \ldots$, are arbitrary integers.

We can apply this theorem to some compatible classes in order to construct all possible rows for a reservation table that supports a particular cycle.

In our example, one compatible class is $\{0, 1\}$. Considering the original reservation table, the first row has two marks at times 0 and 4. When the positions of these marks are matched against the compatible class $\{0,1\}$, the first mark (position 0) matches, but not the second. Adding $2 * p$ (i.e., 4) to the second element (i.e., 1) gives us $\{0, 5\}$, so we can delay the second mark by one time unit. For the second row, we add $1 * p$ (i.e., 2) to each element $\{0, 1\}$, so the new positions for the marks become 2 and 3.

Figure 3.21.a represents a modified reservation table. This table is based on the assumption that input data to the stage 3 is independent from the result of stage 2. Figure 3.21.c represents an alternative solution in which there is assumed to be dependency between stages 2 and 3. The state diagram for these reservation tables is shown in Figure 3.21.b.

BIBLIOGRAPHIC NOTES

The reference [DUB 91] presents a model for comparing different branch techniques. [KOG 81] gives a detailed explanation on pipeline architecture. [LIL 88] presents a good survey of branch prediction techniques.

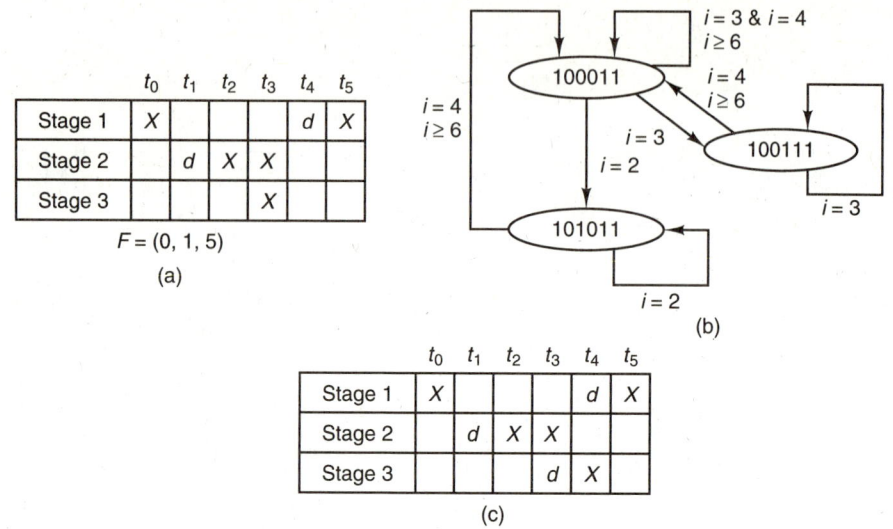

Figure 3.21 Reservation tables with MAL of 2.

REFERENCES

[BAS 91] BASHTEEN, A., I. LUI, AND J. MULLAN, "A Superpipeline Approach to the MIPS Architecture," *IEEE Proc. 36th COMPCON*, 1991, pp. 8–12.

[COL 88] COLWELL, ROBERT P., ET AL., "A VLIW Architecture for a Trace Scheduling Compiler," *IEEE Trans. Computers*, 37(8), 1988, pp. 967–979.

[DIG 92] "DECChip 21064-AA RISC Microprocessor," Hardware, Reference Manual, Digital Equipment Co., 1992.

[DUB 91] DUBEY, PRADEEP K., AND M. J. FLYNN, "Branch Strategies: Modeling and Optimization," *IEEE Trans. Computers*, 40(10), 1991, pp. 1159–1167.

[FIS 83] FISHER, J.A., "Very Long Instruction Word Architectures and the ELI-512," *IEEE Proc. 10th Symp. Computer Architecture*, June 1983, pp. 140–150.

[HAY 78] HAYES, JOHN P., *Computer Architecture and Organization*. New York: McGraw-Hill Book Co., 1978.

[HEN 90] HENNESSY, JOHN L., AND DAVID A PATTERSON, *Computer Architecture, A Quantitative Approach*. San Francisco, California: Morgan Kaufmann Publishers, 1990.

[HWA 93] HWANG, KAI, *Advanced Computer Architecture, Parallelism, Scalability, Programmability*, New York: McGraw-Hill Book Co., 1993.

[HWU 89] HWU, W. M., T. M. CONTE, AND P. P. CHANG, "Comparing Software and Hardware Schemes for Reducing the Cost of Branches," *Proc. 16th Annual Intern. Sympo. Computer Architecture*, May 1989, pp. 224–233.

[IBM 90] "Special Issue: RISC System/6000," *IBM J. Research Develop.*, 34(1), 1990.

[JOU 89] JOUPPI, N. P., AND D. W. WALL, "Available Instruction-level Parallelism for Superscalar and Superpipelined Machines," *Proc. ASPLOS III, Third Conf. Architectural Support for Programming Languages and Operating Systems*, 1989, pp. 272–282.

[KOG 81] KOGGE, PETER M., *The Architecture of Pipelined Computers*. New York: McGraw-Hill Book Co., 1981.

[LAR 73] LARSON, A. G., "Cost-effective Processor Design with an Application to FFT," Technical Report SU-SEL-73-037, Stanford University; Stanford, CA: August 1973.

[LEE 84] LEE, J. K., AND A. J. SMITH, "Branch Prediction Strategies and Branch Target Buffer Design," *Computer*, 17(1), 1984, pp. 6–22.

[LIL 88] LILJA, DAVID J., "Reducing the Branch Penalty in Pipelined Processors," *Computer*, 21(7), July 1988, pp. 47–55.

[LIL 94] LILJA, DAVID J., "Exploiting the Parallelism Available in Loops," IEEE *Computer*, 27(2), 1994, pp. 13–26.

[MAN 82] MANO, M. MORRIS, *Computer Systems Architecture*, 2nd Ed. Upton Saddle River, NJ: Prentice Hall, 1982.

[OEH 91] OEHLER, RICHARD R., AND MICHAEL W. BLASGEN, "IBM RISC System/6000: Architecture and Performance," *IEEE Micro*, 11(3), June 1991, pp. 14–17 56–62.

[PAN 92] PAN, SHIEN-TAI, K. SO, AND J. T. RAHMEH, "Improving the Accuracy of Dynamic Branch Prediction Using Branch Correlation," *ACM-SIGPLAN*, September, 1992, pp. 76–84.

[THO 64] THORNTON, J. E., "Parallel Operation in the Control Data 6600," *Proc. AFIPS Fall Joint Computer Conf.*, Part 2, 1964, pp. 33–40.

[THO 70] THORNTON, J. E., *Design of a Computer—The Control Data 6600*. Glenview, IL: Scott, Foresman & Company, 1970.

[TOM 67] TOMASULO, R. M., "An Efficient Algorithm for Exploring Multiple Arithmetic Units," *IBM J. Research Develop.*, 11(1), 1967, pp. 25–33.

[WOL 91] WOLF, M. E., AND M. S. LAM, "A Loop Transformation Theory and an Algorithm to Maximize Parallelism," *IEEE Trans. Parallel Distributed Systems*, 2(10), 1991, pp. 452–471.

PROBLEMS

3.1. Assume that we have a pipeline with four stages that performs an add operation on two input numbers. The pipeline has a delay of two units of time for each stage. Also, assume that there are adequate memory and buffers. Also, ignore storage time, memory access time, time to set up the pipeline control circuit, and so on. It is necessary to sum 16 numbers by this pipeline. Describe a method that gives the minimum possible time to perform the sum of the numbers. Write the total time required by your method.

3.2. Show that $m_o = \sqrt{\dfrac{(t_{seq} * c_g)}{(t_l * c_i)}}$ is the maximum value of the following equation:

$$\text{PCR} = 1/\{[(t_{seq}/m) + t_l](c_g + mc_l)\}.$$

3.3. Indicate the type of data hazards (RAW, WAR, and WAW) that exist between the following instructions.

i_1 Add R_1, R_2, R_3 --$R_1 = R_2 + R_3$
i_2 Add R_4, R_1, R_4 --$R_4 = R_1 + R_4$
i_3 Add R_3, R_1, R_2 --$R_3 = R_1 + R_2$
i_4 Add R_1, R_1, R_4 --$R_1 = R_1 + R_4$

3.4. Compare Tomasulo's method with the scoreboard approach. Describe the advantages and disadvantages of each.

3.5. Calculate the throughput for a pipelined instruction in which $p_b = 0.1$, $p_t = 0.4$, and $c = 4$. Assume that we use a branch prediction technique to improve the pipeline. What will be the new throughput for when $p_r = 0.7$ and $d = 1$?

3.6. Discuss the advantages and disadvantages of superscalar and superpipeline design. Considering cost and technology, which design is better? Why? [Your comment should be very precise, justified (possibly with citation), and complete.]

3.7. Consider the design of the simple microcomputer in Chapter 2. Using VHDL, design an instruction pipeline for the processor of this machine. The instruction pipeline has three stages: inst_fetch, decode_opfetch, and execute_opwrite. In other words, rewrite the VHDL codes in Figures 2.9 through 2.12 such that, when the inst_fetch process is fetching an instruction, at the same time the decode_opfetch process and the execute_opwrite process are working on different instructions. Define any extra buffers and registers that you may need. Explain your modifications by using block diagram.

3.8. Design a pipeline that efficiently multiplies a stream of 4-bit numbers $A_1, A_2, A_3, \ldots,$ with a constant 4-bit number B. Assume that $A_i = 0.a_3a_2a_1a_0$ and $B = 0.b_3b_2b_1b_0$ are positive binary fractions.

3.9. Assume that we have a pipeline that can perform addition or multiplication operations. It consists of k stages, and, each stage has a delay of $1/k$ time units. When switching between operations (from + to $*$, or from $*$ to +), the pipeline should be drained before the data for the new operation can be applied to the pipeline. Assume that there are adequate memory and buffers. Also, ignore storage time, memory access time, time to set up the pipeline control circuit, and so on. Determine the minimum time required to multiply two n-by-n matrices (where $n>k$) to produce an n-by-n matrix product.

3.10. Consider the following reservation table for a static pipeline:

a. Write the forbidden list.
b. Draw the state diagram.
c. Find the MAL.

	0	1	2	3	4
Stage 1	X				X
Stage 2		X		X	
Stage 3			X		

3.11. Consider the following reservation tables for a dynamic pipeline:

a. Write the collision matrices
b. Draw the state diagram

	0	1	2	3	4
Stage 1	A			A	
Stage 2			A		A
Stage 3		A			

	0	1	2	3	4
Stage 1		B	B		
Stage 2				B	
Stage 3	B				B

3.12. Consider the following reservation table for a static pipeline:

a. Write the forbidden list
b. Draw the state diagram
c. Find the MAL

	0	1	2	3	4
Stage 1	X		X		X
Stage 2		X		X	

d. Is it possible to make MAL 2 by adding delays to the reservation table? If it is, show the new reservation table; otherwise, say why it is not.

4

RISC versus CISC Architecture

4.1 INTRODUCTION

Computer architectures, in general, have evolved toward progressively greater complexity, such as larger instruction sets, more addressing modes, more computational power of the individual instructions, more specialized registers, and so on. Recent machines falling within such trends are termed *complex instruction set computers* (CISCs). However, one may reach a point where the addition of a complex instruction to an instruction set affects the efficiency and the cost of the processor. The effects of such an instruction should be evaluated before it is added to the instruction set. Some of the instructions provided by CISC processors are so esoteric that many compilers simply do not attempt to use them. In fact, many of these instructions can only be utilized through a carefully handwritten assembly program. Even if such powerful instructions could be used by compilers, it is difficult to imagine that they would be used very frequently. Common sense tells us that useless (or seldom used) instructions should not be added to the instruction set. This basic concept of not adding useless instructions to the instruction set has invoked an increasing interest in an innovative approach to computer architecture, the *reduced instruction set computer* (RISC). The design philosophy of the RISC architecture says to add only those instructions to the instruction set that result in a performance gain. RISC systems have been defined and designed by different groups in a variety of ways. The first RISC machine was built in 1982 by IBM, the 801 minicomputer. The common characteristics shared by most of these designs are a limited and simple instruction set, on-chip cache memories (or a large number of registers), a compiler to maximize the use of registers and thereby minimize main memory accesses, and emphasis on optimizing the instruction pipeline.

This chapter discusses the properties of RISC and CISC architectures. Some of the causes for increased architectural complexity associated with CISCs are analyzed in terms of their effect on the development of the architectural features of RISC. The characteristics of RISC and CISC designs are discussed. In addition, the main elements of some of the RISC- and CISC-based microprocessors are explained. The included microprocessors are Motorola 88110, Intel Pentium, Alpha AXP, and PowerPC.

4.2 CAUSES FOR INCREASED ARCHITECTURAL COMPLEXITY

There are several reasons for the trend toward progressively greater complexity. These include support for high-level languages, migration of functions from software into hardware, and upward compatibility. Each of these factors is explained next.

Support for high-level languages. Over the years the programming environment has changed from programming in assembly language to programming in high-level languages, so manufacturers have begun providing more powerful instructions to support efficient implementation of high-level language programs [SUB 89]. These instructions have added not only to the size of the instruction set but also to its complexity due to their relatively high computational power.

Migration of functions from software into hardware. A single instruction that is realized in hardware will perform better than one realized by a sequence of several simpler instructions due to the larger number of memory accesses and the disparity between the speeds of CPU and memory. To increase the processing speed of computers, one observes the phenomenon of migration of functions from software to firmware and from firmware to hardware. (Firmware is a sequence of microinstructions.) This migration of functions from the software domain into the hardware domain will naturally increase the size of the instruction set, resulting in increased overall complexity of the computer.

Upward compatibility. Upward compatibility is often used by manufacturers as a marketing strategy in order to project their computers as being better than other existing models. As the result of this marketing strategy, sometimes manufacturers increase the number of instructions and their power, regardless of the actual use of this complex instruction set. Upward compatibility is a way to improve a design by adding new and usually more complex features (i.e., a new computer should have all the functional capabilities of its predecessors plus something more). As a result, the new instruction set is a superset of the old one.

4.3 WHY RISC

Computer designers have different viewpoints, but the following two criteria are universally accepted goals for all systems:

Sec. 4.3   Why RISC

1. To maximize speed of operation or minimize execution time
2. To minimize development cost and sale price

One way of accomplishing the first goal is to improve the technology of the components, thereby achieving operation at higher frequencies. Increased speed can be achieved by minimizing the average number of clock cycles per instruction and/or executing several instructions simultaneously. To accomplish both goals, the original designers of RISC focused on the aspect of VLSI realization. As a result of fewer instructions, addressing modes, and instruction formats, a relatively small and simple circuit for the control unit was obtained. This relative reduction in size and complexity brought about by VLSI chips yields some desirable results over CISC, which are discussed next.

Effect of VLSI. The main purpose of VLSI technology is to realize the entire processor on a single chip. This will significantly reduce the major delay of transmitting a signal from one chip to another. Architectures with greater complexity (larger instruction set, more addressing modes, variable instruction formats, and so on) need to have more complex instruction fetch, decode, and execute logic. If the processor is microprogrammed, this logic is put into complex microprograms, resulting in a larger microcode storage. As a result, if a CISC is developed using the VLSI technology, a substantial part of the chip area may be consumed in realizing the microcode storage [SUB 89]. The amount of chip area given to the control unit of a CISC architecture may vary from 40% to 60%, whereas only about 10% of the chip area is consumed in the case of a RISC architecture. This remaining area in a RISC architecture can be used for other components, such as on-chip caches and larger register files by which the processor's performance can be improved. As VLSI technology is improved, the RISC is always a step ahead compared to the CISC. For example, if a CISC is realized on a single chip, then RISC can have something more (i.e., more registers, on-chip cache, etc.), and when CISC has enough registers and cache on the chip, RISC will have more than one processing unit, and so forth.

Several factors are involved when discussing RISC advantages: computing speed, VLSI realization, design-time cost reliability, and high-level language support. As for computing speed, the RISC design is suited more elegantly to the instruction pipeline approach. An instruction pipeline allows several instructions to be processed at the same time. The process of an instruction is broken into a series of phases, such as instruction fetch, instruction decoding, operand fetch, execution, and write back. While an instruction is in the fetch phase, another instruction is in decoding phase, and so on. The RISC architecture maximizes the throughput of this pipeline by having uniform instruction size and duration of execution for most instructions. Uniform instruction size and execution duration reduce the idle periods in the pipeline.

VLSI realization relates to the fact that the RISC control unit is implemented in the hardware. A hardwired-controlled system will generally be faster than a microprogrammed one. Furthermore, a large register file and on-chip caches will certainly reduce memory accesses. More frequently used data items can be kept in the registers. The registers can also hold parameters to be passed to other procedures. Because of the progress in VLSI technology, many commercial microprocessors have their own on-chip cache. This cache is typically smaller than the onboard cache, and serves as the first level of caches. The onboard cache, which is adjacent to the processor's chip, serves as the second level of caches. Generally, these two levels of caches improve performance when compared to one level of cache. Furthermore, the cache in each level may actually be organized as a hierarchy of caches. For example, the Intel P6 processor contains two levels of on-chip caches. Finally, sometimes each cache in higher levels is split into two caches: instruction cache and data cache. Processors that have separate caches (or storage) for instructions and data are sometimes called *Harvard-based* architectures after the Harvard Mark I computer. The use of two caches, one for instructions and one for data, in contrast to a single cache can considerably improve access time and consequently improve a processor's performance, especially one that makes extensive use of pipelining, such as the RISC processor.

Another advantage of RISC is that it requires a shorter design period. The time taken for designing a new architecture depends on the complexity of the architecture. Naturally, the design time is longer for complex architectures (CISCs), which require debugging of the design and removal of errors from the complex microprogrammed control unit. In the case of RISC, the time taken to test and debug the resulting hardware is less because no microprogramming is involved and the size of the control unit is small. A shorter design time decreases the chance that the end product may become obsolete before completion. A less complex architecture unit has less chance of design error and therefore higher reliability. Thus the RISC design yields cheaper design costs and design reliability benefits.

Finally, the RISC design offers some features that directly support common high-level language (HLL) operations. The programming environment has changed from programming in assembly language into programming in high-level languages, so the architectures have had to support this change of environment, with additional instructions that are functionally powerful and semantically close to HLL features. Therefore, it has always been desirable for RISCs (the same as CISCs) to support HLL. However, loading the machine with a high number of HLL features may turn a RISC into a CISC. It is therefore a good idea to investigate the frequency of HLL features by running a series of benchmark programs written in HLLs. Based on these observations, only those features are added to the instruction set that are frequently used and produce a performance gain.

A group from University of California at Berkeley directed by Patterson and Sequin studied the characteristics of several typical Pascal and C programs and discovered that procedure calls and returns are the most time consuming of the high-level language statement types [PAT 82a]. More specifically, a CISC machine with a small set of registers takes a lot of time in handling procedure calls and returns because of the need to save registers on a call and restore them on return, as well as the need to pass parameters and results to and from the called procedure. This problem is further exacerbated in RISCs because complex instructions have to be synthesized into subroutines from the available instructions. Thus one of the main design principles of the RISC architecture is to provide an efficient means of handling the procedure call/return mechanism.

This leads to a larger number of registers that can be used for the procedure call/return mechanism. In addition to the large number of registers, the Berkeley team implemented the concept of overlapping register windows to improve efficiency. In this process, the register file is divided into groups of registers called windows. A certain group of registers is designated for global registers and is accessible to any procedure at any time. On the other hand, each procedure is assigned a separate window within the register file. The first window in the register file, the window base, is pointed to by the *current window pointer* (CWP), usually located in the CPU's status register (SR). Register windowing can be useful for efficient passing of parameters between caller and callee by partially overlapping windows. A parameter can be passed without changing the CWP by placing the parameters to be passed in the overlapping part of the two windows. This makes the desired parameters accessible to both caller and callee. Register windowing is done on both RISCs and CISCs, but it is important to note that a CISC control unit can consume 40% to 60% of the chip area, allowing little room for a large register file. In contrast, a RISC control unit takes up only 10% of the chip area, allowing plenty of room for a large register file.

A RISC machine with 100 registers can be used to explain the concept of overlapping register windows. Of these registers, 0 through 9 (10 registers) are used as global registers for storing the shared variables within all procedures. Whenever a procedure is called, in addition to the global registers, 20 more registers are allocated for the procedure. These include 5 registers termed incoming registers to hold parameters that are passed by the calling procedure, 10 registers termed local registers to hold local variables, and 5 registers termed output registers to hold parameters that are to be passed to some other procedure. Figure 4.1 shows the allocated registers for three procedures X, Y, and Z. Notice that procedures X and Y (Y and Z) share the same set of registers for outgoing parameters and incoming parameters, respectively.

In summary, one main motivation behind the idea of the RISC is to simplify all the architectural aspects of the design of a machine so that its implementation can be made more efficient. The goal of RISC is to include simple and essential instructions in the instruction set of a machine.

In general, a RISC architecture has the following characteristics:

1. Most instructions access operands from registers except a few of them, such as the LOAD/STORE, which accesses memory. In other words, a RISC architecture is a load-store machine.

2. Execution of most instructions requires only a single processor cycle, except for a few of them, such as LOAD/STORE. However, with the presence of on-chip caches, even LOAD/STORE can be performed in one cycle, on average.

3. Instructions have a fixed format and do not cross main memory word boundaries. In other words, instructions do not have extension words.

4. The control unit is hardwired. That is, RISC architectures are not microprogrammed. The code generated by the compiler is directly executed by the hardware; it is not interpreted by microprogramming.

5. There is a low number of instruction formats (often less than 4).

6. The CPU has a large register file. An alternative to a large register file is an on-chip cache memory. These days manufacturers have put the cache on the pro-

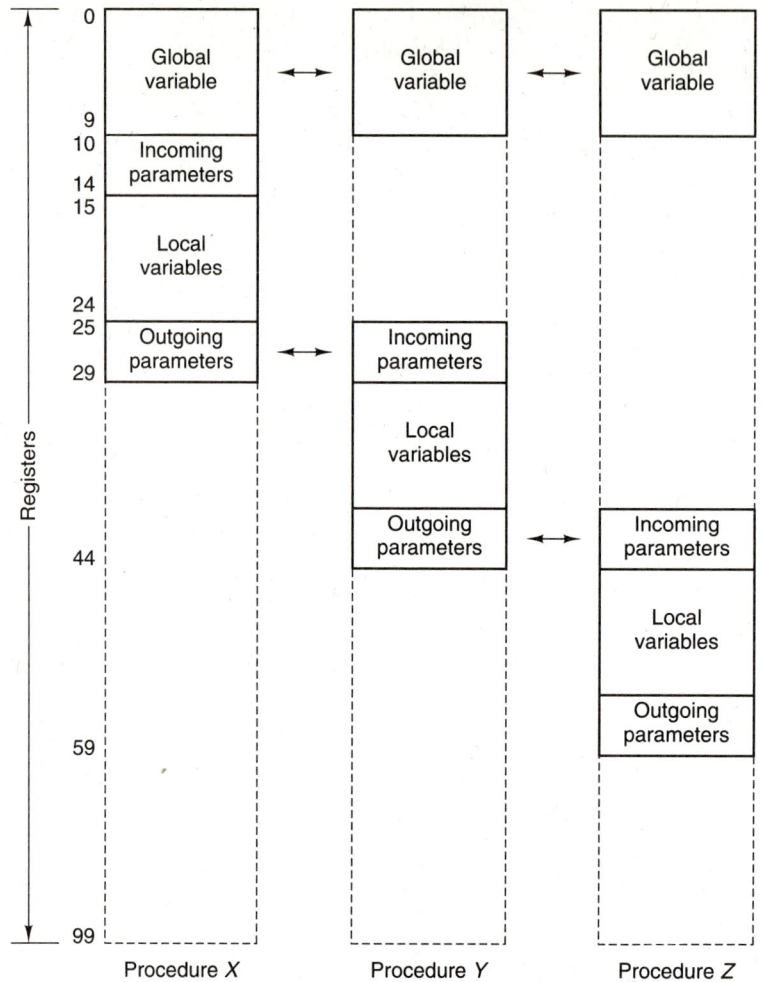

Figure 4.1 Overlapping of register windows: *X* calls *Y*, and *Y* calls *Z*.

cessor chip to accommodate higher speed. Since the area on the processor chip is limited, a small-sized cache may actually be placed on the chip. To support such on-chip caches, a larger cache can be placed off the chip. In general, a hierarchy of caches is used. All data at the highest level (on-chip cache) are present at the lower levels (off-chip caches) so that, after a cache miss, the on-chip cache can be refilled from a lower-level cache, rather than making an unneeded memory access.

7. **Complexity is in the compiler.** For example, the compiler has to take care of delayed branching. It is possible to improve pipeline performance by automatically rearranging instructions within a program so that branch instructions occur later than when originally intended.

8. There are relatively few instructions (often less than 150) and very few addressing modes (often less than 4).

9. It supports high-level language operations by a judicious choice of instructions and by using optimizing compilers.

10. It makes use of instruction pipelining and approaches for dealing with branches, such as multiple prefetch and branch prediction techniques.

4.4 RISC DESIGN VERSUS CISC DESIGN

In general, the time taken by a processor to complete a program can be determined by three factors: (1) the number of instructions in the program, (2) the average number of clock cycles required to execute an instruction, and (3) the clock cycle time. The CISC design approach reduces the number of instructions in the program by providing special instructions that are able to perform complex operations. In contrast, the RISC design approach reduces the average number of clock cycles required to execute an instruction. Both the CISC and RISC approach take advantage of advancements in chip technology to reduce the clock cycle time.

RISC architectures are load-store types of machines; they can obtain a high level of concurrency by separating execution of load and store operations from other instructions. CISC architectures may not be able to obtain the same level of concurrency because of their memory register type of instruction set.

Most of the negative points of RISC are directly related to its good points. Because of the simple instructions, the performance of a RISC architecture is related to compiler efficiency. Also, due to the large register set, the register allocation scheme is more complex, thus increasing the complexity of the compiler. Therefore, a main disadvantage of a RISC architecture is the necessity of writing a good compiler. In general, the development time for the software systems for the RISC machine is longer than for the CISC (potentially). Another disadvantage is that some CISC instructions are equivalent to two or maybe three RISC instructions, causing the RISC code sometimes to be longer. Thus, considering the good points of both RISC and CISC architectures, the design of a RISC-based processor can be enhanced by employing some of the CISC principles that have been developed and improved over the years.

4.5 CASE STUDIES

There are a number of RISC and CISC processors on the market. Some of the RISC processors are Mips R4000, IBM RISC System/6000, Alpha AXP, PowerPC, and the Motorola 88000 series. They provide a variety of designs and varying degrees and interpretations of RISCness. The Mips R4000 microprocessor is based on the superpipelining technique, and the IBM RISC System/6000, Alpha AXP, PowerPC, and Motorola 88000 series are based on the superscalar approach. One CISC processor is the Intel Pentium which is also based on the superscalar approach. In the following sections, the architecture of Motorola 88110, Intel Pentium, Alpha AXP, and PowerPC are described.

4.5.1 Case Study I: Motorola 88110 Microprocessor

The Motorola 88110 is the second generation of the 88000 architecture [DIE 92]. [The first generation, 88100/200, consists of three chips, one CPU (88100) chip and two cache (88200) chips.] The idea behind designing the 88110 was to produce a general-purpose microprocessor for use in low-cost personal computers and workstations. The design objective was to obtain good performance at reasonable cost. Good performance included implementation of interactive software, user-oriented interfaces, voice and image processing, and advanced graphics in a personal computer. The 88110 is a single-chip superscalar microprocessor implemented in CMOS technology. It is able to execute two instructions per clock cycle.

Figure 4.2 represents the main components of the 88110. It contains three caches, two register files, and ten execution units. One cache is used for storing the

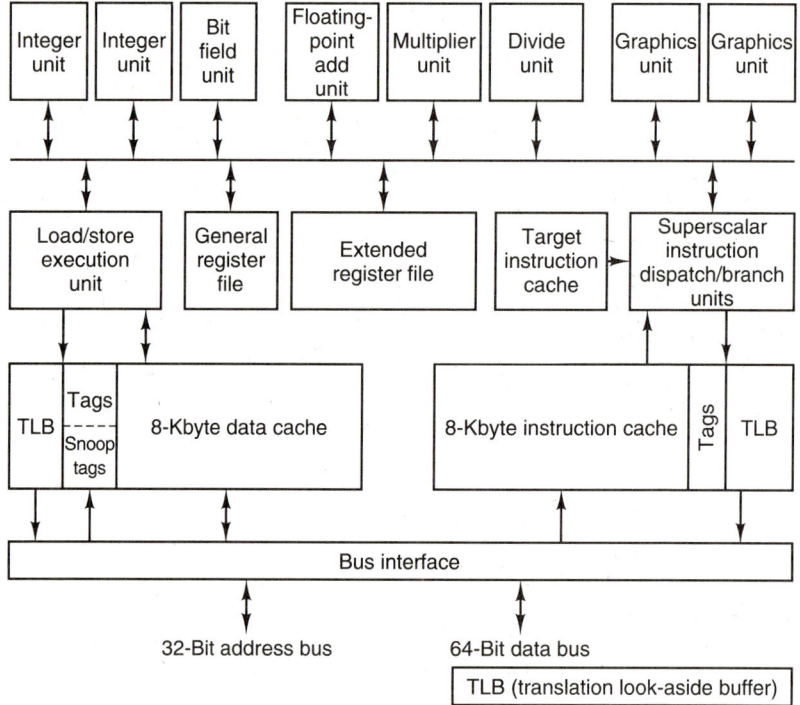

Figure 4.2 Main components of the 88110 (from [DIE 92]). Reprinted with permission, from "Organization of the Motorola 88110 Superscalar RISC Microprocessor" by K. Diefendorff and M. Allen which appeared in IEEE Micro, April, 1992, pp. 40–63, © 1992 IEEE.

Sec. 4.5   Case Studies   **147**

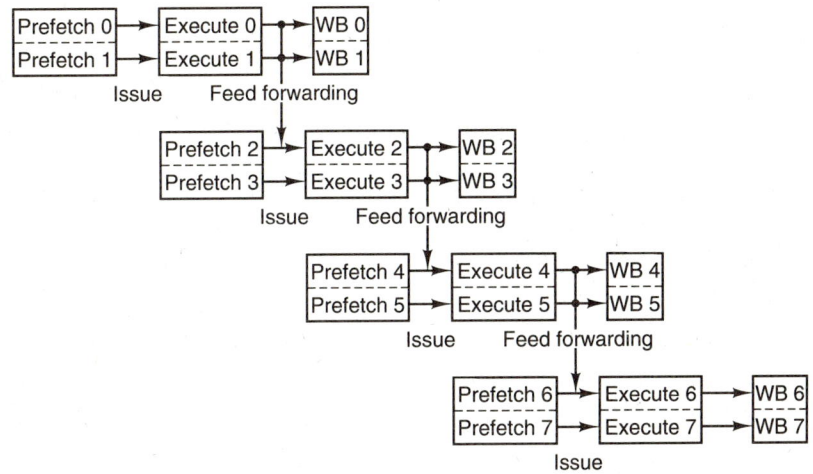

Figure 4.3   Instruction prefetch and execute timing (from [MOT 91]). Reprinted with permission of Motorola.

branch target instructions, and the other two are used for storing instructions and data. The 88110 stores instructions in one cache and the data in the other cache. In other words, it is able to fetch instructions and data simultaneously. The ten execution units in the 88110 are instruction unit, load/store, floating-point adder, multiplier, divider, two integer, two graphics, and bit-field unit. The function of each of these units is explained next.

Instruction unit.   The 88110 is able to execute more than one instruction per clock cycle. This is achieved by including many performance features such as pipelining, feed forwarding, branch prediction, and multiple execution units, all of which operate independently and in parallel. As shown in Figure 4.3, the main instruction pipeline has three stages that complete most instructions in two and a half clock cycles. In the first stage, *the prefetch and decode stage*, a pair of instructions is fetched from the instruction cache and decoded, their operands are fetched from the register files, and it is decided whether or not to issue them (send to the required execution unit) for execution. An instruction will not be issued for execution when one of the required resources (such as source operands, destination register, or execution unit) is not available, when there is data dependency with previous instructions, or when a branch causes an alternative instruction stream to be fetched. In the second stage, *the execute stage*, the instruction is executed. This stage takes one clock cycle for most of the instructions; some instructions take more than one cycle. In the third stage, *the write-back stage*, the results from the execution units are written into the register files.

The instruction unit always issues instructions to the execution units in order of their appearance in the code. It generates a single address for each prefetch operation, but receives two instructions from the instruction cache. The instruction unit always tries to issue both instructions at the same time to the execution units. If the first instruction in an issue pair cannot be issued due to resource unavailability or data dependencies, neither instruction is issued and both instructions are stalled. If the first

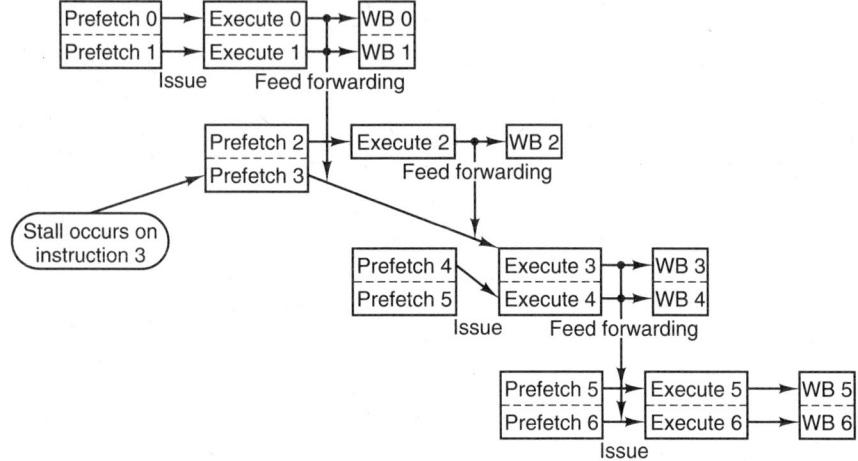

Figure 4.4 Instruction execution order (from [MOT 91]). Reprinted with permission of Motorola.

instruction is issued but the second is not, the second instruction will be stalled and paired with a new instruction for execution. Figure 4.4 represents an example for this latter case. In this example, instruction 3 is stalled and then issued as the first instruction in the next cycle. Instruction 4 is issued as the second instruction. Notice that, since instruction 5 was not issued with instruction 4, it is again prefeteched in the next cycle. However, the cost of the first-time prefetching is zero since it was done in parallel with instruction 4.

To avoid the hazard of data dependency, the scoreboard technique is used. The scoreboard is implemented as a bit vector; each bit corresponds to a register in the register files. Each time an instruction is issued for execution, the instruction's destination register is marked busy by setting the corresponding scoreboard bit. The corresponding scoreboard bit stays set until the instruction completes execution and writes back its result to the destination register; then it is cleared. Therefore, whenever an instruction (except store and branch instructions) is considered for issuing, one condition that must be satisfied is that the scoreboard bits for all the instruction's source and destination registers be cleared (or be zero during the issue clock cycle). If some of the corresponding scoreboard bits are set, the issuing of the instruction is stalled until those bits become clear. To minimize stall time, the feed-forwarding technique is used to forward the source data directly to the stalled instruction as soon as it is available (see Figure 4.4). Once an execution unit finishes the execution of an instruction, the instruction unit writes the result back to the register file, forwards the result to the execution units that need it, and clears the corresponding scoreboard bits. The forwarding of the result to the execution units occurs in parallel with the register write back and clearing of the scoreboard bits.

Although the instruction unit always issues instructions in order of their appearance in the code, a few instructions may not be executed in the same order that they were issued. For example, branch and store instructions may be issued even though their source operands are not available. These instructions stay in the queue of their respective execution units until the required operands become available. Furthermore, since the 88110 has more than one execution unit, it is possible for instructions to complete execution out of order. However, the 88110 maintains the appearance in the user software that instructions are issued and executed in the same order as the code. It does this by keeping a first-in, first-out queue, called a history buffer, of all instructions that are executing. The queue can hold a maximum of 12 instructions at any time. When an instruction is issued, a copy is placed at the tail of the queue. The instructions move through the queue until they reach the head. An instruction reaches to the head of the queue when all the instructions in front of it have completed execution. An instruction leaves the queue when it reaches the head and it has completed execution.

The 88110 employs design strategies such as delayed branching, the target instruction cache, and static branch prediction to minimize the penalties associated with branch instructions. When a branch instruction is issued, no other instruction will be issued in the next available issuing slot; this unused slot is called a delay slot. However, the delayed branching option (.n) provides an opportunity to issue an instruction during the delay slot. When option (.n) is used with a branch (like bcnd.n), the instruction following the branch will be unconditionally executed during the penalty time incurred by the instruction.

The target instruction cache (TIC) is a fully associative cache with 32 entries; each entry can maintain the first two instructions of a branch target path. When a branch instruction is decoded, the first two instructions of the target path can be prefetched from TIC in parallel with the decode of the branch instruction. The TIC can be used in place of, or in conjunction with, the delayed branching option.

The static branch prediction option provides a mechanism by which software (compiler) gives hints to the 88110 for predicting a branch path. When a conditional branch instruction enters the main instruction pipeline, a branch path (sequential path or target path) is predicted based on its opcode. The instructions are prefetched from the predicted path and are executed conditionally until the outcome of the branch is resolved. (In the case when the target path is predicted, the first two instructions are prefetched from the target instruction cache to reduce branch penalty.) If the predicted path was incorrect, the execution process will backtrack to the branch instruction, undoing all changes made to the registers by conditionally executed instructions. Then, the execution process will continue from the other path. The 88110 has three conditional branch instructions: *bb0* (branch on bit clear) *bb1* (branch on bit set), and *bcnd* (conditional branch). The software defines the predicted path based on these branch instructions. When the 88110 encounters (decodes) a bb0 instruction, the sequential path is predicted. When a bb1 instruction is encountered, the target path is predicted. When the 88110 encounters a bcnd instruction, a path is predicted based on the instruction's condition code (cc). If the condition code is greater than zero, greater than or equal to zero, or not equal to zero, the target path is predicted. Otherwise, the sequential path is predicted.

Operand types. The 88110 supports eight different types of operands: byte (8 bits), half-word (16 bits), word (32 bits), double word (64 bits), single-precision floating point (32 bits), double-precision floating point (64 bits), double-extended-precision floating point (80 bits), and bit field (1 to 32 bits in a 32-bit register). The 88110 requires that double words be on modulo 8 boundaries, single words on modulo 4 boundaries, and half-words on modulo 2 boundaries.

The ordering of bytes within a word is such that the byte whose address is "*x...x00*" (in hex) is placed at the most significant position in the word. This type of ordering is often referred to as *big endian*. An alternative to big endian is known as *little endian;* the byte whose address is "*x...x00*" is placed at the least significant position in the word. Therefore, in big endian addressing, the address of a datum is the address of the most significant byte, while in little endian, the address of a datum is the address of the least significant byte. Although the 88110 uses big endian, the programmer is able to switch it to little endian. This switching ability allows the users to run the programs that use little endian addressing.

The 88110 supports the IEEE standard floating-point formats (ANSI/IEEE Standard 754—1985). It supports single-, double-, and double-extended precision numbers. Each of these numbers is divided into three or four fields, as follows:

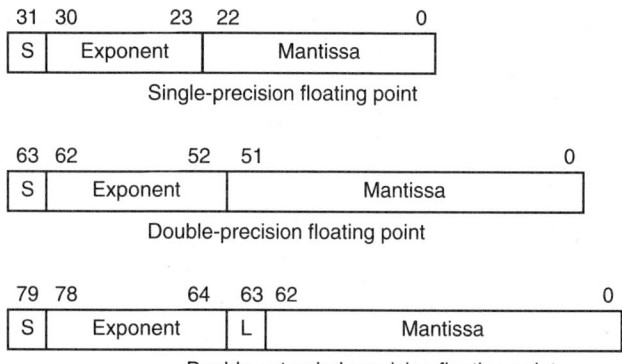

The sign bit S determines the sign of the number; if S is zero, then the number is positive; otherwise, it is negative.

The exponent field is represented in excess 127 for single-precision numbers, in excess 1023 for double-precision numbers, and in excess 16,383 for double-extended precision. In other words, the exponent of the single-precision numbers is biased by 127, the exponent of the double-precision numbers is biased by 1023, and the exponent of the double-extended precision by 16,383. For example, the excess 127 for actual exponent 0 would be 127, and for −2 it would be 125.

The leading bit L represents the integer part of a floating-point number. For single- and double-precision numbers this bit is hidden, and it is assumed to be a 1 when the exponent is a nonzero number and a 0 when the exponent is 0. When the biased exponent is a nonzero (but not all 1's) and the leading bit is 1, the number is normalized. When the biased exponent is a 0 and the mantissa is nonzero (or mantissa 0 and leading bit 1), the number is said to be denormalized. The denormalized representation can be used when a number is too small to be represented as a normalized number. For example the smallest normalized number that can be represented in a single-precision number is $1.0 * 2^{-126}$. Therefore, a smaller number, such as $1.0 * 2^{-128}$, cannot be represented as a normalized number. However, $1.0 * 2^{-128}$ can be represented as a denormalized number $0.01 * 2^{-126}$, or

31	30	23	22	0
0	00000000		01 000000000000000000000	
+	–126		0.01	

In addition to normalized and denormalized representations, the double-extended-precision format can also represent a number as unnormalized. When the biased exponent is nonzero (but not all 1's) and the leading bit is 0, the number is said to be unnormalized. This makes it possible for the double-extended-precision numbers to have more than one representation for a given number. For example, 1101.0 can be represented as the normalized number $1.101 * 2^3$, or as the unnormalized number $0.1101 * 2^4$.

The mantissa field represents the fractional binary part of a floating-point number. The mantissa is represented in 23 bits for single-precision numbers, 52 bits for double-precision numbers, and 63 bits for double-extended-precision numbers. A biased exponent zero, mantissa zero, and leading bit 0 represent a zero value.

Instruction set. Following RISC design characteristics, the 88110 has a fixed size and simple, short instructions. All instructions are 32 bits long. The following list contains most of the instructions. Each instruction (or group of instructions) has its own subdivision, which contains a short description for that instruction. In the list, the destination register for an instruction is denoted as d, and the source registers are denoted as s1 and s2.

DATA TRANSFERS

ld d, s1, s2	*Load register from memory*
ld d, s1, Imm16	It loads the contents of a memory location into register d. s1 contains the base address. To s1, the ld instruction either adds the index contained in the register s2 or the immediate index Imm16.
st s, d1, d2	*Store register to memory*
st s, d1, Imm16	It stores the contents of register s in the memory. The register d1 contains the base address. To d1, the st instruction either adds the index contained in the register d2 or the immediate index Imm16.
xmem d, s1, s2	*Exchange register with memory*
xmem d, s1, Imm16	It exchanges (load and store) the contents of the register d with a memory location. The register s1 contains the base address. To s1, the xmem instruction either adds the index contained in the register s2 or the immediate index Imm16. The xmem is an atomic instruction; that is, once it gets started, nothing can stop it. It cannot be inter-

rupted by external interrupts, exceptions, or bus arbitration. It can be used to implement semaphores and shared-resource locks in multiprocessor systems.

ARITHMETIC AND LOGICAL

add, addu, fadd
Signed add, unsigned add, floating-point add

add d, s1, s2
add d, s1, Imm16
Adds source 1 to source 2.

sub, subu, fsub
Signed subtract, unsigned subtract, floating-point subtract

sub d, s1, s2
sub d, s1, Imm16
Subtracts source 2 from source 1.

mul, fmul
Integer multiply, floating-point multiply

mul d, s1, s2
mul d, s1, Imm16
Multiplies source 1 by source 2

div, divu, fdiv
Signed divide, unsigned divide, floating-point divide

div d, s1, s2
div d, s1, Imm16
Divides source 1 by source 2

cmp, fcmp
Integer compare, floating-point compare

cmp d, s1, s2
Compares source 1 and source 2.

cmp d, s1, Imm16
The instruction returns the evaluated conditions as a bit string in the d register.

and d, s1, s2
and d, s1, Imm16
Logical and of source 1 and source 2.

or d, s1, s2
or d, s1, Imm16
Logical-or of source 1 and source 2.

xor d, s1, s2
xor d, s1, Imm16
Logical exclusive-or of source 1 and source 2.

CONTROL

bb0, bb1
Branch on bit clear, branch on bit set

bb0 Bp5, s1, Disp16
It checks the $Bp5^{th}$ bit of the register s1; if the bit is 0, it branches to an address formed by adding the displacement Disp16 to the address of bb0 instruction.

bcnd cc, s1, Disp16
Conditional branch
It compares the contents of register s1 to 0, and then branches if the contents of s1 meet the condition code cc.

br Disp26	*Unconditional branch*
	It branches to an address formed by adding the displacement Disp26 to the address of br instruction.
bsr Disp26	*Branch to subroutine*
	It branches to an address formed by adding the displacement Disp26 to the address of bsr instruction. The return address is saved in register 1.
jmp s2	*Unconditional jump*
	It jumps to the target address contained in the register s2.
jsr s2	*Jump to subroutine*
	It jumps to the target address contained in the register s2. The return address is saved in register 1.

GRAPHICS

padd d, s1, s2	*Add fields*
psub d, s1, s2	*Subtract fields*
ppack d, s1, s2	*Pixel pack*
punpk d, s1	*Pixel unpack*
pmul d, s1, s2	*Multiply*
prot d, s1, s2	*Rotate*
pcmp d, s1, s2	*Z compare*

SYSTEM

ldcr d, CR	*Load from control register*
	It loads the contents of the control register, CR, to the general register d.
rte	*Return from exception*

Instruction and data caches. The 88110 microprocessor has separate on-chip caches for instructions and data. The instruction cache feeds the instruction unit, and the data cache feeds the load–store execution unit. Each of these caches is an 8-Kbyte, two-way, set-associative cache. The 8 Kbytes of each cache memory are logically organized as two memory blocks, each containing two 128 lines. Each line of the data cache contains 32 bytes (eight 32-bit words), a 20-bit address tag, and 3 state bits. Each line of the instruction cache contains 32 bytes, a 20-bit address tag, and 1 valid bit. Both caches use a random replacement strategy to replace a cache line when no empty lines are available.

The 3 state bits of the data cache determine whether the cache line is valid or invalid, modified or unmodified, and shared or exclusive. The valid state indicates that the line exists in the cache. The modified state means that the line is modified with respect to the memory copy. The exclusive state denotes that only this cache line holds valid data that are identical to the memory copy. The shared state indicates that at least one other caching device also holds the same data that are identical to the memory copy.

There is an address translation lookaside buffer (TLB) attached to each of the data and instruction caches. The TLB is a fully associative cache with 40 entries and supports a virtual memory environment. Each TLB entry contains the address translation, control, and protection information for logical-to-physical (page or segment) address translation. As shown in Figure 4.5, the caches are logically indexed and physically tagged. The 12 lower bits of a logical (virtual) address determine the possible location of an instruction or data inside the cache. The (20 or 13) upper bits of the logical address are fed to the TLB where they will be translated to a physical address. An entry of TLB that matches this logical page address is used to provide the corresponding physical address. The resulting physical address is compared with the two cache tags to determine a hit or miss.

The 88110 contains hardware support for three memory update modes: write-back, write-through, and cache-inhibit. In the write-back mode, used as the default mode, the changes on the cacheable data may not cause an external bus cycle to update main memory. However, in the write-through mode the main memory is updated any time the cache line is modified. In the cache-inhibit mode, read/write operations access only main memory. If a memory location is defined to be cache inhibited, data from this location can never be stored in the data cache. A memory

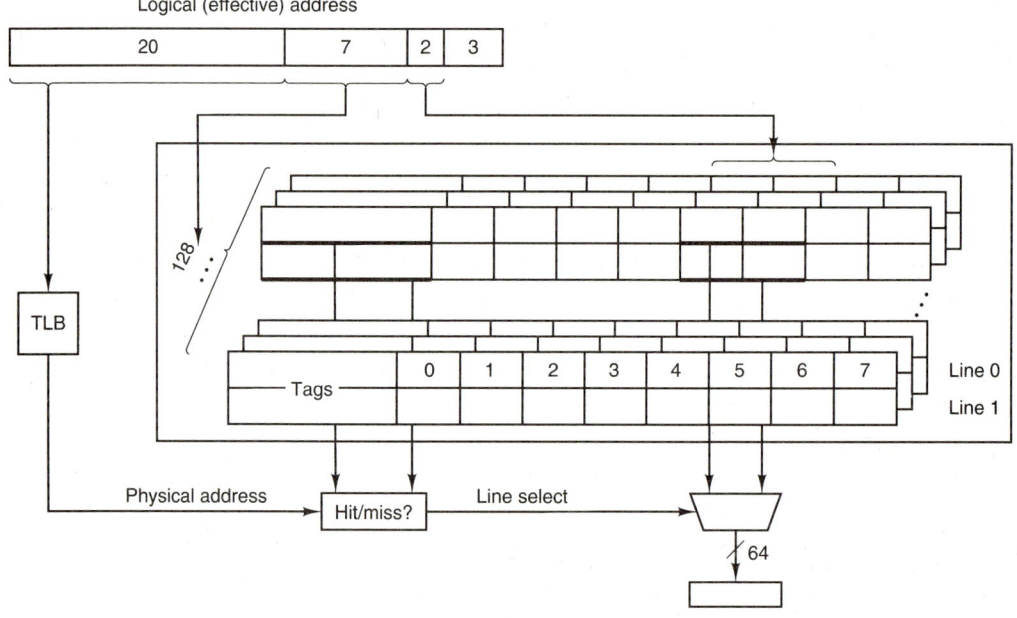

Figure 4.5 Organization of instruction and data caches (from [DIE 92]). Reprinted, with permission, from "Organization of the Motorola 88110 Superscalar RISC Microprocessor" by K. Diefendorff and M. Allen which appeared in IEEE Micro, April, 1992, pp. 40-63, © 1992 IEEE.

location can be declared cache inhibited by setting a bit in the corresponding TLB entry.

The data cache can provide 64 bits during each clock cycle to the load/store unit.

Internal buses. The 88110 contains six 80-bit buses: two source 1 buses, two source 2 buses, and two destination buses. The source buses transfer source operands from registers (or from 16-bit immediate values embedded in instructions) to the execution units. The destination buses transfer the results from execution units to the register files. Arbitration for these buses is performed by the instruction unit. The instruction unit allocates slots on the source buses for the source operands. When an execution unit completes an instruction, it sends a request for a slot on a destination bus to the instruction unit, which allocates a slot for the request. Since there are only two destination buses, the instruction unit prioritizes data transfers when it receives more than two requests at once.

Register files. The 88110 contains two register files, one for integer values and address pointers and the other for floating-point values. Figure 4.6 represents the format of these register files. The integer register file has thirty-two 32-bit registers, and the floating-point register file contains thirty-two 80-bit registers. Each can hold a floating-point number in either single, double, or double-extended format. As shown in Figure 4.7, both register files have eight ports: six output ports and two input ports. Four of the output ports are used to place the source operands on the source buses simultaneously. This allows two instructions to be executed per clock cycle. The other two output ports are used to write the contents of the current instruction's destination

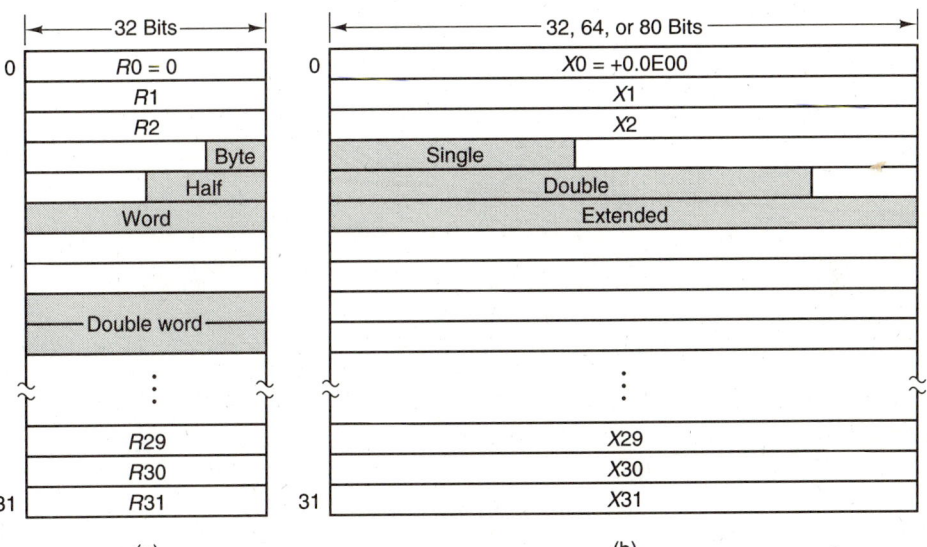

Figure 4.6 Register files: (a) general and (b) extended or floating point (from [DIE 92]). Reprinted, with permission, from "Organization of the Motorola 88110 Superscalar RISC Microprocessor" by K. Diefendorff and M. Allen which appeared in IEEE Micro, April, 1992, pp. 40-63, © 1992 IEEE.

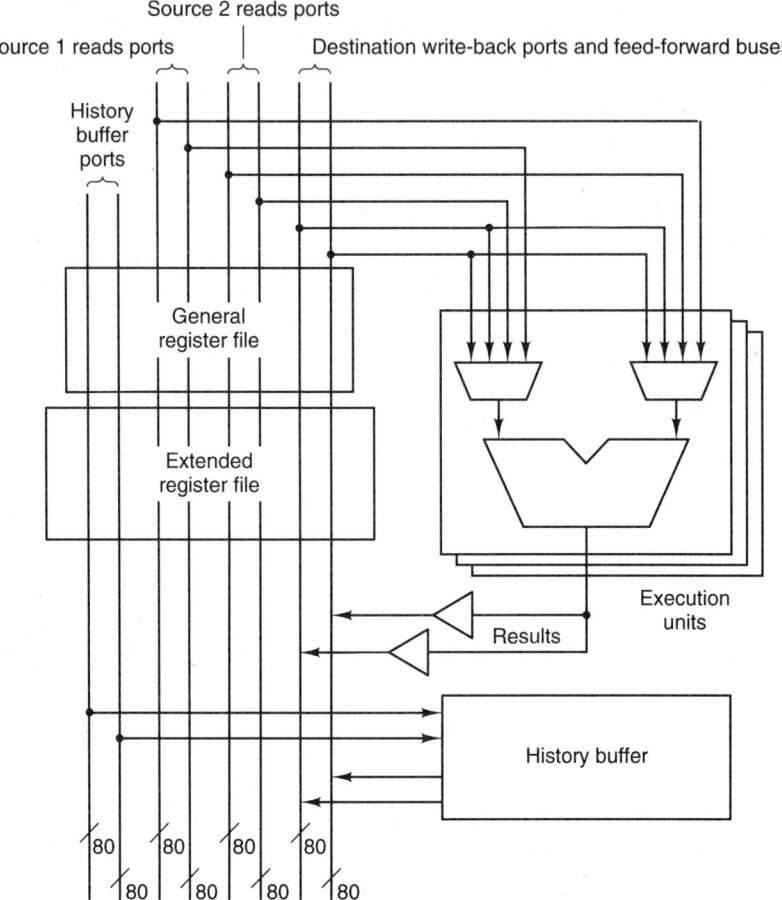

Figure 4.7 Operand data paths (from [DIE 92]). Reprinted, with permission, from "Organization of the Motorola 88110 Superscalar RISC Microprocessor" by K. Diefendorff and M. Allen which appeared in IEEE Micro, April, 1992, pp. 40-63, © 1992 IEEE.

registers into the history buffer. The input ports are used to transfer the results on the two destination buses to the destination registers.

To allow an instruction, waiting in an execution unit, to have access to the result of the previous instruction before the result has been actually written to the output register, a data path around the register files is built. A result returning from an execution unit can be directly fed to the inputs of a waiting execution unit while it is also being written into the register file.

Load/store unit. The load/store unit provides fast access to the data cache. It executes all instructions that transfer data between the register files and the data cache or the memory. When an instruction arrives at the load/store unit, it waits for access to the data cache in either the load queue or the store queue. These queues are managed as FIFO queues and allow normal execution to continue while some instructions are waiting for service by the data cache or memory system. For example, when a store instruction is issued before its store data operand becomes available, it waits in the store queue until the instruction computing the required data completes execution. Then the store instruction resumes the execution. While a store instruction is waiting in the store queue, subsequently issued load instructions can bypass this instruction if they do not refer to the same address as the store instruction.

Floating-point add unit. The floating-point add execution unit handles all floating-point arithmetic instructions (except the multiply and divide), floating-point comparison, and integer/floating-point conversions. The floating-point multiply and divide instructions are handled by the multiply and divide execution units. The floating-point add unit is implemented as a three-stage pipeline, and therefore one operation can be issued in each clock cycle. Its architecture is based on combined carry lookahead and carry select techniques.

Multiplier unit. The multiplier execution unit handles 32- and 64-bit integer multiplies and single-, double-, and extended-precision floating-point multiplies. It is implemented as a three-stage pipeline, and therefore one multiply instruction can be issued in each clock cycle. Its architecture is based on a combined Booth and Wallace tree technique. The Booth method is used to generate the partial products, and the Wallace tree is used to add them.

Divider unit. The divider execution unit handles 32- and 64-bit integer divides and single-, double-, and extended-precision floating-point divides. It is implemented as an iterative multicycle execution unit; therefore, it executes only one divide instruction at any time.

Integer unit. There are two 32-bit integer arithmetic logic execution units. Both units handle all integer and logical instructions. They do not deal with integer multiply and divide; those are handled in other units. Both units have a one-clock-cycle execution latency and can accept a new instruction every clock cycle.

Graphic unit. The process of three-dimensional animation in real time is computationally intensive. The process has five major phases: (1) viewpoint transformation, (2) lighting, (3) raster conversion, (4) image processing, and (5) display. To obtain good performance among these five phases, the raster conversion and image processing phases require hardware support beyond that found in the other execution units. To improve the performance of these phases, the 88110 includes two 64-bit three-dimensional graphics execution units. One handles the arithmetic operations (called pixel add unit), and the other handles the bit-field packing and unpacking instructions (called pixel pack unit). Both units have a one-clock-cycle execution latency and can accept a new instruction every clock cycle.

Bit-field unit. The 32-bit bit-field execution unit contains a shifter/masker circuit that handles the bit-field manipulation instructions. It has a one-clock-cycle execution latency and can accept a new instruction every clock cycle.

4.5.2 Case Study II: Intel Pentium Microprocessor

The Intel Pentium microprocessor is a 66-MHz, 112-MIPS, 32-bit processor. It is a single-chip superscalar microprocessor implemented in BiCMOS(bipolar complementary metal-oxide semiconductor) technology. The BiCMOS technology uses the best features of bipolar and CMOS technology, which provides high speed, high drive, and low power [INT 93a].

Pentium can execute two instructions per clock cycle. It has the properties of both CISC and RISC, but has more characteristics of CISC than RISC. Therefore, it is referred to as a CISC architecture. Some of the instructions are entirely hardwired and can be executed in one clock cycle (a RISC property), while other instructions use microinstructions for execution and may require more than one cycle for execution time (a CISC property). Pentium also has several addressing modes, several instruction formats, and few registers (CISC properties).

Figure 4.8 shows the main components of the Pentium processor [INT 93a]. Pentium has two instruction pipelines, the u-pipeline and the v-pipeline. They are called u- and v-pipelines because u and v are the first two consecutive letters that are not used as an initial for an execution unit. The u- and v-pipelines are not equivalent and cannot be used interchangeably. The u-pipeline can execute all integer and floating-point instructions, while the v-pipeline can execute simple integer instructions and some of

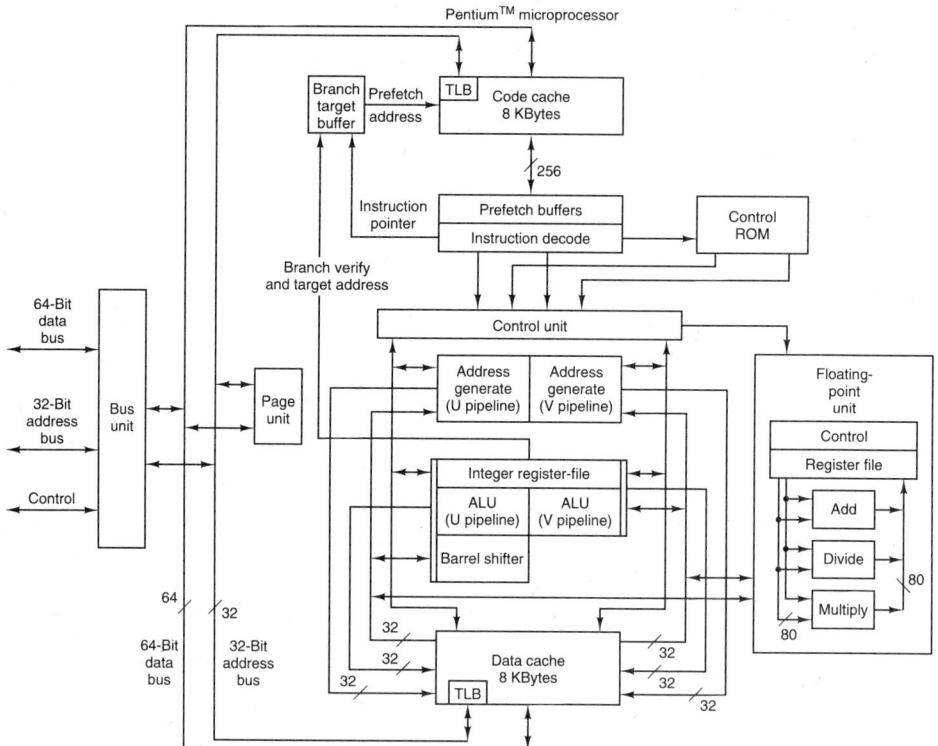

Figure 4.8 Pentium™ processor block diagram (from [INT 93a]). Reprinted with permission of Intel Corporation, Copyright/Intel Corporation 1993.

the floating-point instructions like the floating-point exchange instruction. (A simple instruction does not require any microinstruction for execution; it is entirely hardwired and can be executed in one clock cycle.)

Pentium has two separate 8-Kbyte caches for data and instructions, the data cache and the instruction (code) cache. It also has a branch target buffer, two prefetch buffers, and a control ROM. The instruction cache, branch target buffer, and prefetch buffers are responsible for supplying instructions to the execution units. The control ROM contains a set of microinstructions for controlling the sequence of operations involved in instruction execution.

Each of the data and instruction caches is a two-way, set-associative cache with a line size 32 bytes wide. Each cache has its own four-way, set-associative TLB (translation lookaside buffer) to translate logical addresses to physical addresses. Both caches use the least recently used mechanism to place a new line in them. A least recently used line is selected for replacement based on the value of a bit that is defined for each set of two lines in the cache. For the write operation, the Pentium supports both write-through and write-back update policies.

Pentium contains two units, an integer unit and a floating-point unit. The integer unit has two 32-bit ALUs to handle all the integer and logical operations. Both ALUs have a one-clock-cycle latency, with a few exceptions. The integer unit also has eight 32-bit general-purpose registers. These registers hold operands for logical and arithmetic operations. They also hold operands for address calculations. The floating-point unit (FPU) contains an eight-stage instruction pipeline, a dedicated adder, a multiplier, and a divider. It also has eight 80-bit registers to hold floating-point operands. By using fast algorithms and taking advantage of the pipelined architecture, the FPU provides very good performance. The FPU is designed to accept one floating-point instruction in every clock cycle. Two floating-point instructions can be issued, but this is limited and confined only to a certain set of instructions.

Pentium has a wide, 256-bit internal data bus for the code cache. The integer unit has a 32-bit data bus and the floating-point unit has an 80-bit internal data bus.

A detailed description of the preceding components is given next.

Instruction pipelines. Pentium can execute two integer instructions per clock cycle through the u- and v-pipelines. As shown in Figure 4.9, each of these pipelines consists of five stages (the first two stages are shared). The five stages are *prefetch* (PF), *instruction decode* (D1), *address generate* (D2), *execute*, (EX), and *write back* (WB). In the first stage, PF, instructions are prefetched from the instruction cache or memory.

In the second stage, D1, two sequential instructions are decoded in parallel, and it is decided whether or not to issue them for execution. Both instructions can be issued simultaneously if certain conditions are satisfied [INT 93a]. Two of the main conditions are that the two instructions must be simple, and there should not be any read-after-write or write-after-read data dependencies between them. The exceptions to simple instructions are memory-to-register and register-to-memory ALU instructions, which take 2 to 3 cycles, respectively. Pentium includes some sequencing hardware that lets these exceptions operate as simple instructions.

In the third stage, D2, the addresses of memory operands (if there are any) are calculated. The fourth stage, EX, is used for ALU operations and, when required, data

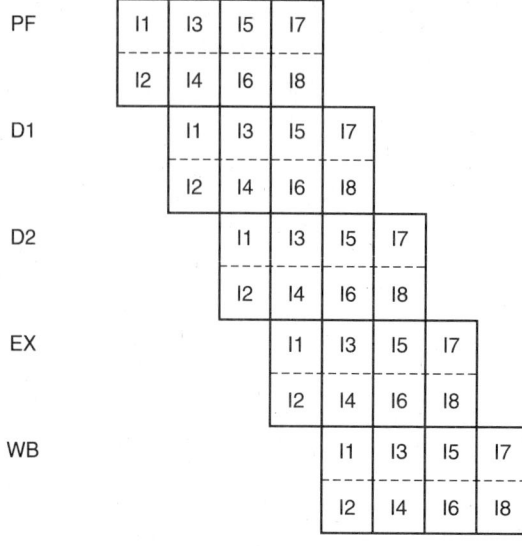

Figure 4.9 Pentium™ processor pipeline execution (from [INT 93a]). Reprinted with permission of Intel Corporation, Copyright/Intel Corporation 1993.

cache access. Instructions requiring both an ALU operation and a data cache access will need more than one cycle in this stage. In the final stage, WB, the registers are updated with the instruction's results.

Pentium always issues instructions and completes their execution in order of their appearance in the program. When an instruction enters the u-pipeline and another instruction enters the v-pipeline, both instructions leave stage D2 and enter the EX stage at the same time. That is, when an instruction in one pipeline is stalled at a stage, the instruction in the other pipeline is also stalled at the same stage. Once the instructions enter the EX stage, if the instruction in the u-pipeline is stalled, the other instruction is also stalled. If the instruction in the v-pipeline is stalled, the other instruction is allowed to advance. In the latter case, if the instruction in the u-pipeline completes the EX stage before the instruction in the v-pipeline, no successive instruction is allowed to enter the EX stage of the u-pipeline until the instruction in the v-pipeline completes the EX stage.

Pentium uses a dynamic branching strategy [ALP 93, INT 93a]. It employs a branch target buffer (BTB), which is a four-way, set-associative cache with 256 entries; each entry keeps a branch instruction's address with its target address and the history used by the prediction algorithm. When a branch instruction is first taken, the processor allocates an entry in the BTB for this instruction. When a branch instruction is decoded in the D1 stage, the processor searches the BTB to determine whether it holds an entry for the corresponding branch instruction. If there is a miss, the branch is assumed not to be taken. If there is a hit, the recorded history is used to determine whether the branch should be taken or not. If the branch is predicted as not taken, the instructions are continued to be fetched from the sequential path; otherwise, the processor starts fetching instructions from the target path. To do this, Pentium has two 32-byte prefetch buffers. At any time, one prefetch buffer prefetches instructions sequentially until a branch instruction is decoded. If the BTB predicts that the branch will not be taken, prefetching continues as usual. If the BTB predicts that the branch

Sec. 4.5 Case Studies

will be taken, the second prefetch buffer begins to prefetch instructions from the target path. The correctness of the branch is resolved in the beginning of the write-back stage. If the predicted path is discovered to be incorrect, the instruction pipelines are flushed and prefetching starts along the correct path. Flushing of pipelines will incur three to four clock-cycle delays, depending on the type of branch instruction.

Although Pentium can execute simple instructions in one clock cycle, it requires three clock cycles for floating-point instructions. A floating-point instruction traverses an eight-stage pipeline for execution. The eight stages are *prefetch* (PF), *instruction decode* (D1), *address generate* (D2), *operand fetch* (EX), *execute stage 1* (X1), *execute stage 2* (X2), *write floating-point result to register file* (WF), and *error reporting* (ER). These eight stages are maintained by the floating-point unit. However, the first five stages are shared with the u- and v-pipelines. (Integer instructions use the fifth, X1, stage as a WB stage.)

Except in a few cases, Pentium can only execute one floating-point instruction at a time. Since the u- and v-pipeline stages are shared with the floating-point unit stages and some of the floating-point operands are 64 bits, floating-point instructions cannot be executed simultaneously with integer instructions. However, some floating-point instructions, like the floating-point exchange instruction, can be executed simultaneously with certain other floating-point instructions, such as floating-point addition and multiplication.

Operand types. The Pentium processor supports several operand types. The fundamental operand types are byte (8 bits), word (16 bits), double word (32 bits), and quad word (64 bits). There are some specialized operand types, such as integer (32 bits, 16 bits, 8 bits), BCD integer, near pointer (32 bits), bit field (1 to 32 in a register), bit string (from any bit position to $2^{32} - 1$ bits), byte string (string can contain 0 to $2^{32} - 1$ bytes), single-precision floating-point (32 bits), double-precision floating-point (64 bits), and extended-precision floating-point (80 bits) [INT 93b].

Similar to the Motorolla 88110, Pentium also uses the IEEE standard floating-point format to represent real numbers. The only difference in the way floating-point operands are implemented in Pentium from that of Motorolla is that the mantissa in double-extended-precision is always normalized except for the value 0. This is shown next, where there is a 1 fixed in the bit position 63. That is, the leftmost bit, which represents the integer part of a floating-point number, is always 1 for non-zero values.

79	78		64	63	62		0
S	Exponent			1	Mantissa		

Instruction set. Following CISC design characteristics, Pentium has variable sizes, and combinations of simple, complex, short, and long instructions. The size of instructions varies from 1 to 12 bytes.

The following list contains some of the instructions. Each instruction (or group of instructions) has its own subdivision, which contains a short description. In the list, the destination register/memory operands are represented as d/md32, d/md16, and d/md8, and the source register/memory operands are represented as s/ms32, s/ms16, and s/ms8. Here d/md32, d/md16, and d/md8 denote a double-word (32 bits), a word (16 bits), and a byte (8 bits) destination register or memory operand, respectively. Similarly, s/ms32, s/ms16, and s/ms8 denote a double-word (32 bits), a word (16 bits), and a byte (8 bits) source register or memory operand, respectively. The d16 and s16 refer to the rightmost 16 bits of the general-purpose registers. The characters L and H are used to denote the low- and high-order bits of the rightmost 16 bits of the general-purpose registers, respectively. That is, Ld8/Ls8 denotes the rightmost 8 bits of d16/s16, and Hd8/Hs8 represents the leftmost 8 bits of d16/s16. An immediate byte value is represented as Imm8, which is a signed number between -128 and $+128$.

DATA TRANSFERS

FLD ms32 — *Load stack from memory*
It loads the contents of the memory location ms to the topmost cell of the FPU stack.

FST md32 — *Store the stack to memory*
It stores the contents of the topmost cell of the FPU stack to the memory location md.

LAR d32,s/ms32 — *Load register/memory to register*
It loads the 32-bit destination register d32 with the 32-bit source register s32 or loads the destination register d32 with the contents of the memory location ms.

XCHG s16,s/ms16
XCHG s/ms16,s16 — *Exchange register/memory with register/memory*
This is basically an exchange between the contents of a 16-bit register and another 16-bit register or a memory location, or an exchange between a 16-bit register or memory location and another 16-bit register. If a memory operand is used, then the execution is treated as an atomic operation as the LOCK is asserted.

ARITHMETIC AND LOGICAL

ADD, ADDC, FADD
ADD Ld/md8, Imm8 — *Add, add with carry, floating-point add*
It adds the immediate byte to the 8-bit destination register/memory and the result is stored in the destination register or memory location.

ADD d16, s/ms16 — It adds the 16-bit destination register to the 16-bit source register or memory, and the result is stored in the 16-bit destination register.

FADD ms32 — It adds the contents of the memory location ms to the stack, and the result is stored in the stack.

Sec. 4.5 Case Studies

SUB, FSUB	*Subtract, floating-point subtract*
SUB Ld/md8, Imm8	It subtracts the immediate byte from the 8-bit register or memory location, and the result is stored in the destination register or memory location.
SUB d16, s/ms16	It subtracts the 16-bit source register or memory location from the 16-bit destination register, and the result is stored in the 16-bit destination register.
FSUB ms32	It subtracts the contents of the memory location ms from the stack and the result is stored in the stack.
MUL, FMUL	*Multiply, floating-point multiplication*
MUL Ls8, Ls/ms8	Unsigned multiply $d16 = Ls8 * Ls/ms8$, where d16 is a 16-bit destination register that stores the result after multiplication.
MUL d16, s/ms16	Unsigned multiply $d'16{:}d16 = d16 * s/ms16$, where $d'16{:}d16$ is a 16-bit destination register pair that holds the result after multiplication.
FMUL ms32	It multiplies the stack with the contents of the memory location ms, and the result is stored in the stack.
DIV, FDIV	*Division, floating-point division*
DIV Ld8, Ls/ms8	Unsigned divide d16 by Ls/ms8 (Ld8=Quotient & Hd8=Remainder).
DIV d16, s/ms16	Unsigned divide $d'16{:}d16$ (d16=Quotient & $d'16$ = Remainder).
FDIV ms32	It divides the stack with the contents of the memory location ms, and the remainder is stored in the stack.
CMP Ls/ms8, Imm8	It compares immediate byte to register Ls8 or memory location. This instruction subtracts the second operand from the first but does not store the result. It only affects flags.
CMP s16, s/ms16	It compares one 16-bit register with another or a memory location.
AND Ls/ms8, Imm8	AND immediate byte to register or a memory location. Here there is a bit-wise manipulation, in which each bit is a 1 if both corresponding bits of the operands are 1 and otherwise 0.
AND s16, s/ms16	AND one 16-bit register with another register or memory location. It is basically used to mask bits.

CONTROL

JMP	*Unconditional jump*
JMP d/md16	The target address for the jump instruction is obtained from the 16-bit destination register or memory location.
JMP Disp16	The target address for the jump instruction is obtained by adding the displacement Disp16 to the address of the instruction following the jump instruction.
Jcc	*Conditional jump*
JNZ Disp16	It checks the zero flag; if the zero flag is 0, it branches to the target address obtained by adding the displacement to the address of the instruction following the jump instruction.
JZ Disp16	It checks the zero flag; if the zero flag is 1, it branches to the target address determined in the above described manner.

SYSTEM

MOV d32 CR	*Load from control register*
	It loads the contents of the control register CR to the general-purpose register.
HLT	*Halt*
	It basically halts the instruction execution and, on interrupt, resumes instruction from the point after halt.

4.5.3 Case Study III: Alpha AXP Microprocessor

The Digital Equipment Corporation (DEC) began the planning and design of the Alpha AXP architecture in 1988, with the knowledge that existing 32-bit architectures would soon run out of address bits. In February 1992, DEC claimed that Alpha is the world's fastest microprocessor. It is also the first 64-bit processor. Alpha runs at 200 MHz, which results in 400 MIPS or 200 Mflops.

Although compatibility with a large existing customer base was a concern, the AXP was designed from the ground up as a new architecture free of the constraints of past hardware compatibility. Unlike the Pentium, which has gone to great lengths to remain compatible with the past line of architecture, DEC decided to avoid past errors and quick fixes by relegating compatibility to software translation [MCL 93]. There are no specific VAX or MIPS features carried directly in the Alpha AXP architecture for compatibility reasons [SIT 93].

Sec. 4.5   Case Studies   **165**

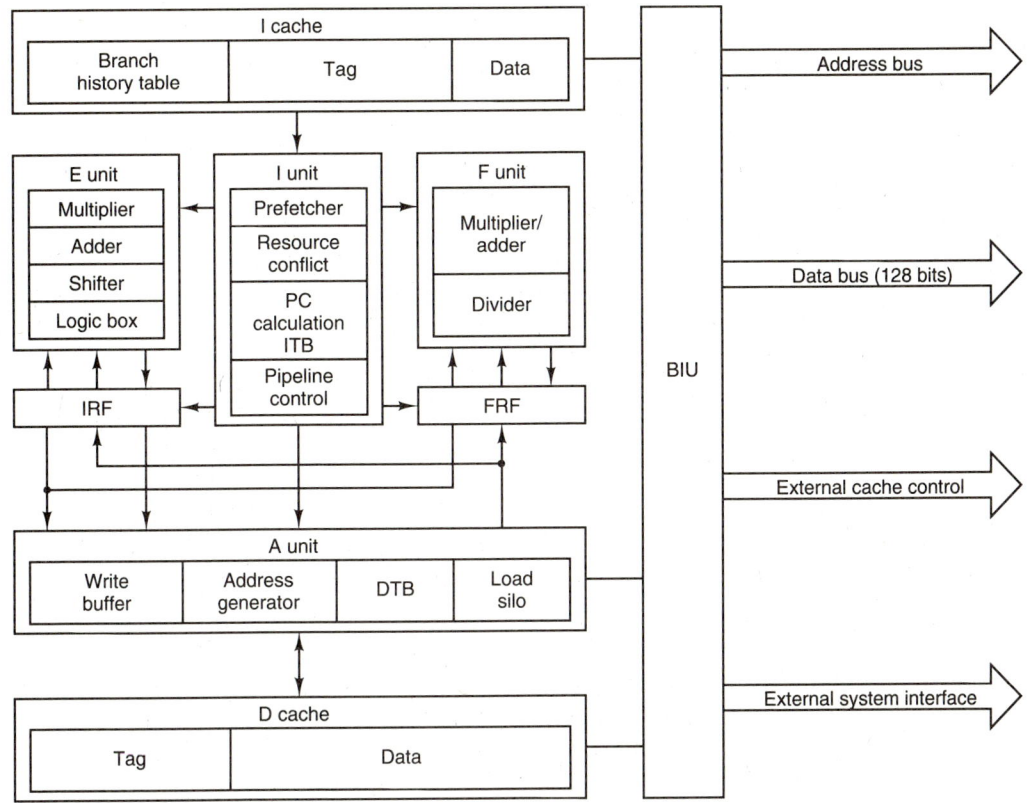

Figure 4.10   Block diagram of the Alpha AXP/210641 (from [DIG 92]). Reprinted with permission of Digital Equipment Corp.

By starting the design from scratch, the Alpha was allowed a clean start, with such features as a full 64-bit linear address space, as opposed to segmented memory or even 32-bit memory with 64-bit extensions evident in other microprocessors. Chip real estate that would have been consumed with components for backward compatibility has been put to better use for things such as enlarged on-chip caches and more execution units. The AXP was designed with a target product longevity of 15 to 25 years in mind.

The Alpha AXP/21064 microprocessor is the first commercial implementation of the Alpha AXP architecture. It is a CMOS chip containing 1.68 million transistors. The AXP/21064 is a RISC architecture. Only LOAD and STORE instructions access memory. All data are moved between the registers and memory without any computation, and all computation is performed on values in the registers. Figure 4.10 shows the main components of the AXP/21064 [DIG 92]. The AXP/21064 consists of an instruction unit (I unit), an integer execution unit (E unit), a floating-point execution unit (F unit), a data cache, an instruction cache, an integer register file (IRF), a floating-point register file (FRF), and an address unit (A unit).

The data cache feeds the A unit, and the instruction cache supplies the I unit. The data cache is an 8-Kbyte, direct-mapped cache with 32-byte line entries. The data cache uses write through for cache coherency. The instruction cache, likewise, is 8 Kbytes in size and organized as direct mapping with 32-byte line entries.

The 64-bit integer execution unit contains an adder, a multiplier, a shifter, and a logic unit. It also has an integer register file (IRF). The integer register file contains thirty-two 64-bit general-purpose registers, R0 through R31. Register R31 is wired to read as zero, and any writes to R31 are ignored. The IRF has six ports; four of these are output (read) ports and two are input (write) ports. These ports allow parallel execution of both integer operations and load, store, or branch operations.

The floating-point unit contains an adder, multiplier, and divider. It also contains a floating-point register file (FRF). The FRF contains thirty-two 64-bit floating-point registers and has five ports (three output and two input ports).

The address unit performs all load and store operations. It consists of four main components: address translation data path, address translation lookaside buffer (TLB), bus interface unit (BIU), and write buffer. The address translation data path has an adder that generates effective logical addresses for load and store instructions. The TLB is a fully associative cache with 32 entries, which translates a logical address to a physical address. The BIU resolves three types of CPU-generated requests: data cache fills, instruction cache fills, and write buffer requests. It accesses off-chip caches to service such requests. The write buffer has four entries; each entry has 32 bytes. It serves as an interface buffer between the CPU and the off-chip cache. The CPU writes data into the write buffer; then the buffer sends the data off-chip by requesting the BIU. In this way, the CPU can process store instructions at the peak rate of one quad word every clock cycle, which is greater than the rate at which the off-chip cache can accept data.

The instruction unit is responsible to issue instructions to the E, F, and A units. The detailed functioning of this unit is discussed next.

Instruction unit. The AXP/21064, through the use of features such as multiple execution units, pipelining, and branch prediction, is able to execute more than one instruction per cycle.

The AXP/21064 has two instruction pipelines, a seven-stage pipeline for integer operations and a ten-stage pipeline for floating-point operations. The seven stages in the integer pipe are instruction fetch (IF), swap dual issue instruction/branch prediction (SW), decode (I0), register file(s) access/issue check (I1), execution cycle 1 (A1), execution cycle 2 (A2), and integer register file write (WR). The ten stages in the floating-point pipe are instruction fetch (IF), swap dual issue instruction/branch prediction (SW), decode (I0), register file(s) access/issue check (I1), floating-point execution cycle 1 (F1), floating-point execution cycle 2 (F2), floating-point execution cycle 3 (F3), floating-point execution cycle 4 (F4), floating-point execution cycle 5 (F5), and floating-point register file write (FWR). The first four stages of the floating-point pipe are shared with the integer pipe; these stages comprise the prefetch and decode stage, and up to two instructions can be processed in parallel in each stage.

In the IF stage, a pair of instructions is fetched from the instruction cache. The SW stage performs branch prediction, as well as instruction swapping. When necessary, the SW stage swaps instruction pairs capable of dual issue. The I0 stage decodes and checks for dependencies. The I1 stage checks for register and execution unit conflicts by using the scoreboard technique and reads the operands to supply data to proper units. Stages A1 and A2 of the integer pipe are used for ALU operations and, when required, data cache access. Most ALU operations are completed in stage A1. Stages F1, F2, F3, F4, and F5 are used for floating-point operations. In F1, F2, and F3, for add/subtract operations, the exponent difference is calculated and mantissa alignment is performed. For multiplication, the multiply is performed in a pipelined array multiplier. In F4 and F5, the final addition and rounding are performed. In the final stage WR (FWR), the integer (floating-point) registers are updated with the final result.

The AXP/21064 allows dual issue of instructions, but there are slight restrictions concerning instruction pairs. In general, the instructions are paired based on the following rules:

Any integer operate can be paired with any floating-point operate.

Any load/store can be paired with any operate.

Any floating-point operate can be paired with any floating-point branch.

Any integer operate can be paired with any integer branch.

There are two exceptions to these rules. The integer store and floating-point operate cannot be paired. Also, the floating-point store and integer operate are disallowed as pairs.

The instruction unit always issues instructions in order of their appearance in the code. If two instructions can be paired and their required resources are available, both instructions are issued in parallel. If the two instructions cannot be paired or the required resources are available for only the first instruction, the first instruction is issued. If the required resources for the first instruction are not available, the second instruction cannot be issued even if its resources are available.

AXP/21064 employs design strategies, such as static and dynamic branch prediction, to minimize the penalties associated with conditional branch instructions. In static branch prediction, branches are predicted based on the sign of their displacement field. If the sign is positive, branches are predicted not to be taken. If the sign is negative, branches are predicted to be taken. In other words, forward branches are predicted as not taken, and backward branches are predicted as taken. In dynamic branch prediction, branches are predicted based on a single history bit provided for each instruction location in the instruction cache. The first time a branch is executed, prediction is done based on the sign of its displacement field. For the next execution of the branch, the history bit can be used for the prediction.

AXP/21064 does not support a delayed branching option. Although this option may increase the performance of architectures that allow dual issue of instructions, it has less effect on performance when many instructions can be issued in parallel. In the development of AXP architecture, every effort was made to avoid options that would not scale well with an increase in the number of instructions issued in parallel. The designers of AXP expect that future versions will be able to issue ten instructions every clock cycle. That is, instead of one instruction, up to nine instructions would be needed in the delay slot. Often, is not possible to schedule the next nine instructions after a branch with instructions that are independent from the branch instruction.

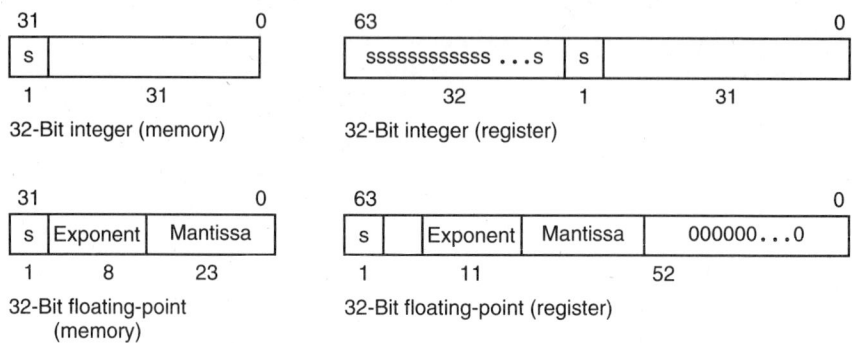

Figure 4.11 Representation of 32-bit integer and floating-point values in 64-bit registers.

Operand types. AXP/21064 supports three different data types: integer, IEEE floating point, and VAX floating point [BRU 91]. Each can be 32 or 64 bits. In AXP/21064, 32-bit operands are stored in canonical form in 64-bit registers. A canonical form is a standard way of representation for redundantly encoded values. As shown in Figure 4.11, the canonical form of a 32-bit integer value, stored in a 64-bit integer register, has the most significant 33 bits all set equal to the sign bit (bit 31). This allows the branch prediction mentioned previously to treat a 32-bit value stored in the 64-bit register just as if it were a 64-bit operand. With a 32-bit canonical value in a 64-bit floating-point register, the 8-bit exponent field is expanded out to 11 bits. Likewise, the 23-bit mantissa field is expanded to 52 bits.

Instruction set. Following the RISC design characteristic, AXP/21064 has a fixed size and simple, short instructions. All instructions are 32 bits long. The instructions fit into four formats: memory, operate, branch, and PALcode (privileged architecture library) [SIT 92]. Figure 4.12 illustrates the instruction formats.

Every instruction is comprised of a 6-bit opcode and 0 to 3 register address fields (Ra, Rb, Rc). The remaining bits contain function, literal values, or displacement fields. The memory format is used to transfer data between registers and memory and for subroutine jumps. A set of miscellaneous instructions (such as fetch and memory barrier) is specified when the displacement field is replaced with a function code. The operate format is used for instructions that perform operations on integer or floating-point registers. Integer operands can specify a literal constant or an integer register using bit 12. If bit 12 is 0, the Rb field specifies a source register. If bit 12 is 1, an 8-bit positive integer is formed by bits 13 to 20. The branch format is used for conditional branch instructions. The PALcode format is used to specify extended processor functions.

There are a total of 143 instructions in the AXP/21064. The following list contains some of the integer instructions. (Similar instructions to those on the list are also available for floating-point numbers.) Each instruction (or group of instructions) has its own subdivision that contains a short description for that instruction.

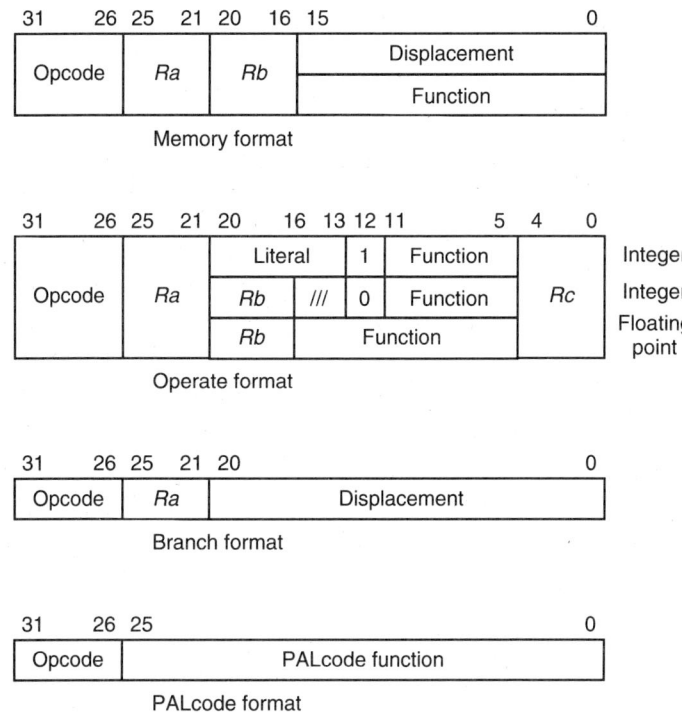

Figure 4.12 Instruction formats of Alpha AXP/21064.

DATA TRANSFERS

LDA Ra, Rb, Disp16	*Load address*
LDAH Ra, Rb, Disp16	*Load address high*
	This instruction loads into Ra, a virtual address created by adding register Rb to the 16-bit displacement field for LDA and 65536 times the 16-bit displacement field for LDAH.
LDL	*Load register with double word from memory*
LDQ	*Load register with quad word from memory*
LDx Ra, Rb, Disp16	This instruction loads into Ra the contents of memory at the virtual address created by adding register Rb to the 16-bit displacement field.
STL	*Store double word from register to memory*
STQ	*Store quad word from register to memory*
STx Ra, Rb, Disp16	Register Ra is stored into the memory location at the virtual address computed by adding register Rb to the 16-bit displacement field.

ARITHMETIC AND LOGICAL

ADDL	*Add double word*
ADDQ	*Add quad word*
ADDx Ra, Rb, Rc	
ADDx Ra, #, Rc	Register Ra is added to register Rb or a literal; sum is stored in register Rc.
SUBL	*Subtract double word*
SUBQ	*Subtract quad word*
SUBx Ra, Rb, Rc	
SUBx Ra, #, Rc	Register Rb or a literal is subtracted from register Ra with the result stored in Rc.
MULL	*Multiply double word*
MULQ	*Multiply quad word*
MULx Ra, Rb, Rc	
MULx Ra, #, Rc	Register Ra is multiplied by Rb or a literal and is stored into register Rc.
UMULH Ra, Rb, Rc	*Unsigned multiply quad word high*
UMULH Ra, #, Rc	Register Ra and Rb or a literal value is multiplied to produce a 128-bit result. The high-order 64 bits are written to register Rc.
CMPEQ	*Compare signed quad word equal*
CMPLE	*Compare signed quad word less than or equal*
CMPLT	*Compare signed quad word less than*
CMPxx Ra, Rb, Rc	
CMPxx Ra, #, Rc	Register Ra is compared to register Rb or a literal value. If the specified condition is true, the value 1 is written to register Rc; otherwise, a 0 is written to register Rc.
AND	*Logical and*
BIC	*Logical and with complement*
BIS	*Logical or*
EQV	*Logical equivalence (XORNOT)*
ORNOT	*Logical or with complement*
XOR	*Logical exclusive-or*
xxx Ra, Rb, Rc	
xxx Ra, #, Rc	These logical instructions perform their respective Boolean functions between registers Ra and Rb or a literal. The result of these functions are placed in register Rc.

Sec. 4.5   Case Studies   171

CMOVEQ	*CMove if register equal to zero*
CMOVGE	*CMove if register greater than or equal to zero*
CMOVGT	*CMove if register greater than zero*
CMOVLBC	*CMove if register low bit is set to zero (bit is clear)*
CMOVLBS	*CMove if register low bit is set to one (bit is set)*
CMOVLE	*CMove if register less than or equal to zero*
CMOVLT	*CMove if register less than zero*
CMOVNE	*CMove if register not equal to zero*
CMOVxx Ra, Rb, Rc	
CMOVxx Ra, #, Rc	Conditional move: register Ra is tested for specified condition. If test outcome is true, then the value of Rb (or literal) is written to register Rc.
SLL	*Shift left logical*
SRL	*Shift right logical*
SxL Ra, Rb, Rc	
SxL Ra, #, Rc	Register Ra is shifted left or right logically up to 63 bits by the value stored in register Rb or by a literal value. The result is stored into register Rc, and zero bits are propagated into the bit positions vacated by shifts.
SRA Ra, Rb, Rc	*Shift right arithmetic*
SRA Ra, #, Rc	Register Ra is right shifted arithmetically up to 63 bits by the value stored in register Rb or by a literal value. The result of the shift is placed in register Rc with the sign bit propagated into the vacant bit positions created by the shift.

CONTROL

BEQ	*Branch if register equal to zero*
BGE	*Branch if register greater than or equal to zero*
BGT	*Branch if register greater than zero*
BLE	*Branch if register less than or equal to zero*
BLT	*Branch if register less than zero*
BNE	*Branch if register not equal to zero*
Bxx Ra, Disp	The value of register Ra is tested for each specified relationship. If the condition is true, the program counter (PC) is loaded with the target virtual address created by shifting the displacement left 2 bits (to address a double-word boundary), sign extending to 64-bits, and adding it to the updated PC. Otherwise, PC points to the next sequential instruction.

BR Ra, Disp	*Unconditional branch*
BSR Ra, Disp	*Branch to subroutine*

The target address is created by taking the displacement, shifting it left 2 bits, sign extending to 64 bits, and adding it to the updated PC. The PC of the following instruction is stored in register Ra; then the target address is stored into the PC. BSR and BR both act identically, except BSR pushes the return address onto the branch prediction stack.

JMP Ra, Rb, hint	*Jump*
JSR Ra, Rb, hint	*Jump to subroutine*
RET Ra, Rb, hint	*Return from subroutine*
xxx Ra, Rb, hint	

The PC of the next instruction is stored in register Ra; then the target virtual address in register Rb is loaded into the PC. These jumps operate the same; however, they behave differently in regards to hints provided for branch prediction. The hint data are stored in the displacement field.

4.5.4 Case Study IV: PowerPC Microprocessor:

The PowerPC family of microprocessors is being jointly developed by Apple, IBM, and Motorola corporation and includes processors such as 601, 603, 604, and 620. Although these processors differ in terms of performance and some architectural features, they all are based on the IBM's POWER processor. This architectural heritage allows the softwares that have been developed for IBM's POWER to be used on the PowerPC family. The changes made to POWER are simplifying the architecture, increasing clock rate, enabling a higher degree of superscalar design, allowing extension to a true 64-bit architecture, and supporting multiprocessor environment [DIE 94]. For compatibility with existing software, the designers of PowerPC retained POWER's basic instruction set. In the following, the architecture of PowerPC 601 is described [MOT 93].

The PowerPC 601 is based on the RISC architecture. It is a single-chip superscalar microprocessor implemented in CMOS technology containing 2.8 million transistors. The PowerPC runs at 60, 66, or 80 MHz. It has a 64-bit data bus and a 32-bit address bus. It can execute three instructions per clock cycle. Figure 4.13 shows the main components of the 601 processor. The 601 has an instruction unit that fetches the instructions and passes them to the proper execution units. There are three execution units, integer unit (IU), floating-point unit (FPU), and branch processing unit (BPU). The IU executes instructions such as integer arithmetic/logical, integer/floating-point load/store, and memory management instructions. The FPU executes all floating-point arithmetic and store instructions. It supports all the IEEE 754 floating-point types. Integer and floating-point units maintain dedicated register files so that they can do computations simultaneously without interference. These register files are 32 gen-

Sec. 4.5 Case Studies

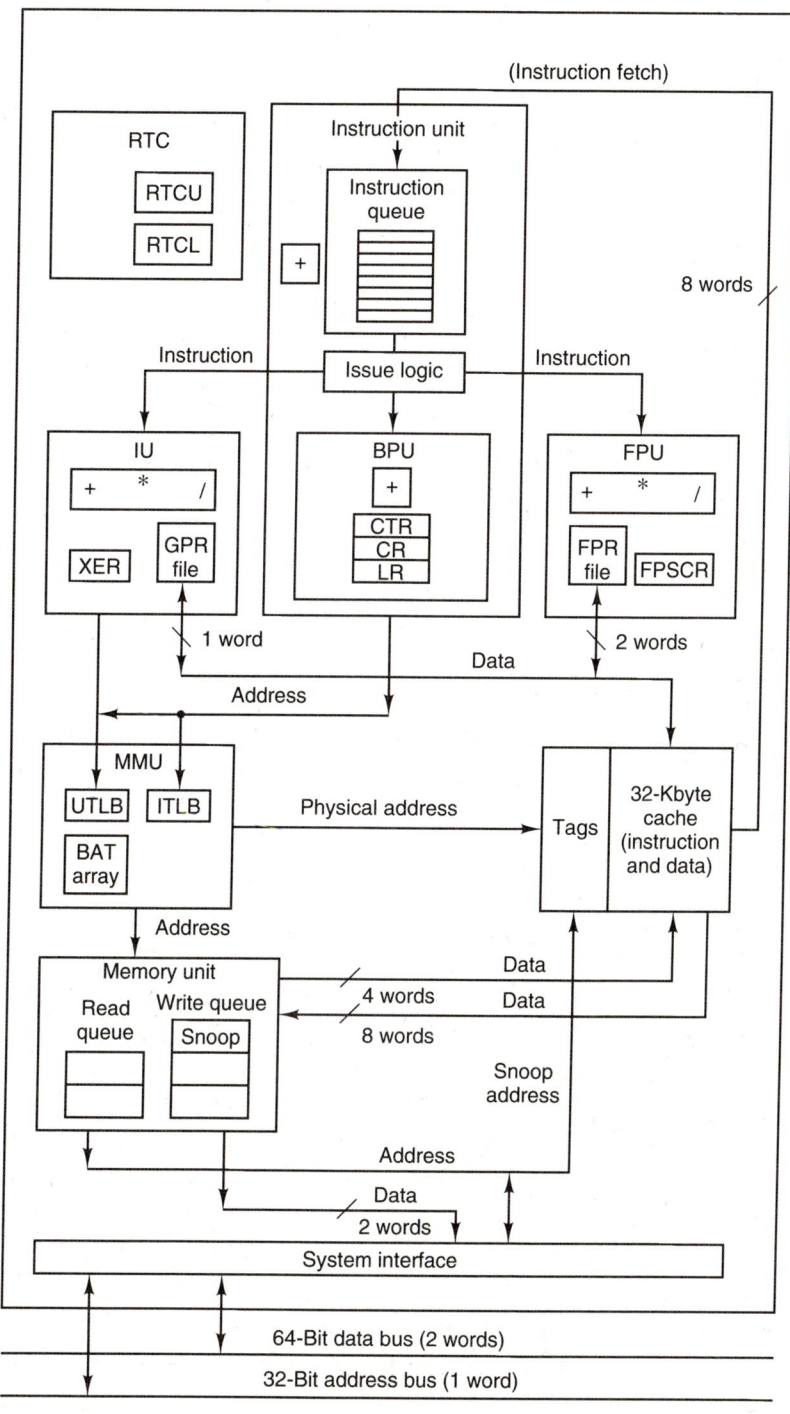

Figure 4.13 Block diagram of the PowerPC (from [MOT 93]). Reprinted with the permission of Motorola and IBM.

eral-purpose registers (GPRs), either 32 bits wide (in a 32-bit implementation) or 64 bits wide (in a 64-bit implementation), and thirty-two 64-bit floating-point registers (FPRs). The BPU calculates branch target address and handles branch prediction and resolution. It contains an adder to compute branch target address and three special-purpose registers: count register (CTR), control register (CR), and link register (LR).

The 601 includes a 32-Kbyte, eight-way, set-associative cache for instructions and data. This cache is logically organized as eight memory blocks, each containing 64 lines. Each line contains two sectors (each sector has 32 bytes), a 20-bit address tag, 4 state bits (two per sector), and several replacement control bits. Cache reload operations are done on a sector basis. Least recently used (LRU) policy is used for replacing cache sectors. At any given time, each cache sector is in one of the states of modified, exclusive, shared, or invalid. The cache can operate in either write-back or write-through mode.

The 601 also has a memory management unit (MMU) that translates the logical address generated by the instruction unit into the physical address. The MMU supports 4 petabytes (2^{52}) of virtual memory and 4 gigabytes (2^{32}) of physical memory. It implements demand paged virtual memory system.

Instruction unit. The instruction unit, which contains the BPU and an instruction queue (IQ), determines the address of the next instruction to be fetched based on the information from a sequential fetcher and the BPU. The instruction unit also performs pipeline interlock and controls forwarding of the common data bus. The IQ can hold up to eight instructions (8 words) and can be filled from the cache during one clock cycle. The sequential fetcher computes the address of the next instruction based on the address of the last fetch and the number of the instructions in the IQ.

As shown in Figure 4.14, an instruction in the IQ may be issued to BPU, IU, or FPU under certain circumstances. The BPU looks through the first four instructions of the IQ for conditional branch instructions. When it finds one, it tries to resolve it as soon as possible. Meanwhile, it uses static branch prediction strategy to predict the branch path (sequential or target). The instruction unit fetches from predicted path until the conditional branch is resolved. Instructions provided beyond the predicted path are not completely executed until the branch is resolved; thus sequential execution is achieved.

The fetch arbitration (FA) stage generates the address of the next instruction(s) to be fetched and sends that to cache system (memory subsystem). The cache arbitration (CARB) stage is responsible for arbitration between the generated addresses (or memory requests) and the cache system. Memory requests are ordered in terms of their priorities. For most operations, this stage is overlapped with the FA stage. During the cache access (CACC) stage, data/instructions are read from the cache. When instructions are read, they are loaded into the instruction queue in the dispatch stage (DS). On every clock cycle, the DS stage can issue as many as three instructions, one to each of the processing unit IU, FPU, and BPU. The issued instructions must be from instruction queue entries IQ0 to IQ7. The entry IQ0 can be viewed as part of the integer decode stage of the integer unit.

The integer unit consists of five stages: integer decode (ID), integer execute (IE), integer completion (IC), integer arithmetic write back (IWA), and integer load write

Sec. 4.5   Case Studies   175

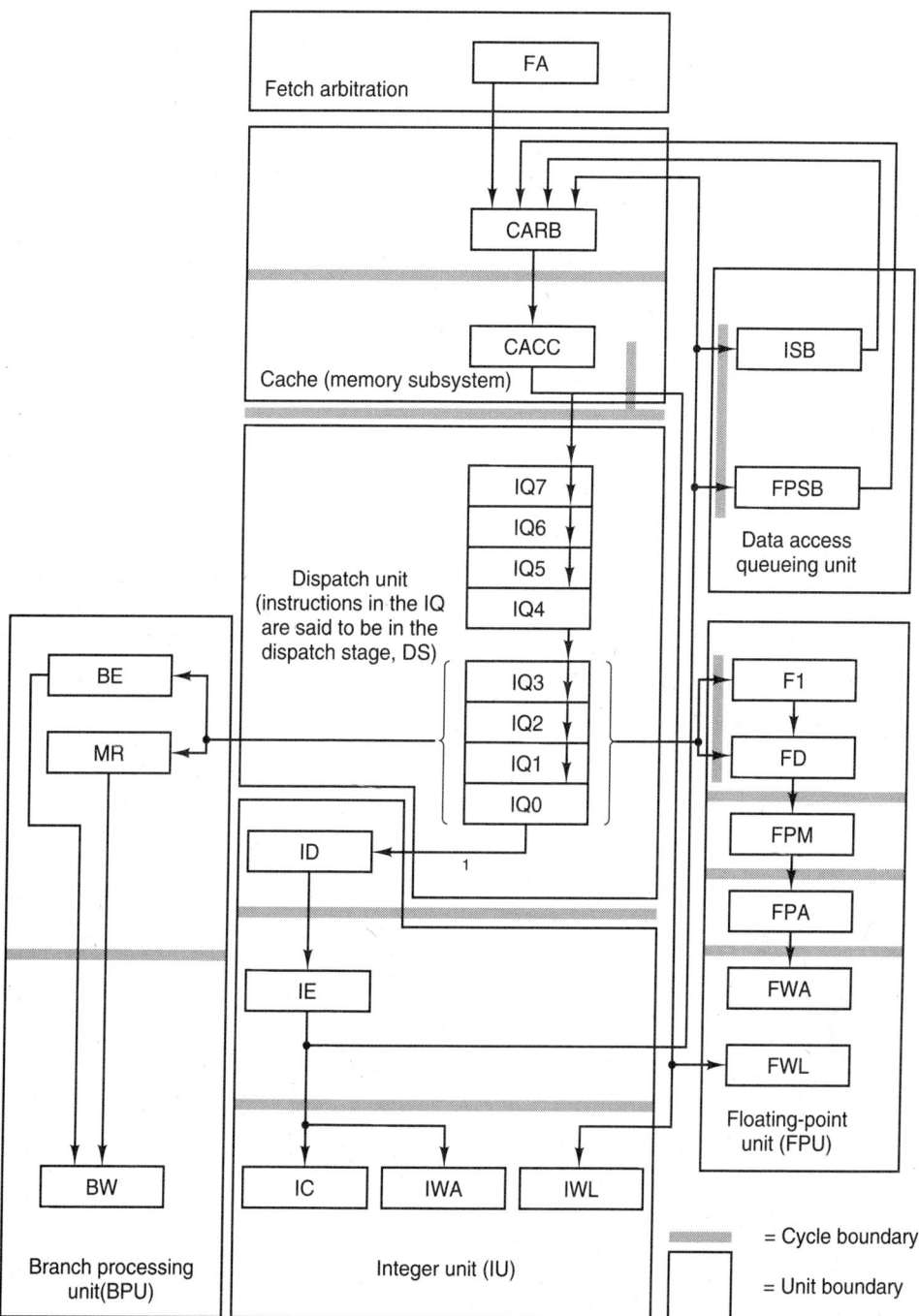

[1]An integer instruction can be passed to the ID stage in the same cycle in which it enters IQ0.

Figure 4.14 Pipeline diagram of the PowerPC processor core (from [MOT 93]). Reprinted with permission of Motorola and IBM.

back (IWL), where the stages IC, IWA, and IWL are overlapped. During the ID stage, integer instructions are decoded and the operands are fetched from general-purpose registers. The IE executes one integer instruction per cycle. In this stage, forwarding technique is sometimes used to provide operands for an instruction. That is, the results produced in the IE stage can be used as source operands for the instruction that enters IE in the next cycle. An instruction that leaves the IE stage enters the IC stage in parallel with entering some other stages (such as CACC for load/stores and IWA for arithmetic operations). The IC stage indicates that the execution of the instruction is completed, even though its results may not have been written into the registers or cache. The results of the instruction are made available to the other units. The instructions that enter CACC stage for cache access after completing the IE stage also enter the integer store buffer (ISB). The ISB stage holds such instructions until they can succeed to access the cache. [The floating-point store buffer (FPSB) is used for floating-point instructions.] In this way, the ISB allows the instruction to free up the IE stage for another instruction. In the IWA stage, the results of integer arithmetic instructions are written in the general-purpose registers. In the IWL stage, as the results of integer load instructions, data values are loaded into the general-purpose registers from cache or from memory.

The floating-point unit consists of six stages: floating-point instruction queue (FI), floating-point decode (FD), floating-point multiply (FPM), floating-point add (FPA), floating-point arithmetic write back (FWA), and floating-point load write back (FWL). The stages FI and FD are overlapped, and also the stages FWA and FWL are overlapped. The FI stage is a single buffer that keeps a floating-point instruction that has been issued but cannot be decoded because the FD is occupied with a stalled instruction. During the FD stage, floating-point instructions are decoded and the operands are fetched from floating-point registers. The FPM stage performs the first part of a multiply operation. (The multiply operation is spread across the FPM and FPA.) On average, it takes one cycle to perform a single-precision multiply operation and two cycles for a double-precision multiply operation. The FPA stage performs an addition operation or completes a multiply operation. In the FWA stage, the results of instructions are normalized, rounded, and written in the floating-point registers. In the FWL stage, as the results of floating-point load instructions, data values are loaded into the floating-point registers from cache or from memory.

The branch processing unit consists of three stages: branch execute (BE), mispredict recovery (MR), and branch write back (BW); the stages BE and MR are overlapped. During the BE stage, for a given branch instruction, the branch path is either determined or predicted. When a branch is conditional, it enters the MR stage in parallel with the BE stage. The MR stage keeps the address of the nonpredicted path of the conditional branches until the branch is resolved. If the branch path was predicted incorrectly, the MR stage lets the fetch arbitration stage start fetching the correct path. During BW stage, some branches update the link register (LR) or count register (CTR).

Operand types. The PowerPC 601 processor supports several operand types. The fundamental operand types are byte (8 bits), word (16 bits), double-word (32 bits), and quad word (64 bits). There are some specialized operand types, such as integer (32

Sec. 4.5 Case Studies

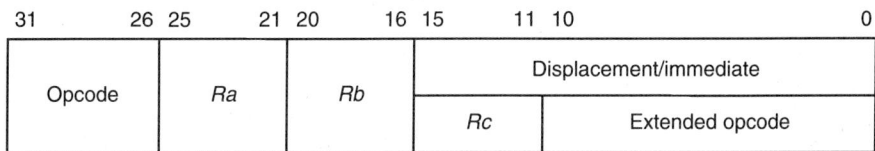

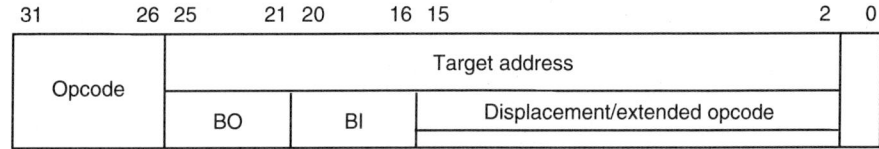

Branch format

BO field specifies options for the branch conditional instructions.

BI field specifies the bit in the condition register to be used as the condition of a branch conditional instruction.

Figure 4.15 Instruction formats of PowerPC 601.

bits, 16 bits), single-precision floating point (32 bits), double-precision floating point (64 bits), and extended-precision floating point (80 bits).

Instruction set. Following the RISC characteristics, the PowerPC 601 has a fixed size and simple short instructions. All instructions are 32 bits long. The 601 for load and store operations supports three simple addressing modes. They are register indirect mode, base register mode, and register indirect with indexing mode. For base register mode, the contents of a general-purpose register are added to an immediate value to generate the effective address. For register indirect with indexing mode, the contents of the two general-purpose registers are added to generate the effective address. Figure 4.15 illustrates the formats for most of the instructions. Most instructions are comprised of a 6-bit opcode and 0 to 3 register address fields (Ra, Rb, Rc). The remaining bits contain immediate, displacement, target address, condition code, or extended opcode.

The following list contains some of the instructions that are used by the PowerPC 601 processor. Each instruction (or group of instructions) has its own subdivision, which contains a short description. In the list, destination register is specified by d and source registers are specified by s, s1, and s2. The immediate address is specified by the operand Imm and the displacement by Disp.

DATA TRANSFERS

lbz, lhz, lwz   *Load byte, load half-word, load word*
lfs, lfd   *Load floating point single precision,*
                  load floating point double precision

lbz d, s1, Disp16

lbzx d, s1, s2	Load a byte from the addressed memory location into register d. The register s1 contains the base address. To s1, either the 16-bit displacement field or the index contained in the s2 is added.
stb, sth, stw	*Store byte, store half-word, store word*
stfs, stfd	*Store floating point single precision, store floating point double precision*
stb s, s1, Disp16	
stbx s, s1, s2	Store the contents of register s into the byte in the addressed memory location. The register s1 contains the base address. To s1, either the 16-bit displacement field or the index contained in the s2 is added.
lhbrx, lwbrx	*Load half-word byte reverse indexed, load word byte reverse indexed*
lhbrx d, s1, s2	Bits 0 to 7 of the half-word in memory are loaded into d[24-31] and bits 8 to 15 are loaded into d[16-23]. The rest of the bits are cleared to 0.
sthbrx, stwbrx	*Store half-word byte reverse indexed, store word byte reverse indexed*
sthbrx s, s1, s2	s[24-31] are stored at bits 0 to 7 of the half-word in memory and bits s[16-23] are stored at bits 8 to 15 in the memory.

ARITHMETIC AND LOGICAL

add, addi	*Add, add immediate*
subf, subfic	*Subtract from, subtract from immediate carrying*
mul, div	*Multiply, divide*
fadd, fsub	*Floating-point add, floating-point subtract*
fmul, fdiv	*Floating-point multiply, floating-point divide*
fmadd	*Floating-point multiply–add*
fmadd d, s1, s2, s3	The following operation is performed: d = (s1) * (s2) + (s3)
fmsub	*Floating-point multiply–subtract*
fmsub d, s1, s2, s3	The following operation is performed: d = (s1) * (s2) −(s3)
and, nand, nor, or, xor	*AND, NAND, NOR, OR, XOR*
and d, s1, s2	The contents of s1 are ANDed with the contents of s2, and the result is placed into register d.
andi, ori, xori	*AND Immediate, OR Immediate, XOR Immediate*
andi d, s, Imm16	The contents of s are ANDed with x'0000' ‖ Imm16, and the result is placed into d. The notation ‖ indicates concatenation operation, and

Sec. 4.5 Case Studies

                                      x'0000' represents the value 0 in hexadecimal format.

cmp, cmpi	*Compare, compare immediate*
fcmpo, fcmpu	*Floating-point compare ordered, floating-point compare unordered*
cmp crfd, s1, s2	The contents of s1 are compared with the contents of s2, treating the operands as the signed integers. The result of the comparison is placed into the CR (condition register) field specified by operand crfd.
slw, srw	*Shift left word, shift right word*
slw d, s1, s2	The contents of s1 are shifted left the number of bits specified by s2[27-31]. The vacated positions on the right are filled with 0. The 32-bit result is placed into d.
rlwinm, rlwnm	*Rotate left word immediate, then AND with mask; rotate left word, then AND with mask*
rlwinm d, s, SH, MB, ME	The contents of the register s are rotated left by the number of bits specified by operand SH. A mask is generated having 1 bits from the bit specified by operand MB through the bit specified by the operand ME and 0 bits elsewhere. The rotated data are ANDed with the generated mask and the result is placed into the register d.

CONTROL

b, bc	*Branch, branch conditional*
b target-address	Branch to the address computed as the sum of the target address and the address of the current instruction.

SYSTEM

sc	*System call*
rfi	*Return from interrupt*
mfcr d	*Move from condition register*
	The contents of the condition register, CR, are placed into register d.
mtsr d, s	*Move to segment register*
	The contents of register s are placed into segment register specified by the operand d.

4.5.5 Summary of the Case Studies

Table 4.1 summarizes some of the important features of the microprocessors that were discussed in this section.

TABLE 4.1 FEATURES OF MOTOROLA 88110, ALPHA AXP 21064, PENTIUM, AND POWERPC 601 MICROPROCESSORS

	Motorola 88110	Alpha AXP 21064	Pentium	Power PC 601
Company	Motorola Inc.	Digital Equipment Corp.	Intel Corp.	IBM Corp. and Motorola, Inc.
Introduction date	–/91	2/92	3/93	4/93
Architecture type	RISC	RISC	CISC	RISC
Integer register type	32	32	64	32
On-chip cache, Kbytes (instruction/data)	8/8	8/8	8/8	32
Number of registers (general purpose/FP)	32/32	32/32	8/8	32/32
Instruction issue rate per cycle	2	2	2	3
Number of pipeline stages (integer/FP)	NS	7/10	5/8	4/6
Multiprocessing support	No	Yes	Yes	Yes
Technology	CMOS	0.68 um CMOS	0.8 um BiCMOS	0.65 um CMOS
Die size, mm	15 by 15	15.3 by 12.7	17.2 by 17.2	11 by 11
Transistors, millions	1.3	1.68	3.1	2.8
number of metal layers	3	3	3	4
operating voltage, V	5	3.3	5	3.6
Clock, MHz	33	200	66	80

N.S: not specified.

From the architectures of the processors discussed in this section, it is reasonable to conclude that most of the commercial microprocessors are either based on RISC architecture or based on both RISC and CISC architectures. Because of the progress in VLSI technology many microprocessors have their own on-chip caches. Usually, there are separate caches each of 8 Kbytes or more for instructions and data. The use of two caches, one for instructions and one for data, in contrast to a single cache, can considerably improve the access time and consequently improve a processor's performance. Furthermore, pipelining techniques are also used to increase the processor's performance. There are two types of pipelines, instruction pipeline and arithmetic pipeline. To improve the throughput of an instruction pipeline, three main hazards should be addressed: structural harzard, data hazard, and control hazard.

To address the structural hazard, most processors follow the superscalar approach, which allows multiple instructions to be issued simultaneously during each cycle. These processors are often implemented in CMOS technology, because in CMOS implementation the circuit density has increased at a much faster rate than the circuit speed. However, some processors (such as Intel Pentium) use BiCMOS technology, which provides high speed, high drive and low power.

Most processors use the scoreboarding scheme for handling data hazard. The scoreboard is implemented as a bit vector for which each bit corresponds to a register in the register files and is marked busy when an instruction issued for execution uses that register as a destination register.

To handle control hazard, most processors employ design strategies, such as delayed branching and static and dynamic branch prediction, to minimize the penalties associated with branch instructions.

BIBLIOGRAPHIC NOTES

The reference [DIE 92] presents a good description of the Motorola 88110 and was used for explaining the main components of the 88110. The reference [HAP 92] evaluates the performance of a processor with a two-level cache using simulation techniques. The reference [JOH 91] is used for CISC versus RISC. The references [DOB 92], [DIG 92], and [MCL 93] describe the Alpha AXP architecture. [MOT 93] was used for description of PowerPC 601.

REFERENCES

[ALP 93] ALPERT, DONALD, AND DROR AVNON, "Architecture of the Pentium Microprocessor," *IEEE Micro, 13*(3), June 1993, pp. 11–21.

[BAS 91] BASHTEEN, A., I. LUI, AND J. MULLAN, "A Superpipeline Approach to the MIPS Architecture," *IEEE Proc. 36th COMPCON*, 1991, pp. 8–12.

[BRU 91] BRUNNER, R., ED., *VAX Architecture Reference Manual*, 2nd ed. Bedford, MA: Digital Press, 1991.

[COL 88] COLWELL, ROBERT P., ET AL., "A VLIW Architecture for a Trace Scheduling Compiler," *IEEE Trans. Computers, 37*(8), 1988, pp. 967–979.

[DIE 92] DIEFENDORFF, KEITH, AND MICHAEL ALLEN, "Organization of the Motorola 88110 Superscalar RISC Microprocessor," *IEEE Micro*, April 1992, pp. 40–63.

[DIE 94] Diefendorff, Keith, Rich Oehler, and Ron Hochsprung, "Evolution of the PowerPC Architecture," *IEEE Micro, 14*(2), April 1994, pp. 34–49.

[DIG 92] "DECChip 21064-AA RISC Microprocessor," Hardware, Reference Manual, Digital Equipment Co., 1992.

[DOB 92] Dobberpuhl, Daniel W., et al., "A 200-MHz 64-Bit Dual-issue CMOS Microprocessor," *IEEE Solid-state Circuits, 27*(11), 1992, pp. 1555–1567; also reprinted in *Digital Technical J., 4*(4), 1992, pp. 35–50.

[FIS 83] Fisher, J. A., "Very Long Instruction Word Architectures and the ELI-512," *IEEE Proc. 10th Symp. Computer Architecture*, June 1983, pp. 140–150.

[HAP 92] Happel, L. P., and A. P. Jayasumana, "Performance of a RISC machine with Two Level Caches," *IEEE Proc.*, 139(3), 1992, pp. 221–229.

[IBM 90] "Special Issue: RISC System/6000," *IBM J. Research Develop., 34*(1), 1990.

[INT 93a] "Pentium Processor User's Manual—Volume 1: Pentium Processor Data Book," Intel Corp., 1993.

[INT 93b] "Pentium Processor User's Manual—Volume 3: Architecture and Programming Manual," Intel Corp., 1993.

[JOH 91] Johnson, Mike, *Superscalar Microprocessor Design*. Upper Saddle River, Prentice Hall, 1991.

[JOU 89] Jouppi, N. P., and D. W. Wall, "Available Instruction-level Parallelism for Superscalar and Superpipelined Machines," *Proc. ASPLOS III, Third Int. Conf. Architectural Support for Programming Languages and Operating Systems*, 1989, pp. 272–282.

[MCL 93] McLellan, Edward, "The Alpha AXP Architecture and 21064 Processor," *IEEE Micro, 13*(3), June 1993, pp. 36–47.

[MOT 91] Motorola, "MC88110—Second Generation RISC Microprocessor User's Manual," Motorola, Inc., 1991.

[MOT 93] Motorola, "PowerPC 601—RISC Microprocessor User's Manual," Motorola, Inc., 1993.

[OEH 91] Oehler, Richard R., and Michael W. Blasgen, "IBM RISC System/6000: Architecture and Performance," *IEEE Micro, 11*(3), June 1991, pp. 14–17, 56–62.

[PAT_82a] Patterson, D., and C. Sequin, "A VLSI RISC," *IEEE Computer, 15*(9), September 1982, pp. 8–21.

[SIT 92] Sites, Richard L., ed., *Alpha Architecture Reference Manual*. Bedford, MA: Digital Press, 1992.

[SIT 93] Sites, Richard L., "Alpha AXP Architecture," *Communications of the ACM*, 36(2), 1993, pp. 33–44.

[SUB 89] Subrata Dasgupta, *Computer Architecture—A Modern Synthesis*, Vol. 1. New York: John Wiley & Sons, 1989.

[THO 64] Thornton, James E., "Parallel Operation in the Control Data 6600," *Proc. Fall Joint Computer Conference*, 26, Part II, 1964, pp. 33–40.

[TOM 67] Tomasulo, R. M., "An Efficient Algorithm for Exploiting Multiple Arithmetic Units," *IBM J. Research Develop. 11*(1), 1967, pp. 25–33.

PROBLEMS

4.1. What are the main differences between RISC and CISC architectures? Considering cost and technology, which design is better? Why? [Your comment should be very precise, justified [possibly with citation], and complete.]

4.2. In this chapter it was mentioned that "As VLSI technology is improved, the RISC is always a step ahead compared to the CISC." Explain your own views and elaborate on this statement.

4.3. Compare the Harvard architecture with a single-cache architecture. What are the advantages and disadvantages of having two small caches (one for data and one for instruction) instead of having a single large cache (for data and instruction)?

4.4. What are the main advantages of having on-chip cache rather than having off-chip cache?

4.5. You are given a choice of two design strategies, one to have a large set of registers and a small cache on the processor's chip and the other to have a small set of registers and a large cache. Which one do you use? Why?

4.6. You are given the task of designing a hybrid architecture that involves a combination of RISC and CISC architectures. Considering cost and performance, what properties of RISC and CISC will you adapt in your hybrid design?

(Your answer should be precise and justified.)

4.7. In a superscalar design, it is possible for instructions to complete execution out of program order. Describe some of the techniques that have been used by the microprocessors to ensure in order execution completion of instructions. Your answer should be based on the architectures of the microprocessors that were discussed in this chapter.

4.8. In a superscalar design, one problem that should be addressed is data hazards. Describe techniques that have been employed in Motorola 88110, Pentium, and Alpha to avoid the hazard of data dependency.

4.9. Describe the function and structures of the following units:

  a. Target instruction cache (TIC) in Motorola 88110.

  b. Translation lookaside buffer (TLB) in Motorola 88110.

  c. u- and v-pipelines in Pentium.

  d. Branch target buffer (BTB) in Pentium.

  e. Integer pipeline in Alpha.

  f. Branch processing unit (BPU) in PowerPC.

  g. Instruction and data cache in PowerPC.

5

Interconnection Networks

5.1 INTRODUCTION

Networking strategy was originally employed in the 1950s by the telephone industry as a means of reducing the time required for a call to go through. Similarly, the computer industry employs networking strategy to provide fast communication between computer subparts, particularly with regard to parallel machines.

The performance requirements of many applications, such as weather prediction, signal processing, radar tracking, and image processing, far exceed the capabilities of single-processor architectures. Parallel machines break a single problem down into parallel tasks that are performed concurrently, reducing significantly the application processing time.

Any parallel system that employs more than one processor per application program must be designed to allow its processors to communicate efficiently; otherwise, the advantages of parallel processing may be negated by inefficient communication. This fact emphasizes the importance of interconnection networks to overall parallel system performance. In many proposed or existing parallel processing architectures, an interconnection network is used to realize transportation of data between processors or between processors and memory modules.

This chapter deals with several aspects of the networks used in modern (and theoretical) computers. After classifying various network structures, some of the most well known networks are discussed, along with a list of advantages and disadvantages associated with their use. Some of the elements of network design are also explored to give the reader an understanding of the complexity of such designs.

5.2 NETWORK TOPOLOGY

Network topology refers to the layouts of links and switch boxes that establish interconnections. The links are essentially physical wires (or channels); the switch boxes are devices that connect a set of input links to a set of output links. There are two groups of network topologies: *static* and *dynamic*. Static networks provide fixed connections between nodes. (A node can be a processing unit, a memory module, an I/O module, or any combination thereof.) With a static network, links between nodes are unchangeable and cannot be easily reconfigured. Dynamic networks provide reconfigurable connections between nodes. The switch box is the basic component of the dynamic network. With a dynamic network the connections between nodes are established by the setting of a set of interconnected switch boxes.

In the following sections, examples of static and dynamic networks are discussed in detail.

5.2.1 Static Networks

There are various types of static networks, all of which are characterized by their node degree; node degree is the number of links (edges) connected to the node. Some well-known static networks are the following:

Degree 1: *shared bus*
Degree 2: *linear array, ring*
Degree 3: *binary tree, fat tree, shuffle-exchange*
Degree 4: *two-dimensional mesh (Illiac, torus)*
Varying degree: *n-cube, n-dimensional mesh, k-ary n-cube*

A measurement unit, called *diameter*, can be used to compare the relative performance characteristics of different networks. More specifically, the diameter of a network is defined as the largest minimum distance between any pair of nodes. The minimum distance between a pair of nodes is the minimum number of communication links (hops) that data from one of the nodes must traverse in order to reach the other node.

In the following sections, the listed static networks are discussed in detail.

Shared bus. The shared bus, also called *common bus*, is the simplest type of static network. The shared bus has a degree of 1. In a shared bus architecture, all the nodes share a common communication link, as shown in Figure 5.1. The shared bus is the least expensive network to implement. Also, nodes (units) can be easily added to

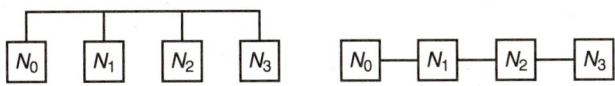

Figure 5.1 Shared bus.   **Figure 5.2** Linear array.

or deleted from this network. However, it requires a mechanism for handling conflict when several nodes request the bus simultaneously. This mechanism can be achieved through a bus controller, which gives access to the bus either on a first-come, first-served basis or through a priority scheme. (The structure of a bus controller is explained in the Chapter 6.) The shared bus has a diameter of 1 since each node can access the other nodes through the shared bus.

Linear array. The linear array (degree of 2) has each node connected with two neighbors (except the far-end nodes). The linear quality of this structure comes from the fact that the first and last nodes are not connected, as illustrated in Figure 5.2. Although the linear array has a simple structure, its design can mean long communication delays, especially between far-end nodes. This is because any data entering the network from one end must pass through a number of nodes in order to reach the other end of the network. A linear array, with N nodes, has a diameter of $N - 1$.

Ring. Another networking configuration with a simple design is the ring structure. A ring network has a degree of 2. Similar to the linear array, each node is connected to two of its neighbors, but in this case the first and last nodes are also connected to form a ring. Figure 5.3 shows a ring network. A ring can be unidirectional or bidirectional. In a unidirectional ring the data can travel in only one direction, clockwise or counterclockwise. Such a ring has a diameter of $N - 1$, like the linear array. However, a bidirectional ring, in which data travel in both directions, reduces the diameter by a factor of 2, or less if N is even. A bidirectional ring with N nodes has a diameter of $\lfloor N/2 \rfloor$. Although this ring's diameter is much better than that of the linear array, its configuration can still cause long communication delays between distant nodes for large N. A bidirectional ring network's reliability, as compared to the linear array, is also improved. If a node should fail, effectively cutting off the connection in one direction, the other direction can be used to complete a message transmission. Once the connection is lost between any two adjacent nodes, the ring becomes a linear array, however.

Binary tree. Figure 5.4 represents the structure of a binary tree with seven nodes. The top node is called the root, the four nodes at the bottom are called leaf (or terminal) nodes, and the rest of the nodes are called intermediate nodes. In such a network, each intermediate node has two children. The root has node address 1. The addresses of the children of a node are obtained by appending 0 and 1 to the node's

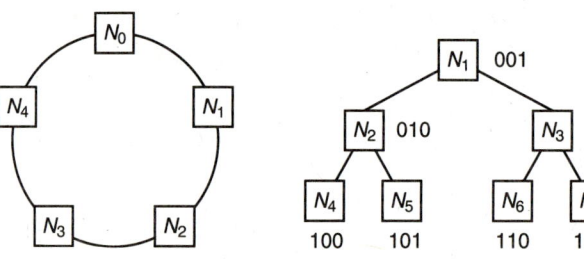

Figure 5.3 Ring.   **Figure 5.4** Binary tree.

address; that is, the children of node x are labeled $2x$ and $2x + 1$. A binary tree with N nodes has diameter $2(h - 1)$, where $h = \lceil \log_2 N \rceil$ is the height of the tree. The binary tree has the advantages of being expandable and having a simple implementation. None-the-less, it can still cause long communication delays between faraway leaf nodes. Leaf nodes farthest away from each other must ultimately pass their message through the root. Since traffic increases as the root is approached, leaf nodes farthest away from each other will spend the most amount of time waiting for a message to traverse the tree from source to destination.

One desirable characteristic for an interconnection network is that data can be routed between the nodes in a simple manner (remember, a node may represent a processor). The binary tree has a simple routing algorithm. Let a packet denote a unit of information that a node needs to send to another node. Each packet has a header that contains routing information, such as source address and destination address. A packet is routed upward toward the root node until it reaches a node that is either the destination or ancestor of the destination node. If the current node is an ancestor of the destination node, the packet is routed downward toward the destination.

Fat tree. One problem with the binary tree is that there can be heavy traffic toward the root node. Consider that the root node acts as the single connection point between the left and right subtrees. As can be observed in Figure 5.4, all messages from nodes N_2, N_4, and N_5 to nodes N_3, N_6, and N_7 have no choice but to pass through the root. To reduce the effect of such a problem, the fat tree was proposed by Leiserson [LEI 85]. Fat trees are more like real trees in which the branches get thicker near the trunk. Proceeding up from the leaf nodes of a fat tree to the root, the number of communication links increases, and therefore the communication bandwidth increases. The communication bandwidth of an interconnection network is the expected number of requests that can be accepted per unit of time.

The structure of the fat tree is based on a binary tree. Each edge of the binary tree corresponds to two channels of the fat tree. One of the channels is from parent to child,

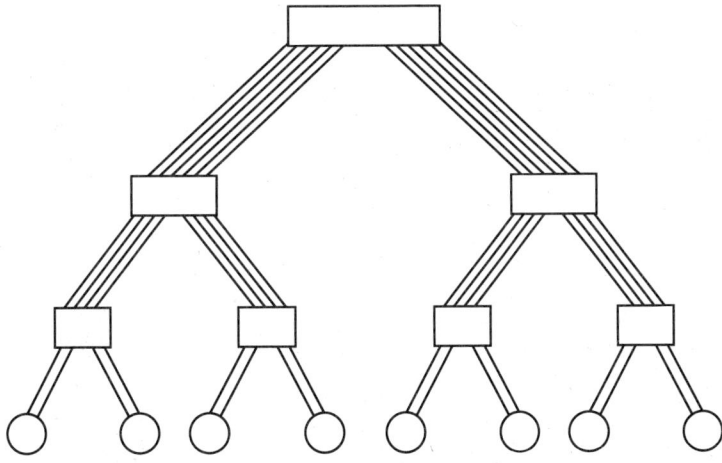

Figure 5.5 Fat tree.

and the other is from child to parent. The number of communication links in each channel increases as we go up the tree from the leaves and is determined by the amount of hardware available. For example, Figure 5.5 represents a fat tree in which the number of communication links in each channel is increased by 1 from one level of the tree to the next. The fat tree can be used to interconnect the processors of a general-purpose parallel machine. Since its communication bandwidth can be scaled independently from the number of processors, it provides great flexibility in design.

Shuffle-exchange. Another method for establishing networks is the shuffle–exchange connection. The shuffle–exchange network is a combination of two functions: *shuffle* and *exchange*. Each is a simple bijection function in which each input is mapped onto one and only one output. Let $s_{n-1}s_{n-2} \ldots s_0$ be the binary representation of a node address; then the shuffle function can be described as

$$\text{shuffle}(s_{n-1}s_{n-2} \ldots s_0) = s_{n-2}s_{n-3} \ldots s_0 s_{n-1}.$$

For example, using the shuffle function for $N = 8$ (i.e. 2^3 nodes) the following connections can be established between the nodes.

Source	Destination	Source	Destination
000	$\longrightarrow$ 000	100	$\longrightarrow$ 001
001	$\longrightarrow$ 010	101	$\longrightarrow$ 011
010	$\longrightarrow$ 100	110	$\longrightarrow$ 101
011	$\longrightarrow$ 110	111	$\longrightarrow$ 111

The reason that the function is called shuffle is that it reflects the process of shuffling cards. Given that there are eight cards, the shuffle function performs a perfect playing card shuffle as follows. First, the deck is cut in half, between cards 3 and 4. Then the two half decks are merged by selecting cards from each half in an alternative order. Figure 5.6 represents how the cards are shuffled.

Another way to define shuffle connection is through the decimal representation of the addresses of the nodes. Let $N = 2^n$ be the number of nodes and i represent the decimal address of a node. For $0 \leq i \leq (N/2) - 1$, node i is connected to node $2i$. For $N/2 \leq i \leq N - 1$, node i is connected to node $2i + 1 - N$.

The exchange function is also a simple bijection function. It maps a binary address to another binary address that differs only in the rightmost bit. It can be described as

$$\text{exchange}(s_{n-1}s_{n-2} \ldots s_1 s_0) = s_{n-1}s_{n-2} \ldots s_1 \overline{s_0}.$$

Figure 5.7 shows the shuffle–exchange connections between nodes when $N = 8$.

The shuffle–exchange network provides suitable interconnection patterns for implementing certain parallel algorithms, such as polynomial evaluation, fast Fourier transform (FFT), sorting, and matrix transposition [STO 71]. For example, polynomial evaluation can be easily implemented on a parallel machine in which the nodes (processors) are connected through a shuffle–exchange network.

In general, a polynomial of degree N can be represented as

$$a_0 + a_1 x + a_2 x^2 + \ldots + a_{N-1} x^{N-1} + a_N x^N,$$

Sec. 5.2 Network Topology

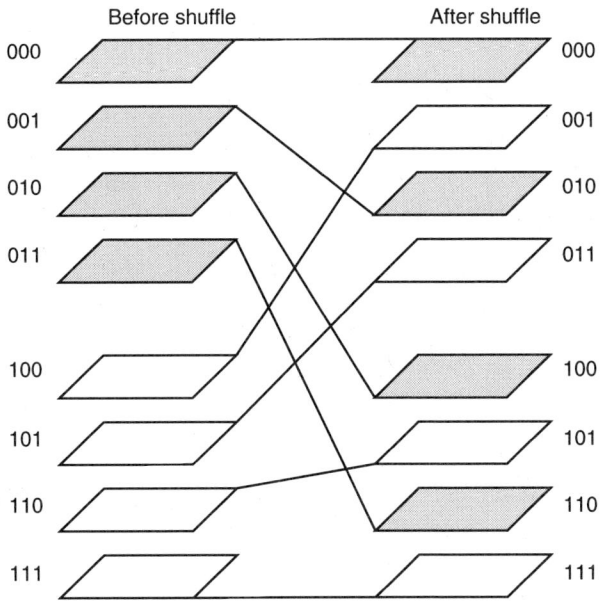

Figure 5.6 Card shuffling.

where $a_0, a_1, ... a_N$ are the coefficients and x is a variable. As an example, consider the evaluation of a polynomial of degree 7. One way to evaluate such a polynomial is to use the architecture given in Figure 5.7. In this figure, assume that each node represents a processor having three registers: one to hold the coefficient, one to hold the variable x, and the third to hold a bit called the mask bit. Figure 5.8 illustrates the three registers of a node.

The evaluation of the polynomial is done in two phases. First, each term $a_i x^i$ is computed at node i for $i = 0$ to 7. Then the terms $a_i x^i$, for $i = 0$ to 7, are added to produce the final result.

Figure 5.9 represents the steps involved in the computation of $a_i x^i$. Figure 5.9a shows the initial values of the registers of each node. The coefficient a_i, for $i = 0$ to 7, is stored in node i. The value of the variable x is stored in each node. The mask register of node i, for $i = 1, 3, 5,$ and 7, is set to 1; others are set to 0. In each step of computation, every node checks the content of its mask register. When the content of the mask

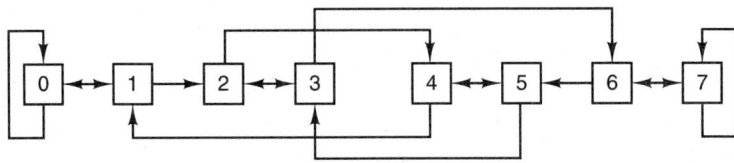

Figure 5.7 Shuffle–exchange connections.

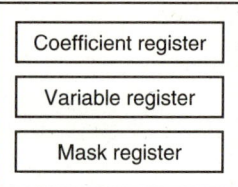

Figure 5.8 A shuffle–exchange node's registers.

register is 1, the content of the coefficient register is multiplied with the content of the variable register, and the result is stored in the coefficient register. When the content of the mask register is zero, the content of the coefficient register remains unchanged. The content of the variable register is multiplied with itself. The contents of the mask registers are shuffled between the nodes using the shuffle network. Figures 5.9b, c, and d show the values of the registers after the first step, second step, and third step, respectively. At the end of the third step, each register contains $a_i x^i$.

At this point, the terms $a_i x^i$ for $i = 0$ to 7 are added to produce the final result. To perform such a summation, exchange connections are used in addition to shuffle connections. Figure 5.10 shows all the connections and the initial values of the coefficient registers.

In each step of computation the contents of the coefficient registers are shuffled between the nodes using the shuffle connections. Then copies of the contents of the coefficient registers are exchanged between the nodes using the exchange connections. After the exchange is performed, each node adds the content of its coefficient register to the value that the copy of the current content is exchanged with. After three shuffle and exchanges, the content of each coefficient register will be the desired $\sum_{i=0}^{7} a_i x^i$. The chart on page 192 shows the three steps required to obtain this result.

As you can see in the chart, after the third step, the value $\sum_{i=0}^{7} a_i x^i$ is stored in each coefficient register. From this example, it should be apparent that the shuffle–exchange network provides the desired connections for manipulating the values of certain problems efficiently.

Two-dimensional mesh. A two-dimensional mesh consists of $k_1 * k_0$ nodes, where $k_i \geq 2$ denotes the number of nodes along dimension i. Figure 5.11 represents a two-dimensional mesh for $k_0 = 4$ and $k_1 = 2$. There are four nodes along dimension 0, and two nodes along dimension 1. As shown in Figure 5.11, in a two-dimensional mesh network each node is connected to its north, south, east, and west neighbors. In general, a node at row i and column j is connected to the nodes at locations $(i-1, j)$, $(i+1, j)$, $(i, j-1)$, and $(i, j+1)$. The nodes on the edge of the network have only two or three immediate neighbors.

The diameter of a mesh network is equal to the distance between nodes at opposite corners. Thus, a two-dimensional mesh with $k_1 * k_0$ nodes has a diameter $(k_1 - 1) + (k_0 - 1)$.

In practice, two-dimensional meshes with an equal number of nodes along each dimension are often used for connecting a set of processing nodes. For this reason in most literature the notion of two-dimensional mesh is used without indicating the

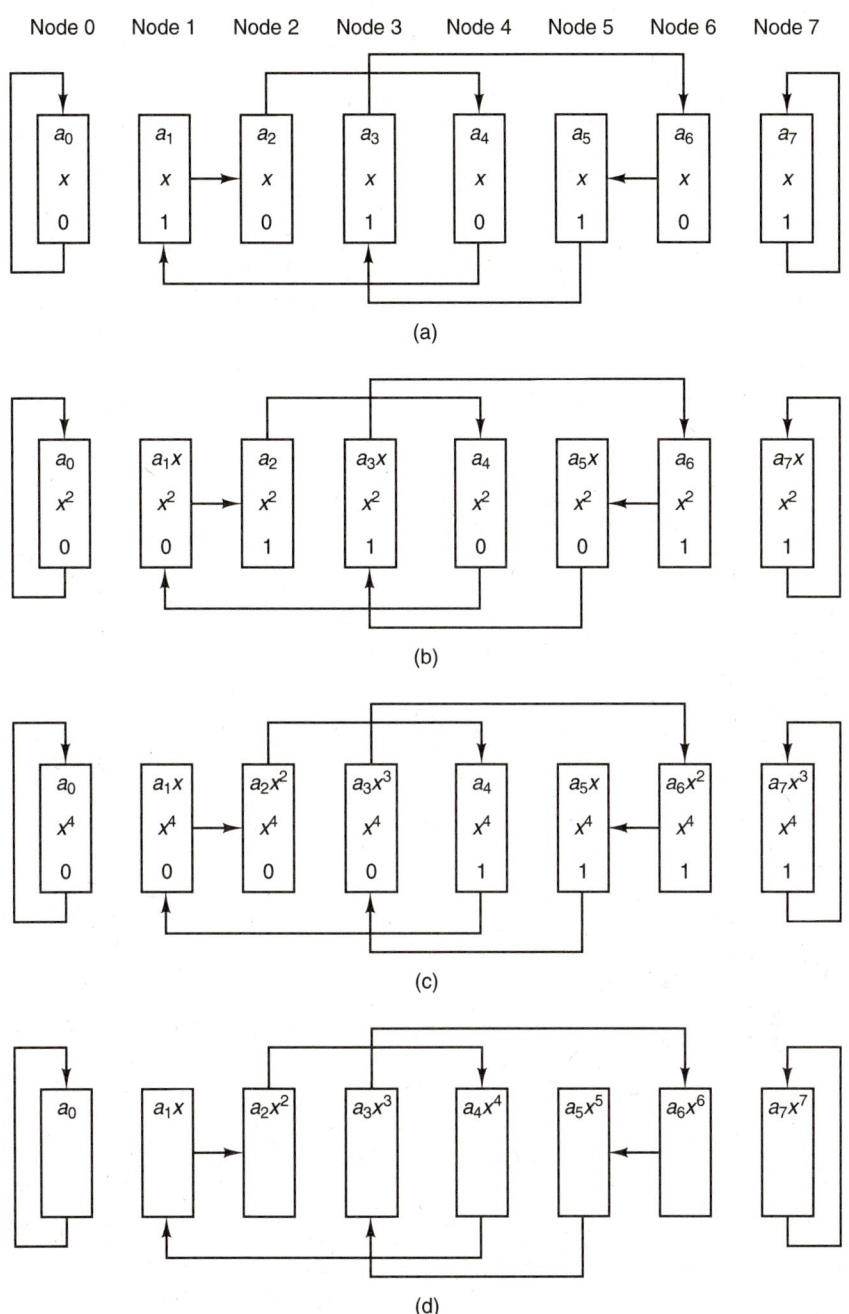

Figure 5.9 Steps for the computation of the $a_i x^i$. (a) Initial values. (b) Values after step 1. (c) Values after step 2. (d) Values after step 3.

	Node 0	Node 1	Node 2	Node 3	Node 4	Node 5	Node 6	Node 7
Initial values	a_0	a_1x	a_2x^2	a_3x^3	a_4x^4	a_5x^5	a_6x^6	a_7x^7
Step 1 Shuffle	a_0	a_4x^4	a_1x	a_5x^5	a_2x^2	a_6x^6	a_3x^3	a_7x^7
Exchange	$a_0 + a_4x^4$	$a_0 + a_4x^4$	$a_1x + a_5x^5$	$a_1x + a_5x^5$	$a_2x^2 + a_6x^6$	$a_2x^2 + a_6x^6$	$a_3x^3 + a_7x^7$	$a_3x^3 + a_7x^7$
Step 2. Shuffle	$a_0 + a_4x^4$	$a_2x^2 + a_6x^6$	$a_0 + a_4x^4$	$a_2x^2 + a_6x^6$	$a_1x + a_5x^5$	$a_3x^3 + a_7x^7$	$a_1x + a_5x^5$	$a_3x^3 + a_7x^7$

	Node 0	Node 1	Node 2	Node 3
Exchange	$a_0 + a_4x^4 + a_2x^2 + a_6x^6$	$a_0 + a_4x^4 + a_2x^2 + a_6x^6$	$a_0 + a_4x^4 + a_2x^2 + a_6x^6$	$a_0 + a_4x^4 + a_2x^2 + a_6x^6$
	Node 4	Node 5	Node 6	Node 7
Step 3.	$a_1x + a_5x^5 + a_3x^3 + a_7x^7$	$a_1x + a_5x^5 + a_3x^3 + a_7x^7$	$a_1x + a_5x^5 + a_3x^3 + a_7x^7$	$a_1x + a_5x^5 + a_3x^3 + a_7x^7$
	Node 0	Node 1	Node 2	Node 3
Shuffle.	$a_0 + a_4x^4 + a_2x^2 + a_6x^6$	$a_1x + a_5x^5 + a_3x^3 + a_7x^7$	$a_0 + a_4x^4 + a_2x^2 + a_6x^6$	$a_1x + a_5x^5 + a_3x^3 + a_7x^7$
	Node 4	Node 5	Node 6	Node 7
	$a_0 + a_4x^4 + a_2x^2 + a_6x^6$	$a_1x + a_5x^5 + a_3x^3 + a_7x^7$	$a_0 + a_4x^4 + a_2x^2 + a_6x^6$	$a_1x + a_5x^5 + a_3x^3 + a_7x^7$

	Node 0	Node 1
Exchange	$a_0 + a_4x^4 + a_2x^2 + a_6x^6 + a_1x + a_5x^5 + a_3x^3 + a_7x^7$	$a_0 + a_4x^4 + a_2x^2 + a_6x^6 + a_1x + a_5x^5 + a_3x^3 + a_7x^7$
	Node 2	Node 3
	$a_0 + a_4x^4 + a_2x^2 + a_6x^6 + a_1x + a_5x^5 + a_3x^3 + a_7x^7$	$a_0 + a_4x^4 + a_2x^2 + a_6x^6 + a_1x + a_5x^5 + a_3x^3 + a_7x^7$
	Node 4	Node 5
	$a_0 + a_4x^4 + a_2x^2 + a_6x^6 + a_1x + a_5x^5 + a_3x^3 + a_7x^7$	$a_0 + a_4x^4 + a_2x^2 + a_6x^6 + a_1x + a_5x^5 + a_3x^3 + a_7x^7$
	Node 6	Node 7
	$a_0 + a_4x^4 + a_2x^2 + a_6x^6 + a_1x + a_5x^5 + a_3x^3 + a_7x^7$	$a_0 + a_4x^4 + a_2x^2 + a_6x^6 + a_1x + a_5x^5 + a_3x^3 + a_7x^7$

values for k_1 and k_0; rather, the total number of nodes is defined. A two-dimensional mesh with $k_1 = k_0 = n$ is usually referred to as a *mesh* with N nodes, where $N = n^2$. For example, Figure 5.12 shows a mesh with 16 nodes. From this point forward, the term

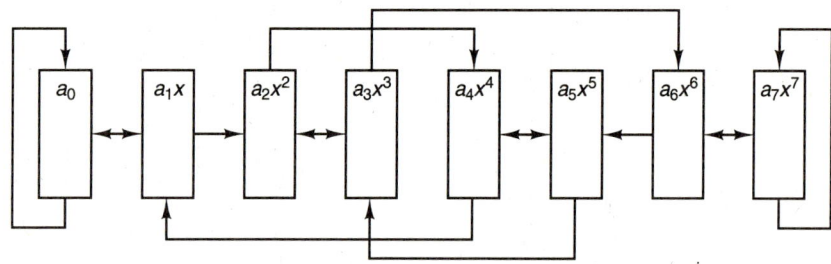

Figure 5.10 Required connections for adding the terms $a_i x^i$.

Sec. 5.2   Network Topology   193

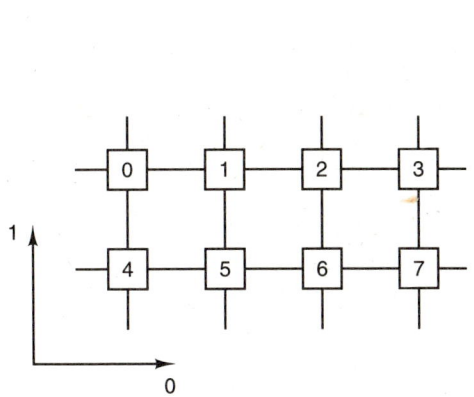

Figure 5.11 A two-dimensional mesh with $k_0 = 4$ and $k_1 = 2$.

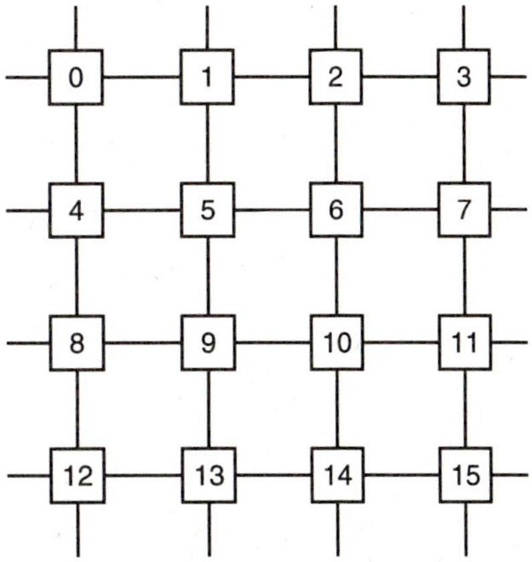

Figure 5.12 A two-dimensional mesh with $k_0 = k_1 = 4$.

mesh will indicate a two-dimensional mesh with an equal number of nodes along each dimension.

The routing of data through a mesh can be accomplished in a straightforward manner. The following simple routing algorithm routes a packet from source S to destination D in a mesh with n^2 nodes.

1. Compute the row distance R as

    $R = \lfloor D/n \rfloor - \lfloor S/n \rfloor$.

2. Compute the column distance C as:

    $C = D \pmod{n} - S \pmod{n}$.

3. Add the values R and C to the packet header at the source node.
4. Starting from the source, send the packet for R rows and then for C columns.

The values R and C determine the number of rows and columns that the packet needs to travel. The direction the message takes at each node is determined by the sign of the values R and C. When R (C) is positive, the packet travels downward (right); otherwise, the packet travels upward (left). Each time that the packet travels from one node to the adjacent node downward, the value R is decremented by 1, and when it travels upward, R is incremented by 1. Once R becomes 0, the packet starts traveling in the horizontal direction. Each time that the packet travels from one node to the adjacent node in the right direction, the value C is decremented by 1, and when it travels in the left direction, C is incremented by 1. When C becomes 0, the packet has arrived at the destination. For example, to route a packet from node 6 (i.e., $S = 6$) to node 12 (i.e., $D = 12$), the packet goes through two paths, as shown in Figure 5.13. In this example,

$R = \lfloor 12/4 \rfloor - \lfloor 6/4 \rfloor = 2,$
$C = 0 - 2 = -2.$

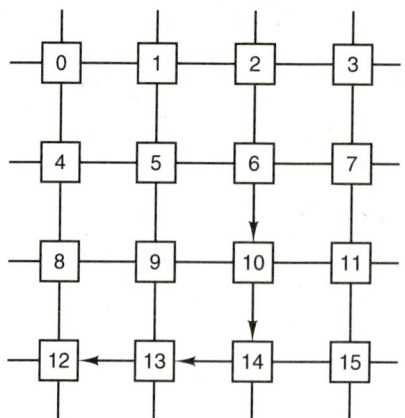

Figure 5.13 Routing path from node 6 to node 12.

It should be noted that in the case just described the nodes on the edge of the mesh network have no connections to their far neighbors. When there are such connections, the network is called a *wraparound two-dimensional mesh,* or an *Illiac* network. An Illiac network is illustrated in Figure 5.14 for $N = 16$.

In general, the connections of an Illiac network can be defined by the following four functions:

$$\begin{aligned}
\text{Illiac}_{+1}(j) &= j + 1 \ (\text{mod } N), \\
\text{Illiac}_{-1}(j) &= j - 1 \ (\text{mod } N), \\
\text{Illiac}_{+n}(j) &= j + n \ (\text{mod } N), \\
\text{Illiac}_{-n}(j) &= j - n \ (\text{mod } N),
\end{aligned}$$

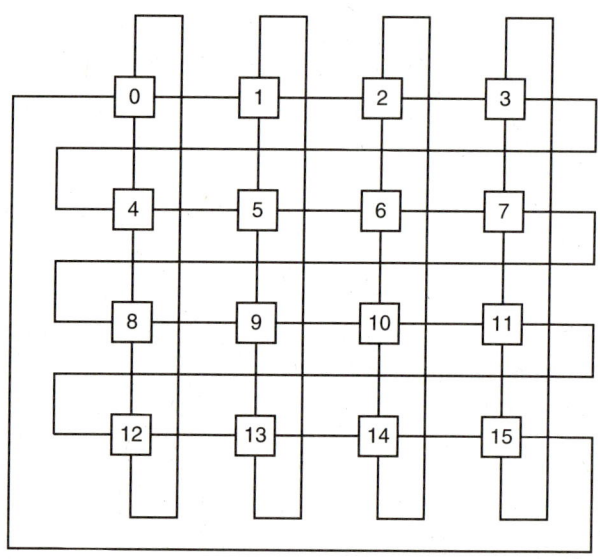

Figure 5.14 A 16-node Illiac network.

where N is the number of nodes, $0 \leq j < N$, n is the number of nodes along any dimension, and $N = n^2$. For example, in Figure 5.14, node 4 is connected to nodes 5, 3, 8, and 0, since

$$\begin{aligned}
\text{Illiac}_{+1}(4) &= (4 + 1) \,(\text{mod } 16) = 5, \\
\text{Illiac}_{-1}(4) &= (4 - 1) \,(\text{mod } 16) = 3, \\
\text{Illiac}_{+4}(4) &= (4 + 4) \,(\text{mod } 16) = 8, \\
\text{Illiac}_{-4}(4) &= (4 - 4) \,(\text{mod } 16) = 0.
\end{aligned}$$

The diameter of an Illiac with $N = n^2$ nodes is $n - 1$, which is shorter than a mesh. Although the extra wraparound connections in Illiac allow the diameter to decrease, they increase the complexity of the design. Figure 5.15 shows the connectivity of the nodes in a different form. This graph shows that four nodes can be reached from any node in one step, seven nodes in two steps, and four nodes in three steps. In general, the number of steps (recirculations) to route data from a node to any other node is upper bounded by the diameter (i.e. $n - 1$).

To reduce the diameter of a mesh network, another variation of this network, called torus (or two-dimensional torus), has also been proposed. As shown in Figure 5.16a, a torus is a combination of ring and mesh networks. To make the wire length between the adjacent nodes equal, the torus may be folded as shown in Figure 5.16b. In this way the communication delay between the adjacent nodes becomes equal. Note that both Figures 5.16a and b provide the same connections between the nodes; in fact, Figure 5.16b is derived from Figure 5.16a by switching the position of the rightmost two columns and the bottom two rows of nodes. The diameter of a torus with $N = n^2$ nodes is $2\lfloor n/2 \rfloor$, which is the distance between the corner and the center node. Note that the diameter is further decreased from the mesh network.

The mesh network provides suitable interconnection patterns for problems whose solutions require the computation of a set of values on a grid of points, for which the value at each point is determined based on the values of the neighboring points. Here we consider one of these class of problems: the problem of finding a steady-state temperature over the surface of a square slab of material whose four edges are held at different temperatures. This problem requires the solution of the following partial differential equation, known as Laplace's equation:

$$\partial^2 U / \partial x^2 + \partial^2 U / \partial y^2 = 0,$$

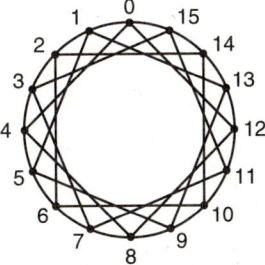

Figure 5.15 Alternative representation of a 16-node Illiac network.

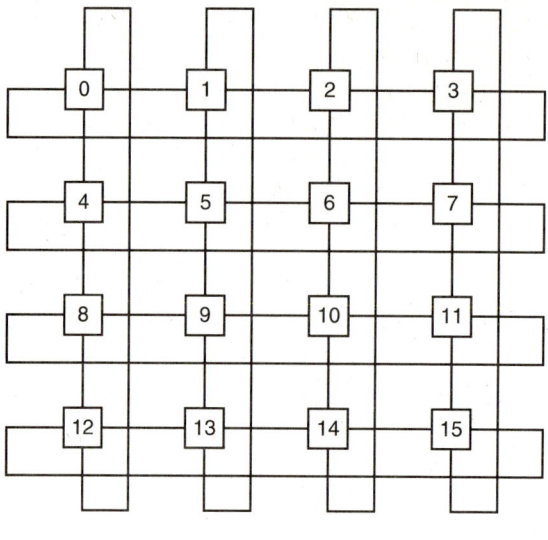

(a)

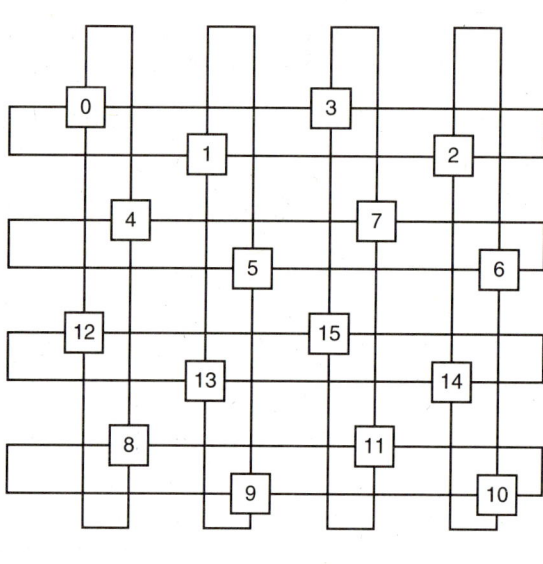

(b)

Figure 5.16 Different types of torus network. (a) A 4-by-4 torus network. (b) A 4-by-4 torus network with folded connection.

where U is the temperature at a given point specified by the coordinates x and y on the slab.

The following describes a method, given by Slotnick [SLO 71], to solve this problem. Even if unfamiliar with Laplace's equation, the reader should still be able to follow the description. The method is based on the fact that the temperature at any point on the slab tends to become the average of the temperatures of neighboring points.

Sec. 5.2 Network Topology

Assume that the slab is covered with a mesh and that each square of the mesh has h units on each side. Then the temperature of an interior node at coordinates x and y is the average of the temperatures of the four neighbor nodes. That is, the temperature at node (x, y), denoted as $U(x, y)$, equals the sum of the four neighboring temperatures divided by 4. For example, as shown in Figure 5.17, assume that the slab can be covered with a 16-node mesh. Here the value of $U(x, y)$ is expressed as

$$U(x, y) = [U(x, y + h) + U(x + h, y) + U(x, y - h) + U(x - h, y)]/4.$$

Figure 5.18 illustrates an alternative representation of Figure 5.17. Here the position of the nodes is more conveniently indicated by the integers i and j. In this case, the temperature equation can be expressed as

$$U(i, j) = [U(i, j + 1) + U(i + 1, j) + U(i, j - 1) + U(i - 1, j)]/4.$$

Assume that each node represents a processor having one register to hold the node's temperature. The nodes on the boundary are arbitrarily held at certain fixed temperatures. Let the nodes on the bottom of the mesh and on the right edge be held at zero degrees. The nodes along the top and left edges are set according to their positions. The temperatures of these 12 boundary nodes do not change during the computation. The temperatures at the 4 interior nodes are the unknowns. Initially, the temperatures at these 4 nodes are set to zero. In the first iteration of computation, the 4 interior node processors simultaneously calculate the new temperature values using the values initially given.

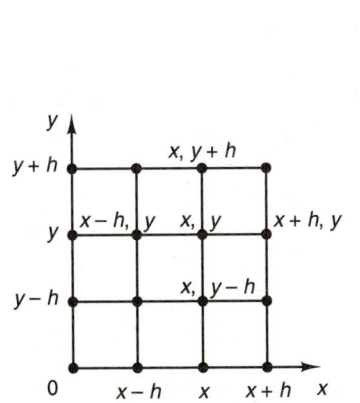

Figure 5.17 Covering a slab with a 16-node mesh.

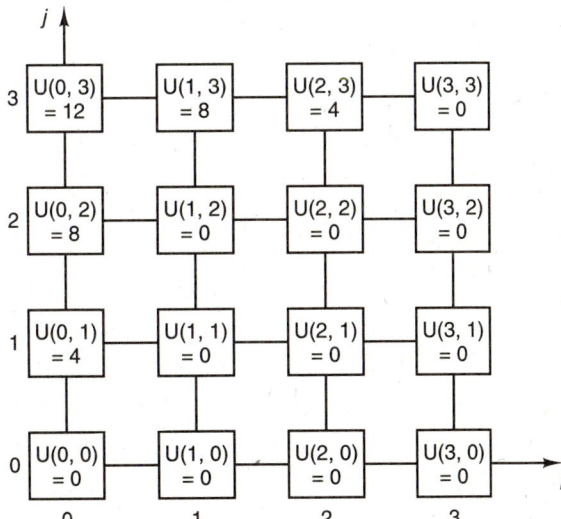

Figure 5.18 Initial values of the nodes.

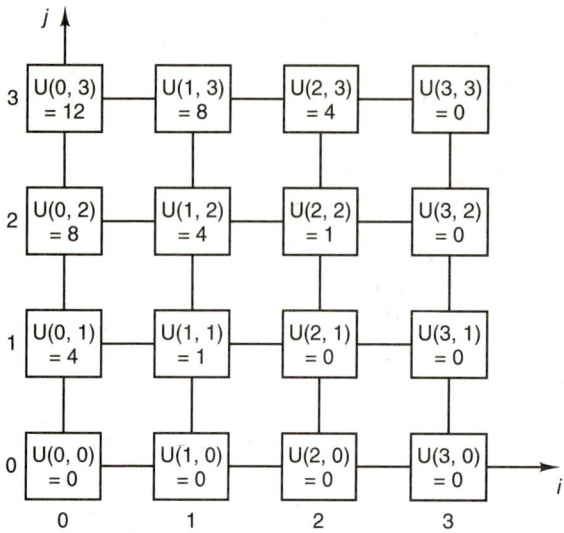

Figure 5.19 Values of the nodes after the first iteration.

Figure 5.19 represents the new values of the interior nodes after the first iteration. These values are calculated as follows:

$$U(1, 2) = [U(1, 3) + U(2, 2) + U(1, 1) + U(0, 2)]/4 = [8 + 0 + 0 + 8]/4 = 4;$$
$$U(2, 2) = [U(2, 3) + U(3, 2) + U(2, 1) + U(1, 2)]/4 = [4 + 0 + 0 + 0]/4 = 1;$$
$$U(1, 1) = [U(1, 2) + U(2, 1) + U(1, 0) + U(0, 1)]/4 = [0 + 0 + 0 + 4]/4 = 1;$$
$$U(2, 1) = [U(2, 2) + U(3, 1) + U(2, 0) + U(1, 1)]/4 = [0 + 0 + 0 + 0]/4 = 0.$$

In the second iteration, the values of $U(1, 2)$, $U(2, 2)$, $U(1, 1)$, and $U(2, 1)$ are calculated using the new values just obtained:

$$U(1, 2) = [8 + 1 + 1 + 8]/4 = 4.5;$$
$$U(2, 2) = [4 + 0 + 0 + 4]/4 = 2;$$
$$U(1, 1) = [4 + 0 + 0 + 4]/4 = 2;$$
$$U(2, 1) = [1 + 0 + 0 + 1]/4 = 0.5.$$

This process continues until a steady-state solution is obtained. As more iterations are performed, the values of the interior nodes converge to the exact solution. When values for two successive iterations are close to each other (within a specified error tolerance), the process can be stopped, and it can be said that a steady-state solution has been reached. Figure 5.20 represents a solution obtained after 11 iterations.

n-Cube or hypercube. An n-cube network, also called hypercube, consists of $N = 2^n$ nodes; n is called the *dimension* of the n-cube network. When the node addresses are considered as the corners of an n-dimensional cube, the network connects each node to its n neighbors. In an n-cube, individual nodes are uniquely identified by n-bit addresses ranging from 0 to $N - 1$. Given a node with binary address d, this node is connected to all nodes whose binary addresses differ from d in exactly 1 bit. For example, in a 3-cube, in which there are eight nodes, node 7 (111) is connected

nodes $X = (x_{n-1}, x_{n-2}, ..., x_0)$ and $Y = (y_{n-1}, y_{n-2}, ..., y_0)$ are said to be neighbors if and only if $y_i = x_i$ for all i, $0 \leq i \leq n - 1$, except one, j, where $y_j = x_j + 1$ or $y_j = x_j -1$. That is, a node may have from n to $2n$ neighbors, depending on its location in the mesh. The corners of the mesh have n neighbors, and the internal nodes have $2n$ neighbors, while other nodes have n_b neighbors, where $n < n_b < 2n$. The diameter of an n-dimensional mesh is $\sum_{i=0}^{n-1}(k_i - 1)$. An n-cube is a special case of n-dimensional meshes; it is in fact an n-dimensional mesh in which $k_i = 2$ for $0 \leq i \leq n - 1$. Figure 5.27 represents the structure of two three-dimensional meshes: one for $k_2 = k_1 = k_0 = 3$ and the other for $k_2 = 4$, $k_1 = 3$, and $k_0 = 2$.

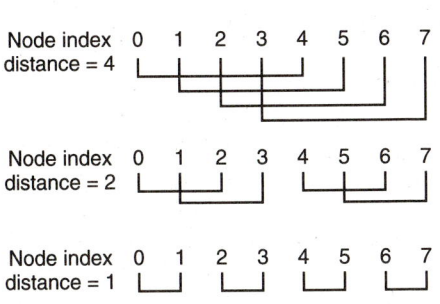

Figure 5.25 Descending class.

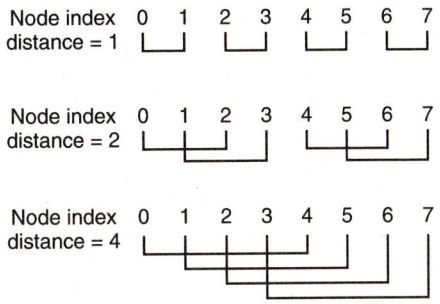

Figure 5.26 Ascending class.

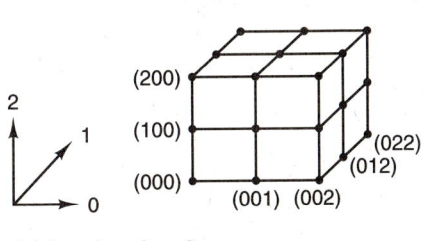

(a) $k_2 = k_1 = k_0 = 3$.

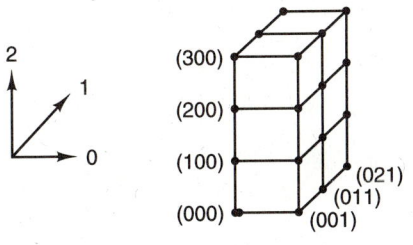

(b) $k_2 = 4$, $k_1 = 3$, and $k_0 = 2$.

Figure 5.27 Three-dimensional meshes.

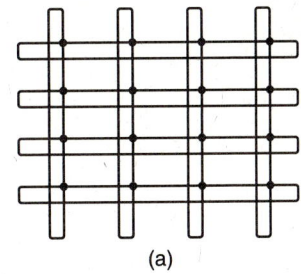

(a)

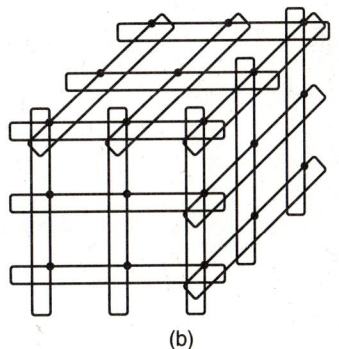

(b)

Figure 5.28 (a) 4-Ary 2-cube and (b) 3-ary 3-cube networks.

k-Ary n-cube. A k-ary n-cube consists of k^n nodes such that there are k nodes along each dimension. Each node X is identified by n coordinates, $x_{n-1}, x_{n-2}, \ldots, x_0$, where $0 \leq x_i \leq k - 1$ for $0 \leq i \leq n - 1$. Two nodes $X = (x_{n-1}, x_{n-2}, \ldots, x_0)$ and $Y = (y_{n-1}, y_{n-2}, \ldots, y_0)$ are said to be neighbors if and only if $y_i = x_i$ for all i, $0 \leq i \leq n - 1$, except one, j, where $y_j = (x_j + 1) \bmod k$, or $y_j = (x_j -1) \bmod k$. That is, in contrast to the n-dimensional mesh, a k-ary n-cube has a symmetrical topology in which each node has an equal number of neighbors. A node has n neighbors when $k = 2$ and $2n$ neighbors when $k > 2$. The k-ary n-cube has a diameter of $n \lfloor k/2 \rfloor$. An n-cube is a special case of k-ary n-cubes it is in fact a 2-ary n-cube. Figure 5.28 represents the structure of two k-ary n-cubes: one for $k = 4$, $n = 2$ and the other for $k = n = 3$. Note that a 4-ary 2-cube is actually a torus network.

Routing in n-dimensional meshes and k-ary n-cubes. One of the routing algorithms that can be used for routing the packets within an n-dimensional mesh or a k-ary n-cube is called *store-and-forward routing* [TAN 81]. Each node of the network contains a buffer equal to the size of a packet. In store-and-forward routing, a packet is transmitted from a source node to a destination node through a sequence of intermediate nodes. Each intermediate node of the network receives a packet in its entirety before transmitting it to the next node. When an intermediate node receives a packet, it first stores the packet in its buffer; then it forwards the packet to the next node when the receiving node's buffer is empty.

Store-and-forward routing is easy to understand and simple to implement. However, it requires a transmission time proportional to the distance (the number of hops or channels) between the source and the destination nodes to deliver a packet. (Channels are actually electrical connections between nodes and are arranged based on the network topology.) To reduce transmission time and make this task almost independent of the distance between source and destination nodes, a hardware-supported routing protocol, called *wormhole routing* (or *direct-connect routing*) is often used.

In wormhole routing, a packet is divided into several smaller data units, called *flits*. Only the first flit (the leading flit) carries the routing information (such as the destination address), and the remaining flits follow this leader. Once a leader flit arrives at a node, the node selects the outgoing channel based on the flit's routing information and begins forwarding the flits through that channel. Since the remaining flits carry no routing information, they must necessarily follow the channels established by the header for the transmission to be successful. Therefore, they cannot be interleaved (alternated or mixed) with the flits of other packets. When a leader flit arrives at a node that has no output channel available, all the flits remain in their current position until a suitable channel becomes available. Each node contains a few small buffers for storing such flits.

At each node, the selection of an outgoing channel for a particular leading flit depends on the incoming channel (the channel that was used by the flit to enter the node) and the destination node. This type of dependency can be represented by a channel dependency graph. A channel dependency graph for a given interconnection network together with a routing algorithm is a directed graph such as shown in Figure 5.29b. The vertices of the graph in Figure 5.29b are the channels of the network, and the edges are the pairs of channels connected by the routing algorithm. For example,

Sec. 5.2 Network Topology

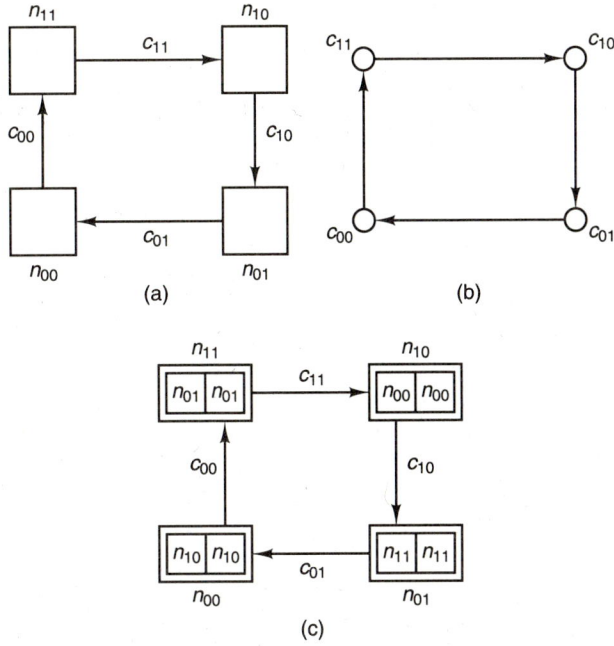

Figure 5.29 A simple network with four nodes. (a) Network. (b) Dependency graph. (c) Deadlock.

consider Figure 5.29a, where a network with nodes $n_{11}, n_{10}, ...,$ and n_{00} and unidirectional channels $c_{11}, c_{10}, ...,$ and c_{00} is shown. The channels are labeled by the identification number (id) of their source node. A routing algorithm for such a network could advance the flits on c_{11} to c_{10}, on c_{10} to c_{01}, and so on. Based on this routing algorithm, Figure 5.29b represents the dependency graph for such a network.

Notice that the dependency graph consists of a cycle that may cause a deadlock in the network. A deadlock can occur whenever no flits can proceed toward their destinations because the buffers on the route are full. Figure 5.29c presents a deadlock configuration in the case when there are two buffers in each node.

To have reliable and efficient communication between nodes, a deadlock-free routing algorithm is needed. Dally and Seitz [DAL 87] have shown that a routing algorithm for an interconnection network is deadlock free if and only if there are no cycles (a route that reconnects with itself) in the channel dependency graph. Their proposal is to avoid deadlock by eliminating cycles through the use of virtual channels. A virtual channel is a logical link between two nodes formed by a physical channel and a flit buffer in each of the two nodes. Each physical channel is shared among a group of virtual channels. Although several virtual channels share a physical channel, each virtual channel has its own buffer. With many (virtual) channels to choose from, cycles, and therefore deadlock, can be avoided.

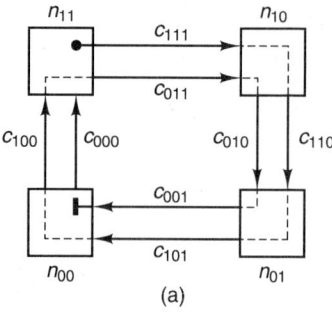

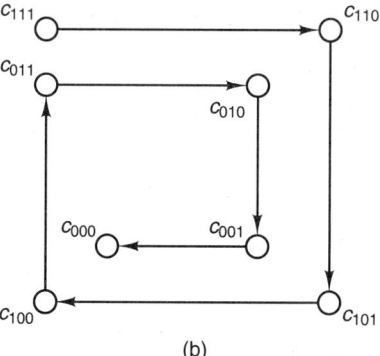

Figure 5.30 (a) Virtual channels and (b) dependency graph for a simple network with four nodes.

Figure 5.30a represents the virtual channels for a network when each physical channel is split into two virtual channels: lower virtual channels and upper virtual channels. The lower virtual channel of c_x (where x is identified as the source node) is labeled c_{0x}, and the upper virtual channel is labeled c_{1x}. For example, the lower virtual channel of c_{11} is numbered as c_{011}.

Dally and Seitz's routing algorithm routes packets at a node with a label value less than the destination node on the upper virtual channels and routes packets at a node labeled greater than their destination node on the lower channels. This routing algorithm restricts the packets' routing to the order of decreasing virtual channel labels. Thus there is no cycle in the dependency graph and the network is deadlock free (see Figure 5.30b).

Wormhole routing is based on a method of dividing packets into smaller transmission units called flits. Transmitting flits rather than packets reduces the average time required to deliver a packet in the network, as shown in Figure 5.31.

For example, assume that each packet consists of q flits, and T_f is the amount of time required for each flit to be transmitted across a single channel. The amount of time required to transmit a packet over a single channel is therefore $q * T_f$. With store-and-forward routing, the average time required to transmit a packet over D channels will be $D * q * T_f$. However, with wormhole routing, in which the flits are forwarded in a pipeline fashion, the average transmission time over D channels becomes $(q + D - 1) * T_f$. This means that wormhole routing is much faster than store-and-for-

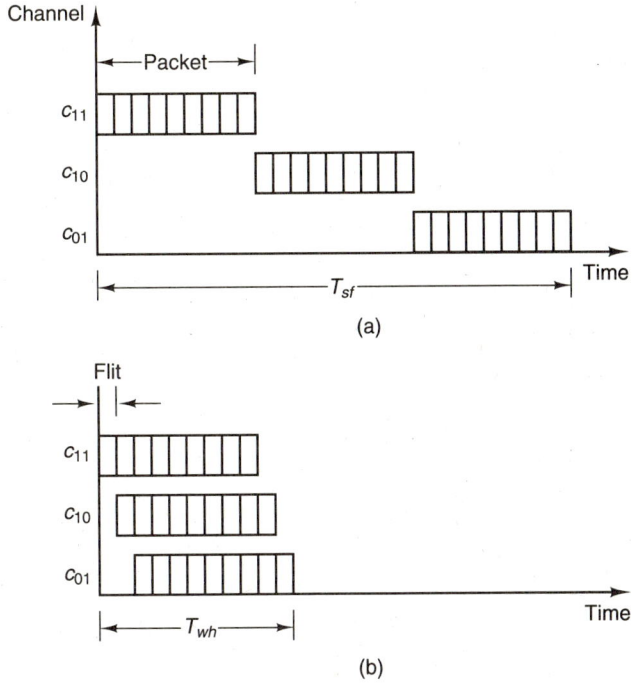

Figure 5.31 Comparing (a) store-and-forward routing with (b) wormhole routing. T_{sf} and T_{wh} are average transmission time over three channels when using store-and-forward routing and wormhole routing, respectively.

ward routing. Furthermore, wormhole routing requires very little storage, resulting in a small and fast communication controller. In general, it is an efficient routing technique for k-ary n-cubes and n-dimensional meshes.

In literature, several deadlock-free routing algorithms, based on the wormhole routing concept, have been proposed. These algorithms can be classified into two groups: deterministic (or static) routing and adaptive (or dynamic) routing. In deterministic routing, the routing path, which is traversed by flits, is fixed and is determined by the source and destination addresses. Although, these routings usually select one of the shortest paths between the source and destination nodes, they limit the ability of the interconnection network to adapt itself to failures or heavy traffic (congestion) along the intended routes. It is in this case that adaptive routing becomes important. Adaptive routing algorithms allow the path taken by flits to depend on dynamic network conditions (such as the presence of faulty or congested channels), rather than source and destination addresses. The description of these algorithms is beyond the scope of this book. The reader can refer to [NI 93] for a survey on deterministic and adaptive wormhole routing in k-ary n-cubes and n-dimensional meshes.

Network Latency. Here, based on the work of Agarwal [AGA 91] and Dally and Seitz [DAL 87], we focus on deriving an equation for the average time required to transmit a packet in k-ary n-cubes that uses wormhole routing. A similar analysis can also be carried out for n-dimensional networks. We assume that the networks are embedded in a plane and have unidirectional channels.

The network latency, T_b, refers to the elapsed time from the time that the first flit of the packet leaves the source to the time the last flit arrives at the destination. Hence, ignoring the network load, T_b can be expressed as

$$T_b = (q + D - 1) * T_f,$$

where D denotes the number of channels (hops) that a packet traverses. Let T_f be represented as the sum of the wire delay $T_w(n)$ and node delay T_s, that is, $T_f = T_w(n) + T_s$. Hence

$$T_b = (q + D - 1)[T_w(n) + T_s].$$

The number of channels, D, can be determined by the product of the network dimension and the average distance (k_d) that a packet must travel in each dimension of the network. Assuming that the packet destinations are randomly chosen, the average distance a packet must travel is given by

$$k_d = (k - 1)/2.$$

Hence

$$T_b = [q + n(k - 1)/2 - 1][T_w(n) + T_s].$$

To determine $T_w(n)$, we must find the length of the longest wire of an n-dimensional network embedded in a plane. The embedding of an n-dimensional network in a plane can be achieved by mapping $n/2$ dimensions of the network in each of the two physical dimensions. That is, the number of nodes in each physical dimension is $k^{n/2}$. Thus each additional dimension of the network increases the number of nodes in each physical dimension by $k^{1/2}$. Assuming that the distance between the physically adjacent nodes remains fixed, each additional dimension also increases the length of the longest wire length by a factor of $k^{1/2}$. Assume that the wire delay depends linearly on the wire length. If we consider the delay of a wire in a two-dimensional network [i.e., $T_w(2)$] as a base time period, the delay of the longest wire is given by

$$T_w(n) = (k^{1/2})^{n-2} T_w(2) = k^{(n/2 - 1)}.$$

Hence

$$T_b = [q + n(k - 1)/2 - 1][k^{(n/2 - 1)} + T_s].$$

Agarwal [AGA 91] has extended this result to the analysis of a k-ary n-cube under different load parameters, such as packet size, degree of local communication, and network request rate. [The degree of local communication increases as the probability of communication with (or access to) various nodes decreases as a function of physical distance.] Agarwal has shown that two-dimensional networks have the lowest latency when node delays and network contention are ignored. Otherwise, three or four dimensions are preferred. However, when the degree of local communications becomes high, two-dimensional networks outperform three- and four-dimensional networks. Local communication depends on several factors, such as machine architec-

Sec. 5.2 Network Topology

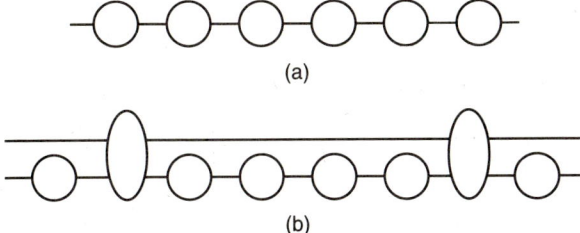

Figure 5.32 Express cube. (a) Regular k-ary 1-cube network. (b) k-Ary 1-cube network with express channels.

ture, type of applications, and compiler. If these factors are enhanced, two-dimensional networks can be used without incurring the high cost of higher dimensions.

Another alternative for enhancing local communication is to provide short paths for nonlocal packets. The k-ary n-cube network can be augmented by one or more levels of express channels that allow nonlocal messages to bypass nodes [DAL 91]. The augmented network, called *express cube,* reduces the network diameter and increases the wire length. This arrangement allows the network to operate with latencies that approach the physical speed-of-light limitation, rather than being limited by node delays. Figure 5.32 illustrates the addition of express channels to a k-ary 1-cube network. In express cubes the wire length of express channels can be increased to the point that wire delays dominate node delay, making low-dimensional networks more attractive.

5.2.2 Dynamic Networks

Dynamic networks provide reconfigurable connections between nodes. The topology of a dynamic network is the physical structure of the network as determined by the switch boxes and the interconnecting links. Since the switch box is the basic component of the network, the cost of the network (in hardware terms) is measured by the number of switch boxes required. Therefore, the topology of the network is the prime determinant of the cost.

To clarify the preceding terminology, let us consider the design of a dynamic network using simple switch boxes. Figure 5.33 represents a simple switch with two inputs (x and y) and two outputs (z_0 and z_1). A control line, s, determines whether the input lines should be connected to the output lines in straight state or exchange state. For example, when the control line $s = 0$, the inputs are connected to the outputs in a straight state; that is, x is connected to z_0 and y is connected to z_1. When the control line $s = 1$, the inputs are connected to outputs in an exchange state; that is, x is connected to z_1 and y is connected to z_0.

Now let's use this switch to design a network that can connect a source x to one of eight possible destinations 0 to 7. A solution for such a network is shown in Figure 5.34. In this design, there are three stages (columns), stages 2, 1, and 0. The destination address is denoted bit-wise by $d_2d_1d_0$. The switch in stage 2 is controlled by the most significant bit of the destination address (i.e., d_2). This bit is used because, when $d_2 = 0$, the source x is connected to one of the destinations 0 to 3 (000 to 011); otherwise, x is

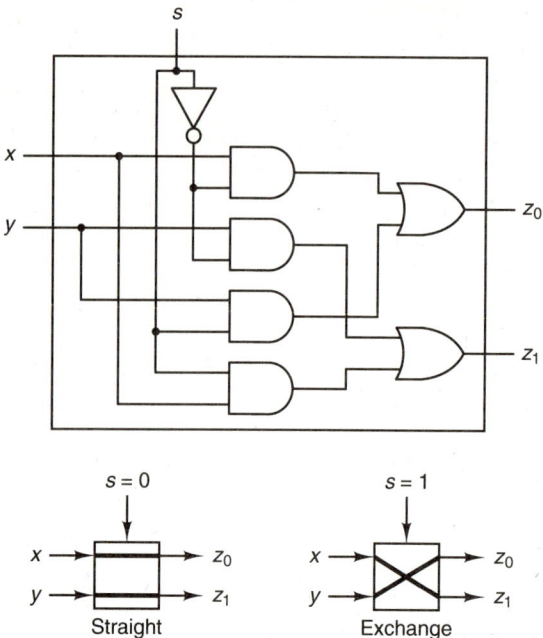

Figure 5.33 A simple two-input switch.

connected to one of the destinations 4 to 7 (100 to 111). In a similar way, the switches in stages 1 and 0 are controlled by d_1 and d_0, respectively.

Now let's expand our network to have eight sources instead of one. Figure 5.35 represents a solution to such a network constructed in the same manner as the design in Figure 5.34.

Note that, in this network, the destination address bits cannot be used to control switches for some connections, such as, connecting source 1 to destination 5. Therefore, at this point, let's assume there is some kind of mechanism for controlling switches. Based on this assumption, the network is able to connect any single source

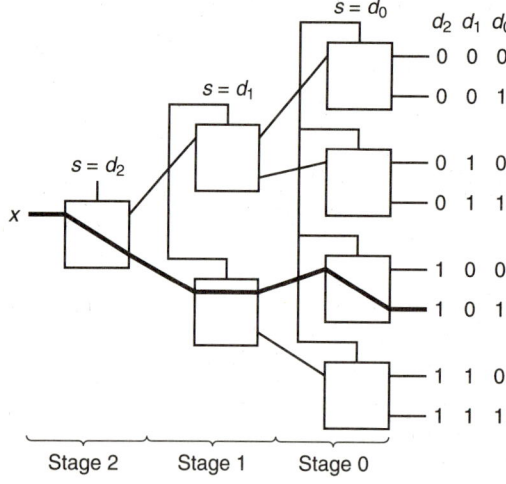

Figure 5.34 A simple 1-to-8 interconnection network.

Sec. 5.2   Network Topology

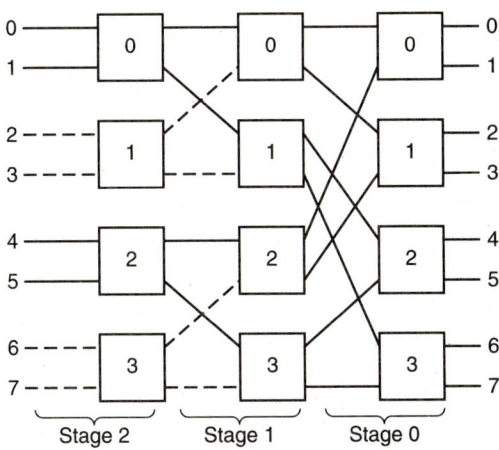

Figure 5.35 A simple 8-to-8 interconnection network.

to any single destination. However, it is not able to establish certain connections with multiple sources and multiple destinations. Describing such multiple connections requires the use of the term *permutation*. A permutation refers to the connection of a set of sources to a set of destinations such that each source is connected to a single destination. A permutation $[(s_0, d_0), (s_1, d_1), ..., (s_7, d_7)]$ means that source s_0 is connected to d_0, s_1 to d_1, and so on. The network of Figure 5.35 cannot establish particular permutations. For example, a permutation that requires sources 0 and 1 to be connected to destinations 0 and 1, respectively, cannot be established at the same time. However, by changing the position of some of the switches, such a permutation becomes possible. Figure 5.36 represents the same network after switching the position of the connections of inputs 1 and 4 to the switches 0 and 2 of stage 2. This new network is able to connect 0 to 0 and 1 to 1, simultaneously, and establish the permutation. Nevertheless, there are many permutations, such as [(0, 1),(1, 2),(2, 3),(3, 4),(4, 5),(5, 6),(6, 7),(7, 0)], that cannot be established by this new network. Later in this chapter, better networks that can provide the necessary permutations for many applications are represented.

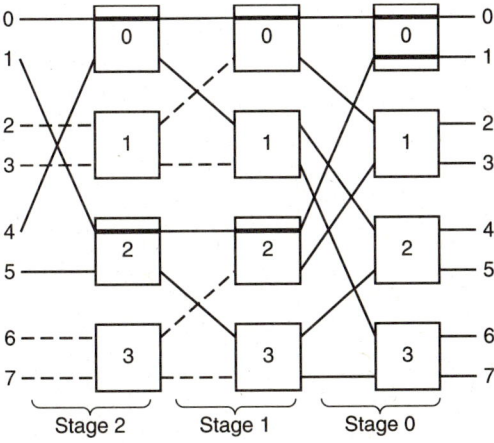

Figure 5.36 An alternative design for an 8-to-8 interconnection network.

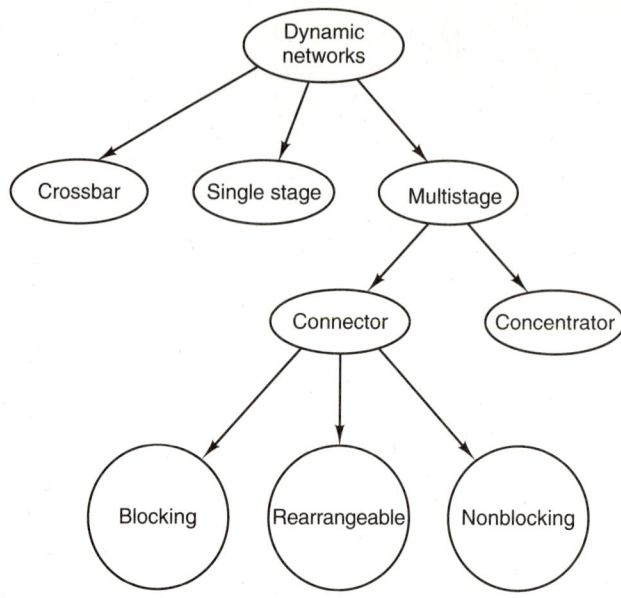

Figure 5.37 Classification of dynamic networks.

To provide a perspective on the various dynamic network topologies and to aid in organizing the later sections, a dynamic networks taxonomy is presented in Figure 5.37. At the first level of the hierarchy are the *crossbar switch, single-stage,* and *multistage* networks.

The crossbar switch can be used for connecting a set of input nodes to a set of output nodes. In this network every input node can be connected to any output node. The crossbar switch provides all possible permutations, as well as support for high system performance. It can be viewed as a number of vertical and horizontal links interconnected by a switch at each intersection. Figure 5.38 represents a crossbar for connecting N nodes to N nodes. The connection between each pair of nodes is established by a crosspoint switch. The crosspoint switch can be set on or off in response to application needs. There are N^2 crosspoint switches for providing complete connec-

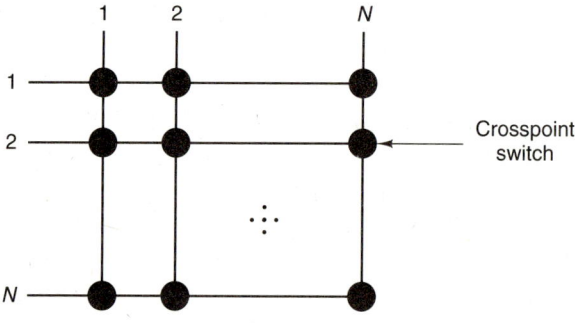

Figure 5.38 Crossbar switch.

Sec. 5.2   Network Topology   213

tions between all the nodes. The crossbar switch is an ideal network to use for small N. However, for large N, the implementation of the crosspoint switches makes this design complex and expensive and thus less attractive to use.

Single-stage networks, also called recirculating networks, require routing algorithms to direct the flow of data several times through the network so that various connections and permutations can be constructed. Each time that the data traverse the network is called a *pass*. As an example, Figure 5.39 represents a single-stage network based on the shuffle–exchange connection. Multistage networks, such as the one in Figure 5.36, are more complex from a hardware point of view, but the routing of data is made simpler by virtue of permanent connections between the stages of the network. Because there are more switches in a multistage network, the number of possible permutations on a single pass increases; however, there is a higher investment in hardware. There is also a possible reduction in the complexity of routing functions and the time it takes to generate the necessary permutations.

Multistage networks are further divided into *concentrators* and *connectors*. Both of these technologies were established in the 1950s by Bell Labs. A concentrator interconnects a specific idle input to an arbitrary idle output. One way to specify a concentrator is by a triplet of integers (I, O, C), where $I > O \geq C$, and where I is the number of inputs, O is the number of outputs, and C is the capacity of the concentrator. The capacity of a concentrator is the maximum number of connections that can be made simultaneously through the network. Thus a concentrator (I, O, C) is capable of interconnecting any of the $\binom{I}{K}$ choices of inputs ($K \leq C$) to some K of the outputs, where $\binom{I}{K} = \left(\frac{I!}{K!(I-K)!}\right)$.

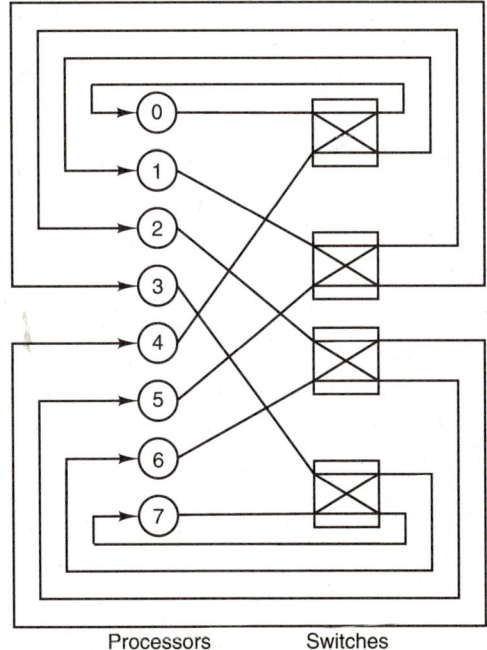

Processors   Switches   **Figure 5.39** A single-stage network.

For example, Figure 5.40 represents a (6, 4, 4) concentrator, called Masson's binomial concentrator. In this network, the crosspoint switches connecting the inputs to the outputs consist of all the possible $\binom{4}{2}$ choices of two switches per input line. There are six possible different matchings between six input and four output lines with two switches per input line. Often concentrators are used for connecting several terminals to a computer.

A connector establishes a path from a specific input to a specific output. In general, connector networks can be grouped into three different classes: *nonblocking, rearrangeable,* and *blocking* networks. In a nonblocking network, it is always possible to connect an idle pair of terminals (input/output nodes) without disturbing connections (calls) already in progress. This is called "nonblocking in the strict sense" simply because such a network has no blocking states whatsoever. These type of networks are said to be *universal* networks since they can provide all possible permutations.

The rearrangeable networks are also universal networks; however, in this type of network it may not always be possible to connect an idle pair of terminals without disturbing established connections. In a rearrangeable network, given any set of connections in progress and any pair of idle terminals, the existing connections can be reassigned new routes (if necessary) so as to make it possible to connect the idle pair at any time. In contrast, in a blocking network, depending on what state the network may be in, it may not be possible to connect an idle pair of terminals in any way.

For each group of connectors, a class of dynamic networks is shown in the following discussion.

Nonblocking networks. Clos has proposed a class of networks with interesting properties [CLO 53]. Figure 5.41 shows one example of such a network. This particular network is called a three-stage Clos network. It consists of an input stage of $n \times m$ crossbar switches, an output stage of $m \times n$ crossbar switches, and a middle stage of $r \times r$ crossbar switches. This class of networks is denoted by the triple $N(m, n, r)$, which determines the switches' dimensions.

Clos has shown that for $m \geq 2n - 1$, the network $N(m, n, r)$, is a nonblocking network. For example, the network $N(3, 2, 2)$ in Figure 5.42 is a nonblocking network. This network requires 12 crosspoint switches in every stage, or 36 switches in all. Note that a crossbar switch with the same number of inputs and outputs (i.e., 4) requires 16 switches. Thus in this case it is more economical to design a crossbar switch than a

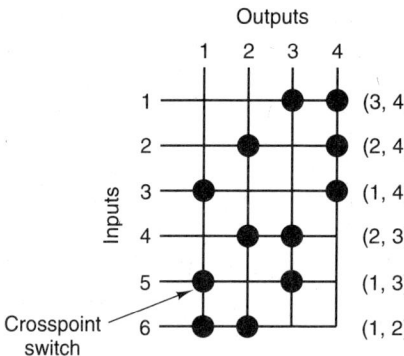

Figure 5.40 A concentrator with six inputs and four outputs.

Sec. 5.2   Network Topology   215

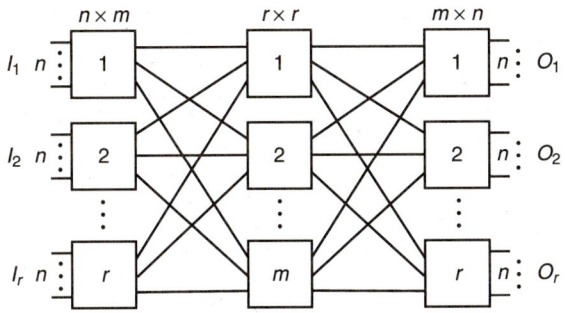

Figure 5.41   A nonblocking network

Clos network. However, when the number of inputs, N, increases, the number of switches becomes much less than N^2, as in the case of the crossbar. For example, for $N = 36$, only 1188 switches are necessary in a Clos network, whereas in the case of a crossbar network 36^2, or 1296, switches are required.

There should be at least $2n - 1$ switches in the middle stage of the Clos network in order to become a nonblocking network. To demonstrate the necessity of this condition, let's consider the following example. Figure 5.43 represents a section of a Clos network in which each input (output) switch has three inputs (outputs). Let's assume that we want to connect input C to output F. In this example, four middle switches are required to permit inputs other than C (i.e., A and B) on a particular input switch and outputs other than F (i.e., D and E) on a particular output switch to have connections to separate middle switches. In addition, one more switch for the desired connection between C and F is required. Thus five middle switches are required (i.e., $2 * 3 - 1$ switches). A similar argument can be given for a general network $N(m, n, r)$, in order to show that N is nonblocking when $m = 2n - 1$.

The total number of switches for a three-stage Clos network $N(2n - 1, n, n)$ can be obtained by analyzing the number of switches in each stage. Assuming that the network has N input terminals, where $N = n^2$, then

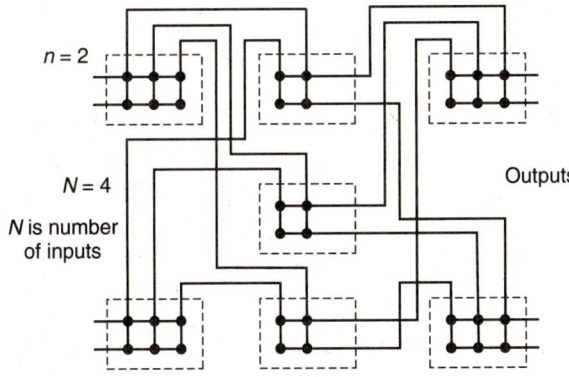

Figure 5.42   A Clos network with $n = 2$, $r = 2$, and $m = 3$.

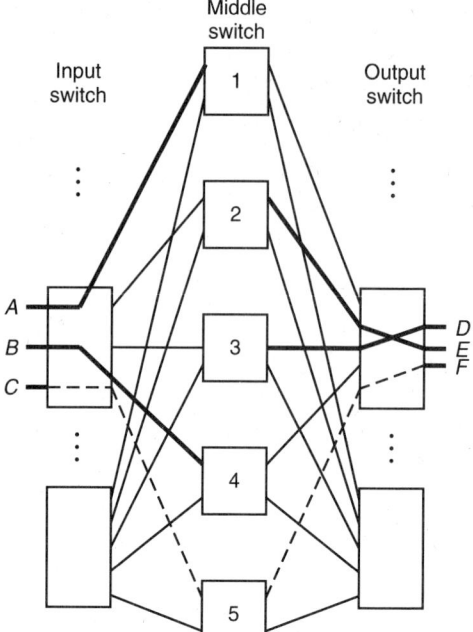

Figure 5.43 A portion of a Clos network in which each input/output switch has three terminals.

The input stage contains $n^2(2n-1)$ switches.
The middle stage contains $n^2(2n-1)$ switches.
The output stage contains $n^2(2n-1)$ switches.

Therefore, the total number of switches, $C(3)$, is

$$C(3) = (2n-1)(3n^2) = 6n^3 - 3n^2.$$

In a similar way, the total number of switches for a five-stage Clos network, shown in Figure 5.44, is

$$C(5) = (2n-1)(6n^3 - 3n^2) + 2n^2 * n(2n-1)$$
$$= 16n^4 - 14n^3 + 3n^2.$$

Rearrangeable networks. Slepian and Duguid showed that the network $N(m, n, r)$ is rearrangeable if and only if $m \geq n$ [BEN 62, DUG 59]. Later, Paull demonstrated that when $m = n = r$ at most $n - 1$ existing paths must be rearranged in order to connect an idle pair of terminals [BEN 62, PAU 62]. Finally, Benes improved Paull's result by showing that a network $N(n, n, r)$, where $r \geq 2$, requires a maximum of $r - 1$ paths to be rearranged [BEN 62].

Construction of Rearrangeable Networks. The development of a rearrangeable network depends largely on the design of the switches and the permutation functions used to connect them. The following method is a generic approach to developing

Sec. 5.2 Network Topology 217

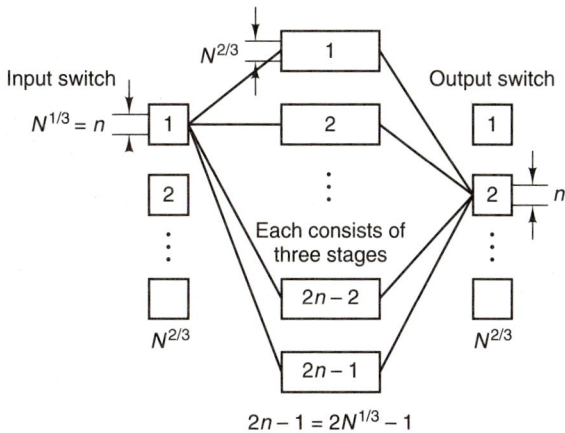

Figure 5.44 A five-stage Clos network; each of the middle-stage boxes is a three-stage Clos network with $N^{2/3}$ inputs/outputs.

such networks. To construct a rearrangeable network with an odd number of stages, the following structure can be used:

$$S_1 \, \alpha_1 \, S_2 \ldots \alpha_{s-1} \, S_s,$$

where S_i represents the switches of ith stage,
  α_i represents the connection between stage S_i and S_{i+1}, and
  $s \geq 3$ represents number of stages.
This network should have the following properties. Let n_i, for $i = 1, \ldots (s+1)/2$, denote the number of inputs (outputs) for every switch in stage S_i. This number is chosen such that

$$\prod_{i=1}^{(S+1)/2} n_i = N$$

where $n_i \geq 2$, and N is the total number of inputs to the network.

The network should also satisfy the following symmetric condition:

$$\alpha_i = \alpha_{s-i}^{-1} \text{ for } i = 1, \ldots, (s-1)/2,$$

$$S_i = S_{s-i+1} \text{ for i} = 1, \ldots, (s-1)/2,$$

where α_{s-i}^{-1} is inverse of the α_i connection.
In other words, the entire network will be symmetrical at the middle stage. To the left of the middle stage the connections $\alpha_1, \ldots, \alpha_{(s-1)/2}$ will connect stages $S_1, \ldots, S_{(s+1)/2}$. To the right of the middle stage the inverse of these connections will connect the stages $S_{(s+1)/2}, \ldots, S_s$.

To define the connection α_i (for $1 \leq i \leq (s-1)/2$), take the first switch of S_i and connect each of its outputs to the input of one of the first n_i switches of S_{i+1}; go on to the second switch of S_i and connect its n_i outputs to the input of each of the next n_i switches of S_{i+1}. When all the switches of S_{i+1} have one link on the input side, start

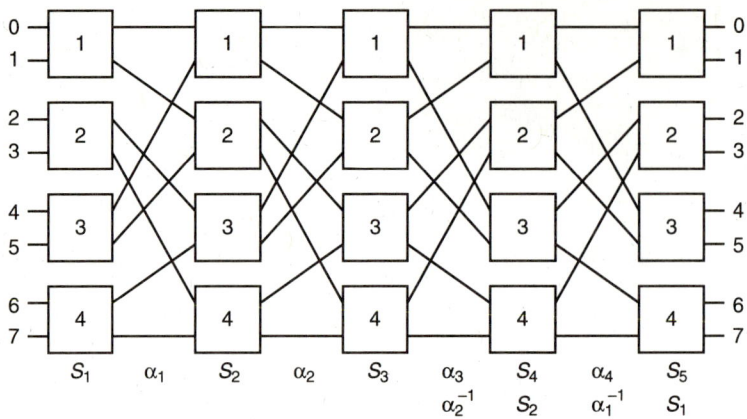

Figure 5.45 An 8-to-8 rearrangable network.

again with the first switch. Proceed cyclically in this way until all the outputs of S_i are assigned. Figure 5.45 represents a rearrangable network, called an eight-input Benes network. Note that $n_1 = n_2 = 2$. An alternative representation of Benes network is shown in Figure 5.46. This representation is obtained by switching the position of switches 2 and 3 in every stage except the middle one.

In general a Benes network can be generated recursively. Figure 5.47 represents the structure of an $N = 2^n$-input Benes network. The middle stage contains two subblocks; each subblock is an $N/2$-input Benes network. The construction process can be recursively applied to the subblocks until subblocks of size 2 inputs are reached. Since the Benes network is a rearrangable network, it is possible to connect the inputs to the outputs according to any of $N!$ permutations.

Blocking networks. Next, two well-known multistage networks, *multistage cube* and *omega*, are discussed. These networks are blocking networks, but they provide necessary permutations for many applications.

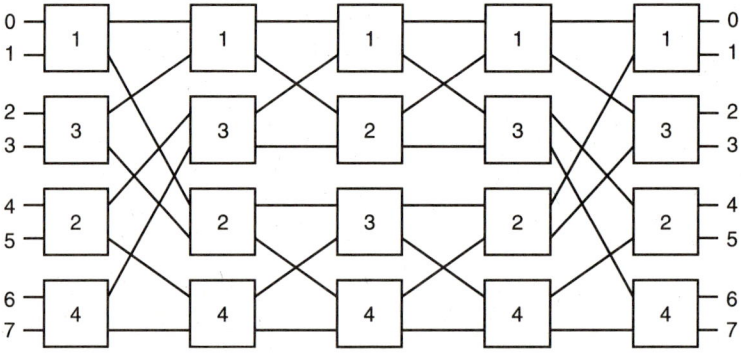

Figure 5.46 An eight-input Benes network.

Sec. 5.2 Network Topology

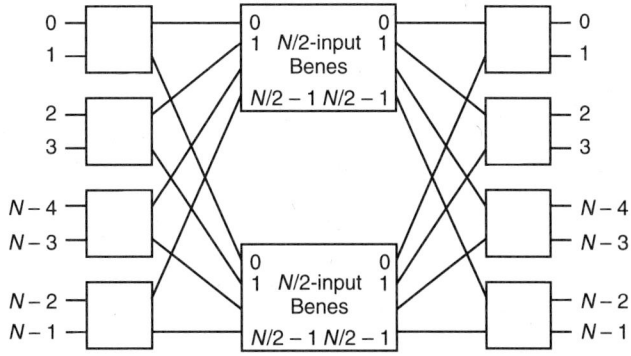

Figure 5.47 Recursive structure of Benes network.

Multistage Cube Network. The multistage cube network, also known as the *inverse indirect n-cube* network, provides a dynamic topology for an *n*-cube network. It can be used as a processor-to-memory or as a processor-to-processor interconnection network. The multistage cube consists of $n = \log_2 N$ stages, where N is the number of inputs (outputs). Each stage in the network consists of $N/2$ switches. Each switch has two inputs, two outputs, and four possible connection states, as shown in Figure 5.48. Two control lines can be used to determine any of the four states. When the switch is in upper broadcast (lower broadcast) state, the data on the upper (lower) input terminal are sent to both output terminals.

As an example, Figure 5.49 represents a multistage cube network when $N = 8$. The connection pattern between stages is such that at each stage the link labels to a switch differ in only 1 bit. More precisely, at stage i the link labels to a switch differ in the ith bit. The reason that such a network is called multistage cube is that the connection patterns between stages correspond to the n-cube network. As shown in Figure 5.50, for $N = 8$, the pattern of links in stages 2, 1, and 0 correspond, respectively, to vertical, diagonal, and horizontal links in the 3-cube.

There are many simple ways for setting the states of the switches in a multistage cube network with $N = 2^n$ inputs. Let's assume that a source S (with address $s_{n-1} s_{n-2} \ldots s_0$) has to be connected to a certain destination D (with address $d_{n-1} d_{n-2} \ldots d_0$). Starting at input S, set the first switch [in the $(n-1)^{th}$ stage] that is connected to S to the straight state when $d_{n-1} = s_{n-1}$; otherwise, set the switch to the exchange state. In the same way, bits d_{n-2} and s_{n-2} determine the state of the switch located on the next stage. This process continues until a path is established between S and D. In general, the state

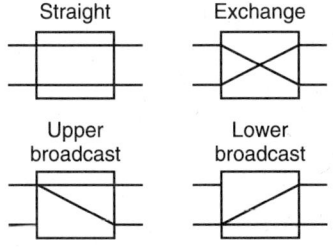

Figure 5.48 The four possible states of the switch used in the multistage cube.

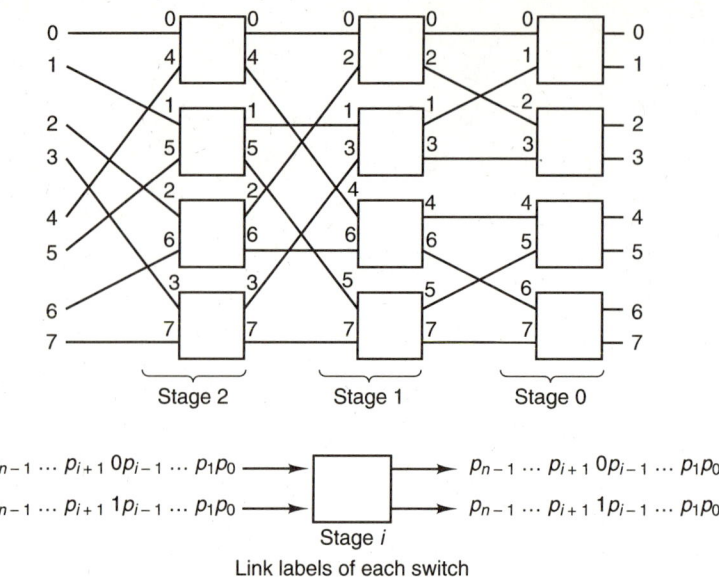

Figure 5.49 An eight-input multistage cube network.

of the switch on the ith stage is straight when $d_i = s_i$; otherwise, the switch is set to exchange. Figure 5.51 represents a path between source 2 (i.e., $S = 010$) and destination 6 (i.e., $D = 110$). In this figure, note that the inputs of the switch on stages 2, 1, and 0 are connected to the output links $d_2 s_1 s_0$, $d_2 d_1 s_0$, and $d_2 d_1 d_0$, respectively.

In the preceding method the differences between the source and destination addresses can be stored as a tag, T, in the head of the packet.

That is, $T = S \oplus D = t_{n-1} \ldots t_0$ determines the state of the switches on the path from source to destination. Once the packet arrives at a switch in stage i, the switch examines t_i and sets its state. If $t_i = 0$, the switch is set in the straight state; otherwise, it is set in the exchange state. Another way is to add destination D as a tag to the header. In this way, the input of the switch on the ith stage is connected to the upper output when $d_i = 0$, otherwise, to the lower output.

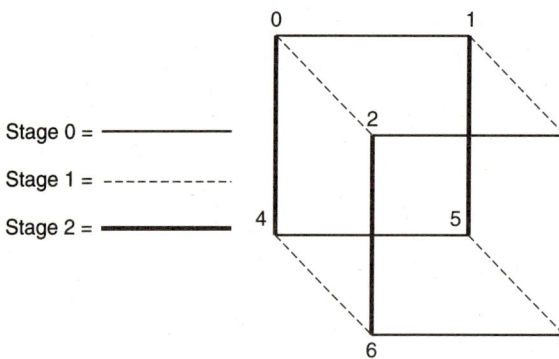

Figure 5.50 Correspondence between the connection patterns of multistage cube and 3-cube networks.

Sec. 5.2 Network Topology

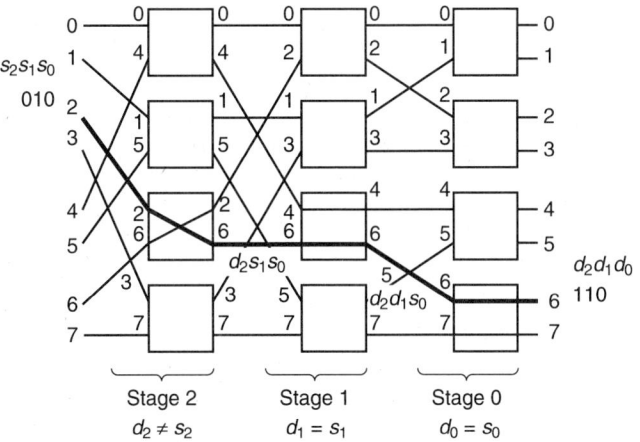

Figure 5.51 Routing in a multistage cube.

A multistage cube supports up to N one-to-one simultaneous connections. However, there are some permutations that cannot be established by this kind of network. For example, as shown in Figure 5.51, a permutation that requires sources 3 and 7 to be connected to destinations 1 and 0, respectively, cannot be established. In addition to one-to-one connections, the multistage cube also supports one-to-many connections; that is, an input device can broadcast to all or a subset of the output devices. For example, Figure 5.52 represents the state of some switches for broadcasting from input 2 to outputs 4, 5, 6, and 7.

Omega Network. The omega network was originally proposed by Lawrie [LAW 75] as an interconnection network between processors and memories. The network allows conflict-free access to rows, columns, diagonals, and square blocks of matrices [LAW 75]. This is important for matrix computation. The omega network provides the necessary permutations (for certain applications) at a substantially lower cost than a crossbar, since the omega requires fewer switches.

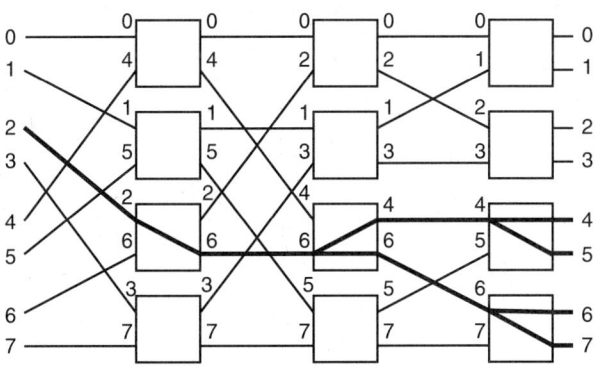

Figure 5.52 Broadcasting in a multistage cube.

The omega network consists of $n = \log_2 N$ stages, where N is the number of inputs (outputs). Each stage in the network consists of a shuffle pattern of links followed by a column of $N/2$ switches. As an example, Figure 5.53 represents an omega network when $N = 8$. Similar to the multistage cube, each switch has two inputs, two outputs, and four possible connection states (see Figure 5.48). Each switch is controlled individually. There is an efficient routing algorithm for setting the states of the switches in the omega network. Let's assume that a source S (with address $s_{n-1} s_{n-2} \ldots s_0$) has to be connected to a certain destination D (with address $d_{n-1} d_{n-2} \ldots d_0$). Starting at input S, connect the input of the first switch [in the $(n-1)^{th}$ stage] that is connected to S to the upper output of the switch when $d_{n-1} = 0$; otherwise, to the lower output. In the same way, bit d_{n-2} determines the output of the switch located on the next stage. This process continues until a path is established between S and D. In general, the input of the switch on the ith stage is connected to the upper output when $d_i = 0$; otherwise, the switch is connected to the lower output. Figure 5.53 represents a path between source 2 (i.e., $S = 010$) and destination 6 (i.e., $D = 110$).

The omega network is a blocking network; that is, some permutations cannot be established by the network. In Figure 5.53, for example, a permutation that requires sources 3 and 7 to be connected to destinations 1 and 0, respectively, cannot be established. However, such permutations can be established in several passes through the network. In other words, sometimes packets may need to go through several nodes so that a particular permutation can be established. For example, when node 3 is connected to node 1, node 7 can be connected to node 0 through node 4. That is, node 7 sends its packet to node 4, and then node 4 sends the packet to node 0. Therefore, we can connect node 3 to node 1 in one pass and node 7 to node 0 in two passes. In general, if we consider a single-stage shuffle–exchange network with N nodes, then every arbitrary permutation can be realized by passing through this network at most $3(\log_2 N) - 1$ times [WU 81].

In addition to one-to-one connections, the omega network also supports broadcasting. Similar to the multistage cube network, the omega network can be used to

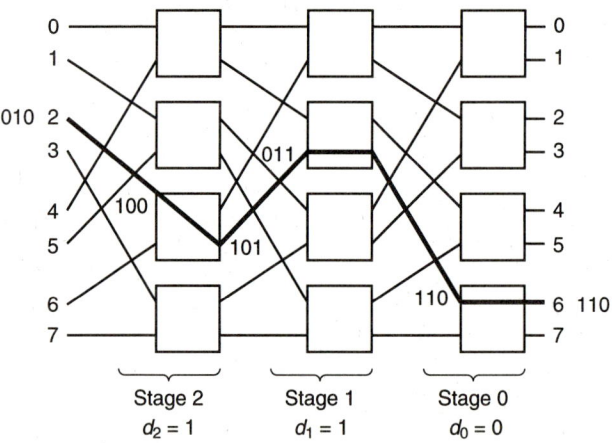

Figure 5.53 An eight-input omega network.

Sec. 5.2 Network Topology

broadcast data from one source to many destinations by setting some of the switches to the upper broadcast or lower broadcast state.

In general, the omega network is equivalent to a multistage cube network; that is, both provide the same set of permutations. In fact, some argue that the omega network is nothing more than an alias for a multistage cube network. Figure 5.54 demonstrates, for $N = 8$, why this assertion may be true. By switching the position of switches 2 and 3 in stage 1 of the multistage cube network, the omega network can be obtained.

Another way to show equivalency (under certain assumptions) between the omega and multistage cube networks is through the representation of allowable permutations for each of them. Any permutation in a network with N inputs, where $N = 2^n$, can be expressed as a collection of n switching (Boolean) functions. For example, consider the following permutation for $N = 8$:

$$[(0, 0),(1, 2),(2, 4),(3, 6),(4, 1),(5, 3),(6, 5),(7, 7)].$$

Let $X = x_2 x_1 x_0$ denote the binary representation of a source. Also, let $F(X) = f_2 f_1 f_0$ denote the binary representation of the destination that X is connected to. Then, the preceding permutation can be represented as follows:

X			connected to	$F(X)$		
x_2	x_1	x_0		f_2	f_1	f_0
0	0	0	→	0	0	0
0	0	1	→	0	1	0
0	1	0	→	1	0	0
0	1	1	→	1	1	0
1	0	0	→	0	0	1
1	0	1	→	0	1	1
1	1	0	→	1	0	1
1	1	1	→	1	1	1

Each of the switching functions f_0, f_1, and f_2, therefore, can be expressed as

$$f_0 = x_2 \bar{x}_1 + x_2 x_1 = x_2,$$
$$f_1 = \bar{x}_2 x_0 + x_2 x_0 = x_0,$$
$$f_2 = \bar{x}_2 x_1 + x_2 x_1 = x_1.$$

Thus, in general, every permutation can be represented in terms of a set of switching functions. In the following, the switching representation of omega and multistage cube networks is derived. Initially, representations of basic functions, such as shuffle and exchange, are derived. These functions are then used to derive representations of omega and multistage cube networks.

Shuffle (σ).   The shuffle function σ is defined as

$$\sigma(x_{n-1} x_{n-2} \ldots x_0) = x_{n-2} x_{n-3} \ldots x_0 x_{n-1}.$$

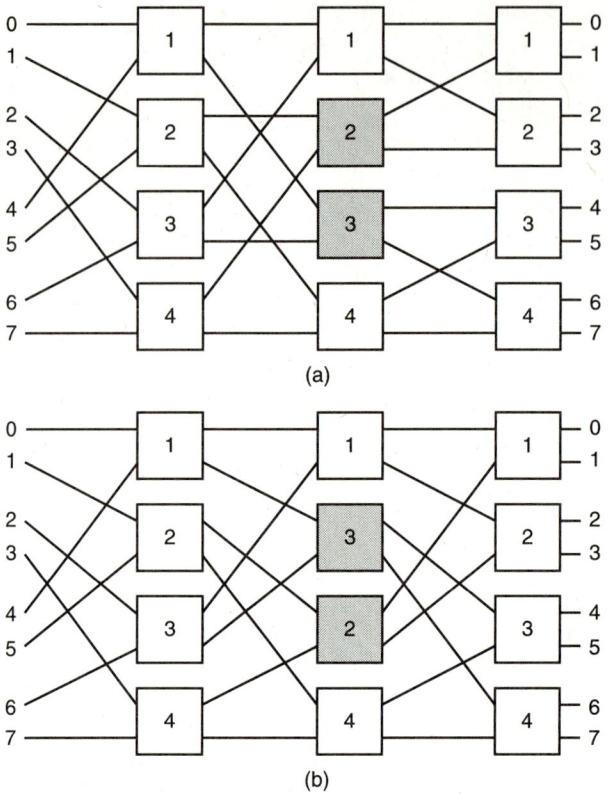

Figure 5.54 Mapping (a) a multistage cube network to (b) an omega network.

This function can also be represented as a set of switching functions, such as

$$f_i = x_{n-1} \quad i = 0$$
$$= x_{i-1} \quad 1 \leq i \leq n-1$$

Exchange (E). The exchange function E is defined as

$$E(x_{n-1}x_{n-2} \ldots x_0) = x_{n-1}x_{n-2}\ldots \overline{x_0}.$$

This function can also be represented as a set of switching functions, such as

$$f_i = \overline{x_0}, \quad i = 0$$
$$= x_i \quad 1 \leq i \leq n-1$$

Omega Network (Ω). Recall that the omega network with n stages is a sequence of n shuffle–exchange functions. That is, $\Omega = E(\sigma(E \ldots \sigma(E(\sigma()))\ldots))$. Thus, to determine to which destination a given source $X = x_{n-1}x_{n-2}\ldots x_1x_0$ is connected, we must first apply function σ, then E, next again σ, and so on. As shown below, after applying σ and E n times to the source X, the switching functions can be obtained. First we apply σ:

$$\sigma(X) \quad \rightarrow \quad x_{n-2} \ldots x_0 \, x_{n-1}.$$

Sec. 5.2 Network Topology

Next, we apply E to $x_{n-2} \ldots x_0 \, x_{n-1}$

$$E(\sigma(X)) \quad \rightarrow \quad x_{n-2} \ldots x_0 \, x_{n-1} \oplus c_{n-1},$$

where the bit c_{n-1} represents the control signal to the switches of the $(n-1)^{th}$ stage, and $\oplus$ denotes the Boolean XOR function. It is assumed that one control signal c_i goes to all the switches of the stage i, and each switch can have two states, straight ($c_i = 0$) and exchange ($c_i = 1$). Note that the bit x_{n-1} is exclusive- or'ed with c_{n-1}, rather than complemented. This is because the bit c_{n-1} determines whether a switch is in the straight state or the exchange state, if a switch is in exchange state then the exchange function should be applied.

Now we apply σ and then E to $x_{n-2} \ldots x_0 \, x_{n-1} \oplus c_{n-1}$

$$E(\sigma(E(\sigma(X)))) \quad \rightarrow \quad x_{n-3} \ldots x_{n-1} \oplus c_{n-1} \, x_{n-2} \oplus c_{n-2},$$

where the bit c_{n-2} represents the control signal to the switches of the $(n-2)^{th}$ stage. Finally,

$$\Omega(X) \quad \rightarrow \quad x_{n-1} \oplus c_{n-1} \ldots x_1 \oplus c_1 \, x_0 \oplus c_0.$$

Thus

$$f_i = x_i \oplus c_i, \quad \text{for } 0 \leq i \leq n-1.$$

Multistage Cube (C). The multistage cube can be represented as

$$C = E(\alpha_0(\cdots E(\alpha_{n-2}(E(\sigma(\,))))\cdots)),$$

where α_i represents the connection between the switches of stage $i+1$ and i, and n is the number of stages. The function α_i is defined as

$$\alpha_i(x_{n-1} x_{n-2} \ldots x_{i+1} \ldots x_0) = x_{n-1} x_{n-2} \ldots x_0 \ldots x_{i+1}.$$

First we apply σ and then E:

$$E(\sigma(X)) \quad \rightarrow \quad x_{n-2} \ldots x_0 \, x_{n-1} \oplus c_{n-1},$$

where the bit c_{n-1} represents the control signal to the switches of the $(n-1)^{th}$. It is assumed that one control signal c_i goes to all the switches of stage i, and each switch can have two states, straight ($c_i = 0$) and exchange ($c_i = 1$).

$$E(\alpha_{n-2}(E(\sigma(X)))) \quad \rightarrow \quad x_{n-1} \oplus c_{n-1} \, x_{n-3} \ldots x_0 \, x_{n-2} \oplus c_{n-2},$$

$$E(\alpha_{n-3}(E(\alpha_{n-2}(E(\sigma(X)))))) \quad \rightarrow \quad x_{n-1} \oplus c_{n-1} \, x_{n-2} \oplus c_{n-2} \, x_{n-4} \ldots x_0 \, x_{n-3} \oplus c_{n-3}.$$

Finally,

$$C(X) \quad \rightarrow \quad x_{n-1} \oplus c_{n-1} \, x_{n-2} \oplus c_{n-2} \ldots x_0 \oplus c_0.$$

Thus

$$f_i = x_i \oplus c_i, \quad \text{for} \quad 0 \leq i \leq n-1.$$

Note that the omega network also has the same set of switching functions; therefore, it is equivalent to the multistage cube.

5.3 INTERCONNECTION DESIGN DECISIONS

A major problem in parallel computer design is finding an interconnection network capable of providing fast and efficient communication at a reasonable cost. There are at least five design considerations when selecting the architecture of an interconnection network: operation mode, switching methodology, network topology, a control strategy, and the functional characteristics of the switch.

Operation mode. Three primary operating modes are available to the interconnection network designer: synchronous, asynchronous, and combined. When a synchronous stream of instructions or data is required by the network, a synchronous communication system is required. In other words, synchronous communication is needed for establishing communication paths synchronously for either data manipulating functions or for a data instruction broadcast. Most SIMD machines operate in a lock-step fashion; that is, all active processing nodes transmit data at the same time. Thus synchronous communication seems an appropriate choice for SIMD machines.

When connection requests for an interconnection network are issued dynamically, an asynchronous communication system is needed. Since the timing of the routing requests is not predictable, the system must be able to handle such requests at any time.

Some systems are designed to handle both synchronous and asynchronous communications. Such systems are able to do array processing by utilizing synchronous communications, yet are also able to control less predictable communication requests by using asynchronous timing methods.

Switching methodology. The three main types of switching methodologies are circuit switching, packet switching, and integrated switching. Circuit switching establishes a complete path between source and destination and holds this path for the entire transmission. It is best suited for transmitting large amounts of continuous data. In contrast to circuit switching, packet switching has no dedicated physical connection set up. Hence it is most useful for transmitting small amounts of data. In packet switching, data items are partitioned into fixed-sized packets. Each packet has a header that contains routing information, and moves from one node in the network to the next. The packet switching increases channel throughput by multiplexing various packets through the same path. Most SIMD machines use circuit switching, while packet switching is most suited to MIMD machines.

The third option, integrated switching, is a combination of circuit and packet switching. This allows large amounts of data to be moved quickly over the physical path while allowing smaller packets of information to be transmitted via the network.

Network topology. To design or select a topology, several performance parameters should be considered. The most important parameters are the following:

1. *VLSI implementable.* The topology of the network should be able to be mapped on two (or three) physical dimensions so that it can produce an efficient layout for packaging and implementation in VLSI systems.

Sec. 5.3   Interconnection Design Decisions

2. *Small diameter.* The diameter of the network should grow slowly with the number of nodes.
3. *Neighbor independency.* The number of neighbors of any node should be independent of the size of the network. This allows the network to scale up to a very large size.
4. *Easy to route.* There should be an efficient algorithm for routing messages from any node to any other. The messages must find an optimal path between the source and destination nodes and make use of all the available bandwidth.
5. *Uniform load.* The traffic load on various parts of the network should be uniform.
6. *Redundant pathways.* The network should be highly reliable and highly available. Message pathways should be redundant to provide robustness in the event of component failure.

Control strategy and functional characteristics of the switch. All dynamic networks are composed of switch boxes connected together through a series of links. The functional characteristics of a switch box are its size, routing logic, the number of possible states for the switch, fault detection and correction, communication protocols, and the amount of buffer space available for storing packets when there is congestion. Most of the switches provide some of these capabilities, depending on implementation requirements relating to efficiency and cost.

In general, states of the switches of a network can be set by a central controller or by each individual switch. The former is a centralized control system, while the latter is a distributed one.

Centralized control can be further broken down into individual stage control, individual box control, and partial stage control. Individual stage control uses one control signal to set all switch boxes at the same stage. Individual box control uses a separate control signal to set the state of each switch box. This offers higher flexibility in setting up the connecting paths, but increases the number of control signals, which, in turn, significantly increases control circuit complexity. In partial stage control, $i + 1$ control signals are used at stage i of the network.

In a distributed control network, the switches are usually more complex. In multistage interconnection networks, the switches have to deal with conflict resolution, as well as with changes in routing due to faults or congestion. Switches utilize protocols for handshaking to ensure that data may be correctly transferred. Large buffers enable a switch to store data that cannot be sent forward due to congestion. This allows increased performance of the network by decreasing the number of retransmissions.

BIBLIOGRAPHIC NOTES

[AGA 91] provides a good performance analysis of k-ary n-cube under various constraints. [FEN 81] was used for explaining design considerations when selecting an interconnection network. [DAL 87] describes wormhole routing and its deadlock-free routing property. [LES 93] was used for writing the diameter and some characteristics of static networks.

REFERENCES

[AGA 91] AGARWAL, ANANT, "Limits on Interconnection Network Performance," *IEEE Trans. Parallel and Distributed Systems*, 2(4), 1991, pp. 398–412.

[BEN 62] BENES, V. E., "On Rearrangeable Three-stage Connecting Networks," *Bell System Tech. J.,* 41(5) 1962, pp. 1481–1492.

[CLO 53] CLOS, C., "A Study of Non-Blocking Switching Networks," *Bell System Tech. J.,* 32, 1953, pp. 406–424.

[DAL 87] DALLY, WILLIAM J., AND CHARLES L. SEITZ, "Deadlock-free Message Routing in Multiprocessor Interconnection Networks," *IEEE Trans. Computers,* C-36(5), 1987, pp. 547–553.

[DAL 91] DALLY, W. J., "Express Cubes: Improving the Performance of *k*-ary *n*-cube Interconnection Networks," *IEEE Trans. Computers,* 40(9), 1991, pp. 1016–1023.

[DUG 59] DUGUID, A. M., "Structural Properties of Switching Networks," Brown University Progress Report BTL-7, 1959.

[FEN 81] FENG, TSE-YUN, "A Survey of Interconnection Networks," *IEEE Computer*, December 1981, pp. 12–27.

[GLA 92] GLASS, C. J., AND L. M. NI, "The Turn Model for Adaptive Routing," *IEEE Proc. 19th Interm. Symp. Computer Architecture*, pp. 278–287.

[LAW 75] LAWRIE, DUNCAN H., "Access and Alignment of Data in an Array Processor," *IEEE Trans. Computers*, C-24(12), 1975, pp. 1145–1155.

[LEI 85] LEISERSON, CHARLES E., "Fat-Trees: Universal Networks for Hardware-efficient Supercomputing," *IEEE Trans. Computers*, C-34(10), 1985, pp. 892–901.

[LES 93] LESTER, BRUCE P., *The Art of Parallel Programming*. Upper Saddle River, NJ: Prentice Hall, 1993.

[NI 93] NI, LIONEL M., AND PHILIP K. MCKINLEY, "A Survey of Wormhole Routing Techniques in Direct Networks," *Computer*, February 1993, pp. 62–76.

[PAU 62] PAULL, M. C., "Reswitching of Connection Networks," *Bell System Tech. J.,* 41, 1962, pp. 833–855.

[SLE 52] SLEPIAN, D., "Two Theorems on a Particular Crossbar Switching Network," unpublished manuscript, 1952.

[SLO 71] SLOTNICK, D. L., "The Fastest Computer," *Scientific American*, 224(2), February 1971, pp. 76–87.

[STO 71] STONE, HAROLD S., "Parallel Processing with the Perfect Shuffle," *IEEE Trans. Computers*, C-20(2), 1971, pp. 153–161.

[TAN 81] TANENBAUM, ANDREW S., *Computer Networks*. Upper Saddle River, NJ: Prentice Hall, 1981.

[WU 80] WU, CHUAN-LIN, AND TSE-YUM FENG "On a Class of Multistage Interconnection Network," *IEEE Trans. Computers*, C-29(8), 1980, pp. 694–702.

[WU 81] WU, CHUAN-LIN, AND TSE-YUN FENG, "The Universality of the Shuffle–Exchange Network," *IEEE Trans. Computers*, C-30(5), 1981, pp. 324–332.

PROBLEMS

5.1. Discuss the advantages and disadvantages of the following networks:
   a. Shared bus
   b. Linear array
   c. Ring
   d. Binary tree
   e. Fat tree.

5.2. Write a routing algorithm for a bidirectional ring network with n nodes.

5.3. Consider a complete binary tree T (where each nonleaf node has two children) of height d (for $d > 0$). Write an algorithm for finding the number of links between a given source node S and a given destination D.

5.4. In this chapter it was shown how a shuffle–exchange network can be used to evaluate a polynomial. Follow the same steps to evaluate the following polynomial:

$$5 - 3x + 6x^2 + 7x^3 + 2x^4 - 5x^5 + x^6, \text{ for } x = 2.$$

Show the contents of the registers at each step.

5.5. In this chapter, a routing algorithm was given for an n-by-n mesh. Use this routing algorithm to show the routing path from source node 15 to destination node 5 in a 4-by-4 mesh.

5.6. Write a routing algorithm for an n-by-n torus network.

5.7. A complete binary tree T (where each nonleaf node has two children) of height d (for $d > 0$) can be embedded in a hypercube C of degree $d + 1$ in such a way that the adjacencies of nodes T are preserved. A complete binary tree T of height d has $2^d - 1$ nodes. A hypercube of degree $d + 1$ has 2^{d+1} nodes, and each node has $d + 1$ neighbors. For example, the tree of height 2 in Figure P5.7 can be embedded in a hypercube of degree 3. In a sim-

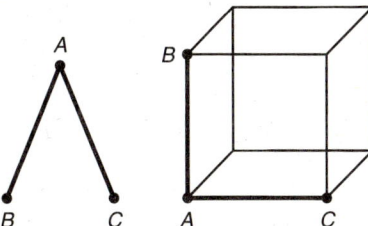

Figure P5.7

ilar way, show that a tree of height 3 can be embedded in a hypercube of degree 4.

5.8. Draw the structure of the following interconnection networks. Also, determine the diameter of each network.
   a. Three-dimensional mesh in which $k_i = 2$ for $0 \le i \le 2$
   b. Three-dimensional mesh in which $k_2 = 3$, $k_1 = 2$, and $k_0 = 4$
   c. A 3-ary 2-cube
   d. A 3-ary 4-cube
   e. A 8-by-8 torus with folded connections.

5.9. Parallel processing of certain applications often requires a processor to broadcast a result to all other processors. A broadcast is defined as the operation of distributing a copy of a message from one node in a network to all the other nodes in the network. For each of the following network topologies, describe an optimal broadcast algorithm for node 0 to distribute a copy of a message to every other node. Assume that each switch has the capability to duplicate data items coming from one of the inputs. By using arrows, show the paths that the data should take when $n = 3$. Also, based on your algorithm derive a formula for the total time required for broadcasting. Assume that the time for transmitting a message through a communication link between any two nodes is τ time units. Furthermore, explain how your algorithm can broadcast more than one message to every other node in an efficient way.

a. An n-by-n mesh network

b. An n-by-n torus network

c. An n-cube

d. A three-dimensional mesh for $k_2 = k_1 = k_0 = 3$.

5.10. Consider a modified mesh network topology called an eight-nearest-neighbor mesh with $N(\geq 2)$ nodes. As shown in Figure P5.10, each node is connected to its north, northwest,

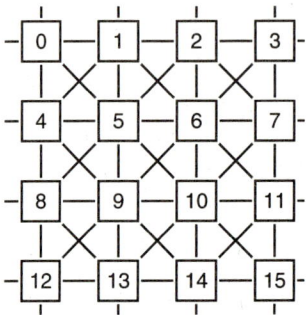

Figure P5.10 An eight-nearest neighbor mesh with 16 nodes.

west, southwest, south, southeast, east, and northeast neighbors. In general, the node at row i and column j is connected to the nodes at locations $(i-1, j)$, $(i-1, j-1)$, $(i, j-1)$, $(i+1, j-1)$, $(i+1, j)$, $(i+1, j+1)$, $(i, j+1)$, $(i-1, j+1)$, with the exception of edge nodes, which may have only three or five neighbors.

a. What is the diameter of this network?

b. Develop a routing algorithm for the eight-nearest-neighbor mesh. The algorithm should be able to route a packet from source S to destination D. Show the steps of your algorithm on a network with 16 nodes. Let S be node 7 and D be node 12.

5.11. In the literature, there are several proposed methods for performing Batcher's bitonic sort on a mesh with n by n PEs (processor elements). The PEs may be indexed quite differently from one method to another, depending on how the sorted result will be used in later steps of an application. As shown in Figure P5.11A, there are three commonly used indexing methods: row major, snakelike row major, and shuffled row major. In row-major indexing, the PEs are indexed left to right and top to bottom. In snakelike row-major indexing, the PEs on even rows are indexed left to right, and the PEs on odd rows are indexed right to left. In shuffled row-major indexing, the PEs are indexed by shuffling their corresponding row-major index. For example, if the row-major index in binary is $x_7x_6x_5x_4x_3x_2x_1x_0$, then its shuffled index is $x_7x_3x_6x_2x_5x_1x_4x_0$.

Here, let's consider the algorithm by D. Nassimi and S. Sahni. This algorithm sorts the n by n elements into row-major order; its main steps are as follows:

Problems

1. Initially, $K = S = 1$, where K is the size of block and S represents the pass number.
2. Subdivide the mesh into blocks, each block with a K by $2K$ PEs.
3. Do HORIZONTAL_MERGE(K, 2K) on each block in parallel.
4. Treat two adjacent blocks (upper and lower) as one block and do VERTICAL_MERGE(2K, 2K) on each new block in parallel.
5. $K = 2 * K$, $S = S + 1$, go to step 2 while $K < n$.

The HORIZONTAL_MERGE sorts a bitonic sequence arranged in two blocks with the increasing order on the left block and the decreasing order on the right block, or vice versa. Similarly, the VERTICAL_MERGE sorts a bitonic sequence arranged in two blocks with the increasing order on the upper block and the decreasing order on the lower block, or vice versa.

At each iteration, a SIGN function determines the order into which a block gets sorted, where + is for nondecreasing order and − for nonincreasing order. The sign will be determined by SI (the shuffled row-majored index of the PE) and S (the pass number).

```
procedure SIGN (SI, S)
        IF ⌊SI/2ˢ⌋ is even then return ("+")
                        else return ("-");
```

A complete example of sorting a 4 by 4 mesh is shown in Figure P5.11B. Initially, PEs contain the randomized numbers (part a) and the sign needed by the next step. After the first HORIZONTAL_MERGE pass, the elements in 1-by-2 block are sorted with the order determined by the signs in part (a). By doing the VERTICAL_MERGE pass, we get four 4 by 4 sorted blocks. After another HORIZONTAL_MERGE pass and another VERTICAL_MERGE pass, the 4 by 4 mesh is completely sorted in the row-major order.

Write a procedure to perform the VERTICAL_MERGE on two J by K blocks.

5.12. Consider an interconnection network with channel bandwidth W (bits/second). Let D be the number of channels traversed by a packet, L be the packet length (in bits), and F be the flit length (in bits).

   a. Derive equations for communication latency of store-and-forward routing and wormhole routing on this network, respectively.

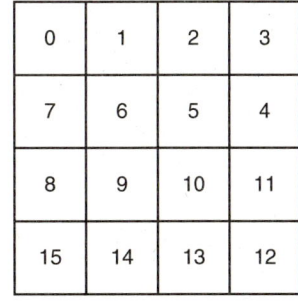
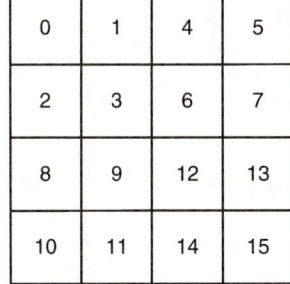

Figure P5.11A

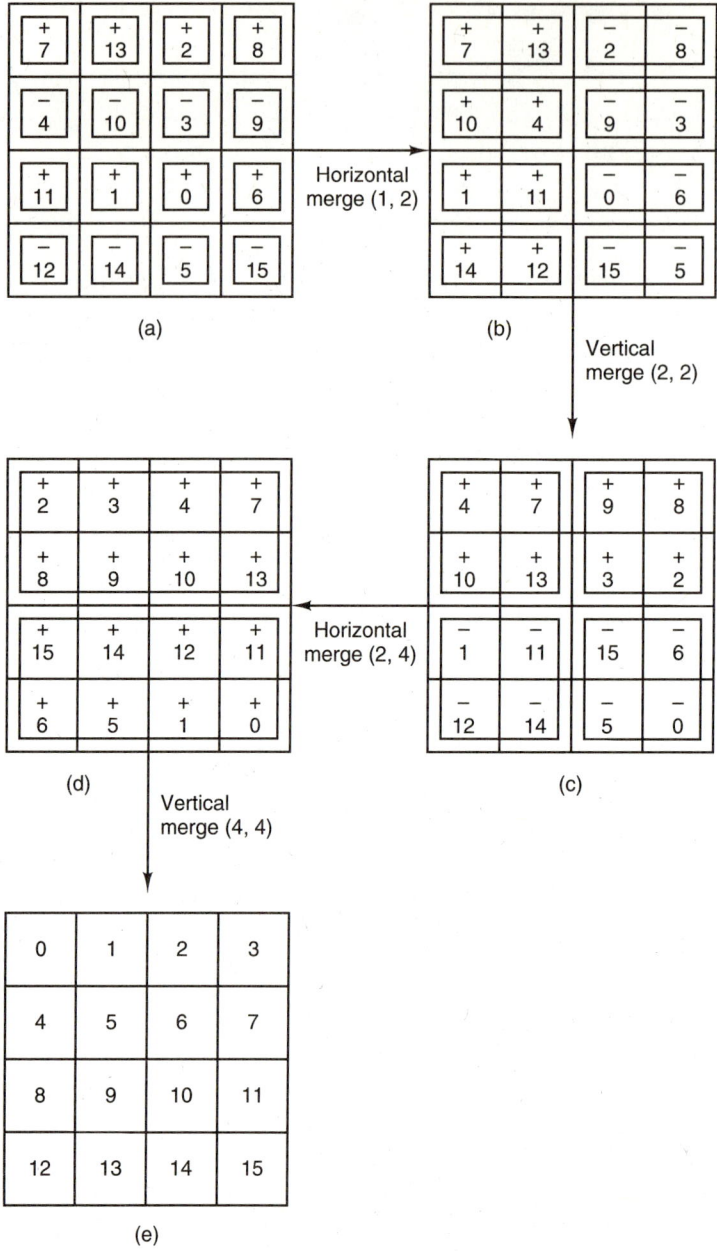

Figure P5.11B

b. Let $W = 200$ million bits/sec, $L = 1024$ bits, $F = 8$ bits, and $D = 10$. Use the equations in part (a) to compute the latency for each routing technique.

5.13. The turn model is a deadlock-free adaptive wormhole routing [GLA 92, NI 93]. Since deadlocks are caused by cyclic dependency among the nodes, the turn model disallows certain directions that the packet can turn in a network. The turn model treats each physical channel in a particular direction as a virtual direction and identifies all possible turns from one virtual direction to the other. The cycles that are caused due to the turns are found and prevented by disallowing one turn from each of the cycles. For example, in a two-dimensional mesh, the possible cycles can be grouped into two abstract cycles as shown in Figure P5.12A.

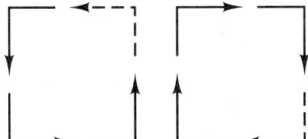

Figure P5.12A.

One turn from each cycle must be prohibited to prevent deadlock. In the figures, the prohibited turns are the two to the west. Therefore, to travel west, a packet must start out in that direction. That is, first route the packet west, if necessary, and then adaptively south, east, and north. Use this method to draw routing paths from S_1 to D_1, S_2 to D_2, and S_3 to D_3 in the 8 by 8 mesh of Figure P5.12B. State the reason of your choice of the routing

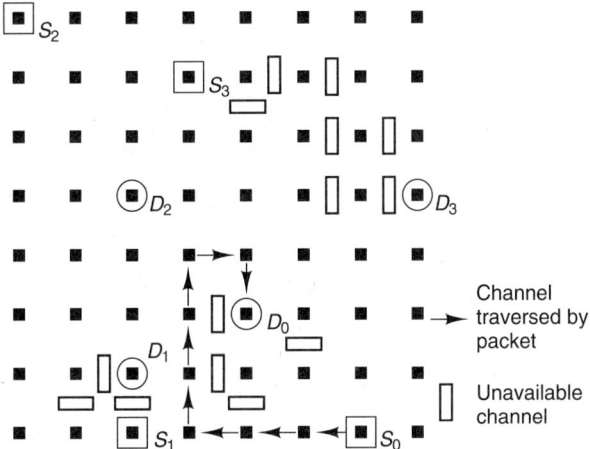

Figure P5.12B.

paths. As an example, a routing path is shown from source S_0 to destination D_0. Note that the channels that are either faulty or being used by other packets are marked as unavailable channels.

5.14. Write a wormhole routing algorithm for k-ary n-cube networks. Explain your scheme for labeling virtual channels and your algorithm on a hypercube with eight nodes (i.e., 2-ary 3-cube).

5.15. Draw the first stage of an omega network with 16 input nodes.

5.16. Draw a multistage cube network with 16 input nodes.

5.17. Prove that the Clos network $N(m, n, r)$, where $m = 2n - 1$, is a nonblocking network.

5.18. A sort network is a network that can accept n unordered numbers and produce an n-ordered output. For example, in a four-input sort network that sorts in descending order (see Figure P5.18A), if the inputs are 2, 8, 6, and 7, then the outputs will be sorted as 8, 7, 6, and 2.

Figure P5.18A

The sort network consists of a set of two-input/two-output identical switches. As shown in Figure P5.18B, the value of the inputs to a switch will determine the connections between inputs and outputs of that switch.

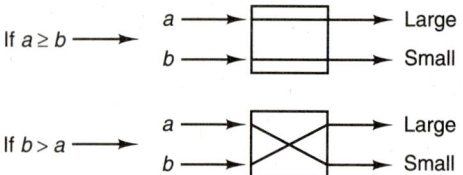

Figure P5.18B

Now, use five of the switches to construct a sort network with four inputs and four outputs.

5.19. Is the network in Figure P5.19 a rearrangeable network? Why?

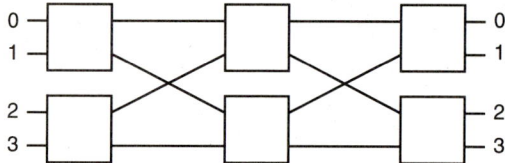

Figure P5.19

5.20. The network in Figure P5.20A is called a modified Benes network. The only difference between this network and the Benes network is that the input terminals are relabeled.

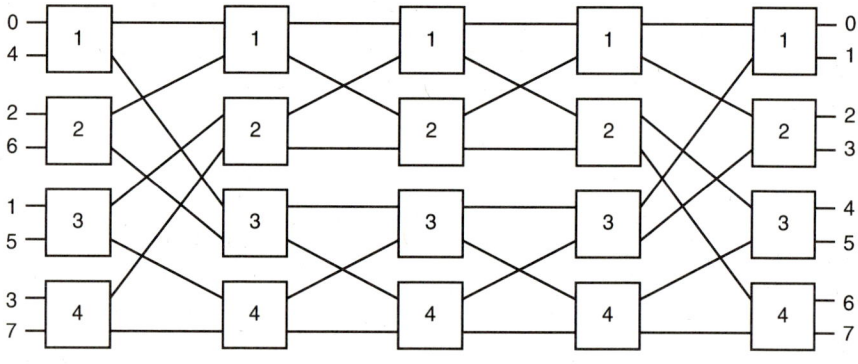

Figure P5.20A

a. Show that the modified Benes network is a rearrangeable network.

b. Consider the network in Figure P5.20B, where the number of inputs is $N = 2^n = 8$. The first three stages of this network constitute an omega network (Ω), and the last two

Problems

stages constitute a network (M) formed by cascading two shuffle–exchange stages. The connection pattern between the first three stages and the last two stages is a bit switch permutation δ. The bit switch permutation can be defined as

$$\delta(x_{n-1}x_{n-2} \ldots x_0) = x_1x_2 \ldots x_{n-2}x_{n-1}x_0, \text{ for } n > 1,$$

where $x_{n-1}x_{n-2}\ldots x_0$ is the binary representation of the input.

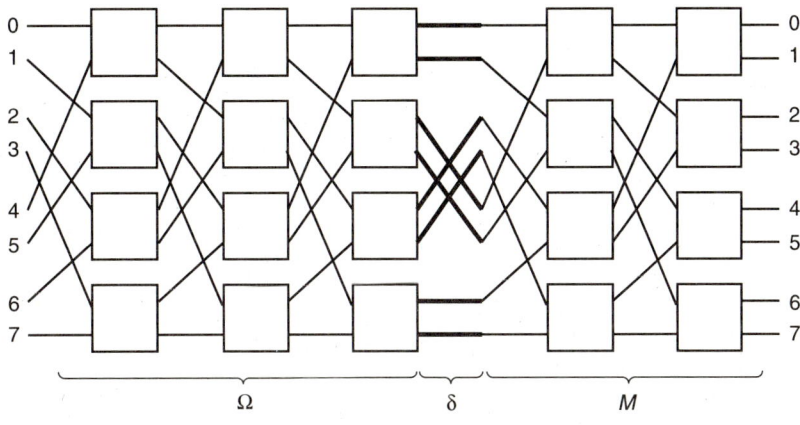

Figure P5.20B

Show that the network of Figure P5.20B is a rearrangeable network. *Hint:* Change the position of some of the switches in the modified Benes network to obtain the above network.

    c. For $N = 8$, show that the bit switch permutation can be realized in two omega passes.

    d. Show that an eight-input network formed by cascading eight shuffle–exchange stages is a rearrangeable network. *Hint:* use parts (b) and (c) to show that such a network is equivalent to a modified Benes network.

5.21. Derive the switching functions for the following networks.

    a. Inverse omega: This network can be represented as

$$\sigma_{n-1}^{-1}(\ldots \sigma_1^{-1}(E(\sigma_0^{-1}(E()))) \ldots),$$

where σ^{-1} is the inverse of a shuffle connection, and n is the number of stages. If a connection connects i to j, then its inverse connects j to i.

    b. Inverse multistage cube: This network can be represented as

$$\sigma^{-1}(E(\alpha_{n-2}^{-1}(\ldots \alpha_1^{-1}(E(\alpha_0^{-1}E())) \ldots))).$$

    c. Baseline network: Defined in Figure P5.21A.

    d. Banyan network: Defined in Figure P5.21B.

    e. Inverse baseline: This network can be represented as

$$E(\beta_{n-2}^{-1} \ldots (E(\beta_0^{-1}(E()))) \ldots).$$

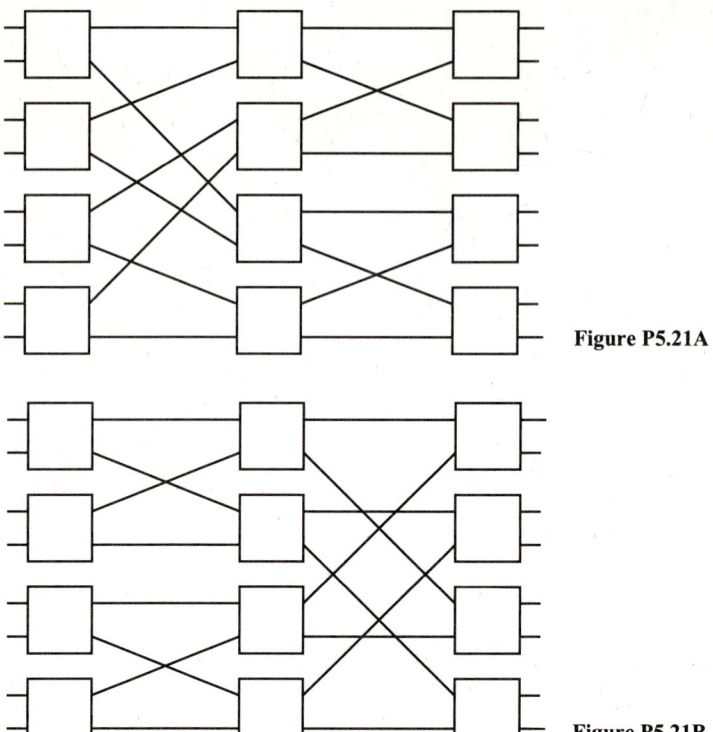

Figure P5.21A

Figure P5.21B

6

Multiprocessors and Multicomputers

6.1 INTRODUCTION

As the demand for more computing power at a lower price continues, computer firms are building parallel computers more frequently. There are many reasons for this trend toward parallel machines, the most common being to increase overall computer power. Although the advancement of semiconductor and VLSI technology has substantially improved the performance of single-processor machines, they are still not fast enough to perform certain applications within a reasonable time. Examples of such applications include biomedical analysis, aircraft testing, real-time pattern recognition, real-time speech recognition, and solutions of systems of partial differential equations.

Due to rapid advances in integration technology, culminating in current VLSI techniques, vast gains in computing power have been realized over a relatively short period of time. Similar gains in the future are unlikely to occur, however. Further advancements in VLSI technology will soon become impossible because of physical limitations of materials. Furthermore, there is a limit to the maximum obtainable clock speed for single-processor systems. These limits have sparked the development of parallel computers that can process information on the order of a trillion (10^{12}) floating-point operations per second (FLOPS). Such parallel computers use many processors to work on the same problem at the same time to overcome the sequential barrier set by von Neumann architecture.

The connection of multiple processors has led to the development of parallel machines that are capable of executing tens of billions of instructions per second. In addition to increasing the number of interconnected processors, the utilization of faster microprocessors and faster communication channels between the processors can easily be used to upgrade the speed of parallel machines. An alternative way to build these types of computers (called *supercomputers*) is to rely on very fast components and highly pipelined operations. This is the method found in Cray, NEC, and Fujitsu supercomputers. However, this method also results in long design time and very expensive machines. In addition, these types of machines depend heavily on the pipelining of functional units, vector registers, and interleaved memory modules to obtain high performance. Given the fact that programs contain not only vector but also scalar instructions, increasing the level of pipelining cannot fully satisfy today's demand for higher performance.

In addition to surmounting the sequential barrier, parallel computers can provide more reliable systems than do single processor machines. If a single processor in a parallel system fails, the system can still operate (at some diminished capacity), whereas if the processor on a uniprocessor system malfunctions, catastrophic and fatal failure results. Finally, parallel systems provide greater availability than single-processor systems. (The availability of a system is the probability that a system will be available to run useful computation.)

The preceding advantages of parallel computers have provided the incentive for many companies to design such systems. Today numerous parallel computers are commercially available and there will be many more in the near future. Designing a parallel machine involves the consideration of a variety of factors, such as number of processors, the processors' speed, memory system, interconnection network, routing algorithm, and the type of control used in the design. Consideration must also be given to the reliable operation of the parallel machine in the event of node and/or link failure. Fault tolerance addresses this reliability concern.

We must also decide on the level of parallelism, which specifies the size of the subtasks that an original task is split into. Different design philosophies favor different sizes. Each design philosophy has its own strengths and weaknesses. In one of the simpler implementations, numerous relatively simple processors work on different sets of the data, performing the same set of instructions on each set. These processors must interact often in order to synchronize themselves. Alternatively, processors can work independently, interacting only briefly and not very often. These processors can be geographically distant from one another. Another approach consists of medium-power processors that are physically close together so that they may communicate easily via dedicated links or communication paths, but that, at the same time, work relatively independently of one another.

Another factor in designing a parallel machine is scalability. This is really a hardware issue that deals with expanding the processing power of the parallel systems, just as sequential architectures have become expandable with respect to memory capacity. More precisely, we would like to plug more processors into a parallel machine to improve its performance.

Considering all these requirements for different applications, the common characteristics that are strongly desired by all parallel systems can be summarized as follows:

1. High performance at low cost: use of high-volume/low-cost components fit to the available technology
2. Reliable performance
3. Scalable design

There are many types of parallel computers; this chapter will concentrate on two types of commonly used systems: *multiprocessors* and *multicomputers*. A conceptual view of these two designs was shown in Chapter 1. The multiprocessor can be viewed as a parallel computer with a main memory system shared by all the processors. The multicomputer can be viewed as a parallel computer in which each processor has its own local memory. In multicomputers the memory address space is not shared among the processors; that is, a processor only has direct access to its local memory and not to the other processors' local memories. The following sections detail the architectures of multiprocessors, multicomputers, and multi-multiprocessors. To present some of the most common interconnections used, the architectures of some state-of-the-art parallel computers are discussed and compared.

6.2 MULTIPROCESSORS

A multiprocessor has a memory system that is addressable by each processor. As such, the memory system consists of one or more memory modules whose address space is shared by all the processors. Based on the organization of the memory system, the multiprocessors can be further divided into two groups, *tightly coupled* and *loosely coupled*.

In a tightly coupled multiprocessor, a central memory system provides the same access time for each processor. This type of central memory system is often called *main memory*, *shared memory*, or *global memory*. The central memory system can be implemented either as one big memory module or as a set of memory modules that can be accessed in parallel by different processors. The latter design reduces *memory contention* by the processors and makes the system more efficient. Memory contention refers to situations where many processors request access to memory within a very short time interval, resulting in unreasonable memory access delays.

In addition to the central memory system, each processor might also have a small cache memory. (A cache memory is a fast type of memory that sits between the processor and the interconnection to main memory in order to make the accessing faster.) These caches also help reduce memory contention and make the system more efficient.

In a loosely coupled multiprocessor, in order to reduce memory contention the memory system is partitioned between the processors; that is, a local memory is attached to each processor. Thus each processor can directly access its own local memory and all the other processors' local memories. However, the access time to a remote memory is much higher than to the local memory.

Regardless of the type, a multiprocessor has one operating system used by all the processors. The operating system provides interaction between processors and their tasks at the process and data element level. (The term *process* may be defined as a part of a program that can be run on a processor.) Each processor is capable of doing a large task on its own. The processors are usually of the same type. A multiprocessor that has the same processors is called *homogeneous*; if the processors are different, it is called *heterogeneous*. Any of the processors can access any of the I/O devices, although they may have to go through one of the other processors.

As discussed in the introduction, a number of problems complicates the task of multiprocessor design. Two of these problems are *choice of an interconnection network* and *updating multiple caches*. Unfortunately, there are no simple answers to these problems. Like every other design, the trade-off between cost and performance plays an important role in choosing a suitable solution, as the following sections demonstrate.

6.2.1 Common Interconnection Networks

One of the first decisions that must be made when designing a multiprocessor system is the type of interconnection network that will be used between the processors and the shared memory. The interconnection must be such that each processor is able to access all the available memory space. When two or more processors are accessing memory at the same time, they should all be able to receive the requested data.

Shared bus. One commonly used interconnection is the shared bus (also called common bus or single bus). The shared bus is the simplest and least expensive way of connecting several processors to a set of memory modules (see Figure 6.1). It allows compatibility and provides ease of operation and high bandwidth.

Some of the available commercial multiprocessors based on the shared bus are the Sequent Symmetry series and the Encore Multimax series. The Sequent Symmetry system 2000/700 can be configured with up to 15 processor units and up to 386 Mbytes of memory, which are attached to a single-system bus [SEQ 91]. Each processor unit includes two Intel 80486 microprocessors that operate independently, two 512-Kbyte two-way, set-associative caches, and the combined supporting circuitry. The supporting circuitry plays a crucial role in isolating the processors from the mundane tasks associated with cache misses, bus arbitration, and interrupt acceptance. The system bus is a 10-MHz bus with a 64-bit-wide data path. Hence the system bus has a bandwidth of 80 Mbytes/sec. Address and data information are time multiplexed, with address information going out on every third bus cycle. In every three cycles, up to 16 bytes of information can be sent. This represents a data transfer rate of

$$(16 \text{ bytes}/3 \text{ cycles}) * (10 \text{ Mcycles/sec}) = 53.3 \text{ Mbytes/sec}.$$

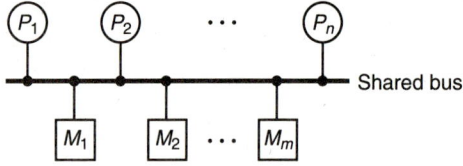

P: Processor
M: Memory module

Figure 6.1 Bus-based multiprocessor.

Sec. 6.2   Multiprocessors

In parallel with the system bus, there is a single line called the system link and interrupt controller (SLIC) bus. The SLIC bus is used to send interrupts and other low-priority communications between the units on the system bus.

The Encore Multimax system is configured around a single bus with a bandwidth of 100 Mbytes/sec. It can be configured with up to 20 processor units and up to 160 Mbytes of memory. Each processor unit includes a National Semiconductor CPU, an AS32381 floating-point unit, a memory management unit, and a 256 Kbytes cache memory.

The main drawback of the shared bus is that its throughput limits the performance boundary for the entire multiprocessor system. This is because at any time only one memory access is granted, likely causing some processors to remain idle. To increase performance by reducing the memory access traffic, a cache memory is often assigned to each processor. Another disadvantage of the shared bus design is that, if the bus fails, catastrophic failure results. The entire system will stop functioning since no processor will be able to access memory.

Bus-based computing also entails bus contention, that is, concurrent bus requests from different processors. To handle bus contention, a bus controller with an arbiter switch limits the bus to one processor at a time. This switch uses some sort of priority mechanism that rations bus accesses so that all processors get access to the bus in a reasonable amount of time. Figure 6.2 represents a possible design for such a bus. All processors access the bus through an interface containing a request, a grant, and a busy line. The busy line indicates the status of the bus. When there is a transmission on the bus, the busy line is active (1); otherwise, it is inactive (0). Every interface (under the control of a processor) that wants to send (or receive) data on the bus first sends a request to the arbiter switch. This switch receives the requests, and if the bus is inactive, the switch sends a grant to the interface with the highest priority.

To determine the highest priority, different mechanisms may be used. One priority mechanism assigns unique static priorities to the requesting processors (or devices in general). Another uses dynamic priority. For example, a bus request that fails to get access right away is sent to a waiting queue. Whenever the bus becomes idle, the request with the longest waiting time gets access to the bus.

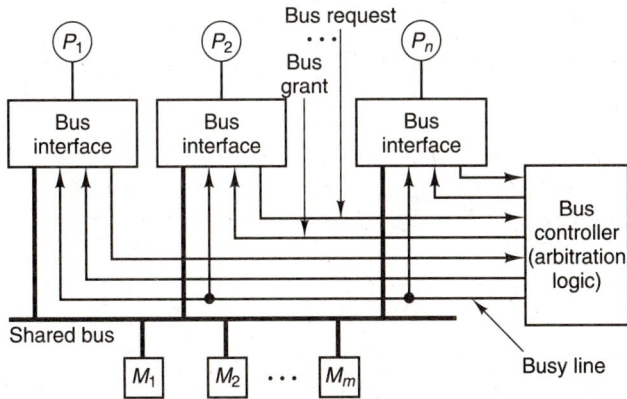

Figure 6.2 A simple bus configuration.

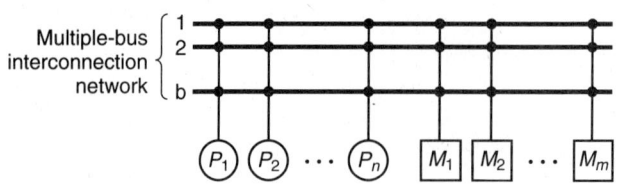

Figure 6.3 One dimensional multiple-bus-based multiprocessor.

Finally, the transmission rate of the bus limits the performance of the system. In fact, after a certain number of processors, adding one more processor may substantially degrade the performance. This is why the shared bus is usually used in small systems (systems with less than 50 processors). To overcome these drawbacks, one can use multiple-bus architecture, as explained next.

Multiple bus. In a multiple-bus architecture, multiple buses are physically connected to components of the system. In this way, the performance and reliability of the system are increased. Although the failure of a single bus line may degrade system performance slightly, the whole system is prevented from going down. There are different configurations of the multiple-bus architecture for large-scale multiprocessors. They fall into three classes: one dimension, two or more dimensions, and hierarchy.

Figure 6.3 represents a one-dimensional multiple-bus architecture with b buses. This architecture is able to resolve conflicts that occur when more than one request for the memory modules exist. It can select up to b memory requests from n possible simultaneous requests. It allocates a bus to each selected memory request. The memory conflicts can be resolved by implementing a 1-of-n arbiter per memory module. From among the requests for a particular memory module, the 1-of-n arbiter allows only one request access to the memory module. In addition to m 1-of-n arbiters, there is a b-of-m arbiter that selects up to b requests from the memory arbiters. Many researchers have studied the performance of the one-dimensional multiple-bus through analysis and simulation [MUD 86, MUD 87, TOW 86, BHU 89]. The results show that the number of read/write requests that successfully get access to the memory modules increases significantly by an increase in the number of buses.

Figure 6.4 represents a two-dimensional multiple-bus architecture. This architecture can be extended to higher dimensions with a moderate number of processors per bus. The memory can also be distributed among the processor nodes. This provides scaling to a large number of processors in a system.

Figure 6.5 represents a hierarchy of buses. This architecture has a tree structure with processors at the leaves, the main memory at the root, and the caches in between.

In general, multiple-bus architecture provides high reliability, availability, and system expandability without violating the well-known advantages of shared bus designs. It has the potential to support the construction of large multiprocessors that have the same performance as systems with multistage networks.

Crossbar switch. Another type of interconnection network is the crossbar switch. As shown in Figure 6.6, the crossbar switch can be viewed as a number of vertical and horizontal links connected by a switch at each intersection. In this network, every processor can be connected to a free memory module without blocking another.

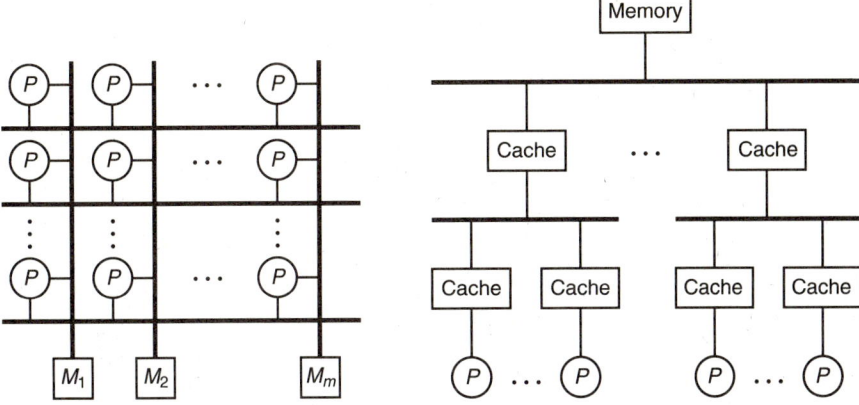

Figure 6.4 Two-dimensional multiple-bus-based multiprocessor.

Figure 6.5 Hierarchical multiple-bus-based multiprocessor.

The crossbar switch is the ultimate solution for high performance. It is a modular interconnection network in that the bandwidth is proportional to the number of processors.

Like multiple buses, crossbar switches provide reliability, availability, and expandability. In an architecture that uses a crossbar switch, the shared memory is divided into smaller modules so that several processors can access the memory at the same time. When more than one processor wishes to access the same memory module, the crossbar switch determines which one to connect.

The main drawback of the crossbar switch is its high cost. The number of switches is the product of the number of processors and the number of memories. To overcome this cost, various multistage networks, such as the multistage cube and the omega, are preferred for large-sized multiprocessors. These networks lessen the overall cost of the network by reducing the number of switches. However, the switch latency, the delay incurred by a transmission passing through multiple switch stages, increases. Switch latency becomes unacceptable when the number of processors (or number of inputs) approaches 10^3 [SUA 90].

A connection similar to the crossbar switch can be obtained by using multiport memory modules. This design gives all processors a direct access path to the shared memory and shifts the complexity of design to the memory. Each memory module in

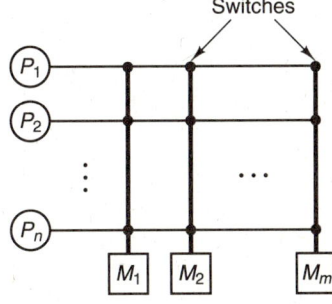

Figure 6.6 Crossbar switch based multiprocessor.

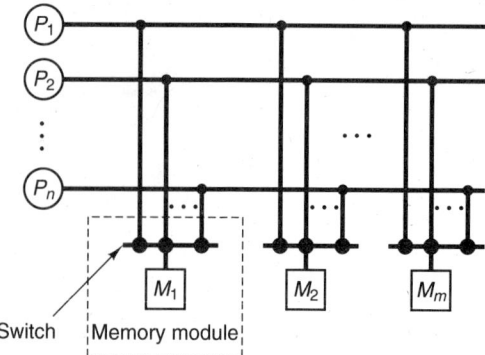

Figure 6.7 Multiport-memory-based multiprocessor.

this type of system has several input ports, one from each processor, as in Figure 6.7. The memory module then has the job that the crossbar switch had of deciding which processor to be allowed to access the memory. In other words, in this arrangement, connection logic is located at the memory module rather than the crossbar switches. The additional logic, of course, increases the cost of the memory module.

In a crossbar, when there is no more than one processor request for each memory module (in other words, when there is no memory contention), all requests can be filled at the same time. When there is memory contention, some of the requests are rejected in order to have at most one request per memory module. In practice, the rejected requests will be resubmitted in the next cycle. However, as suggested in [BHA 75] and [BHU 89], performance analysis becomes easier while keeping reasonable accuracy if it is assumed that a memory request generated in a cycle is independent of the requests of the previous cycles. That is, a processor whose request is rejected discards the request and generates a new independent request at the start of the next cycle.

To analyze the performance of an interconnection network, a common performance parameter, called *memory bandwidth*, is often used. Memory bandwidth can be defined as the mean number of successful read/write operations in one cycle of the interconnection network. In a system with n processors and m memory modules (where $n \leq m$), the memory bandwidth of a crossbar (reviewed in [BHU 89]) can be expressed as

$$BW_c = m\,[1 - (1 - p/m)^n],$$

where p is the probability that a processor generates a request in a cycle. The following explains how this formula is derived:

> p/m is the probability that a processor requests a particular memory module in a cycle. It is assumed that a generated request can refer to each memory with equal probability.
>
> $(1 - p/m)^n$ is the probability that none of the n processors requests a particular module in a cycle.
>
> $[1 - (1 - p/m)^n]$ is the probability that at least one processor has requested a particular module in a cycle.

Stated another way, BW_c denotes the expected number of distinct modules being requested in a cycle.

The preceding bandwidth analysis can be extended to determine the memory bandwidth of a system with a multiple-bus network [MUD 87]. Let b represent the number of buses in the system, and let BW_b denote the memory bandwidth of the multiple bus. It is clear that when $b \geq m$, the multiple bus performs the same as a crossbar switch; that is, $BW_b = BW_c$. However, when $b < m$, which is the case in practice, further steps in the analysis are necessary.

Let q_j be the probability that at least one processor has requested the memory module M_j, shown previously to be $q_j = 1 - (1 - p/m)^n$. Based on the assumption that the q_js are independent, the probability that exactly i of the memory modules receive a request, denoted as r_i, is

$$r_i = \binom{m}{i} q_j^i (1 - q_j)^{m-i}.$$

When $i \leq b$, there are sufficient buses to handle requests for the i memories and therefore none of the requests will be blocked. However, in the case where $i > b$, $i - b$ of the requests will be blocked. Thus BW_b can be expressed as

$$BW_b = \sum_{i=1}^{b} i r_i + \sum_{i=b+1}^{m} b r_i.$$

Ring. Kendall Square Research has designed a parallel computer system, called KSR1, that is expandable to thousands of processors and programmable as shared memory machines [ROT 92]. The KSR1 system achieves scalability by distributing the memory system as a set of caches, while providing a shared memory environment for the programmer. That is, KSR1 is a multiprocessor that combines the programmability of single-address-space machines with the scalability of message-passing machines.

The KSR1 system can be configured with up to 1088 64-bit RISC-type processors, all sharing a common virtual address space of 1 million megabytes (2^{40} bytes). This system can provide a peak performance from 320 to 43,520 MFLOPS'. The memory system, called ALLCACHE memory, consists of a set of 32-Mbyte local caches, one local cache per processor. As shown in Figure 6.8, the data blocks are transferred between caches via a two-level hierarchy of unidirectional rings. Each ring of level 0 contains 8 to 32 processor/local cache pairs and a ring interface. Each processor/local cache pair is connected via an interface to the ring. The interface contains a directory in which there is an entry for each block of data stored in the cache. The ring interface contains a directory in which there is an entry for every data block stored on every local cache on the ring. The ring of level 1 contains 2 to 34 ring interfaces, one for each ring of level 0. Each of these interfaces contains a copy of the directory of the corresponding level 0's ring-interface directory. When a processor p references an address x, the local cache of the processor p is searched first to see whether x is already stored there. If not, the local caches of the other processors, on the same ring as p, are searched for x. If x still is not found, the local caches of other rings are searched through the ring of level 1, the details of which are explained later in this chapter.

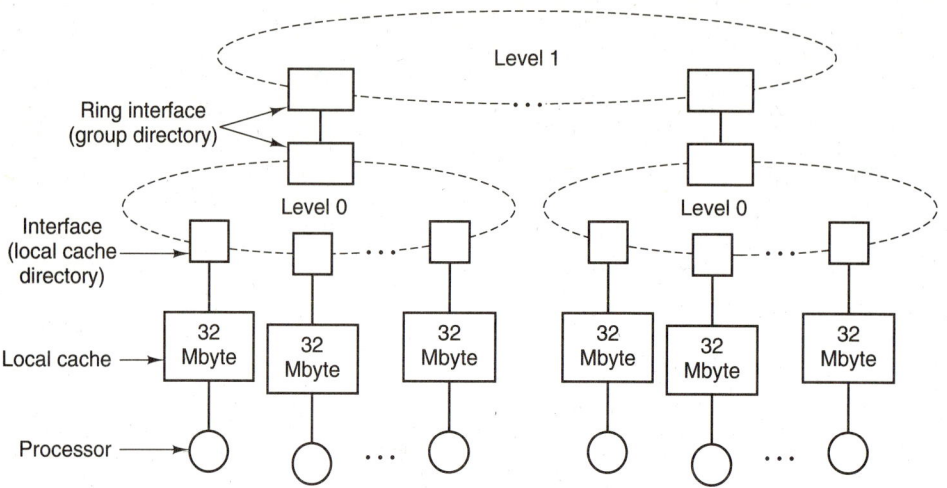

Figure 6.8 The KSR1 architecture.

6.2.2 Cache Coherence Schemes

As the speed and number of processors increase, memory accessing becomes a bottleneck. Cache memory is often used to reduce the effect of this bottleneck. In a uniprocessor, a cache memory is almost always used. Similarly, in a multiprocessor environment, each processor usually has a cache memory dedicated to it. Whenever a processor wants access to a data item, it first checks to see if that item is in its cache. If so, no access of (shared) main memory is necessary. When a processor wants to update the value of a data item, it changes the copy in its cache and later that value is copied out to the shared memory. This process greatly reduces the number of accesses to the shared memory and, as a result, improves the performance of the machine. Unfortunately, problems are caused by this method of updating the data items.

The most common problem is the *cache coherence problem*, that is, how to keep multiple copies of the data consistent during execution. Since a data item's value is changed first in a processor's cache and later in the main memory, another processor accessing the same data item from the main memory (or its local cache) may receive an invalid data item because the updated version has not yet been copied to the shared memory.

To illustrate this type of inconsistency, consider a two-processor architecture with private caches as shown in Figure 6.9.

In the beginning, assume that each cache and the shared memory contain a copy of a data block x. Later, if one of the processors updates its own copy of x, then the copies of x in the caches become inconsistent. Moreover, depending on the memory update policy used in the cache, the copies in the caches may also become inconsistent with the shared memory's copy. As shown in Figure 6.10, a write-through policy updates the memory after any change and therefore keeps the cache and memory consistent.

Sec. 6.2 Multiprocessors

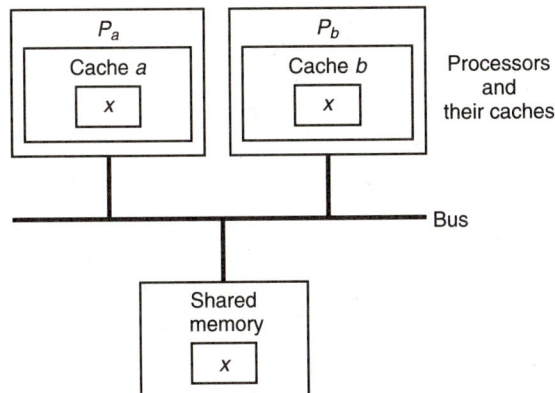

Figure 6.9 A two-processor configuration with copies of data block x.

However, a write-back policy, in contrast, updates the memory only when the data block is replaced or invalidated. Therefore, the memory may not be consistent with the cache at the time of update, as shown in Figure 6.11.

A mechanism must be established to ensure that, whenever a processor makes a change in a data item, that item's copies are updated in all caches and in the main

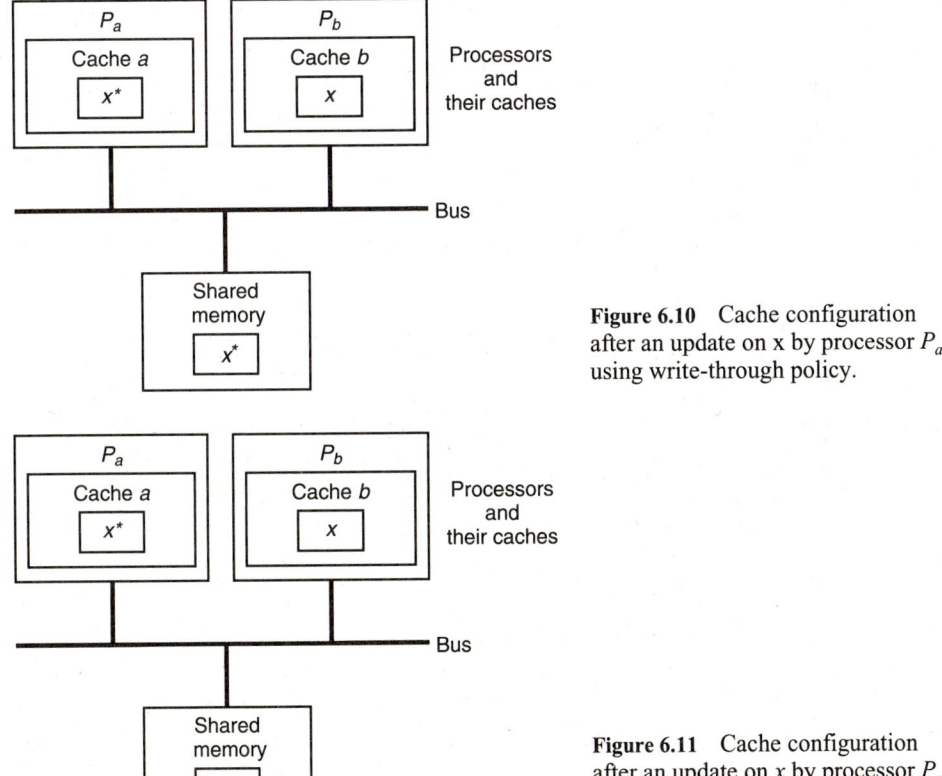

Figure 6.10 Cache configuration after an update on x by processor P_a using write-through policy.

Figure 6.11 Cache configuration after an update on x by processor P_a using write-back policy.

memory before any attempt is made by another processor to use that item again. To establish such a mechanism, a large number of schemes has been proposed. These schemes rely on hardware, software, or a combination of both. Stenstrom [STE 90] presents a good survey of these solutions. Here, some of them are reviewed.

Hardware-based schemes. In general, there are two policies for maintaining coherency: *write invalidate* and *write update*. In the write-invalidate policy (also called the dynamic coherence policy), whenever a processor modifies a data item of a block in cache, it makes all other blocks' copies stored in other caches invalid. In contrast, the write-update policy updates all other cache copies instead of invalidating them.

In these policies, the protocols used for invalidating or updating the other copies depend on the interconnection network employed. When the interconnection network is suitable for broadcast (such as a bus), the invalid and update commands can be broadcast to all caches. Every cache processes every command to see if it refers to one of its blocks. Protocols that use this mechanism are called *snoopy cache protocols*, since each cache "snoops" on the transactions of the other caches. In other interconnection networks, where broadcasting is not possible or causes performance degradation (such as multistage networks), the invalid/update command is sent only to those caches having a copy of the block. To do this, often a centralized or distributed directory is used. This directory has an entry for each block. The entry for each block contains a pointer to every cache that has a copy of the block. It also contains a dirty bit that specifies whether a unique cache has permission to update the block. Protocols that use such a scheme are called *directory protocols*.

To demonstrate the complexity of these protocols in an understandable way, a simplified overview is given in the following sections. More detailed descriptions of these protocols can be found in [STE 90, ARC 86, CHA 90].

Snoopy Cache Protocol. We will look at two different implementations of the snoopy cache protocol, one based on the write-invalidate policy and the other based on the write-update policy.

Write-invalidate snoopy cache protocol. One well-known write-invalidate protocol called *write-once protocol* was proposed by Goodman [GOO 83]. The protocol assigns a state (represented by 2 bits) to each block of data in the cache. The possible states are *single consistent, multiple consistent, single inconsistent*, and *invalid*. The single-consistent state denotes that the copy is the only cache copy and it is consistent with the memory copy. The multiple-consistent state means that the copy is consistent with the memory and other consistent copies exist. The single-inconsistent state denotes that the copy is the only cache copy and it is inconsistent with the memory copy. The invalid state means that the copy cannot be used any longer. A copy in the invalid state is considered as useless copy that no longer exists in the cache.

The transitions between the states can be explained by the actions that the protocol takes on processor read or write commands. These actions are based on the write-back-update policy. When a processor reads a data item from a block that is already in its cache (i.e., when there is a read hit), the read can be performed locally without changing the block's state. The action taken on the read misses, write hits, and write misses are explained in the following three cases. Note that a read (or write) miss occurs when a processor generates a read (or write) request for data or instructions that are not in the cache.

CASE 1: READ MISS

If there are no copies in other caches, then a copy is brought from the memory into the cache. Since this copy is the only copy in the system, the single-consistent state will be assigned to it.

If there is a copy with a single-consistent state, then a copy is brought from the memory (or from the other cache) into the cache. The state of both copies becomes multiple consistent.

If there are copies with a multiple-consistent state, then a copy is brought from the memory (or from one of the caches) into the cache. The copy's state is set to multiple consistent, as well.

If a copy exists with a single-inconsistent state, then the cache that contains this copy detects that a request is being made for a copy of a block that it has modified. It sends its copy to the cache and the memory; that is, the memory copy becomes updated. The new state for both copies is set to multiple consistent.

CASE 2: WRITE MISS

If there is a single-inconsistent copy, then this copy is sent to the cache; otherwise, the copy is brought from the memory (or other caches). In both cases, a command is broadcast to all other copies in order to invalidate those copies. The state of the copy becomes single inconsistent.

CASE 3: WRITE HIT

If the copy is in the single-inconsistent state, then the copy is updated (i.e., a write is performed locally) and the new state becomes single inconsistent.

If the copy is in the single-consistent state, the copy is updated and the new state becomes single inconsistent.

If the copy is in the multiple-consistent state, then all other copies are invalidated by broadcasting the invalid command. The copy is updated and the state of the copy becomes single inconsistent.

As an example, consider the cache architecture in the Sequent Symmetry 2000 series multiprocessors. In these machines, a 512-Kbyte, two-way, set-associative cache is attached to each processor [SEQ 90]. This cache is in addition to the 256-Kbyte on-chip cache of the processors, Intel 80486s. To maintain consistency between copies of data in memory and the local caches, the Symmetry system uses a scheme based on the write-invalidate policy. Figure 6.12 demonstrates how the Symmetry's scheme operates. Although this scheme is not exactly like the write-invalidate protocol, it includes many of its features. Whenever a processor, P_1, issues a read request to an address that is not in its own local cache or any other cache, a 16-byte data block will

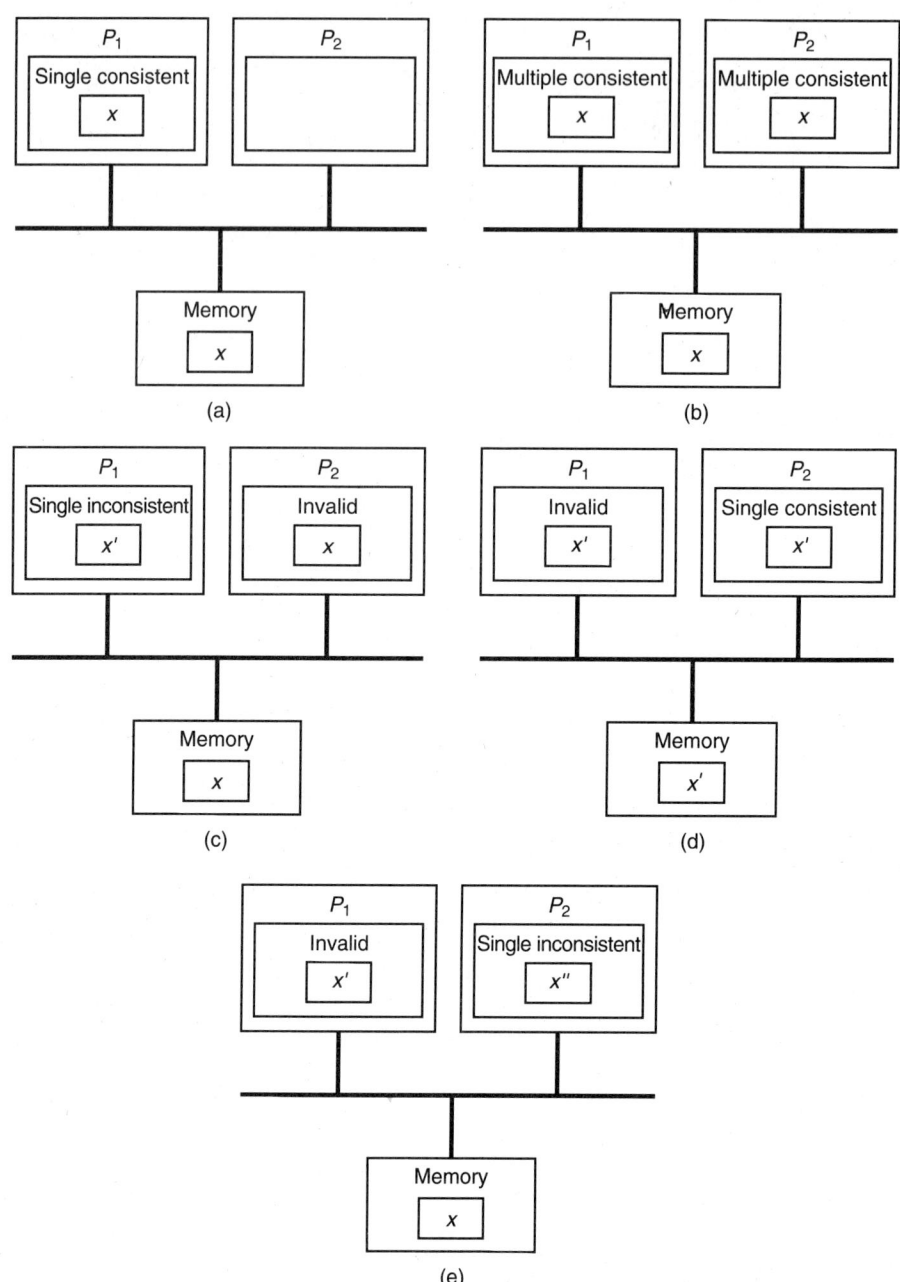

Figure 6.12 Cache coherence scheme in Sequent Symmetry.

be fetched from the memory. This new copy of the data block replaces the least recently used block of the two possible options in a two-way, set-associative cache. The copy is then tagged as single consistent; that is, the state of the copy is initially set to single consistent (see Figure 6.12a). Now suppose that processor P_2 issues a read request to the same data block. At this time, another copy will be fetched from the memory for P_2. During this fetching process, P_1 sends a signal to P_2 to inform it that the data block is now shared. Each copy is then tagged as multiple consistent, (see Figure 6.12b). Now suppose that P_1 needs to modify its copy. To do this, it first sends invalid commands through the system bus to all other caches to invalidate their copies (see Figure 6.12c). Next it changes the state of its copy to single inconsistent and updates the copy. At this point, if P_2 issues a read or write request, a read or write miss will occur. In either of these cases, P_1 puts its copy on the bus and then invalidates it. In the case of a read miss, P_2 receives the copy from the bus and tags it as single consistent. The memory system also receives a copy from the bus and updates the data block (see Figure 6.12d). In the case of a write miss, P_2 receives the copy from the bus and tags it as single inconsistent. Finally, P_2 modifies the copy (see Figure 6.12e).

Note that in the preceding example, when P_1 contains a single inconsistent copy and P_2 issues a read request, P_1 invalidates its copy and P_2 sets its copy to the single-consistent state. An alternative to this procedure could be that both P_1 and P_2 set their copies to multiple consistent. The latter procedure follows the write-invalidate policy, which was explained previously.

Write-update snoopy cache protocol. To clarify the function of a write-update protocol, we will consider a method that is based on a protocol, called Firefly (reviewed in [STE 90] and [ARC 86]).

In this protocol, each cache copy is in one of three states: *single consistent, multiple consistent*, or *single inconsistent*. The single-consistent state denotes that the copy is the only cache copy in the system and that it is consistent with the memory copy. The multiple-consistent state means that the copy is consistent with the memory and other consistent copies exist. The single-inconsistent state denotes that the copy is the only cache copy and it is inconsistent with the memory copy. The write-update protocol uses the write-back update policy when it is in single-consistent or single-inconsistent state, and it uses write-through update policy when it is in multiple-consistent state. Similar to the protocol for the write-invalidate policy, state transitions happen on read misses, write misses, and write hits. (Read hits can always be performed without changing the state.) The actions taken on these events are explained in the following three cases:

CASE 1: READ MISS

If there are no copies in other caches, then a copy is brought from the memory into the cache. Since this copy is the only copy in the system, the single-consistent state will be assigned to it.

If a copy exists with a single-consistent state, then the cache in which the copy resides supplies a copy for the requesting cache. The state of both copies becomes multiple consistent.

If there are copies in the multiple-consistent state, then their corresponding caches supply a copy for the requesting cache. The state of the new copy becomes multiple consistent.

If a copy exists with a single-inconsistent state, then this copy is sent to the cache and the memory copy is also updated. The new state for both copies is set to multiple consistent.

CASE 2: WRITE MISS

If there are no copies in other caches, a copy is brought from the memory into the cache. The state of this copy becomes single inconsistent.

If there are one or more copies in other caches, then these caches supply the copy, and after the write, all copies and the memory copy become updated. The state of all copies becomes multiple consistent.

CASE 3: WRITE HIT

If the copy is in the single-inconsistent or the single-consistent state, then the write is performed locally and the new state becomes single inconsistent.

If the copy is multiple consistent, then all the copies and the memory copy become updated. The state of all copies remains multiple consistent.

Directory Protocols. Snoopy cache protocols require architectures that provide for broadcasting; a bus architecture is an example. Although buses are used in several of today's commercially available multiprocessors, they are not suitable for large-scale multiprocessors. For multiprocessors with a large number of processors, other interconnection networks (such as k-ary n-cubes, n-dimensional meshes, and multistage networks, as discussed in Chapter 5) are used. However, such networks do not provide an efficient broadcast capability. To solve the cache coherency problem in the absence of broadcasting capability, directory protocols have been proposed.

Directory protocols can be classified into two groups: *centralized* and *distributed*. Both groups support multiple shared copies of a block to improve processor performance without imposing too much traffic on the interconnection network.

Centralized directory protocols. There are different proposed implementations of centralized directory protocols. One of them, the full-map protocol, as proposed by Censier et al. [CEN 78] and reviewed by Chaiken et al. [CHA 90], is explained.

The full-map protocol maintains a directory in which each entry contains a single bit, called the *present bit*, for each cache. The present bit is used to specify the presence of copies of the memory's data blocks. Each bit determines whether a copy of the block is present in the corresponding cache. For example, in Figure 6.13 the caches of processors P_a and P_c contain a copy of the data block x, but the cache of processor P_b does not. In addition, each directory entry contains a bit, called a *single-inconsistent bit*. When this bit is set, one and only one present bit in the directory entry is set, and only that cache's processor has permission to update the block. Each cache associates 2 bits with each of its copies. One of the bits, called the *valid bit* (v in Figure 6.13), indicates whether the copy is valid or invalid. When this bit is cleared (0), it indicates

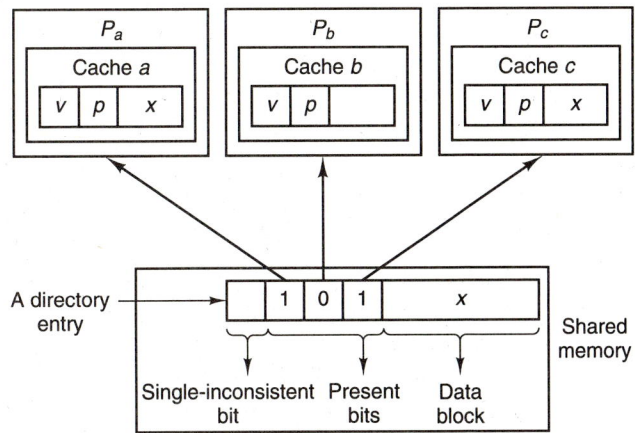

Figure 6.13 Full-map protocol directory.

that the copy is invalid; that is, the copy is considered to be removed from the corresponding cache. The other bit, called a *private bit* (p in Figure 6.13), indicates whether the copy has write permission. When this bit is set (1), it indicates that the corresponding cache has write permission and is the only cache that has a valid copy of the block.

The actions taken by the protocol on the read misses, write misses, and write hits are explained in the following three cases. (Read hits can always be performed.)

CASE 1: READ MISS

Cache c sends a read miss request to the memory.

If the block's single-inconsistent bit is set, the memory sends an update request to the cache that has the private bit set. The cache returns the latest contents of the block to the memory and clears its private bit. The block's single-inconsistent bit is cleared.

The memory sets the present bit for cache c and sends a copy of the block to c.

Once cache c receives the copy, it sets the valid bit and clears the private bit.

CASE 2: WRITE MISS

Cache c sends a write miss request to the memory.

The memory sends invalidate requests to all other caches that have copies of the block and resets their present bits. The other caches will invalidate their copy by clearing the valid bit and will then send acknowledgments back to the memory. During this process, if there is a cache (other than c) with a copy of the block and the private bit is set, the memory updates itself with the copy of the cache.

Once the memory receives all the acknowledgments, it sets the present bit for cache c and sends a copy of the block to c. The single-inconsistent bit is set.

Once the cache receives the copy, it is modified, and the valid and private bits are set.

CASE 3: WRITE HIT

If the private bit is 0, c sends a privacy request to the memory. The memory invalidates all the caches that have copies of the block (similar to case 2). Then it sets the block's single-inconsistent bit and sends an acknowledgment to c. Cache c sets the block's private bit.

One drawback to the full-map directory is that the directory entry size increases as the number of processors increases. To solve this problem, several other protocols have been proposed. One of these protocols is the *limited directory protocol*.

The limited directory protocol binds the directory entry to a fixed size, that is, to a fixed number of pointers, independent of the number of processors. Thus a block can only be copied into a limited number of caches. When a cache requests a copy of a block, the memory supplies the copy and stores a pointer to the cache in the corresponding directory entry. If there is no room in the entry for a new pointer, the memory invalidates the copy of one of the other caches based on some pre-chosen replacement policy (see [AGA 88] for more details).

Distributed directory protocols. The distributed directory protocols realize the goals of the centralized protocols (such as full-map protocol) by partitioning and distributing the directory among caches and/or memories. This helps reduce the directory sizes and memory bottlenecks in large multiprocessor systems. There are many proposed distributed protocols, some, called *hierarchical directory protocols*, are based on partitioning the directory between clusters of processors, and others, called *chained directory protocols,* are based on a linked list of caches.

Hierarchical directory protocols are often used in architectures that consist of a set of clusters connected by some network. Each cluster contains a set of processing units and a directory connected by an interconnection network. A request that cannot be serviced by the caches within a cluster is sent to the other clusters as determined by the directory.

Chained directory protocols maintain a singly (or doubly) linked list between the caches that have a copy of the block. The directory entry points to a cache with a copy of the block; this cache has a pointer to another cache that has a copy, and so on. Therefore, the directory entry always contains only one pointer, a pointer to the head of the link.

One protocol based on a linked list is the coherence protocol of the IEEE Scalable Coherent Interface (SCI) standard project [JAM 90]. The SCI is a local or extended computer *backplane* interface. The interconnection is scalable; that is, up to 64,000 processor, memory, or I/O nodes can effectively interface to a shared SCI interconnection. A pointer, called the *head pointer*, is associated with each block of the memory. The head pointer points to the first cache in the linked list. Also, backward and forward pointers are assigned to each cache copy of a block. Figure 6.14a shows the links between the caches and the main memory for the SCI's directory protocol.

The actions taken by the protocol on the read misses, write misses, and write hits are explained in the following three cases.

Sec. 6.2   Multiprocessors

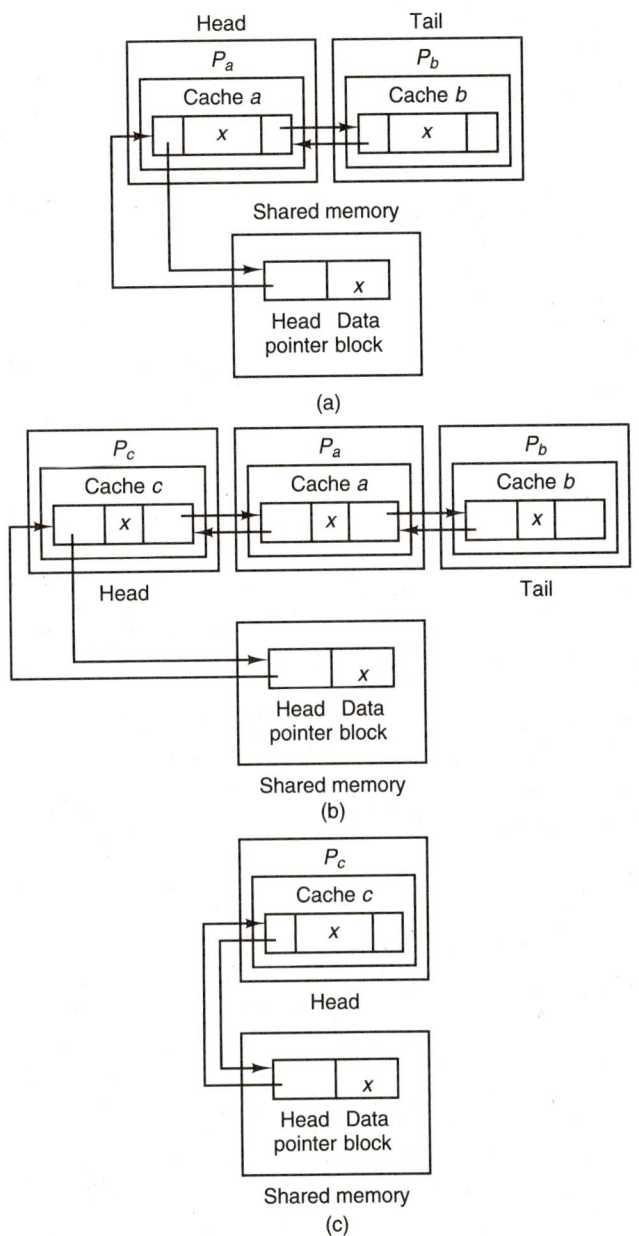

Figure 6.14 Read and write misses in SCI's directory protocol.

CASE 1: READ MISS

Cache c sends a read-miss request to the memory.

If the requested block is in an uncached state (i.e., there is no pointer from the block to any cache), then the memory sends a copy of the requested block to c. The block state will be changed to cached state, and the head pointer will be set to point to c.

If the requested block is in the cached state, then the memory sends the head pointer, say a, to c, and it updates the head pointer to point to c. This action is illustrated by Figure 6.14a and b. Cache c sets its backward pointer to the data block in memory. Next, cache c sends a request to cache a. Upon receipt of the request, cache a sets its backward pointer to point to cache c and sends the requested data to c.

CASE 2: WRITE MISS

Cache c sends a write-miss request to the memory. The memory sends the head pointer, for example a, to c, and it updates the head pointer to point to c. At this point, cache c, as the head of the linked list, has the authority to invalidate all the other cache copies so as to maintain only the one copy. Cache c sends an invalid request to cache a; a invalidates its copy and sends its forward pointer (which points to cache b) to c. Cache c uses this forward pointer to send an invalid request to cache b. This process continues until all the copies are invalidated. Then the writing process is performed. The final state of the pointer system is shown in Figure 6.14c.

CASE 3: WRITE HIT

If the writing cache c is the only one in the linked list, it will proceed with the writing process immediately.

If cache c is the head of the linked list, it invalidates all the other cache copies so as to obtain only one copy. Then the writing process is performed. (The invalidation process is done similarly to the case of write miss.)

If cache c is an element other than the head of the linked list, it detaches itself from the linked list first. Then it interrogates memory to determine the head of the linked list, and it sets its forward pointer to point to the current head of the linked list. The memory updates the head pointer to point to c. At this point, cache c becomes the new head of the linked list. Then, similar to the previous case, c invalidates all the other caches in the linked list and performs the writing process.

Notice that in the case of a write hit the length of the linked list always becomes 1.

In comparing the preceding protocols, it can be seen that the full-map directory protocols often yield higher processor utilization than chained directory protocols, and chained directory protocols yield higher utilization than limited directory protocols. However, a full-map directory requires more memory per directory entry than the other two protocols, and chained directory protocols have more implementation complexity than limited directory protocols.

In comparison with snoopy protocols, directory protocols have the advantage of being able to restrict the read/write requests to those caches having copies of a block. However, they increase the size of memory and caches due to the extra bits and pointers relative to snoopy protocols. The snoopy protocols have the advantage of having less implementation complexity than directory protocols. However, snoopy protocols are not scalable to a large number of processors and require high-performance dual-ported caches to allow execution of processor instructions while snooping on the bus concerning the transactions of the other caches.

Software-based schemes. The software solutions to the cache coherence problem are intended to reduce the hardware cost and communication time for coherence maintenance. In general, they divide the data items into two types: *cacheable* and *noncacheable*. If a data item never changes value, it is said to be cacheable. Also, a data item is cacheable if there is no possibility of more than one processor using it. Otherwise, the data are noncacheable. The cacheable data are allowed to be fetched into the cache by processors, while the noncacheable data are only resident in the main memory, and any reference to them is referred directly to the main memory.

Sophisticated compilers, which can make the cacheable/noncacheable decisions, are needed for these software schemes. One simple way to make this determination is to mark all shared (read/write) data items as noncacheable. However, this method (sometimes referred to as a *static coherence check*) is too conservative, since during a specific time interval some processors may need only to read a data item. Therefore, during that period the data item should be treated as cacheable so that it can be shared between the processors.

A better approach would be to determine when it is safe to update or cache a data item. During such intervals, the data item is marked cacheable. In general, such an approach involves analyzing data dependencies and generating appropriate cacheable intervals. The data dependency analysis conducted by the compiler is a complex task and lies outside the scope of this chapter. Interested readers should refer to [CHE 88], [CHE 90], and [MIN 92].

6.3 MULTICOMPUTERS

In a multicomputer architecture, a local memory (also called private memory) is attached to each processor. Each processor, along with its local memory and input/output port, forms an individual processing unit (node). That is, each processor can compute in a self-sufficient manner using the data stored in its local memory. The processing units are usually of the same type. A multicomputer that has the same processing units is called *homogeneous*; if the processing units are different, it is called *heterogeneous*.

In a multicomputer, a processor only has direct access to its local memory and not to the remote memories. If a processor has to access or modify a piece of data that does not exist in its local memory, a message-passing mechanism is used to achieve this task. In a message-passing mechanism, a processor is able to send (or receive) a block of information to (or from) every other processor via communication channels. The communication channels are physical (electrical) connections between processors and are arranged based on an interconnection network topology. Each processor is connected to a communication channel by a device called a *communication interface.* The communication interface is able to transmit and receive data through a communication channel. It may also be able to perform functions to ensure that the data are sent and received correctly. Before a block of information is sent over a channel, it is packaged together in a message with a header field at the beginning and a checksum field at the end. The header field consists of identification information, including the source address, destination address, and message length. The checksum field consists of several bits for detection of occasional transmission errors. The communication interface, in some implementations, is able to create and decode such header and checksum fields.

6.3.1 Common Interconnection Networks.

The way processors in a multicomputer can be connected to produce maximum efficiency has been studied by many researchers. As a result of these studies, various network topologies have been developed for multicomputers. Most of these topologies try to allow for fast communication between processors, while keeping the design simple and low cost. This section explains some of the important topologies, such as k-ary n-cubes, n-dimensional meshes, crossbar switches, and multistage networks. In particular, emphasis will be given to hypercubes [SEI 85, HAY 89, HAY 86], two- and three-dimensional meshes, and crossbars, which are often used in the multicomputers available on today's market.

k-Ary n-cubes and n-dimensional meshes. A k-ary n-cube consists of k^n nodes with k nodes at each dimension. The parameter n is called the dimension of the cube, and k is called the radix. An n-dimensional mesh consists of $k_{n-1} * k_{n-2} * \cdots * k_0$ nodes, where $k_i \geq 2$ denotes the number of nodes along dimension i. Higher dimensions in k-ary n-cubes and n-dimensional meshes provide lower diameters (which shortens path lengths) and more paths between pairs of nodes (which increases fault tolerance). However, in practice, two- or three-dimensional networks are preferred because they provide better scalability, modularity, lower latency, and greater affinity for VLSI implementation than do high-dimensional networks. Examples of multicomputers that use low-dimensional networks are nCUBE/2 [NCU 90], Caltech Mosaic [ATH 88], Ametek 2010 [SEI 88], and MIT J-machine [DAL 89a, DAL 89b]. The nCUBE/2 uses a 2-ary n-cube network (a hypercube). A two-dimensional mesh is used in Ametek 2010, and a three-dimensional mesh is used in the Mosaic and J-machine. A brief description of these low-dimensional networks and some of the machines that employ them is given next.

n-Cube network (hypercube). Several commercial multicomputers based on a hypercube network have been developed since 1983. Commercial multicomputers available since then are the Intel iPSC/1, Intel iPSC/2, iPSC/860, Ametek S/14, nCUBE/10 and nCUBE/2. Development of these machines was triggered primarily by the development of the Cosmic Cube at California Institute of Technology [SEI 85]. The Cosmic Cube is considered to be the first generation of multicomputers and was designed by Seitz and his group in 1981. It consists of 64 small computers that communicate through message passing using store-and-forward routing scheme. One requirement of the Cosmic Cube was that the method of internode communication must adapt easily to a large number of nodes. A hypercube network satisfies this requirement.

As an example, consider some of the features of *n*CUBE/2. The *n*CUBE/2 is considered as the second generation of multicomputers. It consists of a set of fully custom VLSI 64-bit processors, each with independent memory, connected to each other via a hypercube network. Processors communicate with each other through message passing using a wormhole routing scheme. Each processor is an entire computer system on a single chip. It includes a four-stage instruction pipeline, a data cache of eight operands, an instruction cache of 128 bytes, and a 64-bit IEEE standard floating-point unit. It has a performance of 7.5 MIPS, and 3.5 MFLOPS single-precision (32 bits) or 2.4 MFLOPS double-precision (64 bits). The *n*CUBE/2 supports from 32 to 8,192 such processors, with each processor having a local memory from 1 to 64 Mbytes. The largest configuration of *n*CUBE/2 has a peak performance of 60,000 MIPS and 27,000 scalar MFLOPS.

n-Dimensional mesh network.

Another type of interconnection network that has received recent attention is the mesh network. A few years after the designing of the Cosmic Cube, Seitz and his group started to develop design criteria for the second generation of multicomputers [SUA 90]. Their main goal was to improve message-passing performance. They intended to decrease message-passing latency by a factor of 1000 for short, nonlocal, messages. The rationale behind this was that they wanted to increase the generality of multicomputers so as to become more efficient for certain commonly needed applications, such as searching and sorting, AI, signal processing, and distributed simulation. These types of applications tend to generate a large number of short, nonlocal, messages. Another motivation was that they wanted to simplify the programming task by allowing the programmer to worry only about load balancing and not about communication overhead.

These goals were mainly achieved in the design of the Ametek's Series 2010 medium-grain multicomputer, which was introduced in 1988. The Ametek's Series 2010 uses a two-dimensional mesh network for interprocessor communication. As shown in Figure 6.15, the two-dimensional mesh network consists of a mesh-routing chip (MRC) at each node. To each MRC, a single-processor node is connected. The processor node contains up to 8 Mbytes of memory and a Motorola 68020/68882 processor. The MRC performs the routing and flow control of the messages. The wormhole routing techniques are used for routing.

Another example of a mesh-based machine is the MIT J-machine [NOA 90]. The J-machine can be configured with up to 65,536 processing nodes connected by a three-dimensional mesh network. A 4-Knode prototype J-machine is organized as a three-dimensional cube of $16 \times 16 \times 16$ processing nodes divided into four chassis of $8 \times 8 \times 16$ each. Every node is connected directly to its six nearest neighbors using

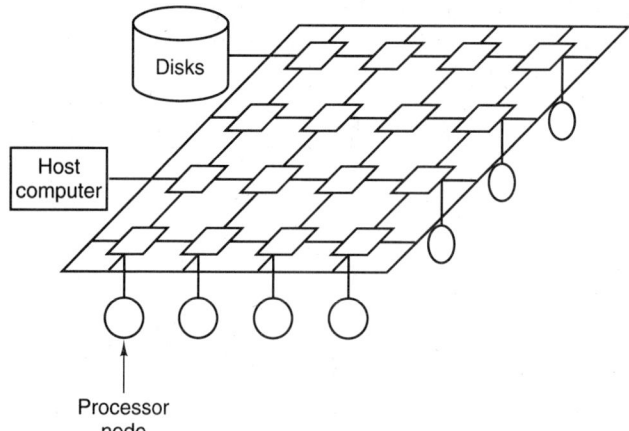

Figure 6.15 A mesh-based multicomputer

9-bit-wide bidirectional channels. These channels are used twice per clock cycle to pass 18-bit flow digits (flit) at a rate of 20 Mflits per second. Each processing node contains a memory, a processor, and a communication controller. The communication controller is logically a part of network, but is physically part of a node. The memory contains 4-K by 36-bit words. Each word of the memory contains a 32-bit data item and a 4-bit tag.

In the J-machine, communication mechanisms are provided that permit a node to send a message to any other node in the machine in less than 2 µs. The processor is message driven, and executes user and system code in response to messages arriving over the network. This is in contrast to the conventional processor, which is instruction driven.

Crossbar network. An example of a multicomputer based on crossbar switches is the *Genesis*. Genesis is a European supercomputer development project that aims to generate a high-performance, scalable parallel computer [BRU 91]. Genesis is a multicomputer in which the nodes are connected by crossbar switches. In the second phase of development, each node of a Genesis consists of three processors sharing a memory system. The three processors are a scalar processor (using an Intel i870), a vector processor, and a communication processor (using an Intel i870). In addition, each node has a network link interface (NLI) for communicating with other nodes. The communication processor controls the NLI and sends/receives messages to/from other nodes. The NLI supports all necessary hardware for wormhole routing and provides several bidirectional links. Each link has a data rate of approximately 100 Mbytes per second. The nodes are connected by a two-level crossbar switch. As shown in Figure 6.16, each crossbar in level 1 connects several nodes as a cluster. The crossbars in level 2 provide communication between clusters. Ideally, only a one-level crossbar switch would be used. In practice, however, a one-level crossbar switch network can only be economically implemented for at most 32 nodes [BRU 91]. Therefore, to interconnect a large number of nodes, we must employ multilevel crossbar switches.

In summary, considering cost optimization, the two-dimensional mesh, which is simple and inexpensive, provides a good structure for applications that require strong

Sec. 6.3   Multicomputers   261

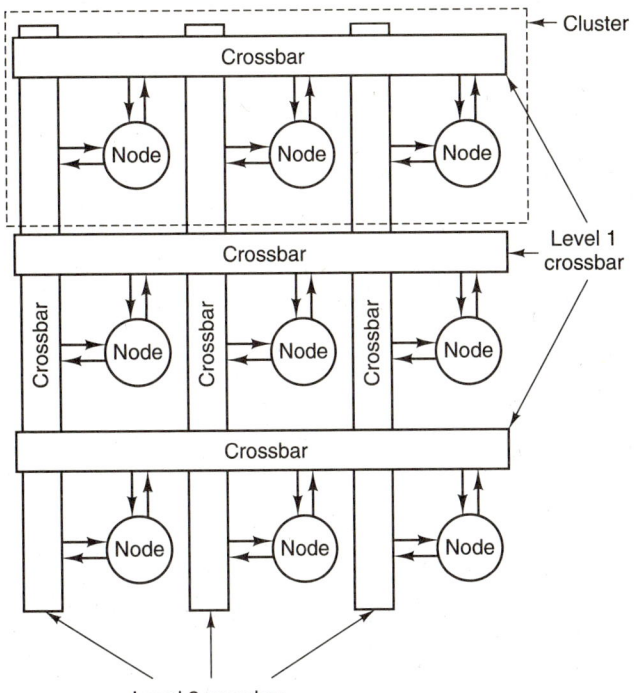

Figure 6.16 Block diagram of a Genesis architecture.

local communication. When there is strong global communication, networks with a higher degree of connectivity, such as the hypercube and the crossbar, may be considered.

Fat-tree network. The fat tree is based on the structure of a complete binary tree. As we go up from the leaves of a fat tree to the root, the number of wires (links) increases and therefore the communication bandwidth increases. Since its communication bandwidth can be scaled independently from the number of processors, it provides great flexibility in design. It also provides a routing network whose size does not require any changes in an algorithm or code. Thus it makes it easy for users to program the network, and delivers good performance. It can also be scaled up to a very large size.

An example of a multicomputer based on a fat-tree network is the Connection Machine Model CM-5. The CM-5 can have from 32 to 16,384 processing nodes. Each processing node consists of a 32-MHz SPARC processor, 32 Mbytes of memory, and a 128-MFLOPS vector-processing unit. In addition to processing nodes, there is one to several tens of control processors (which are Sun Microsystem workstations) for system and serial user tasks. Figure 6.17 represents the organization of the CM-5. Although the CM-5 is a multicomputer, it can perform as a SIMD machine as well. That is, when a parallel operation is applied to a large set of data, the same instruction can be broadcast to a set of processors in order to be applied to the data simultaneously.

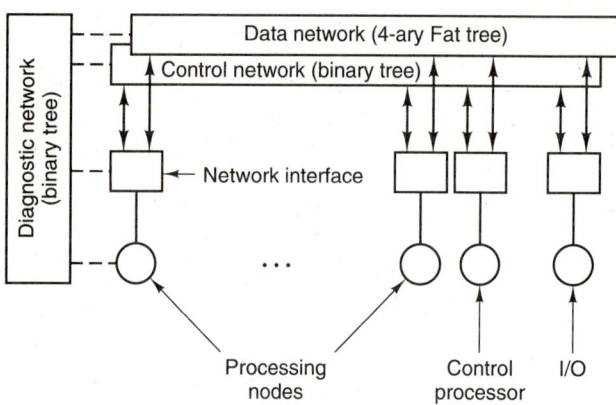

Figure 6.17 Structure of the CM-5.

As shown in Figure 6.17, the CM-5 has three networks: a data network, a control network, and a diagnostic network [LEI 92]. The data network is a fat-tree network that provides data communications between system components. Figure 6.18 shows the interconnection pattern of such a network. Each internal node consists of several router chips, each with four child connections and either two or four parent connections [LEI 92]. That is, the network provides alternative paths for a message to travel. Once a message leaves the source processor toward the destination processor, it goes up the tree until it reaches the routing chip, which is the least common ancestor of the source and destination processors, and it takes the single available path down to the destination. While the message is going up the tree, it may have several alternative links to take at each routing chip. The choice is made randomly among the links that are not blocked by other messages.

The control network is a binary tree that provides broadcasting, synchronization, and system management operations. It provides a mechanism to support both SIMD and MIMD types of architectures in CM-5.

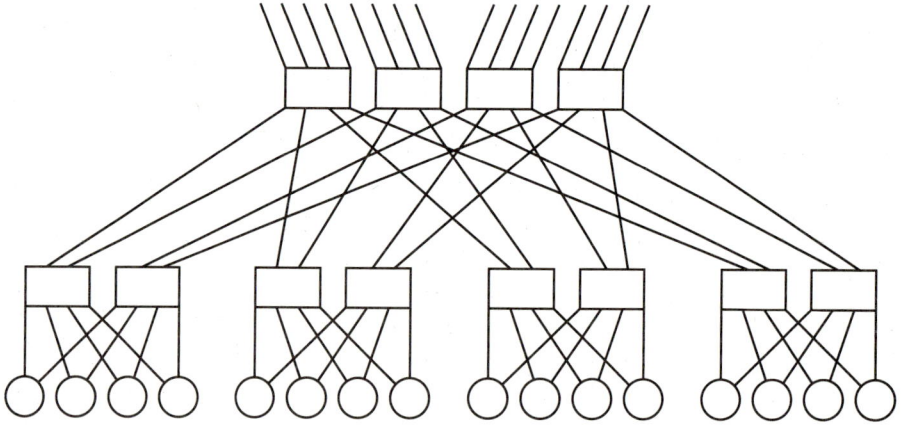

Figure 6.18 The CM-5 data network.

The diagnostic network is a binary tree with one or more diagnostic processors at the root. Each leaf of the tree is connected to a component of the system, such as a board. The diagnostic network is able to detect and ignore the components that are faulty or powered down.

6.4 MULTIPROCESSORS VERSUS MULTICOMPUTERS

A fundamental design issue in parallel computer design relates to multiprocessors and multicomputers. In a multiprocessor system, as the number of processors increases, designs must avoid bus-based systems since a bus is a shared resource and a mechanism must be provided to resolve contention. Although bus organization using the conflict-resolution method is reliable and relatively inexpensive, it introduces a single critical component in the system that can cause complete system failure as a result of the malfunction of any of the bus interface circuits. Also, expanding the system by adding more processors or memory increases the bus contention, which degrades the system throughput and increases logic complexity and cost. The total overall transfer rate within the system is limited to the bandwidth and speed of the single bus. Hence the use of switching networks, which still supports a shared memory model, is highly recommended. Generally, multiprocessors are easier than multicomputers to program and are becoming the dominant architecture in small-scale parallel machines.

According to Seitz [SUA 90], multiprocessors will be preferred for machines with tens of processors and multicomputers for message-passing systems that contain thousands or millions of processing nodes. Multicomputers are a solution to the scalablity of the multiprocessors. In general, as the number of processors increases, multicomputers become increasingly more economical than multiprocessors. Given the observation that major performance improvement is achieved by making almost all the memory references to the local memories [STO 91] and findings that scientific computations can be partitioned in such a way that almost all operations can be done locally [FOX 88, HOS 89], multicomputers are good candidates for large-scale parallel computation.

6.5 MULTI-MULTIPROCESSORS

With the advancement of VLSI technology, it is becoming possible to build large-scale parallel machines using high-performance microprocessors. The design of such a parallel machine can combine the desired features of multiprocessors and multicomputers. One design could connect several multiprocessors by an interconnection network, which we refer to as *multi-multiprocessors* (or distributed multiprocessors). That is, a multi-multiprocessor can be viewed as a multicomputer in which each node is a multiprocessor. Figure 6.19 represents the general structure of a multi-multiprocessor. Each node allows the tasks with relatively high interaction to be executed locally within a multiprocessor, thereby reducing communication overhead. Also, to have a multiprocessor as a node reduces the complexity of the parallel programming that

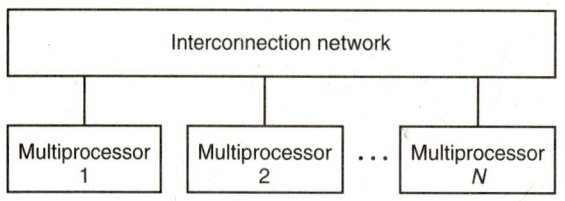

Figure 6.19 General structure of multi-multiprocessors.

exists in a multicomputer environment. The interconnection network allows the multi-multiprocessor to be scalable (similar to multicomputers).

An example of a multi-multiprocessor system is the PARADIGM (stands for PARAllel DIstributed Global Memory) system [CHE 91]. A PARADIGM is a scalable, general-purpose, shared-memory parallel machine. Each node of the PARADIGM system consists of a cluster of processors that are connected to a memory module through a shared bus/cache hierarchy, as shown in Figures 6.20 and 6.21. A hierarchy of shared caches and buses is used to maximize the number of processors that can be interconnected with state-of-the-art cache and bus technologies. Each board consists of a network interface and several processors, which share a bus with an on-board cache. The on-board cache implements the same consistency protocols as the memory module. The data blocks can be transferred between the processor's (on-chip) cache and the onboard cache. One advantage of an onboard cache is that it increases the hit ratio and therefore reduces the average memory access time.

The network interface module contains a set of registers for the sending and receiving of small packets. To transmit a packet, the sender processor copies its packet into the transmit register. When the packet arrives, one of the processors is interrupted to copy the packet out of the receive register.

An interbus cache module is a cache shared by several subnodes. Similar to onboard cache, the interbus cache supports scalablity and a directory-based consistency scheme.

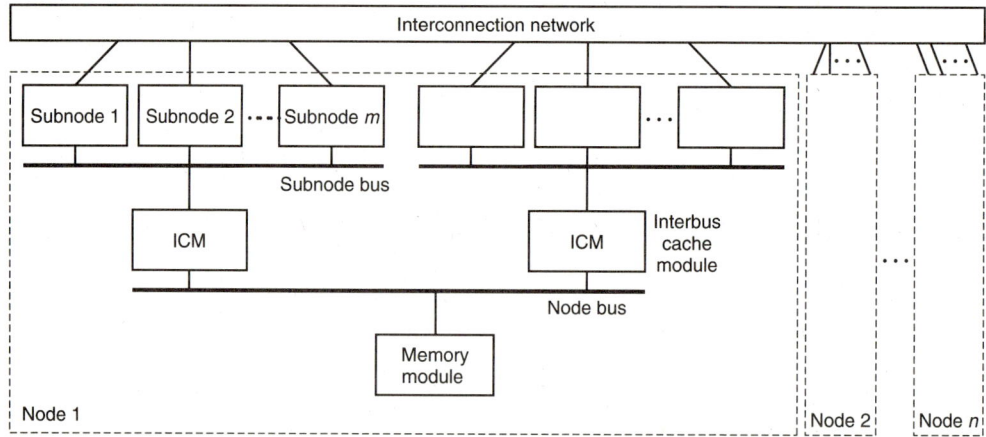

Figure 6.20 PARADIGM architecture.

Sec. 6.5   Multi-Multiprocessors

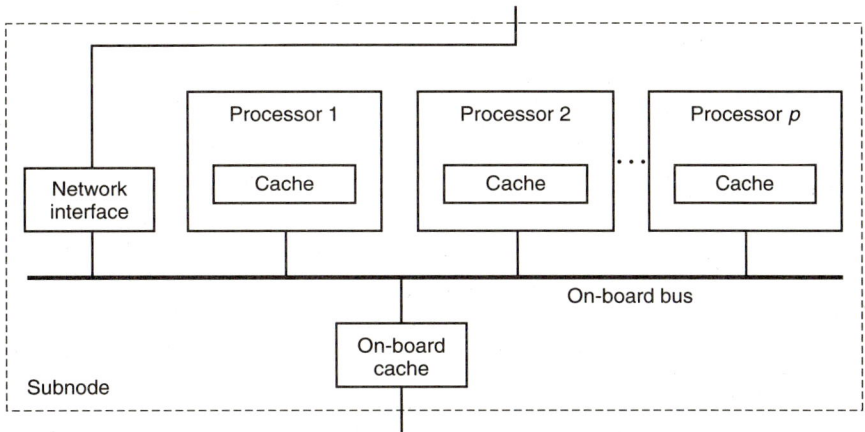

Figure 6.21 A subnode of PARADIGM.

Another example of a multi-multiprocessor system is the Alliant CAMPUS. A fully configured model of this machine has 32 cluster nodes; each cluster node consists of 25 Intel i860 processors and 4 Gbytes of shared memory. As shown in Figure 6.22, within each cluster node, the memory is shared among the processors by crossbar switches. The cluster nodes are connected to each other by crossbar switches for rapid data sharing and synchronization.

The Japanese have developed several parallel inference machines, PIM, as part of their fifth-generation computer project, FGCS [HAT 89, GOT 90]. These machines are developed for the purpose of executing large-scale artificial intelligence software written in the concurrent logic programming language KL1 [UED 86]. Since KL1 programs are composed of many processes that frequently communicate with each other, a hierarchical structure is used in PIMs for achieving high-speed execution. Several

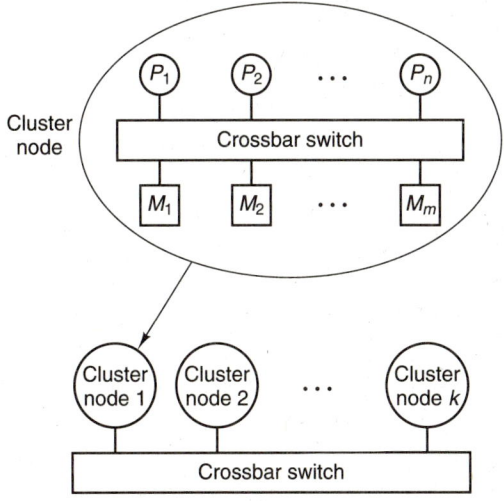

Figure 6.22 The Alliant CAMPUS architecture.

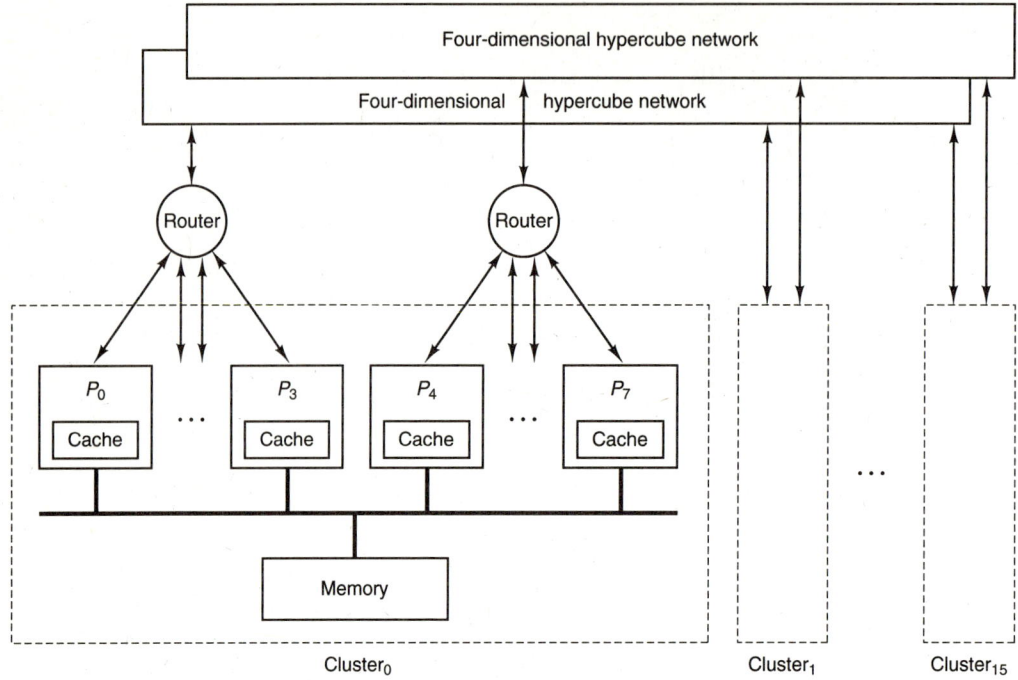

Figure 6.23 PIM/p.

processors are combined with shared memory to form a cluster, and multiple clusters are connected by an intercluster network. Figures 6.23 and 6.24 represent the structure of the types of PIMs, denoted as PIM/p (model p) and PIM/c (model c). The PIM/p

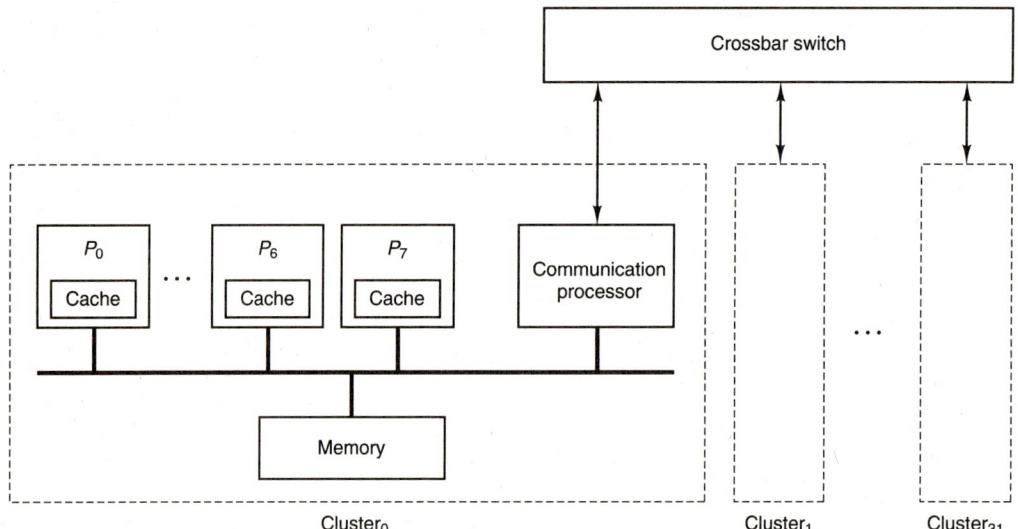

Figure 6.24 PIM/c.

consists of 16 clusters; each cluster is made up of eight processors sharing a memory system. To obtain an intercluster network with throughput of 40 Mbytes/second, two four-dimensional hypercubes have been used. Two network routers are provided for each cluster, one for each four processors. The PIM/c consists of 32 clusters, and each cluster contains eight application processors and a communication processor.

BIBLIOGRAPHIC NOTES

Discussions about synchronization techniques can be found in [DUB 88], [QUI 87], [STO 90], and [BOY 87]. [GIB 91] presents a simple bus configuration. [SUA 90] discusses some of the drawbacks of multiprocessor interconnection networks and also gives a description of the Ameteck. [STE 90] and [CHA 90] provide good surveys on cache coherence protocols. A detailed description of the full-map directory protocol is given in [CEN 78] as an Algol procedure. The paper also presents a performance estimation of this protocol. [CHE 88], [DUB 88], [GOO 89], and [CHE 90] provide different schemes for software solutions to the cache coherence problem. [LEI 92] discusses the different networks used in the CM-5.

REFERENCES

[AGA 88] AGARWAL, A., ET AL., "An Evaluation of Directory Schemes for Cache Coherence," *Proc. 15th Inter. Symp. Computer Architecture.* Los Alamitos, CA: CS Press, Order No. 861, June 1988, pp. 280–289.

[AGA 91] AGARWAL, ANANT, "Limits on Interconnection Network Performance," *IEEE Trans. Parallel and Distributed Systems,* 2(4), 1991, pp. 398–412.

[ARC 86] ARCHIBALD, J., AND J.-L. BAER, "Cache Coherence Protocols: Evaluation Using a Multiprocessor Simulation Model," *ACM Trans. Computer Systems,* 4(4), 1986, pp. 273–298.

[ATH 88] ATHAS, W. C., AND C. L. SEITZ, "Multicomputers: Message-passing Concurrent Computers," *IEEE Computer Mag.,* 21(8), August 1988, pp. 9–24.

[BHA 75] BHANDARKAR, D. P., "Analysis of Memory Interference in Multiprocessors," *IEEE Trans. Computers,* C-24, September 1975, pp. 897–908.

[BHU 89] BHUYAN, L. N., Q. YAND, D. P. AGRAWAL, "Performance of Multiprocessors Interconnection Networks," *IEEE Computer,* 22(2), February 1989, pp. 25–37.

[BOY 87] BOYLE, JAMES, R. BUTTER, T. DISZ, B. GLICKFELD, E. LUSK, R. OVERBEEK, J. PATTERSON, AND R. STEVENS, *Portable Programs for Parallel Processors,* New York, Holt, Rinehart and Winston, 1987.

[BRU 91] BRUENING, U., W. I. GILOI, AND W. SCHROEDER-PREIKSCHAT, "The Architecture of the European MIMD Supercomputer GENESIS," *Distributed Memory Computing,* 2nd European Conference, EDMCC2. Munich, Germany: Springer-Verlag, 1991, pp. 450–462.

[CEN 78] CENSIER, L. M., AND P. FEAUTRIER, "A New Solution to Coherence Problems in Multicache Systems," *IEEE Trans. Computers,* C-27(12), 1978, pp. 1112–1118.

[CHA 90] CHAIKEN, D., C. FIELDS, K. DURIHARA, AND A. AGARWAL, "Directory-based Cache Coherence in Large-scale Multiprocessors," *IEEE Computer,* 23(6), June 1990, pp. 49–58.

[CHE 88] CHEONG, HOICHI, AND A. VEIDENBAUM, "A Cache Coherence Scheme with Fast Selective Invalidation," *Proc. 15th Intern. Symp. Computer Architecture*, 1988, pp. 299–307.

[CHE 90] CHEONG, HOICHI, AND A. VEIDENBAUM, "Compiler-directed Cache Management in Multiprocessors," *IEEE Computer*, 23(6), 1990, pp. 39–47.

[CHE 91] CHERITON, DAVID R., H. A. GOOSEN, AND P. D. BOYLE, "Paradigm: A Highly Scalable Shared-memory Multicomputer Architecture," *IEEE Computer*, 24(2), 1991, pp. 33–46.

[DAL 87] DALLY, WILLIAM J., AND CHARLES L. SEITZ, "Deadlock-free Message Routing in Multiprocessor Interconnection Networks," *IEEE Trans. Computers*, C-36(5), 1987, pp. 547–553.

[DAL 87] DALLY, W. J., *A VLSI Architecture for Concurrent Data Structures.* Kluwer Academic Publishers, Norwell, Massachusetts 1987.

[DAL 89A] DALLY, W. J., ET AL., "The J-Machine: A Fine-grain Concurrent Computer," *Proc. IFIP Congress*, Netherlands 1989, pp.1147–1153.

[DAL 89B] DALLY, W. J., "The J-Machine: System Support for Actors," in *Actors: Knowledge-based Concurrent Computing* (C. Hewitt and G. Agha, eds.). Cambridge, MA: MIT Press, 1989.

[DAL 91] DALLY, W. J., "Express Cubes: Improving the Performance of *k*-ary *n*-cube Interconnection Networks," *IEEE Trans. Computers*, 40(9), 1991, pp. 1016–1023.

[DUB 88] DUBOIS, MICHEL, C. SCHEURICH, AND F. A. BRIGGS, "Synchronization, Coherence, and Event Ordering in Multiprocessors," *Computer*, 21(2), 1988, pp. 9–21.

[FOX 88] FOX, G., M. JOHNSON, G. LYZENGA, S. OTTO, J. SALMON, AND D. WALKER, *Solving Problems on Concurrent Processors*, Vol. 1. Upper Saddle River, NJ: Prentice Hall, 1988.

[GEL 89] GELSINGER, PATRICK P., P. GARGINI, G. PARKER, AND A. YU, "Microprocessors circa 2000," *IEEE Spectrum*, 26(10), October 1989, pp. 43–47.

[GIB 91] GIBSON, GLENN A., *Computer Systems Concepts and Design.* Upper Saddle River, NJ: Prentice Hall, 1991.

[GOO 83] GOODMAN, J. R., "Using Cache Memory to Reduce Processor-memory Traffic," *Proc. 10th Ann. Symp. Computer Architecture*, June 1983, pp. 124–131.

[GOO 89] Goor, A. J. van de, *Computer Architecture and Design.* Reading, MA: Addison-Wesley Publishing Co., 1989.

[GOT 90] GOTO, A., T. SHINOGI, T. CHIKAYAMA, K. KUMON, AND A. HATTORI, "Processor Element Architecture for Parallel Inference Machine: PIM/p," Technical Report 577, Institute for New Generation Computer Technology, Tokyo, Japan, 1990.

[HAT 89] HATTORI, A., T. SHINOGI, K. KUMON, AND A. GOTO, "PIM/p: A Hierarchical Parallel Inference Machine," Technical Report 514, Institute for New Generation Computer Technology, Tokyo, Japan, 1989.

[HAY 86] HAYES, J. P., T. MUDGE, AND Q. STOUT, "A Microprocessor-based Hypercube Supercomputer," *IEEE Micro*, 6(5) October 1986, pp. 6–17.

[HAY 89] HAYES, JOHN, AND TREVOR MUDGE, "Hypercube Supercomputer," *Proc. IEEE*, 77(12), 1989, pp. 1829–1841.

[HOS 89] HOSHINO, T., *PAX Computer*. Reading, MA: Addison-Wesley, 1989.

[JAM 90] JAMES, DAVID V., A. T. LAUNDRIE, S. GJESSING, AND G. SOHI, "Distributed-Directory Scheme: Scalable Coherent Interface," *IEEE Computer*, 23(6), 1990, pp. 74–77.

[LEI 92] LEISERSON, CHARLES E., ET AL., "The Network Architecture of the Connection Machine CM-5," *Proc. 1992 DAGS/PC Symp.*, Dartmouth Institute for Advanced Graduate Studies in Parallel Computation, June 1992, pp. 101–114.

[MIN 92] MIN, SANG LYUL, JEAN-LOUP BAER, "Design and Analysis of a Scalable Cache Coherence Scheme Based on Clocks and Timestamps," *IEEE Trans. Parallel and Distributed Systems*, 3(1), 1992, pp. 25–44.

[MUD 86] MUDGE, T. N., ET AL., "Analysis of Multiple Bus Interconnection Networks," *J. Parallel Distributed Computing,* 3(3), 1986, pp. 328–343.

[MUD 87] MUDGE, T. N., J. P. HAYES, AND D. C. WINSOR, "Multiple Bus Architectures," *IEEE Computer*, 20(6) June 1987, pp. 42–48.

[NCU 90] NCUBE COMPANY, *NCUBE 6400 Processor Manual*, Beaverton, Oregon, 1990.

[NOA 90] NOAKES, M. O., AND W. DALLY, "System Design of the J-Machine," *Proc. Sixth MIT Conf. Advanced Research VLSI.* Cambridge, MA: MIT Press, 1990, pp. 179–194.

[QUI 87] QUINN, MICHAEL J., *Designing Efficient Algorithms for Parallel Computers.* New York: McGraw-Hill, Series in Artificial Intelligence, 1987.

[ROT 92] ROTHNIE, JAMES, "Kendall Square Research Introduction to the KSR1," *Proc. 1992 DAGS/PC Symp.*, Dartmouth Institute for Advanced Graduate Studies in Parallel Computation, June 1992, pp. 200–210.

[SEI 85] SEITZ, CHARLES, "The Cosmic Cube," *Commun. ACM,* 28(1), 1985, pp. 22–33.

[SEI 88] SEITZ, C. L., ET AL., "The Architecture and Programming of the Ametek Series 2010 Multicomputer," *Proc. Third Conf. Hypercube Concurrent Computers Applications,* Vol. I, Pasadena, CA, January 1988, pp. 33–36.

[SEQ 90] SEQUENT COMPUTER SYSTEMS, INC., *Symmetry Multiprocessor Architecture Overview*, Beaverton, Oregon 1990.

[SEQ 91] SEQUENT COMPUTER SYSTEMS, INC., *Symmetry Multiprocessor Architecture Overview*, Beaverton, Oregon 1991.

[STE 90] STENSTROM, PER, "A Survey of Cache Coherence Schemes for Multiprocessors," *IEEE Computer*, 23(6), 1990, pp. 12–24.

[STO 90] STONE, HAROLD S., "High-performance Computer Architecture," 2nd ed. Reading, MA: Addison-Wesley Publishing Co., 1990.

[STO 91] STONE, HAROLD S., AND JOHN COCKE, "Computer Architecture in the 1990s," *Computer*, 24(9), 1991, pp. 30–38.

[SUA 90] SUAYA, ROBERT, AND GRAHAM BIRTWISTLE, EDS., *VLSI and Parallel Computation.* San Mateo, CA: Morgan Kaufmann Publishers, 1990.

[TAN 81] TANENBAUM, A. S., *Computer Networks.* Upper Saddle River, NJ: Prentice Hall, 1981.

[TOW 86] TOWSLEY, D., "Approximate Models of Multiple Bus Multiprocessor Systems," *IEEE Trans. Computers,* C-35, March 1986, pp. 220–228.

[UED 86] UEDA, K., "Guarded Horn Clause: A Parallel Logic Programming Language with the Concept of a Guard," Technical Report 208, Institute for New Generation Computer Technology, Tokyo, Japan 1986.

PROBLEMS

6.1. Describe the advantages and disadvantages of the following:
  a. Write-invalidate snoopy cache protocol.
  b. Write-update snoopy cache protocol.

c. Full-map directory protocol.
   d. SCI directory protocol.
6.2. What are the advantages and disadvantages of the following architectures?
   a. Shared-bus-based multiprocessors.
   b. Hypercube-based multicomputers.
   c. n-Dimensional-mesh-based multicomputers.
   d. Multi-multiprocessors based on parts (b) and (c).
6.3. Consider the equations that are given in the text for memory bandwidth of systems with crossbar switch BW_c and multiple-bus network BW_b. Using the equation

$$BW_b = \sum_{i=1}^{b} i r_i + \sum_{i=b+1}^{m} b r_i$$

show that, when $b \geq m$, $BW_b = BW_c = m[1 - (1 - p/m)^n]$.

6.4. Consider a parallel machine in which 10 processors are connected to 10 memory modules through a network. In this machine, assume that the probability that a processor submits a request to a memory module in a cycle is 0.9, and a generated request can refer to each memory with equal probability. Compute the memory bandwidth for when the network is a
   a. 10-by-10 crossbar switch,
   b. Multiple-bus network with five buses.
6.5. Given the initial configuration in Figure P6.5 of a simplified multiprocessor architecture,

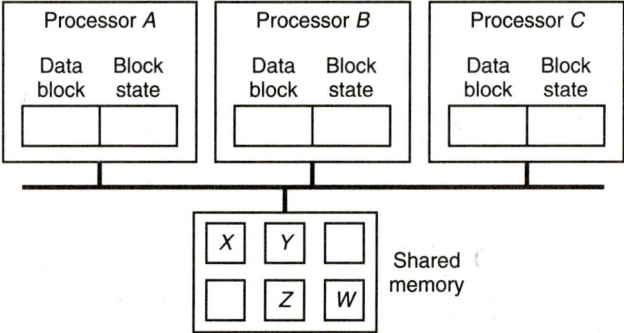

Figure P6.5

show the next state of the system after each of the following requests using the write-update snoopy cache protocol.
   a. At time t_0: processor A issues a write request for data block X.
   b. At time t_1: processor B issues a read request for data block X.
   c. At time t_2: processor C issues a read request for data block Y.
   d. At time t_3: processor B issues a write request for data block X.

$t_3 > t_2 > t_1 > t_0$

Let SC stands for single consistent, SI stands for single inconsistent, and MC stands for multiple consistent.

6.6. Consider a multiprocessor system with two processors (A and B) and each processor has a cache. Also, consider the following sequence of requests. Initially, there is no copy of variable X in any of the caches.

At time t_0: processor A reads variable X.
At time t_1: processor B reads variable X.

At time t_2: processor B updates X; $X = X + 2$.
At time t_3: processor A updates X; $X = X * 2$.
At time t_4: processor B reads variable X.

$t_4 > t_3 > t_2 > t_1 > t_0$

For each of the following protocols, show the state of variable X in caches and memory after each of the preceding statements is executed.

    a. Write-invalidate snoopy cache protocol.
    b. Write-update snoopy cache protocol.
    c. Centralized directory protocol.

6.7. What do you think will be the ideal architecture for a parallel machine? Why?

7

Parallel Programming and Parallel Algorithms

7.1 INTRODUCTION

Algorithms in which operations must be executed step by step are called serial or sequential algorithms. Algorithms in which several operations may be executed simultaneously are referred to as parallel algorithms. A parallel algorithm for a parallel computer can be defined as set of processes that may be executed simultaneously and may communicate with each other in order to solve a given problem. The term *process* may be defined as a part of a program that can be run on a processor.

In designing a parallel algorithm, it is important to determine the efficiency of its use of available resources. Once a parallel algorithm has been developed, a measurement should be used for evaluating its performance (or efficiency) on a parallel machine. A common measurement often used is *run time*. Run time (also referred to as elapsed time or completion time) refers to the time the algorithm takes on a parallel machine in order to solve a problem. More specifically, it is the elapsed time between the start of the first processor (or the first set of processors) and the termination of the last processor (or the last set of processors).

Various approaches may be used to design a parallel algorithm for a given problem. One approach is to attempt to convert a sequential algorithm to a parallel algorithm. If a sequential algorithm already exists for the problem, then inherent parallelism in that algorithm may be recognized and implemented in parallel. Inherent parallelism is parallelism that occurs naturally within an algorithm, not as a result of any special effort on the part of the algorithm or machine designer. It should be noted that exploiting inherent parallelism in a sequential algorithm might not always lead to an efficient parallel algorithm. It turns out that for certain types of problems a better approach is to adopt a parallel algorithm that solves a problem similar to, but different from, the given problem. Another approach is to design a totally new parallel algorithm that is more efficient than the existing one [QUI 87, QUI 94].

In either case, in the development of a parallel algorithm, a few important considerations cannot be ignored. The cost of communication between processes has to be considered, for instance. Communication aspects are important since, for a given algorithm, communication time may be greater than the actual computation time. Another consideration is that the algorithm should take into account the architecture of the computer on which it is to be executed. This is particularly important, since the same algorithm may be very efficient on one architecture and very inefficient on another architecture.

This chapter emphasizes two models that have been used widely for parallel programming: the *shared-memory model* and the *message-passing model*. The shared-memory model refers to programming in a multiprocessor environment in which the communication between processes is achieved through shared (or global) memory, whereas the message-passing model refers to programming in a multicomputer environment in which the communication between processes is achieved through some kind of message-switching mechanism.

In a multiprocessor environment, communication through shared memory is not problem free; erroneous results may occur if two processes update the same data in an unacceptable order. Multiprocessors usually support various synchronization instructions that can be used to prevent these types of errors; some of these instructions are explained in the next section.

In contrast to multiprocessors, in a multicomputer environment updating data is not a problem. Memory is unshared and localized to each processor. However, message-passing is the main concern here, and usually certain communication instructions are implemented for sending and receiving messages.

This chapter discusses the issues involved in parallel programming and the development of parallel algorithms. Various approaches to developing a parallel algorithm are explained. Algorithm structures such as the *synchronous structure*, *asynchronous structure*, and *pipeline structure* are described. A few terms related to performance measurement of parallel algorithms are presented. Finally, examples of parallel algorithms illustrating different design structures are given.

7.2 PROGRAMMING MODELS

In this section, two types of parallel programming are discussed: 1) *parallel programming on multiprocessors* and 2) *parallel programming on multicomputers*.

7.2.1 Parallel Programming on Multiprocessors

To write parallel programs in a particular language in a multiprocessor environment, we need to be able to perform certain operations through the language, such as synchronization. Some of these operations are discussed in depth in the following sections.

Process creation. A parallel program for a multiprocessor can be defined as a set of *processes* that may be executed in parallel and may communicate with each other to solve a given problem. For example, in a UNIX operating system environment, the creation of a process is done with a system call called *fork*. When a process executes the *fork* system call, a new *slave* (or *child*) process will be created, which is a copy of the original *master* (or *parent*) process. The slave process begins to execute at the point after the *fork* call. The *fork* function returns the UNIX process id of the created slave process to the master process and returns 0 to the slave process. The following code makes this concept more clear.

```
return_code = fork ();
if (return_code == 0)
{
    slave ();          --the slave process goes to work here
                       --by calling slave routine
    exit (0);          --slave process returns from work
                       --and terminates
}
else
{
    if (return_code == -1)
        print ("failure in creating a slave process");
    else
                       --master process continues the
                       --execution from this point
}
```

In this code, the *fork* function returns 0 in the slave process's copy of the *return_code*, and returns the UNIX process id of the slave process to the master process's copy of the *return_code*. Note that both processes have their own copy of the *return_code* in separate memory locations.

Synchronization. In a multiprocessor environment, processes usually communicate through shared data. This eliminates the need to make multiple copies of the same data. Having only one copy of data shared by many processes saves memory and also avoids the updating problem usually experienced when multiple copies of the same data item exist. However, shared data are not problem free and, in fact, the programmer must be careful in executing and accessing them. If two processes access the same data at the same time and use that data in a computation and then update the data using the computed result, invalid results may occur. Therefore, access to such shared data must be *mutually exclusive*.

To understand the need for mutual exclusion, let us consider the execution of the following statement for incrementing a shared variable *index*:

```
index = index + 1;
```

This statement causes a read operation followed by a write operation. The read operation gets the old value of the variable index, and the write operation stores the new value. The actual computation of index + 1 occurs between the read and write operations. Now assume that there are two processes, p_1 and p_2, each trying to increment the variable index using a statement like the preceding one. If the initial value of index is 5, the correct final value index should be 7 after both processes have incremented it. In other words, index is incremented twice, once for each process. However, an invalid result can be obtained if one process accesses variable index while it is being incremented by the other process (between the read and write operations). For example, it is possible that process p_1 reads the value 5 from index, and then process p_2 reads the same value 5 from index before p_1 gets a chance to write the new value back to memory. In this case, the final value of index will be 6, obviously an invalid result. Therefore, access to the variable index must be *mutually exclusive*—accessible to only one process at a time. To ensure such mutual exclusion, a mechanism called *synchronization* must be implemented that allows one process to finish writing the final value of the variable index before the other process can have access to the same variable.

Multiprocessors usually support various simple instructions (sometimes referred to as *mutual exclusion primitives*) for synchronization of resources and/or processes. Often, these instructions are implemented by a combination of hardware and software. They are the basic mechanisms that enforce mutual exclusion for more complex operations implemented in software macros. (A macro is a single instruction that represents a given sequence of instructions in a program.) A common set of basic synchronization instructions is defined next.

Lock and Unlock. Solutions to mutual exclusion problems can be constructed using mechanisms referred to as *locks*. A process that attempts to access shared data that is protected with a *locked gate* waits until the associated gate is unlocked and then locks the gate to prevent other processes having access the data. After the process accesses and performs the required operations on the data, the process unlocks the gate to allow another process to access the data. The important characteristic of lock and unlock operations is that they are executed atomically, that is, as uninterruptable operations; in other words, once they are initiated, they do not stop until they complete. The atomic operations of lock and unlock can be described by the following segments of code:

```
Lock(L)
    {
    while (L==1) NOP;    --NOP stands for no operation
    L = 1;
    }
Unlock(L)
    {
    L = 0;
    }
```

In this code, the variable L represents the status of the protection gate. If $L = 1$, the gate is interpreted as being closed. Otherwise, when $L = 0$, the gate is interpreted as being open. When a process wants to access shared data, it executes a Lock(L) operation. This atomic operation repeatedly checks the variable L until its value becomes zero. When L is zero, the Lock(L) operation sets its value to 1. An Unlock(L) operation causes L to be reset to 0. To understand the use of lock and unlock operations, consider the previous example in which two processes were incrementing the shared variable *index* by executing the following statement:

```
index = index + 1;
```

To ensure a correct result, a lock and an unlock operation can be inserted in the code of each process as follows:

```
Lock(L)
index = index + 1;
Unlock(L)
```

Now, each process must execute a Lock(L) instruction before changing the variable index. After a process completes execution of the Lock(L) instruction, the other process [if it tries to execute its own Lock(L) instruction] will be forced to wait until the first process unlocks the variable L. When the first process finishes executing the index = index + 1 statement, it executes the Unlock(L) instruction. At this time, if the other process is waiting at the Lock(L) instruction, it will be allowed to proceed with execution. In other words, the Lock(L) and Unlock(L) statements create a kind of "fence" around the statement index = index + 1, such that only one process at a time can be inside the fence to increment index. The statement index = index + 1 is often referred to as a *critical section*. In general, a critical section is a group of statements that must be executed or accessed by at most a certain number of processes at any given time. In our previous example, it was assumed at most one process could execute the critical section index=index + 1 at any given time.

In general, a structure that provides exclusive access to a critical section is called a *monitor*. Monitors were first described by Hoare [HOA 74] and have become a main mechanism in parallel programming. A monitor represents a serial part of a program. As is shown in Figure 7.1, a monitor represents a kind of fence around the shared data.

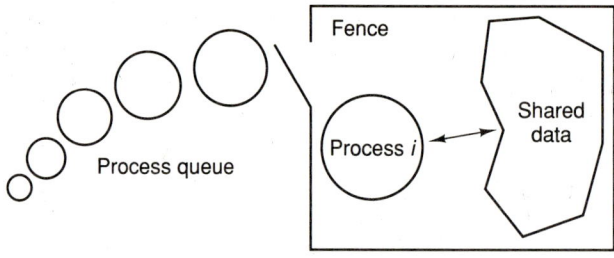

Figure 7.1 Structure of a monitor; it provides exclusive access to a shared data.

Only one process can be inside the fence at a time. Once inside the fence, a process can access the shared data.

The following statements represent the general structure of a monitor.

```
Lock(L)
    <Critical Section>
Unlock(L)
```

A lock instruction is placed before a critical section, and the unlock instruction is placed at the end of the critical section. When a process wishes to invoke the monitor, it attempts to lock the lock variable L. If the monitor has already been invoked by another process, the process waits until the process that initiated the lock instruction releases the monitor by unlocking the lock variable.

Only one process can invoke the monitor; other processes queue up waiting for the process to release the monitor. This limits the amount of parallelism that can be obtained in a program. Therefore, minimizing the amount of code in a critical section will increase parallel performance for most parallel algorithms.

In the preceding implementations of lock, the variable L is repeatedly checked until its value becomes zero. This type of lock, which causes the processor to be tied up in an idle loop while increasing the memory contention, is called *spin lock*. To prevent repeatedly checking the variable L while it is 1, an interrupt mechanism can be used. In this case, a lock is called a *suspended lock*. Whenever a process fails to obtain the lock, it goes into a waiting state. When a process releases the lock, it signals all (or some) of the waiting processes through some kind of interrupt mechanism. One way of implementing such a mechanism could be the use of interprocessor interrupts. Another option could be a software implementation of a queue for enqueueing the processes in the waiting state.

The lock instruction is often implemented in multiprocessors by using a special instruction called *Test&Set*. The Test&Set instruction is an atomic operation that returns the current value of a memory cell and sets the memory cell to 1. Both phases of this instruction (i.e., test and set) are implemented as one uninterruptable operation in the hardware. Once a processor executes such an instruction, no other processor can intervene in its execution. In general the operation of a Test&Set instruction can be defined as follows:

```
Test&Set(L)
{
temp = L;
L = 1;
return temp;
}
Reset(L)
{
L = 0;
}
```

This Test&Set instruction copies the contents of the variable L to the variable temp and then sets the value of L to 1. If a multiprocessor supports the Test&Set instruction, then the Lock and Unlock instructions can be implemented in software as follows:

```
Lock(L)
{
    while (Test&Set(L) == 1) NOP;
}
Unlock(L)
{
    Reset(L)
}
```

In practice, most multiprocessors are based on commercially available microprocessors. Often, these microprocessors support basic instructions that are similar to the Test&Set instruction. For example, the Motorola 88000 processor series supports an instruction, called exchange register with memory (Xmem), for implementing synchronization instructions in multiprocessor systems. Similarly, the Intel Pentium processor provides an instruction, called exchange (Xchg) for synchronization. The Xmem and Xchg instructions exchange the contents of a register with a memory location. For example, let L be the address of a memory location and R be the address of a register. Then Xchg can be defined as follows:

```
Xchg(L,R)
{
    temp = L;
    L = R;
    R = temp;
}
```

In general the exchange instructions require a sequence of read, modify, and write cycles. During these cycles the processor should be allowed atomic access to the location that is referenced by the instruction. To provide such atomic access, often the processors accommodate a signal that indicates to the outside world that the processor is performing a read–modify–write sequence of cycles. For example, the Pentium processor provides an external signal, called lock#, to perform atomic accesses of memory [INT 93a, INT 93b]. When lock# is active, it indicates to the system that the current sequence of bus cycles should not be interrupted. That is, a programmer can perform read and write operations on the contents of a memory variable and be assured that the variable is not accessed by any other processor during these operations. This facility is provided for certain instructions when followed by a Lock instruction and also for instructions that implicitly perform read–modify–write cycles such as the Xchg instruction. When a Lock instruction is executed, it activates the lock# signal during the execution of the instruction that follows.

To implement a spin lock, a processor can acquire a lock with an Xchg (or Xmem) instruction. The Xchg performs an indivisible read–modify–write bus transaction that ensures exclusive ownership of the lock. Therefore, an alternative implementation for Lock and Unlock instructions can be as follows:

```
Lock(L)
{
    R = 1;
    while (R==1) Xchg(L,R);
}
Unlock(L)
{
    L = 0;
}
```

Wait and Signal (or Increment and Decrement). An alternative to Lock and Unlock instructions could be the implementation of *wait* and *signal* instructions (also referred to as increment and decrement instructions). These instructions decrement or increment a specified memory cell (location), and during their execution no other instruction can access that cell. In some situations, when more than one process is allowed to access a critical section, the protection can be obtained with fewer *Wait/Signal* instructions than *Lock/Unlock* instructions. This is because the *Lock/Unlock* instructions operate on a binary value (0 or 1), while the full contents of a variable *Wait/Signal* operate on *semaphore* (*S*).

The atomic operations of wait and signal can be described by the following segment of code:

```
Wait(S)
{
    while (S <= 0) NOP;
    S = S-1;
}
Signal(S)
{
    S = S+1;
}
```

For example, assume that there is a shared buffer of length k, where k processes can operate on separate cells simultaneously. When there are k processes working on the buffer, the $k+1^{th}$ process is forced to wait until one of the (1 to k) processes finishes its operation. A simple way to implement this form of synchronization is to start with an initial value of k in the semaphore variable S. As each process obtains a cell in the buffer, S is decremented by 1. Eventually, when k processes have obtained a cell in the buffer, S will equal 0. When a process wishes to access the shared buffer, it executes the instruction *Wait* (*S*). This instruction spins while $S \leq 0$. If $S > 0$, Wait(S) decrements S and lets the process access the shared buffer. The process executes the instruction *Signal* (*S*) after completing its operation on the shared buffer. Signal (S) increments S, which lets another process have access to the shared buffer.

In summary, as shown in the following statements, in situations when more than one process is allowed to access a critical section, a Wait instruction is placed before the critical section and a Signal instruction is placed at the end of that section.

```
Wait(semaphore)
<Critical Section>
Signal(semaphore)
```

Fetch&Add. One problem with the preceding synchronization methods is when a large number of Lock (or Wait) instructions is issued for execution simultaneously. When n processes attempt to access a shared data simultaneously, n Lock (or Wait) instructions will be executed, one after the other, even though only one process will successfully access data. Although the memory contention produced by the simultaneous access may not degrade the performance so much for a small number of processes, it may become a bottleneck as the number of processes increases. For systems with a large number of processors, for example 100 to 1000, a mechanism for parallel synchronization is necessary.

One such mechanism, which is used in some parallel machines, is called *Fetch&Add*. The instruction Fetch&Add(x,c) increases a shared-memory location x with a constant value c and returns the value of x before the increment. The semantics of this instruction are

```
Fetch&Add(x,c)
    {
    temp = x;
    x = temp + c;
    return temp;
    }
```

If n processes issue the instruction Fetch&Add(x,c) at the same time, the shared-memory location x is updated only once by adding the value $n*c$ to it, and a unique value is returned to each of the n processes. Although the memory is updated only once, the values returned to each process are the same as when an arbitrary sequence of n Fetch&Adds is sequentially executed. To show the effectiveness of the Fetch&Add instruction, let us consider the problem of adding two vectors in parallel.

```
for (i=1; i<=k; i++) {
    Z[i] = A[i] + B[i] ;
}
```

Assuming that there is more than one process, one way of implementing parallelism is to let each process compute the addition for a specific i. At any time, each process requests a subscript, and once it obtains a valid subscript, say i, it evaluates $Z[i]=A[i] + B[i]$. Then it claims another subscript. This continues until the processes exhaust all the subscripts in the range 1 to k.

Each process executes a Fetch&Add on the shared variable, next_index, to obtain a valid subscript (next_index is initially set to 1). The code for each process is as follows:

Sec. 7.2 Programming Models

```
int i;
i = Fetch&Add(next_index, 1);
while (i<=k) {
    Z[i] = A[i] + B[i];
    i = Fetch&Add(next_index, 1);
}
```

Barrier. A barrier is a point of synchronization where a predetermined number of processes has to arrive before the execution of the program can continue. It is used to ensure that a certain number of processes complete a stage of computation before they proceed to a next stage that requires the results of the previous stage.

As an example, consider the following computation on two vectors A and B.

```
sum = 0;
for (i=1; i<=10; i++) {
    sum = sum + A[i];
}
for (i=1; i<=10; i++) {
    B[i] = B[i]/sum;
}
```

Assume that there are two processes, with id 0 and 1, performing the computation in two stages: stage 1 and stage 2. Also, assume that the variable sum and vectors A and B are defined as shared variables and are accessible to both processes. The shared variable sum has been initialized to 0. In stage 1 of the computation, both processes contribute to the calculation of the variable sum. To the variable sum, process 0 adds the values $A[1]$, $A[3]$, $A[5]$, $A[7]$, and $A[9]$, and process 1 adds the values $A[2]$, $A[4]$, $A[6]$, $A[8]$, and $A[10]$. When both processes complete their contribution to the sum, they proceed to the second stage of computation. In stage 2, process 0 computes the new values for $B[1]$, $B[3]$, $B[5]$, $B[7]$, and $B[9]$, and process 1 computes the new values for $B[2]$, $B[4]$, $B[6]$, $B[8]$, and $B[10]$.

The following code gives the main steps of each process.

```
int i, partial_sum;
partial_sum = 0;
for (i=1+id; i<=10; i=i+2) {    --id refers to process id;
                                --it is either 0 or 1.
    partial_sum = partial_sum + A[i];
}
Lock(L)
sum = sum + partial_sum;
Unlock(L)
BARRIER(2)          --none of the processes can continue past
                    --the barrier statement until both
                    --processes have arrived at this
                    --statement
for (i=1+id; i<=10; i=i+2) {
    B[i] = B[i]/sum;
}
```

In this code, each process uses a local variable partial_sum to add five elements of vector A. Once the partial_sum is calculated, it is added to the shared variable sum. To ensure a correct result, a Lock instruction is executed before changing the sum. The BARRIER macro prevents processes updating elements of vector B until both processes have completed stage 1 of computation.

In general, a barrier can be implemented in software using spin locks. Assume that n processes must enter the barrier before program execution can continue. When a process enters the barrier, the barrier checks to see how many processes have already been blocked. (Processes that are waiting at the barrier are called blocked processes.) If the number of blocked processes is less than $n - 1$, the newly entered process is also blocked. On the other hand, if the number of blocked processes is $n - 1$, then all the blocked processes and the newly entered process are allowed to continue execution. The processes continue by executing the statement following the barrier statement.

The following code gives the main steps of a barrier macro for synchronizing n processes:

```
BARRIER(n)
{
    Lock(barrier_lock)
    if(number_of_blocked_processes < n-1 )
        BLOCK
    WAKE_UP
}
```

Let *number_of_blocked_processes* denote a shared variable that holds the total number of processes that have entered the barrier so far. Initially, the value of this variable is set to 0. A process entering the barrier will execute the BLOCK macro when there are not $n - 1$ processes in the blocked stage yet. The BLOCK macro causes the process executing it to be suspended by adding it to the set of blocked processes and also releases the barrier by executing Unlock(barrier_lock). Whenever there are $n - 1$ blocked processes, the nth process entering the barrier executes the WAKE_UP macro and then leaves the barrier without unlocking the barrier_lock. The WAKE_UP macro causes a process (if there is one) to be released from the set of blocked processes. The released process will continue its execution at the point where it was suspended, that is, it executes the WAKE_UP macro and then exits the barrier. This process continues until all the suspended processes leave the barrier. The last process, right before leaving the barrier, releases the barrier by executing Unlock(barrier_lock).

The following code gives a possible implementation for the barrier macro. In this code, the macros BLOCK and WAKE_UP are implemented in a simple form using spin lock.

```
BARRIER(n)
  {
     Lock(barrier_lock)
     if(number_of_blocked_processes < n-1)    --code for BLOCK macro
        {
          number_of_blocked_processes =
             number_of_blocked_processes + 1;
```

```
            Unlock(barrier_lock)
            Lock(block_lock)
        }
    if(number_of_blocked_processes > 0)  --code for WAKE_UP macro
        {
          number_of_blocked_processes =
               number_of_blocked_processes-1;
          Unlock(block_lock)
        }
    else
        Unlock(barrier_lock)
    }
```

To make this code work correctly, the lock variable *barrier_lock* must be initially unlocked, and *block_lock* must be initially locked. The first $n-1$ processes that enter the barrier will increment the variable *number_of_blocked_processes*, and then they will be tied up in an idle loop by executing the statement Lock(block_lock). The last process that enters the barrier will decrement the variable *number_of_blocked_processes* and then will execute the statement Unlock(block_lock) to release a blocked process. Whenever the variable *block_lock* is unlocked, one of the blocked processes will succeed in locking the variable block_lock and continue its execution by releasing another process (if there is one).

Deadlock. Deadlock describes the situation when two or more processes request and hold mutually needed resources in a circular pattern; that is, as shown in Figure 7.2, process 1 holds resource *A* while requesting resource *B*, and process 2 holds resource *B* while requesting resource *A*. Lock variables can be viewed as resources capable of producing such a pattern.

There can be more than one lock variable declared and used in a program. Since lock instructions can be placed almost anywhere in the program and numerous lock variables can exist, it is the responsibility of the programmer to use them with care. Deadlock may occur if a process attempts to lock another critical section while it is working in its own critical section. One possible deadlock scenario is as follows:

At Time	Process 1	Process 2
t_0	Lock(A)	
t_1		Lock(B)
t_2	Lock(B)	
t_3		Lock(A)
.		
.		

It is assumed that time $t_0 < t_1 < t_2 < t_3$. At time t_0, process 1 locks the lock variable *A*. Later, at time t_1, process 2 locks the lock variable *B*. At times t_2 and t_3, processes 1 and 2 attempt to lock the lock variables *B* and *A*, respectively. However, they cannot succeed, since neither has released the previous lock. Therefore, processes 1

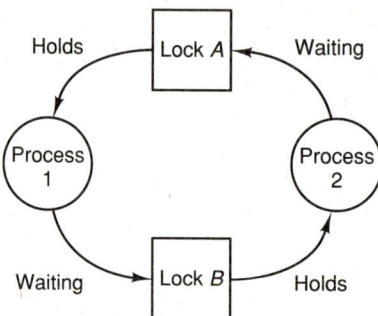

Figure 7.2 Resource allocation diagram for a deadlock situation.

and 2 are both busy waiting at the second lock, each denying the other access to the resources they need. Thus a deadlock situation has occurred.

7.2.2 Parallel Programming on Multicomputers

A multicomputer, also referred to as a message-passing concurrent computer, consists of several processors called *nodes*, which are connected with an interconnection network. Each processor has its own local memory. Thus, in contrast to the shared-memory multiprocessor, there is no global memory. That is, in a multicomputer the nodes are not able to coordinate themselves through global variables, but coordinate their activities by sending messages to each other. The messages are sent and received through communication channels that are implemented in each node.

Similar to the programming in the multiprocessor environment, whenever the master process creates a slave process, a new process id will be produced and will be known to both of the processes. The processes use these ids as addresses for sending messages to each other.

In addition to the process id, the master process also specifies the name of the node that executes the created slave. Once some processes are created, message-passing between them can be initiated. A message may be either a control message or a data message and may contain from 1 byte of information to any size that will fit in the node's memory. The messages may be routed through different routing paths according to their length and/or destination address. However, these differences are invisible to the programmer. Usually, messages may be queued as necessary in the sending node, in transit, and in the receiving node. That is, a message may have an arbitrary delay from sender to receiver. However, their ordering is usually preserved through the network.

Each message carries some additional information, such as the destination process id and message length. In some implementations, it also carries the source process id. Whenever a process wants to send a message, it first allocates a buffer for the message. Once the message has been built in the allocated buffer, the process issues a send command. These are represented as

```
p = mem_allocate (message_length);
            --p points to the allocated buffer
send (p, message_length, source id, destination id);
```

A process can receive a message by issuing:

$$p = receive\_b();$$

The character *b* at the end of *receive_b* indicates that this command is a blocking function, which means it does not return until a message has arrived for the process. The *receive_b* function allocates a buffer equal to the size of the received message and returns *p*, a pointer to the buffer that contains the received message. (This buffer might also be allocated by the user.) If a nonblocking receive command, denoted as *receive*( ), is used, it may return a null pointer if there is no message queued for the process.

In contrast to multiprocessors, in a multicomputer system, processor-to-memory communication is not a problem because memory is localized to each processor in a node. Interprocess message-passing happens less frequently than memory access. Although interprocess communication exhibits a larger delay, it does not present an obstacle to building a system with thousands of nodes [ATH 88].

Although the message-passing model is well suited for multicomputers, we can also implement a message-passing communication environment on a multiprocessor. One way to do this is to implement a communication channel by defining a channel buffer and a pair of pointers to this channel buffer. One pointer indicates the next location in the buffer to be written to by the transmitting process, while the other pointer indicates the next location to be read by the receiving process.

Another way of communication can be as simple as one process writing to a specific memory location, called a mailbox, and another process reading the mailbox. To prevent a message from being overwritten by the transmitting process before it is read by another process, and/or the receiving process reads an invalid message, communication is often implemented by mutually exclusive access to a mailbox.

7.3 PARALLEL COMPUTATION

To make a program suitable for execution on a parallel computer, it must be decomposed into a set of processes, which will then make up the parallel algorithm. Decomposition involves partitioning and assignment. *Partitioning* has been defined as specifying the set of tasks (or work) that will implement a given problem on a specified parallel computer in the most efficient manner[LIN 81]. *Assignment* is the process of allocating the partitions or tasks to processors. Partitioning and assignment are discussed in the following.

7.3.1 Partitioning

The performance of a parallel algorithm depends on program *granularity*. Granularity refers to the size of the task for a process compared to implementation overhead (such as synchronization, critical section resolution, and communication). As the size of each individual task increases, the amount of computation per task becomes much higher than the amount of implementation overhead per task. Therefore, one solution to parallel computation is to partition the problem into several large size tasks. This is referred to as *coarse-granularity parallelism*. However, a large-sized task decreases the number of required processes and therefore reduces the amount of parallelism. An alternative would be to partition a problem into a number of relatively small size tasks that can run in parallel. This is referred to as *fine-granularity parallelism*. In general, a fine-granularity task contains a small number of instructions, which may cause the amount of computation per task to become much smaller than the amount of implementation overhead.

Thus, to improve the performance of a parallel algorithm, the designer should consider the trade-offs between computation and implementation overhead. This is a similar concept to the one for designing a sequential algorithm, for which a designer should consider the trade-offs between memory space and execution time. A general solution for balancing between computation and overhead is *clustering*. The idea of clustering is to form groups of task such that the amount of overhead within groups is much greater than the amount of overhead between groups.

In practice, the number of processors is usually adjusted to the size of the problem in order to keep the run time in a certain desired range. To achieve this goal, it is important that the algorithm utilize all the processors by giving them a task and keeping the ratio of overhead time to computational time low for each task. If this can be accomplished for any number of processors (1 to n), then the algorithm is called *scalable*. It may not be possible to develop a scalable algorithm for some architectures unless the problem holds certain features. For example, to have a scalable algorithm for a problem on a hypercube multicomputer, the nature of the problem should allow localizing communication between neighbor nodes. This is because a hypercube's longest communication path increases as $\log_2 N$, where N is the number of nodes. Some scientific problems that require the solution of partial differential equations can be mapped to a hypercube such that each node needs to communicate only with its immediate neighbors [GUS 88a, DEN 88].

There are two methods of partitioning tasks: *static partition* and *dynamic partition*. The static partition method partitions the tasks before execution. The advantage in this method is that there is less communication and contention among processes. The disadvantage is that input data may dictate how much parallel computation actually occurs at run time and how much of the data is to be given to a process; as a result, some processes may not be kept busy during execution.

The dynamic partition method partitions the tasks during execution. The advantage to dynamic partitioning is that it tends to keep processes busier, and it is not as affected by the input data as is the static partition method. The disadvantage is the amount of communication by processes that is needed in implementing such a scheme.

Processes may be created such that all processes perform the same function on different portions of the data or such that each performs a different function on the data. The former approach is referred to as *data partitioning* (also referred to as *data parallelism*), while the latter is often referred to as *function partitioning* (also referred to as *control parallelism* or sometimes *functional parallelism*). Since data partitioning involves the creation of identical processes, it is also referred to as *homogeneous mul-*

titasking. For a similar reason, function partitioning is sometimes referred to as *heterogeneous multitasking* by which multiple unique processes perform different tasks on data. (The multiplicity of terms is understandably confusing, however, due to the recentness of study in this area, it is also to be expected.)

The data partitioning approach extracts parallelism from the organization of problem data. The data structure is divided into pieces of data, with each piece being processed in parallel. A piece of data can be an individual item of data or a group of individual items. Data partitioning is especially useful in solving numerical problems that deal with large arrays and vectors. It is also a useful method for nonnumerical problems such as sorting and combinatorial search. This approach, in particular, is suited for the development of algorithms in multicomputers, because a processor mainly performs computation on its own local data and seldom communicates with other processors.

The following example illustrates data partitioning and function partitioning. Consider the following computation on four vectors A, B, C, and D.

$$Z[i] = (A[i] * B[i]) + (C[i]/D[i]), \text{ for } i = 1 \text{ to } 10.$$

When data partitioning is applied, this computation is performed as follows: 10 identical processes are created such that each process performs the computation for a unique index i. Here, parallelism has been achieved by computing each $Z[i]$ simultaneously using multiple identical processes.

When function partitioning is applied, two different processes, P_1 and P_2, are created. P_1 performs the computation $x = A[i] * B[i]$ and sends the value of x to P_2. P_2 in turn computes $y = C[i]/D[i]$, and after it receives the value of x from P_1 it performs the computation $Z[i] = x + y$. This is done for each index i. Here, parallelism has been achieved by performing the functions of multiplication and division simultaneously. Generally, in the function partitioning approach the program is organized such that the processes take advantage of parallelism in the code, rather than in the data.

On the whole, data partitioning offers the following advantages over function partitioning:

1. Higher parallelism
2. Equally balanced load among processes (this is because all processes are identical with respect to the computation being performed)
3. Easier to implement

7.3.2 Assignment or Scheduling

In the previous section, the problem of partitioning was discussed. Once a program is partitioned into processes, each process has to be assigned to a processor for execution. This mapping of processes to processors is referred to as *assignment* or *scheduling*. Assignment may be *static* or *dynamic*.

In static assignment, the set of processes and the order in which they must be executed are known prior to execution. Static assignment algorithms require low process communication and are well suited when process communication is expensive.

Also, in this type of assignment, scheduling costs are incurred only once whenever the same program runs many times on different data.

In contrast to static assignment, in dynamic assignment processes are assigned to processors at run time. Dynamic assignment is well suited when process communication is inexpensive. It also offers better utilization of processors and provides flexibility in the number of available processors. This is particularly useful when the number of processes depends on the input size. The drawbacks associated with dynamic assignment are the following:

1. The structure of the program becomes hard to understand.
2. Deadlock detection becomes difficult.
3. Since processes are assigned at run time, the performance analysis of the program sometimes becomes impossible.
4. There is more communication and contention among processes.

7.4 ALGORITHM STRUCTURES

A parallel algorithm for parallel computers can be defined as a collection of concurrent processes operating simultaneously to solve a given problem. These algorithms can be divided into three categories: synchronous, asynchronous, and pipeline structures.

7.4.1 Synchronous Structure

In this category of algorithms, two or more processes are linked by a common execution point used for synchronization purposes. A process will come to a point in its execution where it must wait for other (one or more) processes to reach a certain point. After processes have reached the synchronization point, they can continue their execution. This leads to the fact that all processes that have to synchronize at a given point in their execution must wait for the slowest one. This waiting period is the main drawback for this type of algorithm. Synchronous algorithms are also referred to as *partitioning algorithms*.

Large-scale numerical problems (such as those solving large systems of equations) expose an opportunity for developing synchronous algorithms. Often, techniques used for these problems involve a series of iterations on large arrays. Each iteration uses the partial result produced from the previous iteration and makes a step of progress toward the final solution. The computation of each iteration can be parallelized by letting many processes work on different parts of the data array. However, after each iteration, processes should be synchronized because the partial result produced by one process is to be used by other processes on the next iteration.

Synchronous parallel algorithms can be implemented on both shared-memory models and message-passing models. When synchronous algorithms are implemented on a message-passing model, communication between processes is achieved *explicitly* using some kind of message-passing mechanism. When implemented on a shared-memory model, depending on the type of problem to be solved, two kinds of communication strategies may be used. Processes may communicate *explicitly* using message passing or *implicitly* by referring to certain parts of memory. These communication strategies are illustrated in the following.

Consider the following computation on four vectors *A, B, C,* and *D* using two processors.

```
for (i=1; i<=10; i++){
    Z[i] = (A[i] * B[i]) + (C[i]/D[i]);
}
```

The parallel algorithm used for this computation is straightforward and consists of two processes, process p_1 and p_2. For each index i (for $i = 1$ to 10), p_1 evaluates $x = A[i] * B[i]$ and process p_2 evaluates two statements, $y = C[i]/D[i]$ and $Z[i] = x + y$.

When the processes communicate explicitly, then, for each index i, process p_1 evaluates x and sends a message packet consisting of the value of x to process p_2. Process p_2 in turn evaluates y and, after it receives the message, evaluates $Z[i]$.

When the processes communicate implicitly, no message-passing is required. Instead, process p_2 evaluates y and checks if process p_1 has evaluated x. If yes, it picks the value of x from memory and proceeds to evaluate $Z[i]$. Otherwise, it waits until p_1 evaluates x. When p_2 finishes computation of $Z[i]$, it will start the computation of y for the next index, $i + 1$. At the same time, p_1 starts the computation of x for the next index. This process continues until all the indexes are processed.

The following code gives the main steps of the preceding algorithm when the processes communicate implicitly. In the code, the process p_1 is denoted as the slave process and the process p_2 is denoted as master process.

```
struct global_memory
{                      --creates the following variables as
                       --shared variables
    shared int next_index;.
    shared int A[10],B[10],C[10],D[10],Z[10];
    shared int x;
    shared char turn[6];
}
main()
{
    int y;
    next_index=1;
    turn='slave';
    CREATE(slave)      --create a process, called
                       --slave. This process starts
                       --execution at the slave routine
    while (next_index <= 10){
        y=C[next_index]/D[next_index];
        while (turn == 'slave') NOP;
        Z[next_index] = x+y;
        next_index=next_index+1;
        turn='slave';
```

```
            }
            PRINT_RESULT
    }
    slave()
    {
        while (next_index <= 10) {
            while (turn == 'master') NOP;
            x = A[next_index] * B[next_index];
            turn = 'master';
        }
    }
```

The vectors *A, B, C, D*, and *Z* are in global shared-memory and are accessible to both processes. Once the main process, called the master process, has allocated shared memory, it executes the CREATE macro. Execution of CREATE causes a new process to be created. The created process, called the slave process, starts execution at the slave routine, which is specified as an argument in the CREATE statement.

7.4.2 Asynchronous Structure

Asynchronous parallel algorithms are characterized by letting the processes work with the most recently available data. These kinds of algorithms can be implemented on both shared-memory models and message-passing models. In the shared-memory model, there is a set of global variables accessible to all processes. Whenever a process completes a stage of its program, it reads some global variables. Based on the values of these variables and the results obtained from the last stage, the process activates its next stage and updates some of the global variables.

When asynchronous algorithms are implemented on a message-passing model, a process reads some input messages after completing a stage of its program. Based on these messages and the results obtained from the last stage, the process starts its next stage and sends messages to other processes.

Thus an asynchronous algorithm continues or terminates its process according to values in some global variables (or some messages) and does not wait for an input set as a synchronous algorithm does. That is, in an asynchronous algorithm, synchronizations are not needed for ensuring that certain input is available for processes at various times. Asynchronous algorithms are also referred to as *relaxed algorithms* due to their less restrictive synchronization constraints.

As an example, consider the computation of the four vectors that was given in the previous section. Using two processes to evaluate, we have:

$$Z[i] = (A[i] * B[i]) + (C[i]/D[i]) \qquad \text{for } i = 1 \text{ to } 10. \qquad (7.1)$$

An asynchronous algorithm can be created by letting each process compute expression (7.1) for a specific i. At any time, each process requests an index. Once it obtains a valid subscript, say i, it evaluates: $Z[i] = (A[i] * B[i]) + (C[i]/D[i])$ and then claims another subscript. That is, process p_1 may evaluate $Z[1]$ while process p_2 evaluates $Z[2]$. This action continues until the processes exhaust all the subscripts in the range 1 to 10.

Sec. 7.4 Algorithm Structures

The following code gives the main steps of a parallel program for the preceding algorithm.

```
struct global_memory
{
shared int next_index;
shared int A[10],B[10],C[10],D[10],Z[10];
}
main()
{
        CREATE(slave)   --create a process, called slave
                        --This process starts execution at the
                        --slave routine
        task();
        WAIT_FOR_END    --wait for slave to be terminated
        PRINT_RESULT
}
slave()
{
        task();
}
task()
{
        int i;
        GET_NEXT_INDEX(i)
        while(i>0) {
           Z[i] = (A[i] * B[i]) + (C[i]/D[i]);
           GET_NEXT_INDEX(i)
        }
}
```

The vectors A, B, C, D, and Z are in global shared-memory and are accessible to both processes. Once the master process has allocated shared memory, it creates a slave process. In the slave routine, the slave process simply calls *task*. The master process also calls task immediately after creating the slave. In the task routine, each process executes the macro GET_NEXT_INDEX(i). The macro GET_NEXT_INDEX is a monitor operation, that is, at any time only one process is allowed to execute and modify some statements and the variables of this macro.

Execution of GET_NEXT_INDEX returns in i the next available subscript (in the range 1 to 10) while valid subscripts exist; otherwise, it returns −1 in i. The macro GET_NEXT_INDEX uses the shared variable next_index to keep the next available subscript. When a process obtains a valid subscript, it evaluates $Z[i]$ and again calls GET_NEXT_INDEX to claim another subscript. This process continues until all the subscripts in the range 1 to 10 are claimed. If the slave process receives −1 in i, it dies by returning from *task* to *slave* and then exiting from *slave*. If the master process receives −1 in i, it returns back to the main routine and executes the macro WAIT_FOR_END. This macro causes the master process to wait until the slave process has terminated. This ensures that all the subscripts have been processed.

In comparison to synchronous algorithms, asynchronous algorithms require less access to shared variables and as a result tend to reduce memory contention problems. Memory contention occurs when different processes access the same memory module within a short time interval. When a large number of processes accesses a set of shared variables for the purpose of synchronization or communication, a severe memory contention may occur. These shared variables, sometimes called memory *hot spots*, may cause a large number of memory accesses to occur. The memory accesses may then create congestion on the interconnection network between processors and memory modules. The congestion will increase the access time to memory modules and, as a result, cause performance degradation. Therefore, it is important to reduce memory hot spots. This can be achieved in asynchronous algorithms by distributing data in a proper way among the memory modules.

In general, asynchronous algorithms are more efficient than synchronous for the following four reasons:

1. Processes never wait on other processes for input. This often results in decreasing run time.
2. The result of the processes that are run faster may be used to abort the slower processes, which are doing useless computations.
3. More reliable.
4. Less memory contention problems, in particular when the algorithm is based on the data partitioning approach.

However, asynchronous algorithms have the drawback that their analysis is more difficult than synchronous algorithms. At times, due to the dynamic way in which asynchronous processes execute and communicate, analysis can even be impossible.

7.4.3 Pipeline Structure

In algorithms using a pipeline structure, processes are ordered and data are moved from one process to the next as though through a pipeline. Computation proceeds in steps as on an assembly line. At each step, each process receives its input from some other process, computes a result based on the input, and then passes the result to some neighboring processes.

This type of processing is also referred to as *macropipelining* and is useful when the algorithm can be decomposed into a finite set of processes with relationships as defined in the previous paragraph.

In a pipeline structure, the communication of data between processes can be synchronous or asynchronous. In a synchronous design, a global synchronizing mechanism, such as a clock, is used. When the clock pulses, each process starts the computation of its next step.

In an asynchronized design, the processes synchronize only with some of their neighbors using some local mechanism, such as message passing. Thus, in this type of design, the total computation requires less synchronization overhead than a synchronized design.

Sec. 7.4   Algorithm Structures

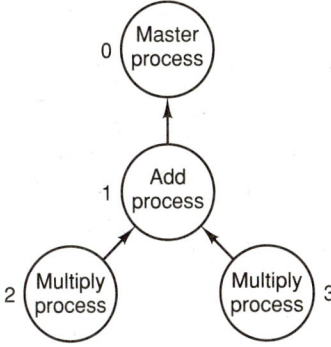

Figure 7.3   Communication of data between processes in a pipeline algorithm.

As an example, consider the computation of $Z[i] = (A[i] * B[i]) + (C[i] * D[i])$ for $i = 1$ to 10, with four processes, including one master and three slaves. The basic communication structure for the processes that cooperate to do this computation is shown in Figure 7.3. The master process simply creates the other three processes, sends off an initial message to each of them, and waits for them to complete their task and send back the result. The processes at the bottom of the figure are multiply processes. For each index i, one multiply process computes $A[i] * B[i]$ and the other process computes $C[i] * D[i]$, and they send their computed values up to an add process. The add process takes two input values and adds them and then sends the result to the master process. The following is an outline of code for each of these types of processes:

The pseudo code for the master process.

```
master: process {
    Initialize the environment and read in data
    create the multiply and add processes
    for each of the multiply processes {
        send the multiply process a pair of vectors to be
        multiplied along with the process id of the add
        process that receives the output of this multiply process
    }
    send to the add process a message that gives it the
        process ids of the multiply processes and the
        process id of the master process.
    while (all of the computed Zs have not been received yet) {
        receive a message from add process and move the Z's
        value into the Z vector
    }
    print the Z vector.
    wait for all of the multiply and add processes to die
}
```

The pseudo code for the multiply process.

```
Multiply: process {
    receive the vectors to be multiplied, along with
```

```
        the process id of the add process.
        Move the received vector into vectors x and y
        for (i=1; i<=10; i++) {
            RESULT = x[i] * y[i];
            Send the RESULT to add process
        }
        send an END MESSAGE to add process
}
```

The Pseudo code for the Add Process.

```
Add:process {
    Receive the message giving the process ids of the two
    producers(multiply processes) and the single consumer
    (master process)
        Receive the first message from the left child,
        and move its value to LEFT_RESULT
        Receive the first message from the right child,
        and move its value to RIGHT_RESULT
        While(an END_MESSAGE has not yet received) {
            RESULT = LEFT_RESULT + RIGHT_RESULT
            Send the RESULT to master process
            Receive the next message from the left child,
            and move its value to LEFT_RESULT
            Receive the next message from the right child,
            and move its value to RIGHT_RESULT
        }
        Send an END_MESSAGE to master process
}
```

7.5 DATA PARALLEL ALGORITHMS

In data parallel algorithms, parallelism comes from simultaneous operations on large sets of data. In other words, a data parallel algorithm is based on the data partitioning approach. Typically, but not necessarily, data parallel algorithms have synchronous structures. They are suitable for massively parallel computer systems (systems with large numbers of processors). Often a data parallel algorithm is constructed from certain standard features called *building blocks* [HIL 86, STE 90]. (These building blocks can be supported by the parallel programming language or underlying architecture.) Some of the well known building blocks are the following:

1. Elementwise operations
2. Broadcasting
3. Reduction
4. Parallel prefix
5. Permutation

Sec. 7.5 Data Parallel Algorithms

Processor	0	1	2	3	4	5	6	7
A	3	0	2	1	5	1	6	3
B	2	2	7	0	1	6	3	2
C	5	2	9	1	6	7	9	5

Figure 7.4 Elementwise addition.

Processor	0	1	2	3	4	5	6	7
A	3	0	2	1	5	1	6	3
B	2	2	7	0	1	6	3	2
C	0	0	0	0	0	0	0	0
Flag	1	0	0	1	1	0	1	1

Figure 7.5 Conditional elementwise addition; each processor sets its flag based on the contents of A and B.

In the following, the function of each of these building blocks is explained by use of examples (these are based on the examples in [HIL 86, STE 90]).

Elementwise operations. Elementwise operations are the type of operations that can be performed by the processors independently. Examples of such operations are arithmetic, logical, and conditional operations. For example consider addition operation on two vectors A and B, that is, $C = A + B$. Figure 7.4 represents how the elements of A and B are assigned to each processor when each vector has eight elements and there are eight processors. The ith processor (for $i = 0$ to 7) adds the ith element of A to the ith element of B and stores the result in the ith element of C.

Some conditional operations can also be carried out elementwise. For example, consider the following if statement on vectors A, B, and C:

$$\text{if } (A > B), \text{ then } C = A + B.$$

First, the contents of vectors A and B are compared element by element. As shown in Figure 7.5, the result of the comparison sets a flag at each processor. These flags, often called a condition mask, can be used for further operations. If the test is successful, the flag is set to 1; otherwise it is set to 0. For example, processor 0 sets its flag to 1 since 3 (contents of $A[0]$) is greater than 2 (contents of $B[0]$). To compute $C = A + B$, each processor performs addition when its flag is set to 1. Figure 7.6 shows the final values for the elements of C.

Broadcasting. A broadcast operation makes multiple copies of a single value (or several data) and distributes them to all (or some) processors. There are a variety of hardware and algorithmic implementations of this operation. However, since this operation is used very frequently in parallel computations, it is worth being supported

Processor	0	1	2	3	4	5	6	7
A	3	0	2	1	5	1	6	3
B	2	2	7	0	1	6	3	2
C	5	0	0	1	6	0	9	5
Flag	1	0	0	1	1	0	1	1

Figure 7.6 Conditional elementwise addition; each processor performs addition based on the contents of the flag.

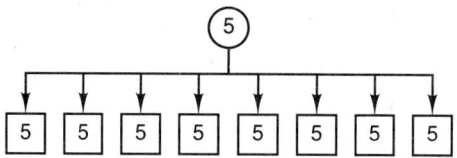

Figure 7.7 Broadcasting the value 5 to eight processors.

directly in hardware. For example, as shown in Figure 7.7, a shared bus can be used to copy a value 5 to eight processors.

Sometimes we need to copy several data to several processors. For example, assume that there are 64 processors arranged in eight rows. Figure 7.8 represents how the values of a vector, which are stored in the processors of row 0, are duplicated in the other processors. The spreading of the vector to the other processors is done in seven steps. At each step, the values of the ith row of processors (for $i = 0$ to 6) are copied to the $(i + 1)^{th}$ row of processors.

When there is a mechanism to copy the contents of a row of processors to another row that is 2^i (for integer $i \geq 0$) away, a faster method can be used for spreading the vector. Figure 7.9 represents how the values of the vector are duplicated in the other

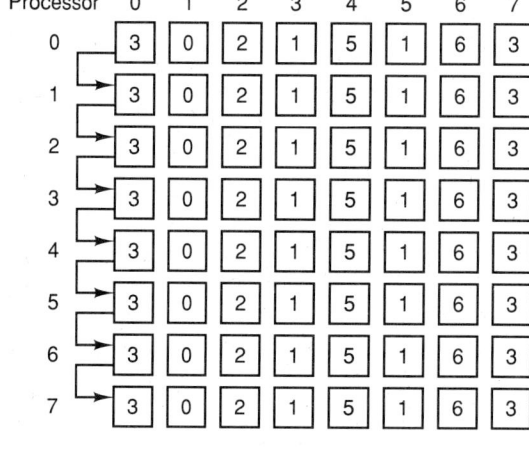

Figure 7.8 Broadcasting the values of a vector in seven steps.

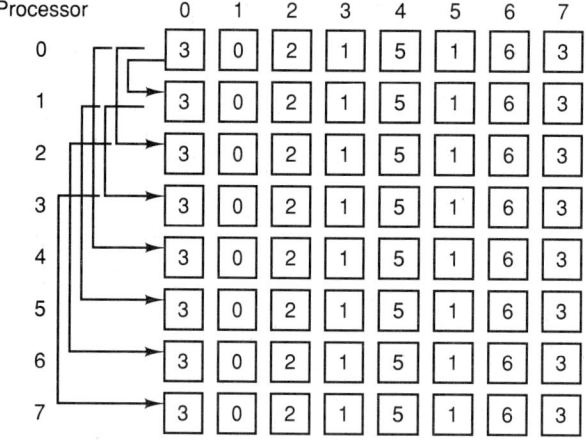

Figure 7.9 Broadcasting the values of a vector in 3 steps.

Sec. 7.5 Data Parallel Algorithms

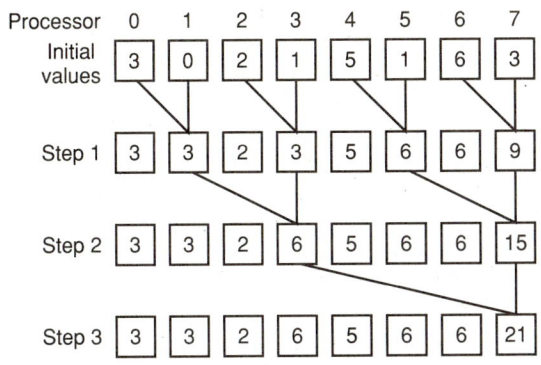

Figure 7.10 Reduction sum operation on the values of eight processors; processor 7 contains the total sum.

processors in three steps. In the first step, the values of row 0 are copied into row 1. In the second step, the values of rows 0 and 1 are copied into rows 2 and 3 at the same time. Finally, in the last step, the top four rows are copied into the bottom four rows.

Reduction. Reduction operation is the inverse of broadcast operation. It converts several values to a single value. For example, consider addition operation on elements of a vector when each element is stored in a processor. One way (a hardware approach) to implement a reduction operation to perform such summation is to have a hardwired addition circuit. Another way (an algorithmic approach) is to perform summation through several steps. Figure 7.10 represents how the elements are added when there are eight processors. In the first step, the processor i (for odd i) adds its value to the value of the processor $i - 1$. In the second step, the value of processor i (for $i = 3$ and 7) is added to processor $i - 2$. Finally, in the third step, the value of processor 3 is added to 7. Besides addition, other choices for reduction operation are product, maximum, minimum, and logical AND, OR, and exclusive-OR.

Parallel prefix. Sometimes, when a reduction operation is carried out, it is required that the final value of each processor be the result of performing the reduction on that processor and its preceding processors. Such a computation is called *parallel prefix* (also referred to as *forward scan*). When the reduction operation is an addition, the computation is called a *sum-prefix* operation since it computes sums over all prefixes of the vector. For example, Figure 7.11 represents how the sum-prefix is per-

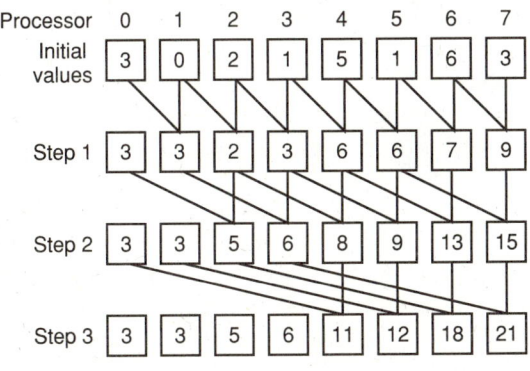

Figure 7.11 Reduction sum operation on the values of eight processors; each processor contains the sum of its value and all the preceding processors.

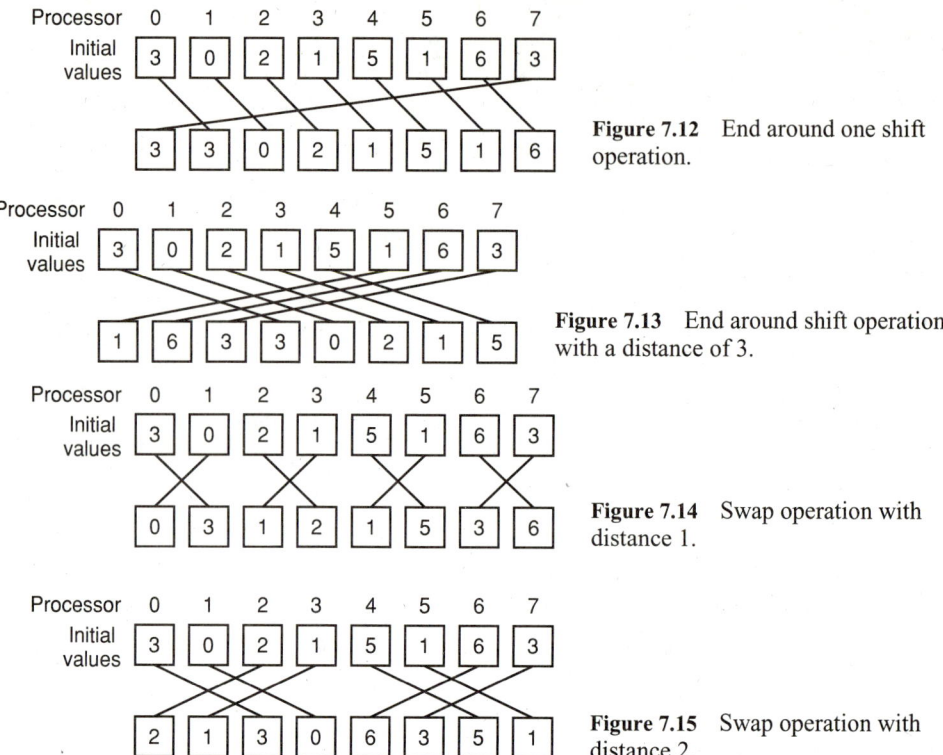

Figure 7.12 End around one shift operation.

Figure 7.13 End around shift operation with a distance of 3.

Figure 7.14 Swap operation with distance 1.

Figure 7.15 Swap operation with distance 2.

formed on our previous example. In the first step, processor i (for $i > 0$) adds its value to the value of processor i-1. In the second step, the value of processor i (for $i > 1$) is added to processor i-2^1. Finally, in the third step, the value of processor i (for $i > 3$) is added to processor i-2^2. At the end of operation, each processor contains the sum of its value and all the preceding processors.

Note that, in the previous solution that was given in Figure 7.10, not all the processors were kept busy during the operation. However, the solution in Figure 7.11 keeps all the processors utilized.

Permutation. The permutation operation moves data without performing arithmetic operation on them. For example, Figure 7.12 represents a simple permutation, referred to as *end around one shift*, on a one-dimensional array that is stored in eight processors. Here, the data in a one-dimensional space are shifted by the distance of 1. Other dimensions and distances may also be possible. Figure 7.13 represent an end around shift operation with a distance of 3.

Another important type of permutation is a *swap* operation. In general, a swap operation with a distance of 2^i (i is an integer) exchanges the values of the processors that are 2^i positions apart. For example, Figures 7.14 and 7.15 show the effect of swap operations with distances 1 and 2, respectively. A swap operation with distance 1 is often referred to as *odd–even swap*. One interconnection network that is well suited for

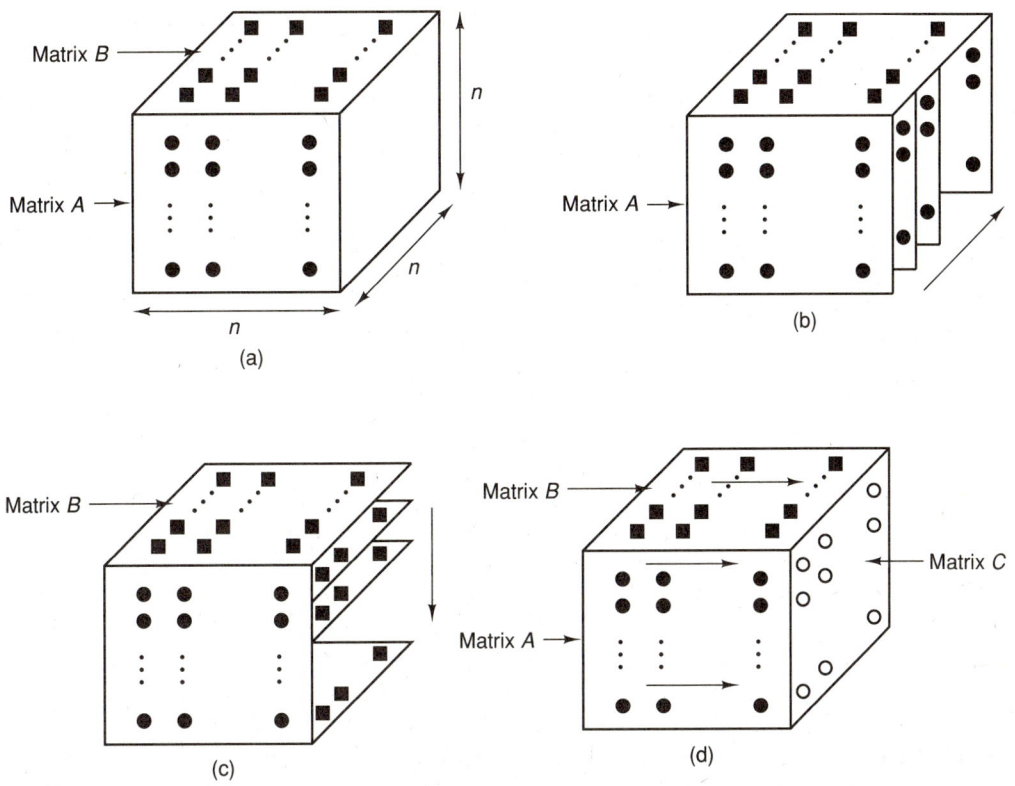

Figure 7.16 Steps of a data parallel algorithm that multiplies two n-by-n A and B matrices. (a) n^3 processors arranged in a cube form; A is loaded on the front n^2 processors, and B is loaded on the top n^2 processors. (b) Broadcasting A. (c) Broadcasting B. (d) Producing C.

swap operations with distance 2^i is the hypercube. In fact the ability to perform swap operations is an important feature of the hypercube.

To represent how the building blocks described can be used to develop a data parallel algorithm, consider the multiplication of two n-by-n A and B matrices. A simple parallel algorithm could be to use broadcast, elementwise multiplication, and reduction sum operations to perform such a task. As shown in Figure 7.16, assume that there are n^3 processors arranged in a cube form. Initially, the matrices A and B are loaded onto the processors on the front and top of the cube, respectively. In the first step of the algorithm, the values of matrix A are broadcast onto the processors. In the second step, the values of matrix B are broadcasted onto the processors. Each of these steps takes $O(\log_2 n)$ time. In the third step, an elementwise multiply operation is performed by each processor. This operation takes $O(1)$ time. Finally, in the fourth step, sum-prefix operation is performed. This operation takes $O(\log_2 n)$ time. Therefore, the total time for the algorithm is $O(\log_2 n)$.

To clarify the preceding operations, consider A and B to be 2-by-2 matrices defined as:

$$\underbrace{\begin{bmatrix} a_{11} & a_{12} \\ a_{21} & a_{22} \end{bmatrix}}_{A} * \underbrace{\begin{bmatrix} b_{11} & b_{12} \\ b_{21} & b_{22} \end{bmatrix}}_{B} = \underbrace{\begin{bmatrix} c_{11} & c_{12} \\ c_{21} & c_{22} \end{bmatrix}}_{C}$$

Figure 7.17 represents the value (or values) of each processor for multiplying these two matrices using the preceding steps.

7.6 ANALYZING PARALLEL ALGORITHMS

In a parallel processing environment, efficiency is best measured by run time rather than by processor utilization. In most cases, this is because the goal of parallel processing is to finish the computation as fast as possible, not to efficiently use processors.

To make the run time smaller, it seems that a solution would be to increase the number of processes for solving a problem. Although this is true (up to a certain point) for most algorithms, it is not true for all algorithms. In fact, for algorithms that are naturally sequential, their performance may degrade on parallel machines. This is due to the fact that there is the time overhead of creating, synchronizing, and communicating with additional processes. Therefore, these implementation overhead issues should be considered when an algorithm is developed for a parallel machine.

To consider the implementation overhead in performance evaluation in general, a measurement, called *speedup*, is used. Speedup is a measure of how much faster a computation finishes on a parallel machine than on a uniprocessor machine. The following section explains how this measure is computed.

7.6.1 Speedup

One way to evaluate the performance of a parallel algorithm for a problem on a parallel machine is to compare its run time with the run time of the best known sequential algorithm for the same problem on the same (parallel) machine. This comparison, called speedup, is defined as

$$\text{speedup} = \frac{\text{run time of the fastest sequential algorithm}}{\text{run time of the parallel algorithm}}.$$

For example, for a given problem, if the best-known sequential algorithm executes in 10 seconds on a single processor, while a parallel algorithm executes in 2 seconds on six processors, a speedup of 5 is achieved for the problem.

Sometimes it is hard to obtain the ideal run time of the fastest sequential algorithm for a problem. This may be due to disagreement about the appropriate algorithm or to inefficient implementation of the serial algorithm on a parallel machine. For example, a serial algorithm that requires too much memory may have an inefficient implementation on a parallel machine in which the main memory is divided between

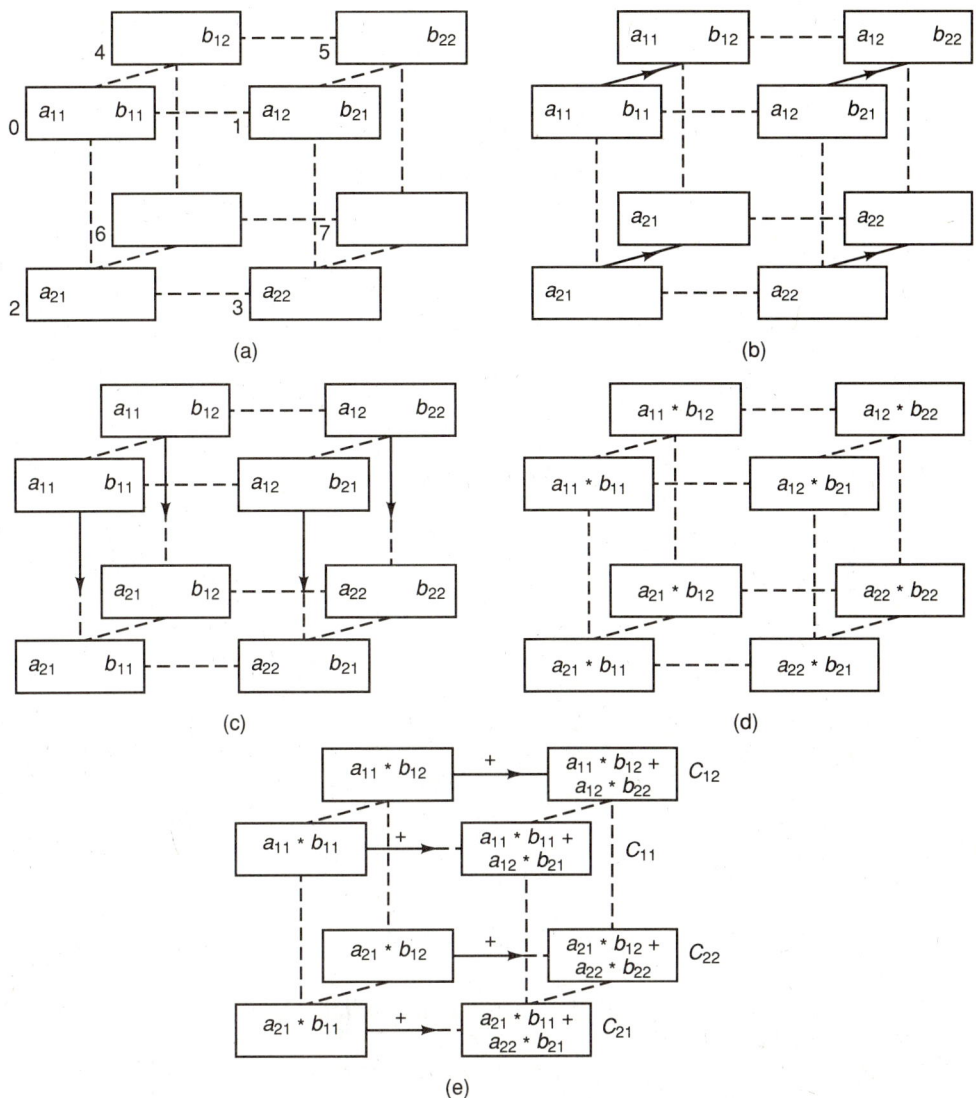

Figure 7.17 Steps of a data parallel algorithm that multiplies two 2-by-2 A and B matrices. (a) Initial values. (b) Broadcasting A. (c) Broadcasting B. (d) Elementwise Multiplication. (e) Parallel sum-prefix.

the processors. Thus, often the speedup of a parallel algorithm on a parallel machine is obtained by taking the ratio of its run time on one processor to that of a number of processors. If the parallel machine consists of N processors, the maximum speedup that can be achieved is N; this is called *perfect speedup*. If there is a constant $c > 0$ such that speedup is always cN for any N, the speedup is called *linear speedup*.

Therefore, it is ideal to obtain a linear speedup with $c = 1$. However, in practice many factors degrade this speedup; some of them are the amount of serialization in the program (such as data dependency, loading time of the program, and I/O bottlenecks), synchronization overhead, and communication overhead. In particular, the amount of serialization is considered by Amdahl [AMD 67] as a major deciding factor in speedup. If s represents the execution time (on single processor) of a serial part of a program, and p represents the execution time (on a single processor) of the remainder part of the program that can be done in parallel, then *Amdahl's law* says that speedup, called *fixed-sized speedup*, is equal to

$$\text{fixed-sized speedup} = \frac{s+p}{s+p/N},$$

where N is the number of processors. Usually, for algebraic simplicity, the normalized total time, $s+p=1$, is used in this expression; thus

$$\text{fixed-sized speedup} = \frac{1}{s+p/N}.$$

Note in this expression that the speedup can never exceed $1/s$ no matter how large N is. Thus, Amdahl's law says that the serial parts of a program are an inherent bottleneck blocking speedup.

In other words, p (or $s=1-p$) is independent of the number of processors. Although this is true when a fixed-sized problem runs on various numbers of processors, it may not be true when the problem size is scaled with the available number of processors. In general, the scaled-sized problem approach is more realistic. This is because, in practice, the number of processors is usually adjusted to the size of the problem in order to keep the run time to a certain desired amount.

Gustafson et al. [GUS 88a, GUS 88b] were able to show that (based on some experiments) for some problems the parallel part of a program scales with the problem size, while the serial part does not grow with problem size. That is, when the problem size increases in proportion to the number of processors, s can be decreased by removing the upper bound $1/s$ for fixed-sized speedup. For example, in [GUS 88b] it is shown that s, which ranges from 0.0006 to 0.001 for some practical fixed-sized problems, can be reduced to a range from 0.000003 to 0.00001 when the problem size is scaled with the number of processors.

Therefore, if s and p represent serial and parallel time spent on N processors (for $N > 1$), rather than a single processor, an alternative to Amdahl's law, called *scaled speedup*, for scalable problems can be defined as

$$\text{scaled speedup} = \frac{s+p*N}{s+p}$$
$$= s + p * N \text{ (assuming that } s+p=1\text{)}$$
$$= N - s * (N-1).$$

where $s + p * N$ is the time required for a single processor to perform the program.

Cost. The cost of a parallel algorithm is defined as the product of the run time and the number of processors:

$$cost = run\ time\ *\ number\ of\ processors\ used.$$

As the number of processors increases, the cost also increases. This is because the initial cost and maintenance cost of a parallel machine increase as the number of processors increases.

7.6.2 Factors Affecting Speedup

In general, it may not be possible to obtain a perfect (linear) speedup for certain problems. Therefore, the alternative goal is to obtain the best possible speedups for these problems. Several reasons may prevent algorithms from reaching the best possible speedup. Some include *algorithm penalty*, *concurrency*, and *granularity*.

Algorithm penalty. This penalty is due to the algorithm being unable to keep the processors busy with work. Overhead costs that cause this penalty are related to distribution, termination, suspension, and synchronization.

Distribution overhead is the cost of distributing tasks to processes. Whenever the partitioning of a task is dynamic, some processes may stay idle until they are assigned a task.

Termination overhead is the overhead of idle processes at the end of computation. In some algorithms (such as binary addition), as the computation nears completion there will be an increasing number of idle processes. This idle time represents the termination overhead.

Suspension overhead is the total time a process is suspended while it waits to be assigned tasks. In general, the suspended overhead serves to show to what extent processes are utilized.

The synchronization overhead occurs when some processes, after completing a predetermined part of their task, become idle while waiting for some (or all) of the other processes to reach a similar point of execution in their tasks.

Concurrency. The speedup factor is affected by the amount of concurrency in the algorithm. The amount of concurrency is directly affected by the code in the area enclosed by locks. When a section of code is enclosed by locks, only one process can enter. This serves to indirectly synchronize processes by sequentializing those wishing to enter that critical section. As discussed previously, contention for entry into the critical section will arise. (Software lockout is the term used to describe such a condition [QUI 87].) The critical section would then represent a sequential part of the program that affects speedup.

Granularity. The performance of an algorithm depends on the program *granularity*, which refers to the size of the processes. Fine granularity, although providing greater parallelism, leads to greater scheduling and synchronization overhead cost. On the other hand, coarse granularity, although resulting in lower scheduling and synchronization overhead, leads to a significant loss of parallelism. Obviously, both of these situations are undesirable. To achieve high performance, we must extract as much parallelism as possible with the lowest possible overhead.

7.7 EXAMPLES

In this section we consider some well-known algorithms for multiprocessors and multicomputers.

7.7.1 Asynchronous Algorithms for Multiprocessors

Matrix multiplication. Consider the problem of multiplication of two $M \times M$ matrices A and B ($C = A * B$) on N processes. One main issue that must be considered in developing such an algorithm is that the algorithm should be independent of the number of available processors on the machine. That is, the algorithm should give the same result when it runs on one processor or more than one processor. It should achieve as good or better performance when running on multiple processors as it does running on one. To achieve these goals, the algorithm for a given number of processes will produce a pool of tasks (or work) in order to keep each process as busy as possible. These tasks are independent of each other. That is, once a process is assigned to a task, it does not need to communicate with other processes.

The question that remains to be addressed is, "What is a task?" The following definition answers this question using the array C and its index k, as shown in the following code segment. A task can be the computation of an element of C or the elements in a column of C. When N is very small compared to M^2, it is better to have a large size task (such as a column of C) in order to reduce the synchronization overhead cost. As N increases, it is better to have a smaller-sized task. The following algorithm represents a task for each process when the task is the computation of C's column. A task is identified by the variable k, where $k = 1$ to M. (In a similar way, an algorithm can be given when the task is the computation of C's element.)

```
struct global_memory
{
    shared float A(M,M), B(M,M), C(M,M);
}
task ()
{
    int k;
    GET_NEXT_INDEX (k)
                --returns in k the next available subscript
                --(in the range 1 to M) while there exist valid
                --subscripts, otherwise it returns -1 in k
    while (k > 0) {
        for (i=1; i <= M; i++) {
            C[i,k] = 0;
            for (j=1; j <= M; j++)
                C[i,k] = C[i,k] + A[i,j] * B[j,k] ;
        }
        GET_NEXT_INDEX (k)
    }
}
```

Sec. 7.7   Examples

Quicksort. The *quicksort*, also known as *partition-exchange sort*, was proposed by Hoare [HOA 62] and has become an attractive sort technique for parallel processing because of its inherent parallelism. Quicksort assumes, correctly, that any list of size 1 is automatically sorted. The basic idea behind quicksort, then, is to repeatedly partition the data until they become a series of single-element, sorted lists. The algorithm then recombines the single-element lists, retaining the sorted order.

Given a list of numbers, one element from the list is chosen to be the partition element. The remaining elements in the list are partitioned into two sublists: those less than the partition element and those greater than or equal to it. Then a partition element is selected for each sublist, and each sublist is further partitioned into two smaller sublists. This process continues until each sublist has only one element. As an example, consider the following list of numbers:

$$4$$
$$3$$
$$9$$
$$8$$
$$1$$
$$5$$
$$6$$
$$8$$

As shown in Figure 7.18, in the beginning the first element (here 4) is selected as the partition element. In step 1, the value 4 is compared with the last element (here 8) of the list. Since 8 > 4, the next-to-last element (here 6) is compared with the partition element (step 2). This comparison continues until a value less than 4 is found (steps 3 and 4). In step 4, since 1 < 4, the partition element exchanges position with value 1. Then, the comparison with the partition element proceeds from opposite direction (i.e., top down); 4 is compared with 3 (step 5). Next 4 is compared with 9; since 9 > 4, an exchange occurs (step 6). This exchange causes the comparison to change direction again to bottom up (step 7). At step 8, the partition element is in its final position and divides the list into two sublists. One of the sublists has elements less than 4 (sublist 1), and the other has elements greater than 4 (sublist 2). The same process is repeated for dividing each of these sublists into smaller sublists. Consider sublist 2. As shown in step 9 through step 13, this sublist is divided into sublists 2.1 and 2.2. Furthermore sublist 2.1 is sorted by selecting 6 as the partition element and switching its position with 5 (steps 14 and 15). The rest of the sublists can be sorted in a similar manner. The last step in Figure 7.18 represents the final sorted list by putting all the sorted sublists together.

One obvious way to implement quicksort in a multiprocessor environment is to create a pool of tasks. Initially, the pool of tasks includes only one task, which is partitioning of the input list. There is a monitor called *GET_NEXT_TASK*. Each process enters this monitor to find a task to do. One of the processes becomes successful get-

306 Parallel Programming and Parallel Algorithms Chap. 7

ting the first task (which is the original list) and partitioning it into two sublists. Then it puts one of the sublists into the pool of tasks and repeats the partitioning process for the other sublist. In this way, very soon all the processes become busy by doing some task. When none of the processes can find a task to do, the quicksort ends; at this point the list is sorted. Figure 7.19 presents the task of each process for our quicksort example.

Gaussian elimination. Gaussian elimination is a method used to solve systems of linear equations. For example, Figure 7.20a represents a system with three equations and three unknown variables, x_1, x_2, and x_3. A system of equations can be stored as a matrix. The coefficients of the equations are stored in the matrix, with the constant values on the right side of the equal sign forming the rightmost column of the matrix, as shown in Figure 7.20b.

Gaussian elimination consists of two parts, elimination and back substitution. The elimination step converts the matrix into an upper triangular format. A matrix in

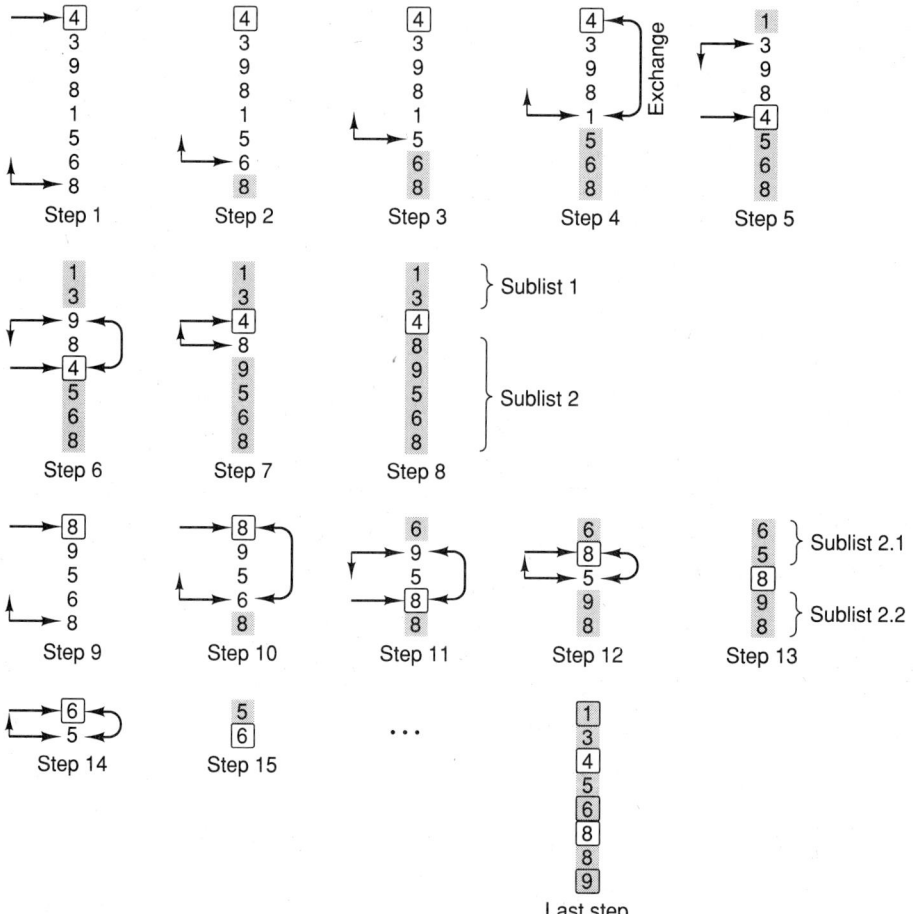

Figure 7.18 Quicksort steps.

Sec. 7.7 Examples

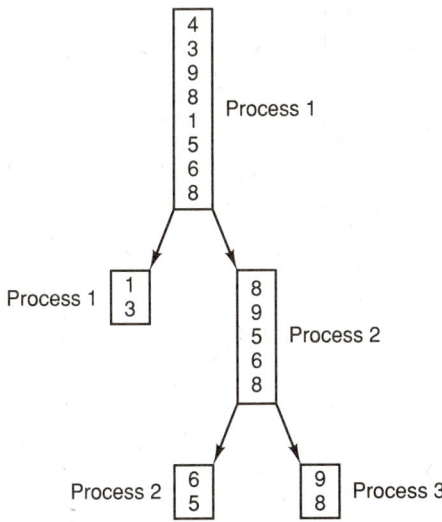

Figure 7.19 Process 1 generates two sublists; one sublist is taken by process 1 and the other is taken by process 2. Furthermore, process 2 partitions the sublist into two sublists; one is taken by itself and the other is taken by process 3.

the upper triangular format is defined such that the kth row of the matrix has zeros in the first $k-1^{th}$ entries, and the kth entry is nonzero. Elimination is performed by starting with the first row and adding a multiple of it to the rows below such that the first column of each of the remaining rows becomes zero. In Figure 7.20c, the multiplier value to be used for the first row when it is added to the second row is $-a(2, 1)/a(1, 1) = -2$. This process is repeated for all of the successive rows in turn except the last, resulting in Figure 7.20d. The selected row that is added to the other rows is called the *pivot row*.

The preceding process is called Gaussian elimination without interchanges; alternatively, if the matrix has zero in the kth element of the pivot row, the rows need to be swapped for the method to work. This is known as Gaussian elimination with interchanges. The Gaussian elimination with interchanges chooses the unpivoted row with the largest element in the currently selected column. If this row is not the pivot row, it is swapped to become the new pivot row. The example has no zero elements, so it uses the method without interchanges.

When the matrix is in upper triangular format, back substitution is used to solve for the unknown variables. Starting at the bottom row and working upward, the variables are solved one at a time and then substituted in the rows above (see Figure 7.20e).

$$\begin{aligned} x_1 + 2x_2 - x_3 &= -7 \\ 2x_1 - x_2 + x_3 &= 7 \\ -x_1 + 2x_2 + 3x_3 &= -1 \end{aligned}$$
(a)

$$\begin{bmatrix} a(1,1) & a(1,2) & a(1,3) & a(1,4) \\ a(2,1) & a(2,2) & a(2,3) & a(2,4) \\ a(3,1) & a(3,2) & a(3,3) & a(3,4) \end{bmatrix} = \begin{bmatrix} 1 & 2 & -1 & -7 \\ 2 & -1 & 1 & 7 \\ -1 & 2 & 3 & -1 \end{bmatrix}$$
(b)

$$\begin{bmatrix} 1 & 2 & -1 & -7 \\ 0 & -5 & 3 & 21 \\ 0 & 4 & 2 & -8 \end{bmatrix}$$

(c)

$$\begin{bmatrix} 1 & 2 & -1 & -7 \\ 0 & -5 & 3 & 21 \\ 0 & 0 & 4.4 & 8.8 \end{bmatrix}$$

(d)

$$\begin{aligned}
4.4x_3 &= 8.8 &&\rightarrow & x_3 &= 2 \\
-5x_2 + 3*2 &= 21 &&\rightarrow & x_2 &= -3 \\
x_1 + 2*(-3) - 1*2 &= -7 &&\rightarrow & x_1 &= 1
\end{aligned}$$

(e)

Figure 7.20 Gaussian elimination steps in solving a system of linear equations.

An analysis of the number of operations performed for Gaussian elimination shows that for an $n \times n$ matrix there are $n-1$ pivot rows selected, each pivot row is added once to all the rows below it, and each nonzero element of the pivot row is multiplied by the multiplier value. This results in $O(n^3)$ multiplication operations. The back-substitution step requires at most n multiplications per row for n rows, giving $O(n^2)$ computations. Because the Gaussian elimination step requires a higher order of computations, it will gain the most by parallelization.

To implement Gaussian elimination on a multiprocessor, the first row is selected as the initial pivot row. Each processor selects a row to work on by obtaining an index number using the Fetch&Add instruction. The processors have shared read access to the pivot row and exclusive write access to their allocated row. When a processor completes a row, it allocates another, if there are still more rows to work on. When all rows have been assigned, the processors wait at a barrier until all are finished. Processor 1 increments the pivot row and the loop repeats.

```
#define       NUMPROCS          --the number of processors
struct global_memory
{
    shared float a(n,n);        --coefficient matrix
    shared int p=0, next_row;   --p points to next pivot row,
                                --and next_row points to the
                                --next available row
}
task()
{
    int  k;                     --the row currently being
                                --considered by a processor
    while (p < n-1) {
        if (proc_id==1) {       --processor 1 updates the pivot
                                --row, and the next available row
```

```
                p=p+1;
                next_row=p+1;
        }
        BARRIER(NUMPROCS);       --processors wait here until all
                                 --are ready
        k=Fetch&Add(next_row, 1); --return index to next
                                 --available row. If no more
                                 --rows are available, wait
                                 --at barrier
                while (k <= n) {  --while the rows are not all
                                 --allocated
                mult =- a(k,p)/a(p,p);
                for (i=p; i<=n; i++)
                    a(k,i) = a(k,i) +mult * a(p,i);
                k=Fetch&Add(next_row, 1);
                }
        }
    }
```

7.7.2 Synchronous Algorithms for Multicomputers

Often, in a multicomputer environment, the data are partitioned between the processors; that is, one processor may have access to some data much easier than others. Therefore, in developing an algorithm for a multicomputer, it is important for each processor to keep most of its memory references local. (Note that this is also true in the case of multiprocessors, when most of the memory references for a processor are kept in its cache memory.)

Matrix multiplication. In the case of matrix multiplication, one attractive way to partition the data is to take advantage of block matrix multiplication [FOX 88, QUI 87]. Given two $M \times M$ matrices A and B, in block matrix multiplication, the matrices A and B are identically decomposed into subblocks and the product is computed as if the subblocks were single elements of the matrices. (It is assumed that the subblocks are square; however, the algorithm can be easily extended for rectangular subblocks.)

For example, when A and B are decomposed to four subblocks (each $M/2 \times M/2$), C can be defined as follows:

$$C = \begin{bmatrix} C_{11} & C_{12} \\ C_{21} & C_{22} \end{bmatrix} = \begin{bmatrix} A_{11} & A_{12} \\ A_{21} & A_{22} \end{bmatrix} \begin{bmatrix} B_{11} & B_{12} \\ B_{21} & B_{22} \end{bmatrix}$$

$$= \begin{bmatrix} A_{11}*B_{11} + A_{12}*B_{21} & A_{11}*B_{12} + A_{12}*B_{22} \\ A_{21}*B_{11} + A_{22}*B_{21} & A_{21}*B_{12} + A_{22}*B_{22} \end{bmatrix}$$

A natural way to do a block matrix multiplication is to compute each C's subblock by a distinct process. Then, a question that remains to be addressed is "How are the data partitioned?"

310 Parallel Programming and Parallel Algorithms Chap. 7

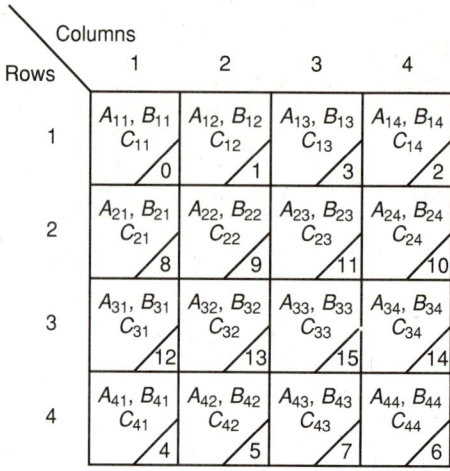

Figure 7.21 Stored blocks in each local memory.

If the local memory is large enough to store a row of A's subblocks (such as A_{11} and A_{12}) and a column of B's subblocks (such as B_{11} and B_{21}), then the computation is straightforward and there is no need for communication between processors. Otherwise, when local memory is small, a subblock of A and a subblock of B are stored in a local memory. To discuss the steps of the algorithm for the latter case, consider a situation where A, B, and C are divided into 16 subblocks (each $M/4 \times M/4$). Assuming

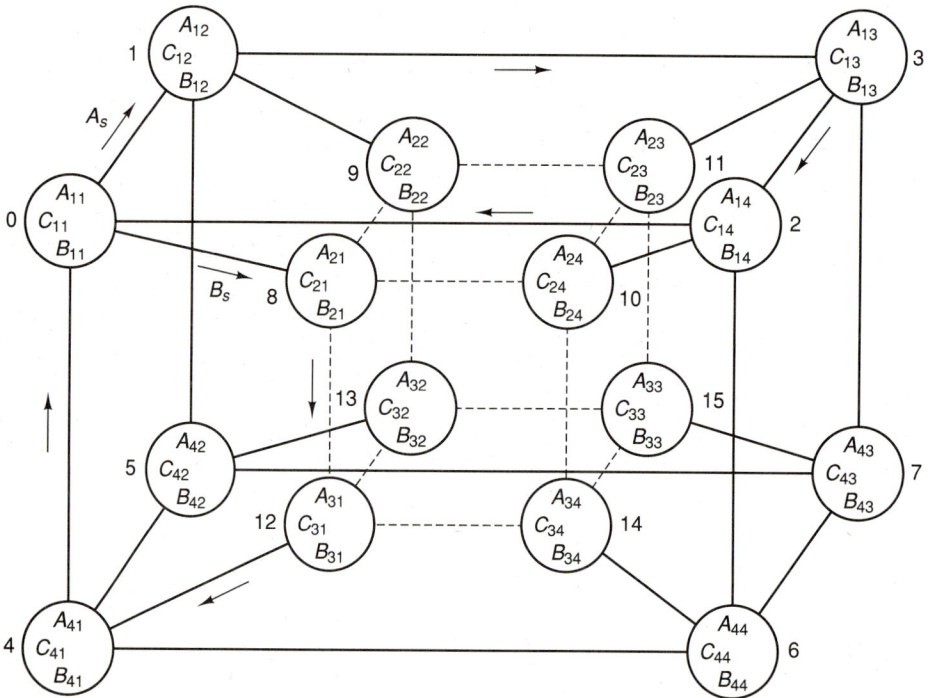

Figure 7.22 Assigned block to the nodes of a 4-cube Multicomputer.

Sec. 7.7 Examples

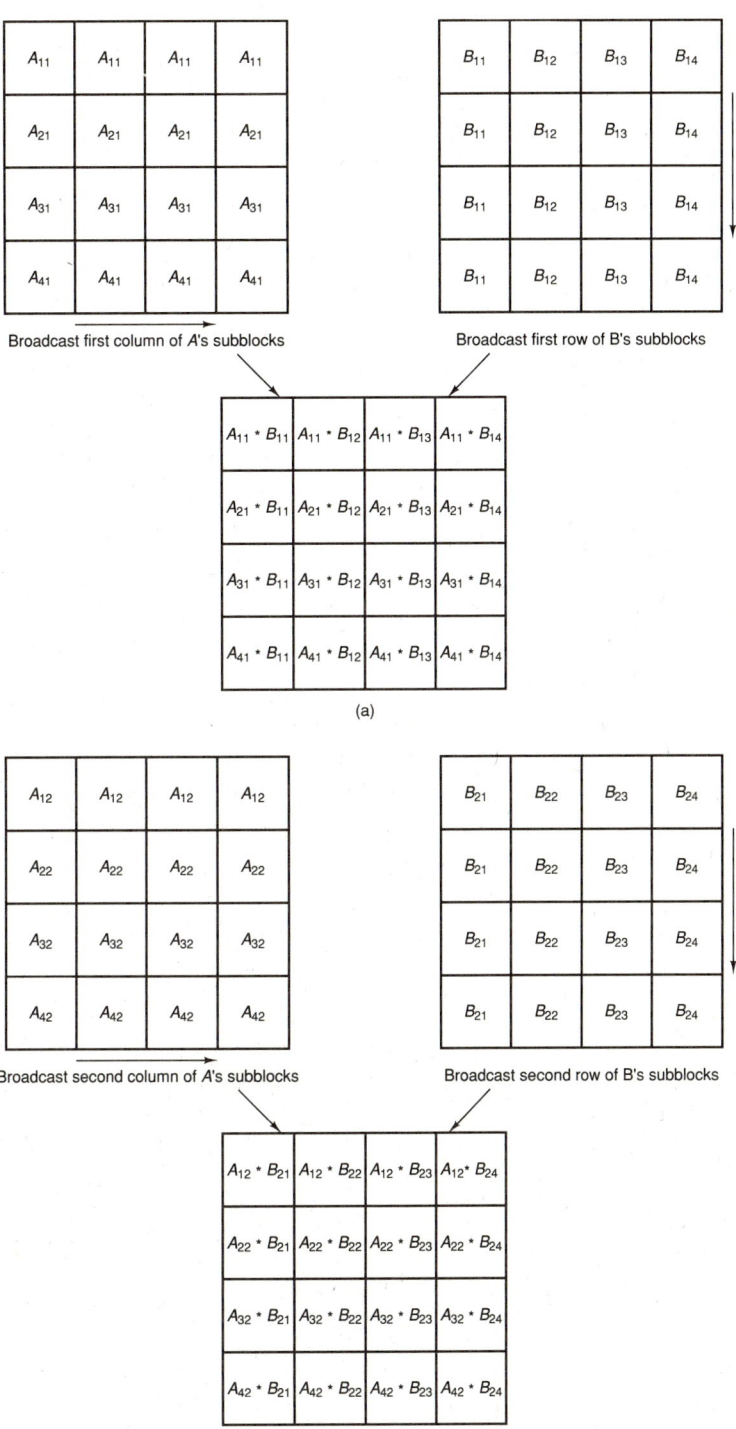

Figure 7.23 Block matrix multiplication steps. (a) Steps for $i = 1$. (b) Steps for $i = 2$.

that there are 16 processors, Figure 7.21 represents the subblocks stored in each. Figure 7.22 shows the assignment of each processor to a node of a hypercube. (To show correspondence between Figures 7.21 and 7.22, a label is assigned to each node.) The main steps of the algorithm are as follows:

```
for i = 1 to √M    __√M * √M is total number of subblocks
{
 a-  The subblocks of A in the i^th column are broadcast in a
     horizontal direction such that all processors in the first
     row receive a copy of A_{1i}, all processors in the second row
     receive a copy of A_{2i}, and so on. (See Figure 7.23.)
 b-  The subblocks of B in the i^th row are broadcast in a vertical
     direction such that all processors in the first column
     receive a copy of B_{i1}, all processors in the second column
     receive a copy of B_{i2}, and so on. (See Figure 7.23.)
 c-  The broadcast of A subblocks is multiplied by the broadcast
     of B subblocks and the results are added to the  partial
     results in the subblock of C. (See Figure 7.23.)
}
```

BIBLIOGRAPHIC NOTES

Some good comments about programming in multiprocessor and multicomputer environments are given in [FOX 88], [BOY 87], and [ATH 88]. In particular, [BOY 87] gives some practical routines for parallel programming. The reference [KUN 76] gives a good discussion and some examples of synchronous and asynchronous algorithms in a multiprocessor environment. The references [AMD 67], [GUS 88a], [GUS 88b], and [DEN 88] discuss the calculation of speedup. Several parallel algorithms for some practical problems are given in [GUS 88b]. These algorithms are implemented on the hypercube to disprove the limitation proposed on speedup by Amdahl's law. (I recommend you read this paper.) Algorithms for matrix multiplication are given in [FOX 88] and [QUI 87]. The paper by Trono [TRO 94] was used for writing an exercise in concurrency.

REFERENCES

[AMD 67] AMDAHL, G. M., "Validity of the Single-processor Approach to Achieving Large-scale Computer Capabilities," *AFIPS Conf. Proc.*, Vol. 30, 1967, pp. 483–485.

[ATH 88] ATHAS, WILLIAM C., AND C. L. SEITZ, "Multicomputers: Message–passing Concurrent Computers," IEEE *Computer*, 21(8) August 1988, pp. 9–24.

[BOY 87] BOYLE, JAMES, R. BUTTER, T. DISZ, B. GLICKFELD, E. LUSK, R. OVERBEEK, J. PATTERSON, AND R. STEVENS, *Portable Programs for Parallel Processors.* New York: Holt, Rinehart and Winston, 1987.

[DEN 88] DENNING, PETER J., "Speeding Up Parallel Processing," *Amer. Scientist*, 76, July–August 1988, pp. 347–349.

[DUB 88] DUBOIS, MICHEL, C. SCHEURICH, AND F. BRIGGS, "Synchronization, Coherence, and Event Ordering in Multiprocessors," *Computer*, 21(2), 1988, pp. 9–21.

[FOX 88] FOX, G., M. JOHNSON, G. LYZENGA, S. OTTO, J. SALMON, D. WALKER, *Solving Problems on Concurrent Processors,* Vol. 1. Upper Saddle River, NJ: Prentice Hall, 1988.

[GUS 88A] GUSTAFSON, J. L., "Reevaluating Amdahl's Law," *Commun. ACM*, 31(5), pp. 532–533.

[GUS 88B] GUSTAFSON, J. L., G. MONTRY, AND R. BENNER, "Development of Parallel Methods for a 1024–Processor Hypercube," *SIAM J. Sci. Stat. Comput.*, 9(4), 1988, pp. 609–638.

[HIL 86] HILLIS, W. DANIEL, AND GUY L. STEELE, "Data Parallel Algorithms," *Commun. ACM*, 29(12), 1986, pp. 1170–1183.

[HOA 62] HOARE, C. A. R., "Quicksort", *Vol. Computer J.*, 5, April 1962, pp. 10–15.

[HOA 74] HOARE, C. A. R., " Monitors: An Operating System Structuring Concept," *Commun. ACM* 17(10), 1974, pp. 549–557.

[INT 93A] *Pentium Processor User's Manual; Volume 1: Pentium Processor Data Book*, Intel, Mt. Prospect, Illinois, 1993

[INT 93B] *Pentium Processor User's Manual; Volume 3: Architecture and Programming Manual*, Intel, Mt. Prospect, Illinois, 1993

[KUN 76] KUNG, H. T., "Synchronized and Asynchronous Parallel Algorithms for Multiprocessors," *Algorithms and Complexity: New Directions and Recent Results*, J. F. Traub, ed. New York: Academic Press, 1976, pp. 153–200.

[LAM 82] LAMPORT, LESLIE, ROBERT SHOSTAK, AND MARSHALL PEASE, "The Byzantine Generals Problem," *ACM Trans. Programming Languages Systems*, 4(3), 1982, pp. 382–401.

[LIN 81] LINT, BERNARD, AND T. AGERWALA, "Communication Issues in the Design and Analysis of Parallel Algorithms," *IEEE Trans. Software Engineering*, SE–7(2), 1981, pp. 174–188.

[QUI 87] QUINN, MICHAEL J., *Designing Efficient Algorithms for Parallel Computers*. New York, McGraw-Hill, Series in Supercomputing and Artificial Intelligence, 1987.

[QUI 94] QUIN MICHAEL J., *Parallel Computing - Theory and Practice,* New York, McGraw-Hill, 1994

[STE 90] STEELE, GUY L., *Data Parallel Algorithms,* Distinguished Lecture Series, Vol. III, Industry Leaders in Computer Science and Electrical Engineering, University Video Communications, Stanford, CA, July 1990.

[STO 90] STONE, HAROLD S., *High - Performance Computer Architecture,* 2nd Ed., Reading, MA: Addison–Wesley Publishing Co., 1990.

[TRO 94] TRONO, JOHN A., "A New Exercise in Concurrency," *SIGCSE Bulletin*, 26(3), 1994, pp. 8–9.

PROBLEMS

7.1. Let's consider a parallel program that consists of two processes sharing the following variables:

```
shared int flag[2] = {0, 0};
shared int turn = 0;
```

Each process competes for access to a critical section using the following mutual exclusion routine. The variable i denotes the process id; it is 0 for one of the processes (p_0) and 1 for the other one (p_1).

```
mutual exclusion routine()
{
    flag[i] = 1;
    while (turn != i) {
        while (flag[(i+1) mod 2] == 1) NOP;
        turn = i;
    }
    <critical section>
    flag[i] = 0;
}
```

Can this code achieve mutual exclusion so that two processes cannot enter their critical sections at the same time? Explain your answer.

7.2. Assume that 10 processors are sharing a critical section. Write a monitor that allows only one processor to access the critical section at any time. The monitor should also set an order between processors. That is, processors get access to the critical section in order of their arrival.

7.3. In a mutiprocessor environment with n processors, write a synchronous parallel program for numerical integration. The problem is to compute the integral from a to b for a given function $f(x)$, represented as

$$\int_a^b f(x)dx.$$

Use the following expression to estimate the value of this integral.

$$d[f(a)/2 + f(a+d) + f(a+2d) + \cdots + f(a+md) + f(b)/2].$$

The value of the integral is approximated by calculating the function f at two points a and b and m sample points, spaced d units apart. Assume that $b > a > 0$.

7.4. Consider an asynchronous parallel algorithm in which each data item is accessed by at most one process during program execution. Can such an algorithm cause memory contention on a multiprocessor based on shared bus? If yes, can you describe a multiprocessor architecture in which the memory contention cannot occur? Explain how or why not.

7.5. Write a parallel program to compute a new vector C by multiplying a vector A with a matrix M. The vector A has n elements, and the matrix M is an n-by-n two-dimensional array. The vector C is computed as follows:

$$C[i] = \sum_{j=1}^{n} A[j] * M[j, i], \quad \text{for } i = 1 \text{ to } n.$$

7.6. (a) Write a parallel program for the producer/consumer problem. The problem concerns two types of processes: producer process and consumer process. The processes communicate through a shared buffer. The producer process creates objects and puts them in the buffer. When the buffer contains at least one object, the consumer removes an object and consumes it. Assume that the producer creates 50 objects in total, and the buffer can hold at maximum 10 objects at one time. Your program must stop when the producer has created all the objects and there is no object in the buffer.

(b) Extend part (a) for when there are two producers and three consumers. As in part (a), all the processes share only one buffer.

7.7. Write a parallel program for the dining philosophers problem. The problem concerns five philosophers sitting at a large round table on which is a plate of Chinese food for each of them. Each philosopher alternatively thinks and eats. A philosopher needs two chopsticks to eat Chinese food. However, there is only one chopstick between every two adjacent philosophers. Therefore, each philosopher must pick up the chopstick on his left and the chopstick on his right. Your program simulates the behavior of the philosophers. The program should ensure that all the philosophers have a chance to eat and finish their food. Note that if all philosophers pick up the chopstick on their left and then wait for chopstick on their right they will all wait forever, and a deadlock situation occurs.

Use random delays to simulate the thinking and eating periods of the philosophers.

7.8. Write a parallel program for the ticketing problem. This problem concerns drawing tickets (numbers) and then waiting for service. For example, most post offices employ a ticketing mechanism to ensure that customers are serviced in order of their arrival. When a customer enters the office, he or she draws a number that is one larger than the number held by the previous customer. Then the customer waits until all the prior customers (the ones holding smaller numbers) have been serviced. To simplify the problem, in your program assume that there are 10 customers and a process is created for each customer. Let the service process be represented by a critical section that contains a dummy loop. Also, let integer variables *ticket* and *next* (that are initially 1) represent the current ticket number that a process should take and the number of the next process that can get service, respectively.

7.9. Write a parallel program for the following yuletide scenario [TRO 94]. Santa Claus sleeps as much as possible so that he can make the marathon flight around the world on Christmas eve. The only time he is allowed to be awakened is if (1) at least three elves need help solving their toy–making problems (if he were awakened each time a single elf needed help, he would never get any sleep at all) or (2) all nine reindeer arrive back at the North Pole (the reindeer vacation on a warm south-sea island until just prior to Christmas).

Some special cases to consider are as follows: If an elf experiences a problem while three elves are already visiting Santa, the elf must wait until all three elves return with their problems solved. The elf can queue up during this time and hope that two other elves will join him so that he can awaken Santa as soon as the first group of elves returns. If Santa is awakened to find that three elves need his attention, but that the last (ninth) reindeer has also arrived back to the North Pole, Santa has decided that the elves will be ignored until after Christmas so that he can begin hitching the reindeer to the sleigh. (It is assumed that the reindeer don't want to leave the tropics, and therefore they stay there until the last possible moment.) The penalty for the last reindeer to arrive is that it must get Santa while the others wait in a warming hut before being harnessed to the sleigh.

(a) Write a parallel program containing a Santa process, several (minimum 5) elf processes, and nine reindeer processes. Be sure to consider the rules regarding elf waiting and reindeer arrival.

(b) Implement your program on a parallel machine (or simulate it on a single processor). Produce a report showing, for each time Santa was awakened, the reason he was awakened, the state of the two queues (elf and reindeer) and the rule used to decide what action Santa should take.

7.10. Write a pipelined algorithm to find the prime numbers among a set of numbers from 1 to n. Assume that there are k processors, and n is an exact multiple of k.

Hint: Divide the numbers equally among the k processors.

7.11. Write a parallel algorithm for the Byzantine generals problem [LAM 82]. The problem refers to a group of generals of the Byzantine army who are camped with their troops outside an enemy city. The generals communicate with each other through messenger. After observing the enemy, the generals (by sending messages to each other) must reach a common agreement to perform an action. The possible actions are attack or retreat. However, some of the generals may be traitors, trying to confuse the others by sending wrong actions. The problem is to find an algorithm to ensure that the loyal generals will reach an agreement. An agreement is reached whenever the following two conditions are satisfied:

1. All loyal generals decide on the same plan of action.
2. A small number of traitors cannot cause the generals to decide on a bad plan of action.

The second condition is hard to satisfy, since a bad plan of action is not well defined. To simplify the Byzantine problem, let one of the generals be considered the commanding general and the others be considered lieutenant generals. The commanding general sends an order (retreat or attack) to the lieutenants. Now, rather than satisfying the preceding conditions, your algorithm should ensure that the following two conditions are satisfied:

1. All loyal lieutenant generals obey the same order.
2. If the commanding general is loyal, then every loyal lieutenant general obeys the order he sends.

Furthermore, make the following assumptions:

1. There are $3n + 1$ (for some integer $n \geq 0$) generals (a commanding general and $3n$ lieutenants) in which at most n of them can be traitors (including the commanding general).
2. Each general is able to send messages directly to every other general. Each message specifies an action and also identifies the names of sender and receiver generals.
3. The messages never get lost or changed.
4. Generals may need to send messages several times in order to reach an agreement.
5. A traitor commanding general may not send any order. In this case, the lieutenants are able to detect the absence of the order and obey some default order. Let *retreat* be a default order.

7.12. Consider a multiprocessor system with n processors and a program that consists of m tasks, where $m > n$. The execution time of each task is four times as long as a single-process creation time on the multiprocessor. Derive an equation for speedup when executing such a program on the multiprocessor by creating n processes and distributing the tasks among them. Assume that all the processes are created by only one processor, and furthermore assume that the execution of tasks starts after all the processes have been created. Find a value for n (in terms of m) that maximizes the speedup.

7.13. Write a parallel program for the quicksort steps discussed in the text.

7.14. Write a data parallel algorithm for the problem of finding a steady–state temperature on the surface of a square slab of material. This problem requires a solution to the Laplace equation. In Chapter 5, a method to solve this equation was described. Base your algorithm on this method. Let M be an 8-by-8 matrix. The elements of M correspond to a mesh that is superimposed on the slab. The values of the elements of M represent the temperature at nodes of the mesh. The nodes on the boundary are held at certain fixed temperatures. The goal is to compute the temperature at the interior nodes. Initially, the temperatures at these nodes are set to zero. On each iteration of computation, a new value for each interior node is computed. The new value of a node is computed by taking the average of the previous values of its four closest neighbors. That is,

$$M[i,j]=(M[i,j+1]+M[i+1,j]+M[i,j-1]+M[i-1,j])/4$$

Your algorithm should stop whenever the new value for every interior node is within some small constant (ε) of its previous value.

7.15. Write a data parallel algorithm to compute the parallel prefix-sum of a linked list with eight elements. Each element of the list is stored in a processor. Processors that form the list are known to each other only by their addresses. The first processor of the list knows the address of the second, the second processor knows the address of the third one, and so on.

7.16. Write a data parallel program for labeling regions in an image with *n*-by-*n* pixels. As shown in Figure P7.16, a region consists of a set of connected pixels that has the same

3	3	3	3	5	8	8	8	8
3	3	3	3	5	5	5	2	8
3	3	5	5	5	6	6	2	8
7	7	1	1	9	9	6	2	8
7	7	1	9	9	6	6	4	4
10	7	1	9	9	6	4	4	4
11	1	1	1	4	4	4	4	4
1	1	1	1	4	4	4	4	4

Figure P7.16

pattern. The problem is to assign a distinct number to each region. (A unique number is assigned to the pixels of a region.) Disconnected regions with the same pattern are considered to be different regions.

7.17 Consider multiplication of two *n*-by-*n* matrices A and B on a mesh SIMD machine. Assume every element of A and B is stored exactly once and no processing node contains more than one element of either matrix. Argue that multiplying A and B requires O(n) data routing steps. A data routing step refers to transmission of data from one processing node to its adjacent node (or nodes).

8

Data Flow and Systolic Array Architectures

8.1 INTRODUCTION

This chapter describes the structure of two parallel architectures, *data flow* and *systolic array*. In the data flow architecture an instruction is ready for execution when data for its operands have been made available. Data availability is achieved by channeling results from previously executed instructions into the operands of waiting instructions. This channeling forms a flow of data, triggering instructions to be executed. An outcome of this is that many instructions are executed simultaneously, leading to the possibility of a highly concurrent computation. The next section details the theory behind the data flow concept and explains one of the well-known designs of a data flow machine, the MIT machine.

In a systolic array there are a large number of identical simple processors or processing elements (PEs). The PEs are arranged in a well-organized structure, such as a linear or two-dimensional array. Each PE has limited private storage and is connected to neighboring PEs. Section 8.3 discusses several proposed architectures for systolic arrays and also provides a general method for mapping an algorithm to a systolic array.

8.2 DATA FLOW ARCHITECTURE

To demonstrate the behavior of a data flow machine, a graph, called a *data flow graph*, is often used. The data flow graph represents the data dependencies between individual instructions. It represents the steps of a program and serves as an interface between

Sec. 8.2 Data Flow Architecture

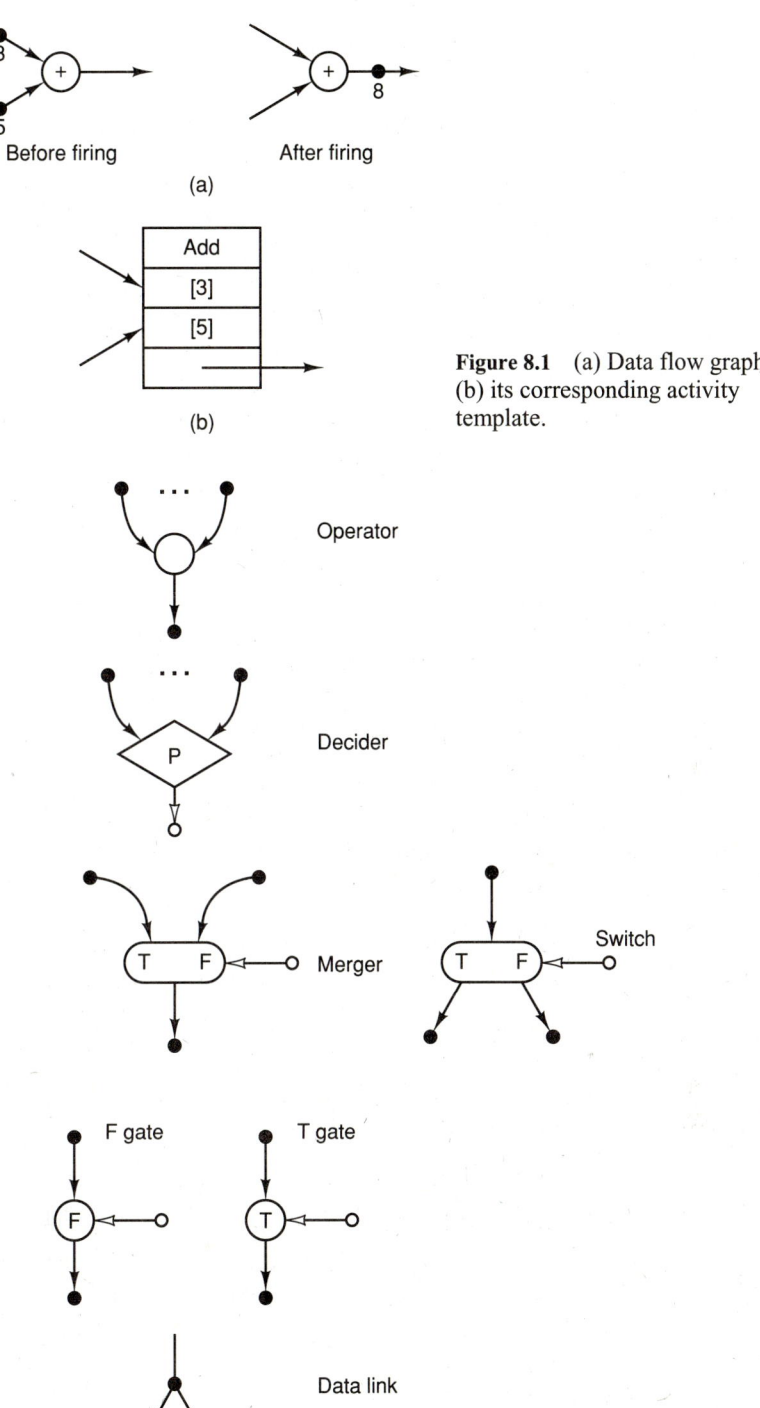

Figure 8.1 (a) Data flow graph and (b) its corresponding activity template.

Figure 8.2 Set of actors for constructing a data flow graph.

system architecture and user programming language. The nodes in the data flow graph, also called *actors*, represent the operators and are connected by input and output arcs that carry tokens bearing values. Tokens are placed on and removed from the arcs according to certain firing rules. Each actor requires certain input arcs to have tokens before it can be fired (or executed). When tokens are present on all required input arcs of an actor, that actor is enabled and thus fires. Upon firing, it removes one token from the required input arcs, applies the specified function to the values associated with the tokens, and places the result tokens on the output arcs (see Figure 8.1a). Each node of a data flow graph can be represented (or stored) as an *activity template* (see Figure 8.1b). An activity template consists of fields for operation type, for storage of input

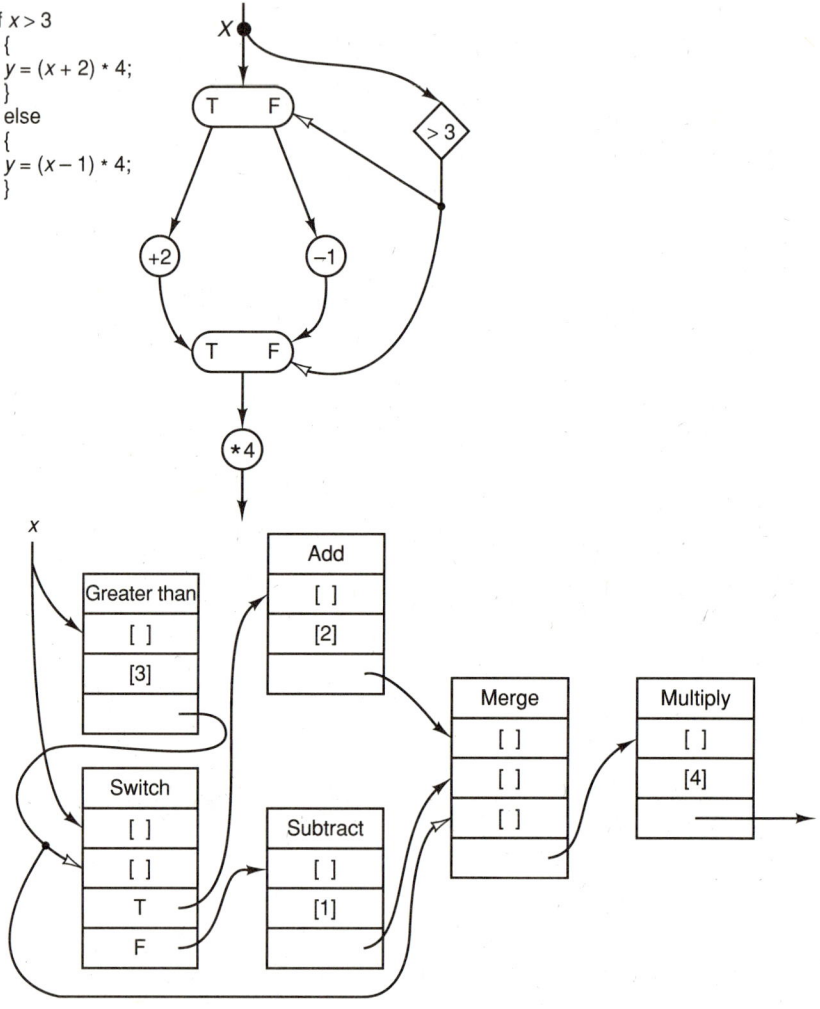

Figure 8.3 A data flow graph and its corresponding activity template for an *if* statement.

Sec. 8.2 Data Flow Architecture

tokens, and for destination addresses. Like a data flow graph, a collection of activity templates can be used for representing a program. Figure 8.2 represents a set of actors that is used in a data flow graph. There are two types of tokens: data tokens and Boolean tokens. To distinguish the type of inputs to an actor, solid arrows are used for carrying data tokens and outlined arrows for Boolean tokens. The switch actor places the input token on one of the output arcs based on the Boolean token arriving on its input. The merge actor places one of the input tokens on the output arc based on the Boolean token arriving on its input. The T gate places the input token on the output arc whenever the Boolean token arriving on its input is true, as the F gate does whenever the Boolean token arriving on its input is false. As an example, Figure 8.3 represents a data flow graph with its corresponding templates for the following *if* statement:

```
if x > 3 { y = (x + 2) * 4; } else { y = (x-1) * 4; }.
```

Another example is shown in Figure 8.4. For a given *N*, the data flow graph represents computation of *N*!. Note in this graph that, the Boolean input arcs to both mergers are initialized to false tokens. At the start this causes the data input token *N* to move to the output of both mergers.

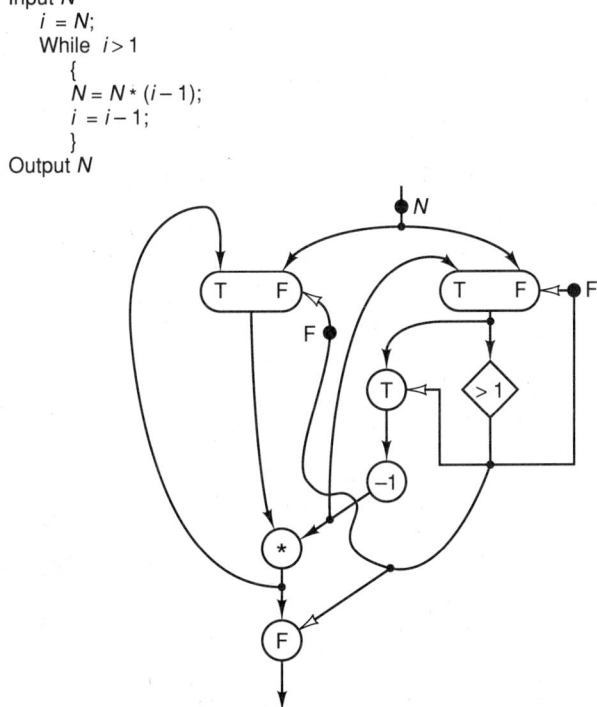

Figure 8.4   A data flow graph for calculating *N*!.

8.2.1 Basic Structure of a Data Flow Computer

To demonstrate the structure of a data flow machine, Figure 8.5 represents the main elements of a data flow machine called the MIT data flow computer [DEN 80]. The MIT computer consists of five major units: (1) the processing unit, consisting of specialized processing elements; (2) the memory unit, consisting of instruction cells for holding the instructions and their operands (i.e., each instruction cell holds one activity template); (3) the arbitration network, which delivers instructions to the processing elements for execution; (4) the distribution network for transferring the result data from processing elements to memory; and (5) the control unit, which manages all other units.

An instruction cell holds an instruction consisting of an operation code (opcode), operands, and a destination address. The instruction is enabled when all the required operands and control signals are received. The arbitration network sends the enabled instruction as an operation packet to the proper processing element. Once the instruc-

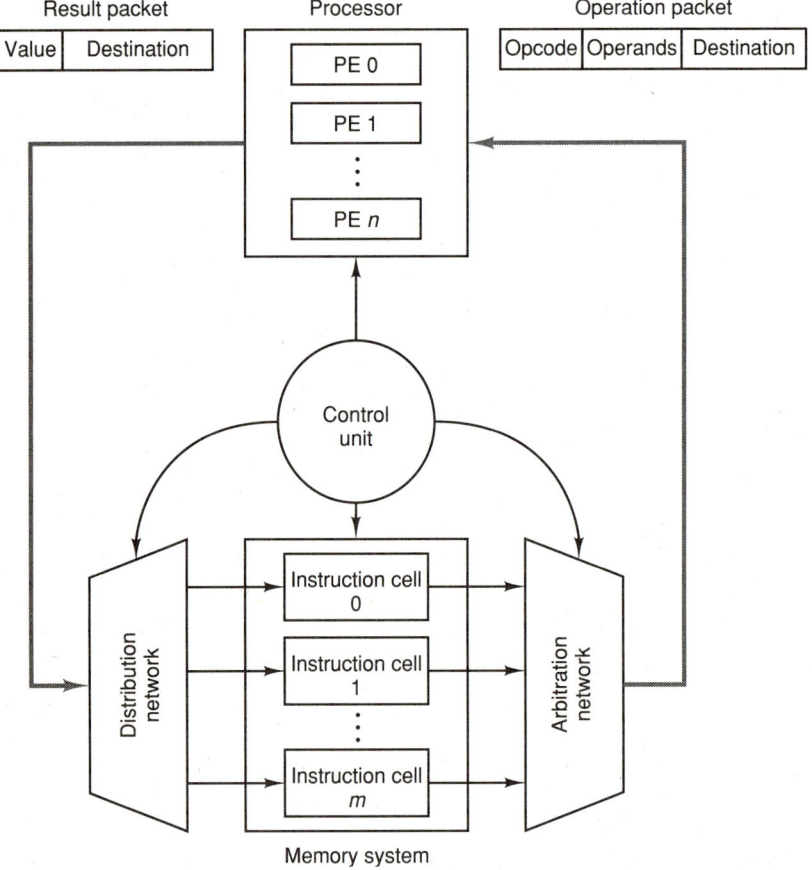

Figure 8.5 A simplified MIT data flow.

Sec. 8.2 Data Flow Architecture

tion is executed, the result is sent back through the distribution network to the destination in memory. Each result is sent as a packet, which consists of a value and a destination address.

Proposed data flow machines can be classified into two groups: *static* and *dynamic*. In a static data flow machine, an instruction is enabled whenever all the required operands are received and another instruction is waiting for the result of this instruction; otherwise, the instruction remains disabled [DEN 80, COR 79]. In other words, each arc in the data flow graph can carry at most one token at any instance. An example of this type of data flow graph is shown in Figure 8.6. The multiply instruction must not be enabled until its previous result has been used by the add instruction. Often, this constraint is enforced through the use of acknowledgment signals.

In a dynamic data flow machine an instruction is enabled whenever all the required operands are received. In this case, several sets of operands may become ready for an instruction at the same time. In other words, as shown in Figure 8.7, an arc may contain more than one token. Compared with static data flow, the dynamic approach allows more parallelism because an instruction need not wait for an empty location in another instruction to occur before placing its result. However, in the dynamic approach a mechanism must be established to distinguish instances of differ-

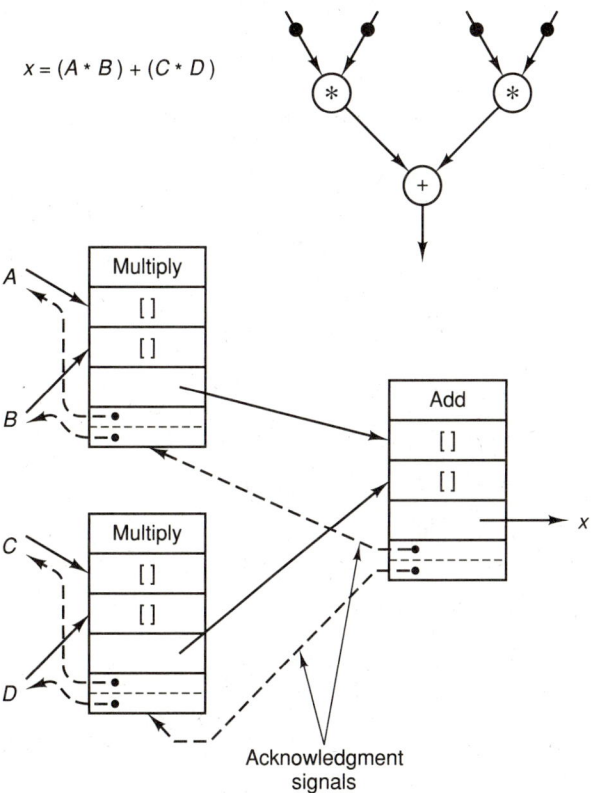

Figure 8.6 An example of a data flow graph for a static data flow machine. Each arc in the data flow graph can carry at most one token at any instance.

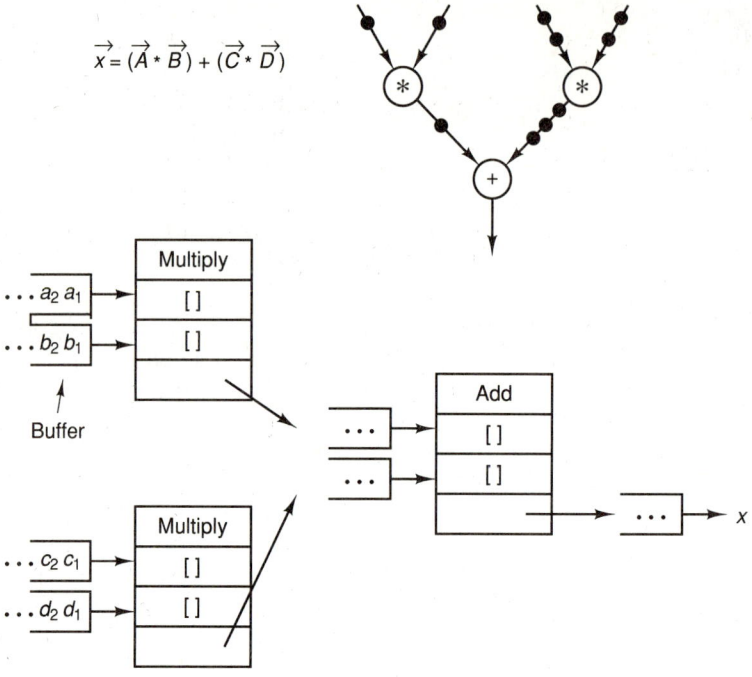

Figure 8.7 An example of a data flow graph for a dynamic data flow machine. An arc in the data flow graph may carry more than one token at any instance.

ent sets of operands for an instruction. One way would be to queue up the instances of each operand in order of their arrival [DAV 78]. However, maintaining many large queues becomes very expensive. To avoid queues, the result packet format is often extended to include a label field; hence matching operands can be found by comparing the labels [ARV 80, GUR 80]. An associative memory, called *matching store*, can be used for matching these labels. As an example, Figure 8.8 represents a possible architecture for a memory unit of a dynamic data flow machine. Each time that a result packet arrives at the memory unit, its address and label fields are stored in the matching store. The result packet's value field is stored in the data store. The matching store uses the address and label fields as its search key for determining which instruction is enabled. In Figure 8.8, it is assumed that three packets have arrived at the memory unit at times t_0, t_1, and t_2. At time t_2, when both operands with the same label for the add instruction (stored at location 100 in instruction store) have arrived, the add instruction becomes enabled.

8.3 SYSTOLIC ARRAYS

In application fields of scientific computing, it is very often necessary to solve simultaneous linear equations, in particular, a large-scale linear system of equations. Finding fast, accurate, and cost-effective methods for solving a large-scale linear system of

Sec. 8.3   Systolic Arrays   325

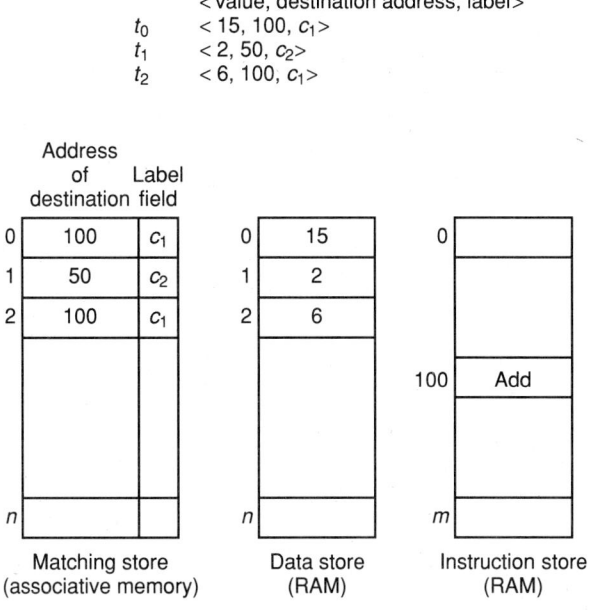

Figure 8.8 A possible memory unit for a dynamic data flow computer.

equations has been greatly needed for centuries, both by scientists and engineers. Nevertheless, we are always dealing with matrix algebra, like LU decomposition, inversion, and multiplication. Due to the lengthy sequences of arithmetic computations, most large-scale matrix algebra is performed on high-speed digital computers using well-developed software packages. But a major drawback in processing matrix algebra on general-purpose computers by software programs is the need for long computation time. Also, in a general-purpose computer the main memory is not large enough to accommodate very large-scale matrices. Thus many time-consuming I/O transfers are needed in addition to the CPU computation time.

To alleviate this problem, the use of parallel computers has been adopted and special-purpose machines have been introduced. One solution to the need for highly parallel computational power is the connection of a large number of identical simple processors or processing elements (PEs). Each PE has limited private storage, and is only allowed to be connected to neighboring PEs. Thus all PEs are arranged in a well-organized structure such as a linear or two-dimensional array. This type of structure, referred to as a *systolic array*, provides an ideal layout for VLSI implementation. Often, interleaved memories are used to feed data into such arrays.

Usually, a systolic array has a rectangular or hexagonal geometry, but it is possible for it to have any geometry. With VLSI technology, it is possible to provide extremely high but inexpensive computational capability with a system consisting of a large number of identical small processors organized in a well-structured fashion. In other words, through progress in VLSI technology, a low-cost array of processors with high-speed computations can be utilized.

Various designs of systolic arrays with different data stream schemes for matrix multiplication have been proposed. Some of the proposed designs are *hexagonal arrays, pipelined arrays, semibroadcast arrays, wavefront arrays*, and *broadcast arrays*. In this section, we will discuss these proposed designs and the drawbacks of each, thereby making a performance comparison among them. Finally, a general method is given for mapping an algorithm to a systolic array.

8.3.1 Basic Terminology and Proposed Arrays of Processors

Before describing various systolic arrays, some terminology common to all designs will be given. First, the processing element primarily used in each design is basically an inner-product step processor that consists of three registers: R_a, R_b, and R_c. These registers are used to perform the following multiplication and addition in one unit of computational time:

$$R_c = R_c + R_a * R_b.$$

The unit of computational time is defined as $t_a + t_m$, where t_a and t_m are the time to perform one addition and one multiplication, respectively.

To compare different proposed arrays of processors, two factors are considered: number of required PEs and turnaround time. Let P denote the number of required PEs. The turnaround time, T, is defined as the total time, in time unit $t_a + t_m$, needed to complete the entire computation.

In the following paragraphs, several proposed architectures for systolic arrays are discussed. The structure of each design is illustrated by an example that performs the computation $C = A * B$, where

$$A = \begin{bmatrix} a_{11} & a_{12} & a_{13} \\ a_{21} & a_{22} & a_{23} \\ a_{31} & a_{32} & a_{33} \end{bmatrix}$$

$$B = \begin{bmatrix} b_{11} & b_{12} & b_{13} \\ b_{21} & b_{22} & b_{23} \\ b_{31} & b_{32} & b_{33} \end{bmatrix}$$

$$C = \begin{bmatrix} c_{11} & c_{12} & c_{13} \\ c_{21} & c_{22} & c_{23} \\ c_{31} & c_{32} & c_{33} \end{bmatrix}.$$

Sec. 8.3 Systolic Arrays

Hexagonal array. The hexagonal array, proposed by Kung and Leiserson [KUN 78], is a good example of the effective use of a large number of PEs arranged in a well-organized structure. In a hexagonal array, each PE has a simple function and communicates with neighbor PEs in a pipelined fashion. PEs on the boundary also communicate with the outside world. Figure 8.9 presents a hexagonal array for the multiplication of two 3-by-3 matrices A and B. Each circle represents a PE that has three inputs and three outputs. The elements of the A and B matrices enter the array from the west and east along two diagonal data streams. The entries of C matrix, with initial values of zeros, move from the south to north of the array. The input and output values move through the PEs at every clock pulse. For example, considering the current situation in Figure 8.9, the input values a_{11} and b_{11}, and the output value c_{11} arrive

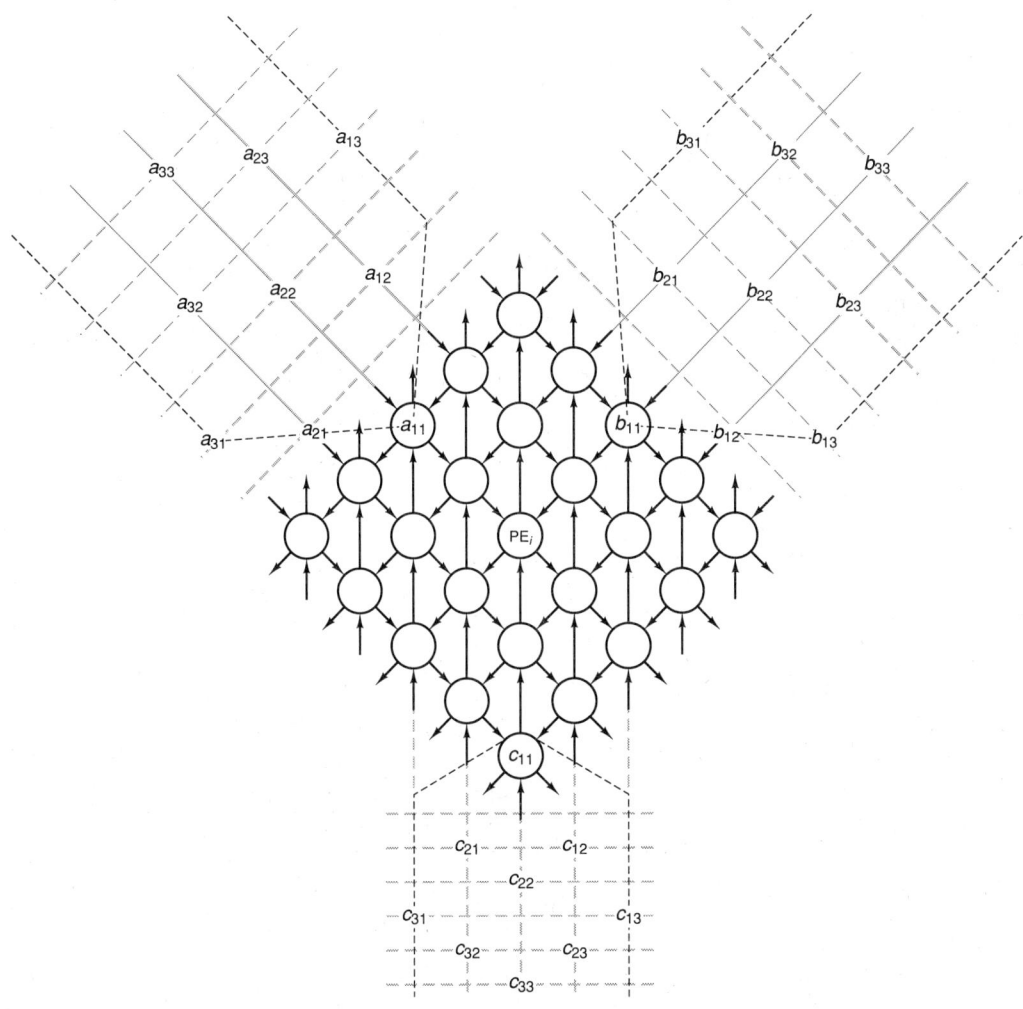

Figure 8.9 Block diagram of a hexogonal array.

at the same processor element, PE_i, after two clock pulses. Once all these values have arrived, the PE computes a new value for c_{11} by performing the following operation:

$$c_{11} = c_{11} + a_{11} * b_{11}.$$

There are 25 PEs in the hexagonal array of Figure 8.9. However, only 19 of them contribute to the computation; those are the PEs on which the elements of matrix C pass through. Assuming that the first element of input data (i.e., a_{11} or b_{11}) enters the array after one unit of time, the turnaround time of such an array is 10 units. In general, for a hexagonal array with two n-by-n matrices, we have the following:

$P = (2n - 1)^2$,
$T = 4n - 2$ when part of the result stays in the array,
$T = 5n - 3$ when the result is transferred out of the array.

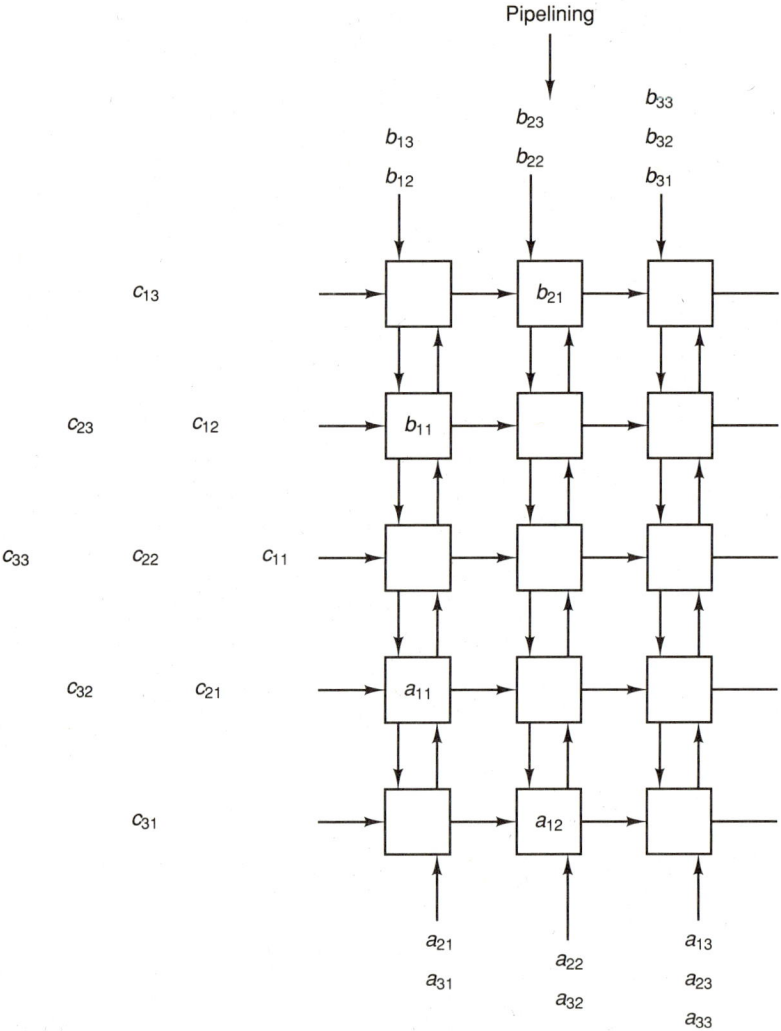

Figure 8.10 Block diagram of a pipelined array.

Sec. 8.3 Systolic Arrays

Note that only $3n^2 - 3n + 1$ out of $(2n-1)^2$ PEs contribute toward the computation. The major drawback of hexagonal arrays is that they do not pipe data elements into every PE in every time unit. This causes the utilization of PEs to be less than 50%. Also, the hexagonal arrays require a large number of PEs. Because of these drawbacks, several other designs, which were intended to make improvements in this area, have been proposed. Some of them are described next.

Pipelined array. The pipelined array was proposed by Hwang and Cheng [HWA 80]. As shown in Figure 8.10, this architecture has a rectangular array design. The elements of matrices A and B are fed from the lower and upper input lines in a pipelined fashion, one skewed row or one skewed column at a time. In general, for a pipelined array with two n-by-n matrices, we have the following:

$$P = n(2n-1),$$
$$T = 4n - 2.$$

The pipelined array has a relatively simple design. The data flow is basically the same as for the hexagonal array, but uses less PEs. However, similar to hexagonal array, it does not pipe data elements into every PE in every time unit. This idles at least 50% of the PEs at any given time.

Semibroadcast array. The semibroadcast array was proposed by Huang and Abraham [HUA 82]. Figure 8.11 represents the structure of a semibroadcast array with

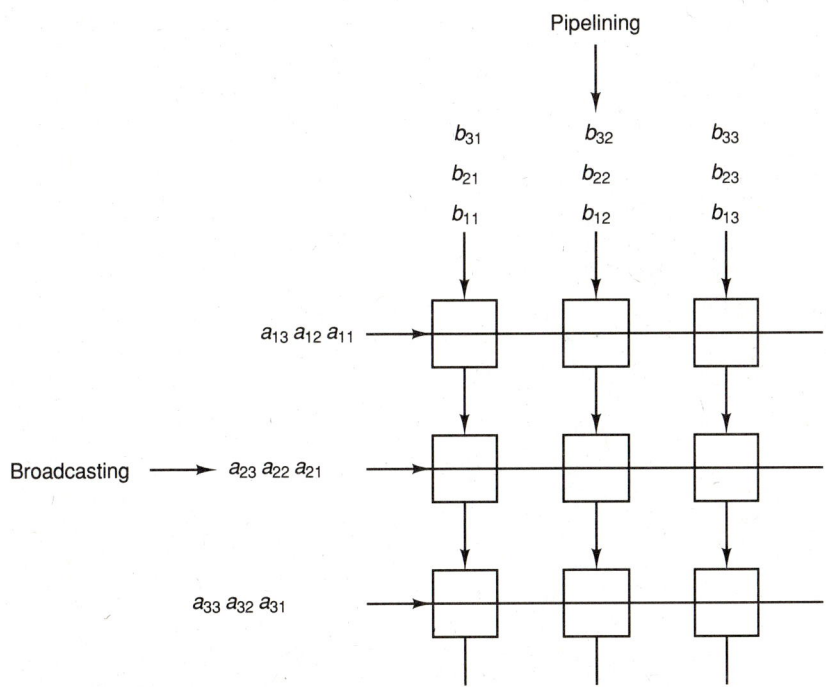

Figure 8.11 Block diagram of a semibroadcast array.

data streams. Here semibroadcast means one-dimensional data broadcasting. For example, in Figure 8.11, only the matrix A is broadcast from the left side of the array, while matrix B is still pipelined into the array from the top edge. The result, matrix C, can be either left in the array or transferred out of the array. In general, for a semibroadcast array with two n-by-n matrices, we have the following:

$$P = n^2,$$

$T = 2n$ when the result stays in the array,

$T = 3n$ when the result is transferred out of the array.

Compared with the previous designs, the semibroadcast array uses less PEs and also requires less turnaround time. The most controversial point is that the propagation delay of the broadcast data transfer may be longer than that for a nonbroadcast array. Therefore, the degree of complexity controlling a semibroadcast array may be higher than that of a pipelined array. This exemplifies the trade-off between cost and time. Probably the most simple implementation of broadcast arrays is made by connecting the PEs using common bus lines. But the cost, compared to pipelined arrays, would be higher. For example, in a VLSI implementation the bus lines require extra layout area.

Wavefront array. The wavefront array was proposed by Kung and Arun [KUN 82]. The structure of a wavefront array with a data stream is shown in Figure 8.12. Given two n-by-n matrices A and B, the matrix A can be decomposed into columns A_i and matrix B into rows B_j. Thus

$$C = A_1 * B_1 + A_2 * B_2 + \ldots + A_n * B_n.$$

The matrix multiplication can then be carried out by the following n iterations:

$$C^{(k)} = C^{(k-1)} + A_k * B_k \quad \text{recursively, for } k = 1, 2, \ldots, n.$$

These iterations can be performed by applying the concept of a wavefront. Successive pipelining of the wavefronts will accomplish the computation of all iterations. As the first wave propagates, we can execute the second iteration in parallel by pipelining a second wavefront immediately after the first. For example, in Figure 8.12, the process starts with $PE_{1,1}$ computing $C_{11}^{(1)} = C_{11}^{(0)} + a_{11} * b_{11}$. The computational activity then propagates to the neighboring processor elements, $PE_{1,2}$ and $PE_{2,1}$. While $PE_{1,2}$ and $PE_{2,1}$ are executing $C_{12}^{(1)} = C_{12}^{(0)} + a_{11} * b_{12}$ and $C_{21}^{(1)} = C_{21}^{(0)} + a_{21} * b_{11}$, respectively, the $PE_{1,1}$ can execute $C_{11}^{(2)} = C_{11}^{(1)} + a_{12} * b_{21}$. In general, for a wavefront array with two n-by-n matrices, we have the following:

$$P = n^2,$$

$T = 3n - 2,$ when the result stays in the array,

$T = 4n - 2,$ when the result is transferred out of the array.

The wavefront array represents a well-synchronized structure. The data flow is basically the same as for a hexagonal array except that it does not pipe elements of matrix C into the array. This implies that it pipes data elements into every PE during computation for some amount of time (at least half of the total turnaround time). However, its

Sec. 8.3 Systolic Arrays

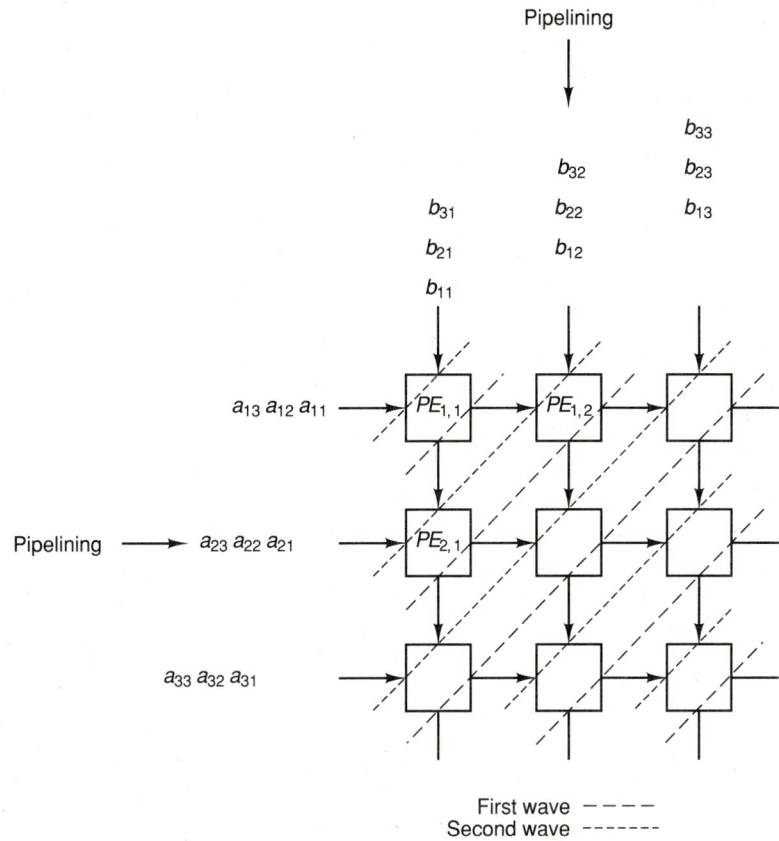

Figure 8.12 Block diagram of a wavefront array.

drawback is that the utilization of PEs is at most 50%. Compared to the previous designs, it uses many fewer PEs than does the pipelined array, but it needs more turnaround time than does semibroadcasting.

Broadcast array. The broadcast array was proposed by Chern and Murata [CHE 83]. The structure of a broadcast array with data stream is shown in Figure 8.13. In this design, a two-dimensional data broadcast scheme is introduced. That is, the data can be broadcast in two directions, by row and by column, across the array. In general, for two n-by-n matrices, we have

$P = n^2,$

$T = n,$ when the result stays in the array,

$T = 2n$ when the result is transferred out of the array.

The broadcast array has less turnaround time than the previous designs. Also, it has higher utilization of PEs. Furthermore, for dense matrix multiplication, no matrix data rearrangement is required. However, the most controversial point about this

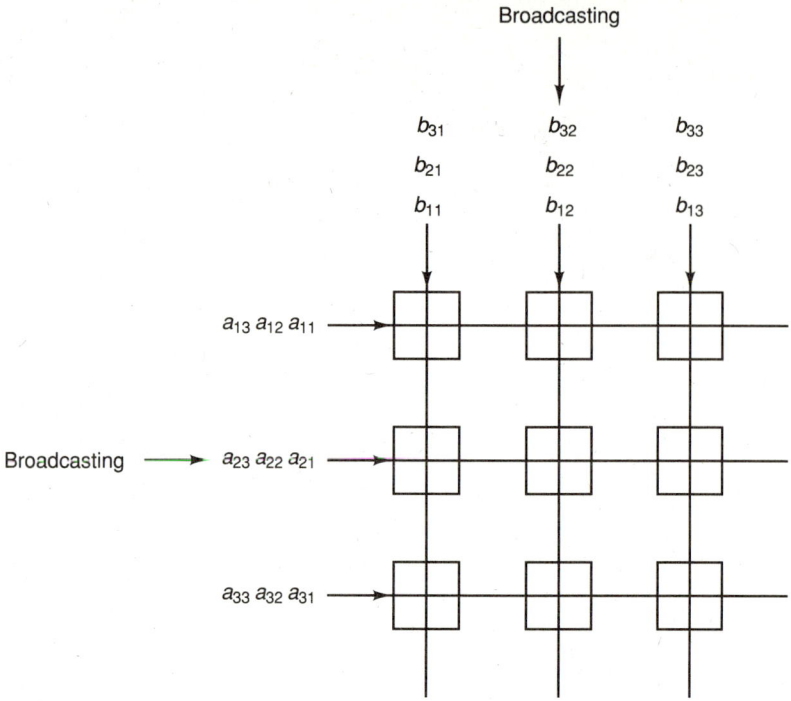

Figure 8.13 Block diagram of a broadcast array.

design is, as with the semibroadcast array, the time delay due to data broadcasting. Again, the degree for complexity for controlling the broadcast array may be higher than that of the pipelined array. The data bus lines needed by broadcast arrays are twice as many as those needed by semibroadcast arrays. Hence they occupy more layout area.

8.3.2 Mapping Algorithm to Systolic Architecture

Kuhn and Moldovan have proposed procedures for mapping algorithms with loops into systolic arrays [KUH 80, MOL 83]. The mapping procedures start by transforming the loop indexes of a given algorithm to new loop indexes, which allows parallelism and pipelining in the algorithm. Buffer variables are introduced in the transformed algorithm to implement the flow of a value of a set of loop indexes, (broadcast data) in a pipelined fashion. The data pipelining makes the algorithm suitable for VLSI design. Once the transformation is done, the transformed algorithm is mapped into a VLSI array. At this step, the function of each PE and the interconnections between them are determined.

    A technique for mapping an algorithm into a systolic array is described next. The following two definitions are given to facilitate the explanation of such a technique.

Sec. 8.3 Systolic Arrays

Definition 1. An algorithm A can be defined as a five tuple $A = (I^n, C, D, X, Y)$, where

I^n is a finite index set of A,
C is the set of computations of A,
D is the set of data dependencies,
X is the set of input variables of A,
Y is the set of output variables of A.

Definition 2. Two algorithms $A = (I^n, C, D, X, Y)$ and $A' = (I'^m, C', D', X', Y')$ are equivalent if and only if

1. Algorithm A is input/output equivalent to A'; that is, $X = X'$ and $Y = Y'$.
2. The index set of A' is the transformed index set of A.
   $I'^m = T(I^n)$, where T is a bijection and monotonic function.
3. Any operation of A corresponds to an identical operation in A', and vice versa; thus $C = C'$.
4. Data dependencies of A' are the transformed data dependencies of A; $D' = T(D)$.

The matrix T is a bijection, and it is also a monotonic function. This is because we need to keep the data dependence of the original algorithm after transformation.

The matrix T is partitioned into two functions as follows:

$$T = \begin{bmatrix} \Pi \\ S \end{bmatrix}$$

where $\Pi: I^n \to I'^k$ $(n > k)$, and $S: I^n \to I'^{m-k}$.

The first k coordinates of elements I'^m can be related to time. The last $n - k$ coordinates can be related to (space) the geometrical properties of the algorithm. In other words, time is associated with the new lexicographical ordering imposed on the elements I'^m, and this is given only by their first k coordinates. The last $n - k$ coordinates can be chosen to satisfy expectations about the geometrical properties of the algorithm. In the remainder of this section, we consider transformed functions for which the ordering imposed by the first coordinate of the index set is an execution ordering. That is,

$$\Pi: I^n \to I'^1$$

$$S: I^n \to I'^{n-1}.$$

The mapping Π is selected such that the transformed data dependence matrix D' has positive entries in the first row. This ensures a valid ordering, that is, $\Pi d_i > 0$ for any $d_i \in D$. Thus a computation indexed by $I \in I^n$ will be processed at time $\Pi * I$.

Steps of the mapping procedure. We use the following steps for the mapping prodedure:

1. Buffer all the variables.
2. Determine the PEs functions by collecting the assignment statements in the loop bodies into m input and n output functions.
3. Apply a linear reindexing transformation T.
4. Find connections between processors and the direction of data flow.

As an example, consider the following algorithm which represents multiplication of two 2-by-2 matrices A and B

```
for (k = 1; k <= 2; k++)
    for (i = 1; i <= 2; i++)
        for (j = 1; j <= 2; j++)
            C(i,j) = C(i,j) + B(k,j) * A(i,k); .
```

Figure 8.14 represents the index set for this algorithm. In this figure, each index element is shown as a three tuple (k, i, j). Note that for both index elements $(k, i, 1)$ and $(k, i, 2)$, the same value of $A(i, k)$ is used; that is, the value $A(i, k)$ can be piped on the j direction. Similarly, values $B(k, j)$ and $C(i, j)$ can be piped on i and k directions, respectively. Based on these facts, the algorithm can be rewritten by introducing buffering variables A^{j+1}, B^{i+1}, and C^{k+1}, as follows:

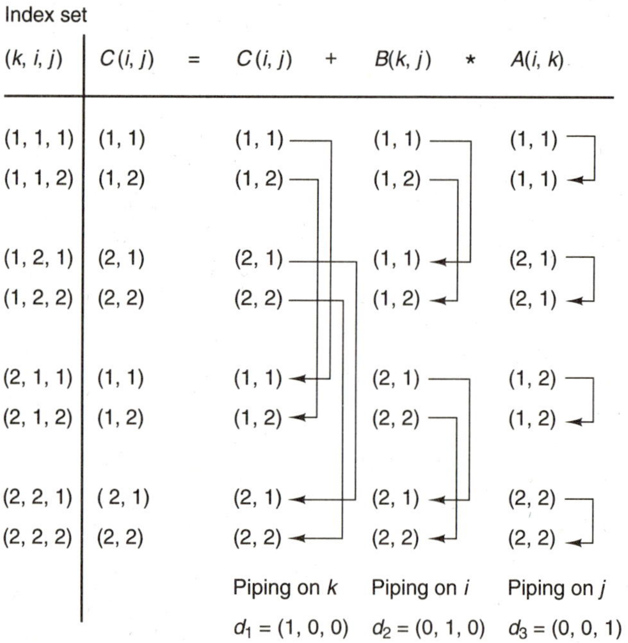

Index set

(k, i, j)	$C(i, j)$	=	$C(i, j)$	+	$B(k, j)$	*	$A(i, k)$
(1, 1, 1)	(1, 1)		(1, 1)		(1, 1)		(1, 1)
(1, 1, 2)	(1, 2)		(1, 2)		(1, 2)		(1, 1)
(1, 2, 1)	(2, 1)		(2, 1)		(1, 1)		(2, 1)
(1, 2, 2)	(2, 2)		(2, 2)		(1, 2)		(2, 1)
(2, 1, 1)	(1, 1)		(1, 1)		(2, 1)		(1, 2)
(2, 1, 2)	(1, 2)		(1, 2)		(2, 2)		(1, 2)
(2, 2, 1)	(2, 1)		(2, 1)		(2, 1)		(2, 2)
(2, 2, 2)	(2, 2)		(2, 2)		(2, 2)		(2, 2)

Piping on k Piping on i Piping on j
$d_1 = (1, 0, 0)$ $d_2 = (0, 1, 0)$ $d_3 = (0, 0, 1)$

Figure 8.14 Index set.

Sec. 8.3 Systolic Arrays

```
for (k = 1; k <= 2; k++)
    for (i = 1; i <= 2; i++)
        for (j = 1; j <= 2; j++)
        {
            A^(j+1)(i,k) = A^j(i,k);
            B^(i+1)(k,j) = B^i(k,j);
            C^(k+1)(i,j) = C^k(i,j) + B^i(k,j) * A^j(i,k);
        }.
```

The set of data dependence vectors can be found by equating indexes of all possible pairs of generated and used variables. In the preceding code, the generated variable $C^{k+1}(i,j)$ and used variable $C^k(i,j)$ give us $d_1 = (k+1-k, i-i, j-j) = (1,0,0)$. Similarly, $<B^{i+1}(k,j)$ and $B^i(k,j)>$ and $<A^{j+1}(i,k)$ and $A^j(i,k)>$ give us $d_2 = (0,1,0)$ and $d_3 = (0,0,1)$, respectively. Figure 8.14 should provide insight in to understanding the logic followed in finding the data dependence vectors. The dependence matrix $D = [d_1 \mid d_2 \mid d_3]$ can be expressed as

$$D = \begin{bmatrix} d_1 & d_2 & d_3 \\ 1 & 0 & 0 \\ 0 & 1 & 0 \\ 0 & 0 & 1 \end{bmatrix}.$$

We are looking for a transformation T that is a bijection and monotonic increasing of the form

$$T = \begin{bmatrix} \Pi \\ S \end{bmatrix}$$

where $\Pi d_i > 0$. Let

$$T = \begin{bmatrix} t_{11} & t_{12} & t_{13} \\ t_{21} & t_{22} & t_{23} \\ t_{31} & t_{32} & t_{33} \end{bmatrix}$$

The condition $\Pi d_i > 0$ (for $i = 1, 2, 3$) implies that

$$(t_{11} t_{12} t_{13}) \begin{bmatrix} 1 \\ 0 \\ 0 \end{bmatrix} > 0 \rightarrow t_{11} > 0,$$

$$(t_{11} t_{12} t_{13}) \begin{bmatrix} 0 \\ 1 \\ 0 \end{bmatrix} > 0 \rightarrow t_{12} > 0,$$

$$(t_{11} t_{12} t_{13}) \begin{bmatrix} 0 \\ 0 \\ 1 \end{bmatrix} > 0 \rightarrow t_{13} > 0.$$

To reduce the turnaround time, we try to choose the smallest values for t_{11}, t_{12}, and t_{13} such as

$$t_{11} = t_{12} = t_{13} = 1; \quad \text{that is,} \quad \Pi = (1, 1, 1).$$

For example, if we chose one index from the index set given in Figure 8.14, say $(1, 1, 2)$, then

$$\Pi \begin{bmatrix} 1 \\ 1 \\ 2 \end{bmatrix} = (1, 1, 1) \begin{bmatrix} 1 \\ 1 \\ 2 \end{bmatrix} = 4.$$

Here, 4 indicates the reference time at which the computation corresponding to index $(1, 1, 2)$ is performed.

Our choice of S will determine the interconnection of the processors. In the selection of mapping S, we are now restricted only by the fact that T must be a bijection and consist of integers. A large number of possibilities exists, each leading to different network geometries. Two of the options are

$$S_1 = \begin{bmatrix} 0 & 1 & 0 \\ 0 & 0 & 1 \end{bmatrix} \quad \text{and} \quad S_2 = \begin{bmatrix} -1 & 1 & 0 \\ 1 & 0 & -1 \end{bmatrix}.$$

Throughout this example, S_1 is selected. Thus

$$T = \begin{bmatrix} 1 & 1 & 1 \\ 0 & 1 & 0 \\ 0 & 0 & 1 \end{bmatrix}.$$

In general, for the multiplication of two n-by-n matrices, 2^n PEs are needed. Thus, for our example, four PEs are needed. The interconnection between these processors is defined by

$$S_1 d_i = \begin{bmatrix} x \\ y \end{bmatrix},$$

where x and y refer to the movement of the variable along the directions i and j, respectively. Thus

$$S_1 d_1 = \begin{bmatrix} 0 \\ 0 \end{bmatrix},$$

means that variable c does not travel in any direction and is updated in time.

$$S_1 d_2 = \begin{bmatrix} 1 \\ 0 \end{bmatrix},$$

means that variable b moves along the direction i with a speed of one grid per time unit. And

$$S_1 d_3 = \begin{bmatrix} 0 \\ 1 \end{bmatrix},$$

means that variable a moves along the direction j with a speed of one grid per time unit.

Sec. 8.3 Systolic Arrays

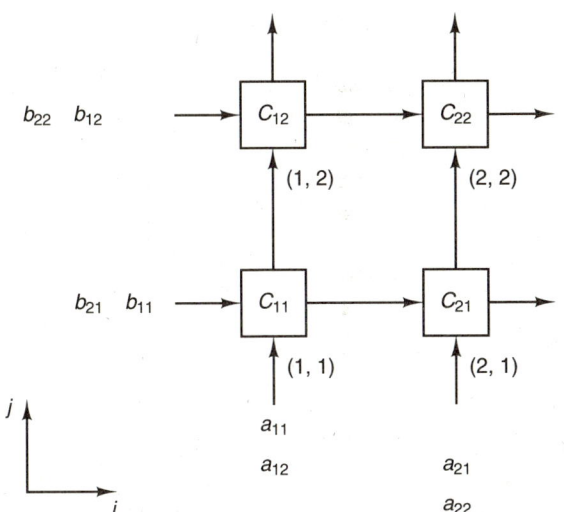

Figure 8.15 Required interconnections between the PEs.

Figure 8.15 represents the interconnections between the PEs. At time 1, b_{11} and a_{11} enter $PE_{1,1}$, which contains variable c_{11}. Then each PE performs a multiply and an add operation; that is, $c_{11} = c_{11} + a_{11} * b_{11}$. At time 2, a_{11} leaves $PE_{1,1}$ and enters $PE_{1,2}$.

Transfer matrix		Original index		Transformed index	C's	A's	B's	Time	PE element
T	*	$[1, 1, 1]^t$	=	$[3, 1, 1]^t$	c_{11}	a_{11}	b_{11}	3	(1, 1)
T	*	$[1, 1, 2]^t$	=	$[4, 1, 2]^t$	c_{12}	a_{11}	b_{12}	4	(1, 2)
T	*	$[1, 2, 1]^t$	=	$[4, 2, 1]^t$	c_{21}	a_{21}	b_{11}	4	(2, 1)
T	*	$[1, 2, 2]^t$	=	$[5, 2, 2]^t$	c_{22}	a_{21}	b_{12}	5	(2, 2)
T	*	$[2, 1, 1]^t$	=	$[4, 1, 1]^t$	c_{11}	a_{12}	b_{21}	4	(1, 1)
T	*	$[2, 1, 2]^t$	=	$[5, 1, 2]^t$	c_{12}	a_{12}	b_{22}	5	(1, 2)
T	*	$[2, 2, 1]^t$	=	$[5, 2, 1]^t$	c_{21}	a_{22}	b_{21}	5	(2, 1)
T	*	$[2, 2, 2]^t$	=	$[6, 2, 2]^t$	c_{22}	a_{22}	b_{22}	6	(2, 2)

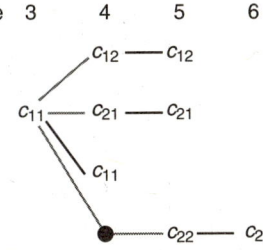

Figure 8.16 Mapping the original index set to the transformed index set.

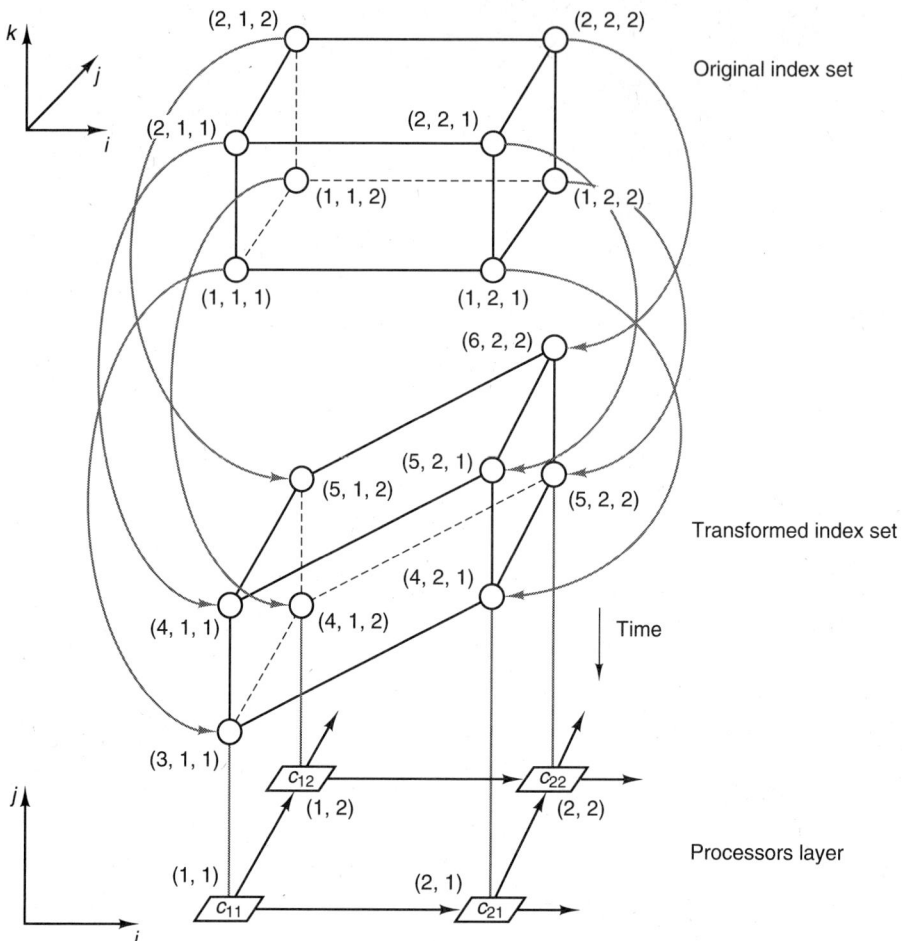

Figure 8.17 The order in which transformed indexes will be computed by the PEs.

At the same time, a_{12} enters $PE_{1,1}$, b_{12} enters $PE_{1,2}$, b_{11} enters $PE_{2,1}$, and b_{21} enters $PE_{1,1}$. Again, each PE performs a multiply and an add operation. Thus

$$c_{11} = c_{11} + a_{12} * b_{21},$$
$$c_{12} = c_{12} + a_{11} * b_{12},$$
$$c_{21} = c_{21} + a_{21} * b_{11}.$$

This process continues until all the values are computed.

Figures 8.16 and 8.17 represent the mapping between original and transformed indexes.

BIBLIOGRAPHIC NOTES

The reference [HWA 84] provides a good description of data flow architectures and systolic arrays.

REFERENCES

[ARV 80] ARVIND, KATHAIL V., AND K., PINGALI, "A Data Flow Architecture with Tagged Tokens," Technical Memo 174, Laboratory for Computer Science, MIT, Cambridge, MA, September, 1980.

[CHE 83] CHERN, M. Y., AND T. MURATA, "Efficient Matrix Multiplications on a Concurrent Data-loading Array Processor," *Proc. Intern Conf. Parallel Processing*, IEEE, New York, 1983, pp. 90–94.

[COR 79] CORNISH, M., ET AL., "The TI Data Flow Architecture: The Power of Concurrency for Avionics," *Proc. Third Digital Avionics Systems Conf.*, November, 1979, pp. 19–25.

[DAV 78] DAVIS, A. L., "The Architecture and System Methodology of DDM1: *A* Recursively Structured Data Driven Machine," *Proc. 5th Annual Symp. Computer Architecture,* 1978, pp. 210–215.

[DEN 80] DENNIS, J. B., "Data Flow Supercomputers," *IEEE Computer*, November 1980, pp. 48–56.

[GUR 80] GURD, J., AND I. WATSON, "Data Driven System for High Speed Parallel Computing," *Computer Design*, Parts I 19(6) and II 19(7), June–July, 1980, pp. 91–100 and pp. 97–106.

[HUA 82] HUANG, K. H., AND J. A. ABRAHAM, "Efficient Parallel Algorithms for Processor Arrays," *Proc. Intern Conf. Parallel Processing*, IEEE, New York, 1982, pp. 271–279.

[HWA 80] HWANG, K., AND Y. H. CHENG, "VLSI Computing Structures for Solving Large-scale Linear System of Equations," *Proc. Interm. Conf. on Parallel Processing*, IEEE, New York, 1980, pp. 217–227.

[HWA 84] HWANG, KAI, AND F. A. BRIGGS, *Computer Architecture and Parallel Processing*. New York: McGraw-Hill Book Co., 1984.

[KUC 78] KUCK, D. J., *The Structure of Computers and Computations*, Vol. 1. New York: John Wiley and Sons, 1978.

[KUH 80] KUHN, R. H., "Optimization and Interconnection Complexity for Parallel Processors, Single Stage Networks and Decision Trees," Ph.D. Dissertation, Department of Computer Science, University of Illinois, Urbana–Champaign, 1980.

[KUN 78] KUNG, H.T., AND C. E. LEISERSON, *Systolic Arrays (for VLSI)*, Society of Industrial and Applied Mathematics, Philidelphia, Pa., 1978, pp. 256–282.

[KUN 82] KUNG, S. Y., AND K. S. ARUN, "Wavefront Array Processor: Language, Architecture, and Applications," *IEEE Trans. Computers*, November 1982, pp. 1054–1066.

[MOL 83] MOLDOVAN, D. I., "On the Design of Algorithms for VLSI Systolic Array," *Proc. IEEE*, 71(1), 1983, pp. 113–120.

PROBLEMS

8.1. Describe the advantages and disadvantages of the following types of design.
   a. Static data flow machine.
   b. Dynamic data flow machine.

8.2. Describe the advantages and disadvantages of the following types of design.
   a. Hexagonal array.
   b. Pipelined array.
   c. Semibroadcast array.
   d. Wavefront array.
   e. Broadcast array.

8.3. For a given n, draw an eqivalent data flow graph for the following series:

$$\text{output} = 1 + 2^2 + 3^2 + \cdots + n^2$$

8.4. What is the output of the dataflow graph in Figure P8.4?

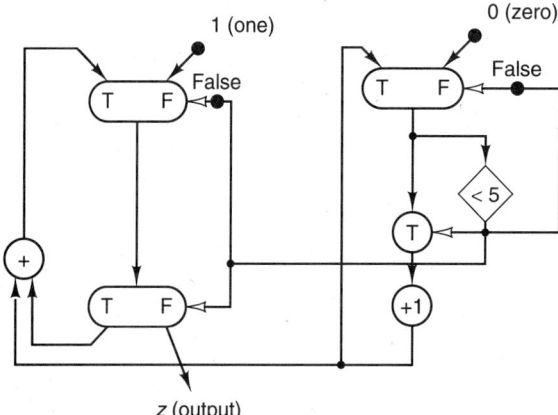

Figure P8.4

8.5. Consider the steps of mapping the matrix multiplication algorithm into a systolic array. Modify the given mapping steps to obtain the following results:
   a. The semibroadcast array given in Figure 8.11.
   b. The broadcast array given in Figure 8.13.
   Show all your work.

9

Future Horizons for Architecture

9.1 INTRODUCTION

The von Neumann computer performs poorly on certain tasks, such as emulating the natural information processing that humans handle routinely. In many real-world applications, the processing of information in a reasonable time requires exploiting the tolerance for imprecision and uncertainty for which von Neumann machines are ill adapted. To overcome this problem, many theories and technologies have been proposed. Zadeh [ZAD 94, ZAD 95] refers to these theories and technologies as *soft computing*. Basically, soft computing is a collection of methodologies that in one way or another aim to exploit the tolerance for imprecision and uncertainty to achieve tractability, robustness, and low solution cost. There are three main classes of methodologies that form soft computing; they are *neural networks, fuzzy logic,* and *probabilistic reasoning*. Although each of these classes of methodologies may be used to resolve certain types of applications, they are in fact complementary to each other, and in many cases it is better to employ them in combination rather than exclusively.

In this chapter, two of the constituents of soft computing that currently offer the most potential for future architectures are discussed. These are neural networks and fuzzy logic. In addition, one subject subsumed by fuzzy logic, multiple-valued logic, is also explained.

Neural networks address the issue of effective information organization and processing. Since biological brains are working examples of massively parallel, densely interconnected, self-organizing computational networks, they represent an ideal prototype after which special-purpose hardwares can be modeled. To extract a design of a machine from a model of the brain's functioning requires an intimate understanding of the brain's most basic processing elements, the neurons, and the dynamics of their operation. This chapter examines the neuron together with the dynamics of neural processing, and surveys some well-known proposed neural networks.

Multiple-valued logic addresses the need to conserve chip area in order to have complex circuits. Multiple-valued logic circuits allow signals with more than two values and therefore provide a significant savings in chip area. This chapter describes the basic features of this logic.

Finally, fuzzy logic attempts to deal effectively with imprecision and approximate reasoning, as opposed to precision and formal reasoning, and it overcomes some of the inconveniences associated with the classical logic. It mimics the remarkable ability of the human mind to summarize data and focus on decision-relevant information. Fuzzy logic has been applied successfully in many cases. This chapter defines fuzzy logic, explains its use in control systems, and discusses the future of this theory.

9.2 NEURAL NETWORKS[*]

As a blueprint for computer architecture, no single source has as much potential or is as challenging as the human brain. The brain's intrinsic relevance to the science of computers lies in its obvious information-processing capabilities and its incorporation of desirable computing characteristics. The most significant computing characteristics that are evident in the structure of the brain include concurrent and distributed data processing, functional modularity, massive parallelism, and a capacity for self-organization. As Vidal [VID 83] has suggested, the incorporation of precisely these characteristics into the design of a computing system is a prerequisite of the successful management of the functional and testing complexity of future VLSI designs.

Since the significance of these characteristics to the development of advanced computer architecture is beyond dispute, the importance of understanding the architecture of the brain that provides for these characteristics is essential. The principal and most evident architectural features of the brain relevant to its processing characteristics are those of layering, modularity, dense interconnections, and distribution of input processing.

> **Layering.** The cells of the brain are grouped into large networks according to a plan of hierarchical superposition, permitting information to be processed in a stratified manner, layer by layer. Fairhurst [FAI 78] describes the brain's mechanism of information-processing in terms of a hierarchically structured model of neural networks.
>
> **Modularity.** Areas of the brain are divided into modules codetermined by the design-integrated considerations of sensory input mapping and functional output.
>
> **Dense interconnections.** Particular cellular interconnections between and within layers provide for data sharing and also serve as feedback and feed-

[*] Portions of Section 9.2 reprinted with permission, from "Neural Petri Nets" by M.R. Zargham and M. Tyman which appeared in Proceedings of Int. Workshop of Timed Perti Nets, Italy, July 1985, pp. 72–77, © IEEE.

forward mechanisms for transmitting data among interconnected regions containing stored data.

Distribution of input processing. Identical or similar input may be differentially represented as it passes through different processing routes (data channels) governed by specific relay mechanisms (category triggers) within the brain.

In the next section the basic terminology and concepts of neurophysiology will be reviewed. The basic concepts of neurophysiology provide a common ground for understanding the neural network models that are introduced later. The development of any model of neural processing requires that the fundamentals of neurophysiology be related to the elements of a computational model. The reader who is not interested in the details of neurophysiology can skip section 9.2.1 and go directly to Section 9.2.2.

9.2.1 Fundamentals of Neurophysiology

The basic brain processing unit is the nerve cell, called the *neuron*. Figure 9.1 shows the main components of a neuron. The output of the neuron, called *axons*, branch out directionally from the cell body, the *soma*, and reach out to terminate on other nerve cell bodies, thus establishing contact between two neurons. The axons are used for transmitting information between neurons. The connection between a neuron and an axon is called a *synapse*. At the synapse the transmission of information from one cell to another occurs.

In each neuron there is a wall-like structure, called the *membrane*, that keeps substances beneficial to the cell in and undesirable elements out. Because of this barrier, the concentration of molecules inside and outside the cell are not equal. Both the

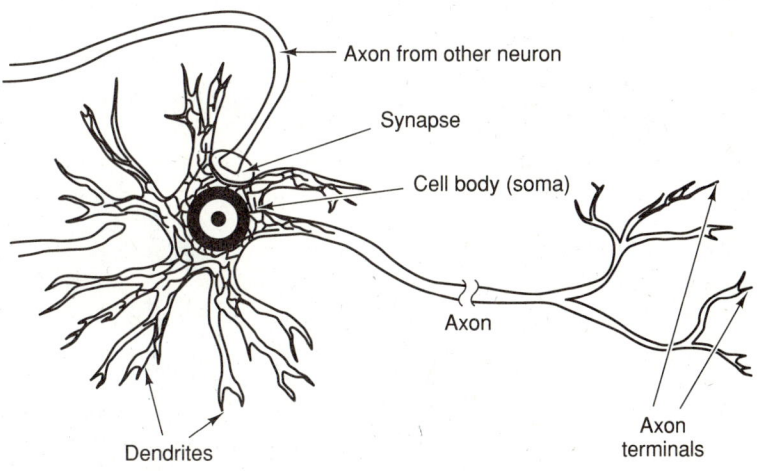

Figure 9.1 Main components of a neuron.

intracellular and the extracellular spaces are filled with a dilute aqueous salt solution that causes most molecules to break down into charged atoms. There are two types of charged atoms, positive (cations) and negative (anions). There is an unequal distribution of charged molecules, particularly small cations, between the inside and outside of the cell. This permits the membrane to be selectively permeable in favor of small cations, setting up an electrical relation called the *membrane potential*. The membrane potential resides in tension or equilibrium in which forces pushing small cations out of the cell are in balance with the forces pushing them back into the cell.

The membrane potential is an essential element for the transfer of information within the central nervous system (CNS). A stimulus disturbs the resting membrane potential of a cell by changing its permeability to certain ions. Whenever the membrane potential change is in the positive direction and reaches a threshold level (the assumption will be made that the threshold value is equivalent in all cells and remains constant), an action potential is generated. The action potential is a stereotyped sequence of depolarizations and hyperpolarizations occurring spontaneously at the membrane surface. The action potential spreads along the membrane surface from the point of stimulation into neighboring regions of the membrane, thus progressing from point to point from the soma down the length of the axon. When the action potential arrives at a synapse it becomes a stimulus, known as a *postsynaptic potential* (PSP), to the next cell, whose effect is to change the permeability of the next cell to small ions.

There are two types of postsynaptic potentials in the CNS: *excitatory postsynaptic* (EPSP) and an *inhibitory postsynaptic* (IPSP). An EPSP causes the membrane potential of the receiving cell to have a more positive value, thus increasing the likelihood of an action potential generation. An IPSP has the opposite effect on the membrane potential, thus making an action potential harder to generate. Each PSP, whether excitatory or inhibitory, has a prespecified life span. Its influence on a cell's membrane potential is greatest at the point and time of arrival, decreasing at a constant rate until it either serves to generate an action potential or disappears.

Typically, the EPSPs are below threshold: they cannot change a membrane potential enough to initiate an action potential. Therefore, two or more EPSPs must combine in an additive relation (sum).

A simple illustration of action potential is shown in Figure 9.2 [GRI 81]. Figure 9.2a shows that excitatory postsynapses (E_1 and E_2) and an inhibitory postsynapse (I) are stimulated at S, and the postsynaptic change is recorded at R. Figure 9.2b shows that E_1 alone cannot produce an action potential, but that the stimulation of both E_1 and E_2 causes an action potential because the summation of E_1 and E_2 exceeds the threshold level. When all three synapses (E_1, E_2, and I) are stimulated, the inhibitory synapse (I) blocks the development of an action potential. The key concept here is that "neurons are analogue devices" [AND 83].

The EPSPs and IPSPs can be represented as digital pulses, with approximately the same height and duration, and can be thought of as binary bits. A pulse at a given synapse may either add to (if it is an EPSP) or subtract from (if it is an IPSP) the membrane potential. This potential can be represented as an analog voltage that corresponds to the algebraic sum of the inputs. When the summed inputs to the cell exceed the threshold level, the cell puts a pulse on the axon. Whenever this occurs, the voltage in the cell body is reset to the initial value.

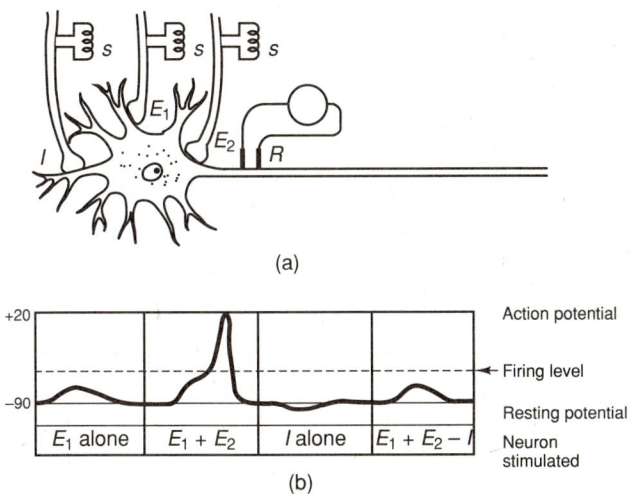

Figure 9.2 Example of neural communication (from [GRI 81]). Reprinted with permission of Simon & Schuster, Inc. from the Macmillan College text "Introduction to Human Physiology" 2/E by Mary Griffiths. Copyright© 1981.

Information-processing in the nervous system. The simple illustration of the flow of information-processing of the brain from the sensory receptors (input) to motor neurons (output) is shown in Figure 9.3. The center box with the question mark, which is primarily composed of the brain, is far less known at present. Input of any sensory signal is performed by receptor cells, and eventually output is transmitted to motor neurons terminating on muscle cells. How a piece of information is processed after the input and before the output is far less known. In this section, each part of the information-processing is examined briefly.

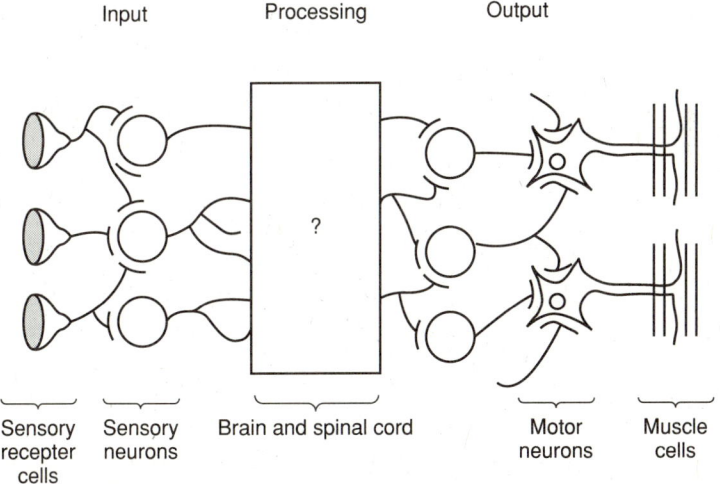

Figure 9.3 Flow of information-processing.

The function of sensory receptors is to transmit information about the internal and external environments to the central nervous system. A receptor responds to a stimulus by developing a generator potential in a sensory neuron. If this potential reaches threshold level, it generates action potentials in the sensory neuron. The greater the generator potential, the greater the frequency of impulses generated and the stronger the sensation or response.

When a sensory neuron sends action potentials to the central nervous system, it branches extensively, making many synaptic contacts. The intensity of a sensation is determined by the frequency of impulses in the sensory neurons and the number of receptors stimulated. Meaning is given to the sensory input, and sensory information may be stored in the central nervous system.

A hierarchy exists in the central nervous system for the control of muscle activities. Simple reflexes are coordinated at the level of the spinal cord, but are modified by impulses from several levels of the brain. Higher functions of the brain depend on the central nervous system. The higher functions include consciousness, learning, memory, language, and thought. The results of the processing are sent to the motor neurons, which terminate at muscle cells.

Most of the activities of information processing in the central nervous system are unknown because of limitations of present technology [PAL 82]. For example, the activities of only a few neurons can be recorded at the same time. Therefore, it is practically impossible to reconstruct a global activity.

Even though the computational principle of models based on the brain rely on the neuron's simple firing mechanism, the methods, purposes, and objects vary from model to model. The following sections review these variations of the brain models.

9.2.2 Artificial Neural Networks

Work on neural net models has a long history. Development of detailed mathematical models began more than 50 years ago with the work of McCulloch and Pitts [MCC 43], Rosenblatt [ROS 62], and Widrow [WID 59, WID 60]. More recent works by Hopfield [HOP 82, HOP 84, HOP 86], Rumelhart and McClelland [RUM 86a], and others have led to a resurgence in the field. This new interest is due to the development of new net methods and algorithms and new VLSI implementation techniques, as well as the growing fascination with the functioning of the human brain. Interest is also increasing because areas of speech and image recognition require enormous amounts of processing to achieve humanlike performance. Artificial neural networks (ANNs) provide one technique for obtaining the processing power required, using large numbers of processing elements operating in parallel.

Although ANNs can be simulated on conventional computers, they are intended to be implemented on special-purpose hardware. ANNs are capable of learning, adaptive to changing environments, and able to cope with serious disruptions.

The artificial neuron was designed to mimic some of the characteristics of the biological neuron. Each neuron has a set of inputs and one or more outputs. A weight is assigned to each input. This weight is analogous to the synaptic strength of a biological neuron. All the inputs are multiplied by their weights and then are summed to determine the activation level of the neuron. Once the activation level is determined,

Sec. 9.2 Neural Networks

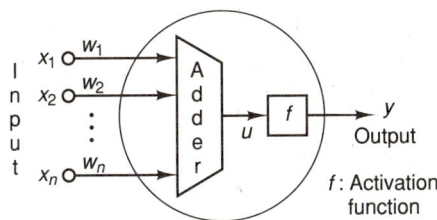

Figure 9.4 Architecture of an artificial neuron.

an activation function is applied to produce the output signal. Figure 9.4 presents an artificial neuron that has n inputs, labeled $x_1, x_2, \ldots x_n$, and one output denoted by y. The output y can be produced as

$$y = f(u),$$

where

$$u = \sum_{i=1}^{n} x_i w_i$$

and f is an activation function.

One simple activation function is the *hard-limiting* function. As shown in Figure 9.5, hard-limiting function is defined as

$$y = \begin{cases} 1, & \text{if } u > T \\ -1, & \text{otherwise} \end{cases}$$

where T is a constant threshold value.

Another activation function is the nonlinear *sigmoid* function. As shown in Figure 9.6, a sigmoid function is expressed as

$$y = 1/(1 + e^{-u}).$$

The sigmoid function is often used because it is differentiable and makes construction of neural network models easier.

Taxonomy of ANN models. ANN models constitute a large class of computational mechanisms that share together the basic features of parallel operation and dense interconnection between the processing elements. At the same time, major differences exist among the individual models regarding their architecture, learning rules, and mode of interaction with the environment. A general taxonomy of these models

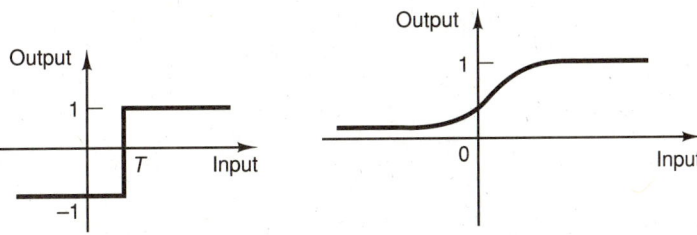

Figure 9.5 Hard-limiting function.   **Figure 9.6** Sigmoid function.

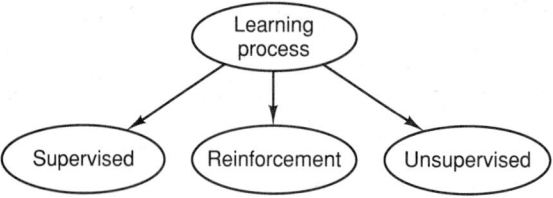

Figure 9.7 Different classes of ANN learning algorithms.

will prove useful in understanding their functionality and fitness to practical applications.

The most general distinction among different ANN models is considered to be the extent to which the environment specifies the input/output mapping that the ANN is supposed to learn. If the environment provides the training examples in the form of input/output pairs of vectors, the mode of operation of the ANN is said to be *supervised*. This mode is also called *learning with a teacher*, since the environment serves as a teacher to the network by providing detailed examples of what is to be learned. If, on the contrary, the environment specifies the input but not the output, the learning is *unsupervised*. In the latter case the network has to discover on its own the solution to the learning problem. Somewhere in between supervised and unsupervised learning lies *reinforcement* learning: some output information is supplied by the environment, but this information is in the form of evaluation of the ANN's performance, rather than in the form of training examples. Sometimes reinforcement learning is called learning with a *critic*, as opposed to learning with a teacher, because the environment does not specify what is to be learned, but only if what is being learned is correct. Figure 9.7 shows the three classes of learning algorithms: supervised, reinforcement, and unsupervised.

Another important distinction among different ANN models is based on their architectures. Here, architecture refers to the type of processing performed by the artificial neurons and the interconnection between them. As shown in Figure 9.8, ANN can be divided into two groups: *deterministic* and *stochastic*.

Deterministic networks always produce the same output result when presented with the same input, while the output for a given input in stochastic networks can vary according to some output probability distribution. Stochastic models are usually harder to analyze and simulate, but at the same time they are more realistic in many applications. For example, if the output of a certain physical system, whose input does

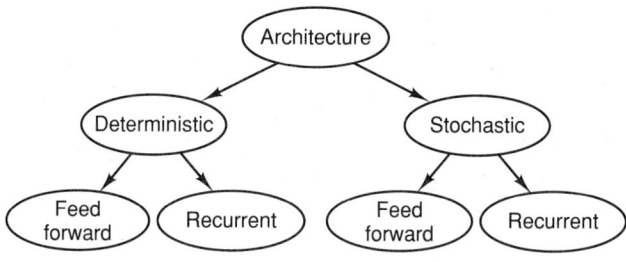

Figure 9.8 Different types of ANN architectures

not change, is to be measured several times with standard measurement devices, the readings will be close to each other, but nevertheless different. In this case it would make much more sense to match the input of the system to the probability distribution of the output rather than to a single hypothetical average of all measurements.

If the directed connectivity graph of an ANN has loops or cycles, the network is said to be *recurrent;* otherwise, it is called feed-forward. (The directed connectivity graph of an ANN is a directed graph in which the vertices correspond to the neurons of the network and edges correspond to the connections between the neurons.) While this distinction does not seem too critical at first glance, the feed-forward networks turn out to be much easier to analyze and train than their recurrent counterparts. At the same time, there are usually restrictions about the type of mappings that strictly feed-forward networks can learn. A recurrent model is always computationally more powerful than its corresponding feed-forward model, because the feed-forward model is a special case of the more general recurrent model.

Based on the learning process criteria, the ANN models in a given group, supervised learning, reinforcement learning, and unsupervised learning, have similar functionality and are usually used in similar applications. These three groups and the principal task that each is applied to are discussed next.

Supervised Learning. Supervised learning models can use either deterministic or stochastic processing elements. The class of deterministic supervised learning algorithms solves the fundamental problem of function approximation. This problem can be divided into two tasks:

1. **Loading task.** Store a set of p pairs of input/output patterns (x^k, y^k), $k = 1$ to p, in such a way that when presented with any input pattern x^k the network responds by producing the correct output pattern y^k. The set of input/output patterns (x^k, y^k) is called the *training* set of the task. The number of elements in the input and output patterns determines the dimensions of the input and output spaces, respectively; these dimensions need not be the same. In this way, the training set defines a function that maps the input space onto the output space.

2. **Generalization task.** When presented with a *new* input pattern, different from any pattern in the training set, the network responds with an *adequate* output, a pattern that depends on the new input in the same manner as the output patterns in the training set depend on their corresponding input patterns.

Algorithms for training feed-forward deterministic supervised networks include, among others, Adaline and Madaline [WID 60, WID 88], back propagation [RUM 86a, RUM 86b], quick propagation [FAH 89], conjugate gradient [KRA 89, MAK 89] and cascade correlation [FAH 90]. A great deal of research in ANN is concentrated on this class of algorithms because of their relatively simple learning rules and their usefulness in practical applications. Deterministic feed-forward supervised models are employed in many successful ANN applications: speech recognition and synthesis [LIP 89], automatic target recognition [GOR 88], car navigation [POM 89], image compression [COT 87], signal prediction and forecasting [LAP 87], handwritten character recognition [LEC 90], and others.

Examples of recurrent deterministic supervised models are Hopfield networks [HOP 82], bidirectional associative memory [KOS 92], mean-field theory [PET 87], recurrent back propagation [PIN 87, ALM 88], real-time recurrent learning [WIL 89] and time-dependent recurrent back propagation [PEA 89]. These algorithms can be used to train ANNs to perform input/output mappings that cannot be learned by feed-forward networks, for example, finite-state machines and sequence recognition. This increase in approximation power is paid for by higher computational costs, which sometimes make the learning and simulation of the problem being investigated infeasible.

If stochastic processing elements are used in the supervised learning paradigm, the function approximation problem can be extended to functions whose result is not a single value, but a probability distribution. The class of models that solves the task of associating input and output probability distributions includes Boltzmann machines [HIN 86], expectation maximization [RED 84], and Cauchy machines [SZU 86]. These models require substantial computational resources even for small problems and typically scale up poorly. In spite of their representational power, they are not likely to be the modeling tool of choice in the future unless their requirements for computational resources decrease dramatically.

Reinforcement Learning. The second largest class of learning algorithms is the well-defined group of reinforcement learning algorithms. The task they try to solve is considerably more difficult than the associative task that supervised learning algorithms tackle. The correct output that corresponds to a given input is not known to the reinforcement learning algorithm. The only possible way for the system to discover the correct output is by trial and error, which requires exploratory behavior on the part of the system. This can be achieved by using stochastic units that produce different outputs for the same input. For example, if the same input vector x is presented to the system two times in a row, the outputs will be two different vectors, $y(1)$ and $y(2)$. The learning algorithm compares the correctness of these two vectors and adjusts the system in order to change the probabilities that these two vectors will be output subsequently: the probability of the more successful output is increased, while the probability of the less successful is decreased.

Essential in this process is the ability of the system to evaluate which of the two vectors is better. The search of the system for the correct output is guided by a single scalar variable called *reinforcement signal* (usually in the range [-1, 1]) that evaluates the correctness of the output that the system has chosen to produce. A value of +1 indicates a perfect guess, while a value of -1 is returned by the environment when the output is completely incorrect. In practice, all reinforcement learning algorithms are optimization schemes that try to maximize the value of the reinforcement signal.

The environment can in its turn be either deterministic or stochastic. In deterministic environments the reinforcement signal is always the same for a given input/output pair. In this way the system is guaranteed a reward each time it makes a successful guess. In stochastic environments, a particular input/output determines only the *probability* of certain reinforcement, while the actual value of the reinforcement comes from a probability distribution. With this type of environment, the system can in fact receive low reinforcement even if the output has been good. This makes clear that learning in stochastic environments is much harder than learning in deterministic ones.

In addition to that, the environment might delay the reinforcement. For example, if a robot balances a broomstick and makes a wrong hand movement, the negative reinforcement will come only after the broomstick has fallen down, before which the robot will have made many more movements. It is very difficult to determine exactly which of these hand movements was wrong and led to the loss of balance so that it can be punished. In this case we have the problem of *temporal* credit assignment in addition to the usual *structural* credit assignment problem. Structural credit assignment deals with determining the change in which connection led to better performance, while temporal credit assignment deals with determining *when* (at which moment in time) correct outputs have been generated and when the outputs have been incorrect.

Examples of reinforcement learning algorithms are associative reward-penalty [BAR 85], TD (λ) [SUT 88], Q-learning [WAT 92], and adaptive heuristic critic and the REINFORCE group of gradient ascent methods [WIL 92].

Unsupervised Learning. The third and last largest class of ANN models is the unsupervised algorithms. Target values are not supplied, nor is reinforcement provided. The network has to discover for itself patterns, features, regularities, correlations, or categories in the input data and code for them in the output. The units and connections must display some degree of *self-organization*. Unsupervised learning algorithms can perform clustering, prototyping, principal component analysis, encoding and feature mapping among other tasks encountered in science and engineering.

Several sorts of regularities can be discovered by unsupervised learning models [HER 91]:

1. **Clustering.** Each input should be classified in one of several groups, or clusters, based on the similarity of the input to the vectors in the corresponding cluster. The output layer of the system has as many units as number of clusters; each unit is responsible for one and only one cluster. If the unit is on, this will mean that the input vector is classified as belonging to the cluster for which this unit is responsible. If the classification is to be unequivocal, only one unit in the output layer should be on at a time. In this way the output units compete with each other to represent the input vector; hence the algorithms that provide this property are called *competitive* learning algorithms.

2. **Prototyping.** One step beyond clustering is prototyping: instead of merely determining the correct cluster, the network is expected to provide a typical example of that cluster.

3. **Familiarity.** The task of the system is to produce a single continuous-valued output that estimates how similar the current input is to the input vectors that the system has observed in the past.

4. **Principal component analysis.** In many cases the measurable variables that constitute the input vector are not independent; rather, a hidden set of independent variables called *factors* or *principal components* exists that actually produces the measurable output of the system. The task of the learning algorithm is to discover this set of factors.

5. **Encoding.** When encoding a certain input vector, the system should reduce the dimensionality of the input without losing too much discriminating information. One way to do that is to use principal component analysis and describe the input vector in the space of the principal components.
6. **Feature mapping.** This problem includes the encoding problem with the additional requirement that the topology of the input space be preserved so that close vectors in the input space remain close in the space of the transformed image.

Examples of unsupervised learning algorithms are self-organizing feature maps [KOH 82], adaptive resonance theory [GRO 87], cognitron [FUK 75], and neocognitron [FUK 80].

The following sections describe some of the fundamental networks, such as Adaline, Madaline, and perceptron networks. The sections introduce each of these networks and describe how they are implemented. The decision space, which describes the network's ability to distinguish between patterns or decisions, will be analyzed for each network. In addition, the Hopfield network is also explained. The Hopfield networks are important because of their direct implementation in hardware.

Adaptive linear neurons. Widrow et al. [WID 60, WID 88] have proposed an artificial neural network with *adaptive linear neurons* called *Adaline*. The neurons are characterized as adaptive because their weights are adjustable and as linear because the function of the neuron is linear.

Many of the proposed ANNs are based on Widrow's Adaline method. This neural method performs very well for classifying linear pattern/decision vector space problems. Its roots are based on the Hebbian rule [HEB 49], which states that a physical change has to take place in a network in order to support learning and that this physical change requires a strengthening of the connections among elements of the network. More specifically, Hebb proposed the following: *Whenever two connected neurons are active at the same time, the strength of the connection between them should be increased.*

This learning rule reflects the principle of *contiguity* that is believed to be the basis of biological learning [OSH 90]. This principle states that, when two events (images, ideas) occur at the same time, they are associated with each other so that, when one of them becomes active in future time, the other will be activated too. For example, let A and B be two neurons, where A is one of the neurons providing input to neuron B. If neuron A's activity tends to be high whenever neuron B's activity is high, the future contribution that the firing of neuron A makes to the firing of neuron B should increase.

The Hebbian rule can be accomplished by changing weights on the inputs of neurons in response to some function of the correlated activity of the connected units. Other networks that are based on the Hebbian rule and related to the Adaline are the Madaline and perceptron networks. As is shown in later sections, these networks, unlike the Adaline, can describe nonlinear decision space, such as the exclusive-or (XOR) function.

Figure 9.9 shows an Adaline neuron with n inputs $x_1, x_2, ..., $ and x_n. Each input can take only one of two binary values, $+1$ or -1. In addition, the neuron also has a

Sec. 9.2 Neural Networks

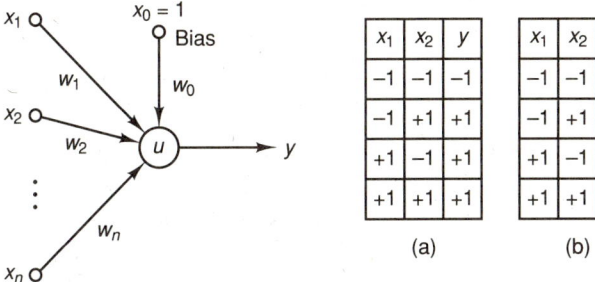

Figure 9.9 An Adaline neuron.

Figure 9.10 Truth tables for the (a) OR and (b) AND functions.

x_1	x_2	y
-1	-1	-1
-1	$+1$	$+1$
$+1$	-1	$+1$
$+1$	$+1$	$+1$

(a)

x_1	x_2	y
-1	-1	-1
-1	$+1$	-1
$+1$	-1	-1
$+1$	$+1$	$+1$

(b)

constant input x_0, which has the value $+1$ all the time. A weight is associated to each input. These weights can take any real number. The weight corresponding to the input x_0 is w_0 and is called the *bias weight*. Later we shall see how this bias weight controls the threshold level. All the inputs are multiplied by their weights and then summed to determine the activation level of the neuron, u. For the output of this neuron, y, to be connected to the input of other neurons, the real value u needs to be converted into a binary value of $+1$ or -1. A hard-limiting activation function does this conversion. The output of the neuron is assigned a value of $+1$ if u is greater than zero and a value of -1, otherwise.

To clarify the operation of an Adaline neuron, let us consider its use in representing some elementary logic functions such as the OR and AND functions. Figure 9.10 shows the desired output y for different combinations of the inputs x_1 and x_2 for these functions.

Figure 9.11 shows a two-input Adaline neuron. Suppose that we want this neuron to represent an OR function. This requires finding the weights w_0, w_1, and w_2, so that the neuron can represent the desired mapping. For example, if $w_0 = 1.5$, $w_1 = +1$, and $w_2 = +1$, then the neuron represents an OR function. (Later we will learn how these weights can be found in general.) A two-input Adaline neuron is also able to represent an AND function; this can be done by choosing $w_0 = -1.5$, $w_1 = +1$, and $w_2 = +1$; see Figure 9.11.

A single neuron divides the input patterns into two classes, one for which the output is $+1$ and the other for which the output is -1. The distinction between outputs $+1$

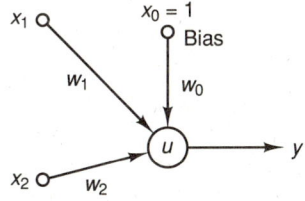

$w_0 = 1.5, w_1 = +1, w_2 = +1$ => OR function
$w_0 = -1.5, w_1 = +1, w_2 = +1$ => AND function

Figure 9.11 A two-input Adaline.

and -1 occurs when the weighted sum u equals 0. For example, in Figure 9.11, we have

$$x_1w_1 + x_2w_2 + x_0w_0 = 0,$$

or

$$x_1w_1 + x_2w_2 + w_0 = 0,$$

or for the AND function,

$$x_1 + x_2 - 1.5 = 0,$$

which is the equation of a straight line. As shown in Figure 9.12, this line divides the input pattern vector space into two parts. Notice that the input pattern $(+1, +1)$ (which generates an output $+1$) is on one side of the line and the other input patterns (which generate an output -1) are on the other side of the line. Also notice that if we have not added the bias weight, w_0, the line equation becomes $x_1 + x_2 = 0$, which always passes through the origin. It is obvious that no lines passing through the origin can separate the input pattern $(+1, +1)$ from other inputs. Therefore, it is necessary to have the bias weight w_0 in order to represent certain functions. However, there still exist some functions that cannot be represented even by addition of the bias weight. For example, in Figure 9.12 it can easily be seen that there is no single line that can put $(+1, +1)$ and $(-1, -1)$ in one class and $(+1, -1)$ and $(-1, +1)$ in another class. This is the XOR function. Thus a single Adaline neuron cannot represent an XOR function.

In general, an N-input Adaline neuron can have 2^N possible input patterns. Each pattern can be classified as $+1$ or -1, so there can be a total of 2^{2^N} possible logic functions for this neuron. However, as we have seen, a single neuron can realize only linearly separable logic functions (decision regions). To realize functions that are not linearly separable, a combination of neurons is required.

Training an Adaline Network. The training process adjusts the weights so that the network produces target (desired) outputs for the given input patterns. Each iteration of the training process adjusts the weights so that the new weights produce an output closer to the target output.

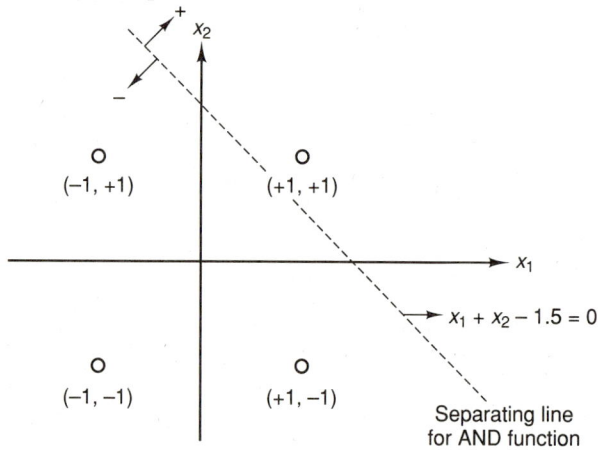

Figure 9.12 Input pattern space for a two-input Adaline.

Sec. 9.2 Neural Networks

Let us assume that t_k denotes the target output and y_k denotes the actual output for the kth input vector. Also let δ_k denote the neuron error, which can be expressed as

$$\delta_k = (t_k - y_k).$$

Notice that each neuron error can only have the values of +2, 0, and −2. (Obviously, when $\delta_k = 0$, the neuron responds correctly to the input pattern x_k.) If $\delta_k = +2$, then the actual output is −1, which is supposed to be +1. Therefore, the weighted sum u should be increased until it becomes greater than 0. To increase u, the weight of positive inputs must be increased while the weight of negative inputs must be decreased. Similarly, if $\delta_k = -2$, then u should be decreased until it becomes less than 0. To decrease u, the weight of negative inputs should be increased while decreasing the weight of positive inputs. These changes can be formalized as follows:

$$W_{new} = W_{old} + \Delta W,$$

where:

$\Delta W = \rho \delta_k x_k$ determines the amount of change, W denotes the vector of weights, and ρ is a positive constant, called the learning rate.

This equation has various names, such as the *Widrow–Hoff learning law*, the *least mean square (LMS) learning law*, and the *delta rule*.

Madaline networks. The single Adaline neuron is not able to represent certain functions, such as XOR. To overcome this incapability the Adaline neurons can be connected in layers, with each layer having a number of such elements. The resulting network is called Madaline (many Adalines). Madalines are used to represent nonlinear (linearly inseparable) functions. Figure 9.13 shows a two-layer Madaline with a total of three Adalines.

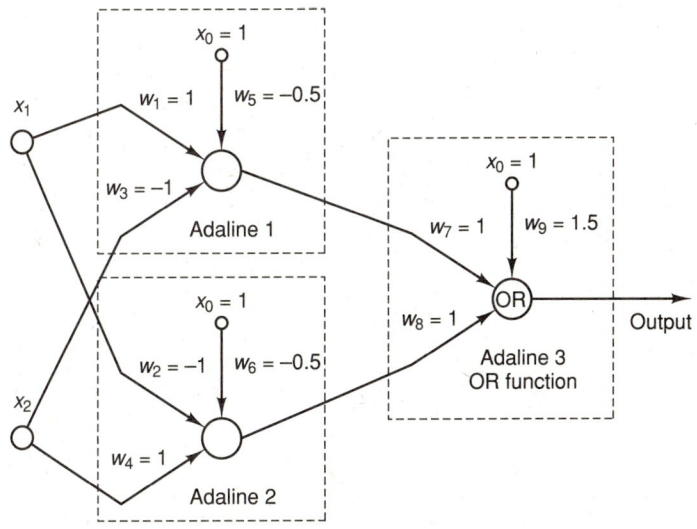

Figure 9.13 A two-layer Madaline model for the XOR function.

The Madaline has an adaptive first layer and fixed threshold functions for the second (output) layer. The neurons in the second layer can consist of AND functions, OR functions, or Majority vote takers.

As you will recall, the Adaline neuron separated the pattern vector space into two categories. The Madaline of Figure 9.13 with two Adalines can further divide the pattern vector space. Figure 9.14 shows the separating boundaries for the exclusive-or problem. Note that the two-layer Madaline has no trouble in classifying this simple nonlinear problem.

Classical perceptron. A classical perceptron neuron is similar to the Adaline neuron. However, the activation function of a perceptron neuron can be linear or sigmoid. Also, in contrast to the Madalines of the 1960s in which the weight of the first layer was adaptive, but not that of the second layer, a perceptron network can have many layers that are all adaptive.

When the activation function is nonlinear, the input patterns are divided into different classes depending on the number of output neurons. By dividing the input pattern space into decision regions, all the input patterns resulting in a particular class can be determined. The decision regions are formed by the number of layers and neurons in the network [LIP 87]. For example, as shown in Figure 9.15a, a single-layer perceptron forms two decision regions separated by a hyperplane. The hyperplane divides the input pattern space into parts, one for which the output is zero and the other for which the output is 1. For the case of a single neuron with two-inputs, the hyperplane separating the two regions is a line. In general, similar to Adaline, the single-layer perceptron can represent the functions that are linearly separable. But if the function is linearly inseparable, it cannot be realized by a one-layer perceptron and thus requires more than one layer.

A two-layer perceptron is able to form simple decision regions of the type shown in Figure 9.15b. Each node in the first layer forms two decision regions separated by a

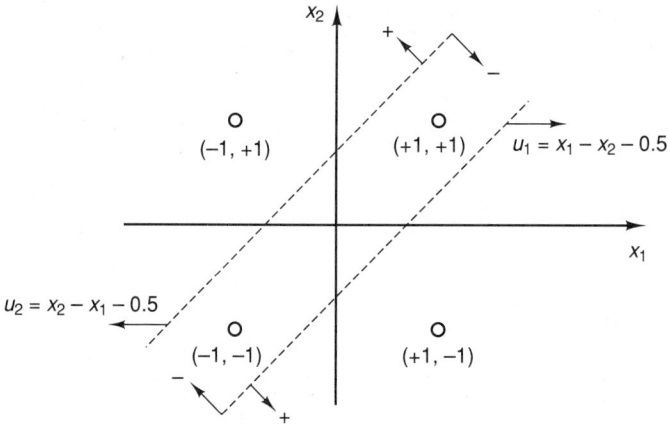

Figure 9.14 Input pattern space for a two-input, two-layer Madaline used to solve the exclusive-or problem.

Sec. 9.2 Neural Networks

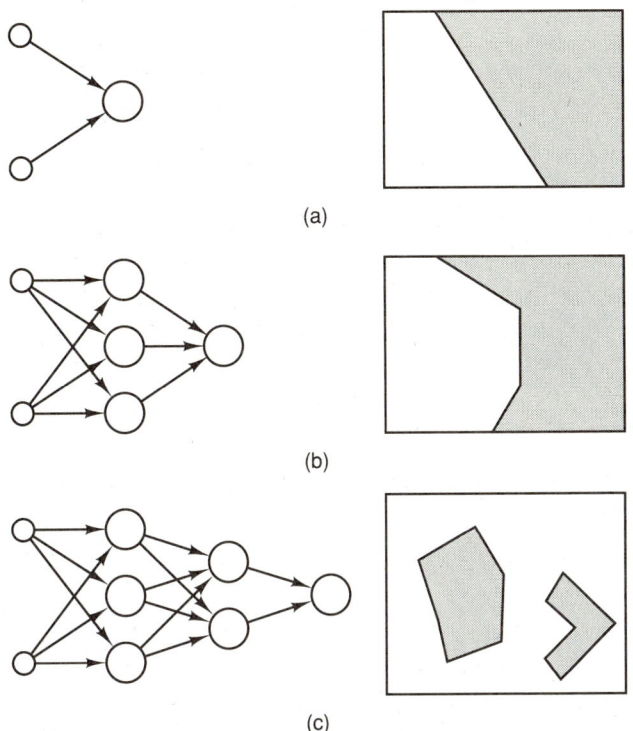

Figure 9.15 Different types of decision regions.

hyperplane. The nodes in the second layer take the intersection of these regions to form (open or closed) convex regions.

A three-layer perceptron can form arbitrary complex decision regions (See Figure 9.15c). Similar to the two-layer perceptron, each node in the second layer indicates whether the input pattern lies in a particular region. Each node in the third layer merges several of these regions in order to construct a bigger region. In general, the layers in a perceptron network can be viewed as the levels of a clustering tree. At each level of a clustering tree, each node represents a class of input patterns in which every input belongs to at least one of its children nodes.

Training Multilayer Perceptrons. Multilayer perceptrons are enhanced versions of single-layer perceptrons. As shown in Figure 9.16, these models have several layers of perceptrons, including one input layer, one output layer, and several *hidden* layers. The outputs of one layer are connected to the inputs of the next layer. To increase the representation capability of these networks, a sigmoid activation function and continuous-valued inputs are often used.

Kolmogorov's mapping neural network existence theorem [NIE 90] says that any continuous function $f: [0, 1]^n \rightarrow R^m$ (R is set of real numbers) can be represented by a two-layer perceptron having *n inputs*, $2n + 1$ neurons in the input layer, and *m* neurons in the output layer. However, it has still not been shown that the multilayer

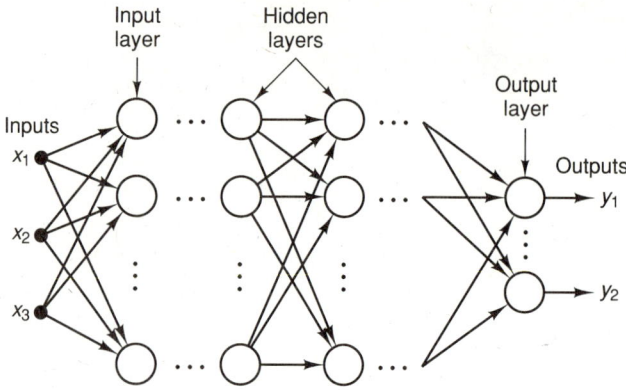

Figure 9.16 Multilayer perceptron.

networks can learn all the functions that they can represent, but in most problems of current interest (like pattern recognition) it has been shown to be possible.

Although it was realized long ago that multilayer perceptrons could realize most of the functions, there was no effective training algorithm for such networks. The reason for this was the difficulty associated with obtaining desired weights for the inputs of the hidden layers. However, in the 1980s this difficulty seemed to be solved as researchers explored new training algorithms. One of these algorithms, which became very popular, is the *back-propagation training algorithm*. This algorithm has been used in many applications and most of the time has produced good results.

Back-propagation Training Rule. Until the mid 1980s there was no proper algorithm or training rule to train multilayer perceptrons. It is very easy to adapt the neurons in the output layer, since the actual response of the network can be compared with the target response for each training input vector. The difficulty lies in changing the weights associated with the neurons in other layers since they do not have a target response. The back-propagation algorithm overcomes this difficulty by propagating the error back through the network.

The back-propagation algorithm was first reported by Werbos [WER 74], then by Parker [PAR 85], and finally by Rumelhart, Hinton, and Williams [RUM 86b]. It is an iterative algorithm in which the actual output gets closer to the target output after each iteration. Each iteration consists of two main passes, *forward pass* and *reverse pass*. The steps in each pass are as follows:

FORWARD PASS

1. Apply an input pattern to the network.
2. Based on the current weights of the network, compute the actual output of the network.

REVERSE PASS

3. Compute the error between the actual output value and the target output value. (Often the mean square error is considered to be the error.)
4. Adjust the weights of the network in such a way that the new weights cause a reduction of the error.

At every iteration of the algorithm, these four steps are repeated for each input pattern. Iterations are repeated until the error for each input pattern becomes less than an acceptable value. In the fourth step (which is the heart of algorithm), the weights are adjusted by propagating the error *backward* in the network. That is, the weights are adjusted layer by layer, starting from the output layer and going toward the first layer. The weights of the output layer are modified similarly to the method used for training an Adaline; that is,

$$w_{ij} = w_{ij} + \Delta w_{ij}$$

where Δw_{ij} amount of change, computed as

$$\Delta w_{ij} = \rho \delta_j y_i$$

w_{ij} = weight from neuron i (in hidden layer) to neuron j (in the output layer).

y_i = output value of neuron i.

δj = error for neuron j in the output layer, computed as $\delta_j = y_j(1-y_j)(t_j-y_j)$.

ρ = learning rate.

y_j = output value of the output neuron j.

t_j = target value for the output neuron j.

Adjusting the weights in the hidden layers involves a little more computation than for the output layer. The only difference is in the computation of the neuron error. In this case the error for a particular hidden layer l is evaluated as

$$\delta_j = y_j(1-y_j)(\sum_{m} \delta_m w_{jm}).$$
neurons in layer $l+1$

For each hidden layer, the error δ is calculated in the same way. The errors of one layer are propagated to the preceding layer. This process continues until the error propagates through the first layer.

The amount of change in the weights of each hidden layer is computed similarly to the output layer case, that is,

$$\Delta w_{ij} = \rho \delta_j y_i$$

However, for the first layer, the output y_i should be substituted by x_i:

$$\Delta w_{ij} = \rho \delta_j x_i$$

In the preceding algorithm, the method used to update the connections is called *on-line* updating. In on-line updating the weight changes are applied after each input pattern is presented. Another option, called *batch* updating, is also used for changing the weights. In batch updating the weight changes are accumulated and applied after *all* patterns have been run through the network. The effect of batch updating is to average the weight changes over the whole set of patterns, thus achieving a smoother movement in weight space. It should be noted that the learning rule for the back-propagation algorithm is derived under the assumption that batch updating is used. However, in many cases it is not practical to provide storage for the accumulation of the weight changes until the whole set is processed; especially if specialized VLSI hardware is used, it is much more convenient to use on-line updating instead.

Neither of these two update modes is superior to the other in terms of speed of convergence; generally, approximately the same number of iterations is needed to train the network in the two modes. This does not mean that the weight change dynamics are the same; it can happen that in one mode the learning process converges, while in the other mode it does not.

In the following, an example is given to clarify the steps of the back-propagation algorithm when using on-line updating.

XOR example. Consider the problem of implementing the XOR function. The activation function for each neuron is the sigmoid function. The output of a sigmoid function can reach the values of 0 and 1 only when the weights are infinitely large. Therefore, it is better to expect outputs other than 0 and 1 from the network. As a result, the truth table has to be changed slightly for the training process. The modified truth table is given in Figure 9.17.

A two-layer perceptron model to implement the XOR with three neurons is shown in Figure 9.18. The network has nine variable weights, as shown.

To start the training, the weights are assigned random numbers in the range [-0.2, 0.2]. The first input pattern is picked (i.e., $x_1 = 0.1$, $x_2 = 0.1$) and applied to the network. The learning coefficient is taken to be 0.5. Let the initial weights be:

$$w_{11} = -0.13, \quad w_{21} = -0.16, \quad w_1 = 0.18,$$
$$w_{12} = 0.15, \quad w_{22} = 0.02, \quad w_2 = -0.18,$$
$$w_{13} = -0.09, \quad w_{23} = 0.10, \quad w_3 = 0.08.$$

The output of neuron N_1 is

$$y_1 = \text{sigmoid}[w_{11} * x_1 + w_{21} * x_2 + (-1.0) * (w_1)]$$

Inputs		Output
x_1	x_2	t
0.1	0.1	0.1
0.1	0.9	0.9
0.9	0.1	0.9
0.9	0.9	0.1

Figure 9.17 Modified truth table for XOR function.

Sec. 9.2 Neural Networks

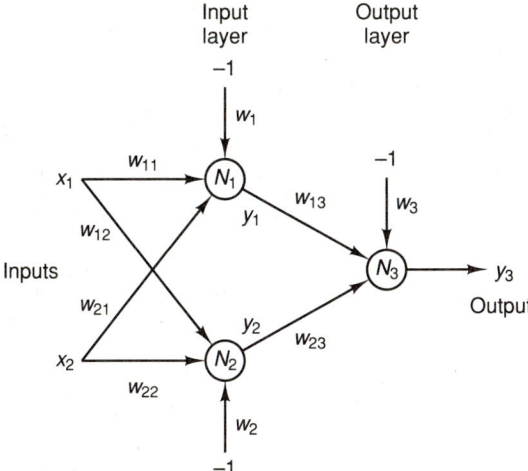

Figure 9.18 Perceptron model for XOR problem.

$$= \text{sigmoid}[(-0.13) * (0.1) + (-0.16) * (0.1) + (-1.0) * (0.18)]$$
$$= \text{sigmoid}[-2.090\text{E}-01] = 1/(1 + e^{2.090\text{E}-01}) = 4.479\text{E}-01.$$

Similarly, the output of neuron N_2 is

$$y_2 = \text{sigmoid}[w_{12} * x_1 + w_{22} * x_2 + (-1.0) * (w_2)]$$
$$= \text{sigmoid}[(0.15) * (0.1) + (0.02) * (0.1) + (-1.0) * (-0.18)]$$
$$= \text{sigmoid}[1.970\text{E}-01] = 1/(1 + e^{-1.970\text{E}-01}) = 5.491\text{E}-01.$$

Finally, the output of the network is

$$y_3 = \text{sigmoid}[w_{13} * y_1 + w_{23} * y_2 + (-1.0) * (w_3)]$$
$$= \text{sigmoid}[(-0.09) * (4.479\text{E}-01) + (0.10) * (5.491\text{E}-01) + (-1.0) * (0.08)]$$
$$= \text{sigmoid}[-6.541\text{E}-02] = 1/(1 + e^{6.541\text{E}-02}) = 4.837\text{E}-01.$$

This represents a simple calculation for the output of the network. Now the error signals can be calculated starting from the outermost layer. Neuron N_3 is an output neuron. The error signal for this neuron is

$$\delta_3 = y_3(1-y_3)(t-y_3),$$

where y_3 is the actual output and t is the target output. Therefore,

$$\delta_3 = 4.837\text{E}-01 * (1.0 - 4.837\text{E}-01) * (0.1 - 4.837\text{E}-01) = -9.581\text{E}-02.$$

Now, the weights of w_{13}, w_{23}, and w_3 can be updated. The new weights are

$$w_{13} = w_{13} + \Delta w_{13} = w_{13} + \rho y_1 \delta_3$$
$$= -0.09 + [0.5 * (4.479\text{E}-01) * (-9.581\text{E}-02)] = -1.115\text{E}-01,$$
$$w_{23} = w_{23} + \Delta w_{23} = w_{23} + \rho y_2 \delta_3$$

$$= 0.10 + [0.5 * (5.491\text{E-}01) * (-9.581\text{E-}02)] = 7.370\text{E-}02,$$
$$w_3 = w_3 + \Delta w_3 = w_3 + \rho * (-1.0) * \delta_3$$
$$= 0.08 + [0.5 * (-1.0) * (-9.581\text{E-}02)] = 1.279\text{E-}01.$$

To calculate the weight changes for the hidden layer, the error must be propagated back toward the input. As such, the error signal for neuron N_1 becomes:

$$\delta_1 = y_1(1 - y_1)(\delta_3 w_{13})$$
$$= [(4.479\text{E-}01) * (1.0 - 4.479\text{E-}01)][(-9.581\text{E-}02) * (-1.115\text{E-}01)]$$
$$= 2.641\text{E-}03.$$

The error δ_1 is used to update the weights coming from the inputs to the neuron N_1. The new weights are:

$$w_{11} = w_{11} + \Delta w_{11} = w_{11} + \rho \delta_1 x_1$$
$$= -0.13 + [0.5 * (2.641\text{E-}03) * 0.1] = -1.299\text{E}-01$$
$$w_{21} = w_{21} + \Delta w_{21} = w_{21} + \rho \delta_1 x_2$$
$$= -0.16 + [0.5 * (2.641\text{E-}03) * 0.1] = -1.599\text{E}-01$$
$$w_1 = w_1 + \Delta w_1 = w_1 + \rho \delta_1 (-1.0)$$
$$= 0.18 + [0.5 * (2.641\text{E-}03) * (-1.0)] = 1.787\text{E}-01$$

The error signal for neuron N_2 becomes

$$\delta_2 = y_2(1 - y_2)(\delta_3 w_{23})$$
$$= [(5.491\text{E-}01) * (1.0 - 5.491\text{E}-01)][(-9.581\text{E}-02) * (7.370\text{E}-02)]$$
$$= -1.748\text{E}-03.$$

Thus the weights w_{12}, w_{22}, and w_2 become

$$w_{12} = w_{12} + \Delta w_{12} = w_{12} + \rho \delta_2 x_1$$
$$= 0.15 + [0.5 * (-1.748\text{E}-03) * 0.1] = 1.499\text{E}-01,$$
$$w_{22} = w_{22} + \Delta w_{22} = w_{22} + \rho \delta_2 x_2$$
$$= 0.02 + [0.5 * (-1.748\text{E}-03) * 0.1] = 1.991\text{E}-02,$$
$$w_2 = w_2 + \Delta w_2 = w_2 + \rho \delta_2 (-1.0)$$
$$= -0.18 + [0.5 * (-1.748\text{E}-03) * (-1.0)] = -1.791\text{E}-01.$$

Using this set of weights, a new output value for the network can be found. Performing the first pass of the back-propagation algorithm gives $y_3 = 4.657\text{E-}01$, which means that the new output is closer to the target output. In the next iteration the second pattern (i.e., $x_1 = 0.1$, $x_2 = 0.9$) is inputted to the network and the weights are updated with new error signals.

This procedure is repeated until the mean square error for each input vector becomes less than a small number (say 0.1). [The mean square error is defined as $(t-y_3)^2$.] The network is then said to be trained for the *XOR* function; that is, the final set of weights of the network will be such that it will give the correct response (output) for each input vector. One such set of weights is shown in Figure 9.19. However, this set of weights is not unique, and there could be many other solutions.

Comments on the back-propagation algorithm. Rumelhart and McClelland [RUM 86a] have expressed the following suggestions for the back-propagation rule:

1. When the initial weights are random and small, the network has a better chance to converge to an optimal solution without getting trapped in local minima.
2. Increasing the learning rate ρ will speed up the back-propagation algorithm. However, ρ should be kept small to avoid diverging oscillations.

The back-propagation algorithm follows the slope of the error surface downward, adjusting the weights until a minimum is reached. However, networks with hidden layers and nonlinear activation functions may have local minima in the error function, causing the algorithm to fail.

In the mid 1980s the back-propagation algorithm was very popular, but, it has recently lost this popularity. Kosko [KOS 92] has mentioned several reasons for this. One is that the back-propagation algorithm has failed to converge to a local minimum even when it was trained with nonlocal information. Also, White [WHI 89a, KOS 92] has shown that the back-propagation algorithm reduces to a special case of stochastic approximation and that there is nothing new about this algorithm. In fact, the back-propagation algorithm simply offers an efficient (parallel) way to implement the estimated gradient descent algorithm.

Another disadvantage of the back-propagation algorithm is that it requires supervision and a lengthy training period. It also requires synchronization between the neurons, which is hard to maintain.

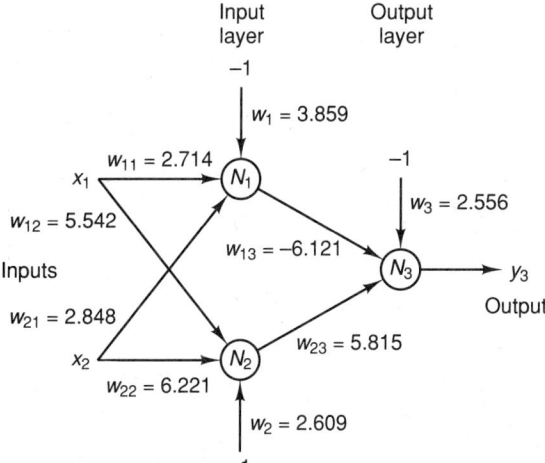

Figure 9.19 Final values of the weights in the XOR mode.

Hopfield network. Hopfield has worked extensively in the field of recurrent neural networks [HOP 82, HOP 84, HOP 85, HOP 86]. Hence, the configurations that he worked with are now called *Hopfield networks*. Hopfield networks can be used to solve certain optimization problems or as an associative memory. Figure 9.20 shows the general structure of a Hopfield network.

Notice that the output values of the neurons are fed back to the inputs. In Hopfield's earlier work [HOP 82, HOP 84], each neuron i has a simple threshold activation function with a fixed threshold value T_i. The network changes state according to the following algorithm. Each neuron changes the value of its output according to the following rule:

$$y_i = \begin{cases} 1 & \text{if } \sum_{j=1}^{n} w_{ji} y_j + x_i > T_i \\ y_i & \text{if } \sum_{j=1}^{n} w_{ji} y_j + x_i = T_i \\ 0 & \text{if } \sum_{j=1}^{n} w_{ji} y_j + x_i < T_i \end{cases}$$

Although each neuron randomly and asynchronously reevaluates its output, the algorithm requires that all neurons change states at the same average rate. Also notice that the algorithm does not have a learning law for adjusting the input weights. The weights are assumed to be determined in advance. For example, to use the Hopfield network as a content addressable memory, the following steps must be performed.

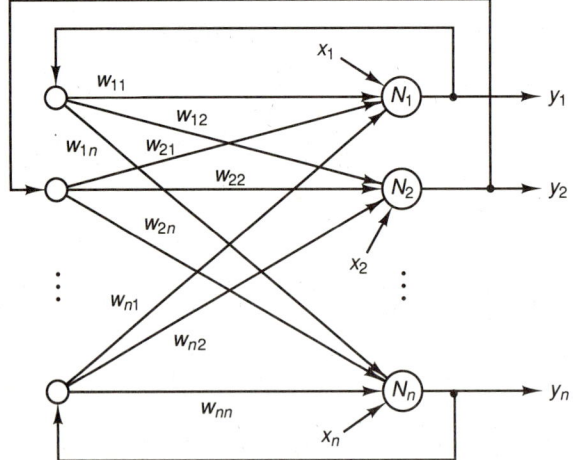

Figure 9.20 A Hopfield network.

Sec. 9.2 Neural Networks

Step 1. Determine connection weights. To store a set of known patterns $Y^1, Y^2, \ldots, Y^m$, the weights can be computed as

$$w_{ij} = \begin{cases} \sum_{s=1}^{m} (2y_i^s - 1)(2y_j^s - 1) & \text{if } i \neq j \\ 0 & \text{if } i = j \end{cases}$$

Step 2. Initialize the network's outputs with the unknown input pattern Y^s, that is, $y_i = y_i^s$ for $i = 1$ to n.

Step 3. Calculate the new output of each neuron and feed it back to the network. Repeat this process until a stable state is obtained.

A stable state is said to be obtained when no more outputs change on successive iterations. The pattern specified by the output values in a stable state represents one of the stored known patterns that matches (or is close to) the unknown input pattern.

Each neuron has two states, 0 or 1. Therefore, a network with n neurons has 2^n distinct states. The network moves from one vertex of an n-dimensional hypercube to another till it reaches a stable state. Hopfield [HOP 82] and Cohen and Grossberg [COH 83] proved that this type of network converges to a stable state when the weight matrix is symmetric and has zeros on its main diagonal; that is, $w_{ij} = w_{ji}$ and $w_{ii} = 0$ for all i and j.

This convergent property can be proved by considering an energy function that never increases with consecutive iterations in the network. Eventually, this function reaches a local minimum, ensuring that the network is stable. *Lyapunov functions* have this property; one such function is defined as

$$E = -1/2 \sum_{i=1}^{n} \sum_{j=1}^{n} w_{ij} y_i y_j - \sum_{i=1}^{n} x_i y_i + \sum_{i=1}^{n} T_i y_i$$

where T_i denotes the threshold of neuron i.

To show that this function decreases with every iteration, let us consider the change in energy ΔE due to a change in some neuron k.

$$\Delta E = E - E',$$

where E is the present energy value and E' is the previous value.

$$\Delta E = -1/2 \sum_{i=1}^{n} \sum_{j=1}^{n} w_{ij} y_i y_j - \sum_{i=1}^{n} x_i y_i + \sum_{i=1}^{n} T_i y_i -$$

$$(-1/2 \sum_{i=1}^{n} \sum_{j=1}^{n} w_{ij} y'_i y'_j - \sum_{i=1}^{n} x_i y'_i + \sum_{i=1}^{n} T_i y'_i).$$

Since $y_i = y'_i$ for all $i \neq k$, and also $w_{ij} = w_{ji}$ and $w_{ii} = 0$, ΔE can be reduced to:

$$\Delta E = -(y_k \sum_{j=1}^{n} w_{kj} y_j) - x_k y_k + T_k y_k + (y'_k \sum_{j=1}^{n} w_{kj} y'_j) + x_k y'_k - T_k y'_k$$

$$= -(y_k - y'_k)((\sum_{j=1}^{n} w_{kj} y_j) + x_k - T_k)$$

$$= -\Delta y_k(u_k), \text{ where}$$

$$\Delta y_k = y_k - y'_k$$

$$u_k = \sum_{j=1}^{n} w_{kj} y_j + x_k - T_k$$

In the preceding expression, Δy_k and u_k always have the same sign; that is ΔE is always negative. When the output value of the neuron k changes from 0 to 1 ($y'_k = 0$ and $y_k = 1$), Δy_k and u_k both become positive. This is because, according to the rules for changing output values, y_k is 1 only when u_k is positive. On the other hand, when the neuron k changes from 1 to 0, Δy_k and u_k both become negative. Thus, any change in E is negative. Since E is bounded, the algorithm leads the network to a stable state that does not change further with time.

Based on the earlier work, Hopfield later represents a model in which inputs and outputs are continuous variables [HOP 84, HOP 86]. The activation function is a continuous and monotone-increasing function like a sigmoid function. The superiority of this model is that it has an electrical circuit implementation, as shown in Figure 9.21.

The amplifiers in the circuit serve as the neurons. The resistors represent the weights and connect each neuron's output to the inputs of all the others. Ordinary positive-valued resistors can be used as weights in spite of the fact that the weights can be negative because the amplifiers have both inverting and noninverting outputs. Such a circuit with symmetric connections ($w_{ij} = w_{ji}$) converges to a stable state that is one of the local minima of the energy function:

$$E = -1/2 \sum_{i=1}^{n} \sum_{j=1}^{n} w_{ij} y_i y_j - \sum_{i=1}^{n} x_i y_i \qquad (9.1)$$

where x_i is the ith component of external input.

Hopfield networks can be used to compute solutions to specific optimization problems. One problem to which Hopfield and Tank [HOP 86] applied their model is a classic optimization problem, the traveling salesman problem, (which is defined as finding the minimum distance of a valid tour of n cities starting from a given city, where a valid tour is defined as visiting each city exactly once.) To map this problem onto the neural network, they have chosen a representation scheme in which the final location of any individual city is specified by the output states of a set of n neurons. Therefore, to represent a complete tour, a total of n^2 neurons, displayed as an nXn square array, has been used. To enable the n^2 neurons to represent a complete tour, the network is described by an energy function in which the lowest energy state (the most stable state of the network) corresponds to the best path. (See [HOP 86] for more detail.) Although, Hopfield networks can be used as special-purpose hardwares for solving certain optimization problems, it turns out they may not even be able to provide local minimum solutions under certain conditions.

Example of a Hopfield Network Application. A Hopfield network can be used for finding a solution to the placement problem in VLSI design. The objective of

Sec. 9.2   Neural Networks

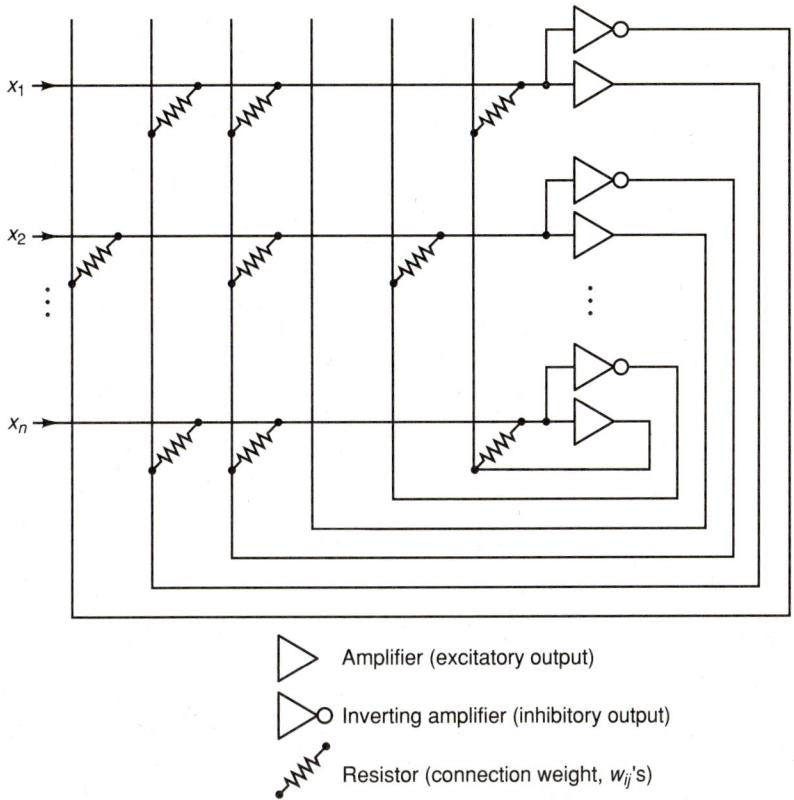

Figure 9.21   General structure of Hopfield's analog circuit.

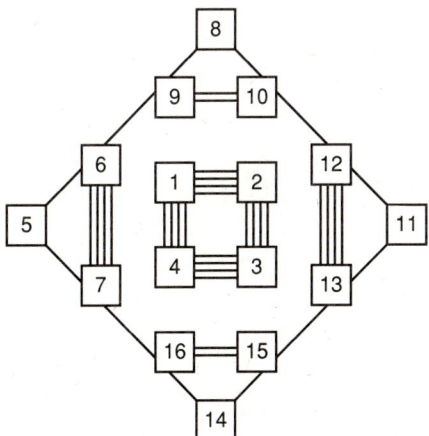

Figure 9.22   A set of cells with their interconnections.

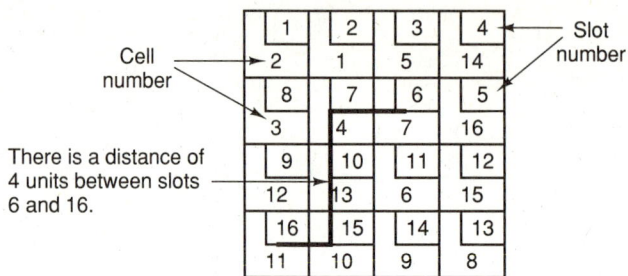

Figure 9.23 A placement solution for the cells of Figure 9.22.

the placement problem is to determine an optimal position on the chip for a set of cells in a way that the total occupied area and total estimated length of connections are minimized. Given that the main cause of delay in a chip is excessive length of the connections, providing shorter connections becomes an important objective in placing a set of cells. A special case of the placement problem is when all the cells are squares and have the same area. In this case the chip area is divided into slots, one for each cell. Here we consider this special case and assume that there are n^2 cells that should be placed in a $n \times n$ slots chip area. Let c_{ij} denote the number of connections between cell i and cell j. Also, let d_{km} denote the distance between slot k and slot m. The d_{km} is the minimum distance from the center of cell k to the center of m considering only horizontal and vertical segments (see Figures 9.22 and 9.23.)

To represent a solution for this problem, we use a neural structure in which the slot location of any individual cell is specified by the output states of a set of $n^2 \times n^2$ neurons. This structure is similar to the one used in [DAT 90]. As an example, let us

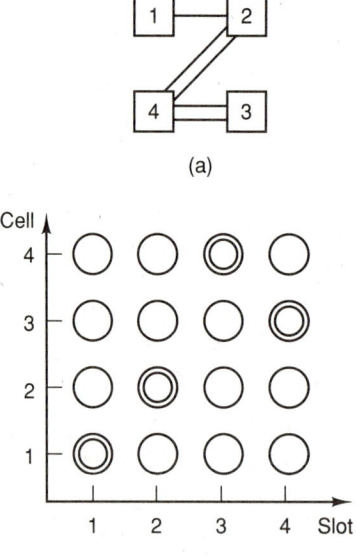

Figure 9.24 Neuron structure for four cells.

Sec. 9.2 Neural Networks

consider the cells given in Figure 9.24a. Since the problem has four cells, it requires a total of 16 neurons. Figure 9.24b represents a neuron structure for this placement problem.

For example, the activated neuron at position (2, 2) (represented by a double circle) represents the assignment of cell 2 to slot 2. In general, an optimum solution must meet (satisfy) the following conditions:

1. Each cell is allocated to exactly one slot.
2. Each slot is assigned to exactly one cell.
3. Total wire length is minimized.

Conditions 1 and 2 mean that, in the array of neurons, exactly one neuron is high in each row (with the rest of them being low), and also exactly one neuron is high in each column (with all others being low). This can be written in terms of two energy functions, one specifying that the sum of neurons in a row (column) is 1 and the second specifying that the cross-product of neurons in a row (column) is 0. The last condition can be written in terms of an energy function that represents the total wire length. Hence

$$E = \frac{A}{2}\sum_i \left[\left(\sum_j y_{ij}\right) - 1\right]^2 \text{, sum of neurons in each row} = 1,$$

$$+ \frac{A}{2}\sum_j \left[\left(\sum_i y_{ij}\right) - 1\right]^2 \text{, sum of neurons in each column} = 1,$$

$$+ \frac{B}{2}\sum_k \sum_i \sum_{j \neq k} y_{ki} y_{kj} \text{, cross-product of neurons in a row} = 0,$$

$$+ \frac{B}{2}\sum_i \sum_k \sum_{j \neq i} y_{ki} y_{ji} \text{, cross-product of neurons in a column} = 0,$$

$$+ \frac{D}{2}\sum_i \sum_k y_{ik} \left(\sum_{j \neq i} \sum_{m \neq k} y_{jm} c_{ij} d_{km}\right) \text{, minimize wire length,} \qquad (9.2)$$

where y_{ij} output of the neuron in row i and column j,

$\quad c_{ij}$ weight of the connection between cell i and cell j,
$\quad d_{km}$ distance between the slot k and slot m,
$\quad A, B, D$ weights for each energy function.

(*Note*: All the summations are to n^2, where n^2 is the number of cells.)

As mentioned before the general energy function for the stable state with a local minimum is

$$E = -1/2 \sum_i \sum_j w_{ij} y_i y_j - \sum_i x_i y_i.$$

In this equation the neurons are labeled in a linear fashion. To address the neurons in a two-dimensional space, the equation can be represented as

$$E = -1/2 \sum_{i=1}^{n^2} \sum_{j=1}^{n^2} \sum_{k=1}^{n^2} \sum_{m=1}^{n^2} w_{ij,km} y_{ij} y_{km} - \sum_{i=1}^{n^2} \sum_{j=1}^{n^2} x_{ij} y_{ij}. \tag{9.3}$$

Equations (9.2) and (9.3) can now be equated to find the weights $w_{ij,km}$ and the bias x_{ij}. By comparing the coefficients of each term in these equations, the values of all w's and x's can be defined as follows:

$$\begin{aligned} w_{ij,km} &= -2A, & \text{if } i = k \text{ and } j = m \\ &= -(A+B), & \text{if } i = k \text{ and } j \neq m \\ &= -(A+B), & \text{if } i \neq k \text{ and } j = m \\ &= -Dc_{ik}d_{jm}, & \text{otherwise,} \\ x_{ij} &= 4A, \text{ for every } i \text{ and every } j. \end{aligned}$$

In practice, to simulate the preceding network on a uniprocessor, the following steps were implemented:

1. Initialize the entries of the weighting matrix W, the vector X, and vector U. Set the interval Δt and the initial maximum number of iteration.
2. For j = 1 to (maximum number of iterations),

{
    a. For i = 1 to N --N denotes number of neurons.

$$u_i = u_i + \left(\sum_{i=1}^{N} \sum_{j=1}^{N} w_{ij} y_i + x_i \right) \Delta t$$

    b. For i = 1 to N
        y_i = 1/2[1 + tanh(u_i/α)]

}

To run this code for the placement problem, which was presented in Figure 9.22, the initial values $A = 1000$, $B = 200$, $D = 40$, $\alpha = 0.05$, and $\Delta t = 0.0001$ were used. Also, initially, random numbers between 0.48 and 0.52 were assigned to every u_i. After 149 iterations, the code was able to produce an optimum solution with the total wire length of 42 (see Figure 9.23).

After running several examples, it was determined that for most small-sized problems a Hopfield network is able to obtain good solutions. However, for larger problems, apart from the known problems of long simulation times, the code is not able to find a solution in many cases.

9.2.3 Implementation of ANNs

In recent years, several neural chips have been developed. However, often neural network models are simulated by software. Whenever an ANN is simulated by software, it is flexible, but it is slow. Therefore, the most promising approach for implementing an ANN is through hardware implementation. In fact, one main reason that ANNs are becoming popular is that they can be realized in a VLSI chip using current technology.

In general, three different technologies are available for hardware implementation of an ANN: *electronic, optical,* and *electro-optical.* Electronic technology itself can be divided into three different implementations: *analog, digital,* and *hybrid.*

In an analog implementation, the quantities can take a value within a fixed range (for example, between 0 and 1). Although this type of implementation reduces the design complexity, it is less accurate and often is unable to obtain an accuracy level of 6 bits. (This is mainly due to the low level of the accuracy of resistors). Many applications require an accuracy level of more than 6 bits.

In contrast to analog designs, the quantities in digital implementation take digital values. The advantage of having digital values is that they provide greater accuracy than analog designs do. However, they often require more area on the chip. A hybrid implementation contains digital and analog elements in order to gain the advantages of both designs.

The connectivity between neurons poses serious problems for electronic circuits because of the delay and space on the chip. Optical technology promises a way to solve this problem. By interconnecting neurons with light beams, no insulation is required between signal paths since light rays can pass through each other without interacting. Also, the signal paths can be made in three dimensions. In addition, all signal paths can be operating simultaneously, which provides a tremendous data rate. Finally, the weights can be stored as holograms. Although optical technology offers an ideal solution in theory, many practical problems are associated with it, the most pressing of which is that the physical characteristics of the optical devices are not compatible with the requirements of neural networks.

In an electro-optical implementation, the interconnections are made optically. Since ANNs are highly interconnected, this method becomes an attractive implementation alternative.

Among the preceding methods, the electronic is currently the most practical. In particular, digital electronics has advanced significantly in recent years. Given that the current state of digital technology is the result of research and development investments of hundreds of billions of dollars over several decades, it would be reasonable to assume that the same level of development for the other two technologies is unlikely to happen in the near future.

In summary, ANNs may not be able to accomplish the wide variety of tasks that researchers have projected. Perhaps, in the near future, they will become more available as special-purpose devices for pattern recognition and home appliances.

9.3 MULTIPLE-VALUED LOGIC

For many years, researchers have questioned the use of the binary system in today's computers. They argue that it does not fully utilize interconnection wires between components, despite the fact that wires realize a large part of any computer system. Interconnections comprise a major part (about 70%) of any VLSI chip. However, by

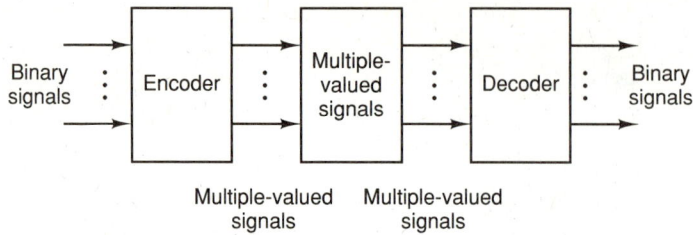

Figure 9.25 Use of a multiple-valued logic circuit as a component in a binary-valued system.

letting each wire carry more than two levels of logic, a significant savings in chip area can be achieved.

The multiple-valued logic circuits allow signals with more than two values. In general, for an r-valued system (radix r), the values can be labeled as 0, 1, 2, ..., and $r - 1$. For example, in a four-valued system (also called quaternary) the possible values are 0, 1, 2, and 3. Usually, the radix r is chosen to be a power of 2, such as 4, 8, and 16. This choice makes the conversion between binary-valued logic and multiple-valued logic very easy and efficient. Given the fact that binary-valued logic currently dominates the design of digital systems and that at present multiple-valued logic can only be used as a subpart of a system, code conversions between binary- and multiple-valued signals are required. Figure 9.25 represents how a multiple-valued circuit can be embedded in a system with binary components. The encoder circuit converts binary inputs to multiple-valued outputs. The decoder circuit converts multiple-valued inputs to binary outputs.

Often binary design techniques (such as a truth table) are used in designing the multiple-valued circuits. The only major difference is that more values must be considered in a multiple-valued design. For example, the truth table for the two-variable, four-valued half-adder shown in Figure 9.26 has 16 rows [SMI 88]. The half-adder adds two-input signals (denoted as A and B), producing a sum signal (denoted as S) and a carry signal (denoted as C).

Based on the available technology, many designs have been presented for the implementation of multiple-valued circuits. These designs are based on MOS technology, CMOS technology, emitter-coupled logic (ECL), integrated injection logic, (I^2L), and charge-coupled device (CCD) technology. One proposed method for implementing a multiple-valued function is based on the use of a universal building block called the T-gate [KAM 87]. As shown in Figure 9.27a, the T-gate is actually a quaternary four-input multiplexer. The function of a T-gate can be defined as

$$Z = x_i, \text{ if } s = i,$$

where s is a four-valued selecting input signal that takes on the values 0, 1, 2, and 3. For $s = 0$, input x_0 is selected; for $s = 1$, input x_1 is selected, and so on. Each input x_i is also a four-valued signal with values 0, 1, 2, and 3. Figure 9.27b presents a more detailed schematic of a T-gate. In this figure, the pass transistors are used as switches

Sec. 9.3 Multiple-Valued Logic

Input		Output	
A	B	C	S
0	0	0	0
0	1	0	1
0	2	0	2
0	3	0	3
1	0	0	1
1	1	0	2
1	2	0	3
1	3	1	0
2	0	0	2
2	1	0	3
2	2	1	0
2	3	1	1
3	0	0	3
3	1	1	0
3	2	1	1
3	3	1	2

Figure 9.26 Truth table of a half adder for four-valued inputs A and B.

for connecting an input signal to the output signal. An input signal appears at the output if the gate voltage of the corresponding pass transistor becomes V_{DD} (i.e., high). The gate voltage of each pass transistor is controlled by a gate, called a *literal gate*. The output voltages of literal gates a, b, c, and d become V_{DD} if the logical value s is 0, 1, 2, and 3, respectively. Otherwise, these voltages are zero. The logical values 0, 1, 2, and 3 of the select line correspond to voltages 0, 2, 4, and 6 volts, respectively. Each literal gate consists of a few transistors (two to three NMOS transistors), and its output increases based on a certain input voltage. For example, when signal s is at 4 volts, the output voltage of literal gate c becomes high, while the output of other literal gates remains low. (This is done by employing transistors with different threshold voltages in different literal gates; for more detail, see [KAM 87].)

The T-gate can be used to design any combinational or sequential circuit. For example, Figure 9.28 presents a block diagram for the sum output(s) of a half-adder with four-valued inputs A and B. The implementation follows the half-adder truth table. Note that the values for s in the truth table are given as the inputs to the T-gates T_1, T_2, T_3, and T_4. One of these inputs appears on the output s, depending on the values of A and B. Although the T-gate provides a structural and generic tool for designing multiple-valued circuits, it often does not lead to an efficient and minimizing design.

In summary, multiple-valued logic may provide a good solution for certain applications, such as memory design, for which it is desirable to reduce the number of lines for parallel transmission of large amounts of data [SMI 88]. In general, multiple-valued logic leads to a reduction in the number of pins. It also reduces the interconnection complexity and increases the data-processing capability per unit area of a chip [KAM 88]. However, multiple-valued logic should not be considered as a competitor to binary-valued logic. In fact, multiple-valued circuits should be used as sub-circuits in the binary-valued world.

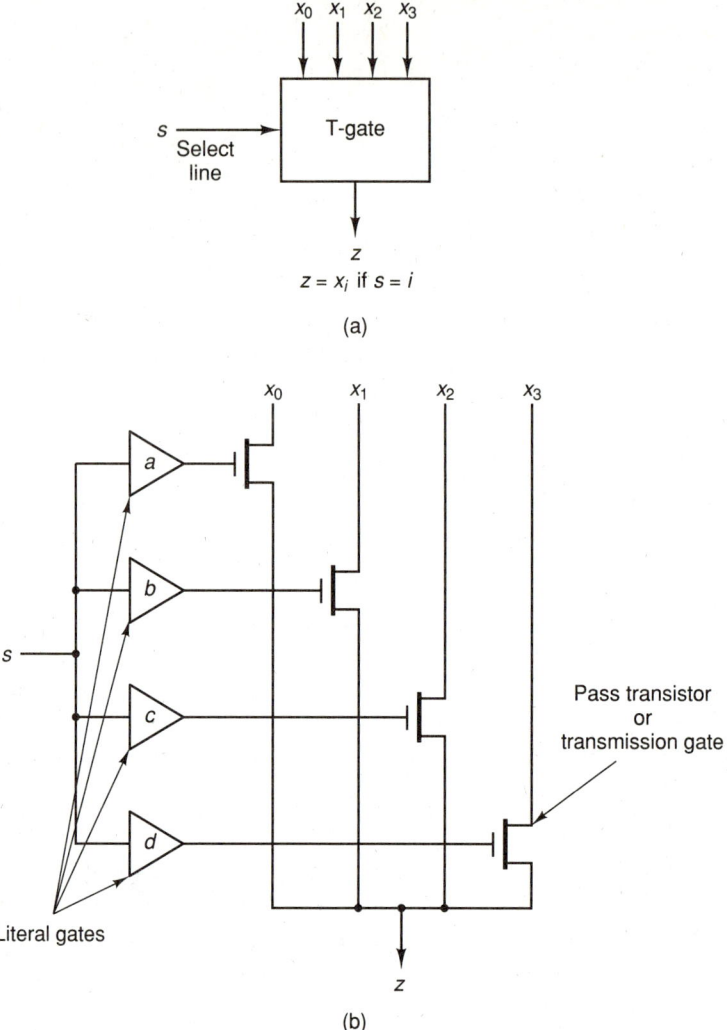

Figure 9.27 Block and circuit diagram of a T-gate.

9.4 FUZZY LOGIC

The basic idea underlying fuzzy logic was suggested by Zadeh [ZAD 65, ZAD 68, ZAD 72]. Zadeh proposed this logic to enhance the use of artifical intelligence (AI) techniques in certain areas such as speech recognition. An assumption is made that the reader is familiar with artificial intelligence theory. However, a brief discussion is given next to show the relationships between traditional AI and fuzzy logic.

There are generally two groups within the study of AI. Those who believe AI should be based on heuristic techniques, and those who believe AI should be based on classical two-valued logic (true or false). Heuristics can best be described as a rule of

Sec. 9.4 Fuzzy Logic   375

thumb to guide one's action. That is, we wish to attain a goal, and a number of possible actions are available at one point in time. A heuristic technique is used to decide which is the best action to achieve this goal. A game of chess is an excellent example. The goal is to checkmate the opponent. At any point in the game, one or more possible moves could be taken. A heuristic is used to decide which move is best to achieve the goal.

The classical two-valued logic represents the meaning of a proposition as true or false. It is able to combine simple propositions through the use of connectives (such as "and," "or," and "not"), into more complex ones. For example, using the "and" connective, the following two propositions

All doctors have a college education.

Brian is a doctor.

can be combined as

All doctors have a college education **and** *Brian is a doctor.*

Whether this new proposition is true or false depends not only on the truth of each simple proposition, but also on the connective "and." For if we change the connective to "or," we may have completely different results. Several propositions may be used to perform reasoning. A simple example of reasoning can be

All doctors have a college education **and** *Brian is a doctor.*

Does Brian have a college education?

The answer is, of course, *true*.

Zadeh believes that we need logic in AI, but the kind of logic we need is not classical logic; it is fuzzy logic. This is because classical logic cannot represent a proposi-

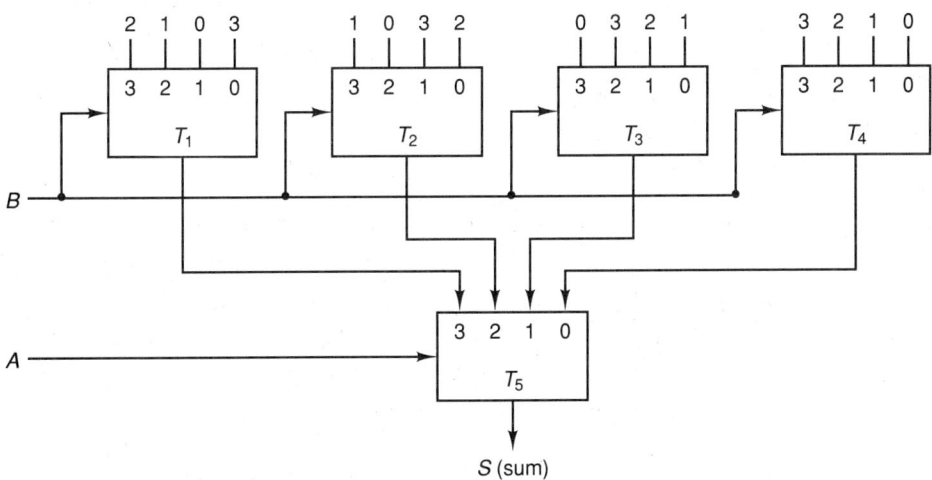

Figure 9.28 Block diagram for the sum output of a half-adder using T-gates.

tion with imprecise meaning. However, in fuzzy logic, which may be viewed as an extension of multiple-valued logic, a proposition may be true or false or have an intermediate value (such as very true). For example, classical two-valued logic cannot address the following questions, but fuzzy logic can:

1. *Most of those who are doctors have high incomes.*
   Brian is a doctor. Is it true to say that he has a high income?
   (Answer: maybe)
2. *Tomoko is much nicer than most of her friends.*
   How nice is Tomoko?
   (Answer: very nice)

In general, fuzzy logic is concerned with formal principles of approximate reasoning, while classical two-valued logic is concerned with formal principles of reasoning [ZAD 88]. Classical two-valued logic considers classes that have sharp boundaries, such as male or female, single or married, and boy or girl. In this way, an object is either a member of a class or not a member of a class. In contrast, fuzzy logic considers classes that do not have sharp boundaries, such as tall, short, nice, and intelligent. Here, a degree indicates the grade of membership of an object to a class. Usually, we have degrees between 0 and 1. For example, we can say Steve is tall to the degree 0.8.

9.4.1 Fuzzy Sets

Let X be a collection of objects denoted generically by x; that is, $X = \{x\}$. A fuzzy set A in X is a set of ordered pairs:

$$A = \{(x, f_A(x)) \mid x \in X\},$$

where $f_A(x)$ is the *membership function* that associates with each $x \in X$ a real number in the interval [0, 1]. The value $f_A(x)$ indicates the grade of membership (or degree of truth) of x in A. When $f_A(x) = 1$, it means that x strongly belongs to A. As the value of $f_A(x)$ gets close to zero, the grade of membership of x in A becomes lower. A value of zero indicates x does not belong to A. (Often, the objects with 0 degree of membership are not listed in A.)

As an example of a fuzzy set, suppose that a fashion dresser wants to characterize the types of models she wishes to have. One characteristic of an ideal model is her height. Let $X = \{5, 5.4, 5.6, 5.7, 6, 6.2, 6.5\}$, represented in feet, be the set of heights of available models. Then the fuzzy set A, denoting the desirable model's height, may be defined as

$$A = \{(5, 0.1), (5.4, 0.4), (5.6, 0.8), (5.7, 1), (6, 0.6), (6.2, 0.4), (6.5, 0.1)\}.$$

For the next example, let X be the set of integers from 0 to 10, that is, $X = \{0, 1, ..., 10\}$. The fuzzy set labeled *small* may be expressed by the membership function

$$f_{small}(x) = \left[1 + \left(\frac{x}{2}\right)^4\right]^{-1}.$$

That is, small = $\{(0, 1), (1, 0.94), (2, 0.5), (3, 0.16), ..., (10, 0.001)\}$

Sec. 9.4   Fuzzy Logic   377

The membership functions should be defined so that they model precisely observed values in the real-world. However, in practice, it is difficult to derive membership functions with such characteristics. In practice, often membership functions are defined based on the data collected from past experiences and a set of well-shaped functions. Some of the commonly used membership functions are

Linear function

$$\begin{aligned} f_L(x) &= 0 & x &\leq a, \\ &= (x-a)/(b-a) & a &\leq x \leq b, \\ &= 1 & x &\geq b. \end{aligned}$$

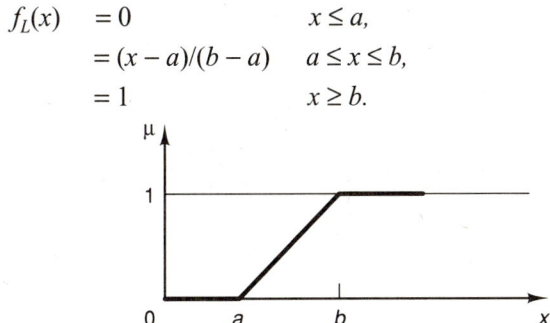

Piecewise linear (or triangular) function

$$\begin{aligned} f_P(x) &= 0 & x &\leq a, \\ &= (x-a)/(b-a) & a &\leq x \leq b, \\ &= (c-x)/(c-b) & b &\leq x \leq c, \\ &= 0 & x &\geq c. \end{aligned}$$

Trapezoidal function

$$\begin{aligned} f_T(x) &= 0 & x &\leq a, \\ &= (x-a)/(b-a) & a &\leq x \leq b, \\ &= 1 & b &\leq x \leq c, \\ &= (d-x)/(d-c) & c &\leq x \leq d, \\ &= 0 & x &\geq d. \end{aligned}$$

S-function

$$f_S(x) = 0 \qquad x \leq a,$$
$$= 2[(x-a)/(c-a)]^2 \quad a \leq x \leq b,$$
$$= 1 - 2[(x-c)/(c-a)]^2 \quad b \leq x \leq c,$$
$$= 1 \qquad x \geq c.$$

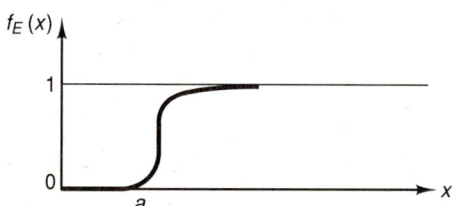

Exponential function

$$f_E(x) = 0 \qquad x \leq a,$$
$$= 1 - e^{-k(x-a)^2} \quad a \leq x,$$

for some $k > 0$.

In the preceding functions a, b, c, and d are some constants, where

$$a \leq b \leq c \leq d.$$

The *complement* of a fuzzy set A is a fuzzy set $\bar{A}$ whose membership function is defined by

$$f_{\bar{A}}(x) = 1 - f_A(x), x \in X.$$

The *union* of two fuzzy sets A and B is a fuzzy set C, written as $C = A \cup B$, whose membership function is defined by

$$f_C(x) = \max \{f_A(x), f_B(x)\}, \qquad x \in X.$$

The *intersection* of two fuzzy sets A and B is a fuzzy set C, written as $C = A \cap B$, whose membership function is defined by

$$f_C(x) = \min \{f_A(x), f_B(x)\}, \qquad x \in X.$$

The fuzzy set C is a *subset* of A, written as $C \subseteq A$, if and only if $f_C(x) \leq f_A(x)$ for all x in X.

The *algebraic sum* of two fuzzy sets A and B is a fuzzy set C, written as $C = A \oplus B$, whose membership function is defined by

$$f_C(x) = f_A(x) + f_B(x) - f_A(x) * f_B(x), \qquad x \in X.$$

Sec. 9.4 Fuzzy Logic

The *algebraic product* of two fuzzy sets A and B is a fuzzy set C, written as $C = A \bullet B$, whose membership function is defined by

$$f_C(x) = f_A(x) * f_B(x), \quad x \in X.$$

The support of a fuzzy set A is a set $S(A)$ such that for every $x \in S(A): f_A(x) > 0$.

For example, let $X = \{5, 5.4, 5.6, 5.7, 6, 6.2, 6.5\}$, $A = \{(5.4, 0.4), (5.7, 1), (6, 0.6), (6.2, 0.4)\}$, and $B = \{(5.4, 0.3), (6.5, 1), (6, 0.5)\}$.

$$\overline{A} = \{(5, 1), (5.4, 0.6), (5.6, 1), (6, 0.4), (6.2, 0.6), (6.5, 1)\},$$

$$A \cup B = \{(5.4, 0.4), (6.5, 1), (5.7, 1), (6, 0.6), (6.2, 0.4)\},$$

$$A \cap B = \{(5.4, 0.3), (6, 0.5)\},$$

$$C \subseteq A = \{(5.4, 0.3), (6, 0.4)\},$$

$$A \bullet B = \{(5.4, 0.12), (6, 0.3)\},$$

$$A^2 = \{(5.4, 0.16), (5.7, 1), (6, 0.36), (6.2, 0.16)\},$$

Fuzzy relation. A fuzzy relation is a fuzzy set defined on the Cartesian product of crisp sets $X_1, X_2, \ldots, X_n$, where tuples $(x_1, x_2, \ldots, x_n)$ may have varying degree of membership within the relation [KLI 88]. When $n = 2$, the relation is called a binary relation. For example, we can define the fuzzy binary relation "very far" on given sets $X = \{$New Delhi, Tokyo$\}$ and $Y = \{$New York, Taipei$\}$ as follows, using real numbers between 0 and 1 as a degree of membership. A degree 1 means that the cities are very far from each other.

$$R(X, Y) = \begin{array}{c} \\ \text{New York} \\ \text{Taipei} \end{array} \begin{array}{cc} \text{New Delhi} & \text{Tokyo} \\ \begin{bmatrix} 0.9 & 1 \\ 0.3 & 0.1 \end{bmatrix} \end{array}$$

Two binary relations can be combined to produce a new binary relation. This process is called composition. Given two binary relations $P(X, Y)$ and $Q(Y, Z)$, their composition $R(X, Z)$ can be represented as

$$R(X, Z) = P(X, Y) \circ Q(Y, Z).$$

The relation $R(X, Z)$ is a subset of the Cartesian product of X and Z, where $(x, z) \in R$ if and only if there exists at least one $y \in Y$ such that $(x, y) \in P$ and $(y, z) \in Q$.

There are different ways for computing the composition of two relations. Among them, the most well known method is the max-min composition. Given $R(X, Z) = P(X, Y) \circ Q(Y, Z)$, the max-min composition can be thought of as the strength of the relational tie between elements of X and Y. In this type of composition, the membership degree for each tuple $(x, y) \in R$ is defined as

$$f_R(x, z) = \max_{y \in Y} \{\min [f_P(x, y), f_Q(y, z)]\} \quad \text{for all } x \in X \text{ and } z \in Z.$$

As an example, let the binary relations $P(x, y)$ and $Q(y, z)$ be defined as follows:

$$P = \begin{array}{c} \\ x_1 \\ x_2 \end{array} \begin{array}{cc} y_1 & y_2 \\ \left[\begin{array}{cc} 0.8 & 0.4 \\ 1 & 0.3 \end{array} \right] \end{array},$$

$$Q = \begin{array}{c} \\ y_1 \\ y_2 \end{array} \begin{array}{cc} z_1 & z_2 \\ \left[\begin{array}{cc} 0.5 & 0.7 \\ 0.1 & 0.9 \end{array} \right] \end{array}.$$

$$f_R(x_1, z_1) = \max \{\min [f_P(x_1, y_1), f_Q(y_1, z_1)],$$
$$\min [f_P(x_1, y_2), f_Q(y_2, z_1)]\} = 0.5.$$
$$f_R(x_1, z_2) = \max \{\min [f_P(x_1, y_1), f_Q(y_1, z_2)],$$
$$\min [f_P(x_1, y_2), f_Q(y_2, z_2)]\} = 0.7$$
$$f_R(x_2, z_1) = \max \{\min [f_P(x_2, y_1), f_Q(y_1, z_1)],$$
$$\min [f_P(x_2, y_2), f_Q(y_2, z_1)]\} = 0.5$$
$$f_R(x_2, z_2) = \max \{\min [f_P(x_2, y_1), f_Q(y_1, z_2)],$$
$$\min [f_P(x_2, y_2), f_Q(y_2, z_2)]\} = 0.7$$

Thus, R can be represented as

$$R = \begin{array}{c} \\ x_1 \\ x_2 \end{array} \begin{array}{cc} z_1 & z_2 \\ \left[\begin{array}{cc} 0.5 & 0.7 \\ 0.5 & 0.7 \end{array} \right] \end{array}.$$

9.4.2 Linguistic Variables and Fuzzy Rules

Two of the main concepts that play an important role in many applications of fuzzy logic are the concepts of *linguistic variable* and *fuzzy if–then rules* [ZAD 73, ZAD 88, ZAD 94]. Linguistic variables are the main concept in exploiting the tolerance for imprecision. A linguistic variable is a variable whose values are words or sentences in a language. For example, height is a linguistic variable when its values are defined to be *tall*, *medium*, and *short*. As shown in Figure 9.29, each of these linguistic values represents a possibility distribution for the height. Each linguistic value is represented as a fuzzy set that is characterized by a membership function. The set of the linguistic values of a linguistic variable is called a *term set*. For example, the term set for linguistic variable age T(age), may be defined as

T(age) = {young, very young, not young, old, very old, not old, extremely old, middle-aged}.

Sec. 9.4 Fuzzy Logic

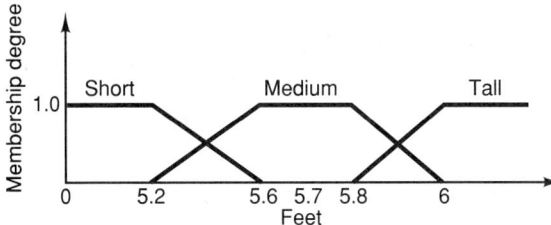

Figure 9.29 Membership functions for the linguistic values short, medium, and tall.

In general, a fuzzy rule can be represented as

if x_1 is A_1 and x_2 is A_2 and ... x_n is A_n then

y_1 is B_1 and y_2 is B_2 and ... y_m is B_m,

where $x_1, x_2, ..., x_n, y_1, y_2, ..., y_m$ are linguistic variables, and $A_1, A_2, ..., A_n, B_1, B_2, ..., B_m$ are their respective linguistic values. For example,

if age is old and height is short then modeling-rate is not good.

9.4.3 Control System

Fuzzy logic has been applied to many applications, such as process control, image understanding, robotics, and expert systems. Fuzzy control is the first successful industrial application of fuzzy logic. A fuzzy controller is able to control systems that previously could only be controlled by skilled operators. Japan has achieved significant progress in this area and has applied it to variety of products, such as cruise control for cars, video cameras, rice cookers, and washing machines [SAN 91]. Researchers in Japan are now tackling the problem of integrating sophisticated human knowledge into a fuzzy framework [LIF 91]. After solving this problem based on fuzzy logic, they intend to make more intelligent and higher-speed computers. These computers will be able to process fuzzy logic at high speeds.

Fuzzy logic is very effective in nonlinear control processes because it models the experience of a human operator, rather than the process itself. In general, a fuzzy logic controller consists of four units: condition interface, rule base, computational unit, and action interface (see Figure 9.30). The condition interface observes the current state of the process and expresses that in terms of linguistic values. The rule base unit determines which rules are to be applied under which conditions. The computational unit performs the fuzzy computations. The action interface transforms the output control linguistic values into control action.

To represent how fuzzy logic can be used in a control system, an example for moving a robot toward a track is discussed. This example is based on a more complex example, which involves backing up a truck, discussed in [KOS 92]. In the truck example, the goal is to move a truck backward to a particular loading zone at a right angle. Here, we will consider a robot that moves forward toward a track, and once it is on the track it moves toward the north direction. Figure 9.31 shows the robot and the track that the robot should go on. Figure 9.32 shows that the position of the robot is determined by two linguistic variables, the direction angle, denoted as α, and the distance from the center line of the track, denoted as x. The direction of the robot move-

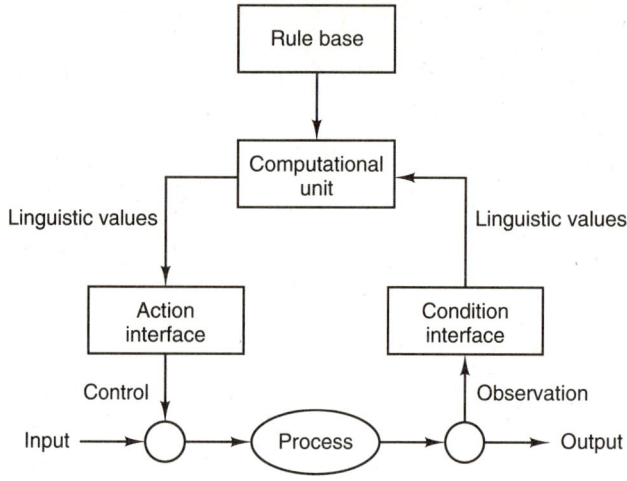

Figure 9.30 Structure of a fuzzy logic controller.

ment, denoted as β, is determined by the angle of the front wheel. For a given initial robot position within a specified area, the goal is to move the robot toward the center of the track. The desired final position is to let the robot move on the track toward the north.

Let's assume the ranges of the linguistic variables x, α, and β, are as follows:

$$-15 \leq x \leq 15,$$
$$0 \leq \alpha \leq 360,$$
$$-15 \leq \beta \leq 15.$$

Notice that the rotation of the front wheel is limited to 15 degrees. Positive values of β represent a right turn of the front wheel, and negative values represent a left turn.

To each of these linguistic variables, a set of linguistic values are assigned as follows:

DISTANCE X (INPUT VARIABLE)
L: left side of the track
C: center of the track
R: right side of the track

DIRECTION ANGLE α (INPUT VARIABLE)
N: North
W: West
S: South
E: East

FRONT WHEEL ANGLE B (OUTPUT VARIABLE)
TR: turn right
ST: straight
TL: turn left

Sec. 9.4 Fuzzy Logic

Figure 9.31 A robot and a track that the robot should go on.

As shown in Figure 9.33, a range of numerical values can be assigned to each linguistic value of a linguistic variable. In this figure, each graph, called a membership function, indicates the degree to which an input value belongs to a particular linguistic value. Such a degree of membership ranges from 0 to 1. The value 0 indicates no membership, and the value 1 represents full membership. A value between 0 and 1 represents partial membership. For example, $x = -10$ belongs to fuzzy value L with degree 1 and to C with degree 0. Similarly, $\alpha = 89°$ belongs to N with degree 0.988 and to E with degree 0.01.

Next, similar to an expert system, a set of rules must be defined. In general, each rule produces some output linguistic values based on some input linguistic values. For example, in the robot case, some of the rules can be defined as

$$\text{if } (\alpha = S \text{ and } x = L) \text{ then } \beta = TL$$

$$\text{if } (\alpha = S \text{ and } x = C) \text{ then } \beta = TL$$

$$\text{if } (\alpha = S \text{ and } x = R) \text{ then } \beta = TR$$

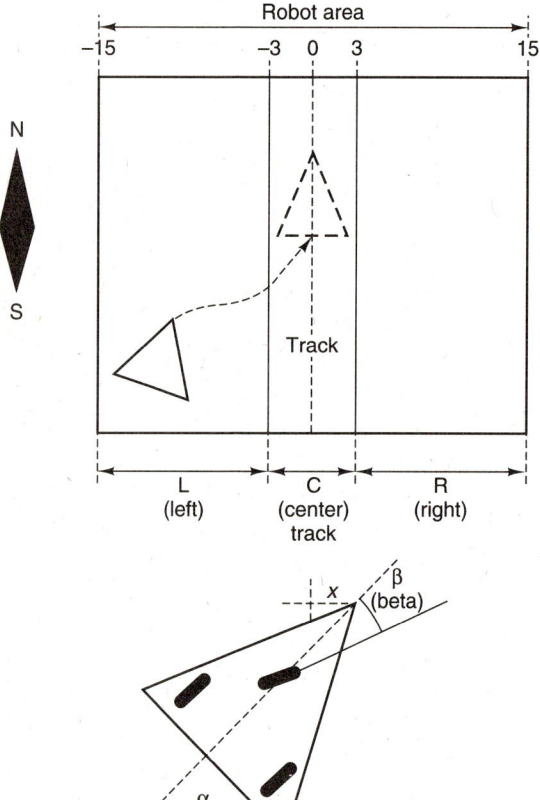

Figure 9.32 The measurements x and α are used to determine the position of the robot with respect to the center of track, and β is used to determine the angle of the front wheel.

Sec. 9.4 Fuzzy Logic

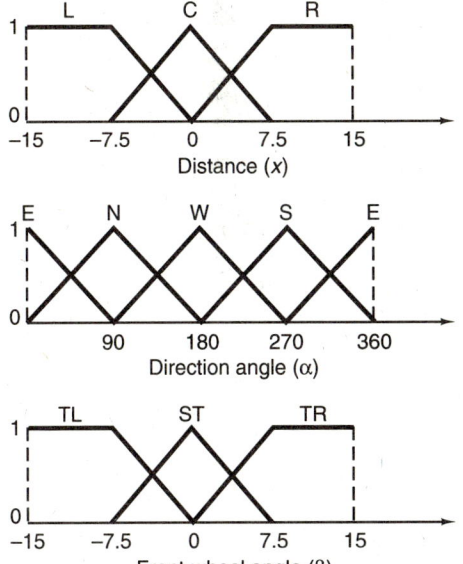

Figure 9.33 Membership functions for the distance, direction angle, and front-wheel angle.

These rules can be extended to consider all the possible values for α; thus there will be 12 rules in all. Figure 9.34 represents all these rules, often called *fuzzy associative memory* (*FAM*) rules, in a table. The preceding three rules are shown in the first row of the table.

The linguistic values of the *if* part of a rule are referred to as *antecedents*, and the values of the *then* part are referred to as *consequents*. For example, in the rule

$$\text{if } (\alpha = S \text{ and } x = L) \text{ then } \beta = TL,$$

S and L are antecedents and TL is the consequent.

For given input values for x and α, the controller should determine an output value for β, the angle of the front wheel. First, for each input value the controller determines the membership degree of its corresponding linguistic values. Next, for each rule, the minimum of the membership degrees of its antecedents is chosen as a membership degree for the rule's consequent. This membership degree is considered as a weight for the rule's consequent. When there is more than one membership degree for

		Distance x		
		L	C	R
Direction α	S	TL	TL	TR
	E	ST	TL	TL
	N	TR	ST	TL
	W	TR	TR	ST

Figure 9.34 Set of rules to determine robot movement.

a consequent, the maximum degree is chosen for that consequent. Hence, at this point, a membership degree is assigned to each linguistic output value. To compute the output value for β, defuzzification is performed. The purpose of defuzzification is to combine the effects of all the linguistic output values into a single output value.

Often the *centroid defuzzification* method is used for defuzzification [KOS 92]. This method provides a weighted average of all linguistic output values. The complexity of the centroid defuzzification depends on the shape of the output membership functions. A simplified calculation is

$$\frac{\sum_{i=1}^{n}(c_i * L_i)}{\sum_{i=1}^{n} L_i},$$

where the L_i's are the weights of linguistic output values and the c_i's are the weighting factors.

As an example, let the initial starting point of our robot be at $x = -10$ and $\alpha = 89$. For these initial values, the membership degree of the linguistic input values are

$x = -10 \longrightarrow f_L(-10) = 1$ $[f_L(-10)$ denotes the degree of L]
$\qquad\qquad\qquad f_C(-10) = 0$
$\qquad\qquad\qquad f_R(-10) = 0,$

$\alpha = 89 \longrightarrow f_E(89) = 0.01$
$\qquad\qquad\qquad f_N(89) = 0.988$
$\qquad\qquad\qquad f_W(89) = 0$
$\qquad\qquad\qquad f_S(89) = 0.$

Now, for each rule we calculate a membership degree for its consequent. As shown next, the consequent's membership degree is the minimum of the membership degrees for α and x. This is because there is an *and* operation between α and x.

Rule No.	Input 1 α	Degree		Input 2 x	Degree	Output, β	Degree (*Minimum of degrees*)
1	S	0	and	L	1	TL	0
2	E	0.01	and	L	1	ST	0.01
3	N	0.988	and	L	1	TR	0.988
4	W	0	and	L	1	TR	0
5	S	0	and	C	0	TL	0
⋮	⋮	⋮	⋮	⋮	⋮	⋮	⋮

Sec. 9.4   Fuzzy Logic   387

	L	C	R
S	$f_{TL}(\cdot) = 0$	$f_{TL}(\cdot) = 0$	$f_{TR}(\cdot) = 0$
E	$f_{ST}(\cdot) = 0.01$	$f_{TL}(\cdot) = 0$	$f_{TL}(\cdot) = 0$
N	$f_{TR}(\cdot) = 0.988$	$f_{ST}(\cdot) = 0$	$f_{TL}(\cdot) = 0$
W	$f_{TR}(\cdot) = 0$	$f_{TR}(\cdot) = 0$	$f_{ST}(\cdot) = 0$

Figure 9.35 Membership degree for each rule when the initial starting point of the robot is at $x = -10$ and $\alpha = 89$.

Figure 9.35 represents a membership degree for each rule's consequent. Note that there are four degrees for the consequent TR. Among these degrees, the maximum degree, 0.988, is chosen for TR. In the same way, degrees 0.01 and 0 are chosen for ST and TL, respectively. Based on these degrees, the system output value can be evaluated as

$$\beta = \frac{(-15.0 * MAX(f_{TL}(\cdot))) + (0.0 * MAX(f_{ST}(\cdot))) + (15.0 * MAX(f_{TR}(\cdot)))}{MAX(f_{TL}(\cdot)) + MAX(f_{ST}(\cdot)) + MAX(f_{TR}(\cdot))}$$

$$= \frac{(-15.0 * 0.0) + (0.0 * 0.01) + (15.0 * 0.988)}{0.998}$$

$$= 14.8.$$

That is, the front wheel of the robot will turn to the right $14.8°$. The robot moves for a short distance and then the process repeats for the new position. Figure 9.36 represents the track of the movement of the robot after 100 iterations.

In practice, fuzzy logic is applied to variety of products. For example, a group at Sanyo Corporation [SHI 91] has applied fuzzy logic to the cooking process in a rice cooker and obtained promising results. Their rice cooker is able to adjust itself appropriately to several factors (such as the water temperature and the rice quantity) to ensure delicious rice. In general, there are four states in making good rice.

1. Water absorption. The rice should absorb about 25% of the water.
2. Boiling water. Bringing the water to boil should take about 10 minutes.
3. Cooking after boiling starts. The rice is kept at a temperature above $98°C$ for more than 20 minutes.
4. Water evaporation. The extra water on the surface should evaporate.

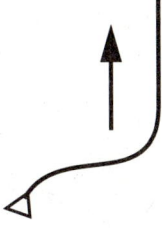

Figure 9.36 Movement of the robot for when $x = -10$ and $\alpha = 89$.

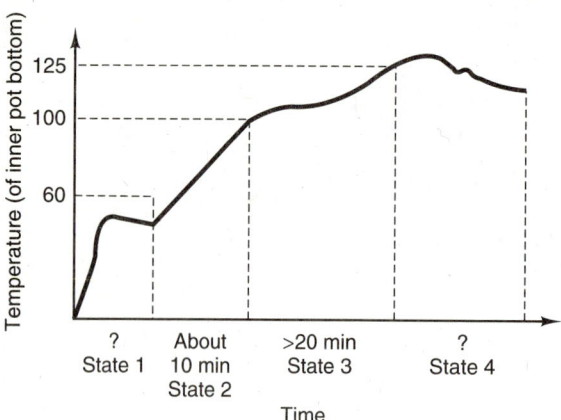

Figure 9.37 States of rice cooking.

Figure 9.37 represents the change of temperatures in these four states. Among these states, state 2 is more complex and is harder to implement. This is so because raising the temperature requires an assessment of the amount of rice and the amount of water. However, the surrounding environment, such as room temperature, water temperature, current of electricity, and shape of the interior pot, makes this process difficult. Hence the conventional type of control circuit becomes too complex. Fuzzy logic makes this process less complex and more implementable.

Fuzzy logic can also control the electric power for heating based on the differences between standard (stored) data and actual data on the amount of rice, water, and temperature. For example, Figure 9.38 represents fuzzy values and their ranges for two of the variables, the difference in temperature and the difference in the amount of water. There are a number of rules for controlling this heating process. For example, a rule might be that if the differences in temperature and the amount of water are both positive then power should be increased.

In summary, fuzzy logic is making its way through many applications, ranging from home appliances to decision-support systems. Fuzzy logic makes the development of a decision-support system easier, less complex, inexpensive, faster, and more

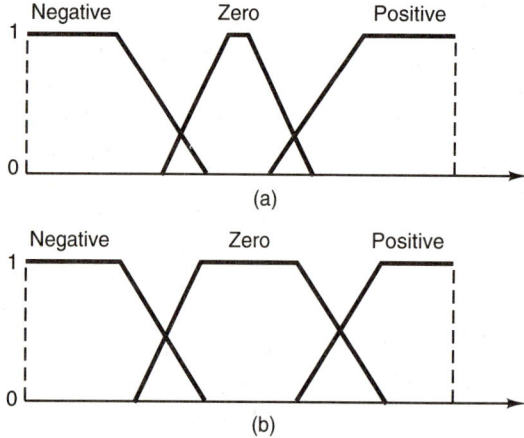

Figure 9.38 Membership functions for the rice cooking controller.
(a) Difference in temperature.
(b) Difference in amount of water.

Sec. 9.4 Fuzzy Logic

reliable. In a mathematical model, if one equation is wrong, the whole system process fails. Fuzzy output is the effect of multiple rules, so even if one rule is faulty, the others will often compensate.

Although software implementation of fuzzy logic provides good results for some applications, dedicated fuzzy processors, called fuzzy logic accelerators, are required for implementing high-performance applications. In recent years, several fuzzy logic accelerators have been developed. Some of them are American Neurology, Inc., NLX-230, Togai Infralogic FC110, and VLSI Technology VY86C500. The general architecture of a fuzzy logic accelerator is explained in the following section.

9.4.4 Architecture of a Fuzzy Logic Accelerator

In general, there are five main units in a fuzzy logic accelerator [VLS 93]: membership function unit, rule evaluation unit, defuzzification unit, storage unit, and control unit. The function of each of these units is explained next.

Membership function unit. The membership function unit computes the degree of membership for each input value. There are different ways to implement such a unit. One way is to implement a lookup table for each input variable. Each lookup table holds the degrees of membership for possible values of an input variable. Another way is to design a unit that supports certain membership functions, such as piecewise linear, trapezoidal, and *S*-function. The degrees of membership are computed according to these predefined functions.

Rule evaluation unit. The rule evaluation unit evaluates the contribution of each rule on the output variables. It supports fuzzy operations such as *and, or,* and *not*.

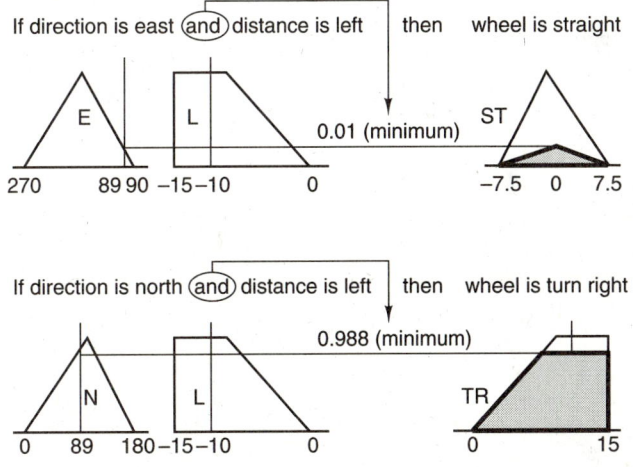

Figure 9.39 Rule evaluation steps.

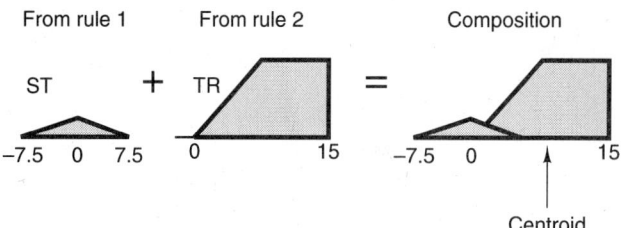

Figure 9.40 Defuzzification steps.

To understand the function of this unit, let's consider our robot example. In this example, two of the rules were

Rule 1: if(α = E and x = L) then β = ST.
Rule 2: if(α = N and x = L) then β = TR.

Suppose that we have input values 89 and -10 for direction α and distance x, respectively. The output of each rule for these input values is represented in Figure 9.39. This figure illustrates the function of the rule contribution unit. Note that the *and* operation is performed by taking the minimum of the membership degrees. The rule minimum membership degrees are used to scale the output membership functions of the output variables that are affected by the rules. The affected output membership functions are scaled in the y-direction.

Defuzzification unit. The defuzzification unit performs the defuzzification step on the scaled output membership functions. Often, the centroid defuzzification method is implemented in fuzzy logic accelerators. As illustrated in Figure 9.40, the centroid method adds the scaled output membership functions to form a composition and then computes the center of mass on the composition.

Storage unit. The storage unit holds the rules of the fuzzy control system. It is also used to store temporary and permanent results of the rule evaluations.

Control unit. The control unit organizes the data flow between separate units of the fuzzy logic accelerator and determines the execution order of instructions. Basically, it is responsible for all control activities in the accelerator chip.

REFERENCES

[ALM 88] ALMEIDA, L.B., "Backpropagation in Perceptrons with Feedback," *Neural Computers* (Neuss 1987), eds. R. Eckmiller and Ch. von der Malsburg. Berlin: Springer-Verlag, 1988, pp. 199–208.

[AND 83] ANDERSON, J., "Cognitive and Psychological Computations with Neural Models," *IEEE Trans. Systems Man Cybernetics*, SMC–13(5), pp. 799–815 September/October 1983.

[BAR 85] BARTO, A. G. AND P. ANANDAN, "Pattern Recognizing Stochastic Learning Automata," *IEEE Trans. Systems Man Cybernetics*, SMC–15(3), 360-375.

[BUT 88] BUTLER, JON T., "Multiple-valued Logic," *Computer*, 12(4), 1988, pp. 13–14.

[COH 83] COHEN, M. A., AND S. G. GROSSBERG, "Absolute Stability of Global Pattern Formation and Parallel Memory Storage by Competitive Neural Networks," *IEEE Trans. Systems Man Cybernetics* SMC–13(5), September October 1983, pp. 815–826.

[COT 87] COTTRELL, G. W., P. MUNRO, AND D. ZIPSER, "Learning Internal Representations from Gray-scale Images: An Example of Extensional Programming," *Proceedings of the Ninth Annual Conference of the Cognitive Science Society*. Hillsdale, NJ: Erlbaum, 1987, pp. 462–473.

[DAT 90] DATE, HIROSHI, M. SEKI, AND T. HAYASHI, "LSI Module Placement Methods Using Neural Computation Networks," International Joint Conference on Neural Networks, June1990, pp. 831–836.

[FAH 89] FAHLMAN, S. E., "Fast-learning Variations on Back-propagation: An Empirical Study," in *Proceedings of the Connectionist Models Summer School*, eds. D. Touretzky, G. Hinton, and T. Sejnowski. San Mateo, CA: Morgan Kaufmann, 1989, pp. 38–51.

[FAH 90] FAHLMAN, S. E. AND C. LEBIERE, "The Cascade-correlation Learning Architecture," in *Advances in Neural Information-processing Systems II*, ed. D. S. Touretzky. San Mateo, CA: Morgan Kaufmann, 1990, pp. 524–532.

[FAI 78] FAIRHURST, M. C., "A Hierarchically Structured Model of Information-Processing in Neural Networks," *Intern J. Bio-Medical Computing,* 9(3), May 1978. pp.181–190.

[FUK 75] FUKUSHIMA, K., "Cognitron: A Self-organizing Multilayered Neural Network," *Biological Cybernetics* 20,(3/4), May 1975, pp. 121–136.

[FUK 80] FUKUSHIMA, K., "Neocognitron: A Self-organizing Neural Network Model for a Mechanism of Pattern Recognition Unaffected by Shift in Position," *Biological Cybernetics* 36(4), April 1980, pp. 193–202.

[GOR 88] GORMAN, R. P. AND T. J. SEJNOWSKI, "Analysis of Hidden Units in a Layered Network Trained to Classify Sonar Targets," *Neural Networks* 1(1), 1988, pp.75–89.

[GRI 81] GRIFFITHS, MARY, *Introduction to Human Physiology*. New York: Macmillan Publishing Co., 1981.

[GRO 87] GROSSBERG, S., "Competitive Learning: From Interactive Activation to Adaptive Resonance," *Cognitive Science* 11(1), January-March 1987, pp. 23–63.

[HEB 49] HEBB, D. O., *The Organization of Behavior*. New York: John Wiley & Sons, 1949.

[HER 91] HERTZ, J. A., R. G. PALMER, AND A. S. KROGH, *Introduction to the Theory of Neural Computation*. Redwood City, CA: Addison-Wesley Publishing Co., 1991.

[HIN 86] HINTON, G. E., AND T. J. SEJNOWSKI, "Learning and Relearning in Boltzmann Machines," *Parallel Distributed Processing*, Vol. 1, Chap. 7. Cambridge, MA: MIT Press, 1986.

[HOP 82] HOPFIELD, J. J., "Neural Networks and Physical Systems with Emergent Collective Computational Abilities," *Proc. Natl. Acad. Sci.* 79, April 1982, pp. 2554–2558.

[HOP 84] HOPFIELD, J. J., "Neurons with Graded Response Have Collective Computational Properties Like Those of Two-state Neurons," *Proc. Natl. Acad. Sci. USA,* 81, May 1984, pp. 3088–3092.

[HOP 85] HOPFIELD, J. J., AND D. W., TANK, "Neural Computation of Decisions in Optimization Problems," *Biological Cybernetics*, 52(3), July 1985, pp.141–152.

[HOP 86] HOPFIELD, J. J., AND D. W., TANK, "Computing with Neural Circuits," *Science,* 233(4764), August 1986, pp. 625–633.

[KAM 87] KAMEYAMA, MICHITAKA, T. HANYA, AND T. HIGUCHI, "Design and Implementation of Quaternary NMOS Integrated Circuits for Pipelined Image Processing," *IEEE J. Solid-state Circuits*, SC-22(1), 1987, pp. 20–27.

[KAM 88] KAMEYAMA, MICHITAKA, S. KAWAHITO, AND T. HIGUCHI, "A Multiplier Chip with Multiple-valued Bidirectional Current-mode Logic Circuits," *Computer*, 12(4), 1988, pp. 43–56.

[KLI 88] KLIR, GEORGE J., AND TINA A. FOLGER, *Fuzzy Sets, Uncertainty, and Information.* Upton Saddle River, NJ: Prentice Hall, 1988.

[KOH 82] KOHONEN, T., "Self-organized Formation of Topologically Correct Feature Maps," *Biological Cybernetics,* 43(1), Jan.1982, pp. 59–69.

[KOH 84] KOHONEN, T., *Self-organization and Associative Memory.* Berlin: Springer-Verlag, 1984.

[KOS 92] KOSKO, BART, *Neural Networks and Fuzzy Systems, A Dynamical Systems Approach to Machine Intelligence.* Upper Saddle River, NJ: Prentice Hall, 1992.

[KRA 89] KRAMER, A. H., AND A. SANGIOVANNI-VINCENTELLI, "Efficient Parallel Learning Algorithms for Neural Networks," *Advances in Neural Information-Processing Systems I*, ed. D. S. Touretzky. San Mateo, CA: Morgan Kaufmann. 1989, pp. 40–48.

[LAP 87] LAPEDES, A., AND R. FARBER, "Nonlinear Signal Processing Using Neural Networks: Prediction and System Modelling," Technical Report LA-UR-87-2662, Los Alamos National Laboratory, Los Alamos, NM, 1987.

[LEC 90] LE CUN, Y., B. BOSER, J. S. DENKER, D. HENDERSON, R. E. HOWARD, W. HUBBARD, AND L. D. JACKEL, "Handwritten Digit Recognition with a Back-Propagation Network," *Advances in Neural Information-Processing Systems II*, ed. D. S. Touretzky. San Mateo, CA: Morgan Kaufmann, 1990. pp. 396–404.

[LIF 91] LIFE Technical News, Laboratory for International Fuzzy Engineering Research, Japan, 2(1), May 1991.

[LIP 87] LIPPMANN, R., "An Introduction to Computing with Neural Nets," *IEEE ASSP Magazine,* 4(2) April 1987, pp. 4–22.

[LIP 89] LIPPMANN, R. P., "Review of Neural Networks for Speech Recognition," *Neural Computation* 1(1), Spring 1989, pp. 1–38.

[MAK 89] MAKRAM-EBEID, S., J. – A. SIRAT, AND J.-R. VIALA, "A Rationalized Back-propagation Learning Algorithm," *International Joint Conference on Neural Networks*, Washington, DC, 1989, Vol. II, New York: IEEE, pp. 373–380.

[MCC 43] MCCULLOCH, W. S., AND W. H. PITTS, "A Logical Calculus of the Ideas Imminent in Nervous Activity," *Bull. Math. Biophysics* 5, 1943, pp. 115–133.

[NIE 90] HECHT-NIELSEN, ROBERT, *Neurocomputing.* Reading, MA: Addison-Wesley Publishing Co., 1990.

[OSH 90] OSHERSON, DANIEL N., AND EDWARD E. SMITH (EDS.). *Thinking, An Invitation to Cognitive Science*, Vol. 3. Cambridge MA: MIT Press, 1990.

[PAL 82] PALM, GUNTHER, *Neural Assemblies: An Alternative Approach to Artificial Intelligence.* New York: Springer-Verlag, 1982.

[PAR 85] PERKER, D. B., "Learning-logic," Technical Report TR-47, Center for Computational Research in Economics and Management Science, MIT, Cambridge, MA, April 1985.

[PEA 89] PEARLMUTTER, B. A. "Learning State Space Trajectories in Recurrent Neural Networks," *Neural Computation*, 1(2), Summer 1989, pp. 263–269.

[PET 87] PETERSON, C., AND J. R. ANDERSON, "A Mean Field Theory Learning Algorithm for Neural Networks," *Complex Systems,* 1(5), Oct.1987, pp. 995–1019.

[PIN 87] PINEDA, F. J. "Generalization of Back-propagation to Recurrent Neural Networks," *Physical Rev. Letters,* 59(19), Nov. 1987, pp. 2229–2232.

[POM 89] POMERLEAU, D. A., "ALVINN: An Autonomous Land Vehicle in a Neural Network," in *Advances in Neural Information-processing Systems I,* ed. D. S. Touretzky. San Mateo. CA: Morgan Kaufmann, 1989, pp. 305–313.

[RED 84] REDNER, R. A., AND H. F. WALKER, "Mixture Densities, Maximum Likelihood and the EM Algorithm," *SIAM Review,* 26(2), April 1984, pp. 195–239.

[ROS 62] ROSENBLATT, R., *Principles of Neurodynamics,* Washington, D.C.: Spartan Books, 1962.

[RUM 86a] RUMELHART, D., AND J. MCCLELLAND, *Parallel Distributed Processing: Explorations in the Microstructure of Cognition.* Cambridge, MA: MIT Press, 1986.

[RUM 86b] RUMELHART, D. E., G. E. HINTON, AND R. J. WILLIAMS, "Learning Internal Representations by Error Propagation," in *Parallel Distributed Processing,* Vol. 1, Chap. 8. Cambridge, MA: MIT Press, 1986.

[RUM 87] RUMELHART, D. E., AND D. ZIPSER, *"Parallel Distributed Processing,* Vols. I and II. Cambridge, MA: MIT Press, 1987.

[SAN 91] *SANYO Technical Review,* Japan, 23(2), 1991.

[SHI 91] SHIMOZAWA, MASAYUKI, ET AL. "Rice Cooking Control by Fuzzy Logic," *Sanyo Technical Review,* 23(2), 1991, pp. 43-49 (in Japanese).

[SIB 91] SIBIGTROTH, JAMES M., "Creating Fuzzy Micros," *Embedded Systems Programming,* December, 1991, pp. 20–34.

[SMI 88] SMITH, KENNETH C., "A Multiple-Valued Logic: A Tutorial and Appreciation," *Computer,* 21(4), 1988, pp. 17–27.

[STE 90] STEVENSON, M., R. WINTER, AND B. WIDROW, "Sensitivity of Feedforward Networks to Weight Errors," *IEEE Trans. Neural Networks,* March 1990, pp. 71–80.

[SUT 88] SUTTON, R. S. "Learning to Predict by Methods of Temporal Difference," *Machine Learning* 3(1), Aug. 1988, pp. 9–44.

[SZU 86] SZU, H., "Fast Simulated Annealing," in *Neural Networks for Computing* (Snowbird 1986), ed. J. S. Denker, New York: American Institute of Physics, 1986, pp. 420–425.

[TAN 86] TANK, D. W. AND J. J. HOPFIELD, "Simple 'Neural' Optimization Networks: and A/D Converter, Signal Decision Circuit, and a Linear Programming Circuit," *IEEE Trans. Circuits Systems,* CAS-33(5), 1986, pp. 533–541.

[VID 83] VIDAL, J. J., "Silicon Brains: Whither Neuromimetic Computer Architectures," *Proceedings of International Conference on Computer Design: VLSI in Computers,* IEEE, 1983, pp. 17–20.

[VLS 93] VLSI TECHNOLOGY, INC., "VY86C500 Data Sheet—12-Bit Fuzzy Computational Acceleration Core," January 1993.

[WAS 89] WASSERMAN, P., *Neural Computing: Theory and Practice.* New York: Van Nostrand Reinhold, 1989.

[WAT 92] WATKINS, C. J. C. H., AND P. DAYAN, "Q-Learning," *Machine Learning,* 8, May 1992, pp. 279–292.

[WER 74] WERBOS, P. J., "Beyond Regression: New Tools for Prediction and Analysis in the Behavioral Sciences," Doctoral Dissertation, Applied Mathematics, Harvard University, Cambridge, MA, 1974.

[WHI 89a] WHITE, H., "Learning in Artificial Neural Networks: A Statistical Perspective," *Neural Computation*, 1(4), 1989, pp. 425–469.

[WHI 89b] WHITE, H., "Neural Network Learning and Statistics," *AI Expert*, December 1989, pp. 48–52.

[WID 59] WIDROW, BERNARD, "Adaptive Sampled-data Systems," *Wescon Convention Record, Part IV*, 1959, pp. 74–86.

[WID 60] WIDROW, B., AND M. E. HOFF, "Adaptive Switching Circuits," in *IRE WESCON Convention Record*, Part 4. New York: IRE, 1960, pp. 96–104.

[WID 88] WIDROW, H., M. HOFF, AND R. BAXTER, "Layered Neural Nets for Pattern Recognition," *IEEE Trans. Acoustics Speech Signal Processing*, 36(7), July 1988, pp. 1109–1118.

[WIL 89] WILLIAMS, R. J. AND D. ZIPSER, "A Learning Algorithm for Continually Running Fully Recurrent Neural Networks," *Neural Computation*, 1(2), Summer 1989, pp. 270–280.

[WIL 92] WILLIAMS, R. J. "Simple Statistical Gradient-following Algorithms for Connectionist Reinforcement Learning," *Machine Learning*, 8(3-4), May 1992, pp. 229–256.

[ZAD 65] ZADEH, L. A., "Fuzzy Sets," *Information and Control*, June 1965, pp. 338–353.

[ZAD 68] ZADEH, L. A., "Communication: Fuzzy Algorithms," *Information and Control*, 12, Feb.1968, pp. 94–102.

[ZAD 72] ZADEH, L. A., "A Rationale for Fuzzy Control," *J. Dynamic Systems Measurement Control*, 94(G), 1972, pp. 3–4.

[ZAD 73] ZADEH, L. A., "Outline of a New Approach to the Analysis of Complex Systems and Decision Processes," *IEEE Trans. Systems Man Cybernetics*, SMC-3(1), 1973, pp. 28–44.

[ZAD 88] ZADEH, LOFTI A., "Fuzzy Logic," *Computer*, 21(4), 1988, pp. 83–93.

[ZAD 94] ZADEH, LOFTI A., "Soft Computing and Fuzzy Logic," *IEEE Software*, 11(6), Nov. 1994, pp. 48–56.

[ZAD 95] ZADEH, LOFTI A., AND MO JAMSHIDI, "Soft Computing and Fuzzy Logic: Toward High MIQ Systems," *Intern. J. Intelligent Automation Soft Computing*, 1(1), 1995, pp. 1–30.

PROBLEMS

9.1. What characterizes a neural network?

9.2. Draw and describe a simple biological neuron. Roughly, how many neurons are in the human brain?

9.3. Given the Adaline network in Figure P9.3, train the network in order to perform the AND function. Assume that the initial values are

$$w_0 = 1.50$$
$$w_1 = 5.00$$
$$w_2 = 2.00$$
$$\rho = 1.25$$

Show your work and write the final values for the weights.

9.4. In Figures P9.4A and P9.4B, how many (if there is a need for) neurons in the hidden layer are necessary to separate the class marked by × from the class marked by O?

9.5. Design a feed-forward network with the decision regions shown in Figure P9.5.

Problems

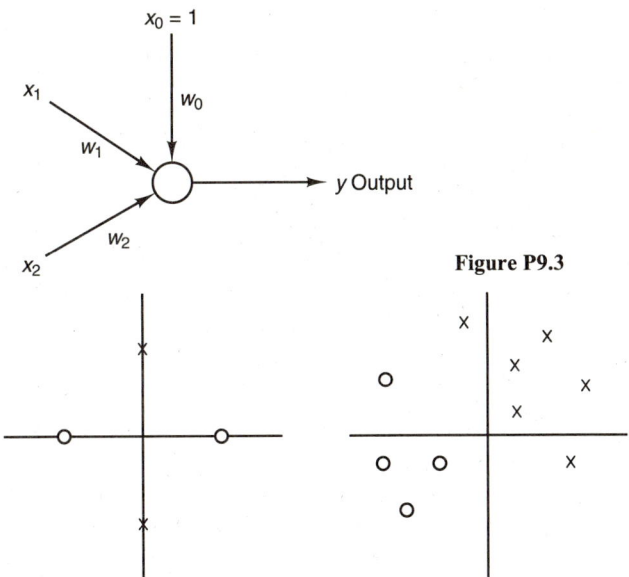

Figure P9.3

Figure P9.4A **Figure P9.4B**

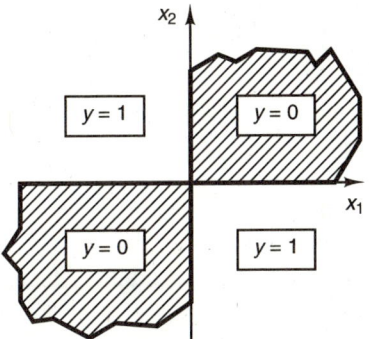

Figure P9.5

9.6. Design a feed-forward network with hard-limiting neurons to achieve the following mapping.

Inputs			Outputs	
x_1	x_2	x_3	y_1	y_2
1	0	0	1	1
0	1	0	1	0
0	0	1	0	1

9.7. Show that the network in Figure P9.7 cannot satisfy the decision regions shown.

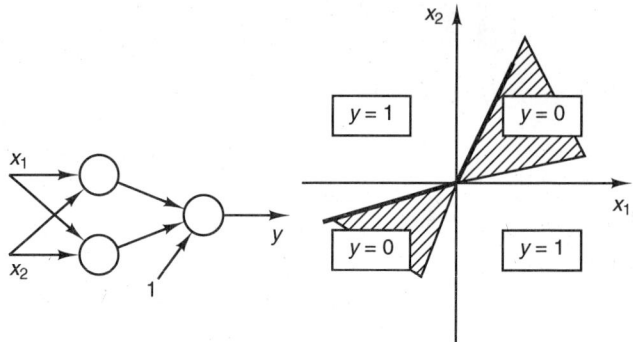

Figure P9.7

9.8. Find the weights in the network of Figure P9.8 such that they satisfy the decision regions shown. Note that each neuron has a hard-limiting activation function.

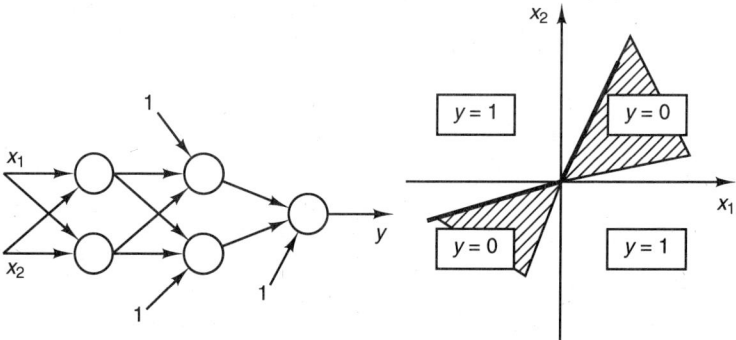

Figure P9.8

9.9. Find the decision regions on the (x_1, x_2) plane in terms of y for the network of Figure P9.9. Note that the neuron has a hard-limiting activation function.

$$y = f(w_1 x_1 + w_2 x_2 + w_3), \quad \text{where } f(\alpha) = 1, \quad \text{if } 0 \leq \alpha,$$
$$= 0, \quad \text{otherwise.}$$

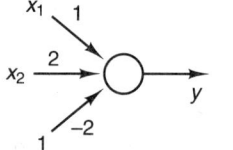

Figure P9.9

9.10. Design a feed-forward network with the decision regions shown in Figure P9.10. Use a minimum number of layers in your design.

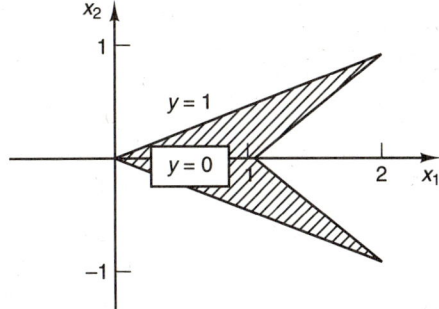

Figure P9.10

9.11. Find the weight factors, using the back-propagation learning law implemented by a computer program, for the following networks. The nonlinear function for each unit is the logistic function $f(x) = 1/[1 + \exp(-x)]$. Choose the initial weights as uniformly distributed random numbers over (-0.5 to $+0.5$). Assume each neuron has a bias input.

    a. Two-input/one-output network with one layer. Use the input/output set of Figure P9.11A.

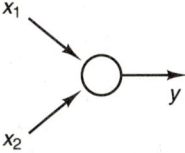

x_1	x_2	y
0.1	0.1	0.1
0.9	0.1	0.1
0.1	0.9	0.1
0.9	0.9	0.9

Figure P9.11A

b. Two-input/one-output network with two-layers. Use the input/output set of Figure P9.11B.

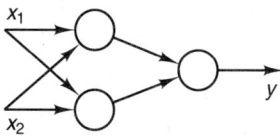

x_1	x_2	y
0.1	0.1	0.1
0.9	0.1	0.9
0.1	0.9	0.9
0.9	0.9	0.1

Figure P9.11B

9.12. Develop and simulate a neural network for a full-adder circuit. Your report should include the network structure, the code, and the input and output of all possible input patterns.

9.13. What are the problems with the back-propagation algorithm? Explain in detail your claims.

9.14. Choose the correct answer for the following questions.

  a. Which of the following models can learn a finite-state automaton?
   1. Hopfield networks
   2. Adaline
   3. Madaline
   4. None of the above

  b. A critic is used in which of the following models?
   1. Supervised learning
   2. Unsupervised learning
   3. Reinforcement learning
   4. None of the above

  c. The opposite of reinforcement is
   1. Reward
   2. Punishment
   3. Stimulations
   4. Excitations

9.15. Are the following statements true or false?

  a. One hidden layer only is enough to represent functions with nonconvex class regions.
  b. Increasing the number of adjustable parameters will always result in better generalization.
  c. Reinforcement learning can learn from probabilistic environments.
  d. Conjugate gradient descent will always perform better than plain back-propagation, no matter what the error surface is.

Problems

9.16. Describe the main advantage and disadvantage of the Hopfield network.

9.17. Let $X = \{1, 2, \ldots, 10\}$. Determine the complement, union, intersection, algebraic sum, and algebraic product of the following fuzzy sets.

$$A = \{(2, 0.4), (3, 0.6), (5, 1), (7, 0.6), (8, 0.4)\},$$
$$B = \{(2, 0.4), (4, 0.8), (5, 1), (7, 0.6)\}.$$

9.18. Given the following relations $P(X, Y)$ and $Q(Y, Z)$, compute the max-min composition, $R(X, Z) = P(X, Y) \circ Q(Y, Z)$.

$$P(X, Y) = \begin{array}{c} x_1 \\ x_2 \\ x_3 \end{array} \begin{array}{ccc} y_1 & y_2 & y_3 \\ \left[0.3 \right. & 0.5 & \left. 0.7 \right] \\ \left[0.0 \right. & 0.7 & \left. 0.9 \right] \\ \left[0.4 \right. & 0.6 & \left. 0.5 \right] \end{array}$$

$$Q(Y, Z) = \begin{array}{c} y_1 \\ y_2 \\ y_3 \end{array} \begin{array}{ccc} z_1 & z_2 & z_3 \\ \left[0.4 \right. & 0.1 & \left. 0.3 \right] \\ \left[0.5 \right. & 0.9 & \left. 0.5 \right] \\ \left[0.6 \right. & 0.5 & \left. 0.2 \right] \end{array}$$

9.19. Find a set of values for P that satisfies the following fuzzy relation equation.

$$P \circ \begin{bmatrix} 0.4 & 0.9 & 0.0 \\ 0.2 & 1.0 & 0.1 \\ 0.6 & 0.4 & 0.0 \end{bmatrix} = \begin{bmatrix} 0.2 & 0.5 & 0.1 \end{bmatrix}$$

9.20. Consider the robot example that was discussed in this chapter.

    a. Simulate a fuzzy controller for the robot using the following rule table.

		Distance x		
		L	C	R
Direction α	S	TL	TL	TR
	E	ST	TL	TL
	N	TR	ST	TL
	W	TR	TR	ST

    b. Let direction angle α have the following linguistic values: N, NW, W, SW, S, SE, E, and NE. Define a membership function for each of these linguistic values. Design a new rule table. Simulate a fuzzy controller for the robot using the new rule table.

    c. Repeat part a using a defuzzification process other than the one used previously. Can you get a better result? Why?

Note: You should submit a report that includes your design, comments about your simulation, source program, and output of simulation. Your output should include a figure (which represents movement of the robot) for each of the following set of inputs:

$$x = -10 \text{ and } \alpha = 89,$$
$$x = 12 \text{ and } \alpha = 0,$$
$$x = -8 \text{ and } \alpha = 220.$$

9.21. The purpose of this problem is to build an expert system from past experience. The system should be able to predict the value of IBM stock considering the previous values. In the following, 240 stock values are listed. These values are monthly, starting from May 1993 and going back to June 1973. Use the last 200 values to train your system and the first 40 values to test your system by predicting the future values.

    a. Implement your system by a neural network.
    b. Implement your system by using a set of fuzzy rules.
    c. Compare results of parts a and b.

Note: You should submit a report that includes your design, comments about your simulation, source program, and output of simulation. For each part a and b, the output should include a figure that represents the true value and the estimated value for the first 40 values.

52.75 (May 1993) 48.63 50.88 54.38 51.50 50.38 68.25 66.88 80.75 86.63 94.75 97.88 90.75 90.75 83.50 86.88 90.00 89.00 92.50 98.25 103.63 96.88 101.25 97.13 106.13 103.00 113.88 128.75 126.75 113.00 113.63 105.38 106.38 101.88 111.50 117.50 120.00 109.00 106.13 103.88 98.63 94.13 97.63 100.25 109.25 117.13 115.00 111.88 109.63 114.00 109.13 121.50 130.63 121.88 118.50 122.63 115.38 111.50 125.75 127.38 112.50 113.38 107.63 117.50 112.38 115.50 110.75 122.50 150.75 168.38 161.00 162.50 160.00 160.13 150.13 139.50 128.75 120.00 127.13 123.63 134.50 138.75 132.50 146.50 152.38 156.25 151.50 150.88 151.50 155.50 139.75 129.88 123.88 126.63 131.38 123.75 128.63 126.50 127.00 134.00 136.38 123.13 121.75 124.63 124.25 123.75 110.75 105.75 107.75 113.75 114.00 110.25 114.13 122.00 117.38 126.75 126.88 119.50 120.38 120.25 111.25 117.00 101.75 99.00 98.88 96.25 86.50 79.88 73.38 70.50 65.63 60.63 61.50 64.25 59.75 61.88 63.63 56.88 54.50 51.50 54.13 55.13 56.13 57.88 58.75 58.63 62.38 64.25 64.38 67.88 68.13 66.63 64.13 65.50 65.25 58.75 55.38 54.88 55.75 63.50 68.63 64.38 65.25 62.38 67.75 70.00 69.75 73.38 76.00 78.56 78.88 75.00 77.19 74.63 67.38 66.06 69.25 72.97 70.25 64.31 64.56 66.50 58.88 62.81 66.38 68.38 66.00 64.31 65.25 67.09 67.03 66.00 61.38 64.69 69.13 69.00 68.81 69.78 67.75 67.94 70.34 68.41 68.03 69.19 64.16 63.34 65.50 63.91 64.44 56.06 56.59 53.06 47.06 46.56 47.56 52.25 53.75 52.47 51.66 53.88 47.06 42.00 44.31 47.28 39.75 48.00 50.41 53.19 53.13 56.81 58.94 59.47 61.31 61.69 66.25 70.06 64.50 75.25 78.63 79.25 (June 1973).

Appendix A
Basic Components of VLSI Design

A.1 INTRODUCTION

As a result of improvements in fabrication technology, very large scale integrated (VLSI) electronic circuitry has become so dense that a single silicon VLSI chip may contain millions of transistors. VLSI electronics presents a challenge, not only to those involved in the development of fabrication technology, but also to computer scientists and computer engineers. The ways in which digital systems are structured, the procedures used to design them, the trade-offs between hardware and software, and the design of computational algorithms will all be greatly affected by the coming changes in integrated electronics. Presently, this is one of the most active areas in computer science, computer engineering, and electrical engineering.

There are two major research areas relative to producing VLSI chips. One is VLSI technique, which deals with the kinds of functions that should be implemented on VLSI chips and the problem of how to realize these *functions*. The other research area centers around the support systems for the computer-aided design and fabrication of VLSI chips, that is, intelligent VLSI CAD systems, also called *silicon compilers*. CAD systems will translate a behavioral description of what the new chip is supposed to do into the chip layout. A *layout* is a complete geometric representation (a set of rectangles) from which the latest fabrication technologies directly produce reliable, working chips.

We might ask why VLSI CAD systems are needed. Without CAD tools, the design process can cost millions of dollars, and a year or more may elapse while moving from the initial characterization of the chip to a working design. By the time the design is completed, it is already a year behind the state of the art. This is exactly the kind of thing the industries cannot afford. They need designs with correct functionality, low turnaround times, and economic feasibility. VLSI CAD systems are able to simplify this otherwise impossible task by hiding the low-level circuit theory and device physics details from the designer and allowing him or her to concentrate on the functionality of his or her design and ways of optimizing it. This kind of approach also means that VLSI designers can come from backgrounds other than electrical engineering or physics, typically computer science.

In general, a VLSI CAD system consists of several layers of software. Each layer simulates the design at a particular level of description and also translates it to a lower level of description. The main layers from top to bottom are hardware design language, gate (Boolean logic), and layout. The design engineers working on different parts of the circuit create a design, usually described in a hardware design language (such as VHDL). Once the design is complete, the description is transformed into a gate-level circuit and then to a layout.

A variety of CAD systems has emerged from industry and academia that tends to give good solutions to some design problems. Surprisingly, the effort needed to provide complete automation is considerably less than that needed for a majority of subproblems tackled independently. Some industries have taken various approaches in designing the CAD subsystem, depending on whether the integrated circuits (IC) are to be semicustomized or fully customized.

Semicustomized systems start with general programmable logic circuits (like field programmable gate arrays [SHE 92]), which are then customized according to the circuit designer's intent. The inherent advantage is in terms of the short manufacturing turnaround time and low development cost. However, certain disadvantages may include high power requirements and large chip areas, which could offset the advantages.

On the other hand, a fully customized chip is one in which the IC is developed starting with cell design, placing the cells on chip, connecting the terminals of the cells, testing the design, and so on, for the specific design. The advantages are in terms of good performance through tailored logic, high yields, and low power consumption. Penalties are paid in terms of long manufacturing turnaround time and high development costs for designing all aspects of logical and electrical functions.

The preceding approaches are suited for a production environment. Another approach, which is less automated and needs the designer's interaction during the course of the design, is hand-layout systems. In these systems, a few tools are developed to aid the designer in producing the design file.

Before using such a system, the designer must complete the circuit diagram and an overall geometry of the chip, its cells, and subsystems. The designer first transforms the designs into a geometrical layout using a *layout editor*. A layout editor is a software package that accepts certain graphics commands to perform functions such as drawing lines and boxes, moving objects on the design, and erasing unwanted objects from the design. The output of this editor is a layout.

Due to the human interface needed in converting the designer's intent into a graphical layout, errors can be expected. Hence the designer *iterates* several times between the design and layout. Most automated systems provide the designer with a

Sec. A.2 Basic VLSI Components and Fabrication Techniques

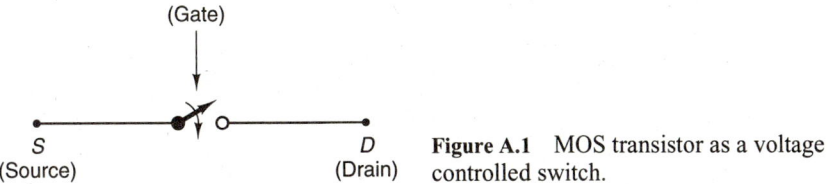

Figure A.1 MOS transistor as a voltage controlled switch.

rule checker, which detects errors in the layout design. The output after the layout stage is in the form of a design file that describes the layout. A standard format for these files that is accepted by the industry is the Caltech Intermediate Form (CIF), which efficiently and unambiguously describes the layout geometry.

To be able to understand a layout, we must first understand the basic components, such as the MOS transistor and the CMOS inverter. These components and their fabrication process are described briefly in the following section. The last section explains some of the main issues that are relevant in layout design.

A.2 BASIC VLSI COMPONENTS AND FABRICATION TECHNIQUES*

The MOS transistor. The most basic component of a modern-day digital VLSI circuit is the *MOS* (metal oxide semiconductor) transistor. Simply expressed, the MOS transistor is a voltage-controlled switch. As shown in Figure A.1, the transistor

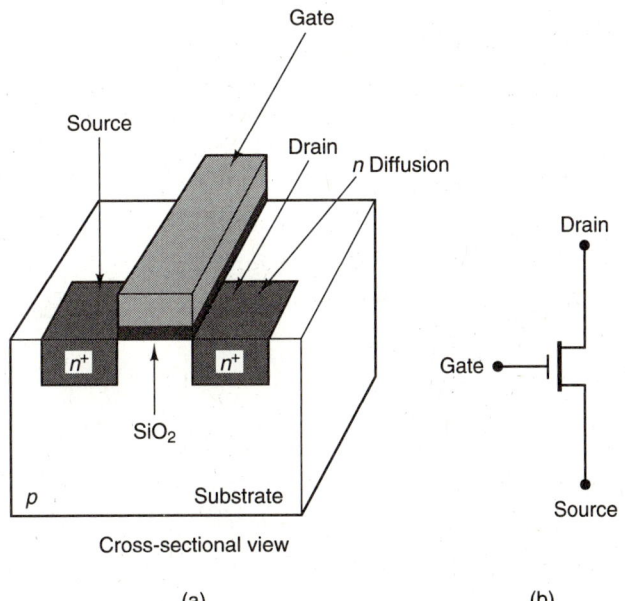

(a)   (b)

Figure A.2 An nMOS transistor. (a) Implementation. (b) symbolic representation.

---

* Portions of Sections A.2 and A.3 reprinted, with permission, from "Layout, Placement, and Routing" by M. R. Zargham and S. Tragoudas which appeared in *The Electrical Engineering Handbook,* Edited by R. C. Dorf, CRC, 1993, pp. 581–590.© CRC Press, Inc.

is closed when the voltage at the terminal marked *G* is within a certain range, and open otherwise. It can basically be of two types, the nMOS and the pMOS.

The nMOS transistor is fabricated on a silicon wafer by making two regions of highly doped n-type material on the two ends, as illustrated in Figure A.2. The term doping means injecting impurities into a pure silicon substrate. n-Type doping implies that the dopant has an excess of negatively charged particles such as electrons, and p-type doping implies an excess of positively charged holes. The substrate in the nMOS transistor is usually p-type doped and tied to zero voltage. The two n-type regions are called the *source* and the *drain,* respectively, and the substrate region in between is the *channel*. There is a silicon layer on top of the channel, called the *gate*, that is electrically insulated from the channel by a silicon oxide material. These three regions, the source, the gate, and the drain, form the three electrical terminals of the MOS transistor. When a positive voltage above a certain threshold level is applied to the gate, the channel becomes conducting due to induced negative charges. If the drain is positive with respect to the source, which it usually is, current flow can occur from source to drain, and the transistor is said to be *on*. If, on the other hand, a voltage less than the threshold is applied to the gate, the channel remains nonconducting, and no current flows from source to drain. The transistor is *off* in this case. It can thus be seen that the gate acts as a controller for the transistor switch.

The pMOS is functionally the inverse of the nMOS. As shown in Figure A.3, the substrate in this case is doped n-type and tied to the supply voltage; the source and drain regions are p-type. The transistor is on when a negative voltage, below a certain threshold, is applied to the transistor. Positive charges are induced in the channel in

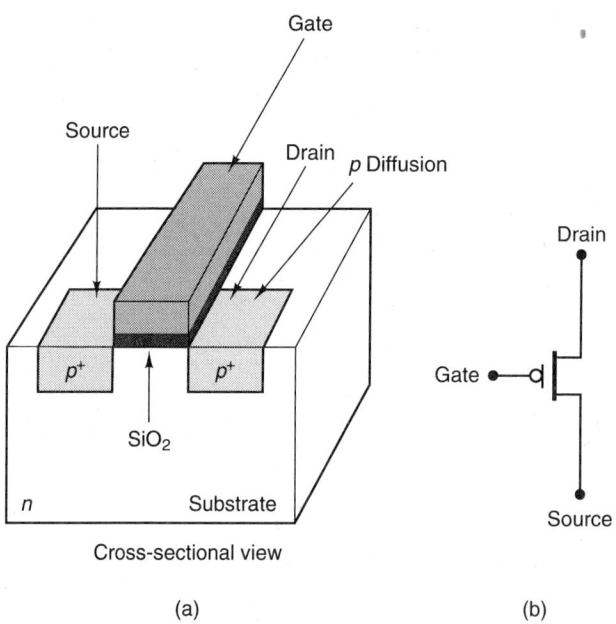

Figure A.3 A pMOS transistor, a) Implementation, b) Symbolic representation.

Sec. A.2 Basic VLSI Components and Fabrication Techniques

this case, and current flow can occur if the drain is at a negative voltage with respect to the source. If the gate voltage is more positive than the threshold, the transistor is off. (An in-depth description of MOS transistors can be found in [WES 93].)

Based on the pMOS/nMOS transistors, there are different technologies for designing digital circuits. Two of the commonly used ones are CMOS and BiCMOS. In CMOS technology (which stands for complementary metal oxide semiconductor) both types of transistors (nMOS and pMOS) are used to design a circuit. This technology provides good circuit density. BiCMOS technology (which stands for bipolar and CMOS) includes bipolar [WES 93], pMOS, and nMOS transistors. The bipolar transistors are used to improve the speed of CMOS technology.

The Inverter. After the MOS transistor, the most basic component of a VLSI circuit is an inverter. An inverter produces an output voltage that is the logical inverse of its input. For example, an input of 1 produces an output of 0, and vice versa.

As shown in Figure A.4a, an inverter in the CMOS technology consists of two MOS transistors, a pMOS and an nMOS. The gates of the two transistors are connected together and tied to the input voltage. When the input is 1 (5 volts), the lower nMOS is on, but the upper pMOS is off, and the output is an electrical short to ground through the nMOS, as illustrated in Figure A.4b. If, on the other hand, the input voltage is 0, the pMOS is on, the nMOS is off, and the output finds a charge-up path through the pMOS to the positive supply (Figure A.4c). Inversion is thus achieved.

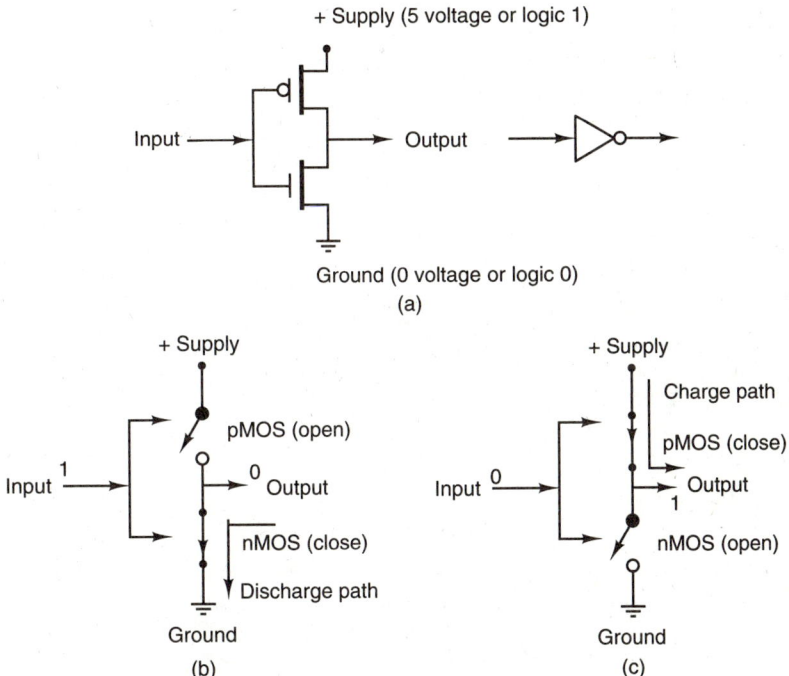

Figure A.4 Different states of a CMOS inverter. (a) A CMOS inverter. (b) State of transistors when the input is 1. (c) State of transistors when the input is 0.

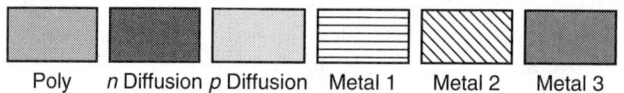

Figure A.5 Different layers used in a VLSI layout.

A.3 LAYOUT-LEVEL DESCRIPTION

For a specific circuit, a layout specifies the position and dimension of the different layers of materials as they would be laid on the silicon wafer. However, the layout description is only a symbolic representation that simplifies the description of the actual fabrication process. For example, the layout representation does not explicitly

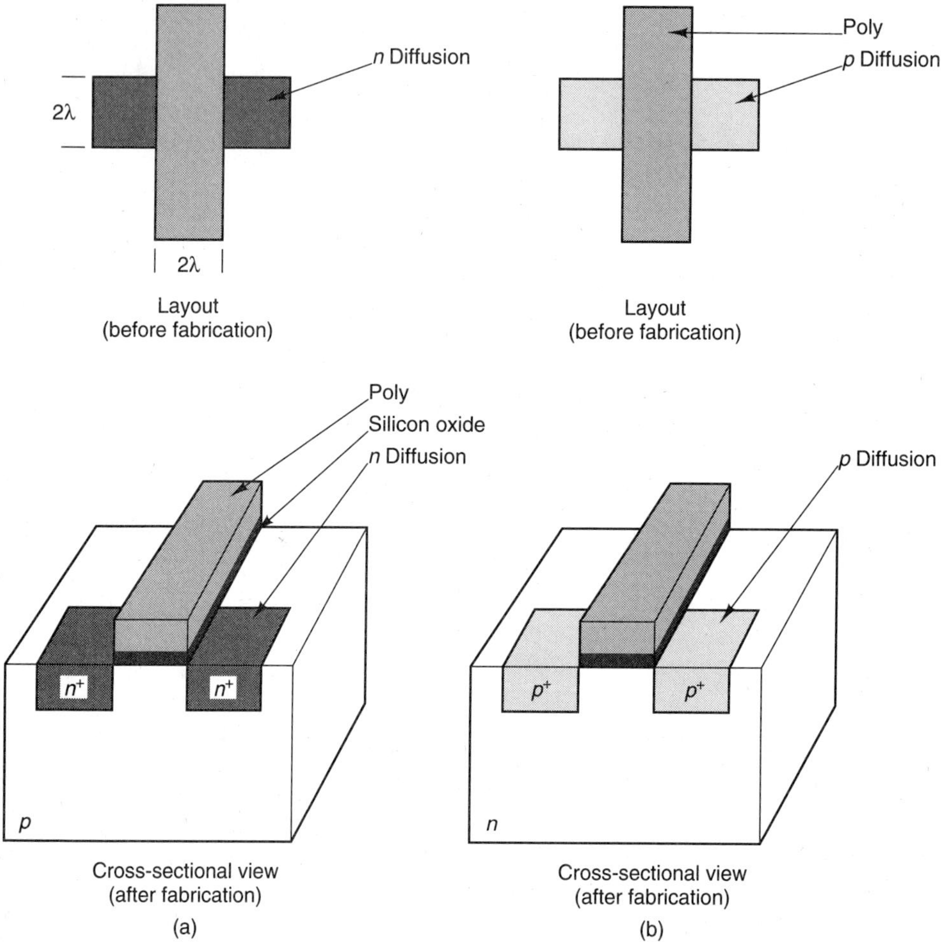

Figure A.6 Layout and fabrication of MOS transistor. (a) nMOS transistor. (b) pMOS transistor.

Sec. A.3 Layout-Level Description

indicate the thickness of the layers, thickness of oxide coating, amount of ionization in the transistors channels, and so on; these factors are determined during the fabrication process. Some of the main layers used in any layout description are n-diffusion, p-dif-

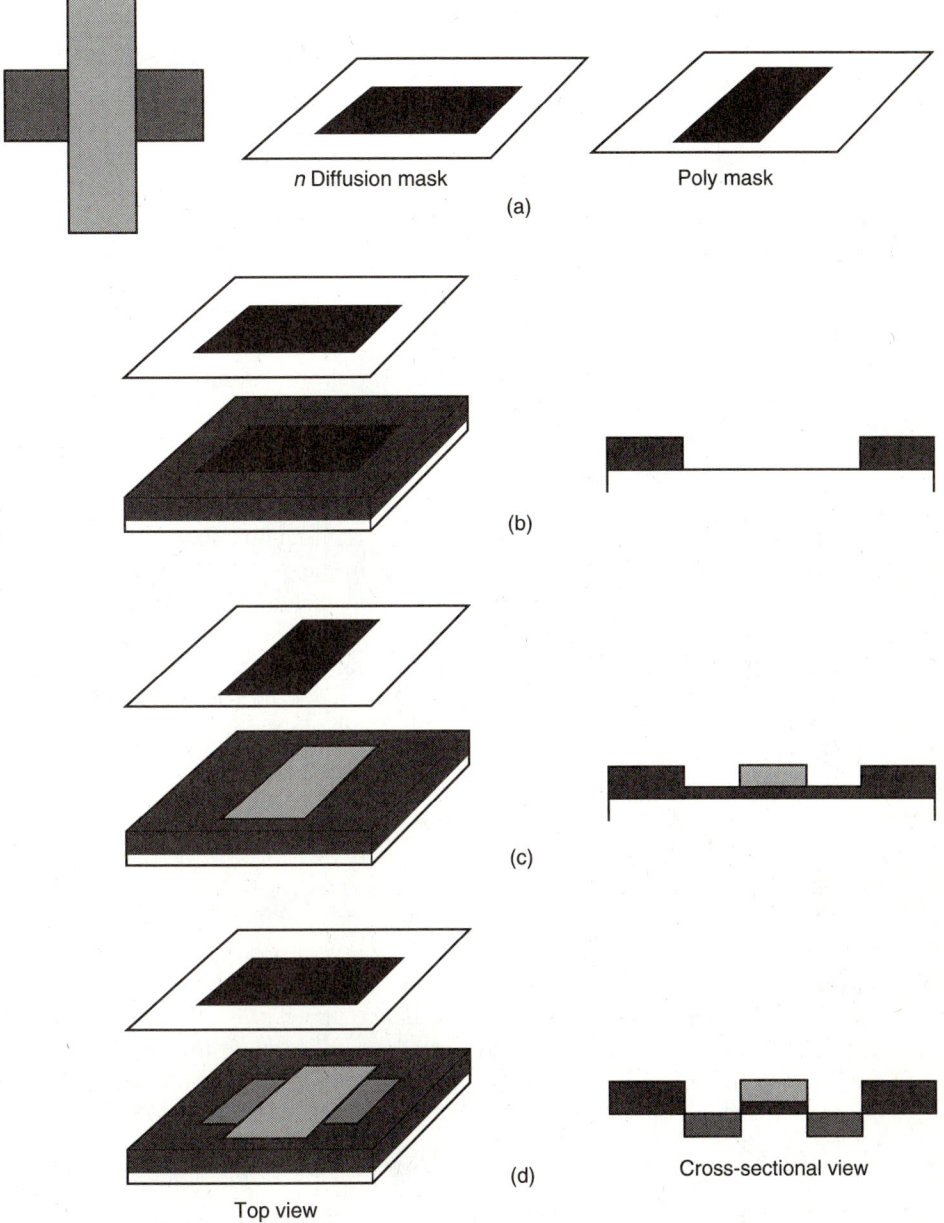

Figure A.7 Fabrication steps for an nMOS transistor.

fusion, poly, metal-1, metal-2, and metal-3. Each of these layers is represented by a polygon of a particular color or pattern. As an example, Figure A.5 presents a specific pattern for each layer, which will be used throughout the rest of this section.

As shown in Figure A.6, an n-diffusion layer crossing a poly layer implies an nMOS transistor, and a p-diffusion crossing poly implies a pMOS transistor.

Note that the widths of diffusion and poly are represented with a scalable parameter called λ (lambda). These measurements, referred to as *design rules,* are introduced to prevent errors on the chip, such as avoiding malfunctioning transistors and thin lines from opening (disconnecting).

Implementing the design rules based on λ makes the design process independent from the fabrication process. This allows the design to be rescaled as the fabrication process improves. For example, a unit of λ could be 0.6 micrometer for a given year and then, by progress in the fabrication process, may be reduced to 0.4 micrometer in a couple of years.

Metal layers are used as wires for connections between the components. This is because metal has the lowest propagation delay compared to the other layers. However, sometimes a poly layer is also used for short wires in order to reduce the complexity of the wire routing. Any wire can cross another wire without getting electrically affected as long as they are in different layers. Two different layers can be electrically connected together using *contacts*. The fabrication process of the contacts depends on the types of the layers that are to be connected. Therefore, a layout editor supports different types of contacts by using different patterns.

The actual chip is fabricated from the circuit layout. Based on the layers in the layout, various layers of materials, one on top of the others, are laid down on a silicon wafer. Typically, the processing of laying down each of these materials involves several steps, such as masking, oxide coating, lithography, and etching [MEA 80]. For example, as shown in Figure A.7a, for fabricating an nMOS transistor, first two masks, one for poly and one for n-diffusion, are obtained from the circuit layout. Next, the n-diffusion mask is used to create a layer of silicon oxide on the wafer (see Figure A.7b). The wafer is covered with a thin layer of oxide in places where the transistors are supposed to be placed, as opposed to a thick layer in other places. The poly mask is used to place a layer of polysilicon on top of the oxide layer to define the gate terminals of the transistor (see Figure A.7c). Finally, the n-diffusion regions are made to form the source and drain terminals of the transistor (see Figure A.7d).

To better illustrate the concept of layout design, the design of an inverter in the CMOS technology is shown in Figure A.8. An inverter produces an output voltage that is the logical inverse of its input. Considering the circuit diagram of Figure A.8a, when the input is 1, the lower nMOS is on, but the upper pMOS is off. Thus the output becomes 0 by becoming connected to the ground through the nMOS. On the other hand, if the input is 0, the pMOS is on and the nMOS is off, so the output must find a charge-up path through the pMOS to the supply and therefore becomes 1. Figure A.8b represents a layout for such an inverter. As can be seen from this figure, the problem of a layout design is essentially reduced to drawing and painting a set of polygons. Layout editors provide commands for drawing such polygons. The commands are usually entered at the keyboard, or with a mouse and, in some menu-driven packages, can be selected as options from a pull-down menu.

Sec. A.3 Layout-Level Description

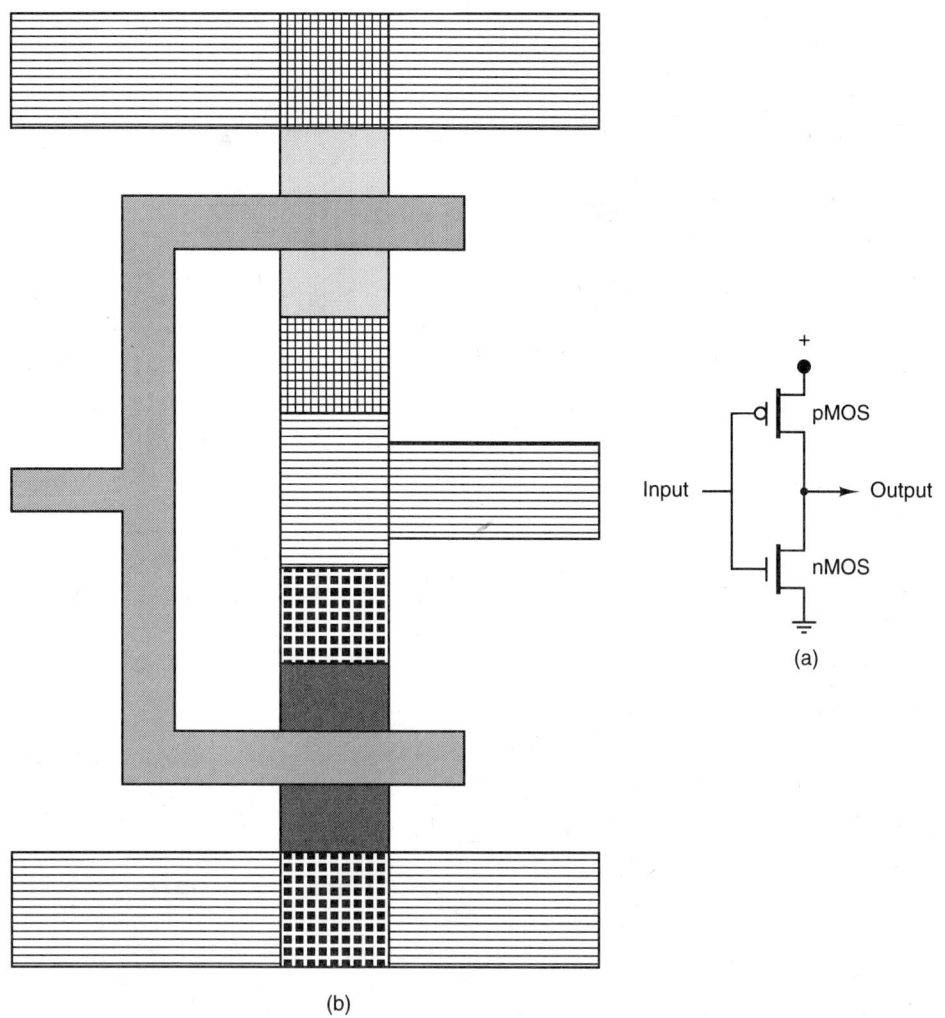

Figure A.8 The circuit diagram and layout of an inverter.
(a) Circuit diagram. (b) Layout.

In addition to the drawing commands, often a layout system provides tools for minimizing the overall area of the layout (i.e., size of the chip). Today a VLSI chip consists of many individual cells with each one laid out separately. A cell can be an inverter, a NAND gate, a multiplier, a memory unit, and so on. The designer can make the layout of a cell and then store it in a file called the *cell library*. Later, each time the designer wants to design a circuit that requires the stored cell, he or she simply copies the layout from the cell library. A layout may consist of many cells. Most of the layout systems provide routines, called *placement* and *routing* routines, for placing the cells and then interconnecting them with wires in such a way as to minimize the layout area. As an example, Figure A.9 presents the placement of three cells. The area between the cells is used for routing. The entire routing surface is divided into a set of rectangular

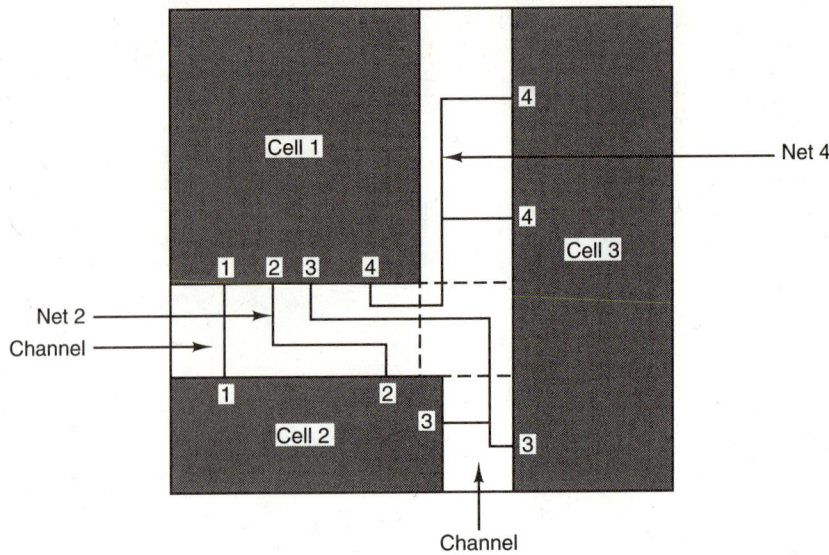

Figure A.9 Placement of routing of three cells.

routing areas called *channels*. The sides of each channel consist of a set of terminals. An id is assigned to each terminal. The terminals that should be connected to each other have the same id. In Figure A.9, the ids are numbers 1 to 4. A wire that connects the terminals with the same id is called a *net*. The router finds a location for the wire segments of each net within the channel.

Today, in order to reduce the design complexity of the layout of an IC, the *divide-and-conquer* approach is used. In this approach, a large problem is recursively subdivided into smaller problems until their size becomes manageable. For instance, the designer can make the layout of a NAND gate and then store it in the cell *library*. Later, each time the designer wants to design a circuit that requires NAND gates, he or she can simply copy the layout from the cell library.

The most common cell library approaches are gate array, sea of gates, field programmable gate arrays, standard cell, and macro/custom cell. Each of these approaches is briefly explained next.

Figure A.10a shows the general layout image of a gate array chip. In this type of layout, predefined patterns of transistors (basic cells such as NAND gates) are fabricated in several rows. The customization of the chip for a specific function is done by connecting some of the cells through metal layers. Current technology allows three and sometimes four layers of metal for interconnection. As the chips have become denser, a serious drawback in the use of gate arrays has led to the new design style called the *sea of gates*. Gate arrays assign large channels between rows for routing. This leads to a waste of chip area as the number of rows increases. As shown in Figure A.10b, the sea of gates eliminates the need for these channels by allowing over-the-cell routing in three or four metal layers. Although this makes better use of the silicon area, it radically increases the complexity of the placement and routing problem.

Sec. A.3 Layout-Level Description

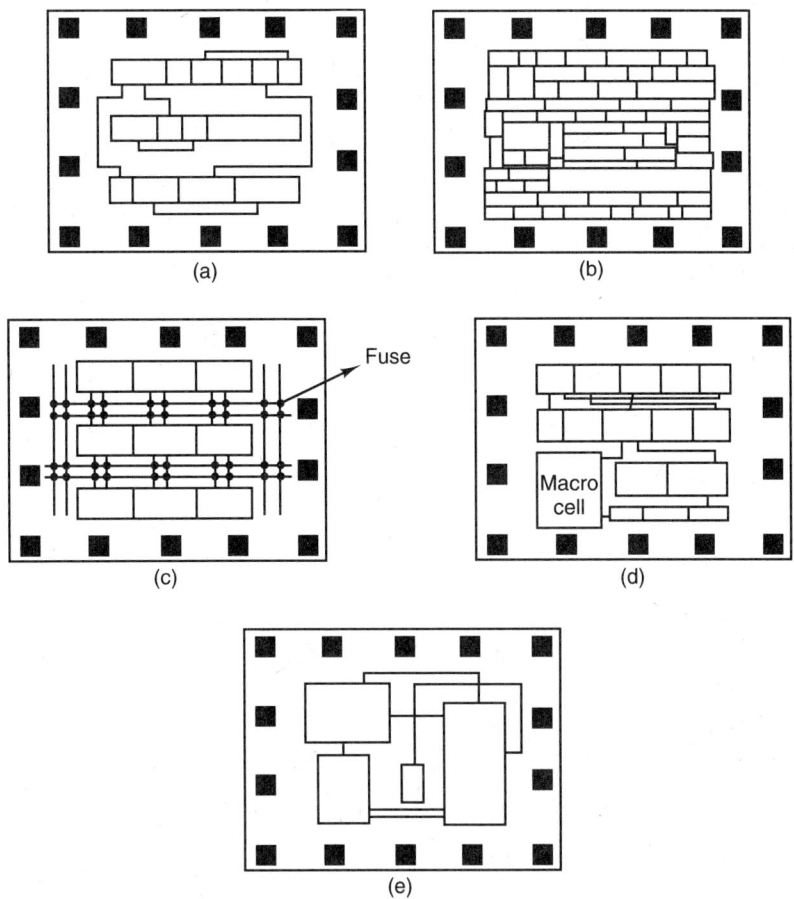

Figure A.10 Different types of chip layout. (a) Gate array. (b) Sea of gates. (c) Field programmable gate array. (d) Standard cell. (e) Macro/custom cell.

The field programmable gate array (FPGA) consists of horizontal rows of simple cells that can be programmed and interconnected by the user. A cell, in its simplest form, is a small memory block that can be programmed to store the truth table of a function (that is, a cell can be considered as a look-up table). As shown in Figure A.10c, the rows of cells are separated by channels that contain predefined horizontal and vertical wiring segments of fixed lengths. Connection between these segments is provided through fuses. To connect two segments, a high voltage is applied across the fuse that lies between these two segments. The high voltage blows the fuse, which provides a low resistance bidirectional connection between two wiring segments.

The standard cell approach also has a row-based layout image similar to a gate array. However, in this approach basic cells are customized from the beginning of fabrication and, in addition to basic cells, macro cells are also allowed on the same chip (see Figure A.10d). (Macro cells include more complex circuits than basic cells.) Since only the needed cells are fabricated, the standard cell approach results in greater silicon efficiency than that of the gate array approach.

In contrast to the gate array and standard cell approaches, as shown in Figure A.10e, the macro/custom cell technique allows us to have any rectilinear-shaped cell on the chip. A cell may be a macro cell, which means it has a fixed geometry and pin locations, or the cell could be a custom cell, which has an estimated geometry and pins that need to be placed.

REFERENCES

[MEA 80] MEAD, C., AND L. CONWAY, *Introduction to VLSI Systems*. Reading MA: Addison-Wesley Publishing Co, 1980.

[SHE 92] SHERWANI, N. A., *Algorithms for VLSI Physical Design Automation*. Norwell, MA: Kluwer Academic Publishers, 1992.

[WES 93] WESTE, N., AND K. ESHRAGHIAN, *Principles of CMOS VLSI Design: A Systems Perspective*. Reading MA: Addison-Wesley Publishing Co., 1993.

PROBLEMS

A.1. Draw the circuit diagram for the following gates using CMOS technology.
  a. NAND gate.
  b. NOR gate.
  c. AND gate.
  d. XOR gate.

A.2. Design a half-adder at transistor level. Use CMOS technology, and also try to use a minimum number of transistors.

A.3. Design a circuit that accepts a 3-bit number $A=a_2a_1a_0$ and generates an output binary number $F=f_1f_0$ such that:

$$F = \lfloor A/3 \rfloor.$$

  a. Obtain the truth table.
  b. Derive the Boolean expressions.
  c. Simplify the Boolean expressions.
  d. Draw the circuit at the transistor level using CMOS technology.

A.4. Using CMOS technology, draw a layout for a NAND gate.

Appendix B
Combinational and Sequential Circuits

B.1 COMBINATIONAL CIRCUITS

A combinational circuit has several inputs and outputs in which outputs are entirely determined by the current inputs. In the following, we will introduce some frequently used combinational circuits, such as multiplexer, demultiplexer, decoder, and encoder.

Multiplexer and demultiplexer. Figure B.1 represents a situation in which a transmission line is shared between four nodes (computers). The line is assigned for transmitting data from A to B for a certain period of time and then is switched for transmission between C and D. This process repeats until A and C send all their data. The circuit that selects one of several signal source lines at the transmitting end is referred to as a *multiplexer* (MUX) and at the receiving end, a *demultiplexer* (De MUX).

In general, a multiplexer with 2^n inputs has n select lines and one output line. The idea is to share the output among the inputs. At any time, only one of the inputs, determined by the select lines, is connected to the output. As an example, Figure B.2 represents a block diagram and a logic diagram for a 2-by-1 (two inputs and one output)

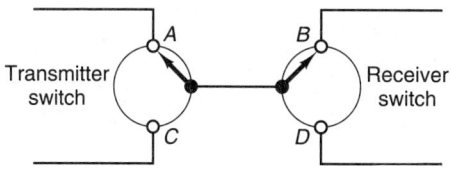

Figure B.1 Time-division multiplexing: one way to send several digital signals on one transmission line.

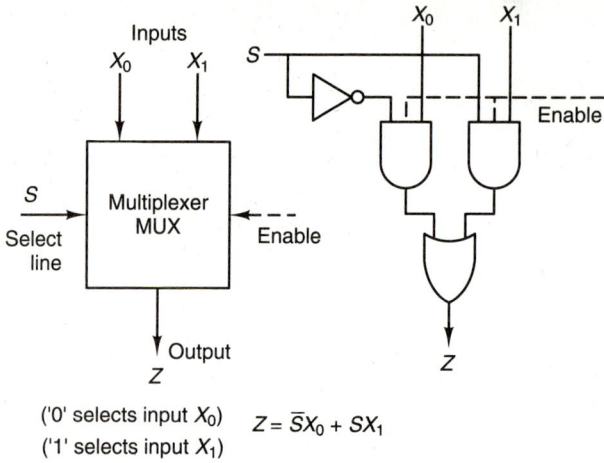

Figure B.2 Block diagram and logic diagram of a 2-by-1 multiplexer.

multiplexer. In this design the enable line works like an on/off switch. When the select line S is zero and the enable line is 1, the input X_0 is connected to the output Z. When both the select and enable lines are 1, the input X_1 is connected to the output Z. Otherwise (i.e., when the enable line is 0), the output is always zero.

The 2-by-1 multiplexer can be used for designing larger multiplexers. For example, as shown in Figure B.3, an 8-by-1 multiplexer can be constructed by seven 2-by-1 multiplexers.

If there are n inputs and each input has m bits, then the multiplexer is referred to as an n-input m-bit multiplexer. The number of output signal lines is also m. Figure B.4 shows a block diagram for such a multiplexer.

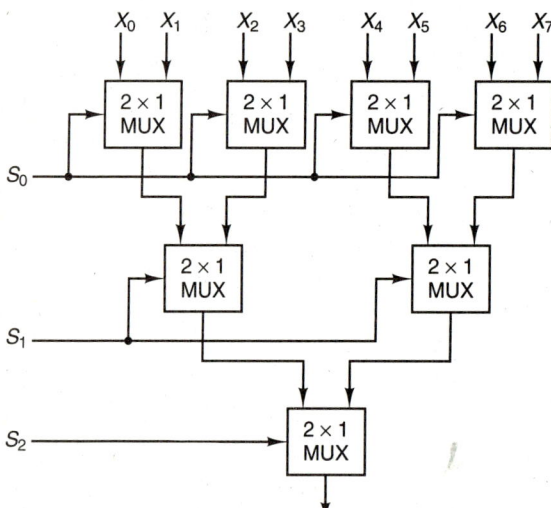

Figure B.3 Design of an 8-by-1 multiplexer by using 2-by-1 multiplexers.

Sec. B.1   Combinational Circuits

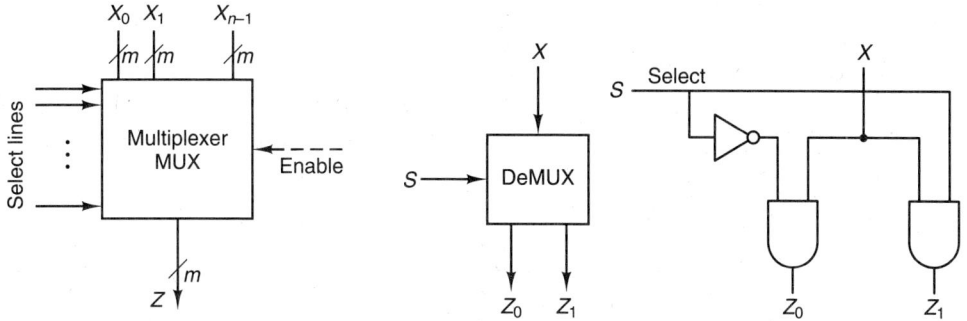

Figure B.4 Block diagram of an n-input m-bit multiplexer.

Figure B.5 Block diagram and logic diagram of a 1-by-2 demultiplexer.

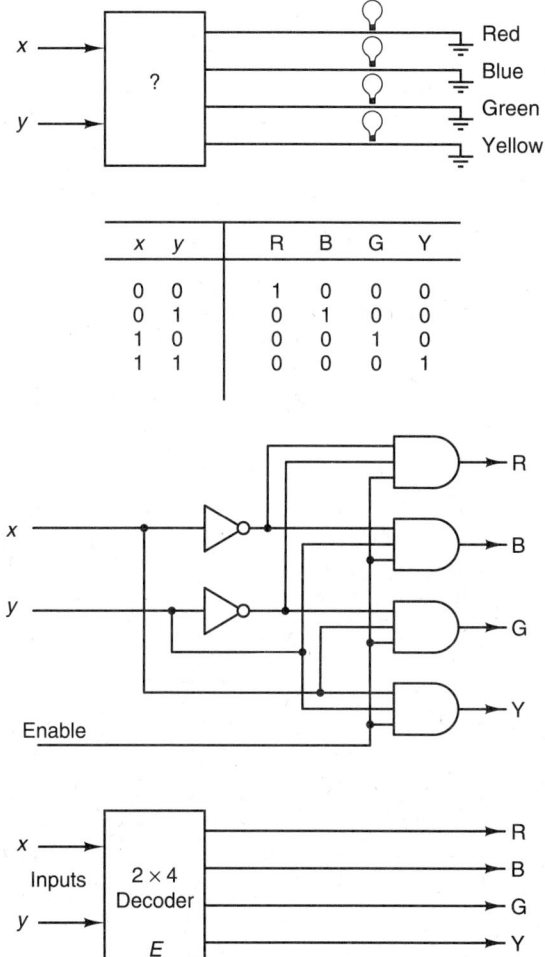

x	y	R	B	G	Y
0	0	1	0	0	0
0	1	0	1	0	0
1	0	0	0	1	0
1	1	0	0	0	1

Figure B.6 Block diagram and logic diagram of a 2-by-4 decoder. The output lines of the decoder are used to turn on one of the four lamps.

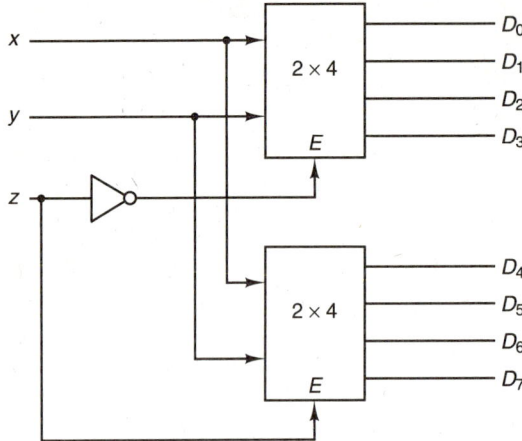

Figure B.7 Design of a 3-by-8 decoder by using 2-by-4 decoder.

The demultiplexer works in reverse of a multiplexer. It has one input, several outputs, and several select lines. The input is routed to one of the outputs according to the select lines. Here again there is an enable line that affects the outcome. A block diagram and a logic diagram for a 1-by-2 demultiplexer are shown in Figure B.5.

Decoder and encoder. Another common application of a demultiplexer is in that of addressing, where the n select lines are interpreted as an address in order to select one of 2^n output lines. This is called a *decoder*. In general, a decoder has n input lines and 2^n output lines. It sets one of the outputs to 1 based on the binary information from the input lines. An example of designing a 2-by-4 decoder is shown in Figure B.6. In this figure, the outputs of the decoder are connected to four lamps: red, blue, green, and yellow. At any time either all the lamps are off or only one of them is on. For example, when the inputs $x = 1$ and $y = 0$ and the enable line is high, the green lamp is turned on. The 2-by-4 decoder can be used for designing larger decoders. Figure B.7 shows a 3-by-8 decoder, which is constructed by using two 2-by-4 decoders.

Although often in a decoder only one output is high at a time, but there are situations where more than one output might be 1. For example, in a BCD-to-seven-segment decoder, more than one output can be high. (BCD stands for binary coded decimal.) The BCD-to-seven-segment decoder is a combinational circuit that accepts a decimal digit in BCD and generates the appropriate output for the selection of segments in a display indicator used for displaying the decimal digit.

Another frequently used combinational circuit is *encoder*. An encoder produces a reverse operation from that of a decoder. It has 2^n input lines and n output lines. Unlike a decoder, which uses an input address to activate one output line, an encoder generates the address or name of an active input line. A 4-by-2 encoder is shown in Figure B.8. In this figure, the additional input-active control line is used to indicate the presence or absence of an active input line. Given that when none of the inputs is active the output is 00 and the fact that when the input x_0 is active the output is also 00, the input-active control line is necessary to distinguish between these two situations. In other words, this line is necessary to show that whether the input x_0 is active.

Sec. B.1 Combinational Circuits

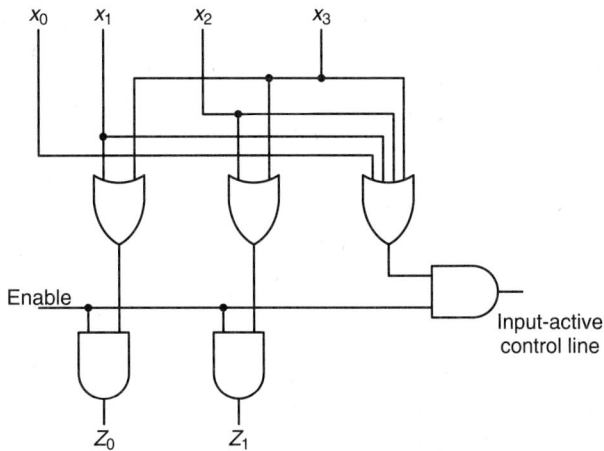

Figure B.8 Logic diagram of a 4-by-2 encoder.

In an encoder, if more than one input goes high, the output is invalid. For example, if x_1 and x_2 go high at the same time, the input x_3 will be selected. To avoid this problem, it is useful to assign priorities to the input lines and design the encoder so that the output address is always that of the active input line with the highest priority. Figure B.9 shows a 4-by-2 priority encoder. In this figure, for each $i > j$, x_i and x_j are connected so that a 1 on the higher priority line x_i effectively blocks a 1 on the lower-priority line x_j.

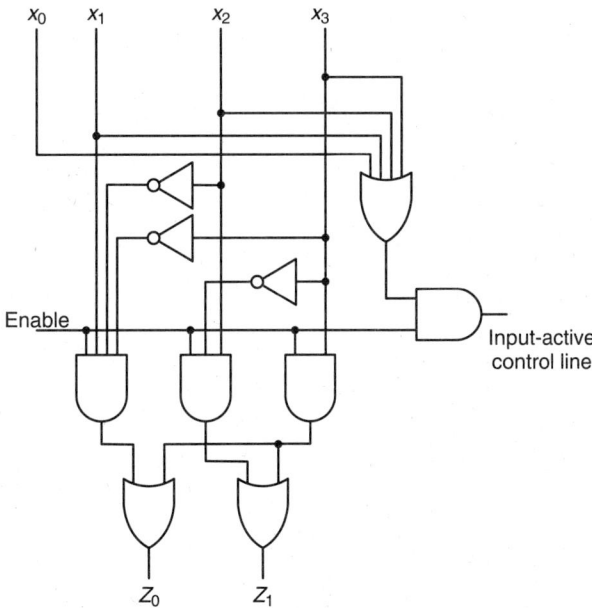

Figure B.9 Logic diagram of a 4-by-2 priority encoder.

Multiplexers and decoders can be used as basic cells to implement Boolean functions. For example, Figure B.10 represents different ways for implementing the function $F(A, B, C, D) = \overline{A}\,\overline{B}\,\overline{C}\,\overline{D} + \overline{A}B\overline{C}D + ABCD + A\overline{B}C\overline{D}$.

In Figure B.10a, a 16-input multiplexer is used to generate the function F. In this implementation, the input variables A, B, C, and D are connected to the select lines; four of the input lines (0, 5, 10, and 15) are connected to 1; and the other input lines are connected to 0. Since the input values $A = 0$, $B = 0$, $C = 0$, and $D = 0$, generate an output of one, the input line 0 is connected to 1. For the same reason, the input lines 5, 10,

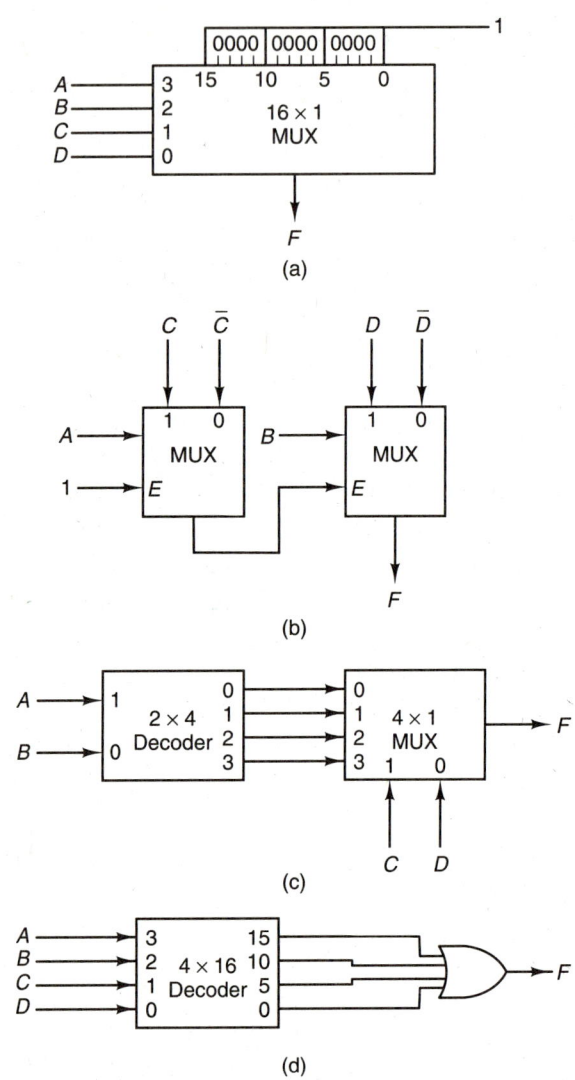

Figure B.10 Different ways for implementing the function $F(A, B, C, D)$ $= \overline{A}\,\overline{B}\,\overline{C}\,\overline{D} + \overline{A}B\overline{C}D + ABCD + A\overline{B}C\overline{D}$.

Sec. B.1   Combinational Circuits   419

and 15 are set to 1. In general, any n-variable Boolean function F can be generated by a 2^n-by-1 multiplexer.

In Figure B.10b, two 2-by-1 multiplexers are used to generate F. This is done by rewriting F as:

$$F = \overline{A}\,\overline{C}(\overline{B}\,\overline{D} + BD) + AC(BD + \overline{B}\,\overline{D})$$
$$= (\overline{A}\,\overline{C} + AC)(\overline{B}\,\overline{D} + BD)$$

The first multiplexer generates the term $(\overline{A}\,\overline{C} + AC)$, and is always enabled. The output of this multiplexer depends on the input variables A and C, where A is connected to the select line and C is connected to the input lines. When $A = 1$ and $C = 1$, or, $A = 0$ and $C = 0$, the output is 1; otherwise, the output is 0. An output of 1 makes the second multiplexer enable. Depending on the values of B and D, the second multiplexer generates the final value of F.

In Figure B.10c, a 4-by-1 multiplexer and a 2-by-4 decoder are used to generate F. From the Boolean function F, we see that there are four cases that make F high;

1. $AB = 00$ and $CD = 00$,
2. $AB = 01$ and $CD = 01$,
3. $AB = 11$ and $CD = 11$,
4. $AB = 10$ and $CD = 10$.

If $AB = 00$, the output line 0 of the decoder will go high. Then, if $CD = 00$, this output will be connected to F and makes $F = 1$. This is the reason why output line 0 of the decoder is connected to the input line 0 of the multiplexer. For the same reason, other connections are established.

Finally, Figure B.10d uses a 4-by-16 decoder and an external OR gate to generate F. When $ABCD = 0000, 0101, 1111$, or 1010, output lines 0, 5, 10, or 15, will go high, respectively. The OR gate generates an output 1 whenever one of these four lines is high.

Programmable logic array.   The programmable logic array (PLA) is a type of VLSI circuit for forming the sums of the products. The PLA is basically a combinational circuit that can be programmed to implement the specific logic functions specified by the user. The word *programmable* refers to the specific connections that can be built after the basic circuit structure has been defined.

The PLA has a simple and rectangular structure that requires a reasonable amount of area on a chip. The structure is based on the fact that any combinational circuit can be realized by three levels of NOTs, ANDs, and ORs. Figure B.11 represents these three levels for any given function f [VLS 82]. Figure B.12 shows an alternative implementation for f. To reduce the required amount of area on the chip, the position of the gates in this implementation can be rearranged as shown in Figure B.13. This new structure, called a folded structure, is used as a floor plan for the PLA. To illustrate the detail of such a folded structure at the transistor level, we design a PLA for the following Boolean functions:

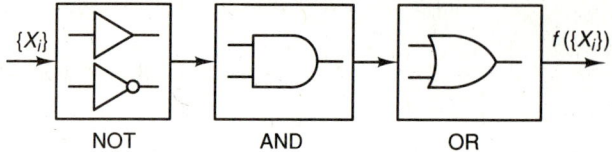

The notation ─▷─ denotes a driver and can be realized as ─▷○─▷─

Figure B.11 General structure of any combinational circuit.

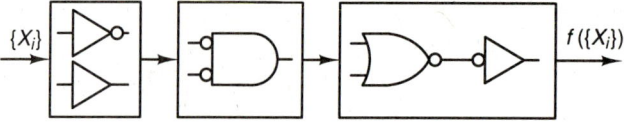

Figure B.12 An alternative structure for the design of any combinational circuit.

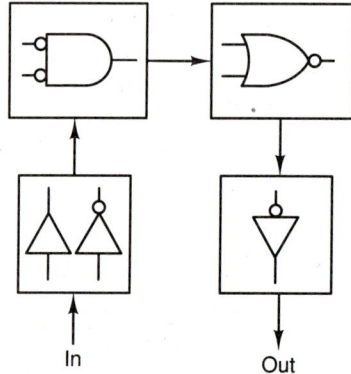

Figure B.13 PLA basic floor plan.

$$Z_1 = \overline{A}B\overline{C} + ABC + A\overline{B},$$
$$Z_2 = A + BC + \overline{A}B\overline{C}.$$

Figure B.14 represents the structure of the PLA for these functions. There is a horizontal line for each term in the functions. Initially, each line is set to 1 by connecting it to the supply through a resistor. Each line might be pulled down to zero subject to the values of the variables in its coresponding term. For example, the first line, R_1, represents the term ABC, which means that whenever $A = 1$, $B = 1$, and $C = 1$ this line will stay high. If one of the input lines, say A, changes to 0, R_1 will be pulled down to 0. This is because the gate of transistor T_1 becomes 1, which causes it to connect line R_1 to ground (i.e., 0).

In addition to horizontal lines, there is an output line for each function. Each output line contains a transistor for each term in its corresponding function. For example, output Z_1 contains three transistors for three terms ABC, $\overline{A}B\overline{C}$, and $A\overline{B}$. Whenever any of these terms changes to 1 (say ABC), the gate of its corresponding transistor becomes 1 (gate of T_2), which produces an output equal to 1 ($Z_1 = 1$).

Sec. B.2 Sequential Circuits

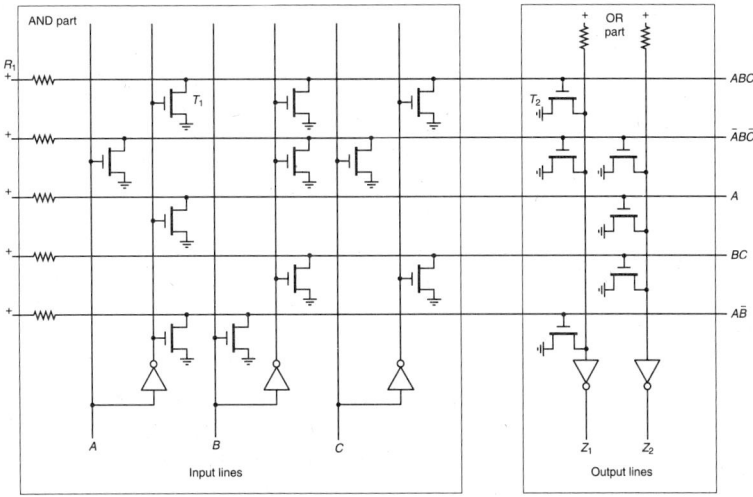

Figure B.14 Structure of a PLA at transistor level.

B.2 SEQUENTIAL CIRCUITS

In sequential circuits, the output signals are functions not only of the present input signals, but also of the past input signals. Thus, as illustrated in Figure B.15, in these types of circuits there is a memory that keeps the present state of the circuit based on past input signals. The memory element values represent the present state of the circuit. Any changes on output signals will be based on the present changes on input signals and the present state of the circuit. Since input signals have different propagation delays, it is desirable to have a synchronization mechanism such that the circuit operation can be executed at a time that all signals are in their proper places. The synchronization is achieved by a sequence of pulses, called *clock*. Figure B.16 shows a series of clock pulses over a period of time.

There are many ways to implement a memory element. Two of the common implementations are flip-flop and latch. A *flip-flop* is a memory element that changes output during the clock transition from 0 to 1 or from 1 to 0. A *latch* is a memory ele-

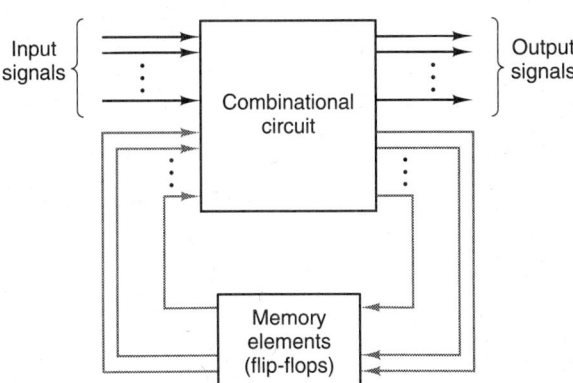

Figure B.15 Basic elements of a sequential curcuit.

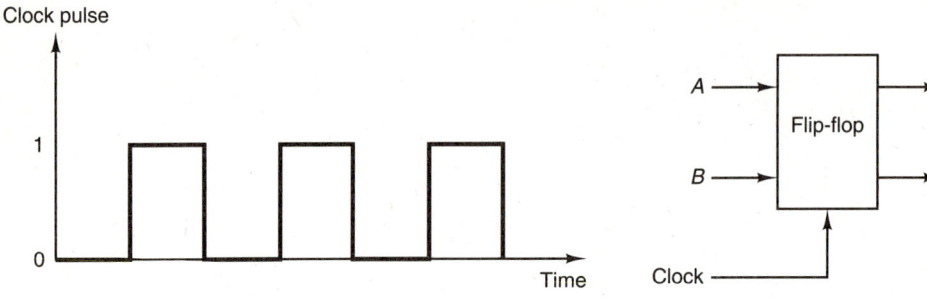

Figure B.16 Clock pulse.

Figure B.17 Block diagram of a flip-flop.

ment that changes output within the period that clock is 1. In other words, a flip-flop is edge triggered, whereas a latch is level triggered. In this appendix we only consider flip-flops for designing sequential circuits. Similar design process can be used for latches.

The block diagram for a flip-flop is shown in Figure B.17. The inputs A and B will determine the output of flip-flop Q when the clock pulse changes from 0 to 1. In addition to output Q, a flip-flop has another output, $\overline{Q}$, which is the complement of Q. The availability of the output $\overline{Q}$ sometimes simplifies the design, as illustrated in a later example.

Figure B.18a shows the logic diagram for a RS flip-flop. (R stands for reset and S stands for set.) In this circuit, the output of the two AND gates remains at 0 as long as the clock pulse (CP) is 0, regardless of the S and R values.

When the clock pulse (CP) changes from 0 to 1, output Q reacts to inputs R and S as indicated in the truth table given in Figure B.19b. In this truth table, Q^n refers to the state

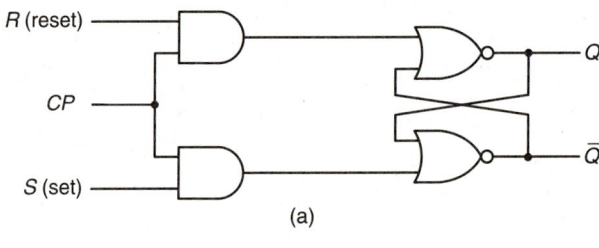

(a)

S	R	Q^{n+1}
0	0	Q^n
0	1	0
1	0	1
1	1	Undefined

(b)

Figure B.18 Clocked RS flip-flop. (a) Logic diagram for RS flip-flop. (b) Truth table for RS.

Sec. B.2 Sequential Circuits

of the flip-flop before the clock pulse occurs, and Q^{n+1} refers to the state after the transition of the clock pulse.

One problem with the *RS* flip-flop is that Q is not defined when $R = 1$ and $S = 1$. The *JK* flip-flop solves this problem by feeding back the output values to the input of the AND gates (see Figure B.19). In this flip-flop, Q will be complemented whenever $J = 1$ and $K = 1$, and a clock pulse occurs.

To verify the cases in the truth table, we take one of them and trace it on the logic diagram. Let's consider the case when $K = 1$ and $J = 0$. In this case the outputs Q and $\overline{Q}$ become 0 and 1, respectively. There are two possible present output states: (1) $Q = 0$ and $\overline{Q} = 1$, and (2) $Q = 1$ and $\overline{Q} = 0$. Each case is considered next.

Case 1: When $Q = 0$ and $\overline{Q} = 1$. When the clock pulse is at 0, the output of gates A_1 and A_2 is 0, the output of N_1 is 0, and the output of N_2 is 1. When the clock pulse changes from 0 to 1, the outputs A_1, A_2, N_1, and N_2 stay the same as those with the clock pulse at 0; that is $Q = 0$ and $\overline{Q} = 1$ stay unchanged.

Case 2: When $Q = 1$ and $\overline{Q} = 0$. When the clock pulse is at 0, the output of gates A_1 and A_2 is 0, the output of N_1 is 1, and the output of N_2 is 0. When the clock pulse changes from 0 to 1, the output of A_1 becomes 1, A_2 becomes 0, N_1 becomes 0, and N_2 becomes 1. Therefore, the outputs Q and $\overline{Q}$ will be changed to 0 and 1, respectively.

Using the preceding flip-flops, any sequential circuit can be realized. The following examples represent the main steps involved in designing a sequential circuit by using *JK* flip-flops. (A similar process can be used for other types of flip-flops.)

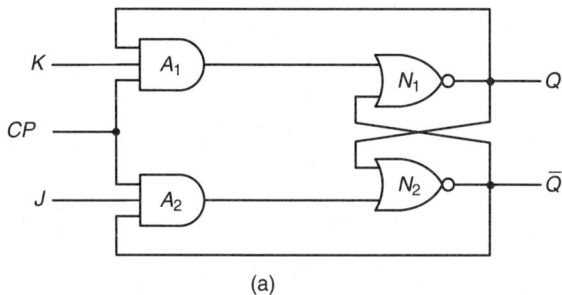

(a)

J	K	Q^{n+1}
0	0	Q^n
0	1	0
1	0	1
1	1	$\overline{Q^n}$

(b)

Figure B.19 Clocked *JK* flip-flop. (a) Logic diagram for *JK* flip-flop. (b) Truth table for *JK*.

Example 1

The purpose of this example is to represent the steps involved in designing a serial 2's complementer sequential circuit using *JK* flip-flops. The circuit has a serial input and a serial output, where the output is the 2's complement of input signal.

In the first step we draw the state diagram for the problem. From the 2's complement converting algorithm we know that we can just copy the leading 0's starting from the least significant bit until the first 1 is encountered, and then the subsequent bits are complemented. That is,

$$\text{input} \rightarrow 1\ 0\ 0\ 1\ 1\ 0\ |\ 1\ 0\ 0$$
$$\text{output} \rightarrow 0\ 1\ 1\ 0\ 0\ 1\ |\ 1\ 0\ 0$$
$$\text{complement}\ |\ \text{copy}$$

As shown in Figure B.20, we need two states for this converting algorithm. They are the copy state and complement state, denoted as *A* and *B*, respectively. In state *A* (copy), whatever comes in will come out until encountering the first 1. At this point the circuit moves into state *B* (complement). In state *B*, we just complement the input bits: 0 to 1 and 1 to 0.

In step 2, we find the number of flip-flops needed in the circuit. Let *n* be the number of needed flip-flops and *s* be the number of states. Then *n* can be obtained by using the following equation:

$$n = \lceil \log_2 s \rceil.$$

In our example, $n = \lceil \log_2 2 \rceil = 1$. Thus only one flip-flop is needed. Next, we assign a unique binary number to each state. In the actual circuit the output of the flip-flops represents these numbers. Therefore, the number of flip-flops determines the number of bits in each number. Here, since we need only one flip-flop, 1 bit should be enough to distinguish between the states. The binary number 0 can be assigned to represent the state *A*, and 1 to represent the state *B*. In other words, whenever the output of the flip-flop is 0, it means that the circuit is in state *A*; otherwise it is in state *B*.

In step 3, we obtain the state table, considering all the possible combinations of input values and states. To obtain such a table, first we need to derive a table, called an excitation table, for *JK* flip-flop. This table shows the values that should be assigned to *J* and *K* in order to change the output *Q* to a specific value. For example, to change *Q* from

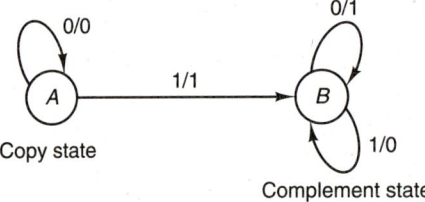

Figure B.20 State diagram of a 2's complement circuit.

Sec. B.2   Sequential Circuits

0 to 1, J should be 1, where K can be 1 or 0. Considering all the possible changes for Q, the following excitation table can be derived from the JK's truth table.

Excitation Table

Q^n	Q^{n+1}	J	K
0	0	0	d
0	1	1	d
1	0	d	1
1	1	d	0

d stands for "don't care" (0 or 1)

From this JK flip-flop excitation table, we can build the following state table:

PS Q	X	NS Q	J	K	Output Z
0	0	0	0	d	0
1	0	1	d	0	1
0	1	1	1	d	1
1	1	1	d	0	0

PS : present state (Q)

NS : next state (Q)

X : input

In step 4, we derive an equation for each flip-flop's input line and for each output line. The Karnaugh map [MAN 84] is used to simplify the equations.

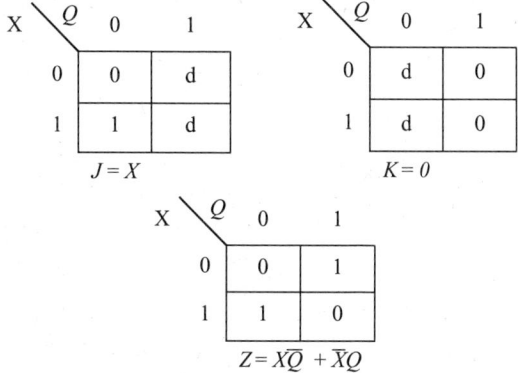

Finally, step 5 we draw the circuit diagram (see Figure B.21).

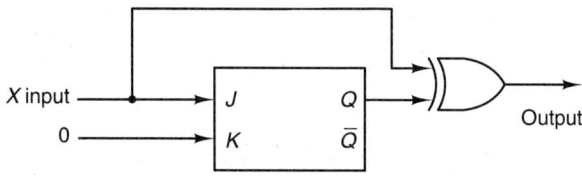

Figure B.21   Two's complement circuit diagram.

Example 2

In this example, we design a counter (using a *JK* flip-flop) that gives a counter state sequence of 3, 1, 0, 3, 1, 0, 3, 1, 0, 3, ... The state diagram for such a counter is shown in Figure B.22. Based on this state diagram, the following state table can be obtained.

PS Q_1Q_0	NS Q_1Q_0	J_0	K_0	J_1	K_1
11	01	d	0	d	1
01	00	d	1	0	d
00	11	1	d	1	d
10	dd	d	d	d	d

From this table, the following equations can be derived.

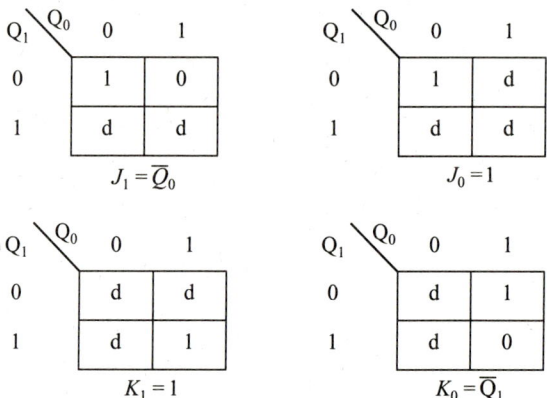

The circuit diagram is shown in Figure B.23.

Design of a sequential circuit by using PLA. In the PLA for combinational circuits, NOT gates (also called buffers) were used on the input and output lines. These gates can also be used as dynamic register cells (or memory elements). Two NOT gates in series can store data for a short period of time. Within this period, the stored data must be refreshed or changed. This is done usually by using the two-phase clocking scheme shown in Figure B.24. As shown in Figure B.25, during phase 1 clock pulse (when Φ_1 is high), the inverted input of the input value will appear on the output of the first NOT gate. When the phase 2 clock pulse goes high, the inverted output of

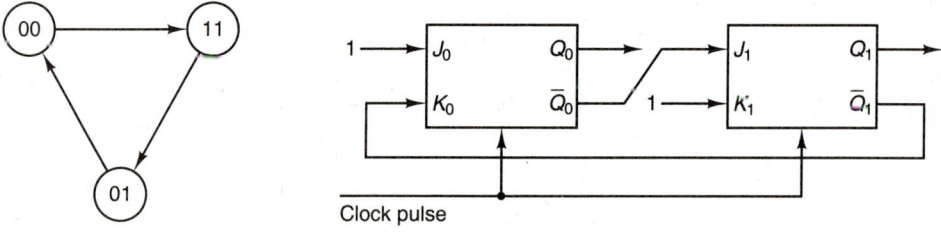

Figure B.22 State diagram for a counter. **Figure B.23** Circuit diagram for a counter.

Sec. B.2 Sequential Circuits   427

first gate will appear on the output of the second gate; that is the original value will appear on the output of the second NOT gate.

Based on these phenomena, an alternative structure for sequential circuits is represented in Figure B.26 [VLS 82]. In this figure, ½R stands for half a register cell and is implemented by a NOT gate. The folded structure of this figure is used as a floor plan for the PLA (see Figure B.27.) This type of PLA can be used for designing any kind of sequential circuit. For example, suppose that we want to design a sequential circuit that detects an input sequence of 000 or 11. An output $Z = 1$ is produced only when three consecutive logic 0 inputs occur or when two consecutive logic 1 inputs occur. A fourth 0 or a third 1 returns the output to logic 0. That is, there is no overlap between the input sequences that generate an ouput of 1. For example,

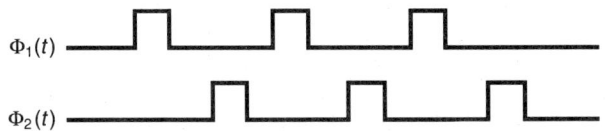

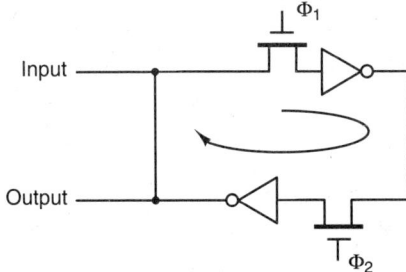

Figure B.24 Two-phase clocks (nonoverlapping clocks).

Figure B.25 Dynamic register cell.

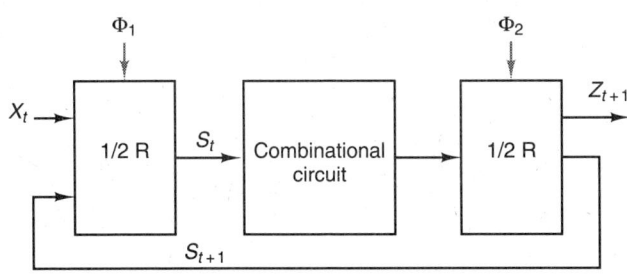

Let S_t = present state
Then S_{t+1} = next state = $f(S_t, X_t)$
and Z_{t+1} = output = $g(S_t, X_t)$

Figure B.26 Alternative structure of a sequential circuit.

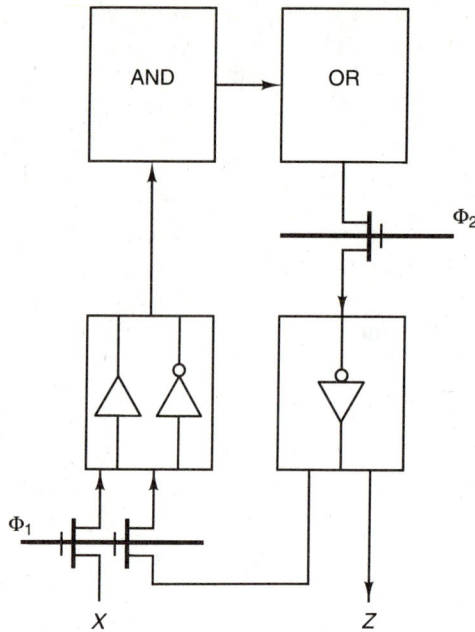

Figure B.27 Floor plan of PLA for sequential circuits.

To design this circuit, first we have to construct the state diagram. Figure B.28 represents such a state diagram. From this state diagram, the following state table can be obtained.

Input X	Present State P_1P_0	Next State N_1N_0	Output Z
0	00	01	0
0	01	10	0
0	10	00	1
0	11	01	0
1	00	11	0
1	01	11	0
1	10	11	0
1	11	00	1

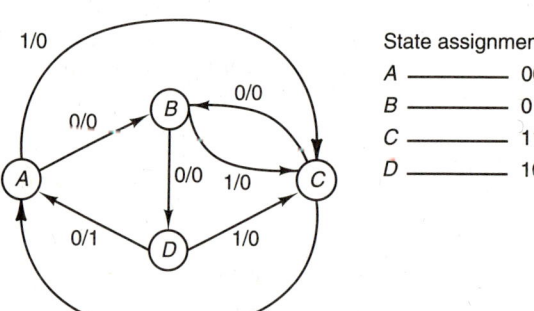

State assignment
A ——— 00
B ——— 01
C ——— 11
D ——— 10

Figure B.28 State diagram for a sequential circuit that detects an input sequence of 000 or 11.

Sec. B.2 Sequential Circuits

Now we can derive the equations for N_0, N_1, and Z, as follows:

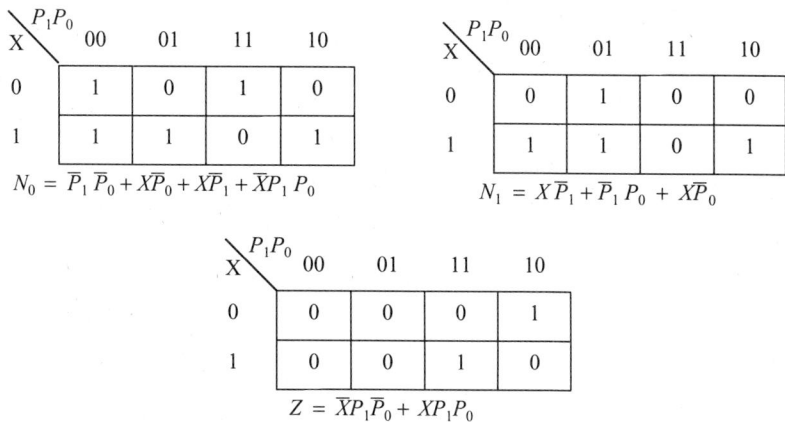

$$N_0 = \overline{P}_1\,\overline{P}_0 + X\overline{P}_0 + X\overline{P}_1 + \overline{X}P_1\,P_0$$

$$N_1 = X\overline{P}_1 + \overline{P}_1 P_0 + X\overline{P}_0$$

$$Z = \overline{X}P_1\overline{P}_0 + XP_1P_0$$

The final PLA is shown in Figure B.29.

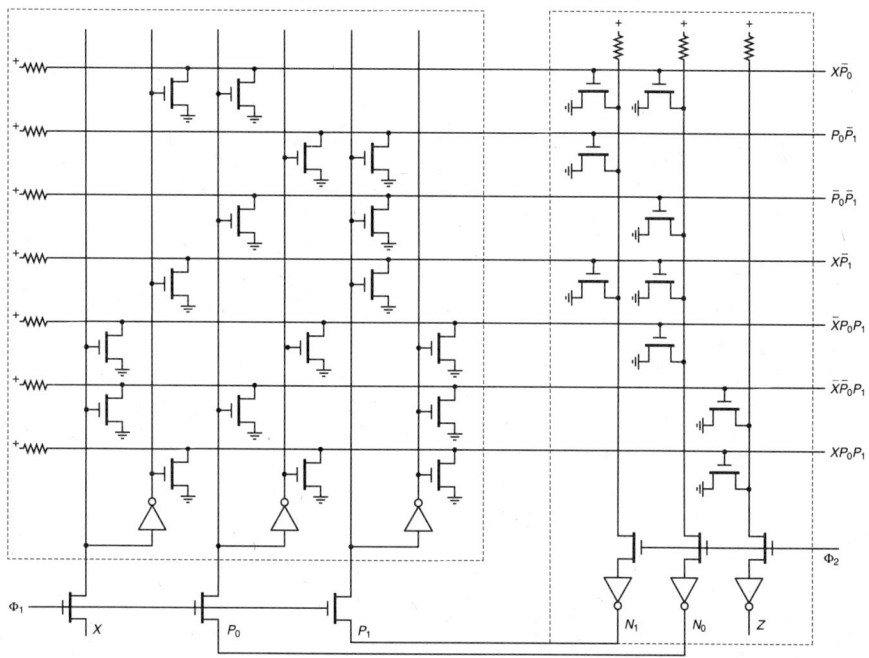

Figure B.29 PLA for a sequential circuit that detects an input sequence of 000 or 11.

REFERENCES

[MAN 84] Mano, M. Morris, *Digital Design*, Upper Saddle River, NJ: Prentice Hall, 1984.
[VLS 82] VLSI Technology, "Introduction to VLSI Systems Design," VLSI Technology, Inc., 1982.

PROBLEMS

B.1. Use the minimum number of 2-by-1 multiplexers to implement the function $F(A, B, C, D) = \overline{A}\,\overline{B}\,\overline{C} + BCD + \overline{A}B\,\overline{C}D$. Label all the inputs and outputs of the multiplexers.

B.2. Show that AND, OR, and NOT gates can be implemented by using NAND gate(s) only.

B.3. Show that AND, OR, and NOT gates can be implemented by using NOR gate(s) only.

B.4. Implement the function
$$F(A, B, C, D) = \overline{A}\,\overline{B}\,\overline{C}\,\overline{D} + \overline{A}BC\overline{D} + ABCD + A\overline{B}C\overline{D}$$
by using a 4-by-1 multiplexer and a 2-by-4 decoder. Label all the inputs and outputs of the multiplexer and the decoder.

B.5. Write out the corresponding output function (or output value) for function F in Figure PB.5.

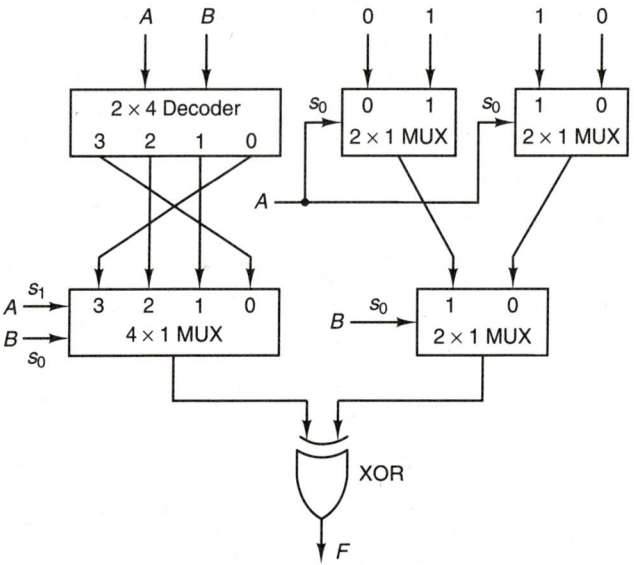

Figure PB.5

B.6. Draw a PLA (at transistor level) for
$$Z_1 = AB\overline{C} + A\overline{B}C + \overline{A}BC$$
$$Z_2 = A\overline{B}C + \overline{A}\,\overline{C}$$

B.7. Design a sequential circuit (using JK flip-flops) that detects an input sequence of 000 or 11. An output $Z = 1$ is produced only when three consecutive logic 0 inputs occur or when two consecutive logic 1 inputs occur. A fourth 0 or a third 1 returns the output to logic 0. For example,
$$X = \ldots 0\ 1\ 0\ 0\ 0\ 0\ 1\ 1\ 1\ 1\ 1\ 0 \rightarrow$$
$$Z = \ldots 0\ 0\ 0\ 1\ 0\ 0\ 0\ 1\ 0\ 1\ 0\ 0 \rightarrow$$

  a. Draw a state diagram for the circuit.
  b. Determine a state table for the circuit.
  c. Draw the circuit diagram.

Problems

B.8. Design a serial incrementer (using PLA). The circuit has one input line X and one output line S, where S is the sum of X and 1 (see Figure PB.8).

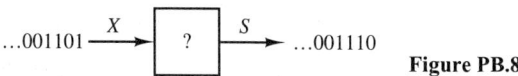

Figure PB.8

   a. Draw a state diagram for the circuit.
   b. Determine a state table for the circuit.
   c. Realize the circuit using PLA.

B.9. Design a serial full adder. The circuit has two input lines X and Y, and one output line S, where S is the sum of X and Y. Assume that X and Y are infinite binary numbers (see Figure PB.9).

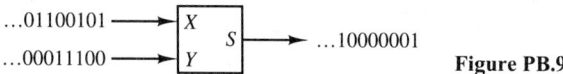

Figure PB.9

   a. Realize the minimize circuit using JK flip-flops.
   b. Realize the minimize circuit using PLA.

B.10. Design a counter (using JK flip-flops) to give a counter state sequence of:

$$0\ 2\ 3\ 0\ 2\ 3\ 0\ 2\ 3\ \ldots.$$

B.11. Design a control logic for a parking area. The controller senses two input signal lines, A and B. Line A is from the entrance gate and is at logic 0 voltage when no car is passing through the gate. When a car enters the parking area, a pulse on line A is generated, that is the line A becomes high (logic 1 voltage) and stays at high for a clock period. Line B is from the exit gate and is at logic 0 voltage when no car is passing through the gate. When a car leaves the parking area, a pulse on line B is generated. Assume that at any given time a maximum of seven cars can park in the parking area. The controller should turn on a FULL light when there are seven cars in the parking space.

Appendix C
Hardware Description Language: VHDL

C.1 INTRODUCTION

We might ask why hardware description languages (HDLs) are needed. The process of designing a single chip, a board of chips, or a series of boards becomes more complex each day. The design process can cost millions of dollars, and a year or more may elapse while moving from the initial characterization of the design to a working device. Often, by the time the design is completed, it is already a year behind the state of the art. Some large chip designs require documentation of more than 100 pages of schematics, making it difficult for designers both to understand all the parts of the design and to communicate with other designers.

The task of designing complex systems involves managing, in some highly structured way, the time-and-space relationships between the various system building blocks. The purpose and intent of these building blocks have to be clearly understood and tailored so as to fit into the overall system structure. Hardware designers need a method that will allow them to model, synthesize, and simulate highly abstract ideas of hardware designs, and this method needs to be standardized throughout industry and government. (The ability to simulate designs allows the designers to test the design on a computer before actually hardwiring the circuit, thereby saving time and money.) Early hardware description languages were too tightly knit into the various hardware manufacturer's automated design tools. To address some of these problems, the U.S. Department of Defense developed a hardware description language for its very high speed integrated circuit (VHSIC) program. In 1983, the Air Force sponsored the initial development of the very high speed integrated circuit description language (VHDL), a

Sec. C.1 Introduction

powerful hardware design language, which is readable by both humans and machines [IEEE 87, ARM 89, BAK 89, BHA 92]. The original version was released by the Defense Department in the summer of 1985. This language was improved for several years, and, finally, version 1076-1987 became an IEEE standard in 1987. About 2 years later, the Defense Department required all military design submissions to be in VHDL. Shortly thereafter, VHDL became the industry standard.

VHDL provides a formal notation for communication between vendors and users of hardware devices, among designers, and among design tools. It supports descriptions of hardware at many levels of abstraction, such as system, subsystem, register, and gate levels. Figure C.1 shows a sample of elements for each level of abstraction. VHDL allows designers to design a hardware device at a highly abstract level and progressively work down to the circuit component level. VHDL also supports verification, synthesis, and testing of the design. Using VHDL, the designer can make sure all the parts work separately before trying to make them work together in the whole

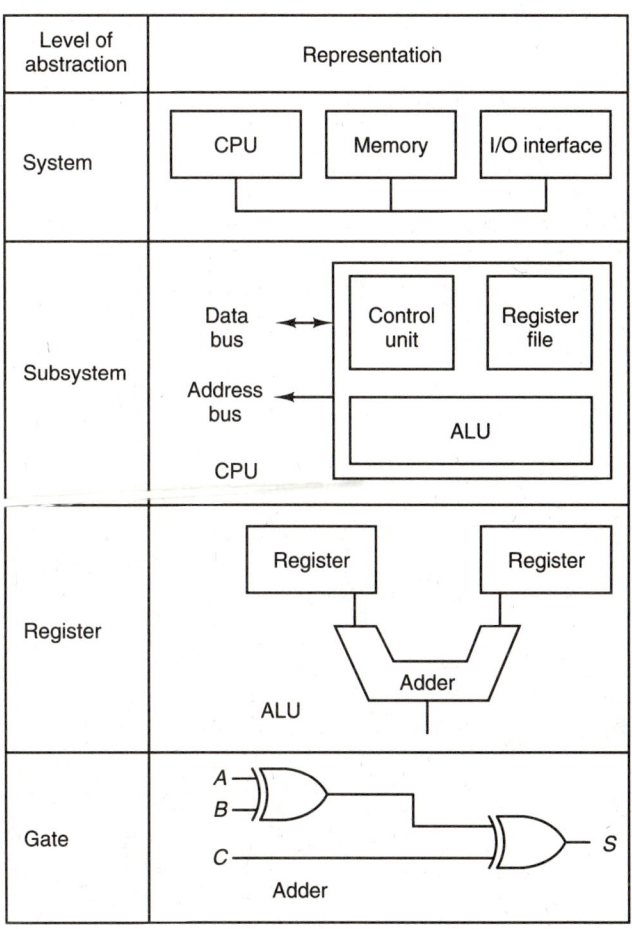

Figure C.1 Levels of hardware description.

design and can make any kind of change in the design without actually having to hard-wire the design. A VHDL simulator makes it possible to find potential problem areas in the design that might not have otherwise been detected. It also shows how the new design will work with other devices.

In general, VHDL, which has a syntax structured after Ada, has many capabilities, including the following:

1. It supports various styles of description, such as structural, data flow, and behavioral. Structural description represents components and their interconnections. Data flow description represents behavior while implying structure. Behavioral description represents behavior without any structural information and is algorithmic.
2. It supports multiple design methodologies, such as top-down (the divide-and-conquer approach), bottom-up (start with small cells and build a bigger cell), and mixed designs. One of VHDL's attractive features is its support for top-down design style. According to this design style, a system is hierarchically divided into a set of subsystems that is easier to design. The subsystems at each level of hierarchy contain more detail than the higher-level subsystems. In bottom-up design methodology, the designer starts with basic components (or subsystems) and proceeds to design a complete system.
3. It supports various digital modeling techniques. These include algorithmic descriptions, which are step-by-step procedures for designing a system in a finite amount of time, Boolean equations, and finite-state machines. A finite-state machine, or finite-state automaton, is a simple mathematical model that has a finite set of inputs and sometimes a finite set of outputs. An automaton goes through a finite set of states based on the order in which inputs are received. It may produce a sequence of outputs in response to the sequence of inputs.
4. It supports various approaches to timing. For example, it supports a synchronous approach in which signal operations take an inherent number of clock cycles. It also supports an asynchronous approach that allows cycles of various lengths.
5. It supports various hardware technologies, including new primitive logic types, new primitive components, and technology-dependent attributes.
6. It supports concurrent statements. VHDL is a concurrent language that can model simultaneous events that occur in hardware by executing several statements at the same time.
7. It allows the user to define new data types, which makes for a higher level of abstraction when describing and simulating new design techniques.

Despite all these capabilities, some designers do not think VHDL works well as a design tool. They emphasize that VHDL is too wordy. The amount of VHDL code needed to describe a design is usually twice that needed by other hardware design languages. In addition, VHDL's wordiness and its inherent parallelism make the debugging process a difficult task, and VHDL does not provide tools for analog design. Finally, VHDL lacks supporting visual representation. Some designers believe that

Sec. C.2   VHDL Views   435

diagrams provide better readability than languages. It is hoped that the new versions of VHDL will solve some of these problems in the near future.

Because VHDL is an extremely large language, it is beyond the scope of this book to cover all its aspects. Therefore, the emphasis will be on some of the most common features of the VHDL, which are used in some examples of this book. The examples stress more on design concepts rather than VHDL syntax; they are not intended to provide executable codes. The reader may refer to [IEEE 87] for detail description of VHDL.

C.2 VHDL VIEWS

A digital system can be viewed as a mathematical function machine or as a black box. One or more input and output lines enter and leave this black box, and a delay is identified with each line. A black box can be represented as an *entity* in VHDL. As discussed earlier, VHDL offers three ways of describing a given entity: the structural view, the data flow view, and the behavioral view [BAK 89]. In each of these three approaches, there are two main elements that describe an entity: the *entity declaration*, which identifies the prime elements of the system, that is, the outside of the black box, and the *architecture body,* which describes the contents of the black box, in other

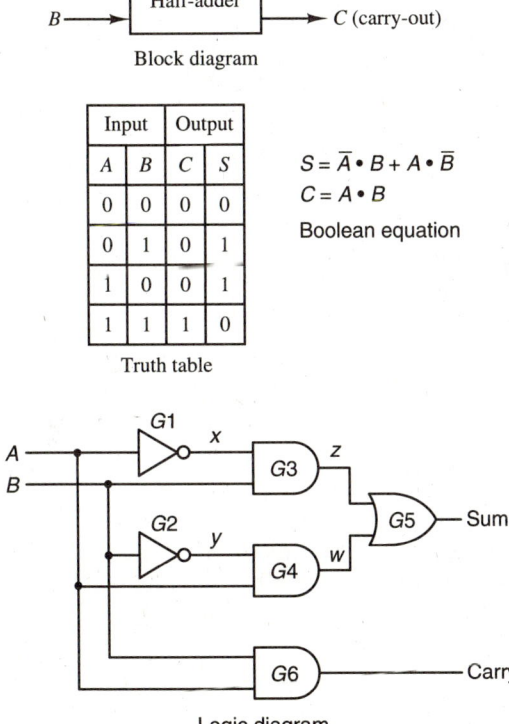

Figure C.2   Different representation of a half-adder.

words, the entity itself. The following sections will give a detailed description of the entity declaration and the architecture body. For the time being it will be sufficient to show the differences between structural, data flow, and behavioral methodologies by describing the design of a half-adder in each style. A half-adder adds two 1-bit inputs and produces a sum bit and a carry bit as outputs.

Figure C.2 shows different representations of a half-adder in digital logic. The logic diagram is used for representing a *structural architecture* (see Figure C.3). In Figure C.3, VHDL key words are represented in bold type. For example, the keyword **entity** begins the description of the interface between the half-adder and its environment. The port statement defines the input signals (*A* and *B*) and output signals (Sum and Carry) of the half-adder. The keyword **architecture** begins the description of the architecture body. The *structure_view* is a name given to this architecture body. The structure_view is divided into two parts: the declaration part, which appears before the keyword **begin**, and the design part, which appears after **begin**. The declaration part consists of three *component statements* and a *signal statement*. The first component statement defines a NOT gate. The second and third component statements define an AND gate and an OR gate, respectively. The signal *I* is the input, and the signal *O* is the output. The signal statement defines a series of signals that is used for interconnecting the components. For example, the signal *x* is used to connect a NOT gate to an AND gate. The design part includes a set of *component instantiation statements*. A component instantiation statement creates an instance of a component. An instance starts with a label followed by the component name and a *portmap*. Each entry of the

```
entity half_adder is
   port (A,B : in bit;-- input ports
        Sum,Carry : out bit); -- output ports
end half_adder;
architecture structure_view of half_adder is
component not_gate
   port (I: in bit; O: out bit);
end component;
component and_gate
   port (I1, I2: in bit; O: out bit);
end component;
component or_gate
   port (I1, I2: in bit; O: out bit);
end component;
signal w, x, y, z: bit;
begin
   G1: not_gate portmap (A,x);
   G2: not_gate portmap (B,y);
   G3: and_gate portmap (x,B,z);
   G4: and_gate portmap (y,A,w);
   G5: or_gate  portmap (z,w,Sum);
   G6: and_gate portmap (A,B,Carry);
end structure_view;
```

Figure C.3 Structural representation from logic diagram.

portmap refers to one of the component's ports or a locally declared signal. A port of a component is connected to a port of another component if they have the same portmap entry. For example, at label G1, A is fed into a NOT gate, with x as the output. At label G3, x and B are fed into an AND gate, with Z as the output.

In general, a structural view can be described by declaring a set of components and connecting them with a set of signals. The components can include NOT gates, AND gates, adders, a memory unit, and any other components that may be needed. If the structural view is compared to a C program, the component definitions are similar to function declarations, and the input and output variables are similar to the parameters for the functions.

The data flow view describes a network of signals in which the flow of signal values is supervised by a set of control elements. For example, at the register level of description, the data flow view presents the description of a circuit in terms of a set of concurrent register and signal assignments. The traffic between the registers is monitored by a set of control elements.

The data flow description does not have to define the components it uses. It often uses the Boolean operators (such as NOT, AND, OR, NAND, and XOR gates) and arithmetic expressions for describing a circuit. Another feature of the data flow view is its ability to show the amount of time elapsed in each element of the circuit. Figure C.4 shows a data flow architecture based on the Boolean equation of our half-adder. The architecture body consists of two signal statements. The first signal statement specifies that the signal connected to port Sum will get the exclusive-or value of the signals connected to port *A* and port *B* after 30 nanoseconds. (The 30 ns can be interpreted as the delay of an XOR gate.) The second signal statement specifies that the Carry signal will get the AND value of the input signals after 10 ns. (In VHDL, the symbol <= distinguishes a signal assignment from a variable assignment as represented in Figure C.4. This will be explained later in this appendix.)

The behavioral approach presents a description similar to most high-level computer programming languages. Like the data flow view, the behavioral view uses Boolean and arithmetic expressions, and it allows for showing elapsed time. However, unlike the data flow view, the behavioral view tends to make more use of control structures such as IF statements and loops. Finally, unlike the structural view, it does not describe the structure of the circuit.

Figure C.5 represents a behavioral architecture based on the truth table of a half-adder. In this figure, the variable *N* stands for the number and position of the 1's

```
entity half_adder is
   port (A,B : in bit ;           -- input ports
         Sum,Carry : out bit);    -- output ports
end half_adder;
architecture data flow_view of half_adder is
begin
   Sum <= (notA and B) or (A and notB) after 30 ns;
   Carry <= A and B after 10ns;
end data flow_view;
```

Figure C.4 Data flow representation from a Boolean equation.

```
entity half_adder is
    port (A,B : in bit ;            -- input ports
          Sum,Carry : out bit);     -- output ports
end half_adder;
architecture behavioral_view of half_adder is
begin
    process
        variable N: integer;
        constant s_vector: bit_vector(0 to 2) := "010";
        constant c_vector: bit_vector(0 to 2) := "001";
    begin
        N := 0;
        if A = '1' then N := N+1; end if;
        if B = '1' then N := N+1; end if;
        Sum <= s_vector(N) after 20ns;
        Carry <= c_vector(N) after 20ns;
        wait on A, B;
    end process;
end behavioral_view;
```

Figure C.5 Behavioral representation from truth table.

in the inputs. The constants *s_vector* and *c_vector* are arrays of bits and are initialized to "010" and "001" respectively. Position 0 is the far left position, and position 2 is the rightmost position. The value of the outputs Sum and Carry are set to the value of the Nth position in the array *s_vector*, respectively. For example, the truth table in Figure C.2 shows that if one of the inputs is 1 and the other is 0, the sum becomes 1 and the carry 0. This fact is represented by the middle bit in vectors s_vector and c_vector, which are referred to by variable N. Because one of the inputs is 1 and the other 0, N becomes 1. Thus

$$Sum = s\_vector(1) = 1,$$

$$Carry = c\_vector(1) = 0.$$

Note that the statements in the architecture body of Figure C.5 are bounded within a process statement. This process statement constructs a process for simulating the half-adder. The wait statement within the process statement causes the process to be suspended until the value of A or B changes. Once a change appears in any of the inputs A or B, the process starts all over again and changes the output values as necessary.

The three VHDL views and their representations are summarized in Table C.1. An architecture may also be described as a mixture of these views.

Before we start to study the detail of the statements in VHDL, it would be helpful to know, in general, how a circuit can be simulated. In the beginning of every simulation process, storage is allocated for all data objects (such as signals, variables, and constants) declared in a VHDL design. Also, initial values are assigned to these objects, and simulation time is reset to 0 ns. Simulation, then, starts adding time to proceed to the next event. Signals that need values at this time are assigned. All design

Sec. C.2 VHDL Views

TABLE C.1 THE THREE VHDL VIEWS

VHDL Description	Represents
Structural	Structural partitioning or Functional decomposition
Data flow	Register transfer level
Behavioral	A Series of sequential statements.

units (processes) whose input signals changed are then executed. This sequence of adding time, signal change, and process execution continues until simulation suspends. Simulation stops when a time limit is reached that the user has specified, or the maximum time allowed by the language is reached. As an example, consider the block diagram of the circuit in Figure C.6. Assume that the signals x, y, v, w, and z are initialized to 0, 1, 1, 1, and 0, respectively. Also assume that a buffer, called the *event queue*, is allocated to schedule the changes to these signals. The initial events in the event queue specify that x should change to 1 at time 0 and also y should change to 0 at the same time. When these changes have been done, the subcircuits that are affected by these signals are determined (i.e., subcircuit 1 and subcircuit 2). The changes on the output of these subcircuits will be determined and added to the event queues. Assume that subcircuit 1 produces 0 for input 1. Since subcircuit 1 has a propagation delay of 10, the event $(v, 0)$ is scheduled for time 10 and is added to the event queue. Also, assume that subcircuit 2 produces 0 for the input 0. Since subcircuit 2 has a propagation delay of 20, the event $(w, 0)$ is scheduled for time 20 and is added to the event queue. After the events at time 0 are processed, the simulation time is incremented by

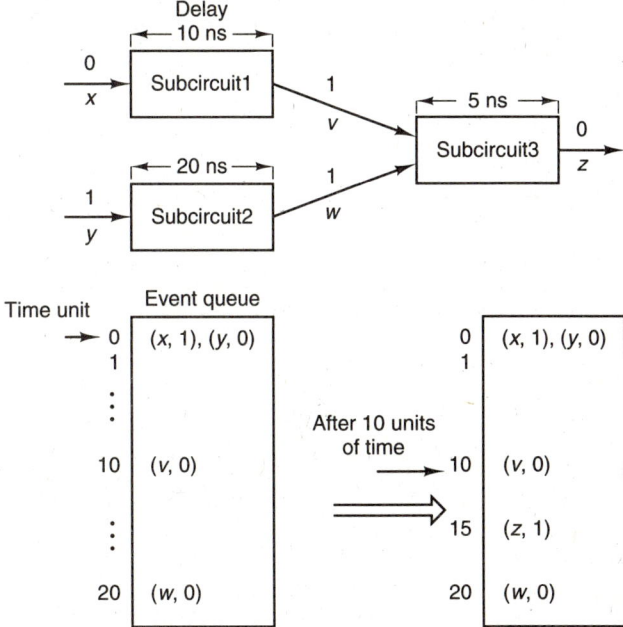

Figure C.6 Simulation process.

1 and the corresponding events are processed. This process continues until it reaches time 10. At that time, event (v, 0) will be processed, which causes event (z, 1) to be scheduled at time 15. The simulation process continues until the event queue becomes empty or reaches some simulation time limit.

C.3 DESIGN ENTITY

In VHDL, a design entity represents a design such as a system, a subsystem, a gate, or any level of design in between. For example, the entire design entity may simply be a half-adder, as illustrated previously, or it could be the entire microprocessor. An entity has two main parts: the entity declaration and the architecture body.

Refer to Figure C.7 as you read this section. A design entity begins with the entity declaration, which first names the design being described (**entity** <name> **is**), followed by a list of the various signals coming in and out of a design [**port (in/out** signal)]. The entity declaration defines the interface (input/output ports) between the entity and the other part of the system. It may also declare common items for its architecture body. Considering the previous example of a half-adder as a design, the entity declaration was defined as follows:

```
entity half_adder is
    port (A,B : in bit;            -- input ports
          Sum,Carry : out bit);    -- output ports
end half_adder;
```

The name of the entity is user-defined. In this instance, the designer used the descriptive name "half_adder"; however any name could have been chosen (for example, number_cruncher or binary_add_circuit). The port statement defined *A* and *B* as input signals and Sum and Carry as output signals. These are the signals coming in to and out from our black box.

The entity declaration may also declare items and statements that are common to each design entity with this interface. For example, an entity declaration for a latch can be defined as

```
entity latch is
    port (Data_in : in bit_vector (0 to 7);
          Data-out : out bit_vector (0 to 7);
          Load, Clock : in bit);
end latch;
```

This latch is an 8-bit latch, which has eight inputs and eight outputs. In addition, it has a load signal and a clock signal as inputs. Figure C.7 represents the main elements of a design entity. Each of these elements is described in the following sections.

The architecture body, which makes up the second part of a design entity, represents the relationship between inputs and outputs of a design entity. The architecture can be expressed in each of the three styles of description, structural, data flow, and

Sec. C.3 Design Entity

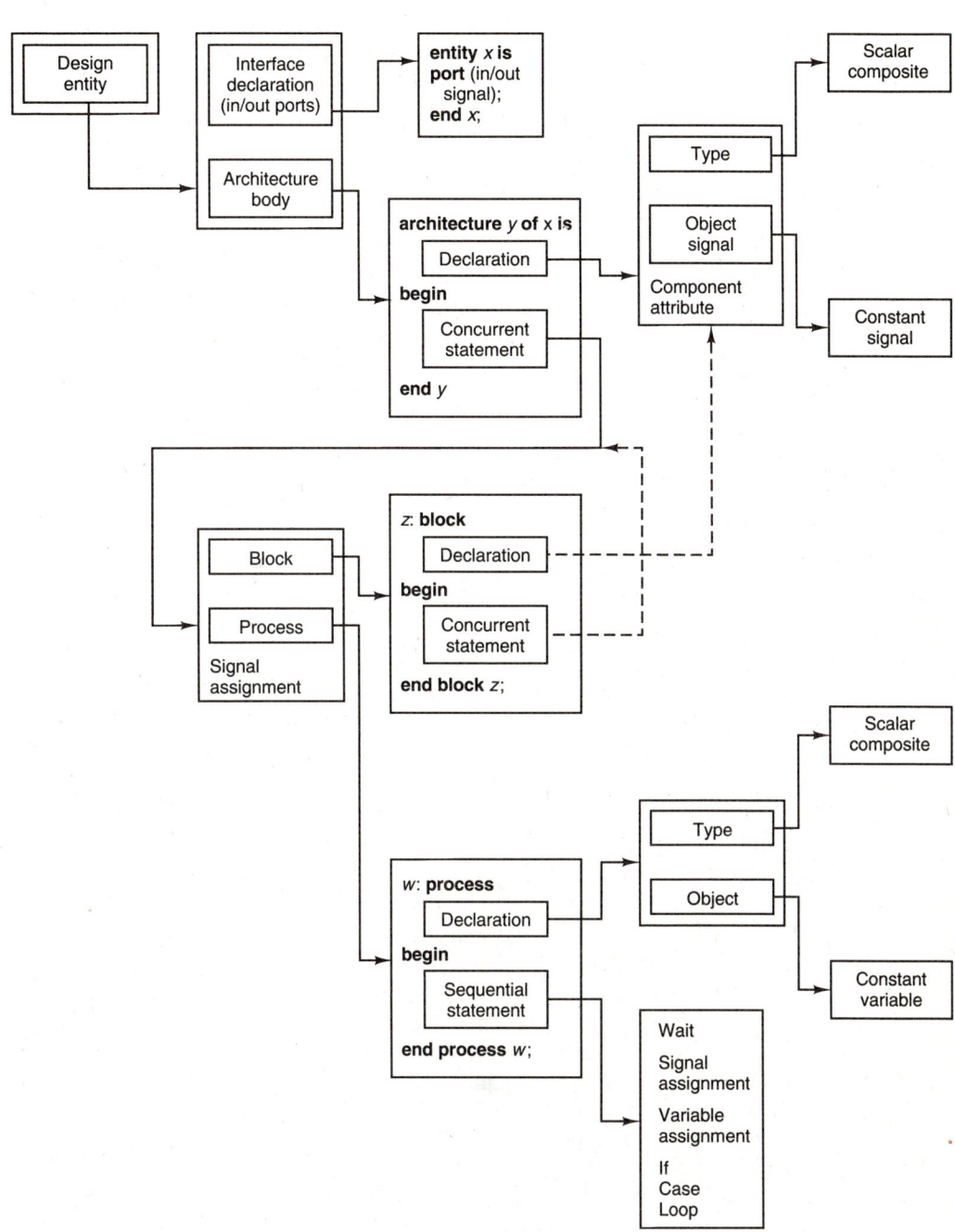

Figure C.7 Main elements of a design entity.

behavioral, or in a combination of these styles. The main parts of an architecture body are as follows:

```
architecture architecture-name of entity-name is
    declaration
begin
    concurrent statement
end architecture-name;
```

As shown here the architecture body is composed of two segments, a **declaration** segment and a **concurrent statement** segment. Just as the entity declaration part begins with an identifying statement, so does the architecture part. However, the statement in the architecture part is named in relation to the entity part:

```
architecture <architecture-name> of <entity-name> is.
```

If the designer wants to show a behavioral representation of the half-adder circuit, a meaningful user-defined architecture name would be

```
architecture behavioral_view of half_adder is.
```

Notice that the name of the entity is repeated in the architecture statement.

```
entity half_adder is
architecture behavioral_view of half_adder is
```

The **declaration** section, the first part of the architecture body, declares numerous signals, components, and attributes that will be used in the sections that follow the declaration. The second part of an architecture body, the concurrent statement segment contained within a **begin ... end** *<architecture-name >* pair, consists of a number of concurrent statements that support the description of both sequential and concurrent behavior in hardware. Some of the commonly used concurrent statements are *block*, *process*, and *signal assignment statements*. The concurrent statement segment can consist of one or more blocks statements, a process statement, or a combination of one or more block statements and a process statement.

A block statement describes a portion of a design and contains a set of concurrent statements. The behavior of a device can be best modeled as a process statement. A process statement groups together a number of sequential statements. A *sensitivity list of signals* may be assigned to a process. Whenever a signal in this list changes, the process is reevaluated by executing its first statement down to the last statement (in order).

A sequential statement could be a control statement, a wait statement, or an assignment statement. Control statements are similar to the programming control statements, such as *if ... then*, *case*, and *loop*. A wait statement can be used to suspend a process until a signal changes. Assignment statements are used to assign certain values to certain variables or signals. To model the amount of time elapsed within components and/or connections (wires), an assignment statement may assign a value to a signal after a given delay.

The chart in Figure C.7 represents the main elements of a design entity and is an invaluable tool that the architecture student can use to design VHDL models. In the following sections the elements of this chart are described in order to provide the reader with the basics of an entity design. Just as a basketball player must master the basics—passing, dribbling, and shooting—and make those basics second nature in order to perform them subconsciously, the computer architect must also master the basics of design. Otherwise, these basics will get in the way.

In the following sections, sometimes, conventional notations are used to describe the syntax of VHDL elements, in particular:

a. The symbol ::== is used to define the sub-elements of an element.
b. The vertical bar | between two elements indicates choice between them.
c. The square brackets [] around an element indicate the element is optional.
d. The braces {} around an element indicate the element may appear zero or more times.

C.4 DECLARATION OF ITEMS WITHIN A DESIGN ENTITY

Various kinds of declarations of items are used within a design entity. This section describes some of the most common ones: type declarations, various object declarations, component declarations, and attribute declarations.

C.4.1 Types

A type defines a set of values that a variable of a given type may take. In VHDL, there are two classes of types: (1) scalar types and (2) composite types. Each class is further divided into several subclasses of types. These subclasses are explained in the next two sections.

Scalar types. A scalar type is a set of distinct values (constants). Scalar types consist of enumeration types, integer types, floating-point types, and physical types. An enumeration type specifies an ordered set of values. A list of identifiers and characters represents the values for an enumeration type. Some examples include the following:

```
type bit       is   ('0','1');
type state     is   (idle, test, busy);
type tri_value is   ('0','1','Z');
type am/pm     is   (am, pm);
```

Integer and floating-point types represent numeric quantities. The types **integer** and **real** are predefined. Additional integer and floating-point types can be declared by defining types whose set of values is specified by a range of integers or floating-points. Some examples include the following:

```
type byte-index      is range  7      downto 0;
type small-integer   is range  0      to     100;
type product         is range -20     to     20;
type delta           is range  0.01   to     0.05;
type alpha           is range -0.25   to     25E-2;
```

The range constraint in the type declaration specifies the range of the values that is defined by the type. The word **downto** specifies a descending range and the word **to** designates an ascending range.

The integer types are defined by using integer literals (such as 0, 7, -20, 1024), and the floating-point types are declared by floating-point literals, which contain a decimal point or a negative exponent (such as 0.01, 25E-2, 0.1E-5). Thus, in the preceding examples, the first three are integer types and the rest are floating-point types.

A physical type defines measurements of some quantity. It specifies a set of measurement units that are defined in terms of some base unit. For example, picosecond (ps) can be defined as a base unit for time. From this base unit, the units *ns, us, ms,* and *sec* can be derived as follows:

```
type time_unit is range 0 to 1E12
    units
        ps;                      -- picosecond
        ns = 1000 ps;            -- nanosecond
        us = 1000 ns;            -- microsecond
        ms = 1000 us;            -- millisecond
        sec = 1000 ms;           -- second
    end units;
```

Composite types. Composite types are used for defining arrays and records of values. An array type specifies a set of elements with the same type. The elements in this set are arranged in a one-dimensional vector, a two-dimensional matrix, or a higher-dimensional structure. These elements may be of any type, but the indexes must be either the integer or enumeration type. For example:

```
type one_byte is array (0 to 7) of bit;
```

This statement defines a byte of memory that has 8 bits. The type *one_byte* is indexed with the integers 0 to 7 and has elements of the type bit. For example, *one_byte* (0) will refer to the least significant bit in this byte.

The following statement defines a memory that contains 1 Kbytes in which each byte has 8 bits.

```
type memory is array (0 to 1023) of one_byte;
```

An array type need not specify the number of elements in the array. For example

```
type bit_vector is array (integer range <>) of bit;
```

Sec. C.4 Declaration of Items within a Design Entity

This statement defines a vector with an undefined number of elements.

The symbol < > stands for an undefined range. It actually defers the specification of the range of indexes. Whenever an object uses this symbol, a specific range for it can be defined, as in the following example:

> **signal** *s_vector: bit_vector* (0 **to** 2);

A record type specifies elements of the same and/or different types. Record types in VHDL are analogous to Pascal records and C structures. Some examples include the following:

```
type time is
    record
        second : small-integer range 0 to 59;
        minutes : small-integer range 0 to 59;
        hour : small-integer range 1 to 12;
        before-after : am/pm;
    end record;

type cell is
    record
        id : integer;
        name : string(1 to 20);
    end record;
```

In addition to these types, there is a small number of predefined types.

C.4.2 Objects

Objects are containers of values and are created when they are declared in a design entity. Every object must be associated with one and only one of the defined (or predefined) types. There are various kinds of objects. These include *constants, variables,* and *signals*.

A constant is an object whose value is established before simulation and cannot be changed during execution. Unlike a constant, a variable has a value that can be changed by assignment statements. A signal's value can also be changed by assignment statements. However, signals have a past history of values, a present value, and a set of predicted future values. Of these values, only the predicted future values can be changed in a signal.

To clarify the meaning and syntax of each of these objects, a series of examples is given next.

CONSTANT:

> **constant** *identifier-list: type-indication* := *expression;*

Examples:

> **constant** *s_vector: bit_vector* (0 **to** 2):="010";
> **constant** *cycle_time: time* := 200 *ns;*

VARIABLE:

variable *identifier-list: type-indication* [*:= expression*];

Examples:

    variable *counter: integer := 0;*
    variable *N: integer;*

SIGNAL:

signal *identifier-list: type-indication* [*:= expression*];

Examples:

    signal *load, enable, shift : bit := '0';*
    signal *Bus_req: tri_value;*

In Figure C.8, signal Bus_req is driven by the bus request signal of both devices. At any given time, only one of the devices can use the data bus for its data transmission. Assume that each device drives Bus_req with a 0 whenever it wants to use the data bus and 1 in all other cases. If one of the devices drives Bus_req with a 0 and the other drives it with a 1, the resulting value of Bus_req will be undefined and will depend on the implementation technology. To resolve this problem, the signal Bus_req is defined to take the values 0, 1, and Z. The value Z represents a disconnect state (or high impedance) of a tri-state output.

C.4.3 Component

A component declaration defines the interface for a component of a design. It specifies the component's name, the component's ports, and the direction of data flows in the ports. For example, the following component statement specifies an AND gate with two input terminals called *input1* and *input2* and an output terminal called *output*.

    component *and_gate*
      port *(input1, input2:* **in** *bit; output:* **out** *bit);*
    end component;

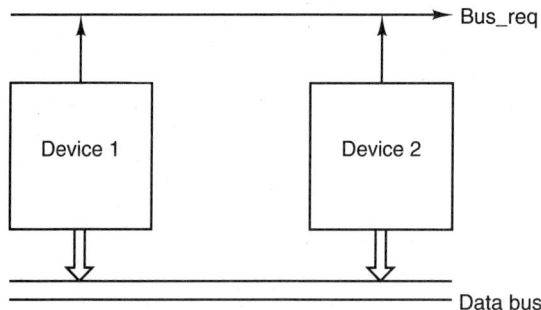

Figure C.8 The data bus is shared between two devices.

C.4.4 Attributes

An attribute is a value type, function, or signal associated with an item. For example, a predefined attribute *STABLE* can be assigned to a signal, such as a clock, in order to detect a change in the clock; this is denoted as *clock'STABLE(T)*. The signal *clock'STABLE(T)* is true if the clock has not been changed within the last *T* units of time; otherwise, it is false. Another example is *output'LAST_EVENT*, which specifies the amount of time that has passed since the last change in the output signal. In addition to the predefined attributes, the user can define new attributes. The format for defining an attribute is:

>   **attribute** *attribute-name: type-indication;*

For example,

>   **type** *small_integer* **is** *range* 0 **to** *100;*
>   **attribute** *positive: small_integer;*

C.5 EXPRESSIONS

At the expression level, VHDL provides logical, relational, and arithmetic operators. Each of these classes of operators is defined next.

C.5.1 Logical Operators

VHDL supports the six logical operations:

>   **not**
>   **and**
>   **or**
>   **nand**
>   **nor**
>   **xor** (exclusive-or)

The operands for these operators have two predefined types, *bit* or *Boolean*. The operands can also be any one-dimensional array whose element type is bit or Boolean. For example,

>   *(A='0'* **and** *B='0')* **or** *(A='1'* **and** *B='1')*
>   *(register_1* **xor** *register_2)* **xor** *register_3*

C.5.2 Relational Operators

Six relational operators are supported in VHDL. They are

=	equal to
/=	not equal to
<	less than
<=	less than or equal to
>	greater than
>=	greater than or equal to

The operands of each relational operator can be of any type, but they must be of the same type. The value that results from evaluating a relational operation will either be *true* or *false*. For example,

```
clock_cycle <= 100 ns
next_state = execute.
```

C.5.3 Arithmetic Operators

The arithmetic operators include

+	addition
−	subtraction or unary minus
*	multiplication
/	division
&	concatenation

The operators +, −, *, and / have their conventional meaning and are defined for operands of integer, floating-point, and physical types. For example, an arithmetic expression is

```
(a + b - (d * c) / a) / (4.5 * b).
```

The operator & is defined for any one-dimensional array type operand. This operator combines two one-dimensional arrays into a one-dimensional array whose length is the sum of the lengths of the two arrays. For example,

```
('0','1','Z')&('1','0') is equal to ('0','1','Z','1','0'),
```

or

```
opcode & reg_add & base & displacement
```

represents an instruction format.

C.6 SEQUENTIAL STATEMENTS

Sequential statements are executed in the order of their appearance in a design. The most common statements are

```
Assignment statement
    Signal assignment statement
    Variable assignment statement
Wait statement
If statement
Case statement
Loop statement
```

C.6.1 Assignment Statements

There are two kinds of assignment statements: signal assignment statements and variable assignment statements. They are used to assign certain values to certain variables or signals. To distinguish between these two, VHDL uses the <= symbol to indicate signal assignment and the := symbol for variable assignment. For example, in the following statements S_1 and S_2 are signal assignments (executed concurrently), while S_3 and S_4 are variable assignments (executed sequentially).

```
X <= Y      or    Z;    --S₁
W <= X      or    Z;    --S₂
X := Y + Z;             --S₃
W := X + Z;             --S₄
```

As an example, Figure C.9 presents a signal assignment statement that describes a particular combinational circuit.

Variable assignment statements. A variable assignment statement assigns a new value to a variable by evaluating an expression. For example,

```
counter_value := counter_value + 1;
```

A variable assignment has the form

```
variable-name := expression;
```

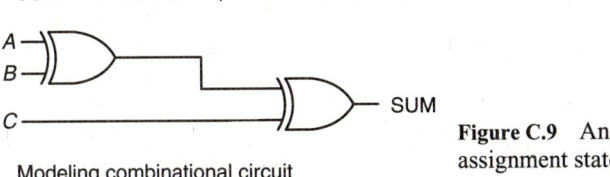

Modeling combinational circuit

Figure C.9 An example of a signal assignment statement.

An instantaneous assignment is made to the variable-name as soon as the statement is executed and the expression is evaluated. These assignments are analogous to Pascal and C variable assignments.

Signal assignment statements. A signal assignment statement may contain an *inertial delay* or *a transport delay*. When an inertial delay is used, the output signal changes if and only if the input signal stays at a certain level for the specified delay time in the statement. In other words, the output signal does not change for an input transient of shorter duration than that of the delay time. This type of delay is common in the real world because, in practice, the input is usually required to stay unchanged for some specified time before it can affect the output. Because of its common use, it has been defined as the default delay; that is, the word *inertial* does not need to appear in the statement.

In contrast to an inertial delay, a transport delay always propagates the changes on input to output. In other words, the transport delay does not require that the input remain unchanged for a specified delay time. For example, when the input and output are connected through a metal wire, any change on the input, no matter how small, can be reflected on the output after a propagation delay. If a statement does not contain a delay time of greater than zero, a small delay, called a *delta delay*, will be assumed.

For example

```
S <= A after 20 ns; -- inertial delay.
```

A change in A will propagate to S if and only if A does not change for 20 ns. This type of delay will prevent the effect of inputs that change too rapidly. Another example is

```
S <= transport A after 20 ns; --transport delay.
```

In this case, any change in A will propagate to S regardless of how long A stays unchanged.

Figure C.10 shows the difference between inertial and transport delay for the following statement.

```
S <= A and B after 10 ns;
```

Figure C.10a represents the schedule of a change in signal S 10 ns after time t_0 when the preceding statement was issued. Figure C.10b shows that the signal S has been changed from what it was in part (a). Note that the same statement is executed at time t_1 and that a new change is scheduled for S. In Figure C.10c the schedule in part (b) is ignored because there has been a change in signal A before the new value for S takes place. That is, the event at time t_1 does not propagate to the output, since the inputs do not remain stable for the entire inertial delay. Figure C.10d demonstrates that the change in signal A does not affect the scheduled value when transport delay is used.

Sec. C.6   Sequential Statements   451

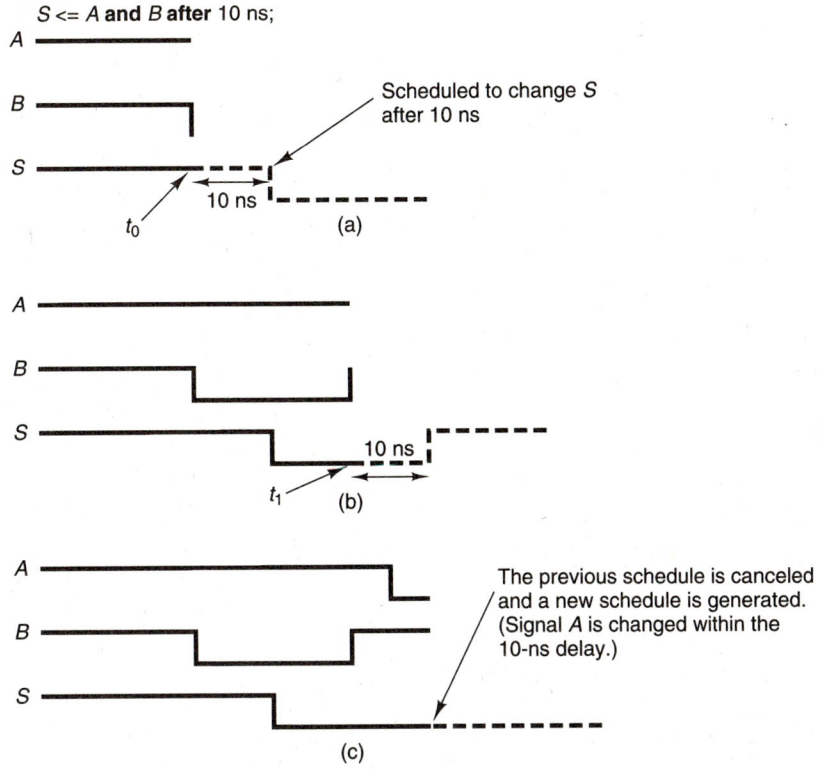

Note that in case of transport delay the previous schedule will not be canceled.

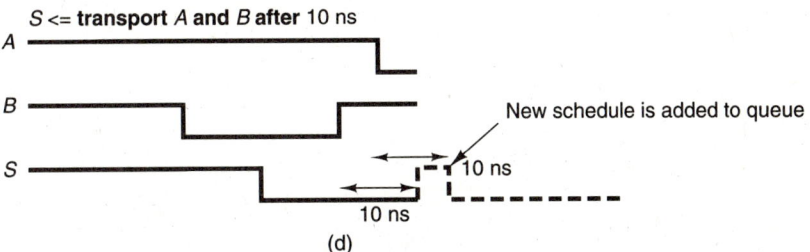

Figure C.10 Inertial and transport delay.

Figures C.11 and C.12 represent signal statements that do not contain delay times. Note that in both figures any change in the input has been reflected in the output after a small delta delay.

C.6.2 Wait Statements

The wait statement suspends a process until certain events or conditions are satisfied. It has the following general format:

```
wait [on sensitivity-list] [until Boolean-expression] [for
                time-expression];
```

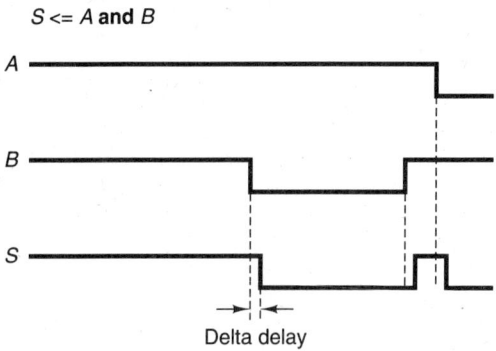

Figure C.11 VHDL modeling of an AND gate.

The sensitivity list defines a set of signals in which the wait statement is waiting for a change. Whenever any of the signals changes its value, the suspended process will continue by executing the next statement.

The Boolean expression defines a condition that must be met for the suspended process to continue execution. The time expression defines a period of time that the process is kept suspended. For example,

```
wait on signal_A, signal_B;
```

When signal_A or signal_B changes, the suspended process will resume, or

```
wait until (clock = 0);
```

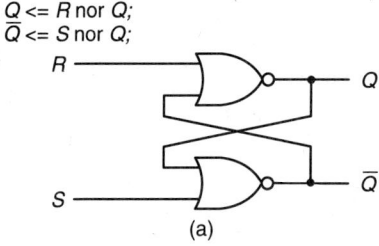

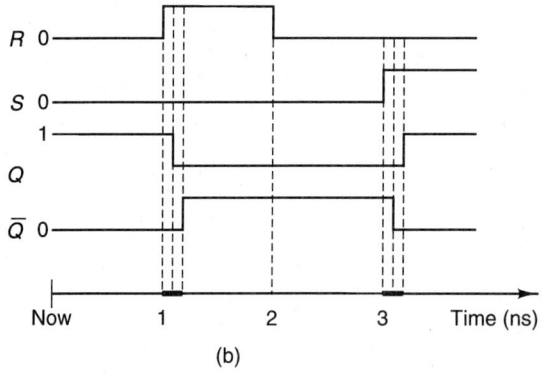

Figure C.12 VHDL modeling of a RS flip-flop. (a) Modeling asyncronous sequential circuit. (b) Timing diagram.

Sec. C.6   Sequential Statements   453

When the clock changes from 1 to 0, the suspended process will resume. Note that since there is no sensitivity list the variable clock is assumed to belong to sensitivity list. Another example is

```
wait for 20 ns;
```

The suspended process will resume after 20 ns. A fourth example is

```
wait on signal_A, signal_B until (clock = 0) for 20 ns;
```

The suspended process will resume whenever one of the following events occurs: (1) signal_A or signal_B changes when the clock is equal to 0, or (2) a delay of 20 ns is passed.

C.6.3 If Statements

An **if** statement executes one or none of its sequence of statements based on the value of a Boolean expression. It has the following format:

```
if Boolean-expression then
       sequence-of-statements-1
[else
       sequence-of-statements-2]
end if;
```

If the expression *Boolean-expression* evaluates to a true value, *sequence-of-statements-1* is executed. If it evaluates to a false value, *sequence-of-statements-1* is skipped. In the latter case, *sequence-of-statements-2* is executed when an **else** clause is included in the **if** statement. A series of *if-then-else* statements can be used to describe the operation of a device. For example, the outputs of an *RS* flip-flop with asynchronous reset (*R*) and set (*S*) inputs can be defined by testing all possible inputs values. Given that *Q* and *Q_Comp* are the output signals, the operation of a *RS* flip-flop can be represented as follows:

```
if (R = '0') and (S = '1') then
    --Set the flip-flop
    Q <= '1' after 20 ns;
    Q_Comp <= '0' after 20 ns;
else
    if (R = '1') and (S = '0') then
        --Reset the flip-flop
        Q <= '0' after 20 ns;
        Q_Comp <= '1' after 20 ns;
    else
        if (R = '1') and (S = '1') then
            --generate unknown outputs
            --x denotes undefined value
            Q <= 'x' after 20 ns;
            Q_Comp <= 'x' after 20 ns;
```

```
                end if;
            end if;
        end if;
```

C.6.4 Case Statements

A case statement executes one of its sequence of statements based on the value of an expression. It has the following format.

```
            case expression is
                case-statement
                {case-statement}
            end case;
            case-statement::==
                when choices =>
                    sequence-of-statements
```

The expression (which appears after the keyword **case**) is evaluated and compared with the consecutive choices. If there is a match, the corresponding sequence of statements is executed. If there is no match, a choice, which is specified as **others**, is executed. Consider the description of a 1-by-2 demultiplexer in the following example:

```
case select is
    when '0' => Output_0 <= Input after 10 ns;
                Output_1 <= '0' after 10 ns;
    when '1' => Output_1 <= Input after 10 ns;
                Output_0 <= '0' after 10 ns;
    when others => Output_0 <= 'x'; --x denotes undefined value
                Output_1 <= 'x';
end case;
```

The **others** choice is optional and may be omitted. However, there should always be one and only one choice that matches the value of the expression. For example,

```
            case (state) is
                when "idle" => state := 'busy';
                when "test" => state := 'idle';
                when "busy" => state := 'test';
            end case;
```

C.6.5 Loop Statements

A loop statement, which executes a sequence of statements repeatedly, has the following format:

```
        [stopping-criteria]
        loop
            sequence-of-statements
```

```
            end loop;
        stopping-criteria::==
            while Boolean-expression |
            for identifier in discrete-range
```

When a **while** condition appears in a loop statement, the Boolean expression is evaluated in the beginning of each iteration. If the evaluated expression is **true**, the sequence of statements is executed; otherwise, the loop is terminated.

When the loop statement must be repeated a certain number of times, a **for** stopping criteria is used. In this case, the sequence of statements is executed once for each value of the discrete range. The following example illustrates different ways that a loop can be constructed.

Given a vector A with $n+1$ bits, each of the following loops computes a new vector, $A\_COMPLEMENT$, which is the complement of A. The **while** clause can be used as a stopping condition for the loop,

```
        i := 0;
        while i <= n loop
            A_COMPLEMENT(i) := A(i) XOR 1;
            i := i+1;
        end loop;
```

or the **for** clause can be used to control the execution of the loop, as in

```
        for i in 0 to n loop
            A_COMPLEMENT(i) := A(i) XOR 1;
        end loop;
```

The following loop is yet another version of the preceding example.

```
        i := 0;
        loop
            A_COMPLEMENT(i) := A(i) XOR 1;
            i := i+1;
            exit when i>n;
        end loop;
```

The **exit** clause causes the loop to be termintated whenever $i > n$.

C.7 CONCURRENT STATEMENTS

Concurrent statements are executed in parallel. The most common statements are

process statement
block statement
conditional signal assignment

concurrent signal assignment
selected signal assignment

C.7.1 Process Statements

Because signals propagate through a logic circuit in parallel, VHDL has a statement, which is known as the process statement, for modeling these signals simultaneously. Each process statement consists of a set of sequential statements that are executed in the order in which they appear. A process statement creates a process for simulating a subcircuit of the logic circuit. During simulation, all processes are executed in parallel. A process statement is often used in conjunction with behavioral descriptions.

For example, the block diagram of the circuit in Figure C.13 is represented by a set of three processes: subcircuit 1, subcircuit 2, and subcircuit 3. Each of the processes subcircuit 1 and subcircuit 2 activates independently when a change is detected in its input set of signals. Once either subcircuit 1 or subcircuit 2 changes its output signals, subcircuit 3 will be activated and will propagate its input changes to its output signals.

A process statement is made up of a declarative part, which defines a set of local variables and signals that are referenced within the process, and a number of sequential statements delimited by a **begin ... end** <process-name> pair. A process statement has the following general format:

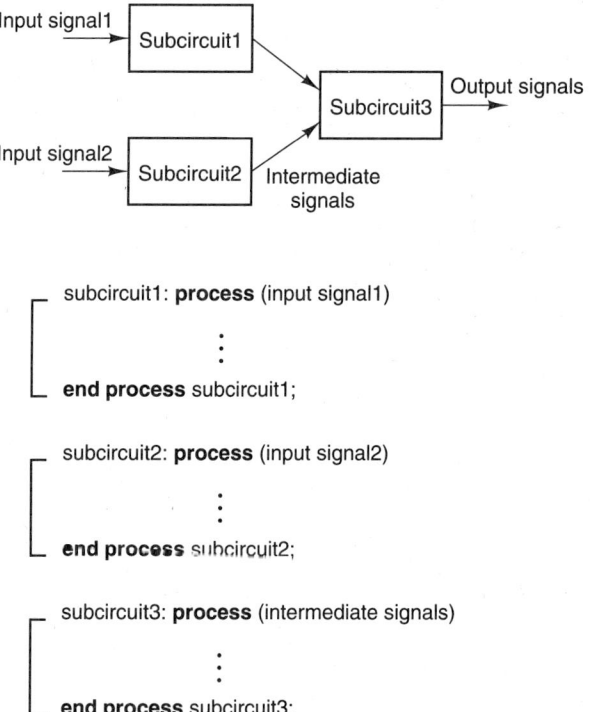

Figure C.13 Three subcircuits; each represented by a process statement.

Sec. C.7 Concurrent Statements

```
[process-name]: process [(sensitivity-list)]
    process-declarative-part
begin
    sequential-statement
end process [process-name];
```

A process statement defines a sequence of statements. The execution of a process starts at the beginning of its sequential statements. Once it reaches the last statement, it immediately returns to the first statement and repeats the process again. If a sensitivity list appears in the statement, then an implicit wait statement is assumed to be the last statement in the *process-declarative-part*. That is, the following statement will be executed as the last statement in each execution iteration waits on *sensitivity-list*.

As an example, the following code represents an architecture for a simple clock pulse generator:

```
entity clock_pulse is
    port (CLOCK: out bit :='0');  --set CLOCK initially to low
end clock_pulse;
architecture behavior of clock_pulse is
begin
        process
        begin
            CLOCK <= '1';       -- set CLOCK to high
            wait for 10ns;      -- wait for duration of high
            CLOCK <= '0';       -- set CLOCK to low
            wait for 10ns;      -- wait for duration of low
        end process;
end behavior;
```

Here is another example in which a behavioral description of a 4-bit counter is given:

```
entity four_bit_counter is
    port (CLOCK, CLEAR: in bit;
          OUTPUT: out bit_vector (3 downto 0));
end four_bit_counter;
architecture behavior of four_bit_counter is
begin
        process (CLOCK, CLEAR)
            variable counter_value:
                    bit_vector (3 downto 0);
            variable previous_clock:
                    bit := '0'; -- initially set to 0
        begin
            if (CLEAR = '1') then
              counter_value := "0000";
            end if;
            if ((CLEAR = '0') and (CLOCK = '1')
                and (CLOCK /= previous_clock) then
                counter_value := counter_value+1;
```

```
            end if;
            previous_clock := CLOCK;
            OUTPUT <= counter_value;
         end process;
   end behavior;
```

A sensitivity list is one method to suspend the execution of a process; however, the wait statement provides an alternative method for the suspension. If a process does not have a sensitivity list, it must have one or more wait statements. If a process has neither a sensitivity list, or wait statements, the process will continue in an infinite loop.

C.7.2 Block Statements

A block statement consists of a set of concurrent statements in which the order of statements is irrelevant and, therefore, it can be executed in parallel. A block statement consists of a declaration part and a number of concurrent statements delimited by a **begin ... end** *<block-name>* pair. Its general format is as follows:

```
block-name: block [(guard-expression)]
      block-declarative-part
begin
      concurrent-statement
end block [block-name];
```

A block statement defines a portion of a design. It may be hierarchically nested to support the design decomposition.

To describe the rule of *guard-expression* in a block statement, the design of a finite-state machine is given next. Figure C.14 shows a state diagram for a serial 2's complement circuit. To find the 2's complement, the circuit scans the zeros on the input signal until it reaches the first 1 in the input. For each of these zeros, the circuit

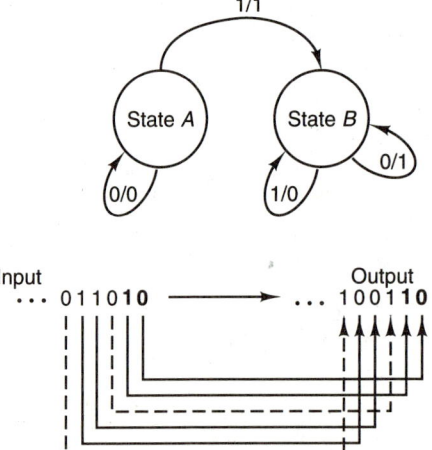

Figure C.14 State diagram for a 2's complement circuit.

Sec. C.7 Concurrent Statements

produces a 0 in the output signal. This is represented in Figure C.14 by an arc from *STATE_A* to itself, which is labeled 0/0 (input/output).

Once the circuit scans the first 1, it produces a 1 in the output and transfers from *STATE_A* to *STATE_B*. Then, for each bit on the input line, its complement is produced in the output line; that is, for an input of 0, an output of 1 is produced, and for an input of 1 an output of 0 is produced. This is shown by the arcs in *STATE_B*.

Figure C.15 represents a VHDL description of the preceding circuit. The guard for outer_block, which is denoted as *(CLOCK='1' and not CLOCK'stable)*, is true when the *CLOCK* signal is 1 and has changed its value. In other words, whenever the *CLOCK* makes a transition from 0 to 1, the guard becomes true. The guard for inner blocks *A* and *B* is the AND of the present_state and the guard of the outer_block. That is, the guard for block *A* is true when present state is *STATE_A* and *CLOCK* makes a 0 to 1 transition. Any statement that is guarded inside block *A* will be executed only when the guard for *A* becomes true. Thus the statement

```
present_state <= guarded STATE_A when INPUT='0'
    else STATE_B;
```

is executed whenever both the present state is *STATE_A* and *CLOCK* makes a 0 to 1 transition.

```
entity 2s_complement is
   port (INPUT, CLOCK: in bit; OUTPUT: out bit);
end 2s_complement;
architecture behavior of 2s_complement is
begin
    outer_block: block (CLOCK = '1' and not CLOCK'stable)
        type state is (STATE_A, STATE_B);
        signal present_state : state := STATE_A;
   begin
        A: block ((present_state = STATE_A) and guard)
          begin
            present_state <= guarded STATE_A when
                INPUT='0' else STATE_B;
        end block A;
        B: block ((present_state = STATE_B) and guard)
          begin
            present_state <= guarded STATE_B;
        end block B;
        OUTPUT<= '0' when present_state = STATE_A and
                INPUT= '0' else
        '1' when present_state = STATE_A and INPUT ='1' else
        '0' when present_state = STATE_B and INPUT ='1' else
        '1';
    end block outer_block;
end behavior; .
```

Figure C.15 VHDL description for a 2's complement circuit.

C.7.3 Concurrent Signal Assignment

Concurrent signal assignments operate in parallel. That is, the order in which they appear in the program is irrelevant, as can be seen in the following example:

```
X <= Y or Z;
W <= X or Z;
```

C.7.4 Conditional Signal Assignment

A conditional signal assignment is performed as a process statement that assigns a value to a signal based on certain conditions. It has the following format:

```
signal-name <= options
   { signal-value when Boolean-expression else }
   signal-value;
   options ::== [guarded] [transport]
```

When there is a change in one of the input lines, the conditions will be evaluated in order of their sequence. The last signal value does not have a condition, because it is the default value and is assigned to the signal whenever none of the conditions is satisfied. For example,

```
SUM <=
  '0' when A ='1' and B ='1' else
  '1' when A ='1' or  B ='1' else
  '0';
```

First, it must be determined whether A and B are both 1's. If this is the case, 0 is assigned to *SUM*. Otherwise, it must be determined whether A or B is 1. In this case, a 1 is assigned to *SUM*. Finally, if none of the these conditions is satisfied, the default value 0 is assigned to *SUM*.

C.7.5 Selected Signal Assignment

The selected signal assignment is performed as a process statement that assigns a value to a signal. This is similar to a case statement. A single expression selects which signal of several transforms is to be applied. The selected signal assignment has the following format:

```
with expression select
signal-name <= options
   {signal-value when Boolean-expression , }
    signal-value when Boolean-expression;
```

Sec. C.7   Concurrent Statements   461

For example:

```
DECODER: with A1 & A0 select
    Z <=
    "0001"        after  10  ns    when "00",
    "0010"        after  10  ns    when "01",
    "0100"        after  10  ns    when "10",
    "1000"        after  10  ns    when "11";
```

REFERENCES

[ARM 89] ARMSTRONG, JAMES R., *Chip-Level Modeling with VHDL,* Upper Saddle River, NJ: Prentice Hall, 1989.

[BAK 89] BAKALAR, KENNETH, AND M. SHAHDAD, "An Introduction to VHDL," DAC 26 tutorial, CAD Language Systems, Inc., 1989.

[BHA 92] BHASKER, JAHRYAM, *A VHDL Primer.* Upper Saddle River, NJ: Prentice Hall, 1992.

[IEEE 87] *"IEEE Standard VHDL Language Reference Manual,"* IEEE Std. 1076-1987. New York: IEEE, 1988.

PROBLEMS

C.1. A majority function is a function that returns a 1 if there are more 1s in the string than 0's. Using VHDL, design a circuit that accepts 3 bits and performs the majority function.
   a. Give a data flow description.
   b. Give a behavioral description.

C.2. Using VHDL, design a circuit for shift-and-add multiplication. The detail of this method is given in Chapter 2. Assume that the input numbers are n-bit 2's complement and are stored in registers M and Q. You can use any description style.

C.3. Using VHDL, design a circuit that generates a two-phase clock pulse. You can use any description style.

C.4. Using VHDL, design a circuit for parking control. The circuit has two inputs, *IN* and *OUT,* and one output, *LAMP*. A change from 0 to 1 on input *IN* indicates that a car has entered the parking area. A change from 0 to 1 on input *OUT* indicates that a car has left the parking area. When there are 10 cars in the parking area, the output *LAMP* becomes 1, indicating that the area is full; at this time, any change on *IN* should be ignored. When there are less than 10 cars in the parking area, *LAMP* is zero. You can use any description style.

C.5. Using VHDL, design a circuit for the signal of Figure PC.5.
   You can use any description style.

C.6. Design a circuit in VHDL that converts the input digits into its 2's complement. After the start signal changes from 0 to 1, subsequent 2-bit sequences on line x are to be interpreted

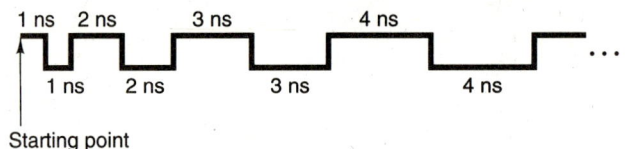

Figure PC.5

as 2-bit numbers. The 2's complement of these digits will appear on the output line z with a delay of one clock period. That is,

... 0 0 1 1 1 1 0 0 → start signal
... 1 1, 0 1, 1 0, 1 1 → input x
... 0, 1 1, 1 0, 0 0 0 → output z

You can design in any description style.

C.7. Using VHDL, design a circuit that accepts two 4-bit unsigned numbers and generates an output binary number equal to the multiplication's of the input numbers.
   a. Give a structural description.
   b. Give a data flow description.
   c. Give a behavioral description.

C.8. A palindrome is a word or series of bits that reads the same forward as backward. For example, 1, 010, 0110, 00100, and 1001 are all palindromes. Using a structural description, design a circuit that will take a string of up to 5 bits and return a 1 if the string is a palindrome. There will have to be a control variable to indicate how many bits are to be input. If more than 5 bits are input, ignore the remaining bits. If 0 bits are input, the output should be 0.

C.9. Using a block statement, give a behavioral description of a circuit that detects an input sequence of 010 or 011. An output $z = 1$ is produced only when these inputs occur.

Index

A
ABC (Atanasoff-Berry Computer), 1
Abort, instruction fault exception, 95
Access
 field, 85
 time, 66
Accumulator, 41
Activation function, of ANNs 11
Activity template, 320
Actors, nodes in data flow, 320
Adaptive linear neurons (Adaline)
 algorithms, 352
 network training, 354
Adaptive routing, 207
Addition function, 43–51
Address
 bus, 19
 field, 85
Algorithm penalty, 303
Algorithm structures, 288–294
 asynchronous, 290
 pipeline, 292
 synchronous, 288
ALLCACHE memory, 245
Alliant CAMPUS, 265

Alpha AXP Microprocessor, 164–172
 instruction set, 168
 instruction unit, 166
 operand types, 168
Amdahl's law, 302
Ametek's Series 2010, 259
ANN (see Artificial neural network)
Approximate reasoning, in fuzzy logic, 12
Architectural complexity, 140
Architecture
 body, in VHDL, 435
 of the brain, 342
 future horizons, 341–390
Arithmetic logic unit (ALU), 2, 18, 43–66
Arithmetic operators, 448
Arithmetic pipeline, 125
Array processor, 8, 9
Artificial neural network (ANN), 11, 346
 hardware, 371
 implementation of, 370
 learning algorithm classes, 348
 models, taxonomy of, 347
Assignment, of processors, 287
Associative memory, 72–74, 77
Associative-mapping cache, 78

463

Asynchronous algorithms, for multiprocessors, 304
Atanasoff-Berry computer, 1
Average latency, of pipeline, 130
Axons, in neurophysiology, 343

B

Back-propagation training algorithm, 358–363
   forward pass, 358
   reverse pass, 359
Bandwidth, of pipeline, 104
Base register addressing, 40
Base, addressing, 92
Batch updating, algorithm, 360
Batcher's bitonic merge algorithm, 201
Baugh-Wooley's algorithm, 57
Benes network, 218
Berry, Clifford, 1
Bias, in exponents, 61
Bias weight, in Adaline, 353
BiCMOS technology, 181
Bidirectional ring, 186
Big endian, in ordering of bytes, 150
Binary word fields, 61
Binary-coded decimal (BCD), 49
   number addition, 49–51
BIPS (billion instructions per second), 13
Bitonic sequence, 201
Block matrix multiplication, 311
Blocked processes, 282
Blocks, of words, 67
Boolean tokens, 321
Booth's technique, 54–57
Branch prediction, 120
Branch target buffer (BTB), 121, 160
Branches, program instructions, 117
Broadcast array, 331
Buffer, 102
Buffers, instruction storage, 20, 102
Building blocks, 294, 299
Bus, signal lines, 19
Bus contention, 241

C

Cache coherence schemes, 246–257
   hardware-based, 248
   software-based, 257
Cache memory, 68, 74–85, 239, 246
   operation, 76
   organization, 77-78, 80
   performance, 83
   replacement, 81-82
Cacheable data items, 257
Card shuffling, technique, 189
Carry lookahead adder, 45–48, 52
Carry save adder, 49, 52
Cell library, in layout design, 409
Central processing unit (CPU), 18, 20, 21, 23, 32, 33, 37, 38
Centralized control system, switches, 227
Centroid defuzzification method, 386
Chained directory protocols, 254
Channel, transistor, 404, 410
Child process, in parallel programming, 274
Circuit switching, 226
CISC processor case studies, 158–164
Classical perceptron neuron, 356
Clock cycles, 12, 421
Clustering, in ANN, 286, 351
CMOS technology, 181
Coarse-granularity parallelism, 286
Collision
   matrices, 131
   vectors, 129, 131
Combinational circuits, 413–419
Common data bus (CDB), 113
Communication
   interface, 258
   processor, 260
Comparison CAM, 72
Compatibility, of computer architecture, 14
Competitive learning algorithms, 351
Completion time, of parallel algorithms, 272
Complex instruction set computers (CISCs), 38, 139
Component declaration, in component design, 446
Component instantiation statement, 21, 436
Composite types, of arrays, 444
Computer architectures, taxonomies, 4
Computer generations, 2
Computer-aided design (CAD) systems, 3
Concurrency, of algorithm, 303
Concurrent execution of instructions, 114
Concurrent statements, 455–461
   block, 458
   concurrent signal assignment, 460
   conditional signal assignment, 460
   selected signal assignment, 460

Index

Condition code registers, 33
Conditional branch, 119
   loop branch, 119
   sequential path, 119
   target path, 119
Connection Machine Model CM-5, 261
Connector networks
   blocking, 218–225
   nonblocking, 214–216
   rearrangeable, 216–218
Content addressable memories (CAM), 72
Contiguity, in biological learning, 352
Control bus, 19
Control hazard, 117
Control parallelism, 10, 11, 286
Control signals, 27, 28, 30, 34
Control unit, 19, 24, 27–37
   hardwired, 27–32
   microprogrammed, 32–37
Control unit (CU), 18
Cosmic cube, 259
Critical section, in processing statements, 276
Current window pointer (CWP), 143
Cycles per instruction (CPI), 12

D

Data bus, 19, 23
Data cache, 142
Data flow
   architecture, 8, 318–324
   computer, structure, 322
   data flow graph, 318
Data hazards
   RAW, read after write, 111
   WAR, write after read, 112
   WAW, write after write, 112
Data parallelism, 10, 286
Data partitioning, 286
Data tokens, 321
Decode_opfetch, 26, 27
Decode_opfetch, function, 29
Decoder, in demultiplexer, 416
Defuzzification, 386
Delay insertion, 133
Delayed branching, 123
Delta rule, 355
Demultiplexer, 413
Design classification, 1–14
Design rules, 408
Destructive-read property, 71

Deterministic networks, 348
Deterministic routing, 207
Digital Equipment Corporation, 164
Dimension, of n-cube network, 198
Direct addressing, 39
Direct-connect routing, 204
Direct-mapping cache, 78, 79
Directory protocols, 248, 252
   centralized, 252–254
   distributed, 254–257
Dirty bit, in word cache, 77, 88
Disk, storage device, 20
Displacement addressing, 40, 91
Distributed control network, switches, 227
Distributed multiprocessors, 263
Divide-and-conquer, in design layout, 410
Drain, transistor, 404
Dummy stages, delays in pipeline, 133
Dynamic assignment, process, 288
Dynamic branch prediction, 167
Dynamic data flow machine, 323
Dynamic dependency checking, 112
   prediction, 120
   scoreboard method, 115–117
   Tomasulo's method, 113–115
Dynamic networks, 185, 209–225
   crossbar switch, classification, 212
   multistage, 213
   single-stage, 213
Dynamic pipelines
   collision matrices, 131
   collision vectors, 131
   forbidden lists, 131
   scheduling, 131–133
   state diagram, 133
Dynamic random access memory (DRAM), 70

E

Eckert, J. Presper, 2
EDSAC (Electronic Delay Storage Automatic Calculator), 2
Effective address, i486 microproceessor, 91
Efficiency, of pipeline, 104
Elapsed time, of parallel algorithm, 272
Encoder, in demultiplexer, 416
Encoding, in ANN, 352
Encore mltimax, 240
ENIAC (Electronic Numerical Integrator and Calculator), 2

Entity declaration, 435
Event queue, 439
Exact match CAM, 72
Exceptions, in instruction faults, 95
Exchange, network connection, 188
Excitatory postsynaptic (EPSP), 344
Execute stage, instruction unit, 147
Execute_opwrite phase, function, 26, 27, 30
Execution (EX), instruction, 106
Execution time, of instruction, 12
Expandability, of computer, 14
Express cube, 209

F

Familiarity, in Ann, 351
Fast Fourier transform (FFT), 188, 201
Faults, exception, 95
Feature mapping, in Ann, 352
Feed-forward network, 349
Feed-forwarding, in ANN, 113
field programmable gate array (FPGA), 411
Fine-granularity parallelism, 286
Firefly protocol, 251
Firmware, 140
Fixed segments, of word, 72
Fixed word size, 69
Fixed-sized speedup, Amdahl's law, 302
Flip-flop, circuit, 421
Flits, in wormhole routing, 204
Floating-point
  addition, 63
  multiplication, 65, 66
  number, 61
  operations, 13
  register file (FRF), 166
  representation, 61–66
  unit (FPU), 159
FLOPS (floating-point operations per second), 13, 237
Flynn's taxonomy, 4-6
Forbidden list, in dynamic pipelines, 129, 131
Fork system call, 274
Formal principles of reasoning, 12
Forward scan, 297
Forwarding technique, 113
Frames, memory pages, 85
Full adder, 43
Full-map protocol, 252
Functional parallelism, 286
Fuzzy associative memory (FAM), 385
Fuzzy logic, 12, 342, 374-390
  accelerators, 389
  applications, 387
  architecture of, 389
  control system, 381–389
  controller, structure of, 381

G

GaAs (gallium arsinide) transistor technology, 125
Gate, transistor, 3, 404
Gaussian elimination, 306
  back substitution, 307
  elimination, 306
Generality, of computer, 14
Generalization task, 349
Genesis, of computer, 260
Gigaflops(GFLOPS), 13
Global memory, 239
Granularity, 285, 303

H

Hard-limiting function, 347
Hardware description languages (HDLs), 432
Harvard Mark I computer, 142
Harvard-based architectures, 142
Head pointer, 254
Heterogeneous
  multicomputers, 257
  multiprocessor, 240
  multitasking, 287
Hexagonal array, 327
Hierarchical directory protocols, 254
High-level language (HLL), 142
  support, 140
Hits, in caches, 76, 84
Hit ratio, 84
Homogeneous
  multicomputers, 257
  multiprocessor, 240
  multitasking, 286
Hopfield network, 364–370
Horizontal microprogramming (HM), 35
Hybrid architectures, 10
  machines, 6

I

IEEE 754 floating-point standard, 63
IEEE Scalable Coherent Interface (SCI), 254
Illiac network, 194, 195
Immediate addressing, 39
Inconsistent bit, 77, 88

Index field, 78
Indexed addressing, 40, 92
Indirect addressing, 39
Inherent parallelism, 272
Inhibitory postsynaptic (IPSP), 344
Input latch, 102
Input/output (I/O), 2
I/O device, 19
I/O interfaces, 19, 20
Instance, 21
Instruction, 166
Instruction and data memory (I&D), 8
    cache, 142
    decoding (ID), 106
    execution process, 26
    fetch (IF), 20, 26, 106
    format, 37
Instruction pipeline, 106–125
    stages, 106, 107
    throughput improvement, 108
Instruction register (IR), 20, 24, 26, 31, 34
Instruction set, 38
Instruction set design, 37–43
    number of, in computer, 37
    opcode size, 37
    type of operand fields, 39
    type of operation, 38
Instructions, types of
    arithmetic, 39
    control, 39
    data transfer, 39
    input/output, 39
    logical, 39
    system, 39
Integer register file (IRF), 166
Integrated circuit (IC) technology, 3
Integrated switching, 226
Intel 486 Microprocessor cache structure, 82
Intel Pentium microprocessor, 158–164
    instruction pipelines, 159
    instruction set, 161
    operand types, 161
Interbus cache module, 264
Interconnection
    crossbar switch, 242–245
    design considerations, 226
    networks, 184–227
    multiple bus, 242
    multiprocessor, 240
    ring, 245
    shared bus, 240–242

Interleaved memory, 71, 72
Interrupts, 93
Inverse indirect n-cube, 219–221
Inverter, transistor gate, 405
Issuing problems
    data hazard, 109
    structural hazard, 109

K
Key segment, of computer word, 72
KSR1 system, 245

L
Laplace's equation, 195
Latch circuit, 421
Latency, in pipelines, 128
Layout editor, circuit design, 402
Learning, in ANN, 11
Least mean square (LMS) learning law, 355
Limited directory protocol, 254
Linear speedup, in algorithm, 301
Lines, in data transfer, 67
Linguistic variable, 380
Literal gate, 373
Little endian, in ordering bytes, 150
Load field, in instructions, 85
Load instruction, 28, 34
Load operation
    horizontal microprogram, 35
    state diagram, 31
    vertical microprogram, 36
Loading task, 349
Load-store machine, 42
Locality of reference, memory, 66
Locked gate, in multiprocessors, 275
Logical addresses, 85
Logical operators, 447
Loosely coupled multiprocessor, 239
LSI (large-scale integration), 3
Lyapunov functions, 365

M
Macropipelining, 292
Madaline networks, 355
Mailbox, in memory, 285
Main memory, 239
Mantissa, of floating point numbers, 61, 62
    alignment, 63
Mapping, of cache, 77
Maskable interrupt, 94
Masson's binomial concentrator, 214

Master process, in parallel program, 274
Matching store, associative memory, 324
Matrix multiplication
   asyncronous algorithms, 304
   syncronous algorithms, 309
Mauchly, John, 2
Maximum speedup, of pipeline, 104
Maximum throughput, of pipeline, 105
Megaflops (MFLOPS), 13
Membership function, 376, 384
Membrane, in neurophysiology, 343
Membrane potential, defined, 344
Memory unit, 19, 69-71
   access time, 14
   address register (MAR), 23, 25, 31, 34
   bandwidth, 14, 244
   cell, 69–71
   contention, 239
   data register (MDR), 23, 26, 31, 34
   hierarchy, 66–68
   management unit (MMU), PowerPC microprocessor, 174
   segment placement, 90, 91
   size, 14
   speeds, 74
   system design, 66–93
Memory data register (MDR), 32
Mesh-based multicomputer, 260
Microcode, 33-34
Microcomputer, 20
   system, 21
   using VHDL, 20–27
Microinstruction, 33
   horizontal design, 34
   vertical design, 34
   word design, 33
Microoperation (MO), 19
Microprogramming, 32, 33
Microword, 33
Migration of functions, 140
MIMD (multiple instruction stream, multiple data stream), machines, 5, 10-11
Minimum average latency (MAL), 130-133
Minimum latency, of pipeline, 131
MIPS (million instructions per second), 12-13
MISD (multiple instruction stream, single data stream), 5, 11
Miss, in caches, 76, 84
Monitor, in parallel program, 276

MOS transistor, 403
Motorola 88110 microprocessor, 146–157
   bit-field unit, 157
   divider unit, 157
   floating-point add unit, 157
   graphic unit, 157
   instruction and data caches, 153
   instruction set, 151
   Instruction unit, 147
   integer unit, 157
   internal buses, 155
   load/store unit, 156
   multiplier unit, 157
   operand types, 149
   register files, 155
MSAR register (microcode storage address register), 34
MSI (medium-scale integration), 3
Multicomputer, 7
Multicomputer interconnection networks, 258–263
   crossbar, 260
   fat-tree, 261
   k-ary n-cubes, 258
   n-dimensional mesh, 258, 259
   n-cube, 258
Multicomputers, 257–267
Multilayer Perceptrons, training, 357
Multi-multiprocessor, 7, 263–267
Multiple prefetching, 123
Multiple-valued logic, 371–373
Multiplexer (MUX), 32, 413
Multiplication function, 52–60
Multiport-memory-based multiprocessor, 244
Multiprocessor, 7, 239–257
   vs. multicomputers, 263
Multistage cube network, 219–221
Multistage networks
   concentrator, 213
   connector, 214
Mutual exclusion, 274
Mutual exclusion primitives, 275
M-way interleaving, 72

N
NaN, not a number, 63
NAND gates, 3

Nervous system, information-processing, 345
Network
  latency, 207
  switching functions, 223
  topology, 185–225
  topology, interconection networks, 226
Neural Networks, 341–371
Neuron, 343
Neurophysiology fundamentals, 343–346
Noncacheable data items, 257
Nondestructive-read property, 71
Nonmaskable interrupt, 94
Nonvectored interrupt scheme, 94
NOP (no operation) instructions, 111
NOR gates, 3
Normalized, floating point number, 62
Normalizing numbers, 64

O
Objects, 445
Omega network, 221
On-chip cache, 76
On-line updating, 360
Opcode, 24, 37
Operand fetch (OF), 106
Operand fields, 24
Operands per operation, 40
Operating system, 19
Operation code, 37
Operation mode, interconection networks, 226
Overflow, of floating point number, 62
Overlays, in virtual memory, 85

P
Packet switching, 226
Pages, in virtual memory, 67, 85
  fault, 86
  table, 85
PARADIGM (PARAllel DIstributed Global Memory) system, 264
Parallel adder, 44
Parallel algorithms, 272, 294–312
  analyzing, 300–303
  broadcasting, 295
  elementwise operations, 295
  parallel prefix, 297
  permutation, 298
  reduction, 297
Parallel computation, 285–288
Parallel computers, 4, 237
Parallel inference machines (PIM), 265
Parallel programming, 272–294
  barrier, 281
  deadlock, 283
  fetch and add, 280
  increment and decrement, 279
  lock, 275–279
  multicomputers, 284
  multiprocessors, 273–284
  process creation, 274
  synchronization, 274
  unlock, 275–279
  wait and signal, 279
Parallel search, 72
Parallelism, types of, 10
Parent process, 274
Partition-exchange sort, 305
Partitioning, 285
Partitioning algorithms, 288
PE (process elements), 10
Pencil-and-paper method of multiplication, 53
Perfect speedup, parallel algorithms, 301
Performance and quality measurements, of a computer, 12–14
Permutation, 211
  end around one shift, 298
  odd-even swap, 298
  swap, 298
Personal computers, 20
Pipeline
  architectures, 5
  control, 128–136
  frequency, 105
  interlock, 110
  performance measures, 103
  reservation table, 128
  scheduling, 128-136
  structure, 102
Pipelined
  array, 329
  carry save multiplier, 127
  vector processor, 6, 9, 10
Pipelining, 102–136
Pivot row, 307
Placement routines, 409
PNs (processing nodes), 9
Portmap, 436
Postsynaptic potential (PSP), 344

PowerPC microprocessor, 172–179
   instruction unit, 174
   istruction set, 177
   operand types, 176
Prefetch and decode stage, 147
Present bit, in director protocols, 252
Principal component analysis, 351
Private bit, 253
Process, defined, 239, 272
   creation of, 274
Processing elements (PEs), 8, 10, 325
Program counter (PC), 4, 23, 25, 40
Programmable logic array (PLA), 32, 419
Prototyping, 351

Q
Quantum, time period, 85
Quicksort, 305, 306

R
R/W (read/write), memory cell, 69
RAM (random-access memory), 2, 19, 21, 23, 70
RAW (read after write), 111
Rearrangeable networks, construction, 216
Recurrent networks, 349
Reduced instruction set computer (RISC), 38, 139
Redundant hardware, 48
Registers, 18, 102
Reinforcement learning process, 348, 350
Reinforcement signal, 350
Relational operators, 448
Relative addressing, 40
Relaxed algorithms, 290
Reliability, of computers, 14
Remington-Rand Corporation, 2
Replacement algorithms, 88
   first in, first out (FIFO), 88
   least recently used (LRU), 89
Response time, 14
Ripple carry adder, 44
RISC architecture
   advantages of, 140–145
   characteristics, 143
   effect of VLSI, 141
   vs. CISC architecture, 139–181
RISC design vs. CISC design, 145
RISC processors, 145–157, 164–181
ROM (read-only memory), 19

Routing routines, 409
Run time, of program, 272

S
Scalability, 238
Scalable algorithm, 286
Scalar processor, 8, 10, 260
Scalar types, 443
Scaled speedup, 302
Scheduling, of processors, 287
Scoreboard tables
   destination register status, 117
   functional unit status, 117
   instruction status, 115
Scoreboard technique, 148
Sea of gates, 410
Segment selector, i486 microproceessor, 91
Segmentation, of memory, 89
Semibroadcast array, 329
Sensitivity list of signals, 442
Sequent Symmetry 2000 multiprocessors, 249
Sequential
   algorithms, 272
   circuits, 421–429
   locality of reference, 67
Sequential statements, 449–455
   case statements, 454
   if, 453
   loop, 454
   signal assignment, 450
   variable assignment, 449
   wait, 451
Serial adder, 51
Serial algorithms, 272
Set-associative cache, 80
Shared memory, 239
Shift-and-add multiplication, 53
Shuffle-exchange network, 188
Sigmoid function, 347
SIMD (single instruction stream, multiple data stream), 5, 11
SIMD machines, 10
Single-inconsistent bit, 252
Single-processor machines, 4
SISD (single instruction stream, single data stream), 4
Slave prosess, 274
Snoopy cache protocols, 248
Soft computing, 341

Soma, cell body in the brain, 343
Source, region in transistor, 404
Spatial locality of reference, 67
Special-purpose processors, 6, 11
Speedup, 104, 300–303
   factors affecting, 303
Spin lock, 277
Spool (simultaneous print operation on line), 2
SSI (small-scale integration), 3
Stack, 41
Stack addressing, 40
   machine, 41
   register, 40
Stage, in pipelines, 102
Stalled instruction, 110
State diagram, 129, 130, 132, 133
   for the load operation, 31
Static
   assignment, 287
   branch prediction, 167
   coherence check, 257
   data flow machine, 323
   partition, 286
   prediction, 120
Static networks, 185, 185–209
   binary tree, 186
   fat tree, 187
   k-ary n-cube, 204
   linear array, 186
   n-cube or hypercube, 198–202
   n-dimensional mesh, 202
   ring, 186
   routing in k-ary n-cubes, 204–209
   routing in n-dimensional meshes, 204–209
   shared bus, 185
   shuffle-exchange, 188–190
   two-dimensional mesh, 190–198
Static pipeline, 128
   scheduling, 129–131
Static random access memory (SRAM), 70
Stochastic networks, 348
Store-and-forward routing, 204
Structural architecture, 436
Structural credit assignment, 351
Sum-prefix, 297
Supercomputers, 238
Supervised learning process, 348, 349
Suspended lock, 277
Switching methodology, interconection
   networks, 226
Synapse, 343
Synchronization, 275
Synchronous algorithms, for multicomputers, 309–312
System link and interrupt controller (SLIC) bus, 241
Systolic array, 5, 6, 10, 324-338

T

Tag field, 78
Target instruction cache (TIC), 121, 149
Temporal credit assignment, 351
Temporal locality of reference, 67
Term set, 380
Test & Set instruction, 277
T-gate, 372
Three-bit scanning, 56
Throughput, of processor 13, 104
Throughput improvement
   bottleneck problem, 109
   fetching problem, 108
   instruction pipeline, 124
   issuing problem, 109
Tightly coupled multiprocessor, 239
Time-slice, 85
TLB (translation lookaside buffer), 87, 159
Tomasulo's method, 113, 124
Torus network, 195
Training set, 349
Transistor technology, 2, 3
Translation lookaside buffer (TLB), 87, 93, 154, 166
Trap, exception, 95
Turnaround time, 14
Two's-complement multiplication, 57
Two-dimensional torus, 195
Two-way set-associative mapping cache, 81
Types, 443

U

Unconditional branch, 118
Underflow, 62
Unidirectional ring, 186
Unsupervised learning process, 348, 351
U-pipeline, 158
Upward compatibility, of processor, 140
Utilization, of processor, 13

V

Valid bit, in directory protocols, 252
Vector processor, 5, 9, 10, 13, 260
Vectored interrupt scheme, 94
Vertical microprogramming (VM), 34, 35
Very high speed integrated circuit description
      language (VHDL), 432-461
  design entity, 440–443
  item delarations, 443–447
  simulation process, 438
  views, 435–440
Virtual
  addresses, 85
  channel, 205
  memory, 85–93
  paging, 85
VLSI (very large-scale integration), 3
  components, 403–405
  design, 401–412
  layout, 406–412
Von Neumann architecture, 11, 18–95, 106
Von Neumann, John, 2, 4
V-pipeline, 158

W

Wallace tree method, 52, 56
WAR (write after read), 112
Wavefront array, 330
WAW (write after write), 112
Widrow-Hoff learning law, 355
Wilkes, Maurice, 2
Word, defined, 20
Wormhole routing, 204, 206
Wraparound two-dimensional mesh, 194
Write invalidate coherency, 248
Write through, operations, 76
Write update coherency, 248
Write-back (WB), 76, 106, 147
Write-invalidate snoopy cache protocol, 248
Write-once protocol, 248
Write-update snoopy cache protocol, 251